"Do you want to know what courage, honor, and dignity actually are and how you can manifest these traits in your own life? If there were a required reading list for being a real man, John Giduck and Sergeant Major John Anderson's *The Green Beret in You* would be #1. As a husband, father, and businessman this is one of the most important books I have ever read. *The Green Beret in You* should be on the nightstand of every American."

Brad Thor

New York Times bestselling author of *The First Commandment*

"Today, America is threatened from within and without. Oklahoma City. Columbine High School. The World Trade Center. Virginia Tech. These are events carved into the cultural awareness of our civilization. In these dark days, and in the trials of the years yet to come, the virtues and values of the Green Beret are needed more than ever. In every aspect of our lives – in family, in business, and in sports – now more than ever, every American needs the total commitment of the Green Beret lifestyle. Hooah!"

Lt. Col. Dave Grossman

Ranger commander, internationally acclaimed speaker
and trainer of military and law enforcement.
Author of *On Killing, On Combat* and
Stop Teaching Our Kids To Kill

"As Special Forces Sergeant Major John Anderson and John Giduck clearly show in this book, being a Green Beret is not just a title, it is a total commitment to living a life with integrity and honor, accepting responsibility for your own actions, accepting responsibility for your job, mission, family, children, friends and teammates. Being a Green Beret is about doing your best every day. It is a lifestyle that every American can adopt, and this book shows you how."

Command Sergeant Major Mel Wick

Founding Cadre Member of the Delta Force

THE GREEN BERET IN YOU

Living with Total Commitment to Family, Career, Sports and Life

JOHN GIDUCK

— WITH —

SPECIAL FORCES SERGEANT MAJOR
JOHN A. ANDERSON (RET.)

Published by Archangel Group Inc.

The Library of Congress has cataloged this edition as follows:
LCCN 2007908337

ISBN 0-9767753-2-8

For information about special discounts for bulk purchases or to purchase
additional copies send an email to info@antiterrorconsultants.org, call Archangel
at 303 215 0779, or fax a request to 303 215 0780 including your name and contact
information or visit www.antiterrorconsultants.org

Designed by Michel Hogan

TABLE OF CONTENTS

This book is dedicated to all of the men
who ever earned the right to wear the green beret.
It is you who gave America a model to emulate.

FOREWORD

– BY –

DELTA FORCE COMMAND SERGEANT MAJOR
MEL WICK (RET.)

What is a "Green Beret?" Ask a dozen people randomly on the street and you will get a dozen different answers, but all will contain an element of awe, an element of mystery, and an element of, "I wish I could be one." What is it about a Green Beret that invokes this reaction? How could this "lifestyle" possibly apply to everyday people? Sergeant Major John "Andy" Anderson (Ret.) and John Giduck have unraveled the mystery and clearly explain the path to finding the "Green Beret" inside yourself.

With over 32 years experience as an active duty Green Beret, and over 22 of those years in Joint and Special Mission Units, I have had the opportunity to observe first hand thousands of Green Berets under a variety of conditions. I have observed and worked with Green Berets everywhere from combat in the jungles of Vietnam to the mean streets of Baghdad; from training combat divers in Thailand to mountain climbing in the Alps; from night combat equipment jumps at 25,000 feet to 40 mile grueling cross country rucksack movements; from eating monkeys with the Montagnards, bugs in Africa, and snakes in Ecuador, to formal dinners with Heads of State; from living in 5-Star hotels to lice and flea-infested mud huts with locals. Through it all, whatever the location or conditions, the Green Beret maintains the same positive attitude, the same level of self discipline, the same level of respect and understanding of the local people. He never deviates from his commitment to integrity, mission accomplishment, and his teammates. As Andy and John clearly show in this book, being a Green Beret is not just a title, it is a total commitment to living a life with integrity and honor, accepting responsibility for your own actions, accepting responsibility for your job, mission, family, children, friends, and teammates. Being a Green Beret is about doing your best every day. A true warrior is a warrior every day, under all circumstances, not just when it is convenient.

Over the years I was involved in the design and conduct of various assessment and selection programs for Green Berets and Special Mission Units, I spent many days with psychologists, psychiatrists and behavioral scientists. I helped these experts complete many in-depth studies, conduct countless surveys, and analyze years of data, all in an effort to try to figure out what it really takes to make a Green Beret.

How can you identify a person with the "heart of a warrior," and how do you develop that inner potential to its fullest? Andy and John have laid out the most accurate, easy to understand explanation I have ever seen. As you read this book, look into your own heart and measure yourself against the standards outlined. Do you find the Heart of a Warrior? Do you have the strength of will and the self discipline? Do you recognize that discipline is doing what is right, even when no one is watching? Having recognized it, can you live up to that standard for the rest of your life, as the men of the Special Forces do every single day? Do you have the character, recognizing that character is what you are like when you are alone in the dark? Do you have what it takes to live your life as a Green Beret?

BIOGRAPHY
MELVIN L. WICK

CSM Wick has more than 32 years experience in the Special Operations community including 16-plus years in Delta Force. He was a founding cadre member, and served as the Command Sergeant Major for Delta, the Joint Special Operations Command (JSOC), the US Army Special Operations Command (USASOC), and the United States Special Operations Command (USSOCOM). He has on the ground combat experience in Vietnam, Desert One in Iran, Grenada, Panama, Somalia, Bosnia, Kosovo, and several other classified operations. He has conducted personal security for US Ambassadors during high threat periods, conducted numerous threat/vulnerability assessments of high-risk facilities and has planned and conducted security operations around the world. His diversified career in Special Operations has built a broad base of experience and expertise in leadership, operations planning, managing complex projects in high threat environments, and building positive working relationships with indigenous personnel. He has planned, designed, and supervised the implementation of advanced special operations training courses from 1 week to 6 months in duration, planned and conducted joint exercises up to JCS level as well as designing, planning and conducting operational tests of special operations unique equipment.

As the Director and Program Manager for the Center for National Response, CSM Wick turned an abandoned highway tunnel into a unique one-of-a-kind, national level, Weapons of Mass Destruction and Counter Terrorism training center, training over 10,000 DOD, Federal, State and local first responders.

Recently Sergeant Major Wick had the leading role in the site selection, design, construction, stand up, and operation of a Security Training Center in Iraq. He was instrumental in the POI development, recruiting and hiring of the instructors and support staff, pre-mission training, instructor evaluations, and on site monitoring and program evaluation. Mel Wick has also supervised the conduct of threat/vulnerability assessments of critical infrastructure in the US and Iraq, security and training operations in Iraq, employee travel through high risk areas and other security related activities.

Mel has a Bachelor of Science degree from Liberty University, Lynchburg, Virginia and is currently the President of Quick Services LLC.

PROLOGUE

- BY -

JOHN A. ANDERSON

SERGEANT MAJOR, U.S. ARMY SPECIAL FORCES

(RETIRED)

When my co-author, John Giduck, first came to me with the idea of writing a book based on the lives of the men in the Special Forces for the benefit of everyday American citizens, I was skeptical. I had spent the vast majority of my adult life – 25 years – in Special Forces, and continue to train our young Green Berets to this day. And while I remain convinced that the commitment, dedication and discipline of those fine men is without peer, and makes them the elite of our society, I did not see how the lives of the Green Berets could have much application to civilians.

Maybe part of my problem was that I had spent too much time in Special Forces, and not enough time in regular society. This is what made John the perfect person to not only develop the idea for this book, but bring to literary life the wonderful gifts that the Special Forces have. Though John had never served in Special Forces, he spent many years with the men of that unit, ultimately serving as an instructor to the Green Berets now fighting America's War on Terror. He also spent many years in Russia with their special forces, and has experienced firsthand that the men of different nations' elite military units often have more in common with each other, than they do citizens of their own countries. In this regard, he walked in both camps; understanding the lives of America's civilians, and the life of the Green Beret. This is what provided him the ability to see how the training, teamwork, operations, tactics and devotions of the Green Berets did have direct application to anyone wishing to live his life to its fullest.

Thus, on the pages that follow you will find many perspectives, beliefs, anecdotes and stories from my life as a Green Beret, in which you will hopefully find some value. For this reason we agreed early on that the book had to be written from my perspective. So, while the words on the pages that follow appear to be written by me, in the first person, just as many of the stories are John's, from his life and others he has known. Most of the words are his, as the writing fell on his shoulders. Regardless of the origin of the stories, though, John and I have both lived the lessons and morals from them all. We believe that every tale is one that reflects the best of the Green Berets, their attitudes on life, and the way they live that makes them so very special.

We realized early on that we were producing a book that would see far more men attracted to its themes, than women. Not that the lessons and encouragement in the chapters are not just as applicable to women, but the responsibility, the dedication, and commitments discussed will likely find their way more readily into the lives of America's men. For this reason, and the difficulty of endlessly repeating the egalitarian reference of "he or she" in the text, most of this book uses the male pronouns "he," "his," and "him." However, where points are of particular poignancy to women, references are in the feminine. We trust this does not offend anyone, but in fact makes the book more reader friendly. If someone takes offense, though, that's tough. I'm a Green Beret, and have pissed off a lot of people throughout my life.

As to the references to the Special Forces units and the men who fill their ranks, we have used the terms *Special Forces*, *SF* and *Green Berets* interchangeably. Though the official term of these units is "Special Forces," the soldiers on the Teams comprising this elite organization modestly refer to themselves merely as "SF." The general public, however, best knows them as "Green Berets." Though they never refer to themselves in this fashion, they recognize that it is the popular label others have placed on them, and they are accepting of it. So, for purposes of readability and for the comfort of the average citizen, the term "Green Beret" is used throughout the text.

Also, in the text of the book, you will find distinctions between America's Special Forces, and similar units from other countries. When capitalized – Special Forces – we are making reference to U.S. Army Special Forces. When appearing in lower case letters – special forces – we are referencing similar units from other nations, that use the same term. Likewise, when "Green Beret" is capitalized, we are referring to the men of Special Forces. Any references to the hat itself – green beret – are in lower case letters.

BALLAD OF THE GREEN BERET

Performed by Special Forces Sgt. Barry Sadler (now deceased)
Written by Barry Sadler and Robin Moore

Fighting soldiers from the sky.
Fearless men who jump and die,
Men who mean just what they say,
The brave men of the Green Beret.

Silver wings upon their chests,
These are men, America's best,
One hundred men will test today.
But only three win the Green Beret.

Trained to live off nature's land.
Trained in combat, hand-to-hand.
Men who fight by night and day.
Courage take, from the Green Beret.

Silver wings upon their chests,
These are men, America's best.
One hundred men will test today.
But only three, win the Green Beret.

Back at home a young wife waits.
Her Green Beret has met his fate,
He has died for those oppressed,
Leaving her his last request:

Put silver wings on my son's chest,
Make him one of America's best,
He'll be a man they'll test one day,
Have him win the Green Beret.

PART 1

FIGHTING SOLDIERS FROM THE SKY

Fighting soldiers from the sky. *Then-Sergeant First Class John Anderson, on right, exiting plane at 25,000 ft during HALO training of Spanish special forces, 1976.*

INTRODUCTION

*...Fighting soldiers from the sky,
Fearless men, who jump and die.*

Consider for a moment the image of the Green Beret. He is a fearless warrior, whose too many days in the sun cause him to take in all that is around him through narrowed eyes. They are the eyes of both predator and prey, of one who knows the horrors of battling the enemy against seemingly impossible odds, yet has a wary respect for that enemy. They are eyes that take in everything. Above them, on his head, can be seen the dark green of the beret for which he is known. It is dressed perfectly in parade fashion, showing the pride with which it is worn, even though he may be deep in the jungle or alone in the desert. His jaw is strong about his handsome face, a face now bearing the scars of the wars he has been asked by his country to fight. His mouth is tight and grim. It is a mouth that says little, but when it utters words they should be listened to, for he is not a man who likes to repeat himself. He does not speak loudly, and never brags, but goes about his business with both a detached air and the singleness of purpose of a true professional.

He does everything this way, as it is the only way he knows. Years of Special Forces training, and even more serving in combat zones throughout the world, have taught him that to not do your job well, to not do it perfectly, is to risk failure. And in his world, failure means death. There is no job he will undertake and not give his all to complete, for he is in the business of accomplishing what lesser men would view as impossible. When he confronts a problem he deals with it, too, in the only way he knows: he hits it head on. He does this whether dealing with a superior enemy force in battle, or just one of life's many challenges. He does not look for trouble, but recognizes that others will bring trouble to him. When this happens he faces them with unflinching eye, and defeats them. He knows that in life there are people you never push. Because when you do, they will take you all the way to the wall whether you want to go there or not. He knows he is such a man.

Thus, he is calm and quiet under the most stressful conditions imaginable, and carries the confidence of that capability with him wherever he goes. This is what people outside of Special Forces notice first. This is what they respond to, and have come to expect from others of his breed. This is the model of the modern soldier of the U.S. Army Special Forces; soldiers known as the Green Berets.

To be sure, the men of Special Forces are an enigma, as much victims of their own press as they are America's elite. Myth, rumor and legend surrounding them have become so inextricably intertwined it is difficult for the uninitiated to separate fact from fiction. Not that these men care one whit what others think of them. In his book *Green Berets: Unconventional Warriors, In Action with America's Elite Fighting Men*, Hans Halberstadt puts these men in some perspective for the rest of the population. He reports that very little is understood about Green Berets by the general public. "First, their proper name, Special Forces, isn't even recognized by most people. But mention Green Berets and women hide and strong men tremble…. It's important to remember that the green beret is a hat, not a unit; it is worn by men in an organization called the Special Forces."[1] Still, the sobriquet of "Green Beret" has become so well used, so universally recognized, that even these elite soldiers have come to tolerate it.

In many ways, these men are the envy of the remainder of the military complex, even the other members of the Special Operations

---

[1] Hans Halberstadt, *Green Berets: Unconventional Warriors, In Action with America's Elite Fighting Men*, (Berkley Books, New York, 1988), 17.

community. Special Operations is the umbrella military command that oversees all Special Operations Forces, which include Special Forces. It is inaccurate to call any of these other units "Special Forces." In addition to actual Special Forces, Special Operations includes Army Rangers; the 160th SOAR (Special Operations Aviation Regiment); Air Force PJs (Parachute Jumpers) and commandos; SEALs; Marine Special Operations (MARSOC); and PsyOps, or Psychological Operations. For many years the Special Forces was the only unit to wear a beret, and they did it in violation of orders for more than a decade. When finally officially awarded their treasured headgear by President John F. Kennedy in 1961, they were alone in the U.S. in the wearing of this symbol of military excellence throughout the world.

So it is, that these men are not only the fascination of so many millions of movie-goers and action-adventure novel enthusiasts, but the envy of the rest of the elite of the military's unconventional forces. They are not revered merely for their combat skills, but for the depth of their knowledge on the issues that drive both war and politics. They are the envy of all for their broad spectrum of skills far outside the tactical realm, and for their unique and unprecedented autonomy in operating throughout the world, for "nowhere else in the military do noncommissioned officers deal so directly with the execution of American foreign policy."[2] A great deal of their missions are political, with no shots fired. Nowhere else in the Armed Forces do you find enlisted men that are multi-lingual, with advanced degrees, often in political science, or junior officers in positions to influence relations between the U.S. and other countries.

Thus, it is from these men, who have set a standard as both warriors and humanitarians, that we have much to learn. The Green Beret - both hat and man - has become a symbol of excellence, of courage in all aspects of life, and of sacrifice for our country and our fellow man that stands as a final bastion of honor in a world gone crazy with material consumption and immorality. The Code of the Green Beret is a standard of honor and propriety in personal conduct

[2] Halberstadt, 18.

that can easily be applied to the life of anyone, and the Green Berets live it, every single day. It is a Code that has been painstakingly developed for more than half a century, always demanding the best from men who were there because they were already the best - America's best. It is a Code we all need to be reminded of and can benefit from applying to our own lives.

The Green Berets believe that inside every man, woman and child, is a warrior: a person of honor, integrity and discipline. Green Berets exist in a world where these qualities are necessary for both success and survival. But then, so do we all. This book is your chance to embrace these qualities in your own life. It is your opportunity to learn the secrets that make the Green Berets so special and their lives so great, so deserving of immortalization in literature, cinema, song, folklore and history. This is your chance to nurture the warrior in you, to live like a Green Beret.

*ODA 124, 1st Special Forces Group, in Okinawa,
1985. Master Sergeant John Anderson is second
from left, second row. In front row, far left, is
Staff Sergeant Ronnie "Beaver" McCann, and to
his right, Sergeant First Class Charles "Mitch"
Conway. Both would go on to become Command
Sergeants Major, with Ronnie McCann serving
as "the" Command Sergeant Major of the
John F. Kennedy Special Warfare School, and
Mitch Conway serving as Command Sergeant
Major of the 10th Special Forces Group
(Airborne). CSM Conway continues to serve
in Special Forces to this day.*

– 1 –

THE MAKING OF A GREEN BERET

…One hundred men will test today,
But only three win the Green Beret.

WHERE DO THEY COME FROM?

Before you can appreciate what the values and ethos of America's Green Berets can bring to your own life – a life most likely spent in the warm embrace of peaceful civilian endeavors – you must first understand just who and what the men of the U.S. Army's Special Forces are. Since Green Berets exploded into the American consciousness, largely as a result of the hit song by Special Forces Sergeant Barry Sadler,[3] the bestselling book *The Green Berets* by Robin Moore[4] and the 1968 movie of the same name starring John Wayne, they have become virtual legends in our country and many others. Even the iconic character Billy Jack, an ex-Green Beret Vietnam veteran fighting an intolerant town to protect a local Indian tribe and teenage children, went far to further their image. Their name, symbols and reputation have become the stuff of modern legend, most recently seen in such caricatures as Sylvester Stallone's *Rambo* movies, and

[3] *Ballad of the Green Berets*, 1966.
[4] Moore Hill Publishing, Concord, Massachusetts, 1965, 2000.

even Mel Gibson's portrayal of a former Green Beret police detective in the *Lethal Weapon* series.

Little boys grow up dreaming of becoming one of the most elite our country can produce, and scores of men – young and old – fabricate their own membership in this exclusive fraternity for the sole purpose of picking up women in bars. Through it all, over the past 40 years of American obsession with the Special Forces, they have been lionized, canonized, and mythologized. At the same time they have been vilified, demonized and defamed by others. I was once warned that the favorite headline of America's print news media starts with "Ex-Green Beret Kills ….," as though lurking just beneath the surface of America's glee that such men exist to keep us all from harm in the dark night, was some sinister fear of their capacity for death, and maybe even evil. Evil that, perhaps, we had instilled in them.

But the question remains, just where does the truth of the Green Beret fit into all of this attention and rhetoric? Just who are these men? What have they been through to earn membership into this secret society, and what do they stand for that the rest of us might have something to learn from them? In answering these questions, it is important for everyone to understand just where these men do come from. Is it possible that one of these fierce, deadly commandos who strikes fear into the hearts of America's enemies was, at one time, just a freckle-faced kid? Could he have once been a little boy with a skewed baseball cap covering a cowlick, and gap-toothed grin, looking for someone to play catch with? Not only is it possible that one, or some, of our elite warriors started out this way, but the truth is they all did.

Green Berets are all part of – and at one time were nothing more than – the common citizenry, for there is no greater resource in the world than Americans. Make no mistake, America is a culture, society and nation founded on the creed and ethos of the warrior. From the early settlers who hacked out a civilization from the wilderness, battling the warrior race they found living there, to modern times, we are a people unalterably devoted to the notion of the warrior. Starting as early as Rogers' Rangers and the French and Indian Wars, to the Minute Men, Daniel Boone and Davy Crockett, through our cowboy era with the romance of a lone self-assured man never hesitating to bring justice with fists or the famed Colt revolver, we have worshipped the warrior. In World War II we had the Big Red One, the elite and courageous Marines of the Pacific Theater, Rangers, the 101st and 82nd Airborne Divisions, and the OSS. All were brave men who picked up arms to do what had to be done in a world gone crazy with murderous lust. In Korea, the Frozen Chosen were among the many who braved the harshest circumstances and environment for the cause of liberty, not only for Americans, but so that everyone could enjoy the freedom and self-determination of America. Then Vietnam brought us the Green Berets, and an entirely new ethos of elite warrior that would sustain us through the turn of the century.[5]

Thus, it is from our warrior culture that we first created the most elite soldiers the world has ever known, and continue to create them every year. For we do not seem to run out of young men who wish to be the best; who wish to be "America's best." But the warrior spirit of America is not found merely in her military during times of war. For the military is nothing more than an organization comprised of common, everyday American citizens, men and women alike. It is those very people who carry the Warrior Code forward. As a country, the United States has, in aggregate, more martial artists, boxers, wrestlers, scuba divers, mountain climbers, sky divers, shooters, extreme skiers, hunters and motorcycle riders than any other. As though these activities – which require a warrior spirit and love of danger – are not enough, we seem to invent more, and ever more dangerous, activities each day. To this very day, more than a quarter of a millennia later, we are a people in search of the constant demands of the warrior lifestyle, forever testing ourselves, our courage and our limits.

It is a testament to the warrior spirit that is alive and well in our people that their fascination of the Green Beret exists to the

5 See John Giduck, *Terror at Beslan: A Russian Tragedy With Lessons for America's Schools*, (Archangel Group Publishing, Golden, Colorado, 2005), 333-334.

degree it does. It is the same with all cultures that rightfully claim warrior roots, as all warriors admire and revere the most elite, the most accomplished and brave of their own. Just as the British worship the SAS, the Russians are fascinated with the Spetsnaz, Germans the GSG-9, and the Dutch the Royal Marines, so, too, have ancient civilizations experienced the same. In centuries past, the Knights of the Round Table went out every day to protect victims of evildoers, earning them the idolatry of the peasants. Both Shaolin monks and Samurai warriors continue to be studied, revered and emulated to this day. In ancient Rome, the Centurions were the soldiers on whom all depended, and in Greece the Spartans. In Africa, the Masai have long been seen as among the bravest, fiercest warriors. In ancient Russia the Cossacks and their elite teams of shock troops called *gaiduks* or *giducks* were chronicled for years.[6] But of all these, none has ever captured the imagination of not only a people, but the entire world, the way that the Green Beret has.

Should you ever happen to see a Special Forces soldier walk down any street in civilian America, you would find onlookers electrified by his presence, by the sudden recognition that such men really do exist and there is one in their midst at that moment. A Hollywood celebrity could pass by and you wouldn't see as many heads turn as when the American citizenry is suddenly confronted with the reality of our warrior elite. That soldier may be walking down the sidewalk thinking the same things as all those around him: "*What will the car repair bill be? How will I get the report on my desk done by its deadline? When will I meet a nice girl and get married?*" Yet his very existence and the iconic presence of that forest green beret, molded so perfectly and worn at a jaunty angle, is enough to remind us all of who we are as a nation, and just who we are at our best. We are drawn to them the way struggling young athletes are magnetized to the world champions of their sport, recognizing that just by being around the best makes them better. And nothing could make us

---

[6] Serge A. Zenkovsky, editor, *Medieval Russia's Epics, Chronicles, and Tales*, (Penguin Books, New York, 1963), 356.

better as a people than having just a few of the qualities of the Green Berets incorporated into our lives.

THE MAKING OF A GREEN BERET

Contrary to popular belief, Green Berets are made and not born. Yes, it is necessary to start with an individual with a solid foundation of self-discipline, commitment, honesty, decent athletic ability and an above-average intellect. But these qualities can be found in many, who ultimately might not make the grade in Special Forces training.

Historically, to get into Special Forces you had to be a three time volunteer. You had to have volunteered for the Army by enlisting, volunteered for Airborne School, and volunteered for Special Forces. SF didn't want someone who just decided to "give it a shot" because he was being drafted anyway. Airborne training is not only an essential component of the necessary combat skills for an SF soldier, it also serves as a litmus test of the courage and discipline required to even enter the Army's *John F. Kennedy Special Warfare School* at Ft. Bragg, North Carolina. As with any cross section of citizens, you will find those with phobias about heights among the Green Berets. The difference is that for them there is no allowance for indulgence in personal insecurities, the way the rest of the world panders to its weaknesses. It is fine that you are afraid of heights; it is even fine that you are terrified to jump out of an airplane. But as a Green Beret you will do it, and you will do it a lot, and you will never hesitate in performing that feat when ordered. Sometimes you will do it voluntarily, on your own, to ensure your skills and mastery of your fear do not wane. That is what sets the men of the Special Forces apart from the rest of the populace.

Typically, to enter Special Forces training you must be at least a buck sergeant. If an officer, you have to be a captain, or first lieutenant promotable to captain. These minimum requirements ensure that SF is not getting a bunch of overly young, immature adrenaline junkies who, due to their youth and physical fitness, manage to get through training. They want mature professionals. They want people who will not act impulsively, or otherwise jeopardize their missions, their Team, or the Special Forces, because of juvenile hijinks.

In SF, the individual soldier must be able to function independently in a foreign, hostile environment. He may be America's sole ambassador of goodwill and assistance to a group of foreigners not entirely convinced of our commitment or motivation in helping them. Thus, SF must have people whose wisdom and judgment can be counted on. It is for this reason that in any graduating class from the SF Qualifications Course,[7] there may be one or several who – though they successfully negotiated the training program – are sent elsewhere as unsuitable for actually serving in the Special Forces. This would be like a law school graduate or doctor, surviving school, the bar exam or med boards, meeting the criteria for their professions in every other way, only to be told that they didn't have what it took and sent home. In Special Forces, the cost of a mistake in who gets put on a Team is often measured in human lives. But, so it is in the legal, medical, fire/rescue and law enforcement professions in the civilian world.

The training that is undergone during the Q Course is, to say the least, daunting. The famous Barry Sadler song laments that one hundred men will test today, but only three win the green beret. However, some classes do not even come close to that number of graduates. Special Forces Command cannot afford to allow unqualified people to get past the selection process just to meet some John Kerry-esque political numbers quota; when during the 2004 presidential campaign, Senator Kerry's answer to the numerous conflicts America was engaged in around the world was simply to triple the numbers of all Special Operations Forces.[8] The commanders at SOCOM[9] know that it is better to send undermanned teams of competent professionals

---

7 "Q" Course or more formally "SFQC."
8 See Chapter 11, Rules of Special Operations Forces, which includes the axiom "Special Forces can't be mass produced."
9 Special Operations Command

into a difficult situation, than rely on mediocre performers to fill the ranks. Simply, mediocrity kills.

Until recently, the actual training of a Green Beret was comprised of three phases, all preceded by a testing phase known as Assessment and Selection (SFAS). In the military, the word "Selection" is a gentle euphemism for putting trainees through the most grueling, difficult - and what would be considered by the outside world as inhuman - treatment possible, in an effort to weed out those who do not belong. This is what Hell Week is all about in the Navy SEALs' BUD/S[10] training program. In Army Special Forces, the selection portion was a torturous 24 days of "Hell on earth," according to Tom Clancy in his book *Special Forces: A Guided Tour of U.S. Army Special Forces*.[11] During this period, the would-be Green Berets endured cruel levels of exercise, traversed countless miles of rugged terrain with overloaded rucksacks,[12] and suffered sleep deprivation, all on little to no food. They were forced to swim great distances under heavy weights and horrible circumstances, perform land navigation and other skills in the dark while exhausted, successfully negotiate obstacle courses, and run until they dropped.

Hans Halberstadt humorously explained the conditions in which this test of worthiness was commenced: "[With] the blessing of your Chain of Command, you can stand in line and wait your turn to visit lovely Camp Mackall in the picturesque rural hills of central North Carolina. Most schools in the Army are housed in rather nice buildings with all the amenities. Not the Q Course. The most prestigious school in the Army is also – in terms of its physical buildings – the most primitive. Phase I is housed behind a chain link and barbed wire fence in a little compound of ragged buildings that look like they ought to be condemned by the local authorities. The buildings are old and covered with tarpaper. The setting is a lot like you

---

[10] Basic Underwater Demolition/SEAL
[11] Tom Clancy and John Gresham, *Special Forces: A Guided Tour of U.S. Army Special Forces*, (Berkley Books, New York, 2001), 71.
[12] Rucksacks are large backpacks in which Special Forces carry every bit of equipment, clothing, weapons, ammunition and other survival gear they need, often weighing close to 100 pounds on operations.

will find in the places where SF is supposed to work. There is a shower; it is cold."[13]

None of this was ever designed to "make" a Green Beret. It was merely to cull out those who did not have what it took to ultimately perform the missions of a Special Forces soldier once they had been properly trained, so time and money was not wasted on them. This arduous process has always taken place at the *Colonel Nick Rowe Special Forces Training Facility* at Camp Mackall, North Carolina situated in the hills west of Ft. Bragg, North Carolina. It is "named after PFC[14] John Mackall, the first U.S. paratrooper killed in combat, a member of the 82nd Airborne Division."[15] Traditionally the Q Course was run seven times a year in the hopes of ultimately producing the 1,000 Green Berets that Army Special Forces needed merely to keep up with attrition from retirement and separation from the military, injuries, wounds and combat deaths.[16] But that was before America went to war after 9-11. Since then, both the demands for, and the attrition rate of, SF are much higher, and the needs for Green Berets ever greater.

Traditionally, those who survived Assessment and Selection, were given a very brief respite, and then began Phase I of the Q Course. This phase was 39 days long and was designed to provide a foundation of common field and combat skills for consistency in all SF soldiers, as they were drawn from various branches of the Army. During this phase the apprentice-commandos underwent intensive training in land navigation, fieldcraft, patrolling, ambush, reconnaissance, and small unit tactics.

Phase II was where a person was trained in the Military Occupational Specialty (MOS) he would have throughout his career in Special Forces. Although everyone entering any branch of the military is given an MOS and specialized training in that area, upon entering SF each soldier gets a whole new identity in terms of the

---

13 Halberstadt, 66.
14 Private First Class
15 Thomas H. Taylor, *The Simple Sounds of Freedom: The True Story of the Only Soldier to Fight for Both America and the Soviet Union in World War II*, (Random House, New York, 2002), 25.
16 Clancy and Gresham, 61.

specialized skills he will have to perform. Whereas the regular Army has hundreds of MOS's, Special Forces has only five, known as the 18-Series designations, as each specialty comes with a corresponding letter that is preceded by the number 18. Because the training time for these MOS's varies, the length of time to complete this phase varies from trainee to trainee. It is not uncommon for soldiers with MOS's that take long periods of time to complete, to end up graduating two or three classes behind the one they entered the Q Course with.

18A is an officer slot, and is six months long. This course takes officers from conventional Army units and turns them into leaders capable of running an ODA. The ODA, or Operational Detachment Alpha, is a twelve-man team that forms the basis of all SF operations, popularly known as an A Team, in the field. 18A students get a heavy dose of unconventional warfare (UW) training, including guerilla warfare and insurgency operations.

18B is the Weapons Specialist, and is held by someone with a sergeant's rank, as are all of the other MOS's. The 18B candidate can operate and maintain every kind of weapon in the world, from pistols to rocket-propelled grenade launchers. This includes our enemies' weapons, as well as our own.

The 18C is the Engineering Sergeant, and is skilled in both building things and blowing them up. This may seem an odd combination of skills, but actually makes a lot of sense for those who may have to build a dam one day on a peacekeeping mission, and then blow up a bridge in combat on another.[17]

The Medical Sergeant is designated 18D, and undergoes the longest of the Phase II training courses, at twelve months, which is simply the finest first-response medical training in the world. These men are the best doctors practicing medicine without a license to be found anywhere.

The 18E Communications Sergeants "are among the most talented and skilled communications personnel in the world."[18] They are experts in everything from Morse code training to advanced

[17] Clancy and Gresham, 80-82.
[18] Ibid.

computer networking and encryption. They can "design and string homemade can wire antennas one day and install computer network routers the next."[19]

But, even getting through all of this intense tactical training and academic schooling – which sees large numbers of candidates drop out – wasn't enough for them to be entitled to wear the beret and the coveted Special Forces shoulder tab, and get assigned to a Team. Phase III was the final test, and a chance to put the unconventional warfare polish on the foundation of skills they had developed. Despite the end finally being in sight, even more trainees regularly failed this final phase.

The 38 days of Phase III training was comprised of such UW skills as intelligence gathering and analysis, airborne operations for both insertion and extraction of teams from hostile areas, unconventional warfare as a discipline, cross-cultural communications, and, finally, the Robin Sage exercise. This was – and continues to be - the bar exam of Special Forces, and the test that required the candidate to draw on all that he had learned since entering the Q Course. In Robin Sage, the candidate had to demonstrate that he was adept at every SF skill, as no one enjoyed the luxury of job specialization. Drawing on the long traditions and early experiences of America's special operators, this test was designed as a reenactment of the very types of behind-the-lines operations conducted by the Jedburgh teams[20] of SF's predecessor OSS[21] during World War II.

The Robin Sage exercise was historically run four times a year in the imaginary country of Pineland. There, the SF candidates linked up with indigenous guerilla fighters and attempted to develop rapport with the leaders. Their objective was to work out an agreement for the Special Forces to train, arm, equip and fund the guerilla

---

19 Ibid.
20 Jedburgh Teams were usually comprised of three men, that were dropped at night into German occupied territory in Europe to coordinate with indigenous partisans and guerillas to fight the Nazis. The name derived from the base in Jedburgh, England, where they trained and prepared for these missions.
21 Office of Strategic Services, a clandestine special activities unit formed and commanded by Wall Street lawyer, and World War I Congressional Medal of Honor recipient, Col. William "Wild Bill" Donovan. OSS is seen as the predecessor to both the CIA and U.S. Army Special Forces.

operations, so long as they did so in accordance with American wishes. The guerillas themselves have always been played by current Special Forces soldiers (the exercise takes dozens of SF soldiers to play their roles), soldiers from other units and even some experienced civilian volunteers. The goal of the guerillas is always to take advantage of the SF soldiers in the negotiations, and get them to give up arms, equipment and money with no reciprocation.

As if this weren't test enough, all the while teams of enemy forces were attempting to locate and capture the SF-neophytes. Despite months – and in some cases almost two years – of arduous training, including successful completion of the grueling hell that is Assessment and Selection; the development of essential combat skills under difficult conditions in Phase I; the honing of expertise in a combat specialty in Phase II; and finally the successful completion of true Unconventional Warfare skills in Phase III, it should come as no surprise that quite a number of SF candidates failed to successfully perform to the standards of Robin Sage.

Post 9-11, the training is even more daunting, including nineteen long days of SERE School. Short for *Survival, Evasion, Resistance and Escape*, this is the cruelest of all military training. In short, it is prisoner-of-war survival. The trainees are dropped into a hostile environment completely controlled by some of the most vicious instructors in the world. Their first task is to evade capture under almost impossible circumstances. That is the survival and evasion part. But these are young Green Berets, and some surprisingly do succeed in not being caught. That does not get them out of the next portion of the school, however. Whether captured or not, at a certain point everyone ends up in the prisoner-of-war phase, called Detention. This next experience is euphemistically referred to as IR or interrogation resistance. In essence, it is a gutcheck to see how well you hold up under torture, and most in the civilian world would be astounded at the physical and psychological abuse heaped on these young men.

For those who survive the almost three weeks of hell that is SERE, there is still much more to go. Language training is interwoven throughout the *pipeline*, as it is called, and varies in length depending upon the languages being learned. As before, the entire SF training program culminates with the Robin Sage Exercise, or what is now officially called the Unconventional Warfare Culmination Exercise or UW CULEX. However, during Robin Sage, today's Green Beret hopefuls may find themselves in places other than Ft. Bragg, attempting to deal with real world scenarios that require their immersion into a foreign culture and the demands of their foreign language proficiency, rather than being afforded the luxury of conducting their operations and conversations in English. This requires them to completely indulge their communications ability and their culture-awareness skills. According to the current command sergeant major of the SF training program, today's Green Berets are getting much more training, under more difficult conditions, than those of my generation.

It is only at this point - and after receiving the nod from the Special Forces command - that a soldier is officially graduated from Special Forces training, receives his beret, SF tab, and Group flash,[22] and is assigned to one of the five operational "Groups" that comprise all Special Forces. The current active duty Groups are the 1st, 3rd, 5th, 7th and 10th. In addition, there are two National Guard SF Groups, the 19th and the 20th. Even then the training is not over. The young, "new-to-Group"[23] Green Berets are viewed by their veteran counterparts as having merely passed the minimum threshold requirements to prove that they are ready to start learning. This is not unlike the martial arts mentality, where first degree black belts are seen as those who have been training long enough that they are finally ready to start being taught some real skills.

Service in a Special Forces Group is a never-ending process of training, new skills acquisition, old skills retention, and self-improvement. From this point forward each of the new Green Berets will never stop working. They will be sent to other military training schools to develop and hone additional combat techniques such as sniper skills,

---

22 A flash is the patch worn on the front of the beret, immediately over the left eye. Each Group has a different, and distinctive, flash identifying the unit to which any Special Forces soldier is assigned.
23 In SF, when you are assigned to a unit or Team, it is referred to as being "in Group."

rappelling, Air Assault from helicopters, and Pathfinders.[24] They will undergo critical skills training in both military schools and through outside civilian instructors, in such disciplines as hand-to-hand combat, tracking, knife fighting, and close quarters combat firearms.

The best of them will be sent to the highly specialized training schools that qualify them for placement on the HALO and Scuba Teams, the elite of the elite. HALO Teams[25] are the units that specialize in covert insertions from aircraft flying as high as eight miles above the ground. These Teams are able to leave an aircraft at altitude, flying their bodies more than 50 miles behind enemy lines with no radar signature or detection as to their presence. The Scuba Teams undergo a grueling four week and four day school on Fleming Key, just north across an isthmus from Key West, Florida, that is designed to give them the waterborne operational capabilities of Navy SEALs.In addition to these critical combat skills, they may receive etiquette training, VIP or bodyguard instruction, air combat liaison indoctrination, mountain climbing training, and more. Through it all, they are required to maintain their high level of physical conditioning by running, heavy rucksack forced marches (called "rucking" or "humping"), weight training and calisthenics. In the midst of the daily preservation of these skills they somehow manage to squeeze in their regular jobs with their units, which typically take up an additional eight hours a day, five days a week.

INDOCTRINATION INTO THE GREEN BERET CODE

Since the start of America's War on Terror, demands for Special Forces operations, and Special Forces soldiers, have been accelerating. This saw the resurrection of a Vietnam-era program for the manufacturing of Green Berets, in which new recruits were carefully vetted and then slotted into an SF training program from the moment they enlisted.

---

[24] Pathfinders is a course that trains soldiers to jump into hostile territory to set up drop zones and helicopter landing zones for the insertion of larger elements.
[25] Really HALO/HAHO for High Altitude Low Opening and High Altitude High Opening.

Now called the 18 X-Ray Program, new, hopeful Green Berets are in a specialized program from their first day in the Army. They go from one mandatory training school to the next, until they have graduated all phases of the Q Course. With necessary breaks between training schools and phases, depending on a trainee's SF MOS this can mean anywhere from one to two full years of training, starting with Basic Training and Advanced Individual Training (AIT), until awarded the cherished beret.

During this long process of grueling physical and academic demands, skills development, and constant performance evaluations, each soldier is molded into the Green Beret philosophy and mentality. Like a lawyer who must be able to tolerate the stresses of zealously representing one guilty of a heinous crime, or a doctor being capable of dealing easily with the sight of blood and gore, a true Green Beret must adopt the right mentality and be able to function with it. The months-long training process is forever reinforcing elements of the Green Beret Code.[26] The indoctrination of young Green Berets into this Code will continue to be enforced, lived by, and exhaustively referenced, throughout their time in Group. The Special Forces has a long tradition of oral history being passed down from Group to Group, Team to Team, and Green Beret to Green Beret. The retelling of stories of missions, failures, techniques, enemy tactics, outlandish behavior, and lessons learned from all of it, is not unlike the oral histories of our own Native Americans. These campfire and barroom sessions are not told for pure enjoyment. Word-of-mouth tales remind them of the courage and bravery of the generations of Green Berets that came before them, and of the lessons that SF has learned through its decades of unconventional warfare. It is also their way of honoring all who sacrificed to give them those lessons.

As I continue to serve as a Special Forces firearms and hand-to-hand combat instructor, it is interesting for me to hear the young men of SF today telling of the exploits of my Teams and contemporaries from Vietnam and years since, as though they are now completed

[26] See Chapter Eleven, Special Forces Code

legends. They tell them with awe-filled wonderment of whether they could possibly be true. They tell them just as my generation of SF soldiers recounted the tales of those who came before us from Korea and World War II, as well as the earlier years of Vietnam; like young boys imagining great battles with dragons, and then musing over whether they really could have happened.

A NATION WITH AMNESIA

The civilian world could benefit greatly from this oral tradition. Too many Americans think the luxury-ridden lives they lead exist in a temporal vacuum. They live as though their families have no history, that there is nothing outside of their cushy existences, and that they were born into such leisure as a matter of right. These folks never stop to think that the life they lead was born of the actions, hard work, sacrifices and risks of those who came before them. Too many American families have long since stopped telling the stories of their own ancestors, of the courage that got them where they are today.

John taught college for several years and was amazed that the young adults in his class had little to no knowledge of the lineage or history of their own families. They didn't have a clue where their families came from, and no knowledge of when they immigrated to America, or who among them made the courageous decision to make that trip, to take so great a risk for their loved ones. Of the students whose grandfathers had fought in World War II and Korea, they knew nothing. Of those whose fathers had fought in Vietnam, they often didn't know what branch of the service they had been in, much less what unit, what battles they had fought, or what all those medals tucked away in shoeboxes beneath beds were for.

To live like this is a mistake. We are all Americans, and seeing ourselves in such a nationalistic context is virtually unprecedented in the world. Lieutenant Colonel Joseph Ruffini (ret.) tells the story of sitting around a campfire in a forest in West Germany during the Cold War. He was commanding a tank battalion during joint Allied

War Games, preparing to defend the Fulda Gap from Soviet and East German invasion. As he was passing the time late one night with his counterpart from the West German Army, they were discussing the national and ethnic identities of people throughout the world. His German colleague observed that when asked what they are or where they're from, only people from the United States respond automatically that they "are American." He said that this was not true for any other nation. He explained to Col. Ruffini that when you ask people from the United Kingdom what they are, they respond that they are Scottish, or Welsh, or from London or Northern Ireland, or are Jordies. The same is true of people from Spain, Germany, Russia and every other country. People from all over the world see themselves first as a member of a clan or tribe, or from a region identified by ethnicity. Only Americans see themselves as Americans first. This is one of the things that made our nation the best in the history of the world.

In almost all cases, being an American means that your family came from someplace else. The convergence of the strengths of so many cultures, histories, languages, religions, cuisines, skills and trades, and value systems into one amalgamated society called "America" is what puts us head and shoulders above every other country. To forget your heritage is to deny America the strength of what your family brought here, and what it gave to our country. Just as the men of a Special Forces Team recognize that their true value is as one part of the overall machinery that is the Team, so must we as American citizens see ourselves. We must realize that the qualities that our forebears brought, are each merely single cogs among many, that make up the great machine that is America.

We can never believe that where we came from is more important than our American-ness, as has become popular in recent decades. In years past, the immigrants arriving in the United States wanted nothing more than to "be American." They were no longer Irish, Italian, German, Polish, Russian or Swedish. They wanted to learn English and insisted that their children learn the language, and every other aspect of American culture, as quickly as possible.

They wanted their children to come home from school and teach them about being American. After all, their desire to assimilate into American society was why they came here. In seeking to immerse themselves into American society, they adopted the motto *E. Pluribus Unum*: From the many, the one.

ASK NOT WHAT YOU CAN
DO FOR AMERICA

Today, immigrants in America seem more set on only retaining the identity of the nation they came here from, than incorporating themselves into American society. We are expected to teach them in their native language, to communicate with and entertain them in a language other than that of the nation that has allowed them the opportunity of a better life. They want to fly the flag of their native land, celebrate its holidays, retain dual citizenship, and demand special legal privileges because of the minority status this gives them. While this may further their own short term selfish interests, it does little to truly benefit them, or America, in the long term. For America to continue to grow and be strong, she requires the donation and complete incorporation of the qualities and strengths of the people who have come to her. This cannot happen if immigrants are holding back and demanding America serve them, rather than they serve her with their gifts. America needs her immigrants and their gifts, more today than ever before.

As a microcosm of America, the Special Forces is the only American military unit that was largely begun with, and for, foreign nationals. When Special Forces was founded in 1952 its purpose was to infiltrate behind the lines of hostile nations, link up with indigenous guerilla forces, and fight the enemy regime. The men of SF had to be able to understand and communicate with the populace of any country. They had to be able to speak the language, know the customs, and even pass themselves off as locals. They had to understand the issues, conflicts and politics of that country, from the national level down to the feuds of clans and families. This could only be accomplished by accepting many foreign nationals (known as DPs for Displaced Persons) into SF under the promise of quick citizenship for their service, and the chance to kill Communists.

Just like America, Special Forces was strengthened because of the membership of these men from countries the world over. The contributions of the DP's would have been reduced had they lost sight of who they were, where they had come from, and why they were in the Special Forces, and America. What value would they have been if they were allowed to forget their native language? Then again, what value would they have had for SF and America, had they never learned English? This is the dilemma America faces today with all of her citizens.

SERVING AMERICA

In the increasingly global nature of business and geo-politics, America also needs citizens who can serve her in dealings with foreign nations, and increasingly with non-state foreign groups (terrorists) that are threats to her. Every other country in the world is either an enemy of America, or a potential enemy. You don't have to look too far back in history to see that relations among nations are fleeting. Virtually all of the countries that were our enemies 50 to 60 years ago are now our friends, and vice versa. In the first half of the 20th century Germany, Italy and Japan started as our enemies, but now are allies. The Soviet Union was our ally, then quickly became our longest-term enemy, as was true for such other nations as Poland, Romania and Bulgaria. China was our ally, but now is a threat to the Free World.

Today, Russia is less the enemy that she was, though relations for the future are tenuous at best. Poland, Hungary, Bulgaria, Ukraine, Estonia, Lithuania and Latvia are allies, as are a number of other former Soviet Republics. The lesson is: Only Americans will always be there to stand for America. In order to do that, they must be American. Indeed, they can, and should, be proud of their heritage and the contributions of that heritage, but there can be no divided loyalties. There can never be any doubt that our citizens' duty, devotion and allegiance is to America. Without the guarantee of that commitment, our nation cannot survive. Though the people of America are the greatest resource in the world, and certainly the greatest asset of our nation, if she cannot depend on her people, she is irrevocably lost.

These are the legacies and traditions that every Green Beret carries with him. He proudly wears the mantle of his membership in the elite society of Special Forces and the entire history of that group. Just as proudly, he wears the honor of his family and its history, and their contribution to America. Finally, each Green Beret is an American, and nothing means more to him. He wears all of these on his sleeve, just as if they were visible among the many stripes; unit patches; SF, Ranger and Airborne tabs; and hash marks. To him, they are there every time he looks at himself in his uniform. This is what every American citizen – civilian and military alike – should see when looking in the mirror: the badges of an American.

John Anderson takes a break during a recon operation.
Green Berets may rest, but they never quit!

— 2 —

THE CHARACTER OF THE GREEN BERET

…Men who mean just what they say,
The brave men of the Green Beret.

DISCIPLINE IN YOUR LIFE

Once the honest, hard working, disciplined and physically fit recruits have been forged into the mentality of the Green Beret, they become men of inestimable character. Though honesty and integrity can be found in many people, and among a number of professions, few combine those qualities with the physical and mental bravery required to do the job of a premier soldier. Courage is ultimately the badge of the Green Beret. His honor is derived from the knowledge that he will risk his life by going into harm's way, not only for his country, but for anyone in trouble. Just as the song says, "Courage take, from the green beret."

In an effort at some emulation of this, it has become popular in America for people to incessantly prattle on and on about how some type of therapy, or some book, or TV talk show host, has made them "feel empowered" to deal with whatever aspects of their lives were intimidating them. Quite honestly, this is bullshit. The notion that someone suddenly *feels empowered* is a complete fiction of personal conviction. In fact it is not conviction at all. No one who is truly confident feels the need to tell others. Insisting that you are empowered is the first sign that you are not. It is impossible for you to be inspired to true courage by a 30-minute daytime TV show, or some other intimidated person's written words, or some psychologist who never performed a brave act in his life.

Moreover, if someone needs to "feel empowered" to deal with some intimidating issue in his life, then he is not ever going to be able to consistently deal with intimidating issues. If you have to feel empowered to do the tough thing, the brave thing, then you are *never* going to be someone who *does* that brave thing when necessary. The things in life that frighten or intimidate most of us are usually nothing more than some loudmouth; an overbearing boss at work; an older sibling, no matter how old we are; a bully at school as a kid; or an argumentative jerk frequently encountered in social circles. When we encounter them, it's usually unexpected, catching us off guard and dissolving our resolve. One of my favorite sayings to come out of Special Forces is:

> *Discipline can be a constant in your life,*
> *whereas courage can never be.*
> *Discipline will get you through the times*
> *when your courage fails.*

Real courage is driven by a sense of bravery that comes from within. But these nuevo-feelings of "empowerment" are merely artifices of confidence designed to convince us that maybe, just maybe, we can handle our own lives. Whether truly felt, or the contrivance of some "empowering" external source, they are transitory. This kind of confidence can be felt profoundly, right up until the threat that had us seeking empowerment confronts us. But disciplining yourself to do the necessary thing each time you face threats will see you through every time. You do not have to have confidence to enter a fight. However, you must have the discipline to enter the fight and fight your hardest, all the way to the end.

Green Berets are seen by others as almost dripping with confidence. While they are, in fact, highly confident men, it is a confidence born of experiences that have taught them that no matter how scared they may be - however unsure of themselves - to trust and follow their training. Experiences in combat, and out, have taught them that to rely on their training, to do their best, to fight their hardest, will always see them through. If it happens to fail, they will die honorably and nobly. For them, this is hardly the worst of the many possible outcomes they face.

For the Green Berets, it comes down to the rational acceptance that sometimes they are scared. But courage is not the absence of fear, it is what you do despite your fear. As author John Eldredge writes, "What makes Maximus or William Wallace so heroic is simply this: They are willing to die to set others free."[27] This is a lesson all of America needs to learn. My good friend, Green Beret Drew Dix, was awarded the Congressional Medal of Honor for numerous trips he made into the town of Chau Doc during the 1968 Tet Offensive in Vietnam. With nothing more than jeeps and light arms, he made trip after trip into the city with a tiny, *ad hoc* fighting force to rescue everyone from an American nurse to the Chief of Police of the city, his wife and children, and many others. He did this in the midst of swarms of VC and NVA soldiers. Despite the indescribable courage demonstrated by Drew on that day, and many others during his years with Special Forces, he told me that he would never criticize another man for being scared to death in combat, saying: "Because I know exactly what that level of fear is like." You see, Drew didn't receive the nation's highest award for valor because he lacked fear. He received it for what he did despite the almost overwhelming fear he must have felt, and despite the fact that the chances of him surviving were virtually non-existent.

[27] John Eldredge, *Wild At Heart: Discovering the Secret of a Man's Soul*, (Nelson Books, Nashville, Tennessee, 2001), 186.

NOTHING TO FEAR, BUT FAILURE TO ACT

This is another of the ways that Green Berets are often differentiated from the regular citizenry. In their line of work, they are not afforded the luxury of acting on their fears. When confronting fear, they do not get to go on *Oprah* or *Dr. Phil* and have their talk show host-protectors confront their nemesis with them, or for them. They don't get to stay home from school, feign illness to avoid a confrontation at work, drop out of college and run home to Mommy and Daddy, or simply have a nervous breakdown, thereby avoiding life's problems. When afraid, the only choice of the Green Beret is simple: pull the straining straps of an overloaded rucksack over his shoulders, pick up a rifle, and go into harm's way. They are no less afraid than every other American, and given the nature of the threats they face, they may very well be more afraid. They just don't get to wallow in their self-pity. They don't get to indulge their fear. They are the last line of defense protecting us, so that we can live weak and self-indulgent lives. That is the character of the Green Beret, and as I enter the latter years of my life I am humbled that our nation continues to produce such men.

Our Special Forces soldiers face these fears every day. Fears for themselves, and their families. Fears that others need never concern themselves with. This is something shared by America's law enforcement officers. As Hans Halberstadt explains, "These people know that they are targets of assassination."[28] One of the most unique aspects of their many activities, thus, is the need for complete secrecy in all that they do.[29] Our police – especially SWAT operators who, in a very real way, are America's domestic special forces – face the same threats to themselves and their families everyday, and these threats will only increase as America's War on Terror continues. Neither the men of SF, nor police departments, are afforded the opportunity to

28 Halberstadt, 15.
29 Ibid.

lean on a host of other people. They don't get the luxury of sharing what they do with others. They do what all of us need to learn to do in life when things get tough, when our problems are at their worst: Stand up, ruck up, and move out. Out west we call this "Cowboying Up," and it's a part of our American heritage everyone would do well to reclaim.

DAMN THE TORPEDOES

The term "self-responsibility" gets used a lot, but I have never seen much evidence that it exists. If it exists at all it is not to be found in many people. The litigation explosion bears testimony to this fact. In decades past, there were very few lawsuits. As recently as the 1970s, an oft-heard refrain from Americans to unwarranted complaints was, "So, sue me." So, Americans did, and in record numbers. Today, the number of lawsuits – and the occurrences over which we invest years of valuable time and untold amounts of money in litigation – are outrageous and an inexcusable waste of U.S. resources. Anytime someone files a lawsuit that is not absolutely necessary, he is saying: "I had a right to a perfect life, free of unpleasant experiences and feelings. Something happened that denied me that perfect life, and I accept no responsibility for that which has happened in my own life. So some other person should pay me a lot of money."

You need only look at the annual list of the most ridiculous jury verdicts to see the degree to which this cancer has taken firm hold on our culture, and managed to metastasize throughout our people. Yearly, I read of enormous jury verdicts for burglars who were injured by dangerous conditions on the property being broken into, of rapists recovering monetary damages for injuries inflicted by their victims, and of carjackers being given money for injuries that they sustained in the vehicles they stole. Not only do these people not live the Green Beret Lifestyle, but neither they, nor the lawyers, experts and juries who are assisting them, live their lives with any measure of honor or decency.

These are the products of what has become a sick culture, believing that becoming rich in any way possible justifies the means by which it was achieved. Evidence of this is seen in every overblown jury verdict for practically any injury, physical or emotional, real or imagined. It is as though Americans are getting on juries wanting to outdo – or not be outdone by – the other juries that are giving millions of dollars to any plaintiff that files a lawsuit. In this way, we have created a nation of contrived victims and creative liars, to whom our legal system gives no incentive whatsoever to get better. The longer you claim physical injuries and their attendant pain, as well as emotional and psychological harm, the more money you get. It is a simple formula that creates obvious scams. Who shows up in court years after the incident that incited the litigation, and says, "Oh, by the way, I got over this a long time ago, I can walk fine now, and the nightmares went away a year ago?" The answer is: No one.

Our once proud justice system, is now merely an administrative process in which integrity is not only absent, but punished. In order to have a chance at winning, you must exaggerate, fabricate evidence, perjure yourself, and solicit experts who prostitute themselves to validate your lies. Do not think that there is one side of this more moral than the other, as it is to be found consistently on both sides of any legal action, and in both civil and criminal proceedings. All of society enables this behavior. And why is this? Because America has long since ceased to teach, motivate, and honor integrity. At best, we pay lip service to the high regard with which we value honesty; right before we go back to prevaricating and advocating the version of events that casts us in the light most favorable to us winning.

You would be hard-pressed to find a Green Beret willingly participating in such moral travesties. Ask all the lawyers, police or judges you know: how many times have they seen a Special Forces soldier involved in any such judicial sleight-of-hand? How many times has anyone ever seen a man in uniform in a court of law; one with rows of ribbons and silver jump wings on his chest, gleaming jump boots, the crossed arrows of the Special Forces on his collar, and a folded green beret in his hand? It is rarely seen, and if seen at all, I can guarantee you it is not because that man decided to exploit the legal system as his own personal lottery, trying to win a million dollars he hadn't worked for.

The men of the Special Forces live by an entirely different set of standards; standards that far surpass those found in civilian America today. As men of courage they - all too often – do not hesitate to make statements adverse to their own interests. If they do something wrong, they admit it quickly. They do not attempt to excuse their behavior, or spread the blame around. They admit their wrong-doing and face the consequences.

It is not as though Green Berets are perfect, and can't get themselves into trouble now and again. We have created the bravest, best trained commandos in the world, and throw them into death defying situations time and again. We make them face the worst horrors of war. Then we bring them home to spend their days jumping out of airplanes seven miles in the air, shooting and running in close-quarters live-fire exercises, scuba diving and mountain climbing, and then expect them to sit home and play video games every night.

Famed author Robin Moore - and the only civilian journalist to ever undergo the Q Course - was still running around with his beloved Green Berets in Afghanistan while in his 70s. In addressing this very issue, he wrote:

> I knew that the men were obligated to obey General Order Number One in Afghanistan, which was a terrible tradition started back in Desert Storm: a ban on drinking alcoholic beverages in defined areas of a war zone. The same thing had been done in the Balkans, and now it had become institutionalized practice, particularly in Muslim nations. It seemed odd to me that

those willing to die couldn't be trusted with an occa-
sional "cold one."

I soon found out it was all hogwash. General Order
Number One in Afghanistan meant as much as [similar
orders] in Vietnam, and El Salvador, and Somalia, and
everywhere else the Green Berets had fought and died.
The simple fact was that the Green Berets would fight
and party hard, no matter where they were, and one
hundred General Orders would not get in the way of
either endeavor.[30]

The truth is that Green Berets are young, tough, fit and proud men,
and at times that can be an unfortunate recipe. On the rare occasion that life's events, and their own decisions, result in a Green Beret
being in trouble, he will be the first to own up to what he did. He'll
admit his wrongdoing and face the consequences of his actions
without excuse.

As observed by Robin Moore, there are times when a Green
Beret might decide that it would be wrong for him to follow an established rule or regulation. He doesn't attempt to hide this ignoring or
flouting of "the law," he simply does it with full knowledge that there
may be consequences. Knowing just how regulation-obsessive the
regular Army could be, and how pedantic its officers often were, one
of the earlier unofficial criteria for acceptance onto a Team after the
Q Course was whether the candidate had at least a couple of Article
15's on his record. We realized that Special Forces troopers were supposed to be exactly that: "Special." In most instances the cloistering
and suffocating environment of the traditional military made SF
candidates claustrophobic. Special Forces soldiers needed to be independent thinkers and creative improvisers, not military automatons

---

[30] Robin Moore, *The Hunt for Bin Laden – Task Force Dagger: On the Ground with the Special Forces in Afghanistan*, (Ballantine Books, New York, 2003), xii.

who followed all rules and orders, regardless of the senseless nature of them.

We realized that in few cases could such men get through one or two tours in the Army without having run afoul of its highly structured, obsequiously obedient environment. In the years I was with SF, an Article 15 was an administrative, non-judicial punishment for an admitted wrongdoing.[31] Even today, when confronted with lower charges, a soldier can demand a full trial by court martial, or take the administrative punishment of a letter of reprimand by simply admitting what he did. For these reasons, we looked for such records that contained things that – to any other unit – would have been blemishes. However, to us they were badges of independent thinking, honesty and integrity.

We wanted men who weren't afraid to buck the system, particularly when they believed doing so was justified. Yet, at the same time, we sought those who made no excuses for their actions and didn't attempt to avoid punishment. We wanted men who willingly admitted what they had done, comfortable in their own hearts and minds with the reasons they acted as they did. This is part of the Green Beret Code.

As a Sergeant Major[32] commanding a company, I expected this level of integrity from all of the men under me, and from all men in Special Forces. When confronted with possible misfeasance on the part of one of my soldiers, I would have never considered the possibility I might get lied to. I respected this level of honesty and honor. But I still dealt with the violation. In most instances I would respect a soldier's honesty by dealing with things in a non-official – and certainly non-judicial – fashion. This might have meant a more serious outcome than an Article 15, and a more painful outcome than even a court martial. "Wall to wall counseling" was not unheard of, nor was it unfair. Nor did it ever result in charges being brought against me.

---

[31] Though non-judicial punishment previously, Article 15's are now misdemeanor criminal convictions.
[32] The second highest non-commissioned officer (NCO) rank in the Army, with the only higher rank being Command Sergeant Major.

My men had too much integrity. On the only occasion I was ever lied to, that man was sent packing to a leg[33] unit the next day.

This approach was exemplified by the best colonel I ever knew. Bo Baker was the overall community and SF commander at Bad Tolz, Germany, where 10th Special Forces Group always maintained a full battalion.[34] He was the ultimate leader, and would talk to you either as an officer to a lower ranking soldier in the Army's prescribed manner, or simply as one GI to another. The latter usually meant you were going to get your ass kicked by this six-feet-four-inch, 250 lb. commando. It was your choice. No one ever complained, nor did anyone ever think he had been treated inappropriately or inequitably. Col. Baker was a true leader, and set an example everyone else could only hope to follow.

No matter how much America changed over the quarter century of my military career, while in SF I was always living in an era when men dealt with things like real men. If a man was wrong he was wrong, and once made to realize it, he admitted it. If a man was wronged, he didn't run to the police, hire a lawyer or cry to his therapist. He simply found the wrongdoer and punched his lights out. If a real man, the wrongdoer admitted his error, shook hands, and everyone went on with their lives. What they didn't ever do was file criminal charges, sue their antagonist, and spend years of their lives tied together while untold amounts of money were funneled into lawyers' pockets over a simple incident that should have been quickly forgotten. Americans - particularly American men - have long ago lost this sense of honor in how they comport their lives. Fortunately, honor is still alive and well in the Special Forces.

RIGHTS VS. MORAL STANDARDS

However, this level of personal honor can sometimes have greater consequences than the simple admission of guilt or fault. Things are

---

33 The term "leg" or "straight leg" is a somewhat derogatory reference to any non-Airborne qualified military personnel. The term comes from the fact that when in a Special Forces, Ranger or Airborne unit, you wear jump boots with your uniform pants tucked – or bloused – into the boots. This is done even in dress uniform, whereas all other units wear low quarter shoes with "straight" pants legs.

34 Today, the base at Bad Tolz has been closed, and 10th Group's battalion operates out of Stuttgart.

easy when men of honor are accused of a wrongful act which they committed. In those instances they don't make excuses or "throw themselves on the mercy of the court." They would be sickened at the thought someone would feel sorry for them, and would shoot themselves before asking someone to do so. They just admit their wrongdoing and stand tall before whatever authority they must face with pride, prepared to suffer whatever consequences come. Knowing that they can endure the worst a vile and vicious enemy can do to them, they have no concerns about their ability to successfully deal with the worst anyone else can mete out.

But when Green Berets believe they did the right thing, that an accusation against them is unjust, they become the proverbial immovable object. Under these circumstances, they are the last people to ever concede, or apologize, for doing what was right or necessary. Should criminal proceedings be instituted they are the last men to seek a plea bargain, and are the first to reject one from a prosecutor, whether civilian or military. To them, a prosecutor who files charges against them, and then offers to reduce those charges in order to avoid the work and risk of losing at trial, is a person without honor. And they will never subordinate themselves to such a pathetic figure.

In such circumstances, Green Berets will demand a trial; they will demand that their accusers face them in court. In effect, to anyone who attacks them in this fashion they will say: "Damn the torpedoes, damn the consequences. If they want to find me guilty and wrong, then I will pay the price, but I will not dishonor myself or the Special Forces by saying I did something wrong when I did not." This was the very moral conflict between a slick talking, deal-making lawyer played by Tom Cruise, and his clients, in the hit movie *A Few Good Men*. By taking that position, two young Marines not only maintained their integrity and honor, but taught what those words meant to their officer-lawyer. Though Marines in that movie, the defendants were living as Green Berets.

Rights mean nothing to the men of Special Forces, especially when the assertion of rights conflicts with their own moral standards or code. We have a lot of rights in America. Among others we have the right to free speech, right of privacy, and the right to never self-incriminate. One of our problems with all of these rights is that we think having them means we need to exercise them all of the time. Though no one will ever take away your right to free speech, how often is what's said of any value? How often is what we have to say publicly better than the silence everyone would have enjoyed but for our insistence on cramming our verbal rights down everyone's throat? We suffer an even greater problem with an unregulated news media, accountable to no one, exploiting the rights it has been given, virtually free to defame noble people with no responsibility.

What is missing in the laundry list of rights all Americans – and others who just happen to find themselves in our country – have, is any kind of moral standard by which we should guide the exercise of those rights. After the Constitution had been ratified in 1787, Thomas Jefferson realized the unprecedented freedoms the citizenry had just been handed. He said, "The success of America will depend upon the morality of the people." Sadly, many Americans have long since lost sight of the morality with which we all need to govern our lives. As for the Green Berets, they care nothing of their rights. In joining the military they voluntarily sacrifice many of the rights of ordinary citizens. In joining the Special Forces they determine that their own moral code and the Code of their unit supersede any rights that they may have, inalienable or otherwise. That is why their reputation precedes them throughout the world.

Many detractors of our military – and especially those who find fault with our Special Forces – propagandize that since these men have no fear of death, they have no reason to follow the law, to behave morally or impose any limitations on themselves. These weak-hearted critics fear that men who regularly brave certain death will amorally try to get away with anything. But that is neither the truth, nor the Code by which they live. To the Special Forces, comfort with facing death does not give them the freedom to do things they know

THE CHARACTER OF A GREEN BERET

are wrong, but to always do what is right with a complete disregard for the consequences. And doing the right thing in tough circumstances often comes with a price.

WHO DARES WINS

To be able to live this way, you must be unafraid of the challenges and consequences life brings. We are all going to end up the same in the end: dead. *How* we live is all that really matters, and the legacy of the lives we lived is all that we, both, leave behind and take with us. John and I have always philosophized that *this is life, and none of us are getting out of here alive; and for most of us death will come long before we're prepared for it.* In recognizing this ultimate reality, the only thing that we should truly be afraid of is bringing dishonor to ourselves, our families and our friends. We must live honestly, with integrity, and with a strong personal moral code.

John once shared with me his anticipation of the day a doctor sadly notifies him that he has a terminal illness. When that happens, he wants to get up with a smile, pat him on the shoulder and say, "Doc, don't let this ruin your day. It's really no big deal, I've been ready for this my whole life." As for me, I've lived a long and adventurous life. I've gotten to truly live, to do the things that others go to the movies to be able to touch ever so tenuously. I have seen a lot of people die and have been around every religion on the planet. Recognizing that they can't all be right in explaining God or gods, or what happens when we die, I can honestly say that I'm looking forward to the ride. Whatever is out there, there are a lot of questions I'll want answered when I arrive.

England's version of the Green Berets is the Special Air Service (SAS). Their motto says it all: "Who Dares Wins." To steal a line from contemporary philosopher Richard Bach, "It is always easy to choose a traditional and safe life."[35] It is only those who risk mightily, who perhaps fail but get up again, always returning to the struggle,

---

[35] Richard Bach, *Messiah's Handbook: Reminders for the Advanced Soul,* (Hampton Roads Publishing Company, Inc., Charlottesville, VA, 2004), no page number.

who are the ultimate winners. President Theodore Roosevelt, whose own life screamed "warrior" in every respect, famously put these sentiments to words that resound in their call to every American:

> *It is not the critic who counts, not the man who points out how the strong man stumbles, or where the doer of deeds could have done them better. The credit belongs to the man in the arena, whose face is marred by dust and sweat and blood, who strives valiantly ... who knows the great enthusiasms, the great devotions; who spends himself in a worthy cause; who at the best knows in the end the triumph of high achievement, and who at the worst, if he fails, at least fails while daring greatly, so that his place shall never be with those cold and timid souls who have never known neither victory nor defeat.*

Others may not understand. In living according to your own personal code - and being not afraid to dare - you may make moral decisions that others will question, or outright hate you for. This happens most often when making tough decisions in difficult circumstances. People you thought were friends may abandon you. Others may despise you. If you don't believe me, try taking a position on any matter that draws adverse news media attention. With your reputation being attacked publicly, see how many invitations you get to parties or Sunday brunches.

But your supposed friends are merely weak, and the rest are afraid of your strength of character and willingness to risk the ridicule or rejection of strangers in order to walk the path that you know to be the right one. They know they would never have the strength or courage to do the same. This, alone, frightens them. If you are true to yourself, when you dare you will ultimately win.

Consider just a few examples from our recent history in which men and women lived their lives according to Green Beret principles. In each case, they did the thing they thought was right and necessary, making no apologies and prepared to suffer the consequences.

In 1988 Marine Lt. Col. Oliver North unwaveringly defended his actions as necessary and appropriate for the national security of our country, and in order to affect the rescue of her citizens who had been taken hostage. Congress had ordered certain things not be done, but he and his president only cared that American lives hung in the balance. When drug before the very Congress that was so willing to see America weaken herself before terrorists, he answered in a straight and forthright manner. Those arrayed against him attempted to destroy both his life and his marriage, as well as the personal life of his young and beautiful assistant, Fawn Hall. She was offered special treatment if she testified against her boss. When they could get nowhere in those efforts, detractors attempted to destroy both of their reputations by accusing them of having an affair. They had not, and their strength of character saw them through a horrible ordeal. Today, Oliver North is a popular author, war correspondent and respected expert on many military and national security matters. Miss Hall returned to her former quiet life.

When Gerald R. Ford ascended to the presidency in 1974, one of his first acts was to pardon Richard Nixon. This decision immediately drew the outrage of many Americans, including much of the press. He was vilified, assailed and accused of being part of the overall Watergate conspiracy. In response, President Ford looked America in the eye and said that he had done this because he believed it necessary in the best interests of the country. He made no excuses and offered no other explanation. Upon his recent death, he is viewed as one of the greatest men of that era, a true patriot who came along at a desperate time in America's evolution and unified the country.

Even Muhammed Ali lived according to this Code. In 1966, when he was subject to induction into the Armed Forces of the United States, he objected on religious grounds. He did not run to Canada in a reckless act of cowardly abandon, as so many thousands of others did before and after him. He stood his ground, looked his accusers in the eye and said, "What I am doing is right, and I will not yield, but will stay here and face whatever the consequences of my decision might be." Those consequences were a criminal conviction on June 20, 1967 and assessed prison term, plus being stripped of the heavyweight boxing title and not being allowed to fight for three years, before being exonerated by the U.S. Supreme Court in 1971. Though I could not have disagreed more with the choice he made, I had to respect the way he stood ready to suffer the consequences of doing what he believed was right. That is the Code.

Whether a Green Beret or an average American citizen, living according to these principles is never easy. However, it can be done by everyone. It is, first, a matter of dedicating yourself to a code of conduct and honor. Next, you must make sure to live according to that code, with every small and seemingly insignificant decision you make and action you take. Finally, you must never deviate from it, and refuse to allow others to exploit your honor and integrity. John Wayne had a personal code by which he lived his life every day, and it came through in both his life and films. I have a wooden plaque with a part of that code in my firearms shop and rarely go a day without stopping to read his words: "I won't be wronged; I won't be insulted; I won't be laid a hand on. I don't do these things to other people, and I require the same of them." It was this code, this standard of irretrievable and uncompromising morality and courage, that made us all love him. Just as the Duke showed us time and again in his movies, the more times you are forced to make difficult but honorable decisions in life, the faster this will become a way of life.

THE SOLDIER

It is the Soldier, not the reporter,
Who has given us the freedom of the press;
It is the Soldier, not the poet,
Who has given us freedom of speech;
It is the Soldier, not the campus organizer,
Who has given us the freedom to demonstrate;
It is the Soldier, not the lawyer,
Who has given us the right to a free trial;
It is the Soldier who salutes the flag,
Serves under the flag,
Whose coffin is draped by the flag,
And who allows protestors to burn the flag.

Author Unknown

– PART 2 –

GREEN BERETS IN EVERYDAY LIFE

John Giduck on Russian Spetsnaz base, 2001.
Note the black eye courtesy of the Russian
special forces.

– 3 –

BUILDING THE GREEN BERET IN YOU

Favored are the warriors who fall in the just fight,
for they shall dwell forever,
in the undying glow of their own glory.

Winston Churchill

THE GREEN BERET IN EVERY MAN

To nurture the Green Beret in yourself, you must imagine who the best person you could be is. Imagine the absolute best version of the "you" that you are now, and then go be that person. If you're not who you want to be, but have met all other goals, your sights were set too low. Establish a set of standards for yourself and then stick to them, but first make sure those standards are high. Like SF soldiers who ultimately decide even that is not enough, and try out for the ultra-elite Delta Force. But improving yourself is important in every aspect of your life, and nothing is too trivial to improve on. If you drink too much, stop. If you're too uptight and need to relax and be human around your friends or employees, maybe you should start drinking if that's what it takes. Or start exercising, doing yoga or immerse yourself in a philosophy like Zen-Buddhism. There is no such thing as a morality police out there for you, no matter how hard some people try to fill that role. You have to be your own morality enforcer. Everyday you must evaluate your behavior against the code you have set for yourself. Become your own grader, just like those SF instructors at Selection: ever vigilant, always looking for a single transgression or failure, with which to dump you out of the program. That is the way of the Green Beret.

Regardless of the attributes you decide are good for you, some are universal. One is being respectful of women. As I examine typical male behavior today, I am struck by the limitlessness and unaccountability with which men comport themselves around ladies. It's clear that many men believe there are no rules restricting their conduct. When I see how they act, I am forced to conclude that women's liberation didn't liberate anyone, except males. They were liberated from being gentlemen; from curbing their language and profanity; from never telling dirty jokes around ladies; from picking women up for dates on time, and in clean vehicles; from holding doors for them; from paying for dates; and, from accepting responsibility for the safety of the woman they were with until she was seen safely through her door. I don't know what freedoms the women got, except to tolerate this inexcusable behavior.

FIRST, BE A MAN

If you are to live your life according to an honorable code, one any Green Beret would be proud to adopt for himself, you must evaluate your own social behavior. It's alright to be rough, crude and rude around other men. But when around women and children, you must demonstrate the highest standards of manhood. These are the same standards of professionalism and elite-ness you should exhibit in every other aspect of your lives. As John Wayne remarked in the movie *McLintock*: "You have to be a man first, before you're a *gentle-man*." There are far too many people in society who do not understand this, and far too few men who are willing to punch the lights out of some jerk whose behavior around women or children is beyond the pale. They are too afraid of being arrested, or sued, or even beaten up themselves to take a stand. Even when it's their own wives and children being abused by disgusting language or obscene behavior, these pseudo-men do nothing. They have never put themselves on the line enough in their lives to know that when you're in the right, you never lose. When you're in the right, the bruises don't hurt that much. In fact they become badges of courage.

This is seen all the time in corporate America. Males there think that because they make a lot of money, or are in positions of power, that they can get away with anything. They convince themselves that acting macho means speaking in the most inappropriate ways to women who have to work around them and can't just walk away, or tell them to shut their mouths. These putative-men continually use foul language and tell dirty jokes around the women they work with, and most likely the women in their social circles as well. There is no excuse for this. There is never an excuse for bad manners. Be like a Green Beret: address every woman as "ma'am" and every man as "sir," and you will automatically experience a sea change in your own behavior and attitude toward others. After all, it is difficult to be inappropriate to someone you are hanging a title of respect on in every sentence. Remember, there is nothing wrong with being the most gentlemanly man in a room.

As to these other poor excuses for manhood, they need to be taught what real power is. It doesn't matter how much money someone makes, how big his house and yacht are, or even how many of them he owns. Nor does it matter how many politicians or celebrities he hobnobs with; or that he may be one himself. Real power is knowing that you could take his life with your bare hands in less than a minute. Real power is knowing that you could take him out with a single bullet from a mile away. Real power is knowing that you could take him on face-to-face in front of a group of people, and make him piss his pants. Every once in a while, men like that – bullies - need to be reminded how powerful they are not. Not only are these oxygen thieves not powerful, but they're not even men.

The mark of a man is not someone unafraid. Everyone has fear. In Green Beret terms, a man is one who only ever allows the fear to creep up as high as his neck. If you ever let the fear get all the way to your head, then you are no longer thinking clearly and you're going to die. Or you're going to stab a friend in the back to save yourself, or take credit for something you don't deserve. You will mostly do these things when you are facing situations where great fear is a reasonable response; but not exclusively.

Doing anything unnatural like skydiving, rappelling, scuba diving, or mountain climbing is a good test of who will do well in combat, and who won't. That is one of the reasons why the Special Forces trains its soldiers in these skills. The same is true for dealing with your fear in all aspects of life and work. For those of you who are young and physically capable, but are wasting your time on the golf course, or watching others live their lives in the NFL, NHL, NBA or MLB, get off your sixes and get in the game. Test yourself, improve yourself; be a better doctor, lawyer, CPA, or business manager through your never-ending efforts to become a stronger and better person. Often this can be accomplished by pushing yourself to your limits and beyond in other pursuits. We can all continue to benefit from this effort. Several years ago, Russian special forces' top hand-to-hand combat instructor, Col. Mikhail Ryabko, told John that he had reached the point where there was nothing more he could teach John about fighting, but from then on he should work on making himself a better person.

Being a top operator in one area, does not necessarily give you the skills or intestinal fortitude to deal well with everything. Having conditioned yourself to excel in one field does not guarantee there will be total transfer of that ability to others. Ranger commander, Col. Dave Grossman tells of a young man he knew who was a Mixed Martial Arts (MMA) fighting champion. He had faced down the toughest men in matches that had virtually no rules and little safety equipment. Yet, when he was thrown into the stresses of something no more threatening than a law enforcement paintball training exercise, his psychological and physiological systems soared into a high red state. Simply put, he was scared.

Being one of the toughest hand-to-hand men in the country didn't help him when he was thrown into a medium of combat he was unfamiliar with – at first. Very quickly, however, his training, mental conditioning and courage born of those gruesome close-quarter experiences allowed him to accelerate beyond others who had been doing both paintball and Sims[36] ammunition exercises for years.

YOUR HIGHEST AND BEST USE

This is part of human nature that can be seen anywhere. Entrepreneurs, who build multi-million dollar companies in just a few years, do not always fare so well managing the huge organizations they created. What makes them great at the one, makes them poor performers at the other. Top athletes on one sports team sometimes have a difficult time adjusting to a new team when traded, even though they're still in the same sport. Trial lawyers often make poor contract attorneys, and vice versa. Heart and lung specialists would not be asked to take on a family medical practice. I have even seen housewives who were extremely popular with all of their neighbors and other parents, end up being pariahs when they moved to a completely different part of the country, with a different culture. In life, as in combat, all we can do is be as ready as possible for whatever we encounter.

The Russian special forces men assure us that there is only one guarantee in combat: something will happen, but it will not be exactly what you prepared for in training. In Special Forces we came to realize that skill level, discipline and fear control did not always transfer completely to other areas. Men who were scuba gods didn't always handle skydiving as well. Guys who became best friends fight-

---

[36] Simunition rounds are low impact bullets that law enforcement and military train with for combat reality. Duty weapons can be modified to shoot these painful, pellet-like projectiles.

ing in the fetid and steamy confines of the jungle wouldn't necessarily see that relationship being as deep when deployed to the desert. For these reasons, everyone must know his limitations and gauge them objectively against the challenges being faced, or the environment they are asked to function in. All of life, both civilian and military, operates on this same principal. But never forget that these prior experiences are never wasted, as the foundation of all that training and all that skill development will ultimately give you an advantage, in every one of life's endeavors.

WHEN THE STRONG ARE ALSO GENTLE

Although no one questions the masculinity of Special Forces, the depiction of them as mean and unapproachable is the worst of caricatures. You will find no greater gentleness than in those who are the strongest. This is one part of the Green Beret character that all men can adopt. I can remember needing to take my wife out one evening many years ago. I had been deployed – or traveling, in civilian-speak - a great deal, and she had been at home juggling all of our life duties, along with taking care of our five year-old daughter, Lisa. I pawned babysitting duties off onto several of the men on my Team, and went out for a nice evening. When we returned late that night, rather than finding a quiet house and a little girl sleeping softly in her bed, we walked into a virtual melee. There was Lisa, yelling at these rough, tough Green Berets, whom she had caught cheating her at the Hungry Hippo Game. It was not lost on me that three of the world's toughest, bravest and most deadly commandos were still so gentle as to be willing to spend their evening sitting on a floor, playing with a little girl; however poorly they were doing it.

But this is always the way with truly tough men. Despite the expectations of many that Green Berets must be mean and frightening – the kind of men who go through life with a scowl, staring others down – I have never lived that way. People are always surprised to find that I am a friendly and approachable person, always ready to treat everyone with respect and to sit and get to know them. John has similar experiences. In early 2007 he was speaking at a statewide school safety conference in Texas. Former Army Ranger Rod Hanks, a school security expert in Huntsville, had heard many people at the conference anticipate that with John's life experiences, he would be a dark, menacing person they would all have to tiptoe around. Mr. Hanks told them that what they would really confront was "the most polite, soft-spoken man they had ever met." When they disagreed, he replied: "This is a guy who has nothing to prove to anyone. He has no reason to act tough." Of course, upon spending several days with John they found that Ranger Hanks did understand men. He did understand warriors.

This is seen even at the top of the Special Forces pyramid. Mel Wick is an almost completed legend in the Special Operations community. After a lifetime in Army Special Forces, he was one of only a handful of founding cadre members of the world's most elite counter-terror unit, the Delta Force. Over sixteen years with that unit, he rose to the esteemed position of the Command Sergeant Major of the entire Delta Counter-Terror Group, known formally as 1st Special Forces Operational Detachment – Delta (1SFOD-D). That put Mel Wick at the top of the food chain among the best counter-terror and hostage-rescue operators the world has ever known, and stories about him have taken on near mythic proportions.

John has the privilege of working regularly with CSM Wick, providing training to America's warriors. Now recently retired from the Army, it is difficult for people to believe that he is among the most intense "kick-ass-and-take-names" soldiers of all elite units. Of average height and build, Mel is a soft-spoken, kind and thoughtful man. He trains his people with a quiet countenance, always suggesting, never ordering. He never screams or bullies his ideas onto others. If such men can find it in themselves to be gentle, polite and respectful toward others, then there is no excuse for the world's pretend-tough guys to behave to a lesser degree. Remember, there is never an excuse for bad manners, no matter who you are or what you're trying to prove.

DON'T HIDE

Many people are compulsive liars. They lie about whether they are busy rather than tell people who invited them somewhere they don't want to go; they dissemble when asked to tell someone the truth about something; and they engage in prevarication when caught underperforming at work. When they know they need to have an honest and forthright discussion with someone that is not going to be pleasant, they say anything and everything except what they need to, or at the very least they put it off for as long as they can. This is no way to live.

No one can be completely honest one hundred percent of the time. But, when you find yourself deviating from the truth, ask yourself why. If you are being dishonest on a small scale solely to prevent another from being hurt, and when doing so is in that person's best interest, you may be forgiven the transgression. For instance, when a soldier tells his buddy's wife or parents that he died quickly and painlessly in battle, when in fact he was shot to ribbons, and died agonizingly waiting for a medical evacuation helicopter that never came, he is only acting in their best interest. But if he tells that same tale, when in fact the team was ambushed as a result of his own screw up, then he is a fraud, only seeking to protect himself from the truth.

EXCUSES ARE LIKE....

One of the pillars of Green Beret-level inner strength and conviction is honesty. Even in situations where being honest may create more difficulties for you than an easy lie, you must be true to your integrity. In the military, when you mess up, or forget to perform a task, your only response is to admit the wrong, followed with: "I have no excuse, sir!" No one likes excuses. But they do respect those who refuse to even attempt to rationalize their own poor behavior. Rather than lie to yourself and others in your everyday life, own up to your mistakes and misdoings. Even if you have a good excuse, keep it to yourself, unless specifically asked for a reason by the person you owed a duty to. If you are ordinarily a person that would not do such a thing - even if it's just being late for a meeting - your past conduct and reputation will go far to mitigate any sanction against you. Your refusal to make excuses will go even further.

Once, when commanding security forces at a nuclear facility, a federal regulation was unintentionally violated that might have exposed my men to radiation. This drew the wrath of everyone from the top management to government officials, the union and lawyers. At a meeting to "investigate" this, I walked in and said it was all my responsibility and they could find no fault in anyone else. As so often happens when people are honest and accept full responsibility for their mistakes without excuse, they didn't know what to do. Their investigation had nowhere else to go, and all of the involved parties knew that I would never lie to them about anything.

MEETING ONE'S DUTY

Our addiction to being passively dishonest is seen in other ways too. In our overly-polite society it has become expected practice to lie to each other about most everything. We act as though we like people when we don't. We don't tell a friend when he's acting like an ass, even though as his friend it's our duty to say something. We don't confront others when they have wronged us. And even when those same people ask us why we seem to have withdrawn from them, we lie. We are afraid of telling people what we feel and letting them bear the burden of the consequences of their actions. We are afraid to let people feel the weight of our personalities and character. Sometimes we are just afraid to tell people the hard truth. Even when asked, we avoid conflict at seemingly any cost.

But when we confront the same behavior in others, we don't understand why they just aren't upfront with us. No one would want his doctor to lie to him about the seriousness of his condition. Sooner or later the reality is going to hit you, and you would have preferred to know early on. You do not want your lawyer to lie to you about how strong your case is. If you did something wrong, and should agree to a settlement, you are only hurt by a lawyer who won't tell you that. If you expect people who have no duty to you, beyond their professional relationship, to always tell you the absolute, unvarnished truth, you would never want anything different from a friend. Nor do your friends want something different from you. If they do, they are not friends. When you realize you need to have a tough conversation with someone, do it right away. Get it over with. These things only get harder with the passing of time. Col. Bo Baker would always say that dirty diapers only got stinkier with age.

If you are not going to be affirmatively honest with the people in your life, especially those who mean something to you and to whom you mean a great deal, what good are you? The people in our group at Archangel are friends as well as workmates. We depend on each other for everything, not the least of which is honesty. John and I, both, have been in situations where we had to tell friends – and sometimes each other – when it was time to stand down, when we were acting inappropriately. In our lives, if someone we have accepted as a friend tells us we are wrong about something, rather than get defensive or argumentative, our initial reaction is to assume that person is right. That's why he is in our lives; that's why we had enough respect and admiration to call him "friend" in the first place. When it comes to your own behavior, trust your friend's judgment over yours.

Years ago when I was a master sergeant and in charge of SF training in Kenya, I was being an excessive micro-manager and constantly correcting minor things my men were doing, without waiting for them to figure out what they had done and fix their own mistakes. Though I was the ranking person there, my men – being typical Green Berets, and with all due respect to my position and authority

– grabbed me and threw me in the river. They made their point, and I was man enough to immediately recognize that they were right, and I was wrong. Even though I wound up in the hospital due to the invasion of my body by various parasites in that filthy water, I never held it against them. After all, when you're wrong, you're wrong. And when you're wrong, you get what you deserve.

NO SUGARCOATING

Those who live the Code of the Green Beret do not euphemize. They never look to couch things in gentle or pretty language to make things easier on themselves. People who try to keep from telling you bad news, or giving you a straight story, are only protecting themselves, not you. Don't be that weak. When you do that, as Col. Grossman says, you are doing little more than pulling the white, fluffy blanket of denial over your head. As the song says, Green Berets are "men who mean just what they say." Dare to be such a person.

With warriors you never have to question where you stand. They will let you know. If they don't like you, they will never pretend that they do. They will not be gratuitously vicious, but will omit you from their lives. If for some reason you aren't sure and ask them, they will look you in the eye and tell you they don't like you. If you ask them why, they will tell you that too; in no uncertain terms. Once again, John Wayne set a standard for all of America. In *Chisum*, he was confronted by a power-mongering rancher looking to be king of the valley. When this antagonist asked John Wayne's character why he wouldn't have a drink with him, the Duke immediately replied: "I don't like you … We may have to be neighbors, but I don't have to be neighborly." I always say to people, "If you really want to know what I think, just give me a couple of beers." Of course, my teammates have long since caught on that this is only a device to get free beer, and that I never stop telling people the truth.

Consider how much simpler, straightforward and pure a life of honesty would be, than what you may be living now. If you feel lost or depressed in your marriage, sit down and talk to your spouse. Odds are she has been feeling the same way, and just didn't know how to bring it up to you. Even if she hasn't, at least the two of you won't be living a lie any longer. If your boss treats you in an insulting or demeaning fashion, sit him down and tell him that you're not going to put up with it. He may be your corporate superior, but he is not your superior as a human being. Being a Green Beret, however, means that you won't be more hurtful than necessary. It means never being gratuitously cruel.

Too often we don't do or say the tough thing with people because we're trying to suck up to those from whom we might be able to exploit some financial advantage or other benefit. If you do this, you are a whore. Even sadder is the fact that you are a whore whose life is not only full of pathetically demeaning behavior, but is also full of people that don't come up to your own low standards. Every single day, life is full of these challenges. The sooner you begin to live as a Green Beret, the sooner you will know that you are not hiding from who you are, but have seized control and are now actually *living* your own life with dignity. You will find a tremendous freedom in that; just ask anyone who has ever gone through the Twelve Steps of Alcoholics Anonymous. Finding people to whom you owe the truth, and telling them, is a wonderfully liberating act.

THE SKY IS FALLING

The other side of this epidemic of euphemizing in America is just the opposite: the need to exaggerate. Americans are imbued with a compulsion to use superlatives in their descriptions of everything. Phrases like *the greatest, the best, the worst, the most beautiful, ugliest, the most unbelievable thing I've ever seen in my life*, and so on, have become so much a part of our cultural lexicon that we're afraid people won't understand our experiences if we don't couch them in such terms. When was the last time someone simply observed that "it was raining," as opposed to "it's pouring," or "a deluge?" All snowstorms, no matter how light, are now blizzards and whiteouts. Being a little hungry is starving to death, cool weather is freezing to death, hot weather means you're dying from heat prostration, moderate winds are like tornados, and any burglary makes the homeowner feel like he was violated. Even a few mosquito bites are being bitten to death or, worse, eaten alive.

There is no room for this affliction of exaggeration in Special Forces. Green Berets must be able to accurately and objectively assess, and then relate, the true state of conditions. And they must be able to do this without a hint of exaggeration. Most of the minor unpleasantries in life that people think are so terrible, the Green Berets must ignore altogether. When surrounded by attacking forces, an A Detachment that is receiving "light fire" from the enemy must be able to accurately communicate that situation (called a SitRep for Situation Report) over the radio. To anyone who has never been in combat, "light fire" would make you feel like Custer in the first minutes at the Battle of the Little Big Horn. It would sound like a crescendo of bullets coming at you, thicker than hail with no end in sight. But they don't get to say, or even think, that.

When forced to endure extreme conditions, allowing them-selves to fall into the trap of exaggerating their situation could result in them feeling overwhelmed, then giving up and dying. If you're out in the ocean and missed your pickup, and have a twelve mile swim back in frigid waters, and you start exaggerating the temperature and its effects on you, you will not make it. This happened to a friend of mine, and he made the whole twelve miles back to shore. In such a situation you can't start telling yourself: "Oh my God, the water is unbelievably cold, people freeze to death in water this cold in twenty minutes!" You have to convince yourself that you can handle it, and will survive. You tell yourself that dolphins are warm-blooded mammals too, that need air to survive. If they can take the rough seas and cold, so can you. You become one with your environment and thereby survive it. But if you exaggerate it instead of minimizing it in your own mind, you're fish food. I never exaggerate. Years ago a young sergeant asked if I had ever been lost in the jungle. I answered, "No, but I was disoriented for three days once."

This tendency toward exaggeration is one of the major factors in the stress everyone thinks they deal with in their lives. Even as people relate the events or circumstances that cause them stress, they exaggerate them. The more they do this, the more convinced they become that things really are as bad as they said. This leads to them believing in, and reacting to, a correspondingly exaggerated stress level, causing them to feel even more stress. It becomes a self-regenerating cycle, and self-fulfilling prophecy.

Just as you couldn't tolerate your lawyer or doctor, plumber, electrician, or any employee, refusing to tell you the truth in lieu of some gentle euphemism, neither would it be appropriate for them to exaggerate a situation. After lab tests show you have a curable form of non-aggressive cancer, imagine a physician telling you that you only have three months to live. As a practicing attorney, John knew many lawyers who would exaggerate how bad a client's case was, just so they could look like heroes when they managed to win, or secure a favorable settlement.

It is no different in our personal lives. In order to live with the detached, existential calm of the Green Beret, you must stop this cycle of escalating exaggeration. When dealing with civilians I have learned one certain test that tells me when someone is about to exaggerate an event, if not outright lie to me. Anytime someone begins a statement with: "And I said, *like.*,…" or "I was *like*….." it is not going to be reliable. Though we typically attribute such vernacular to teenagers, you'd be surprised how many adults have developed this linguistic artifice. Psychologically it gives them the ability to exaggerate what they – or someone else - said or did without actually lying. In their minds, the injection of the preposition "like" relieves them of responsibility for their prevarication. "Like" is a comparison, it is used to describe something similar to what really existed or occurred. Therefore, when someone uses this phrase, he's indicating that what he said was similar to what he is actually telling you. Sadly, it is seldom even that accurate. If I ever had a Green Beret under my command tell me that he had, *like* stood his guard, *like* put out the Claymore mines, *like* test-fired our weapons, or *like* put up a good ambush, I would have probably shot him on the spot.

This tendency to exaggerate things to others, also sees us doing it to ourselves. We have all had times in our lives when we felt so overwhelmed with personal problems and work demands that we were ready to quit everything. These are times when we allowed circumstances to become exaggerated in our own minds. Then along came a friend with a calm and objective mind, and helped put everything in perspective. That person evaluated each problem in the cold light of reality, and through this non-exaggerated analysis showed us that nothing was that bad. He helped us prioritize each problem, showing the ones that could and should be dealt with quickly, and the initial steps to take on the others. He showed us which problems weren't really problems at all, and which ones could be delegated to others. It usually takes no more than an hour for someone to show you how the tidal wave of the stress and dilemmas you thought you were facing were really little more than the product of your own exaggeration.

As you go through your daily life and you are late, don't blame it on traffic that had you waiting for "an hour" when it was ten minutes. Don't say it was a "parking lot" when traffic was moving at 20 mph. Stop relating how someone "yelled" at you, when all he did was say that you were wrong. We normally exaggerate someone else's behavior to cast him in an ill light, because deep down we know that person was right. Never say things were "unbelievable," "the worst you've ever seen," or that you just had the "worst meal you've ever tasted," unless it's true. Don't accuse someone you've had a difference of opinion with of being the "stupidest person" you've ever known. The fact that you may use these descriptors with some frequency smacks of a lack of honesty, and certainly accuracy, in your recitation of any event in your life. Who, then, can trust anything you say? My rule in Special Forces, was that if someone would lie to you about one thing, he'd lie to you about anything. The same is true for chronic exaggerators: they can't be trusted.

YOUR WORD IS YOUR BOND

Another aspect of being a person of integrity in your verbal communication – someone who means just what he says – is the trustworthiness of your commitments. In centuries and generations past, people would orally agree to something, then stick to it. Their word was good, and they would abide by the agreement they made, whether it turned out to be advantageous or not. Today, we dare not agree to anything without first expending money for a lawyer to lock the other side into compliance, while we duplicitously attempt to slip as many loopholes in for ourselves that we can. Having spent my youth going to school as one of a very few white boys on an Indian reservation, I have heard few things that describe this dynamic of American society better than the old lament of the American Indians: "Only the white man insists your words be put down on paper, and then uses them against you."

It is a sad statement of society that outside of complex business or legal matters, anything ever needs to be reduced to writing. Having worked with John for years, including his years as a trial lawyer, I am aware of far too many businessmen and companies who will do nothing they are obligated to do until threatened with litigation, or actually sued. There are far too many people, with far too little integrity, who won't even pay a bill until they get a demand letter from a lawyer. This is even true with large corporations that can easily afford to meet their obligations. The people running these outfits forget that oftentimes their creditors are just small businessmen who did the job they contracted for, and did it well. They cannot afford to wait twelve or twenty months to be paid. There is no excuse for this kind of behavior. There is never an excuse for dishonor.

One of the worst instances depicting this need to involve lawyers and written contracts into every aspect of our personal lives, is the need to have a prenuptial agreement to get married. Lawyers advise everyone about to be wed to enter into a binding legal contract. This is not an agreement of marriage; that one is oral. It is an agreement of divorce. If you plan for a divorce, odds are you're going to get one. It is true that a basic tenet of all Special Operations is to always have an escape plan. In fact, that's the part that gets planned first. If you can't devise a good plan to get your Team out of a hostile situation in enemy territory, you don't send them on the mission in the first place. But, when you are dealing with the one human being you are pledging your life to, and love more than anything, you should not be planning your future in the same way that you would to run a mission into enemy territory.

Whether reduced to writing or not, if you got married with a certain understanding, abide by that agreement regardless of the reason for your divorce. Having emotions is a fact of life, but experiencing them is never an excuse for not living by your word. Do it for yourself, not the other person. Be an individual of your word; make your word mean something, even if your spouse fails to do the same. If you know someone who is going through a divorce, and goes out of his way to destroy his wife (or vice versa), dragging that legal proceeding out for years while viciously attacking the person he was married to, then you've just been given a glimpse into the kind of person he is. If you're thinking of going into business with that person, you've just seen what kind of partner he will be and what you will go through when the partnership ultimately comes to an end, as business relationships eventually do.

Remember, the legacy you leave in life is the most valuable thing your friends, children, grandchildren and other surviving family members will inherit. For many, your friends, not your family, will bear the real weight of the life you lead. That legacy will be based on your honesty and integrity. Be sure that you will be remembered as a person of your word, and that people will remember you were a man who meant just what he said.

PRIDE CAN BE A SIN TOO

People seldom realize that humility is an element of integrity. No matter how good you are at something, how elite, whatever championships you may have won or how beautiful you might be, someday it will change. All such qualities are fleeting and in life the accomplishments of our youth quickly fade into obscurity. Just ask anyone who's ever attended a 25th high school reunion. Top level athletes lose their ability to perform at championship level fairly early in life, being returned to the ordinariness of the rest of us. The great Soviet super-heavyweight Olympic weightlifter Vasilii Alexiev, once said: "All great athletes die two deaths, and the first is the more painful." With time and age, beauty fades and abilities diminish. Even men who are so proud of being tall, will become stooped. Young or old, human beings are lazy by nature. You must discipline yourself, push yourself to be better. How far or hard you push, and at what, will vary and change as you pass through different phases of life. A twenty-plus year veteran colonel must discipline himself to physically train differently than when he was a young captain, or even a sergeant on the Teams. If you recognize these facts of life from the outset, you will pass through your early years with proper humility.

There is nothing wrong with believing, or knowing, that you are the best at something. But it should never be something that you shove down others' throats. Green Berets strive to let others know that their skills, abilities and elite-ness are things they can rely on, not something others should fear or have to defend against; except America's enemies. Just as most men are physically stronger than their wives, but no woman should ever fear her husband's hands. They should be there to protect and comfort her.

BRAIN VS. MUSCLE

In his many years as a competitive weightlifter, John spent some time at the Olympic Training Center in Colorado Springs, and has coached several young men, including his own son, Walter, who won several national championships. What he learned in all those years is that the vast majority of us are born with certain special abilities, but few have it all. When kids start out as young athletes, the most genetically gifted are the stars right away. Those that are naturally biggest and strongest, or have the most speed or coordination, are the quickest out of the gate.

But as time goes on, those athletes with the greatest mental and psychological strength will eventually surpass the ones that merely possessed natural physical ability. The ultimate victors are those who dedicate themselves to their sport, who train in the worst weather, stick to their diets, train through injuries and illnesses, and give all they have. At the Olympic Training Center, the majority of athletes who had made it to that level were the mentally strong ones. Most of the physically gifted – the "gazelles" we called them in SF – had long since fallen by the wayside. Nature ensures that the most physically gifted are usually not also given tremendous mental discipline and drive. Those few who make it all the way to dominate a sport at the world level, are the anomalies born with both.

In Special Forces we needed people with decent athletic ability, but more importantly, the mental strength and mindset to never quit, no matter how bad things were. That is what training was all about. All those prancing, leg shaving, muscled-up pretty boys who could only train in a temperature-controlled environment, with the right music, properly hydrated with their favorite energy drink, were useless to us. That is the difference between the conditioning of athletes, and that of soldiers. Top level athletes will perform far above anyone, even Green Berets. But to do that, training and performance conditions must be perfect. They have to get the proper amount of sleep, with the right diet taken over five meals a day. Their vitamin intake is delicately balanced, and their training sessions monitored and properly spaced. They get massages to help speed the recovery process, with doctors attending to their every medical problem or slight injury.

Soldiers don't have the luxury of functioning under any of these conditions, much less all of them. Special Forces soldiers are expected to succeed in the worst possible situations. In normal training conditions, the best Green Berets may function at only 80 percent of top athletes. But make both groups go without sleep for days on end, no food for five days, no water for three days, living outside in the cold and rain, and the elite soldier will still be performing at 90 percent of his maximum capacity, while the high flying athlete will have dropped to 20 percent of his. As conditions deteriorate, and stresses increase, the Green Beret prevails, while the pampered athlete falls apart. The Green Berets have to continue on, because if they don't, they die. Athletes just go home to get a meal and some sleep. For them, tomorrow is always another day.

NEVER QUIT

Most men who made it into Special Forces were above average athletes, but the majority lacked the size, strength, speed or agility to be competitive at the collegiate or professional levels. In my own case, even though I had been a high school football player and wrestling champion, I wasn't good enough to get a college scholarship in either sport. But that didn't diminish my love of athletics, or my recognition that sports were not only good for my mind and body, but would make me a better soldier.

Though I spent most of my life in Special Forces, I was always involved in sports. In addition to all of the combat-useful sports I had to be adept at for my job, I spent countless hours in the weightroom, ultimately working my way up to a 400-plus pound benchpress, over 500 pound squat and an almost 600 pound deadlift. I was also a competitive motocross racer and tried my best to win a world championship. Eventually, I had to be satisfied with the races that I did win, as it became clear that genetically I lacked the balance, coordination and reflexes of the top performers.

I tried to be the best at everything I did. It didn't matter whether I was better than others, only that I was the best that I could be. This was the attitude that got me through the Q Course and kept me alive in combat. It is also the attitude that has seen me through every other phase of my life. As Olympic weightlifting champion Lee James said to John many years ago: "If you work hard to be the best, always trying to be better than you were before, sooner or later you will be better than everyone else anyway, without ever having wasted time worrying about them."

RIDING WITHOUT TRAINING WHEELS

In trying to develop any skill, I never had to have some expert teach me everything there was to know, follow me around at practice or hold my hand. I just jumped in and figured it out. I learned by watching others, and then applying what I saw. If you want to be good at something, this is the only way it can happen. Among his other talents, John has been an accomplished horseman his entire life. I have seen many instances when people came to him for advice on how to handle their horses. In most cases, these were wealthy people who got into riding late in life, bought a top level animal and had been using riding lessons and instructors like training wheels, never getting on their own horses without supervision.

John's advice was always the same: Take your horse out on your own, learn to ride *the horse* and not the saddle by riding bareback, and spend as many hours as you can doing it. They needed to get away from pretentious and arbitrary English-riding hand and foot positions, which may have been required in a show ring but were not utilitarian. They needed to get comfortable falling, as it is a part of riding; just as falling is a part of life. After months of riding like this every day, they would be able to sit a horse as though born to it. Few people heeded this advice; they just weren't ready to give up their crutches or their excuses as to why they couldn't do what they bought the horse for.

Too many people have come to believe that they can't do anything without some sort of expert consultant. That's ridiculous. No one needs a personal trainer to get, and stay, in shape. Just get your butt in the gym and work. Be responsible for your own training discipline and dedication. You cannot buy those qualities, you must develop them. This is the Green Beret life and philosophy. With regard to America's addiction to needing lessons and lectures in order to do anything from childbirth to jogging, one Russian Spetsnaz colonel was fond of saying that if infants could talk and understand English, they would never learn to walk. Like adults, they would believe they couldn't do it without an instructional class taught by an expert.

Do not think that someone else has to teach you. Use your brain to its fullest. All those muscled up bodybuilders and weightlifters working as athletic trainers are people who just got in the gym and tried to figure it out. They kept their mouths shut and watched and listened to the other guys in the gym who obviously knew what they were about. In doing so, they learned, and got better and stronger. When you rely on someone else to tell you everything, you never learn. What you get is a demonstration, but that does not become a part of you. American Kenpo-Karate master, Ed Parker, always told students that came to him that he would never show them his art, but that he would *share* it with them. "If I show it to you it becomes an exhibition, and in time will be pushed so far into the back of your mind that it will be lost. But by sharing it with you, you will not only retain it forever, but I, too, will improve."[37]

If trainers and consultants are sharing what they know with you, you will be developing your own knowledge base and quickly grow beyond your need for them. Unfortunately, the addiction to consultants is like the damnable cycle of psycho-therapy, where patients continue to undergo treatment for decades, but somehow never get over their problems. People who "show" you what to do for

37 Joe Hyams, *Zen In the Martial Arts*, (J.P. Tarcher, Inc., Los Angeles, 1979), 12.

their living, have no incentive to ever let you walk on your own. You have to do that by yourself; and if you ever want to be good at anything, this is the only way it can happen. After all, no one ever became a cycling champion by keeping the training wheels on.

WHEN IN GREECE

If you want to be the best that you can be, you need to follow the ancient Greek rule of developing your mind, body and spirit. This is not something you ever grow too old to do. Know what's going on in the world and what role you can play in it. Get away from the television set and read something of value, not the pulp trash fiction you might usually waste valuable time on. Develop and maintain a spiritual core in yourself and everything you do. To the surprise of many people, the best philosophers in our society are often military generals who came up through the combat ranks. They are never the mono-faceted, military automatons many expect. You can't survive years in combat, enduring the worst possible experiences imaginable, commanding troops and watching men die for your decisions, and not be affected by it. No one can commit an entire career and lifetime to devising ways to keep his own people safe, while killing as many of the enemy as possible – other human beings – and not have spent many sleepless nights contemplating the enormity of it all. No one can do this without wrestling with notions of good versus evil, human survival, and the meaning of life under horrible circumstances.

In order to deal with the worst experiences life can throw at anyone, and go forward with your sanity in tact, you must find and cling to a spiritual base, a well of wisdom and a fountain of positive energy that tells you that despite all of the suffering you did the right thing. We all need that spiritual foundation to succeed in life with any measure of balance and happiness. The wealthiest people in the world, who have satisfied every possible material want but still don't have this, are also the unhappiest.

WHO YOU ARE TODAY

You have to develop and maintain a sound body. Though you may have been a world class athlete in your youth, this will mean nothing to your overall mental and physical health decades later if you have done nothing in the years since then. Nor will it please your spouse that the lean, hard, fit man she fell in love with has turned into a pathetic, fat, slovenly couch potato. Things change for all of us, and over the course of our lifetimes we learn the transitory nature of everything. Our opinions change, our politics change, and our commitments come and go. We change careers, cars, houses and hobbies. Our bodies change continually, as must our expectations of them. With regard to this point, Bruce Lee once said that the past is an illusion, deal with the body you have now.[38]

  Though I was in peak physical condition for most of my life, I am at an age now where I have to relearn my body, or more accurately learn the body I have today. As of the final writing of this book I am 61 years old, but can still benchpress 350 pounds on a good day. Six days a week I am out of bed and in the gym by 5:00 a.m. I do everything from a half-hour long ladies' abs class - in which I am the only man and certainly the only grandfather - to the free weight room. I train twenty sets per body part and make sure I get there whether I am hurt or tired. Knowing the importance of cycling my training, I go through periods where I will add long distance swimming, walk-running and calisthenics. At times I will still do weighted rucksack marches. I use an elliptical training machine several days a week to ensure my cardiovascular system is being sufficiently worked. And I've lived and exercised like this every day since leaving the Special Forces at age 44.

  Examining myself objectively – and despite my Spartan exercise regimen - I realize that over the ensuing years my gut has grown to reflect that my life today is physically easier than it once was.

[38] Hyams, 36.

Less time spent living on a thousand calories a day in freezing cold or blistering hot conditions for months on end, and having to move up to twenty miles a day with a 90 pound rucksack, has certainly had its effect. Being able to eat what I want, when I want, has resulted in a body that showcases that it sometimes takes in more calories than it expends. But I am still well trained and physically capable. My heart is sound, and my veins clear of congestion. I can outperform many men young enough to be my grandsons, but at the same time I have had to adjust the way I exercise. Despite the hardcore nature of my approach to exercise, a lifetime of injuries and physical depreciation have forced me to use more machines and fewer free weights. I have had to realize that a little flexibility work is tremendously beneficial, and that using the heaviest possible weights is something I do only once in a while, employing high repetition sets and lighter weights most of the time.

This is not part of the aging process, so much as it is a part of the life process. Life's cycle is not something any of us can deny. If there is one thing I learned from the Green Berets I served with over the years, it was that they are the ultimate pragmatists. No matter what happens, they accept it and move forward. I have known men who got both of their legs blown off by land mines in Vietnam. One guy made his teammates help him escape from the hospital the very next day, and take him down to the beach so he could go swimming. One close friend had a foot blown off in addition to being shot in the femur. He waited nine hours for a medevac to arrive so he could be treated. His wounds were so great that he spent one and a-half years in Walter Reed Hospital. When released he headed straight back to the war. Though he would suffer from those injuries for the rest of his life, I never saw him experience a single bad or self-pitying day in his life. He overcame all obstacles.

Another friend of John's and mine, Eric Hollen, had survived years in the Ranger Battalions before moving to Special Forces. A seasoned veteran, one day his spinal cord was crushed in a tractor accident. He is now a young man in a wheelchair for the rest of his life. This has not stopped Eric, or even slowed him down. Tall and blonde, with a long lean face and limp hair that defies efforts at control, he looks like a young John Elway with muscles. Today he is a full time college student, and daily spends an hour in the swimming pool for endurance. He lifts weights for two hours every day, and is working toward a 400 pound benchpress; he has won national shooting championships, and as of the final editing of this book just made the Olympic Pistol Team. Though Eric no longer wears the beret to work every day, he continues to live his life as a Green Beret and is an inspiration to us all.

For all of Eric's courage, he is not a rarity among Green Berets. John and I are both life members of the Special Operations Association, and I am a member of the Special Forces Association. At each year's reunions, I see dozens of our nation's former elite commandos buzzing about in wheelchairs, many without legs that were lost to booby traps or land mines. Some men are missing arms, others live with colostomy bags. There are so many of these men that I start to feel that people like me, who made it out of service relatively unscathed, should be ashamed. I have never seen a single one of them angry or depressed over his condition. Not a single one of them bemoans the unfairness of life, or wants to sue the government over what happened. Many refuse to even apply for disability benefits. None of them had grief counselors or psychological therapists of any kind when they were wounded.

Despite all that these men have endured, no one could meet a better or happier bunch of guys, or anyone as satisfied with their lives as these heroes. They endured the worst pain and injury a human being could suffer, and live. Having lived, they decided to continue living. Today they have gone from warriors hanging on the skids of a helicopter while racing into a hot LZ,[39] to warriors who face every challenge life throws at them from a seated position, but no less brave and no less daring. These men are exemplified by such noble veterans as Charles Berg, one of the directors of the Special

[39] Landing Zone

Operations Association. This is the attitude that got them into and through Special Forces training. This is the attitude that made them the best at their chosen profession and kept their friends alive. This is what made them the admiration of other men, and why we make movies about them. This is what made them Green Berets, and they continue to live that creed every single day.

LEARNING FROM OTHERS

This leads to another aspect of Green Beret philosophy: When it comes to life's lessons, a wise person does not need to reinvent the wheel of errors committed by those that came before him. In Special Forces, a smart man learns from the other guy's mistakes. This is part of the reason we keep our tradition of oral history. This is the way we continually reinforce and teach each other the mistakes that were made in the past, as well as the tactics and ideas that worked. As we all know, this is one of the most frustrating aspects of parenthood: that we see our teenagers making the same mistakes we made, just as we drove our parents crazy by ignoring their advice.

As adults, we are supposed to be wiser and possessed of better judgment than we were as teenagers. In both our personal and professional lives, we can save ourselves a great deal of effort, and pain, by paying careful attention to what others have done and where they have failed. Learning from others' mistakes is the way a Green Beret gets better, and stays alive. It's a way we can all make our own lives better.

DOING WHAT'S NECESSARY

It's always easy to do the things you like, the things that you're naturally good at. But this is not why we live our lives. We live so that we may conclude our lifetimes as better people than we started, making it a process of self-improvement. This is true in all areas, and so long as you are alive and responsible for sustaining yourself and earning a living to support others, you are charged with this continuing duty. It is a duty that doesn't end until you're dead. As Richard Bach wrote: "Here is a test to find whether your mission on earth is finished: if you're alive, it isn't."[40]

If your computer skills are weak, develop them. If your vocabulary or public speaking abilities are insufficient, change them. Even though you may work in an office, if your poor physical condition prevents you from having the energy necessary to function intensely over long hours, fix that too. Be honest with yourself. If you need to break a habit, no matter how addictive or long standing, just break it. Quit whining, making excuses or thinking some TV ad or hypnotist can do it for you. Make a decision, set your mind to it, and allow yourself no excuses. Years ago, while still in the Teams, I was like most SF soldiers of my era: a two pack-a-day smoker and had been for years. On 28 April 1978 I realized I needed to quit; so I quit. I never had another cigarette. I still remember the date.

I had also been an habitual chew or snuff user, seldom going a single waking minute without some tobacco product tucked into my lip. More than a decade after retiring from the military, this habit was worse than ever. As I was getting older and wanted to be around for my wife, and had a daughter trying to bring my first grandbaby into the world, I realized the destructive effect of this behavior. I quit that, too, cold turkey. No excuses. It's now been several years and I have never let myself so much as smell another snuff can. Though I admit it was – and still is – the hardest thing I ever did, I did it in the only way possible.

When you need to make a change in your life, don't do it in steps, and don't wait for New Year's Day to start resolutions you will never stick with. Do it now, today, and do it by yourself. No one else created your habit or dependency. It was the product of decisions you made day after day. No one else can end it, either, *but you*. You won't need support groups, special programs or experts. And don't believe that you quitting an addictive habit should become your spouse's

---

40   Richard Bach, *Illusions: The Adventures of a Reluctant Messiah*, (Dell Publishing, New York, 1977), 159.

problem. If you need to stop drinking because you have a problem, accept responsibility for that. It doesn't mean your wife needs to quit drinking too. Be her designated driver and quit feeling sorry for yourself. As John says, "You can't quit cancer, but you can quit whatever bad habit you have." Or, as we would say in the Teams: Stand up, ruck up, and move out. No one else is going to carry your ruck for you through life. That's a weight you have to bear all on your own.

YOU'RE NEVER TOO GOOD TO PITCH IN

Years ago while based in Bad Tolz, Germany with the 10th Special Forces Group,[41] I was a sergeant first class.[42] My team pulled what was known as "X Duty." That meant we were supposed to support another company in its training. Despite the dramatic sound of "X Duty," what that really meant was we got to do all the scut work for someone else. We hauled mortar rounds for them, cleaned up shooting ranges, and drove their transport vehicles. Any support they needed, we provided them. When they moved us into the training area to begin our stint as these Army butlers, we were put in the same barracks as the post truck drivers. As we hauled our rucks in, there was instant tension. The truck drivers thought that we would be elitist jerks and see them as low-lifes in the military hierarchy where Green Berets reigned supreme.

As our Team sergeant, the first thing I did to alleviate the mounting hostility was to stuff my beret in the cargo pocket of my BDU pants,[43] and without any rank or uniform other than a t-shirt, walked in and sat down with a young Spec 4.[44] I said to him, "Looks like we've got the shit stick for the next couple of weeks and will be pulling all the crap details. Now, you guys have been carting us around for the past ten days while we were training. The question is what can we

---

[41] Not to be confused with the 10th Mountain Division which, while a good unit, is not a Special Forces or Special Operations unit, and is not Airborne qualified.

[42] Sergeant First Class is an E-7 non-commissioned officer rank. It is one rank below Master Sergeant.

[43] Battle Dress Uniform, the camouflaged fatigues all military service personnel wear.

[44] Specialist Fourth Class is one rank below an E-5 or buck sergeant. Sp 4 is the equivalent of the old corporal rank.

do for you to make your jobs easier?" This developed instant rapport, and we all worked great together as a single team for the next ten days.

RANDOM ACTS OF KINDNESS

Everywhere you go, every day of your lives, you shoulder the duty to help your fellow man. Wesley Autrey, the New York man who leapt down onto the subway rails to move a fallen man off the tracks with a train racing toward them, pulled the man into the depression between the rails and covered him with his body as the train raced over them. Though celebrated as a hero by the city of New York and the President of the United States at the January 2007 State of the Union Address, Mr. Autrey insisted that he was no more hero than any other person. "There is a hero inside everyone," he said. "We all need to start loving and caring about each other more." This man epitomizes a common citizen who lives the Green Beret Lifestyle, who accepts his responsibility for the safety of all those around him, every day of his life.

Anyone who wishes to live his or her life as a Green Beret accepts that same duty. One of the rules of the Green Beret is a stolen line from the Boy Scouts motto, "Always Be Prepared." This is found in the Special Forces recon practice of: "Take everything - leave nothing behind." As a citizen, no matter where you go, you should always have minimal life saving tools with you.

BEING PREPARED

A few years ago John had some winter visitors from the flatlands of east Texas. Unaccustomed to both snow and mountains, they wanted to drive over some of the high passes in the Rockies and visit ski resort towns. Though he had no intention of leaving cleared and graded dirt roads traversing the mountain passes, John immediately began tossing gear into the back of his SUV. In went a snow shovel, sleeping bags, food, water, rappelling gear and more. Though he always has at least one firearm in his car, in went a couple of others with extra ammunition. With all of this equipment always packed and ready in his house, this took no more than five minutes. When asked why he was doing this, his answer was that every month people unexpectedly ended up off the roads and stranded in the mountains. Some of those people died. Whether that happened to him and those whose safety he was responsible for, or to someone else he happened to come across, no one was going to die because he was unprepared.

As it turned out, just as they were cresting a high, lonely portion of the road, several men armed with rifles stepped out of the woods into the middle of the road forcing them to stop. Perhaps, for the first time, his guests understood why he had prepared so well, particularly when he reached for a handgun and tucked it between his legs. The men were hunters with no cell reception, whose car battery had died in the night. John met his duty as a citizen and jumped their car, happy that he wasn't the only one in the group without a loaded gun.

TO DEFEND THE DEFENSELESS

Experiences like this require no dramatic heroics, merely an acknowledgement that we are all responsible for coming to the aid of others. This is what Green Berets do all over the world. And just as the Special Forces exist to help in this fashion, sometimes they are called on to help by protecting others with force. You must be prepared, capable and willing to do the same.

When driving in sloppy road conditions caused by melting winter snow, keep one or two gallons of windshield wiper fluid in your car. When you see a woman pulled off the road attempting to rub snow on her filth-smeared windshield, pull over and pour some cleaner into her car's fluid reservoir. You never know who the next person will be that pulls over while she is outside her car and vulnerable. You never know what accident you may have helped her prevent by being able to see.

If you see a woman, or an elderly person, pulled over with a flat tire, get out and change it. If the hood is up on the car, you don't have to be a mechanic to be of assistance. Stop and at least make sure those people have access to a cell phone to call for help and then remain with them until that help arrives. Under such circumstances women should always be concerned for their safety. Don't impose yourself on them. Tell them that you will just wait in your car until their friend or a tow truck arrives.

If you see another car pull over ahead of you to "help" that woman, and the man that gets out does not feel right, pull over yourself. At the very least, you can remain there until you see her safely back on the road. If she becomes the victim of violence, your duty is clear. If you are not ready to meet that duty, then you can join the ranks of those cowardly and weak-hearted people who routinely stand idly by while evil is being done, while innocents are victimized.

BE A SPECIAL FORCES TEACHER

Both John and I have done this on many occasions. In a few instances, John ended up having to drive women to their destinations, or following them to ensure their malfunctioning cars made the trip. Each time he would give the ladies a set of tools to use to ensure their safety, things we routinely taught in women's sex assault defense classes. These were not mechanic's tools, but survival tools. He would produce his driver's license, attorney registration card and other forms of identification. He would then have the women call either someone they knew would answer the phone, or leave a message on someone's voicemail, other than their own home phones. This is necessary, as rapists and murderers end up with a woman's purse, home address and keys. They can force a woman to tell them how to access voicemail and erase any messages.

John would insist the women tell the person they were calling who he was, all of his personal information, and the description and license plate of his car. They would explain where they were, what was wrong and where he was going to take them, being sure to leave the time of the message and the time they should arrive. They would then explain that they would leave another message as soon as they got there safely. He was teaching them skills that would give them the best chance of staying safe in future situations.

This is the duty of every man, and woman, in our country. Could these efforts have ultimately resulted in some unfortunate consequences for John if the woman were a con artist or extortionist? Yes, and unfortunately such people do exist. However, that would never stop a Green Beret from doing the right thing. As a person unafraid of the worst life can throw at him, no warrior would risk having to live with the knowledge that the woman he drove past ended up assaulted or killed in exchange for his own problem-free day.

YOU MAY BE THE ONLY ONE

For years before 9-11 everyone in our group carried pocket knives, called combat folders, when flying. Many would decry this practice, saying that we were paranoid. They thought we had a screw loose, and wanted to know why we felt the need to have knives on planes. At the time, carrying knives on aircraft was legal within the limits of three and one-half inch blades. Sometimes we'd get hassled by airport security screeners for the "special" types of knives we were carrying, but we knew we were within the law and always prevailed. We knew that someday, somewhere, someone was going to try to take an aircraft full of people. We were old enough to remember the plane hijackings in the 1960s and 1970s, and knew that those types of terror attacks had not vanished, merely gone into hibernation. Should it have occurred on a plane we happened to be on, we would have met our duty to the innocent people around us, and the aircraft. Simply, we would have fought.

Consider how different 9-11 might have turned out if every single man on those aircraft had been just as paranoid, had exercised his right to be similarly armed when the hijackers cut the throats of those flight attendants and pilots. How different might things have been if just one man had been so armed? Famed speaker and tactical instructor Dave Grossman always says that the difference between warriors and regular people can be seen in that one example. He relates that after 9-11, the vast majority of people responded to that horror by saying, "Thank God I wasn't on any of those planes." But the warriors in our society, the ones who had found the Green Beret in themselves said, "I wish I had been on one of those planes, I might have been able to make a difference." With no false courage or bragging, I can honestly say that John and I, and everyone we work with – and every warrior in America - wishes he had been on one of those planes that morning.

Living life as a Green Beret means you never turn from trouble. You never fail to help another, even though that help may result in unpleasant consequences for you. If a woman is being assaulted, you may end up hurt or even dead for helping her. So be it; there is no better or nobler way to die. If a child is being kidnapped, it is your duty to do whatever necessary to stop it. If a pit bull is attacking a child and you don't have a knife or a gun (why you wouldn't, I could never understand), stick your arm in that dog's mouth, forcing it to lock on and eliminating further threat to the child. You may lose your arm, but better that than have the dog tear the child's throat out. These are the tradeoffs that must be made in combat. Should it turn out badly for you, for the rest of your life you will be proud every time you look down at that empty sleeve and know that you would do the same thing with the other arm should you encounter that situation again.

YOUR WORST MUST BE BETTER THAN THEIR BEST

In training, the British SAS (Special Air Service or special forces) are continually driving each soldier to develop skills to the point where his worst is better than the enemy's best. This is because when the enemy comes, he always comes when he thinks you are at your worst. And he only comes when he is at his best, when all of the circumstances are in his favor. Civilian life is no different. There are threats out there for everyone, including your loved ones, and those threats will only come when you are at your lowest level of preparedness, unaware or absent entirely. They will come when conditions are perfect for the criminal. The question is: If you are going to build the Green Beret in yourself, what must you prepare for and how must you live?

Safety expert Gavin De Becker points out that, "ordinary citizens can encounter violence at their jobs to the point that homicide is now the leading cause of death for women in the workplace. Twenty years ago, the idea of someone going on a shooting spree at work was outlandish; now it's in the news nearly every week."[45] Women, alone, visit emergency rooms for injuries caused by the men in their lives more often than from car accidents, robberies and rapes together.[46] Despite the fact that danger lurks outside our doors every day, we are manufacturing increasingly passive – if not cowardly – generations of American males. Col. Grossman relates the attitude of famed firearms champion and instructor, Jeff Cooper: "Any man who is a man may not, in honor, submit to threats of violence. But many men who are not cowards are simply unprepared for the fact of human savagery. They have not thought about it (as incredible as this may appear to anyone who reads the papers or listens to the news) and they just don't know what to do. When they look right into the face of depravity or violence they are astonished and confounded."[47]

John Eldredge explains that far too many men in America realize just how lame they are, and how incapable they are of performing as men.

> We are now in the midst of battle without the train-
> ing we really need, and there are few men around to

[45] Gavin De Becker, *The Gift of Fear: Survival Signals That Protect Us From Violence*, (Little, Brown and Company, Boston, 1997), 9.

[46] Ibid.

[47] Dave Grossman, *On Killing: The Psychological Cost of Learning to Kill in War and Society*, (Little, Brown and Company, Boston, 1995), 207.

> show us how to do it. We know how to attend church; we've been taught not to swear or drink or smoke. We know how to be nice. But we don't really know how to fight, and we're going to have to learn as we go. That is where our strength will be crystallized, deepened, and revealed. A man is never more a man than when he embraces an adventure beyond his control, or when he walks into a battle he isn't sure of winning.[48]

This sad reality is made all the worse when people are confronted with the necessity of doing the tough thing when they are in a crowd of others. Psychologists call this "diffusion of responsibility." It occurs when it becomes easy to think that if something should be done, others in the group will do it. This is how we end up with crowds of people standing around watching a young woman being beaten in the middle of jammed rush hour traffic on a bridge, until she leaps to her death, as happened several years ago. This is how we get groups of others standing by allowing elderly World War II veterans to be beaten and robbed, homeless people attacked, women raped and others beaten to death by gangs, without anyone stopping it. Can you imagine a Green Beret standing idly by while such atrocities were being committed in his presence? Do you think he would only take a stand if others were going to help him, or would he throw himself into the fray because it was right and necessary? If a lone Green Beret can make a stand in these every day events, so can you.

In order for every man in America to be ready, willing and able to make that stand when the time comes, he must be prepared. We know that our society produces a plentiful supply of boys, but it seems to produce fewer and fewer men.[49] There are two simple reasons: one, we don't know how to initiate boys into men, and, second, we are not entirely sure we want to. "We want to socialize them, to be sure, but away from all that is fierce, and wild, and passionate. In other words, away from masculinity and toward something feminine. But, as Christina Hoff Sommers says, we have forgotten a

---

[48] Eldredge, 212-213.
[49] Eldredge, 83.

simple truth: 'The energy, competitiveness, and corporal daring of normal, decent males is responsible for much of what is right in the world.' Sommers reminds us that during the Columbine massacre, 'Seth Houy threw his body over a terrified girl to shield her from the bullets; fifteen-year-old Daniel Rohrbough paid with his life when, at mortal risk to himself, he held a door open so others could escape.'[50] Acts such as these can be performed by anyone who has nurtured the Green Beret in himself first; who has lived his life to be a warrior.

According to author Rick Fields:

> The warrior is by definition a fighter, a man or woman of action, a specialist in meeting and resolving conflict and challenge. In most societies, warriors have taken this role quite literally. They seek out battle, fighting is what gives meaning to their lives. In other societies, battle is only a last resort, something to be engaged in only after all other means of resolving conflict have been exhausted. And finally, there is a tradition in which the warrior sees the true battle as an inner or spiritual one, in which the fight is with the enemies of self-knowledge or realization. Though the true warrior is a fighter, he or she does not fight out of aggression. The apparent fierceness of the warrior proceeds from a primary caring for others. Putting others before oneself is the ultimate source of the warrior's courage.[51]

Eldredge believes this strength is so essential to men that it is the one thing that makes them heroes. He writes, "If a neighborhood is safe, it's because of the strength of men. Slavery was stopped by the strength of men, at a terrible price to them and their families. The Nazis were stopped by men. Apartheid wasn't defeated by women. Who gave their seats up on the lifeboats leaving the *Titanic*, so that women and children would be saved? This isn't to say women can't

---

50 Ibid., citing Christina Hoff Sommers, *The War Against Boys: How Misguided Feminism Is Harming Our Young Men*, (Simon & Schuster, New York, 2000), 13.
51 Rick Fields, *The Code of the Warrior: In History, Myth, and Everyday Life*, (Harper Perennial, New York, 1991), 2-3.

be heroic. It's simply to remind us that God made men the way they are because we desperately *need* them to be the way they are. Yes, a man is a dangerous thing. So is a scalpel. It can wound or it can save your life. You don't make it safe by making it dull; you put it in the hands of someone who knows what he's doing."[52]

Seventy year-old Allan Cady is such a man. In February 2007, this retired Marine was on a tour bus in Costa Rica along with a large group of other retirees taking a Carnival cruise. A young man attempted to rob the passengers only to be attacked by Mr. Cady, who ultimately put him in a choke hold, killing him with his bare hands. The robber's two armed accomplices fled in the face of this courageous defense by a would-be victim. This one, lone man, who acted in spite of his fear, is a model for everyone.

As you confront your own anxieties over the threats you may face in your own life, do not be concerned by the fear you are feeling. Fear is not only natural, but a wonderful survival mechanism. You must remember, however, that fear is a great servant when you are under threat, but a terrible master. You must master your fear, just as you have mastered your fears in other aspects of your lives. Initial fear of driving a car when you turned sixteen, eventually went away through committed practice. Fear of exams may never have gone away completely during your academic career, but you mastered it and faced those exams every time, ultimately succeeding. Fear of public speaking – the most common of all fears in society – may have turned you into a competent, if not excellent presenter. But these successes over fear only came with redundancy of performance.

Only when you have failed to rise to your own inner challenges have you allowed fear to control you. I can imagine no worse thing to control my life than fear. If you are afraid of flying, and have therefore sat home, refusing to visit friends and family, you have failed yourself and your loved ones. If you are afraid of injury to your child, and so refused to let him ever do the things that children need to do to learn and grow, you have failed as a parent. If you were afraid of the

---

[52] Eldredge, 83.

water, and so never made yourself learn to swim, you may have just sounded your own death knell, or that of someone you love, should you end up in an emergency around the water.

When I was first in combat in Vietnam I was with a very small recon team deep in enemy territory. I was so afraid I was dysfunctional. I couldn't make myself do the things I'd been trained to do. But I didn't give up on myself, nor did my teammates and superiors give up on me. With time and experience in battle, I went from being *dysfunctionally* scared, to *functionally* scared. I was still terrified, but managed to do my job, to act in accordance with my training. With increasing confidence in my ability to not only survive – but prevail – in combat, I became functionally cool, dispassionate, a true professional. The better I got, and the more I survived, the closer I got to almost becoming a liability. I became over confident. I was at the point that I didn't even contemplate the possibility of being killed.

Ultimately, my combat skills were so good it seemed that everything was happening in slow motion. Not the type of slow motion experience people have when they're terrified, as in a car crash, but the type of slow motion perception experienced by a championship quarterback as he reads a defense and watches the play unfold. For me, my ability to read the battle, anticipate the enemy, take in all of the available information, process and react to it, had become so finely honed that it seemed I had all the time in the world. I had gone from that terrified kid to a true Green Beret, sitting there with enemy soldiers in my sights, thinking to myself, "No don't do that, don't move there, don't make me kill you." This is the point all true warriors ultimately reach. No one wants to kill another human being. You take no pleasure in it, and you do it with no feeling of aggression.

But you also understand that there is evil in the world, and that someone must stop that evil. Often evildoers will give you no choice but to kill them, no matter how much you wish you had an alternative. This is what America is facing today, fighting a war where our terrorist enemies are everywhere. Such vicious people are even here in our country, swimming freely through the pool of our civilian community. And the victims in that pool need someone to protect them, someone to stop those sharks from attacking. That "someone" is a Green Beret. This is what you must nurture, build, train and perfect in your own character. Somewhere, someday, someone will need you to save them. On that day the bugle will sound for you. The only question will be whether you have developed the Green Beret in yourself to the degree that you will move to the sound of the guns to save another. No one can afford a single day in which he does not work on building the Green Beret in himself.

Master Sergeant John Anderson and his Team use their days off over the July 4th, 1982 weekend to keep their mountain climbing skills up in Little Cottonwood Canyon, Utah. Green Berets are forever honing their skills, and will use their limited personal time to make sure they are the best at their jobs.

– 4 –

GREEN BERETS IN THE WORKPLACE

... a symbol of excellence, a badge of courage,
a mark of distinction in the fight for freedom."

John F. Kennedy describing the green beret
on December 10, 1961.

CORPORATE CULTURE

Perhaps the greatest test for anyone trying to live his life with the commitment, purpose and integrity of the Green Beret is found in the private sector workplace. When entering the military, Green Berets have already made the decision that money is not everything. They have committed themselves to a lifetime of nominal financial rewards, knowing they will be rich in the things that matter most in life. For them, commitment, integrity, purpose, comradeship, nobility, honor and courage are the most meaningful aspects of life, and in joining Special Forces they seek out others who feel the same way.

In this way, they are surrounded by a community of people for whom money means very little, a veritable family who all happily survive on relatively small salaries. They each have the comfort and support of others who have turned their backs on American obsessions with celebrity scandals, upscale neighborhoods, expensive cars, excessive jewelry and other aspects of the conspicuous consumption that we are all bombarded with from television, movies, radio and magazines.

When Green Berets perform to their utmost under the very combat conditions they exist to be sent into, the greatest reward they may receive is another stripe on their shoulders, or a small piece of cheap metal or ribbon to adorn their chests. And they don't even care about those. They do not risk their lives for medals or promotions. They do so as part of their "bottom line," which is preserving the lives of their teammates and others whose safety they have been charged with. In making a career in Special Forces, they have already turned their backs on money.

The corporate culture in America has an entirely different bottom line. It is an environment of intense, and often vicious, individual competition. It is an atmosphere that induces employees to believe that every single person must be out for himself. Where trust and trustworthiness are fleeting and tenuous things, if they are to be found at all. It is a culture where the ends – if those ends involve money – always justify the means.

In recent years this is the culture that has seen abuse of power, authority and personal discretion rise to scandalous levels in unprecedented numbers. Leaders of major corporations have been sent to prison for lining their own pockets with tens – and sometimes hundreds – of millions of dollars while their employees and shareholders lost everything, victimized by their lies. It is the culture that has bred both print and TV journalists who plagiarize stories, concocting completely fictional accounts and sometimes accusations resulting in the destruction of the reputations of innocents. It is the very environment which sees paparazzi relentlessly pursuing their prey, then standing by snapping pictures while a princess lay dying.

YOUR MONEY FOR NOTHING

All of this is not to be found exclusively in the corporate world. Indeed, this behavior is as much a product of a shifting of American values as it is a cause of that shift. For we live in a society where our people care more about whether they can afford a Lexus, getting into the most exclusive country club, and how well their investments are doing, than they care about real threats to that way of life. For many, the world is defined by *People Magazine, The View, Desperate Housewives, American Idol, Sex and the City* and other supposed "reality" shows, and it is from these sources that they derive their information about issues critical to our nation. These are people who care more about Ben and Jen, and Jen and Brad, Britney and K-Fed and who got voted off the island last week, than they do about infusing their lives, and that of their families, with core values.

For Americans, much of life has taken on all aspects of a lottery, where it has become not only acceptable but desirable, to sell one's dignity for a little attention and a lot of money. This is seen in the new craze over Las Vegas, where "What happens in Vegas stays in Vegas;" itself an unprincipled bastardization of a Green Beret saying and tradition. It is heard in people bemoaning the fact that they haven't won a million dollars in the lottery, or sacrificing anything to get on any of the innumerable and ridiculous reality shows in the hopes of winning that same million dollars. Even the American legal system – once the iconic symbol of American justice and nobility to the world – has been reduced to little more than another lottery. In that lottery, however, its players look for any opportunity to file a lawsuit, blaming others for the consequences of some decision of their own, ready to take their turn at the litigation wheel and win enough money to retire on. Money they never deserved, and certainly did not earn.

Years ago I read a placard that contained a definition of prosperity: "Spending money you haven't earned, to buy things you don't need, to impress people you don't even like." Sadly, American corporate culture has become imbued with this notion. Managers no longer see themselves as leaders, responsible for setting a good example to their subordinates, or for protecting them from corporate excesses. They no longer care more about their people and the job than they do themselves. Rather, they see their jobs as nothing more than opportunities for manipulating circumstances for their own profit, of maneuvering corporate assets around to achieve their own prosperity. To them, the people under them are nothing more than chattel, little different from any piece of property, subject to being bought, sold or thrown away for a tax write-off the moment it becomes fiscally expedient.

John and I, and others on our team, have had to provide executive protection services to plant managers when corporate executives decided to close plants and lay off all of the employees just before the holidays. In one instance the company big wigs didn't give any thought to either the managers delivering this terrible news, or the workers about to be left with no job and mounting Christmas bills, resulting in the first manager to close a plant being shot to death by a bereft employee. Never forget that the people under you are, in fact, people and deserving of proper treatment.

ONE TIN SOLDIER

The question then becomes how one lone individual, one Green Beret, can manage to maintain his own integrity and honor in the face of such a dauntingly amoral environment. The first, and most important, thing is to decide who and what you are, what you stand for, and what your personal code is. Then, never deviate from it. Do not allow threats or fears of job loss, financial destitution or lack of advancement to seduce you away from those principles. Remember that with SF, if you are willing to face death for someone you care about, or something you believe in, no one can pressure you into compromising yourself and your values with lesser threats.

Years ago, a Green Beret under my command had been inappropriately and unfairly reprimanded for a minor transgression; something the men of SF suffered regularly as the traditional Army was always afraid of us, and constantly tried to "keep us in line" over any infraction they could manufacture. He had been on the list to go to HALO school[53] which was a highly sought training program, but was denied entry due to this petty reprimand. When this came across my desk I went to the commanding officer and told him that if they didn't let him in I was quitting both SF and the Army. This treatment of a good man under my charge was outrageous, and I was not going to stand for it. Sometimes, you just have to be ready to throw yourself on your sword for others who have placed their trust in you.

It is a tremendous strength to never fear losing a job. Part of this strength must be born of you having chosen to live a fiscally wise, frugal life, which gives you the financial freedom to withstand the downfalls life is certain to throw at you. If you have not succumbed to the superficiality of too-expensive houses, cars and lifestyle, you will be fine. Green Berets live every day recognizing that tomorrow they could be wounded in battle or training, and forcibly separated from the Army. Even with maximum disability benefits, they could be facing a life of little income and the physical inability to work. They never lose sight of the fact that this year may be their best financially. They guard against future tragedy, never allowing themselves to become overextended with excessive mortgages, credit cards and expensive toys. This is the attitude every American should adopt. Rather than making spending decisions based on an expectation that every year will be better than the current year, or at least as good, one should always assume that this is your best year and that you will never make this much money again.

Live well, but live wisely; which is within your means. Most Green Berets I have known had a Depression Era mentality when it came to personal finances: recognizing the need to save, not to finance unnecessary things, and always ensuring that they could

---

53 High Altitude Low Opening, and HAHO, or High Altitude High Opening SF skydiving training.

pay all of their monthly bills on a gas station attendant's salary. How many fewer bankruptcies, broken marriages and desperate people would we have if everyone lived as the men of Special Forces, rather than trying to impress others with their four, five and six figure toys? If they seek to impress at all, Green Berets impress others with who and what they are, not what they've bought. Anyone can buy a green beret, they can be found in any military surplus store. What can't be bought at any price, however, is *being* a Green Beret.

The other part of the strength that comes from never fearing being fired can only come from inside of you. In life, "doing the right thing" often comes with a price, and that price may be your job. To all Green Berets, it is better to pay that price in the loss of a job, promotion or money, than to pay it in the loss of personal integrity and pride. When confronted with the moral decision of doing something that you know is right, versus doing something that protects an illegal or unconscionable action of your company or boss, never sacrifice your principles. Most of you will have many jobs in your lifetime. Integrity, once lost, may be gone forever. However, not fearing the loss of your job should never cause you to stop caring about your company, your job, your co-workers and subordinates. It should only free you up to meet all of those duties notwithstanding other pressures being placed on you. It should free you up to be the person you have decided you were meant to be.

Part of the duty you must meet to your company and colleagues requires that you do your very best as an individual within that group environment, to subordinate yourself to the good of the organization. You must care more about your team, your company and your co-workers than you do about yourself. From my first day of SF training to my last day of service at a high non-commissioned rank, I was made to understand that all problems are solved by the simple prioritization of: *Mission, Men,* then *Self.* This is what makes Special Forces so very special, and allows us to accomplish so much with so few people; far more than exponentially greater numbers of conventional military ever could. It is a commandment of SF, as compelling as any of the Ten Commandments that Moses brought down from the mountain, that all missions must be accomplished, no matter what the cost.

To do this, you must first take care of your men. You must provide them with everything necessary to accomplish that mission. That is your job as a leader. If they fail – if they die – it must never be for lack of you fulfilling your obligation to supply, equip, and train them. If you have done these correctly, you never have to worry about yourself, because those under you will realize your commitment and sacrifice to them, and THEY, IN TURN, WILL TAKE CARE OF YOU! If you are a true leader, you never ask your men to do anything you aren't willing to do, and that you haven't shown them you have already done, and would do again. No one will go into harm's way for a commander, just because he tells them to. But they will go to hell and back – and kill the devil himself in the process – for a leader. They will do it, if they know that you would do it too, and that it is killing you that you are not allowed to lead them in every operation.

ADVANTAGES OF THE WOLF PACK

In general, civilians tend to be too individualistic to tolerate much uniformity, though most business organizations could benefit from it. For instance, companies that dictate a dress code will always be more organized and more successful than those that do not. A dress code is nothing more than an SOP[54] establishing a minimal level of personal discipline. Not that SOPs are always about setting minimum standards. They can, and should, be about setting maximum tolerances wherever possible. For example, an employer might set limits on the amount of jewelry worn due to others being intimidated by such displays, or clients being put off by the excessive materialism of those whose salaries their fees are paying.

In other contexts, in the civilian world if everyone kept the "hot" material or exciting project documents – what in Special Forces

[54] Standard Operating Procedure

would be the classified stuff - in the same place, the same drawer of the desk, it would allow other members of the team to pick up for you if you got called away due to a family emergency or some other reason. When running classified recon[55] missions into enemy territory, all members of the Team carried certain items in designated pockets of their uniforms, or parts of their rucksacks. First aid kits and morphine, codes, maps, spare batteries for the radios, spare ammunition - all of the equipment that was critical and might have to be located on the body of a wounded or dead soldier in an instant under fire - was organized and uniformly arranged on every Team member. This saved countless lives and kept a tremendous amount of classified information from falling into enemy hands; which saved even more lives on the Teams running the same missions in the future. This sort of organization, and subordination of the individual to the team, could benefit the business world greatly.

When these organizational decisions are made, the employee should not resent or resist their implementation, as long as they are fair and reasonable. If anticipating resistance, management should approach the situation as a Green Beret top sergeant, by respecting the fact that they are dealing with a motivated, proud and smart group of people (why else would you have them in your company?), and explaining the reason for the decision, taking them into your confidence. It is a delicate balance for leaders to impose necessary behavioral standards onto their people, and yet know when to be flexible enough to tolerate deviations from those standards.

In the Special Forces, these identical situations are encountered. Despite well defined military standards on uniforms, the men of Special Forces have been known to indulge themselves in certain deviations for personal, or Team, pride. At times this has been seen in the wearing of unauthorized patches based on operations they conducted, or Teams they served on, wearing tiger stripe jungle fatigues in unauthorized areas, or the angle at which their berets were worn. Indeed, the very wearing of the green beret itself was

[55] Reconnaissance

something the men of SF did in contravention of orders for years, until it was officially awarded to them by President Kennedy in 1961.

SOMETIMES YOU MUST BEND

As a Green Beret manager, when you confront such resistance to doctrine, try to be understanding of some of the smaller deviations of company regulations. Before pedantically enforcing every little rule, first ask yourself whether that one transgression undermines the purpose of the rule, hurts the organization and destroys morale. Often you will find that winking at certain small violations will go far to improve morale of your overall workforce; something that corporate America – in its pell mell race toward the making of money – often overlooks. Do not forget that it is your workers who ultimately make you all that money, and the better their morale, the better their job performance.

If, after an objective assessment of the transgression, you determine that it cannot be tolerated, do not turn it into a power struggle. Do not redress the errant employee publicly, or demand he follow you to your office in front of others. Sit him down in an informal setting and explain the reason for the rule or the change in policy. Do this over a beer or a cup of coffee. Solicit his help, citing the impact he has on others through his natural leadership qualities and role. This will solve the majority of these kinds of problems. If not successful, you still have the authority for formal sanction, and nothing has been lost by you attempting to bring him into the fold. In fact, you will have gone far to earn even more respect from your subordinates, who will hear of the manner in which you handled the issue.

EVERYONE IS SOMEWHERE IN THE CHAIN OF COMMAND

Regardless of where you are in the Chain of Command, you are always both supervisor and subordinate. We all have others under us, relying on us, and we all have someone that we answer to. This is true even for the CEOs of corporations who answer to boards of directors and shareholders. As subordinates, we owe our employers a duty of loyalty, honesty and doing the best job that we can. As supervisors, we owe the same duty to those above us, but to those below us we owe an even greater duty: that of leadership, support, motivation, fairness and protection. This is far above the mere duty of being a manager. At its most basic level, managers only manage *things*, while leaders *lead people*.

Too many members of the American workforce show up each day only thinking of how little work they can get away with. This is the opposite of the attitude necessary to survive in the world of the Green Beret. It is also the opposite of the commitment necessary to succeed in the civilian corporate world, or just to live life as a person of character and integrity. Each day you go to work, life presents you with a new opportunity to strive mightily, to do your best and to work your hardest.

Green Berets show up every single day early in the morning, knowing that they will be undergoing exhaustive PT,[56] including running, calisthenics, maybe hand-to-hand combat. They will be forced over impossible obstacle courses to make them the best soldiers in the world. They will shoot and practice small unit tactics and combat firearms techniques. They will spend a long day performing their regular duties depending on their MOS. During breaks, they will be in the weightroom, maybe back on the shooting range, or re-run the obstacle course. They know each morning they arrive to work that they may be deployed without warning and not come home again for weeks or even months, without even the ability to say goodbye to their wives and children. And they live this, every day of their careers.

ASSETS AND LIABILITIES

To survive in their environment they know that they must continually strive to be the best. This is what makes them "Special," and is neces-

[56] Physical Training

sary for their own survival and that of their teammates. But, in terms of survival, civilians in the workplace are little different. Over the years since I retired from the Green Berets, I have served on a number of boards of directors, and at times assumed direct supervisory duties of security forces in the private sector. One of the first things I would tell those under me was that companies – like elite military units – do not fire people. People fire themselves.

Absent the rare incidence of a completely inappropriate and unfair supervisor, no organization can afford to give up hard-working, competent and dedicated employees. Private sector corporations function according to a bottom line of monetary profit. No such entity is going to incur the cost of training a replacement employee, only to give up the hardest working – and therefore best profit-generating – worker they have. Companies only fire those who have demonstrated that they are not there for the team, are not committed to doing the best job they can, and make no effort to improve themselves and their work performance. Corporations only get rid of liabilities, never assets. If you fail to live and work according to these principles, you will fail to survive.

CROSS TRAINING

Striving to be the best pays dividends in many areas, inside and outside of the workplace. In Special Forces, your first goal is to teach your job to those under you, and in the course of that effort to select your replacement and ensure he has been adequately prepared to assume your position. Your next task is to learn the job of the person above you, so that you are ready to move up, or step in and ensure the smooth running of the organization if he is absent. Once these two goals have been met, you should make sure that your counterparts in other positions have all been cross-trained in each other's jobs. This cross-training is the very foundation of survival of the Special Forces A Detachment. For the Green Berets, each man must be ready to step in and ensure booby traps are disarmed, communications are up and air support is provided in battle. All of the wounded must receive necessary medical attention, and weapons made operational, in the event any of those specialists are wounded or killed.

While things may not often reach such a dire state in your office, ensuring continued operations does take on the importance of the very survival of your organization. For some agencies, the threat to life is no less than that faced by Special Forces. In private security, law enforcement, intelligence agencies, fire rescue, paramedics, rural search and rescue, diving operations, lifeguarding, and mining operations, the commitment to be the best through each person's ability to perform any task can have life or death consequences, and those men and women can be no less committed than the Green Berets. The lesson learned in Special Forces is just as applicable to the business community: In a small unit, no one can afford the luxury of job specialization. While particularly applicable to small businesses – which are just a different type of small unit – it is equally important to large corporations, where each department is a small unit.

Specialization and sub-specialization may be the growing trend in business, but in firms where everyone is highly specialized, the workers have become disenfranchised from each other. This detracts from any common effort on the part of the workforce, in addition to making it impossible for co-workers to support each other in the best interest of the organization when one "specialist" is unable to perform his job. If any of the people in those organizations are not living according to the Green Beret Code, they have no business asking others to depend on them for anything. Nor do they have any business depending on others. They will quickly find that they cannot do their own jobs, however specialized, without the help of those others.

ALL FOR ONE, AND....

This has been one of the unfortunate consequences of the modern impact of unions on American business. Unions were a necessary creation early in the 20th century. Today they've caused a complete division of employees working together to get the mission accomplished. This is one of the main reasons federal law does not allow unions in the military or critical government agencies. To allow any outside institution to limit the emphasis on completing the mission at all costs, would destroy our national security. Whether in a large, medium or small company, if you have ever found yourself saying, "I don't have to do that, it's not in my job description," you are not worthy of your job or salary. In our own organization, and other private sector agencies we have been responsible for, our rule has always been that the person doing the most important task at the moment was the most important person in the company.

I have seen many times when John's legal assistants or secretaries would be typing frantically to meet a court deadline. At the time, that person was more important than even the most senior partner in the firm. Every lawyer would get that person coffee, babysit her kids, pick up her dry cleaning or run out and get her lunch. They would do anything to help her complete her task. It is the completion of the task, finishing the mission, doing the damn job that is the only focus any team can ever have, whether in Special Forces or business.

Look what has happened to many major corporations that have become paralyzed by union constraints on employees. The workers were so busy worrying about themselves that the corporations either went bankrupt or were forced to move out of the United States to ensure their survival. In business – unlike the military and government – you aren't just handed a new tranche of money to spend at the beginning of each year. In business, you have to earn that money, work hard to do the job that got you that money, and not spend more than you made. When a business is forced to take on too many employees with too many costly benefits at too high a payroll, while productivity of those workers decreases, the future of the organization is dismal. The employees of these businesses care nothing about the mission, about the team, about self-respect, integrity or honor; ultimately to their demise.

BEING ONE OF AMERICA'S BEST

Being the best is not only important in critical, life saving professions. No matter what job you hold, if it is honest work you should be proud of who you are and what you do, and be the very best at it. Over the years I have had many men try to impress me with their elite skills, their supposed "special" military service and the high risk operations they ran. Even in Special Forces people can be found who survived initial training for no reason other than to impress others with their beret, with no intention of ever living and working as true Green Berets. These men do not impress me, and the fact that they wore – or wear - a beret means nothing to me. One of the most impressive men I ever met was working on the security teams at one of the Department of Energy's (DOE) nuclear weapons facilities. He was big and muscular at six feet three inches, and two hundred thirty pounds. He was well trained, a good operator and special response team leader. I knew that he had been in the Marines, and one day after seeing the high level of his training performance I asked him what he had done in the Marines. Looking me straight in the eye, he proudly said, "Sergeant Major, I was a cook."

I was both stunned and impressed by his reply. It was the first time anyone had ever been so candid about his prior service. I asked him, "Were you a good cook?" He responded, "I was the best damn cook in the division." Hearing this told me much about this man. It told me about his code of honesty, and I knew right away that he was a man I could trust and who would never lie to me.

When I was in Special Forces I strove mightily to be the best Green Beret I could be. I wanted to be a Super Soldier, which to me was personified in Green Beret Joe Alderman. This same attitude is what got me through the torturous "Q" or Qualifications Course to earn the cherished green beret. I knew I wasn't going to be the fastest, or have the most endurance, or be the smartest. But I knew I was going to do my best, and no matter what I was never going to quit. This mindset took much of the pressure off of me, as I knew that if I failed it would have been because I continued pushing myself until I passed out or died, or they threw me out. No matter what, it was not going to be because of a conscious decision of my own. Quite literally, I would have run until I dropped.

As I rose in the NCO ranks to Sergeant Major, I sought to train the men under me to be better than I. I would use my own money, curry favors from others and call in favors from those who owed me, to get my men the best training and equipment I could. In return, I expected the men in my company to give me their all. I expected them to be the best individually and, thus, become the best Teams in all of Special Forces. When I did not receive this level of commitment, I didn't hesitate to fire them. Sometimes this meant that men I had become friends with were terminated. That was just the way of it, and the way it always has to be. They no longer placed the Team ahead of themselves, hadn't striven to be the best. Thus, they had breached their duty to me and to their teammates. In reality, I didn't fire them, they fired themselves.

THE LITIGATION BUGABOO

In the business environment you cannot function any differently. Like freeing yourself from fear of being fired, never allow the threat of litigation by an employee to paralyze you from making a necessary management decision. Threats of lawsuits are little more than a legally tolerated form of extortion. The Green Beret does what is right, regardless of the consequences or threats from others. As a business leader, your first priority is to "fill the slot." There are times when you can only hope that the person you are putting in that slot is a quality soldier. Once filled, your next priority as a leader is to do the "Dud Cut." This means that after providing that individual with adequate training, and time to develop into a worthwhile employee, you get rid of him if he fails you. Even if he is giving his best effort, if it becomes clear that will not be enough for him to do the job adequately, you still have to get rid of him. This is part of being a leader. You must make decisions in the best interests of the team, no matter how painful to you or the individual.

In the private sector, you must get rid of the careerists and keep the professionals. Careerists are in their positions for promotions and bragging rights; whereas professionals are there to do the job, irrespective of press coverage, industry notoriety or benefits. The professional wants to be challenged and to be surrounded by others who are just like him. Just like Green Berets.

THE SIREN SONG OF SUPERIORITY

Another consequence of my efforts to ensure my men were the best was that Green Berets from every SF Group around the world, would do anything they could to get onto my Teams. These were the men who wanted to be the best, and when they heard I was the most demanding leader, yet offered the best skills, expertise and training, they wanted to not only be the best, but be with the best. These men would pull every string they could to get to my company. When they arrived, no matter what the mission, I was going to make certain that my Teams were going to be the best at anything we were asked to do. I didn't care if we were going to be burning shit in cans. If that was the mission, we were going to be the best shit burners in all of Special Forces, if not the whole Army.

I have never changed or altered this attitude in any way, or with any group that I have worked with. When in charge of DOE nuclear weapons security forces, I gave them the best training possible and instilled a sense of pride in them for the important, dangerous and elite work they were doing on behalf of America. Even when supervising the security staff of a private corrections service provider, I attempted to accomplish the same thing. I instituted a dress code and got my people uniform shirts. Training was stepped up, including such unprecedented programs as defensive tactics, law, and report writing. I lobbied hard to get them pay increases, tuition reimbursement benefits, and generally forged them into a team that they could be proud of. These efforts quickly paid dividends to the company.

To date, both John Giduck and I, along with others from the Archangel Anti-Terror Group, continue to serve Special Forces through the training we provide. Just as when I was a Green Beret sergeant major, I make certain that the training we are giving them is the best. After years of martial arts training and even more years with the Russian Special Forces, John provides a hand-to-hand combat program that is the best I have ever seen, and I am no dilettante when it comes to this subject, having been a Green Beret and DOE hand-to-hand instructor and court certified use-of-force expert. If this program had been known to me while still in SF, I would have required every single person on my Teams to train it at least two hours every day. If necessary I would have outlawed any other type of PT training to make sure they got its life saving skills worked into their daily schedules.

In my opinion, the integrated close-quarter combat firearms and hand-to-hand combat training we provide Green Berets is the best available. We constantly boast that we have never taught the identical course to SF Teams twice, as we learn something new in every class we teach, then incorporate it to improve the course the next time. We are training men who want to be the best, and we cannot do that if we are not willing to work to reach that pinnacle ourselves.

This is all I have ever cared about in anyone. Whatever job someone has – whether it is a job they are forced by life circumstances to take, or a true calling – I only ever want to know one thing: Are you good at what you do? I have asked this question of people in every position from lawyer, doctor and Green Beret, to lumberjack, plumber, wallpaper hanger and farrier. In most instances, they know I am a retired Special Forces sergeant major and expect me to look down my nose at them for the work they do. In every instance, they have been surprised to find that I am as admiring of them for doing their jobs well, for being the best they can be, as I have ever been of anyone in the military.

The very success and survival of our society depends on millions of different jobs being done by millions of different people. Not everyone can be a Green Beret, SEAL, Ranger, Air Commando, Force Recon Marine, or even a Secret Service agent, FBI Special Agent, Hostage Rescue Team operator, CIA Special Activities Division agent, or a spy. We need doctors and lawyers, plumbers and electricians, painters, computer programmers, ski instructors, school bus drivers, salesmen, construction workers, ditch diggers, snow plowers and farmers. We need convenience store clerks. But what we need most from all of those people in all of those positions is for them to approach their jobs with the mindset of the Green Beret: Being the Best. No one will ever fault you for striving to be the best you can be, and that commitment is necessary for every person to live according to a code of character and personal integrity. Without this integrity, who are we? What can we possibly contribute to anyone in our lives, including ourselves?

HONOR

Personal integrity in meeting your duty to your company must play a role in other areas as well. In both corporations and government agencies, the number one cost of doing business is often employee theft. This usually takes the form of small item theft, but it is theft nonetheless. In Special Forces this behavior was never tolerated on any level. The Special Forces lifestyle was all about PRIDE. During the Vietnam era it became the unofficial standard of a Green Beret to have a Rolex watch. This had a two-fold purpose: One, it set us apart from other, lesser units and was a symbol of our brotherhood; and, two, it provided us with a valuable asset we could trade for assistance or safe passage should we find ourselves in an escape-and-evasion mode in hostile territory. No one gave us these watches; we worked hard, saved our money and paid for them ourselves. In all my years in Special Forces I could take my Rolex off and leave it in the dirt in the middle of a camp and walk away. Within a few hours someone would walk up with it and say, "Hey Top, I think this is yours."

This wouldn't prove to be the case in the regular, leg Army. Once, in Germany, I had to accept a wrestling challenge from a fellow Green Beret. I took my Rolex off and left it on the radiator. By the time I had finished kicking his butt, and dealing with the other SF men who decided to jump on top of me, it was already gone. We had more than a few experiences like that with those outside the Green Beret family. This is the difference between those who live like Green Berets, and those who never will.

Whether you are serving on a Special Forces Team, corporate team, project group, or functioning in any other community, the members of that group must all rely on each other. To do this, you have to be able to trust one another. Unfortunately, for much of America trust – like honor – has become a quaint notion. It has become a notion that Jack Nicholson's character, in the movie *A Few Good Men*, well recognized was being used "as a punch line at parties" by people outside the military. It is not that the Special Forces, and certainly not the military, invented these concepts or has a monopoly on them. It is just that most Americans have moved beyond embracing them as part of their daily lives. Groups like Green Berets, other Special Operations units, and the military in general, attract those Americans who desire a life that is imbued with these principles and standards. For others, honor has faded in the face of a lifestyle where we all try to get away with as much as we can.

When putting a team together and expecting it to function as such, it is axiomatic that if you will steal from me, you will also lie to me. If you will lie to me, you will lie to me about anything. And if you will lie to me about anything, how can I trust you when you say that you will be there for me when we are facing our most difficult challenges? "When the smoke clears I will still be there," is a phrase that people use everyday, but give little thought to. For us, it literally means that when the battle is over, when the bullets have stopped flying and the enemy is lying at your feet, you will still be standing there, facing the threat with me. It means you are tough enough and good enough that you will survive, and brave and committed enough that you will not leave your friends and run.

This was never better represented than by a sergeant first class on one of my Teams. I had been pushing my men up a steep, towering mountain for most of the day, without water or respite of any kind. The men were stringing out below, and I was driving myself to stay in the lead. When I reached the summit there was only this one young sergeant, Benny Pokemire, with me. As we stopped to catch our breath after hours of climbing, he said, "The only difference between me and those guys down there, is that when the smoke clears after a battle, I'll still be standing there with you." Even between Green Berets there are varying levels of commitment and sacrifice. We should all strive to be like that one SF soldier standing atop that mountain summit.

With Americans' indulgence in *blamism*, litigation, lack of self-responsibility, and reality shows where everyone is made a celebrity by being the best manipulator and back-stabber, the civilian world – indeed even some of the regular military – has a long way to go to recapture the highest and most noble traditions of integrity and honor. If your children regularly witness you blaming others for your problems, bringing home company property for personal use, misusing company vehicles or treating rental cars worse than your own; if they see you immersing yourself in any of the vapid and vacuous television shows and magazines that popular culture inundates us with – or looking to sue someone when you should just accept your own responsibility - how honest and honorable will their own lives be? The same is true of your subordinates at work, your co-workers and teammates. Whether you are stealing company property for your own use or damaging the property of another, whether you are seeking to take money from others because some part of your own life didn't work out as well as you thought it should have, it is all theft of some sort. Even the major mass media syndicates are looking to steal from you with their amoral, and often immoral, brainwashing.

These are exactly the things Green Berets do not do. They do not do it to one another, and they do not even do it to people outside the SF community. No one on your team should ever have to steal from you; not your money, your time, or your property. If someone on your team needs something that badly, he should know all he has to do is ask for it and you will give it to him. During my military service, none of us made much money. Occasionally an emergency would come up and one of us would need to buy a plane ticket quickly, though rarely did we have the money. In each instance, everyone would pitch in and come up with the money so that our friend could attend to a family emergency. Never did anyone have to be reminded that the debt was owed. True team members always pay back every penny, as soon as they can.

When someone does steal, the price should be great. Among Green Berets the price for stealing was high, life destroying, and sometimes life-ending. But the punishment was never what kept Green Berets from stealing. They did not do it because they had a sense of pride, a desire to be the best; not only the best at their chosen profession, but the best people they could be. Anyone can adopt this attitude and the code that comes with it.

THE EARNED REPUTATION

The decisions you make in all of these areas will dictate the reputation that you go through life with. It is up to each person to decide what legacy he wishes to leave behind. Unfortunately, few ever give thought to this important aspect of life. They fail to give any real thought to the fact that when we die, the only thing we leave behind are the legacies of our lives, the decisions we made, the lives we lived, and the reputations we forged on the anvil of life's challenges.

In analyzing the person you want to be known as, take a hard and honest look at your own life decisions and ask yourself whether you would trust such a person. Would you, for instance, want to be business partners with a co-worker who constantly helped himself to all the "free" supplies from their employer? Do you want to risk your professional reputation with someone who never shows up for work on time, thus stealing money from his company by being paid a salary for work he was not there to do.

Do you want to risk your financial future – and your family's future – on someone who lies to his clients or his boss about why a project wasn't finished or an important contract lost? How about someone who complains that he doesn't get the training time he needs rather than commit some of his personal time to his own betterment? Do you want to be in business with someone who sues others whenever a deal doesn't work to his advantage? These are the decisions people make every day of their lives. While they always have their reasons, they often fail to recognize that by pandering to their own interests they also pay a price in other areas of their lives

Lisa Tongren is a corrections officer and negotiations team leader. In an unfortunate re-enactment of the famous McDonald's spilled-coffee-in-the-lap case, she was driving down the road with a hot cup of coffee, and while leaning over the passenger seat spilled it down her leg, causing severe burns. She got the necessary medical attention and attempted to forget the incident, only to be overwhelmed by "friends" telling her how stupid she was for not suing the coffee shop, and trying to tempt her with all the money she could get by hiring a lawyer. But Lisa accepted her own responsibility, laughed at her own thoughtless behavior, and moved on. When being seduced by the lure of money she continued to follow her own code and did not attempt to profit from the unfortunate consequences of her own actions. Those who plied her with such well-meaning advice lacked any such code, and certainly no sense of self-responsibility. While they had no honor, she did the honorable thing. The everyday events of our lives are where we face the constant tests of the Green Beret Code. This young lady was living it.

In Special Forces, once your reputation is established there is no place that you can go and not find that it has arrived ahead of you. If that reputation is bad you can only shed it through a lot of hard work, but it will always be like a shadow that never leaves your side, no matter how much you might complain about the unfairness of it all. If that reputation is good, you should still expect to have to earn it all over again, and again after that, anytime you get assigned to a new Group or Team. When I was in Special Forces, we were a unit of approximately 3,500 men[37] out of a one or two million person Army, depending on the era. In that small community, your reputation always preceded you.

The same is true in any corporation or industry in America. Despite the fact that you may have worked hard to earn an excellent reputation, be prepared to re-earn it any time you change departments, units, branch offices or companies. Whether in Special Forces or the civilian world, there is no point in decrying the inequity of this. For when living the Green Beret Lifestyle, whether others are putting you to the test or not, you are living your personal code everyday. You re-earn that good reputation with every action you take and decision you make, whether others are watching or not. A Green Beret is never afraid to be judged by the way he lives.

GREEN BERET TOP SERGEANT AS BUSINESS MANAGER

One of the most difficult things for an SF Team sergeant to do is make twelve smart, physically fit, individualistic (and they are individualistic because that is the type of person that comes to SF) men - men who have accomplished what few others could ever contemplate - *work as a team*. Accomplishing the same with a group of motivated, intelligent, educated and proud young businessmen and women is no less challenging a task, and in some cases may be more difficult. This

---

[57] Full Special Forces complement in recent years has been approximately 8,000, with that number increasing today.

is really the same with any group of people who come to a job with the personal drive to achieve success.

I have found that a simple demonstration conveys the need for teamwork in a very comprehensible way. Hold both of your hands up, palms out, with the fingers of each hand spread out like you're showing them the number ten. Ask them if there is any doubt that if you continue to hold your fingers out, that any one of them could reach out and break any finger he wanted. Of course, there are none; even the smallest-boned females could do it easily. Now make tight fists with both hands and tell them to "break that." Make the point: *that is a team working together,* as opposed to individuals with some superficial connection to each other. Just like the fingers, some of the team members are bigger than others. Some have abilities the others do not. But they are all part of a single unit.

Every person has strengths and weaknesses. Each person knows it, and so will the rest of the team in a short time. But, if every one tries to use his strengths to overcome, and help build on, others' weaknesses, the team cannot be beaten. They will become a true team in every respect, with the whole being greater than the sum of the parts. In Special Forces, the Team sergeant's job is to make sure that this happens. In the private sector, the manager-leader's job is no different. There are no easy answers, as personalities and motivations are different. But experience and lots of Team time have shown that there are a limited number of personalities found in units like Special Forces. The same is true of people who are attracted to almost every profession. The names will change, but you will know what it takes to motivate each person, because you will have seen that person before; maybe in another body and with a different name, but you will have previously seen and dealt with that character makeup.

Another thing that you need to know about building a true team is that only real team members can live in the ultra-close environment that SF operations require. To test this among Green Berets, you need to schedule a mission or training that lasts at least 15 days. That forces everyone in the detachment to live hard in close quarters.

Watch, and you will see the ones that are not team players, the ones that indulge their own weaknesses under the stress of the environment. These people inject conflict into the team to such an extent that an otherwise small personality problem or idiosyncrasy will often develop into a fistfight. This problem can be worked on with some people, but others will have to be moved to a different unit, or a different type of unit. The same is found with people in many high stress environments, such as emergency rooms, police and fire departments, trial law firms, accounting firms during tax season, publishing houses and many others.

No matter what, though, when you are in the Top Sergeant position you must protect your team from those above you. This is even true in the constitution of the team. Never allow those above you to dictate who is on your team. I don't care if he is the general's son-in-law or the CEO's girlfriend, work hard to make sure that if someone is not a real team member he - or she - is out.

It has also been my observation in life that truly smart people are often highly irritable, and can sometimes be short-tempered. This is because they get frustrated by those around them not understanding things that are so obvious to them. They grow tired of what they see as others always asking them to do their thinking for them. They become exasperated when asked to explain how they arrived at certain conclusions, when the questioner has all the same information available and should have quickly come to the same understanding. Sometimes their pique is justified, as people will exploit others who are smarter or work harder. This is a factor in team functioning you must be ready for, and able to resolve. You want smart people on your team, especially in the private sector. You need the smart ones, but also can't afford to allow their temperamentalism to harm the team.

TEAM BUILDING IN THE CORPORATE WORLD

America's corporate culture has attempted to adopt and benefit from military, especially Special Forces, training and team creation. For a number of years now, corporations have taken to spending enormous amounts of money on teambuilding exercises, and supposed team-building consultants. All of this is for the desired result of making their self-serving and disenfranchised office workers meld together as a cohesive and trusting group for the ultimate benefit of the company's bottom line. In this effort they devise all manner of out-of-town trips, ropes courses, camping trips, horseback riding adventures, golf tournaments and outdoor games. Sometimes they do nothing more than sit around in a "retreat" type forum and talk.

What they have failed entirely to realize is that the corporate approach to teambuilding does not work the way it's done, or at least the way it's attempted. Part of the problem is that the so-called experts being paid to arrange all of these events – really little more than elementary school field trips – have never been in the military and have never been part of a real team themselves. Relying on them is like going to a marriage counselor that has been divorced three times, or listening to an expert on child psychology whose own kids are social waste products. In trying to build teams of integrated and committed employees, corporations at best mimic the form, but never the substance, of military teambuilding activities.

The business sector must come to grips with the reality that you can never build a team by doing anything that is fun. If your teambuilding exercise is something people would enjoy doing at a company picnic, it is wasted effort, and all you will have managed to do is give these folks a few days off to ride horses, hike in the woods or golf. The executives in charge of these debacles must realize that there is little similarity between the military teambuilding approach – one that is also seen successfully used with top level sports teams – and what is being done in the civilian corporate world. There are only three ways to build a true team. If you are doing anything else, you are wasting your time, your money, and deluding yourself into believing that you will realize some result that will, in fact, never occur.

1.   Having a small group of people push themselves to their absolute physical limits and beyond, *TOGETHER!* This is most often seen in the training of athletes, and the Selection Phase of Special Operations units and other government agencies such as the Secret Service and FBI.

2.   Having a group of people endure the most extreme, difficult and life threatening environmental circumstances *TOGETHER,* and *SURVIVE.* While Special Forces training incorporates this dynamic as a matter of course, the bonding from this experience among civilians is most often seen in groups that have been lost in the wilderness together, and people who endured natural catastrophes such as hurricanes and earthquakes together. The Outward Bound program attempts to develop the character of the children they oversee through such experiences. Sadly, the Cub Scouts and Boy Scouts used to build the character of America's young men through such worthwhile exercises, but an increasingly weak society, political correctness and fear of litigation have seen such efforts diluted down to undertakings often no more difficult or dangerous than arts and crafts.

3.   Having a group of people face life and death conflict – yes - TOGETHER. This means combat. This is the category where the military, and those fearless civilians working in hot zones around the world, enjoy team bonding that cannot be touched by any other experience.

Other than these three approaches, nothing works. Any other team-building efforts amount to nothing more than superficial efforts to create the form of true team bonding, while shying away from the substance that makes them successful. And you cannot build a team over a weekend either, no matter how difficult that weekend. Decades of experience with men at all levels, and from many countries, has taught me that such efforts are a waste of time. It takes 10 to 16 continuous days in these difficult conditions to become team players, or to learn if they ever can be.

Other efforts at teambuilding have no greater chance of creating a truly cohesive, committed unit, than attempting to build a championship baseball team by taking them to watch Major League games, or training a boxing team by having them sit through a *Rocky* movie marathon. Does anyone honestly believe that our military could create elite Special Operations soldiers by having a group of untrained men watch the movies *Navy SEALs, The Green Berets* with John Wayne, the *Rambo* series, or even *Tears of the Sun* and *Blackhawk Down*? Could this be accomplished by having the men play golf, or play paintball while drinking at a picnic, or doing walking meditation through the woods? Of course not.

If you do not believe we can train elite military operators from such ridiculous experiences, how is it that so many highly paid, successful executives – among the brightest in America – can delude themselves into believing that they can build elite business teams through similar endeavors? They forget that the job of the team is secondary, and no matter what it is, that job can't be done without first *having* a team.

Long before you, as a manager or business owner, waste your time and money in an endeavor that is certain to fail, take five volunteer managers and send them to Iraq or Afghanistan, Kosovo, Chechnya, Sudan or Haiti, to do a month of humanitarian aide. Let them live in squalor together, don body armor every day and carry guns as last ditch personal protection. Let them protect each other, place their lives in the hands of the others, knowing that each other is the only protection they have from kidnapping, beheading, street robbery, mine fields, bad food and giardia-ridden water. Let them do all this in the worst possible circumstances; then bring them home.

Or sign your people up for one of the intense weeks-long, top level bodyguard training schools found around the world; the closest thing to military training without enlisting. Not only would they emerge a team, but one with critical skills for executives working or traveling abroad. If you want to keep them home, have them join groups like the Guardian Angels, go through their training and spend time together patrolling dangerous streets late at night to protect innocent victims from assault. Or sign them up as a security team at a battered women's shelter.

When they have completed whichever program you chose, give them a special pin to wear on their suit coat lapel, or issue them a challenge coin[58] that they will carry, attesting to their courage and special experiences. Then you will have a team. It will be a real team that will function together far beyond the capabilities of every other group in your company. Then watch how others in your organization will clamor to become members of that elite group. Whether a law enforcement, military, athletic or corporate group, you will end up with the same result. In trips John has led to Russia to train with elite Spetsnaz units, he has on occasion taken regular civilians. Over the years he has seen a CPA, cowboy and stockyard worker, business owners and even a female college professor successfully endure training that many in our military would not. But just from this experience, the bond of those who survived that training together is always demonstrable when they are around each other.

Many will not want to endure the experiences, make the sacrifices, and risk the unpleasantness and possible danger, to join such a group. These are not the Green Berets in your organization. That is alright, though, as not everyone can be special or elite. The military needs its conventional units and personnel too. But such a program will allow you to identify the true corporate warriors in your midst, as opposed to those that simply want to work a job and draw a paycheck.

58 In Vietnam the Green Berets started a tradition that was quickly adopted by SEALs and other Special Operations units. The Green Berets from each Group were issued large coins verifying the holder's membership in SF. Each Green Beret was to have his coin with him at all times. If anyone ever challenged his status by showing a coin of his own, the challenged man had ten seconds to produce his own, by slapping it on a table. If he could, the challenger owed him a drink of his choice right then. If he couldn't, the challenger was treated to a drink. Since then, virtually all military units have begun producing their own coins; this practice is now seen with police departments, SWAT teams and even some government agencies.

RAPPORT

No lesson from the Special Forces is more directly applicable to the civilian business environment than that of rapport-building. The establishment and maintenance of rapport with whomever you are working is as important as having a loaded weapon in a gunfight. In Special Forces, you must understand what motivates the people you are working with to risk their lives to complete a mission. You know that you have one of the best trained Teams in the U.S. Army; and by definition one of the very best in the world. Every man not only knows his job, but can also teach it. Every Team member is cross-trained to do at least one other man's job as well; some can do three or four. All are highly motivated hard-chargers with a *can do* attitude, and you are proud of them. With that group, you are often given the mission to train a third world unit in infantry tactics.

If the commander, or even a lowly private, in that other country's army perceives a haughty or superior attitude from any one of your Team members, the mission will not be completed to the standards you or your commander have set. If one of the soldiers we are to train invites me to his home for dinner, and I do not like the food, or do not understand the simplest customs, I will have insulted him and his family. The result will be that this one single incident will destroy the working relationship necessary to build the bonds crucial to the running of successful combat operations, and the possible destruction of a critical U.S. policy toward that nation.

Despite the fact that Green Berets are highly trained commandos, often drawing the most difficult and dangerous missions, in reality they are trained to be teachers. Special Forces are what the military calls "force multipliers." That means the mission of Special Forces – when used as they were designed – is to drop a few Green Berets into a foreign land, have them link up with the indigenous population and begin training them to be a self-sustaining and effective combat unit. The legend is that you can put an A Detachment of twelve Green Berets in a hostile foreign country, come back three months later and find 1,500 highly trained soldiers ready to fight; all this without any of the indigenous trainees needing to know English.

In his inside look at Special Forces, Hans Halberstadt reported, "The work of these men is as much political science as it is combat, and a successful wearer of the green beret is as skilled in interpersonal and cross-cultural relations as he is with firearms."[59] Special Operations Command (SOCOM) understands just how much can hang in the balance of two human beings merely getting along: "The relationship between two such people can influence relations between the countries in the near and distant future, for good or ill. So, the officer had better be skilled in much more than small unit tactics. He is a diplomat in green, and he had better be good."[60]

Many times I was called on to repair the seemingly irretrievable enmity that developed between U.S. military personnel and officers from a host country. Even in SF, there sometimes were men who would not commit to working and playing well with the indigenous soldiers to further U.S. relations and security around the globe. Many of these missions were picked up by the real professionals of Special Forces, and fixed by the establishment of true rapport. The only inviolable rule in such circumstances – whether representing military, government or business – is recognizing and accepting the fact that the people you are dealing with are men, and women, who are human just like you. You are not superior, and your quality of life, or level of education, does not make you better than them.

This cannot be accomplished without empathy for, and understanding of, other peoples' cultures, feelings, customs, religious beliefs and practices, cuisine and even conversational styles. When John and I were in southern Sudan, we quickly found that the Dinka tribesmen were very soft spoken, talking in barely a whisper,

[59] Halberstadt, 18.
[60] Ibid.

especially compared to Americans. Immediately we had to curb the American tendency to be loud and boisterous, frequently talking over others in conversation. By American standards, Russians are often found to be argumentative, and can be insulting in business situations. Many Asian cultures are exceedingly polite, but saving face is a constant concern that you must be sensitive to. No one of these cultures or behaviors is better than another; though some are easier for Americans to deal with than others. They are simply different. You must be able to adjust to the differences, particularly when working with those others is essential to the completion of the mission.

If two dirty soldiers, sitting in dank woods in the middle of nowhere can impact the success of relations between nations, imagine what two businessmen can do to hurt the relations of two companies. In business, this does not mean pandering to every person's insistence that all others change their behavior completely to accommodate his individual beliefs, practices or customs. This cultural hand-wringing has become an American obsession, and has paralyzed both our private and public sector institutions. Being respectful of another belief system only means to treat others with the same respect you would ask from them. It doesn't mean you have to do anything special *for* them.

When dealing with other cultures in everyday life, I believe that we should never do something for others that they aren't ready to do for us. This applies to all of those special interest groups out there demanding that they be pandered to. With the increasing diversity in the workforce, as well as the internationalization of business, cultural awareness is a necessary lesson to be taken from the Special Forces. Just as with the Green Berets, if your respect for others is not reciprocated, then politely and confidently tell them to go screw themselves. If the intransigence of those you are working with is going to keep you from accomplishing the mission under acceptable terms to you, at least leave them respecting – if not fearing – you. Even a Green Beret can only be pushed so far. Make sure your foreign "colleagues" know in their hearts who is the strongest, and that you can always go higher and do better than them to get the job done.

THE MANTLE OF AUTHORITY

When you are in a position of authority, you are on a tight rope. The first thing you must recognize is that the power you have been given can never be used to satisfy personal animosities, jealousies or vendettas. The moment you are elevated to a command position, you must see things differently. You must be harder on yourself than you are on any of those working under you. You must treat the lowliest employee with respect. You must lead from the front.

One of the most important concepts the Green Berets learned from working with Montagnards[61] in Vietnam with regard to the concept of leadership was their saying: "You cannot push a rope." When in a leadership role, those under you are the rope. You can only move that rope by taking a position at the front and pulling them behind you. You can never push those you lead ahead of you. As is commonly said among Green Berets: If you are not leading from the front, you are not leading. Far too many abuses are seen in corporate America because men and women are given power without personal discipline, or recognition of the constructive purpose that must attend the use of that power.

This does not mean that leadership is, by any means, easy. That is one of the problems with the civilian business world today: everyone has abandoned leadership in exchange for management, and they think management can be made easy. This is increasingly seen with the management-by-committee or group approach. But no organization can be run that way. Leading is tough, and it takes a tough person to do it. You will have to make difficult decisions, and implement them even if you don't want to, and even if they make you unpopular. But if you're a good leader, you can make people attack the assigned job with vigor and effort, no matter how much they don't

---

61 Indigenous tribal mountain people found throughout Vietnam and Southeast Asia.

want to do it at all. In SF, I was once told that leadership is being able to tell people to go to hell, and still make them look forward to the trip.

If you are a leader, your subordinates will be able to ask you an honest question about how to do a job or handle a problem in the best way, and know that they will get your best answer. They will, of course, know that the answer may not be a perfect one, but it is the best you are capable of giving. This is critical in forging the loyalty and commitment necessary in any Chain of Command. Your subordinates should never legitimately worry about whether you are setting them up. Even if you would never do such a thing, if they are concerned that you might, you have failed as a leader. If you allow anyone below you in the chain of the command to do such a thing to his subordinates, you have failed doubly as a leader. This is what team integrity is all about.

One way to create trust and dedication to a leader is by that leader never separating himself from his subordinates. This is violated in many industries and professions. It is seen in managers insisting they have the best accommodations when traveling. It is seen in hospitals where physicians insist their co-workers refer to them as "Doctor;" where business executives and lawyers demand their perceived inferiors only address them as "Mister" or "Ms." When John was teaching college he was amused by instructors who would only allow their students to address them as "Doctor" or "Professor," whereas he was always, "John."

In all my years in Special Forces no top leader ever required subordinates to call him by his full rank and name. I never made anyone say, "Sergeant Major Anderson." Although my name is John, I was always just "Andy" to everyone. For others it might have just been "Sarge." This did not imply any lack of respect or loss of discipline. In fact, it represented a level of discipline and respect that far surpassed the superficialities of those insecure souls that had ascended to positions of command and demanded obeisance be paid to them regularly.

This chasm of separation between enlisted ranks and officers in the conventional military, is one of the greatest mistakes made. John has a friend who served in the military with his older brother. When they first met at Ft. Benning, Georgia, John James was a drill sergeant training new recruits. Shortly afterward – and after a number of years as an NCO - he graduated Officer Candidate School. Fifteen years after that, John Giduck and then-Major John James found themselves together in Afghanistan. Despite the fact that he was the son of a highly decorated Army general, and was commanding troops in a war zone, Major James not only refused to make those working under him refer to him by rank, but was often heard to laughingly redress them for not calling him by his familiar nickname: "Jimmy Joe."

This was not an insecure man concerned with the superficial *indicia* of respect, but a top level leader. It was clear to John that the people under Major James trusted him implicitly and would unhesitatingly follow him into battle. That is the highest compliment anyone can ever be paid. Who do you care enough about, respect and honor to such a degree, that you would follow that person into combat, or any life threatening situation? Who have you have been so brave, trustworthy and honorable to, that they might do the same for you?

Special Forces is all about developing such respect and trust that each would follow everyone else into battle. This level of bonding is not the result of superficial acknowledgement of higher rank, or deluding yourself into thinking your rank is a substitute for honor, trustworthiness and courage. Despite the informality among those on my Teams, I can assure you that no one ever doubted the seriousness with which I approached my job or the high standards I set for everyone, myself included. The same is true for John James and many like us. In fact, it is this very obsession with observances of venerated rank that has retarded the evolution of all of the conventional military units in America, and the world. To see the flaw in overall command chain unity, look at the British system and all of the military units they created or trained over centuries. The boundaries between officers and enlisted men continue to be their Achilles' heel.

If you are a business manager who requires your employees to address you as "Mister" or "Director," you suffer the same affliction. If you are afraid that failing to use your title will erode their respect for you, take a quick glimpse in the mirror and accept the fact that they already don't respect you. If they do not respect you, that is something you have earned. Don't delude yourself into believing that you can simply demand respect without earning it. Do not believe for a moment that forcing someone to say the words you want to hear is the same as a member of your team *wanting* to show you more respect than you demand.

John Giduck and I have known each other for many years, yet he will still call me "Sergeant Major" at times, particularly when we are around others. This is his way of subtly communicating to them the level of respect and honor he expects them to show me. This is John being my teammate. When we are both on Special Forces bases, we automatically find ourselves addressing officers many years our junior as "Sir," or top NCOs as "Master Sergeant" or "Sergeant Major." We do this out of respect, despite the fact that we are civilians and they insist we address them by their first names. When training Teams of young Green Berets, they always start off by calling me "Sergeant Major," despite the fact I am retired from the Army. When I finally get them to call me "Andy," they do it in a way that conveys the respect they have for what I was so many years ago; when I was one of them.

For those of you who work under a true leader - one who leads as a Green Beret - even though you may call him "Bill," your respect for him and his position should resonate in your mind and voice every time you address him, every time you say: "Bill." At the same time, those who respect you will immediately default to using your title when in the presence of strangers. They will do this without being asked. They will do it to ensure outsiders who have not earned the right to demonstrate familiarity with you, treat you as you deserve to be treated. No greater respect could ever be shown to any man or woman.

HUMBLY KNOWING YOU'RE THE BEST

One of America's greatest characteristics, now in danger of being destroyed by mass media and pop culture, is the practice of humility. Every day Americans are subsumed into a culture in which crowing that you are *Number 1!, The BEST, the Greatest,* and deserving of becoming a celebrity, while everyone else is inferior, is not only tolerated but lauded. This is seen as much as heard. NFL football players seem incapable of scoring a touchdown without engaging in the all-too-predictable, and mind-numbingly boring, spiking of the ball. The fans who have accomplished nothing more than buying a ticket and fighting traffic to attend the game, are forever thrusting their index fingers into the air in front of television cameras while chanting, "We are number one!" As if they did something noteworthy.

I believe this all began with Cassius Clay; later to become Muhammed Ali. His insistence in publicly proclaiming how great and "pretty" he was, was rejected by many in our society at first, having been used to modest sports and military heroes. Since then this behavior has taken on the characteristics of a runaway train. Between pop psychology, daytime talk shows and an endless stream of books seeking to empower us and build our confidence, no one dares appear modest about anything anymore. Add to this an epidemic on childrearing that requires schools and parents to constantly tell their kids that they are the best, the greatest, and deserving of a four-foot trophy anytime they show up at an athletic event. There seems to be no respite from this attack on humility.

Within the military, Special Forces are not known for the machismo that many might expect from them. They are not men who lower themselves to the showing off seen by other units. Unlike other, lesser, units, they do not even have their own "Special Forces" license plates. They do not brag or boast, preferring to let their accomplishments and reputation of their unit speak for them. Rather than being known for the arrogance or imperiousness seen in many other military units, they are known simply by the moniker "The Quiet Professionals."

While it is true that the men of the Special Forces have been called "commandos," "silent killers," and even "snake eaters" – a name accorded them for their ability to operate in extreme conditions in the jungle – they have never been enamored of these references. They prefer to go about their work quietly, professionally, and with as little fanfare and recognition as possible. Part of this is a matter of operational necessity, as much of what they do is classified. For those things that are not top secret, they are ever aware that their membership in Special Forces is a danger to their wives, children and other family members. For themselves, they care little. This is no different from the risks endured by America's civilian law enforcement and SWAT officers, intelligence officers and other federal agents. The Green Berets do not indulge themselves with public crowing of their greatness or spending millions on their own publicity for one simple reason: they are humble.

Despite the fact that they are the most elite soldiers the world has ever known, the Green Berets are the last to ever be heard self-servingly advocating their own prowess. In most instances, the presence of the forest colored beret itself is enough to convince anyone that they are dealing with someone special. Beyond that, when in proper uniform, the "Special Forces" tabs on their shoulders, jump wings on their chests, and in many cases ribbons attesting to their courage under fire, quell any question of their accomplishments. But the men of Special Forces often reject even these hard-won symbols. Many will wear nothing on their uniforms but their SF tab and jump wings, believing anything else is merely for show, and that is not the business they are in.

When actually worn, however, these symbols of rare bravery and ability are merely reminders of all that they are and have accomplished, earning them an unparalleled reputation. Perhaps this reputation was best summed up for the general population of Americans in the Sylvester Stallone movie *First Blood*, where a deputy tried to warn Sheriff Wil Teasle, played by Brian Dennehy, against pursuing John Rambo into the mountains: "Those Green Berets ... they're real badasses." For, indeed, they are; but you will never hear it from them.

I did a tour with the famed British Special Air Service – the SAS – that country's version of SF and Delta combined, and found them to be much the same. The men of the "Regiment," as they humbly refer to themselves, are forever insisting that they are "just average blokes." John and I have also had the opportunity to spend a good deal of time with Russia's Spetsnaz, or special forces, including members of the ultra-secretive and elite Alpha Counter-Terror Group. While proud of their units and their capabilities, these men are almost shockingly shy. It is no small coincidence that the men of the top units in three of the world's most formidable militaries are like this. For, as with true greatness found in anyone, the better people are and the more they have done, the more they realize what they have not yet accomplished.

There are many other units of lesser reputation that have accomplished much, and are justifiably proud. The ones that are satisfied with the quiet knowledge that they are the best at what they do, live the Green Beret Lifestyle. But many do not. I have worked with many Special Operations-type units in the law enforcement and corrections communities. I have been impressed with many for their sacrifice, work ethic, appetite for training and desire to be the best. I have also seen a number of them lord their membership on a supposedly premiere tactical team over everyone else. They seem to believe that belonging to that group makes them better than other people. This is exactly what Green Berets do not do. Whether you are in a "special" tactical unit in the military or law enforcement, the fact remains it is a small unit. Do not ever be so stupid, or so naïve, as to think that the time will never come when your numbers are not enough. Don't think that you will never be overrun and suddenly in need of the support of those "regular" soldiers, police, corrections officers, or firemen you turned your nose up to.

Whether civilian or military, this behavior usually seems to come from the people or the units that aren't all that good anyway. People should only aspire to joining special units for what they can do for others. Such service gives you an opportunity to work with other warriors to save innocent lives, not because of something you will get out of it, or because it will allow you to treat others with inexcusable arrogance. Almost always, the ones behaving this way didn't have to go through an arduous selection process, don't train that hard, and aren't that skilled. They behave like prima donnas because they are insecure and know deep in their souls that they are substandard. The good ones never have to act that way. If the Special Forces would never behave so stupidly, no one else can justify this type of behavior.

This quiet modesty is a quality that was present in the American people in years past. Consider the men of World War II – the Greatest Generation – who came home after years at war. They are famous for their modesty, in most cases never speaking of what they accomplished, of the medals they won, or the heroic actions that warranted them. Stories are legion of men working in the same factory for decades after the war, becoming and remaining friends for a half century, but never knowing that they had served in the same brigade[62] during the war. They had never met in the service, and since they never talked about their service, were friends all those years without knowing the experiences they shared. Korea, the war that America ignored, saw an equal level of humility from the thousands who fought there. Who has ever heard Korean War veterans bragging of their sacrifices at places like Chosin and Heartbreak Ridge? Jim Beard, who lives just down the block from me, is a perfect example. He received the Navy Cross[63] for his actions at the Chosin Reservoir

---

62 A brigade of infantry is made up of two or three battalions, with each battalion comprised of three companies, of approximately 185 men each, for a total of about 1,000 men.
63 The Navy's second highest medal for valor in combat, with the Medal of Honor the only one higher.

battle. He worked for me for years at DOE, yet I had to learn about it in a book on the Korean War I happened to be reading one day.

The Vietnam veterans were of a similar stripe. Part of this was driven by the rejection and resentment they experienced at the hands of their countrymen upon returning to America. Unlike the public adulation of those who had served in World War II, these men – and women – quickly learned to keep their service and sacrifices to themselves. For years it was unpopular, and sometimes dangerous, to tell anyone what they had done. The other part of this silence was their own modesty; including their regret that they were taken out of a war that they felt was worth winning before that service had been completed.

Lieutenant Colonel Dave Grossman, one of the most compelling public speakers and trainers of our police and military, often asks the rhetorical question: "Is there anyone out there who is better, tougher or braver than the men who stormed the beaches of Normandy and Iwo Jima, or who fought in the Ardennes Forest during the Battle of the Bulge? Is anyone badder than the men who fought in Korea, in such places as the Chosin Reservoir, or in the trenches of World War I? Is anyone tougher than those who fought in the jungles of Vietnam?" Of course not, but if all of these men that have accomplished so much can remain so modest and self-effacing, how is it that so many in the rest of American society can be so impressed with the little that they have done in their lives?

HEROES YOU ARE NOT

I don't understand how men who go through the most grueling training to become elite soldiers, followed by incredible danger in combat operations, end up having to listen to a never-ending series of dilettantes and "virtual" warriors extol their own greatness. It seems that we have become a race of people who revere and worship anyone who ends up with a million dollars (no matter what they did to get it), or who gets himself on some celebrity fantasy television show, or who ends up in a movie or with a music video. Yet, at no time, do we ask ourselves what these people have really accomplished, or what quality of person they are really. We don't ask these things because we do not care. In fact, when the available intel tells us that they are drug addicts, alcoholics, wife-beaters, mental cases, tax cheats, or throw ridiculous tantrums like spoiled children, we idolize them all the more. It is the people who sell their psyches for public attention and money we seem to think most highly of.

We have real heroes in our very midst. I do not mean the casual "all inclusive" definition of hero that has become part of popular culture, where anyone who does some little thing for someone else is called a hero, and gets called to the local TV station or newspaper for some special award. To be a hero, you have to have risked your life under extremely dangerous circumstances to save the life of another human being. That is what a hero is, and any other use of that word does a horrible disservice to the men, and women, who have served – and in some cases died - in such noble endeavors. Yet, instead of recognizing them and paying them the homage they deserve, we either ignore them or, worse, make a mockery of their selflessness. In a nation of 300 million, everyone knows the names and histories of people like Britney Spears, Paris Hilton, Kevin Federline, and others like them. We all are intimately knowledgeable of the often screwed up lives and relationships of Brad Pitt, Angelina Jolie, Jennifer Aniston, Anna Nicole Smith, Maddona and Tom Cruise.

Yet, how is it that we do we not know that John Walton, son of the billionaire Wal-Mart magnate Sam Walton, spent the early years of his life serving as an NCO medic in the Special Forces, receiving the Silver Star for what Green Beret and author John "Tilt" Meyer described as a mission where his six-man recon team was so surrounded by enemy forces that the team leader had to call in air strikes right on top of the team. The strike itself killed one team member, wounded the team leader, and blew the leg off of another Green Beret. John Walton then took command of the team and saved those still alive. Until his death on 27 June 2005, he continued to live according to the Code of the Green Beret, championing many charitable and humanitarian causes, and always supportive of his Special Forces comrades. How is it that we don't know of such men? In my years in Special Forces, I knew a number of other Green Berets who came from extremely wealthy backgrounds, or had Ph.D.'s in fields that would have earned them millions, yet chose to sacrifice the easy life for one of service to their country.

Billy Waugh is one of the most famous Green Berets who ever lived. A friend of John's today, Billy was one of my first commanding NCOs. When I was a young, upstart Special Forces soldier running deep recon missions with CCN, he was the Command Sergeant Major, and already a living legend. CCN was one of three Command and Control groups. This included Command and Control North (CCN), Central (CCC) and South (CCS). These small units ran missions deep into Cambodia, Laos and North Vietnam, and had the highest mortality rate of all military units in the Vietnam War. After decades of decorated service in Special Forces, he then spent many more years defending America in covert operations with the CIA, including conducting surveillance in Sudan on a then-newly evolved terror threat named Usama bin Laden. His service to America is so long and esteemed that bestselling author W.E.B. Griffin often dedicates his books to him, writing about Billy: "A legendary Special Forces command sergeant major who retired and then went on to hunt down the infamous Carlos the Jackal, Billy could have terminated Osama bin Laden in the early 1990s but could not get permission to do so. After fifty years in the business, Billy is still going after the bad guys."[64] At age 71 he was running around Afghanistan with our young Green Berets hunting the Taliban and al Qaeda. Now 78 years old, he continues to train our elite soldiers in Special Forces.

Then there is Rowe Stayton. A top graduate from the Air Force Academy, Rowe had an illustrious career as a jet fighter pilot until his retirement at the rank of major. He then attended law school and built a reputation as a top notch criminal defense attorney. But at age 50, when the War on Terror began after too many years'

---

[64] See for example, W.E.B. Griffin, *The Hunters*, (G.P. Putnam's Sons, New York, 2006), unnumbered page.

separation from the Air Force to fly, he talked his way into a position as a sergeant, commanding a platoon of Arkansas Army National Guardsmen on their way to Iraq. Now, several years after returning from his first tour in Iraq, he is returning there to continue to fight for America.

Despite his name, Gary O'Neal is an Oglalla, Sioux tribal member. Tall and handsome, with an infectious laugh, he is a retired SF soldier with many decorations. Though a lifetime in SF took its toll on his body, he continued to serve America running the Robin Sage culmination exercise outside of Ft. Bragg, North Carolina. When in his late 50s he was challenged by others as to his physical infirmities and ability to continue in that role, he entered and won championships in both bodybuilding and powerlifting. Often playing the role of indigenous warrior chieftain, he ensures that those who graduate the Q Course have been held to the highest standards.

And what of Pat Tillman, the talented multi-million dollar safety for the Arizona Cardinals who answered a calling, giving up all that money and fame – and almost guaranteed longevity as a civilian – to join the Army Rangers? In him America had a young man who realized that we were a nation at war, that we were a people that had been attacked by an enemy that had long before declared war on us.

With more money guaranteed to him annually than most of us could spend in a lifetime, he instead opted to receive maybe one percent of that amount for the privilege of living hungry and dirty out of a rucksack in a war zone, the honor of being shot at, but most importantly, the nobility of serving his country. It is true that Ranger Tillman died during Operation Anaconda in Afghanistan, from friendly fire. But war is dangerous and combat confusing, and "blue on blue" casualties have always been a reality of battle. Still, nothing about the cause of his death in any way diminishes the honor of this man, or the sacrifice he made for our country.

Unfortunately, rather than being revered as a patriot and for setting a standard for all young Americans, his story has been used as an example of a wealthy life squandered, of opportunity flushed down the toilet. Others his age see only a lucrative career sacrificed so he could be killed by his own people. Young men in America look at what he did and tell each other over drinks in crowded bars that they would never be so stupid as to give up their six figure salaries to go die for no reason. What they do not know, is that this elite soldier died serving the country he loved, in combat, surrounded by the men on his Team that he was closer to than any brothers could ever be. No man could ever die wealthier than that. I only wonder what will happen when the few Pat Tillmans, John Waltons, Rowe Staytons, Gary O'Neals and Billy Waughs we produce are gone? Who will fight for us then? What will become of America when the true heroes are gone and all that we have left is a nation of young video game addicts, fantasy football coaches, computer programmers and investment bankers?

This is not a new phenomenon in society. Countries have always had too many of the faint-hearted, and too few of the noble and heroic warriors. This is exactly what Shakespeare was touching on in *Henry V* when the king spoke to his men, mostly wounded, and outnumbered five-to-one at Agincourt. He rallied his troops to the nobility of the battle they had yet to face by reminding them that they were not prideless mercenaries, but a band of brothers. Five hundred years earlier, it was as though he was writing to all of those who would one day choose to live their lives as Green Berets:

> *We few, we happy few, we band of brothers;*
> *For he to-day that sheds his blood with me*
> *Shall be my brother...*
> *And gentlemen in England, now a-bed*
> *Shall think themselves accursed they were not here;*
> *And hold their manhoods cheap whilst any speaks*
> *That fought with us.*

STOP AND SMELL THE ROSES

This is the legacy that the men of the Special Forces leave all of America, every single day. But for their service and their sacrifice to have any meaning, the rest of us have to notice and take heed of their example. It is perhaps a grim reality, but reality nonetheless, that there are things far more important than salaries, golden parachutes, cars, houses, fashionable clothing, celebrities and sports heroes. We have all known others who have been diagnosed with terminal illnesses. For most people, the day they receive such news, everything changes. The popular country song, *Live Like You Were Dying*, by Tim McGraw captures this, where the singer is telling of the time his father was diagnosed with a deadly disease and for the first time began truly living. Throughout the song is the constant refrain that he hopes everyone gets to "live like you were dying." For most people, this is what it takes before they begin to contemplate their lives and ask themselves what is truly important. For the first time they realize that they have paid little to no attention to the glorious intangible things that make life worth living. For the first time, they realize that money does not – and never did – buy happiness.

But people who have lived as Green Berets never suffer the sudden recognition that they wasted so much of their precious lives in driveling and empty pursuits. They never lost sight of what was truly important. They never lost sight of the fact that someday they would die, and when that day came all that would matter would be the way they had spent their time and the things they had committed their lives to. They always knew that the popular saying, "He Who Dies With the Most Toys Wins," was bullshit. For the one who dies with the most toys is still dead, and that person died a child, playing with toys, never looking around at the world and life, and never realizing that we were all put here for something more important.

Among our group at Archangel we live according to an ages-old Warrior Code, which is what all Green Berets do. Each morning we wake up and say to ourselves, "Today is the day that I might die."

Realizing this, we go out and do everything to our utmost, with total mental, physical and spiritual awareness and investment. We do not sit in traffic fuming that we are not two miles ahead of where we are. Whatever we are doing, we do it with complete assimilation of ourselves. If you are driving down the road at breakneck speed because you're late, and you're thinking about all that you have yet to do that day then suddenly die in a car accident, you weren't experiencing life in your last minutes; which means you weren't living.

Do not forget, if you are not where you are, you are nowhere. Whether you are in the shower, or driving down the road, or – as often happens in my case – loading thousands of rounds of ammunition or repairing a gun, do it with full concentration, mental involvement and spiritual connection with what you are doing and experiencing at that moment. If you are living your life in an over-anxious, frenetic and frenzied mental race, worrying over all the things that you are not doing at that moment, you are not living. If you are not living, you cannot possibly do anything well. If you are not living each moment of your life, you are no good to yourself or your family and friends.

You can do this in anything in your life or daily activities. Some cultures do it better than others; indeed, the Japanese, Chinese and Tibetans are known for this level of mental and spiritual investment, this complete immersion in the moment. Authors Charles Gaines and George Butler articulated this type of mental and spiritual investment in the simple act of weightlifting, when they wrote:

> Concentration in bodybuilding means thinking a muscle through what it is doing – forcing it with your mind, and with your eyes if you can stare at it, to work fully. … I remember watching Ed Corney doing dumbbell curls in Baghdad. He was seated on a stool in the middle of the big, strange gym that the city let the Mr. Universe competitors work out in. There must have been thirty or forty Iraqis standing along all four walls, and another fifty or so at the windows looking in. Ed Corney sat in the middle of all those fervid, noisy little people, staring at the sheath of his bicep fill and empty, fill and

empty, his face remote and rapt as a Yogi's, his mind somewhere deep down inside the fibers of that arm.[65]

Former Green Beret and author John "Tilt" Meyer, with whom I served in CCN,[66] describes the importance of this ability at its most dire. In honoring Capt. Thinh Dinh, the bravest South Vietnamese Kingbee helicopter pilot he ever worked with, and who saved his life and the lives of his Teams many times, writes:

> Thinh was a deeply religious man. In his devotion, and the calm it brought him, he was almost mystical. During the flights out to a target area, he would turn the helicopter over to his co-pilot and then enter into a profound state of prayer. ... a separate world or existence he would allow himself to be absorbed into. ... The lumbering old Sikorsky [helicopter] became an extension of himself and an instrument of the Divine Will. [67]

This type of spiritual investment can be accomplished in everything you do. Americans just have too many luxuries, and so fail to pay attention to what they get to experience everyday, instead choosing to complain about what few things they don't have. I spent 30 days on the ground once, and you cannot even begin to appreciate the delight a shower gives you until you've been without. During that same operation three of us shared a single toothbrush that had the handle cut off to conserve space in our overloaded rucksacks. Every time you're in the shower, stop and feel the warm spray on your skin, the tiny rivulets of water as they run down your body, the aroma of the soap and the cleansing texture of a washcloth. Afterward, feel the air touching your skin as the cooling process of evaporation begins. Enjoy the rugged friction of the towel as it is rubbed vigorously across

65 Charles Gaines and George Butler, *Pumping Iron: The Art and Sport of Bodybuilding*, (Simon and Schuster, Inc., New York, 1974, 1981), 43-44.

65 Command and Control North, ran deep penetration reconnaissance teams into North Vietnam and Laos. Though a small team, CCN had the highest casualty rate of all units in the Vietnam War, often exceeding 100 percent as many were wounded several times.

67 John Stryker Meyer and John E. Peters, *On the Ground: The Secret War in Vietnam* (Levin Publishing Group LLC, Oceanside, CA, 2007), 103.

your chilled skin, followed by you shrugging into the warm embrace of a thick robe. While brushing your teeth, delight in the roughness of the bristles across your teeth and gums, and the flavor of the toothpaste bursting in your mouth. There are many in the world that never get to experience such wonders.

When John and I, and our team, came out of the Sudan desert we went straight to a $500-plus a night businessmen's hotel in Nairobi, Kenya. We walked into a marble floored lobby with enormous columns, full of people in black tie and evening gowns, in our desert camouflage. We were filthy, smelly and exhausted. We dumped our 100 pound rucksacks on that pristine floor and told the startled registration clerks that we had reservations. The people around us were aghast and obviously knew we had just come in from the nearby war. A glitch in the reservations meant that John and I had to share a bed. After days on the concrete hard ground of the desert floor, we couldn't have been happier, just falling into clean sheets and a soft bed. We've both had enough experiences like this that we never complain if we have nothing more than a bug free bed to sleep in and a roof over our heads.

We don't see this in America today. Americans seem to do everything possible to keep from truly experiencing and appreciating everyday activities. A friend of John's that I came to know well in recent years is a Russian special forces colonel. One of their premiere hand-to-hand combat practitioners and instructors, Mikhail Ryabko has come to the U.S. to visit us on several occasions. A true warrior, he had some interesting observations about American culture. At one point he noticed that Americans cram too much into their days. After visiting a local health club, he said, "You all lead such busy and stressful lives, then to reduce the stress and stay in shape for good health you go to the gym. But you don't take your time and focus on the exercises you need to help you with that daily stress, or improve your physical condition. Instead, you frantically race on treadmills or stationary bicycles, all the while reading the newspaper as you attempt to listen to CNN, or some nervous system-destroying music, interspersed with important cell phone calls that can't wait. Yet none of that provides the benefits of the very exercise you need." Today if he visited, he would add our addiction to communication via Blackberry to his concerns.

This is the ultimate test of the Green Beret Lifestyle: Do you know what you are living for, before it's too late? Too many people spend a lifetime worrying about their jobs, without really experiencing and enjoying what they do. Then, after decades of complaining about a job which they hate, they drop dead or commit suicide within a year of retirement. They realize all-too-late how much that job gave them. Just think of how much more it could have meant had they opened their minds and their souls to it while actually working.

Or people are too busy worrying about supporting their families, to stop and enjoy them, show their kids they love them and are proud of them, or let their spouses know they are adored. They substitute real love with the parroted rhetoric of "I love you," anytime they hang up with them on the phone. Rather than take the time to show their loved ones how they feel, they are too busy trying to improve their standard of living to remember they have family and friends, and to cherish those relationships. As a Green Beret, when you remind yourself each morning that you may die that day, these are the only things that will matter. Eventually, one morning when you say that to yourself, you will have been right. If you didn't make the time to enjoy the things and people that made your life worth living, then you will have just lived and died with no purpose other than worrying.

New Team leaders after First Sergeant John Anderson
passed the mantle of leadership for ODA 124 to Sergeant
First Class Ronnie McCann in early 1986. SFC McCann
is standing, center. Staff Sergeant Mitch Conway is
standing on far right. Far less than one percent of the
U.S. population ever gets to this level.

– 5 –

THE GREEN BERET TEAM

The average person sees all the events of his life,
as either a blessing or a curse.
The warrior views everything as a challenge,
from which there are lessons to be gained.

Author unknown

TEAMS FOR EVERYDAY LIFE

Most Americans are completely imbued with the notion that they are solitary figures marching bravely through life, handling all of the travails and challenges that life throws at every one of us, completely alone. Men are especially guilty of this, and it is a fallacy to be sure. America has always suffered a cultural obsession with the lone hero, a man with no friends, standing as a last citadel of courage against overwhelming odds. This cultural myth started with notions of the mountain men, living alone for years at a time, forging inroads into a hostile and unforgiving wilderness. From there evolved the iconic notion of the cowboy, often embodied in the form of a single gunfighter, placing himself before certain death, his trusty six gun his only ally. He was a man ready to suffer the horrors of battle to defend those who could not possibly defend themselves. In modern times this has evolved into such models as Rambo, Chuck Norris as *Walker Texas Ranger,* James Bond, Jean Claude Van Damme, the *Die Hard* movies, and the various adventure roles played by Arnold Schwarzenegger.

What these American myths do not tell us, however, is that not only is it extraordinarily rare that any true warrior fights his battles alone, but that none of us gets through a single day's problems without the help of others. The truth is that the mountain men traveled and lived in "brigades" of men for safety and assistance, and rarely did a single lawman make an arrest without backup in the Old West. Few in the civilian world seem to realize that Rambo is a fictional creation of author David Morrell and Hollywood, and the minds of Americans that wanted and needed a hero.

The reality is that no single Special Forces soldier ever operates alone. Green Berets, like SEALs, British SAS, and every one of the world's elite commandos, live and die by "the Team." To them, the Team is everything, and each one of them only thinks of himself in terms of his contribution to that Team. This is not only seen in combat operations, but in every aspect of their daily lives. You cannot possibly forge a Team of men so well integrated, so cohesive and interdependent, that it can survive and succeed against superior numbers of enemy in a hostile environment, solely by having that Team spend time together at work. Members of a Special Forces ODA[68] do everything together. The Teams that do not are never the best, or even good.

Yet in contemporary civilian society, men face ridicule anytime they do anything together, and suffer further attacks on their manhood anytime they are incapable of handling a problem alone. This has been helped along to a large degree by the women's movement in America, where any form of male togetherness is disdained as "male bonding," a term which has come to imply an interminable immaturity of all things male. As a culture, we have come to believe that if you cannot handle the problem by yourself, you are not a man. Yet no man out there feels capable of handling all of life's battles alone,

---

[68] Operational Detachment – Alpha, or the A Team, as it is known outside of SF, is the designation for all Special Forces Teams.

and so we are a nation of males walking about in a state of anxiety and fear, too afraid of our problems, and too afraid of society's condemnation to turn to other men for assistance. It is a sad irony that, while so many men walk about in such a state of emasculated terror, no one of them would fail to hurry to the aid of a friend, if that friend would only say, "I have a problem and it's too big to handle on my own. Will you help?"

It is only in the movies that a lone man can successfully fight off ten or more bad guys with his hands and feet, or can, using only his handgun, fight the entire outlaw gang in the streets, while the timid, manless shames of society cower with the women. John and I have both been trained hand-to-hand combat practitioners and instructors for many years, and it is the truth of combat that no single man can take on a large group, at least not for very long. Exhaustion alone will finish him in the end; and that end comes fast. A single man cannot hold off an outlaw gang any longer than his ammunition, and speed of re-loading, allows him to. After that, he will die. He'll die a hero, but die nonetheless. Dan Haggerty, in the old 1970s television show *Grizzly Adams*, once remarked: "A flock of crows can bring down an eagle, but that don't make the eagle any less."

Look to our Special Forces, the modern heroes of America. They are not fictional Rambos, running about the jungle bare-chested, waging solitary war against enemy masses. They are men, who for all their courage and skill, live by the Team. They know that their lives depend on their teammates, on the group, the clan, the tribe. The Team depends on the friendship which binds its members, that allows them to take on the enemy, however many he may be. It is not that they will not fight alone; indeed, such men will make that stand and die for their cause. But this is a last resort, as it should be for all men. They know that the whole of that Team is far greater than the sum of its parts. Recognizing all this, how can the average man confronting the often frightening issues and problems life forces on us all, do any better than those Green Berets who not only depend on their Teams in combat, but in all aspects of their lives as well?

The best Special Forces soldiers will drive or jog to work together, train together, lift weights together, do PT together, eat together, party together, go to bars together, and share the events and problems of each other's lives, every single day. There is nothing that happens in any of their personal or home lives, which they do not all know. They all know one another's wives, children and parents. They know and respect one another's hobbies, loves, dreams, aspirations and plans for the future. Everything is shared: responsibilities and joys alike. If one of them is away, others on the Team will arrive at his house to see if there are any jobs his wife needs done.

This last reflection of team loyalty is something we have all done our entire lives. For 25 years in the Special Forces I always stepped in to handle typical husbandly chores for teammates called away on other duty, or recovering from wounds in the hospital, just as they did for me. And this has continued in life after SF. For years, we at Archangel continued to travel into war zones around the world. When we did, others were always there to help our wives with any problems or jobs that arose. After the Beslan School siege in September 2004, John was constantly in demand to speak around the country, often being gone every day of the week. When he was away, I called his wife every night to make sure she was alright, and see if there was anything she needed. They lived in a remote area of the Colorado Rockies, and knowing that there were few distractions I would talk to her for some time, trying to break up the monotony of her evenings. Then when our teammate Yuri Ferdigalov – who had been with us to Sudan and the Chechnya Region, and who had responded to the Beslan School Siege in Russia with John – left for Iraq, we did the same for his wife Natasha. This is what friends do for each other. And no one on a Special Forces Team ever has to worry about anything inappropriate happening between a teammate and his wife.[69]

69 See Chapter 11, Rules of Special Operations Forces

This is what it takes to forge a true team. And teams are essential for all of us getting through the toughest parts of our lives. Green Berets do not just fall back on their Teams when operating behind enemy lines, they rely on them every day, in every aspect of their lives, personal and professional, in war and peacetime. Being members of a real Team, where each cares more about his friends than he does himself, they get through all the problems of life together. If the toughest, strongest and bravest members of American society don't stand alone in life, but rely on their teammates every day, how can the rest of society go it alone?

As a nation forged on the anvil of individual rights and freedoms, over time we have devolved into a society where we each attempt to deal with all of the stresses and problems of life on our own. In our march toward our individual "pursuits of happiness" we have become disenfranchised from our support groups, from our teams. Experts in sociology and social anthropology lament the fact that in the past 60 years Americans have lost their sense of community. This can be seen in everything from the abandonment of the traditions of front porch sitting and block parties, to the erection of privacy fences in backyards, the litigation explosion and road rage. The destruction of the extended family and ascendance of the mobile nuclear family are part of this same evolution. We all want to be left alone, and we respond unhappily to unexpected visitors at our homes, telephone calls from well wishers, and invitations to community functions.

Worst of all, is the fact that the vast majority of Americans today have no real friends. And having no real friends, they cannot possibly have a team on which they can rely. As humans we are a community animal, a species that not only functions best *in* a group, but can only function healthily and successfully *with* a group. It is instinctual for us to look to develop these types of relationships with others. At our most basic level, we do this to ensure others are friends and not threats to us, and, also, so that we can belong to something more powerful than we are alone. Look at the human beings around the planet who continue to live in the most natural states possible. Every one of them, from Africa to Asia and the Amazon rain forest, live in tribes. These tribes are tight-knit communities essential for their very survival. They suffer, fight, grow food, hunt, face starvation and natural disasters, all together. And in sharing these life and death struggles as one, they are melded into a cohesive unit that improves the lot of each of its members.

Green Berets are no different, and in many ways exist as little more than modern versions of ancient warrior cultures. If you were to wander into a setting in which members of Special Forces were present, you would be struck by the close, tribal nature of their association. You would recognize that they were intimate with each other, and yet feel their distance from everyone who did not belong. This is not peculiar to Special Forces and other commandos, but can be found with any group that endures hardship together, trains to the extreme limits of human physical ability together, or that has endured life and death situations together. It can be seen among any men or women who have faced battle in the sports arena as a team, or who have prepared each other to face that battle alone.

Just look at the clannish behavior of athletes. We have all observed – and some have taken part in – the group dynamics of a football team out socializing. Even individual sports like wrestling, boxing and gymnastics, will see their members banded together anywhere they can be found, eschewing interaction with others. To them, they are elite, and they set themselves apart from the rest of society. Anyone who ever competed seriously in any form of athletics can drift back to the time when days were spent toiling with comrades who shared your dream, and worked unsparingly to achieve glory. In looking back, you will recall that you were closer to that group of warriors than just about any other people you have since been around. And in recalling, you will feel the primal tug of those relationships, of that bonding; realizing that it has never been replaced.

THE LIFE TEAM

We are all instinctively moved to create these associations. Unfortunately for most, however, they use the worst possible criteria in selecting the people they wish to put on their Life Team. In most instances, people do not even realize that is what they are doing when building relationships with others. They use the most casual and undiscerning of vetting criteria, and then think these are going to be people who can be depended upon when life is at its worst. Then, when life's worst problems do loom on their horizons, they are shocked to see friends flee like bats from the light. When this happens, the poor, hapless fellow who thought he had friends finds himself suddenly ostracized, socially exiled to face his difficulties alone. Just think of how quickly people distance themselves from a "friend" as soon as they find out he has lost his job and might ask to borrow money.

But what did this sad fellow think would be the measure of those men he had brought into his life, those men he had put on his team because they belonged to the same country club, or they all had Harley collections? Did he honestly believe that it was a sign of character that they were all attorneys, accountants, investment brokers, or dentists, and attended the same social functions, or had clubhouse seats at football games together? Could they really be trusted when times got tough because they were in the same fantasy football league? Did the women believe they could trust a friend because their kids went to the same exclusive pre-school, or they lived in the same swanky neighborhood? These are some of the criteria on which people in America base their selections for those they put on their Life Teams. In reality, these are not friendships. They are superficial relationships of social convenience, poorly chosen due to vapid and vacuous selection standards.

Playing golf with a group of guys each week will not make them team members you can rely on. Face your first life-shattering experience, then watch your "friends" crumble, walk or run away, or suddenly define the parameters of your friendship for the first time. After all, you were never really friends: you only played golf together, and that person really had no duty to you. All of the sudden, the "friend" who was never too busy to golf is too busy to help, when it should be just the opposite. But in life, those real friends who are often too busy to have fun, always make time for another in crisis. Stop and imagine the bond of those who have faced danger and death together. Do you think any of them would walk away when a friend suddenly faced the worst that peacetime, civilian society could throw at them? In such circumstances, they stand together without thought, without a moment's hesitation. Having spent a substantial amount of time with Russian special forces soldiers, John and I have come to say, somewhat tongue-in-cheek, that if you're going to be a friend, be a friend like a Russian. For when you call your Russian friend and say, "I just killed this guy," the only question he will ask is whether you need help moving the body.

Few people in life really need teammates who brave automatic weapons' fire and exploding grenades. But the average, everyday catastrophes and problems of life are enough to send the majority of people shrinking off in pathetic devotion to their own lack of character. Few of those we routinely call friends are anything more than casual acquaintances. Nothing can be expected of acquaintances; much can, and should, be expected of friends. Friendship is much like Nietzsche's abyss, where he wrote that when you look into the abyss, the abyss also looks back into you. For when you look at the commitment of your friends, they are also looking at your commitment to them.

MUTUALITY OF COMMITMENT

Every one of us needs a team committed and loyal to us. They must be brave enough to stand with us as we face the worst that life throws at us, and we must do the same for them. Just as Green Berets do for each other. The question must always be asked in our lives, - even our civilian lives - "When we are in trouble, who will come for us? Who will come to our aid?" When our small SF Teams are overrun in enemy controlled territory not only will other SF men grab weapons and go racing to our aid, but the helicopter and fighter pilots seldom let us down. They will race into hell to save us, just as we do for them. Police, firemen and other critical service professions live this interdependence and reliance every day. But in our personal lives, when we are facing our worst problem we still must ask, who is coming for us? Who is coming to help, and could I be depended upon to race to the aid of those that call me "friend?"

At some point in our lives we will all face emotional desperation as personal relationships end. We will confront sickness, injury, the death of family members, divorce, hopeless financial situations, unemployment, threat of legal action, and fear over our children. It is in such times that those we have selected to our Life Team are tested in the crucible of loyalty and strength. Just as we must be ready to face that same test when our friends are in need. Ask yourself: "Have I been that kind of a teammate, that kind of a friend? Have I been worthy of the people whose team I share a place on in my life?"

Many will think that you cannot possibly build that level of loyalty in a group without them having faced combat together. While it is true that combat does forge a bond between survivors unlike anything else, it is not essential that you and your team go to war. Nor do you have to go into the ghetto with hundred dollar bills hanging out of your pockets to have gang bangers try to mug you or shoot you down, just so you can be better friends. The truth of the matter is that until recent years America had gone for a long period with few of its servicemen having any combat experience. This included Green Berets and other Special Operations soldiers. Even without actual combat experience, the members of the SF ODAs still had a devotion to each other that would have seen them safely through combat. For it is the strength of the relationships built through efforts during peacetime preparation that compel them to sacrifice for each other during war.

Every single person can duplicate much of the conditioning that goes into the building of an SF soldier, and the creation of a true combat team; one whose members are ever ready to face the worst horrors together. Teams are built of men, and women, first and foremost. As with chains, a team is only as strong as its weakest link. This is an axiom of life few think of when priding themselves on what good friends they are to others. Most have never been in a life or death struggle in which the slowest, weakest or most afraid was holding the others back, risking lives through their deficiencies. Yet seldom does a year go by that you cannot see a news report where a group of hikers, skiers or mountain climbers became stranded or lost, attempting to survive extreme conditions of thirst, starvation, cold and injury for days. Some of these groups fare better than others. Those who survive by working together share a bond that will never be broken.

LEAVE NO ONE BEHIND

Being a member of a team means no one is left behind. This is one of the mantras of not only SF, but the foundation of all SEAL, Ranger, British SAS and even Russian Spetsnaz Teams. The only thing that makes elite soldiers willing to risk their lives to save one person that is alone and in danger, is the knowledge that their entire Team would do the same for them. Many people decry the loss of two, or five or even ten soldiers to rescue a single fallen comrade, pointing out with actuarial efficiency that it is hard to justify the loss of exponentially greater resources, i.e., soldiers, to save one life. But these are not the people who go willingly into battle. We ask a great deal of our elite warriors in America. We ask them to go into deadly situations under seemingly suicidal conditions. What makes them willing to go bravely into such near certain death, is the knowledge that when things are at their worst, their comrades will come running. Were it not for this willingness in our elite soldiers to risk possible death to save others from certain death, our military would not be nearly so great as it is. It is what sets our warriors (and those of just a few other Free World countries) apart from the rest of the world.

One of the most poignant recent examples of this occurred in the battle for Robert's Ridge during the failed Operation Anaconda in Afghanistan in March 2002. Intelligence had failed to adequately warn small Teams of elite Special Forces and SEALs of the enormous numerical and positional superiority of the enemy Taliban and Al Qaeda. One Team of SEALs, designated RAZOR 3, landed in its helicopter only to come under overwhelming enemy fire. In attempting to evacuate the LZ[70] the helo was severely damaged by light arms and RPG fire. As it was lifting, SEAL Petty Officer First Class Neil C. Roberts, who had led the six man recon Team, was flung from the rear ramp. As Robin Moore details in his book, *The Hunt for Bin Laden*, "Immediately the pilots told the team they were turning around. It didn't matter if everyone died – leave no man behind!"[71]

From that point, all available Special Operations units and aircraft immediately returned to the area under withering enemy fire, to bring back their SEAL brother. Whether dead or alive, he was going home with them. Robin Moore concluded his recounting of this dramatic event with a lesson for everyone who chooses to live life as a Green Beret: "Seven special operators, Army Rangers, and Air Force Tactics airmen had died trying to save a Navy SEAL who was down. Seven men lost their lives trying to recover one man. Several reporters questioned that. Apparently they did not grasp the brotherhood of Special Operations – it was the modern-day version of 'all for one and one for all.'"[72]

For civilians, the "no one gets left" rule will most often apply when traveling, or going out at night. This survival rule is critical for women to adopt. When traveling, you should operate like an ODA in an enemy country. Do not delude yourself: anytime you travel out-

[70] Landing Zone
[71] Moore, 356.
[72] Ibid., 362

side the U.S. you are in a hostile, foreign environment. Even when on leave, Green Berets will travel together, rarely splitting up members of the Team. Even the famed World War II *Band of Brothers* commander, Major Richard Winters, noted this when his men from Easy Company of the 101st Airborne Division, were finally relieved after months of combat and given R&R[73] in Paris. Then one of the Army's most elite groups, his men could only enjoy the sights and distractions of that beautiful city by going everywhere together.[74]

Thousands of vacationing Americans are robbed, raped, beaten, kidnapped and murdered overseas every year, and most often in countries tourists travel happily to. When outside the U.S., go out together and establish your Rules of Engagement (ROEs). It is even a good idea to follow this rule at home. Set up what the British SAS call ERVs, or Emergency Rendezvous points, where everyone will go if someone becomes separated for more than a designated period of time, or in the event of a perceived threat. The most important of your team's rules must be that no one goes home alone, and no one is left behind. This is where commitment and loyalty are most important, as often one person will be completely inebriated and insist on staying at a bar long after everyone else is ready to go in for the night. This person's state is the most compelling reason NOT to leave her alone.

This is what happened with Imette St. Guillen, the beautiful young grad student who was tortured, raped and murdered after being mummified with packing tape in New York City in March 2006. Most likely, a similarly unpleasant fate befell 18 year-old Natalee Holloway in Aruba in May 2005, each a tragedy that occurred when friends allowed young women to go off on their own. This can never be allowed to happen, and it is the team's job to ensure that it does not. This rule applies to families and friends while vacationing, traveling or socializing. Never leave someone behind, even when it's time to catch your flight home. This must be adhered to

---

73 Rest and Recreation.
74 Dick Winters, *Beyond Band of Brothers: The War Memoirs of Major Dick Winters*, (A Berkley Caliber Book, New York, 2006), 161.

even if the missing person was behaving irresponsibly. If the errant team member refuses to go home with the group, either designate one or two others to stay with her, or forcibly remove that person to her home or hotel. It will not be pleasant, and she may be angry with you for a while, but that is a far easier burden to bear than knowing she died because you abandoned her in a dangerous environment.

RULES OF ENGAGEMENT

Predetermine the ROEs for everyone in the group before they start drinking or otherwise abandoning sensible behavior. The first is one of the most crucial rules Green Berets follow: Do not trust anyone outside the team. This is particularly important when out of the country.

No matter how interesting, attractive, rich, smart, funny or charming someone is, do not ever lose sight of the fact that you are in an alien and potentially threatening environment, and must ensure your own safety. For some reason people do not recognize that those who would do you harm first present a set of characteristics that will put you at ease, inducing you to trust them. "Charm" is nothing more than a behavioral device designed to induce another into giving the actor what he wants. It is a psychological ploy that has been used by rapists, murderers and kidnappers, such as Ted Bundy and Jeffrey Dahmer.

But these are only a couple of the more famous cases where innocents were charmed to their deaths, and do not even represent the tip of the iceberg of predators using this type of bait to lure women. Bill Bradford was an amateur photographer who would lure pretty young girls with his clean cut look and friendly demeanor. A serial killer, Bradford strangled his victims, then took bodyparts as souvenirs. Gary Leon Ridgway was similarly inviting. In his own words: "I would talk to her ... and get her mind off anything she was nervous about. She would think, 'Oh, this guy cares.' I just want to get her in the vehicle and eventually kill her." Ronald J. Dominique would meet his victims on the street and charm them into going for a ride with him, or talk them into having sex, which always resulted in their deaths. Finally, Javed Iqbal Mughal would charm boys he met into going off with him. They were then drugged, raped and strangled. No, we are not running out of these people, or the threats they pose.

John and I have a lady friend who related a story that frightened us a number of years ago. A young, attractive woman, she was vacationing in Mexico with her nine-year old daughter. Our friend met a man from the Deep South of the United States. Being a southerner herself, she allowed him to establish quick rapport with her. His southern accent, and their shared heritage, completely disarmed her, to the extent that she accepted his invitation to take her and her daughter over the mountains, alone, to a remote ranch his family owned. To most reading this, the potential danger to our friend and her daughter is obvious. Yet these realities are always easy to recognize when examining the decisions of others. Most people have, at some point or another, succumbed to similar – and equally dangerous – inducements of total strangers whom they had no reason to trust. In the case of our friend and her daughter, they did return unharmed but we made certain she understood the dangers inherent in her decision-making.

TARGETING

All too often, when people are traveling or vacationing, their focus is not on potential dangers, but on having a good time. Though there is nothing wrong with wanting to have fun, the fun stops when one of them is suddenly the victim of a violent crime. Again, this is a Green Beret rule that women in particular violate all the time. In order to evaluate the sensibility of one's own behavior, it must be viewed in the harsh light of reality. Just as Green Berets never delude themselves into thinking situations are safer than they are when operating out of the country, so, too, must every citizen accept the reality of the danger that lurks about them.

Criminals like to target tourists because they are in unknown environments, have no support groups and are usually paying attention to new sights, sounds and experiences, not what is really going on around them. Also, people from other countries, or even other cities and states, make perfect targets because they are unlikely to be around to testify at a trial if the perpetrators are caught. Recognize that most criminals are male, and few will deny themselves the opportunity to rape a woman if she just happens to be targeted for some other crime. In fact, many criminals are only looking to rape women, and these male sexual predators abound all over the world. This is why women can never abandon their teams; nor their teams abandon them. While men are targets of all sorts of crime as well, they don't suffer the extreme vulnerability of women. If a man jeopardizes himself in protecting a woman, so be it. Men should be warriors and accept a warrior's responsibility to protect those weaker, no matter the cost. This is the Code of the Green Beret.

We have a friend who is a flight attendant. Notwithstanding his chosen profession, Kirk Walker has had substantial training in special forces' hand-to-hand combat and other martial arts, and even put himself through one of Britain's elite bodyguard schools. When he is on an overnight layover, he sees the safety of the women who are part of his flight crew as his absolute duty. He not only oversees any socializing and contact with outsiders that might occur, but sleeps with his hotel room door ajar so that the women have a refuge to which they can flee in the event they are threatened in the night. This also helps alert him to possible danger; sounds he might not otherwise hear if his door were shut. To Kirk Walker, these women belong to his team and his duty to them is clear. As the only man on that team, he cares more for his teammates than he does for himself. Does living in hotels like this make him a greater target for a criminal assault and robbery? Absolutely. Is it a worthwhile risk for the safety of the women whose security he accepts the duty of ensuring? Again, the answer to that is, "Absolutely."

PLANNING AHEAD

For all of these reasons, and many others, the rules of Green Berets in working and traveling with their Teams must be followed. This is why Special Forces Teams work hard to plan for every possible contingency, and you should do the same. Establish communications with your group, know how to reach each other and any one else who may be necessary for personal security. If forced to travel alone, schedule contact times for checking in. Leave complete information on hotel, phone numbers, travel group contacts, and a recent photo with someone who you know will come find you no matter where you are.

At times colleagues working in government service would leave all of this information with John and me when traveling or conducting dangerous operations outside the U.S. They knew that if something happened to them we would come find them, even when the danger of rescue prevented others in their organizations from going to their aid, or American diplomatic relations or political expediency made it impossible for the government to send help. This is what Green Berets, and others in government service, do for each other all the time. If these rules are followed religiously by the world's toughest and most elite soldiers, they are essential to everyone.

DUTIES CAN'T BE DELEGATED

The rule of non-delegable duties applies to events far more mundane than the threat of criminal victimization. A short time ago Defense Department Counter-Terror expert and author Lt. Col. Joe Ruffini was working in Washington, D.C. with a lady colleague from one of the federal agencies involved in the War on Terror. They had worked on various projects together for only a short time, and were both out of town and far from home. When it came time to catch his flight home,

Col. Ruffini made a final check on this woman. She failed to answer her room phone or his persistent knocks at the door. Upon learning that she had not checked out of her room, he persuaded management to open her door. There he found her, sick and incapacitated on the floor, suffering from a horrendous bout of food poisoning. Despite his own harried work schedule, he spent the next two days in this lady's room, doctoring her back to health. He could have easily delegated his duty to her by calling someone from her agency. To Lt. Col. Ruffini, however, she was a member of his team and he would not leave her behind, no matter the personal inconvenience.

Another rule of Green Beret Team integrity and survivability, that everyone can benefit by adopting, is never breach the ranks of the team by inviting outsiders, unless approved by everyone on the team. And never let a stranger separate you from your team. If the person you have just met is a decent man, and truly wishes to get to know you better in an honorable fashion, he will be happy to spend his time with you and your team of girlfriends (and possibly trusted male friends), before being given the opportunity to see you in the future. Trust your friends, rely on them, value their assessments, and never allow another to invade the integrity of your team. There is nothing that is going to happen that night that is worth your life. Even in the case of young women who are looking to "hook up" with someone for sex, they should still trust the judgment of their friends when the would-be lucky pursuer is introduced to them. If they don't like him, you shouldn't go with him.

For all of these reasons, in selecting one's Life Team, it is important to be discerning of the true character and nature of each member. These are people in whose hands you will place your safety, if not your life, from time to time. That low golf handicap, a mid-six figure salary, or an expensive car, are never standards against which to judge someone's character. Not that all wealthy people are weak, but socio-economic status is the last indicator of strength in a person. In today's corporate environment it is all-too-possible that many people you encounter will have gained their wealth by acting less than honorably. For those of you who have amassed a significant amount of wealth, do not be afraid to develop friendships with others who could never afford your country club, can't jet off to Paris for a weekend, or who wear a blue – or even camouflage - collar to work. They may just be the best friends you ever had.

SELECTION FOR TEAM MEMBERS

If you are any judge of character, the friends you select will care nothing about your money, and may choose to let you join their team *in spite* of your wealth, not because of it. If you have begun to build an association with someone and it becomes clear that he is motivated by what you and your money can do for him, you must throw him off your team immediately. That is exactly what Green Berets do when a member of their Teams fails to measure up. But the reason you should terminate your association with this person is not to protect your money. It's because in becoming fixated on benefiting from your money, that person has demonstrated that he is not more concerned with his team and his teammates than himself. Anyone who thinks of himself and his own ability to profit from the team will sacrifice the team at critical moments. This is the only currency of a team, whether it be a civilian Life Team or Special Forces A Detachment.

Some of the best people you can ever meet will be found in martial arts dojos, cruddy hard core weight rooms, mountain climbing and rappelling groups, on shooting ranges, or in scuba and skydiving clubs. By the very nature of the sports they choose, they signal that they are adventurous, courageous and disciplined. In these sports, each person must work with, and be responsible for, the safety of others. They immerse themselves in a culture where risk is not something to run from, and for some the prospect of death is a constant companion.

No one who willingly faces a black belt coming at him at high speed with fire in his eye and clenched fists, or a fellow shooter employing rapid fire deadly force right next to him, or a 300 pound benchpress over his head, or leaps from a plane at 10,000 feet, is going to shy away from the everyday troubles we all face and sometimes need help with. It is no small coincidence that these activities are the same ones that Green Berets train in, and from which forge the steel of their Teams. It is through hand-to-hand combat training, physical conditioning and strength training, extreme outdoor survival, mountain climbing, shooting, diving and skydiving that they come to depend upon each other in life threatening circumstances long before they reach combat.

Though you will likely never have to rely on your friends to defend you, or save the lives of your family with fists, strength or bullets, or by jumping out of a plane or diving 200 feet under the ocean, it just may happen. Or the same may be asked of you. I have had more than my share of times when friends' lives were at risk in the civilian world and I stepped in, once while racing up the street in my underwear in the middle of the night, with a .45 caliber Colt semi-automatic handgun. Another time my co-author was in the Caribbean doing a shark-feeding dive. As a scuba instructor, he was given a long, sharp-ended pole to keep the sharks away from the group. A mishap resulted in his wife hitting the bottom, terrified, with him still at the surface. With sharks wheeling around her, he drove for the bottom, bursting his eardrum in the process. The pain was intense, and his mask began filling up with blood from his nose. He knew he could have headed back up alone and relieved the pressure and the pain, but would not leave his wife's side. Nor could he jeopardize the group and clear the blood from his mask amidst them. When the group finally reached the boat some 30 minutes later, he got her out of the water first. Several other men in the group, panicked by the sharks circling about them while treading water at the boat platform, actually crawled over John's back to get into the boat.

Retired Navy Master Chief[74] Keith Mattson has a lifetime of Special Operations experience under his belt. In his sixties, he is a large, muscular man who moves more weight on a daily basis in the

---

[74] Similar to Sergeant Major in the Army, this is the second highest NCO rank in the Navy, with the highest being Command Master Chief.

gym than most men do in a lifetime. As a top scuba diving instruc-tor in Orlando, Florida he is often called upon to ensure the safety of others. One occasion several years ago put his mettle to the test. While working with some students he received word that two divers from an unrelated group had been lost underwater. Despite the fact that his own dives had already left him with maximum nitrogen levels in his body, he made repeated dives to almost 200 feet in an attempt to rescue the victims. Keith was presented with a special award from the mayor for his efforts. I can assure you, however, that while racing to the bottom, almost an eighth of a mile under the surface with the effects of decompression sickness in his body screaming at him to surface, awards were the last thing on his mind. As a warrior, as one who lived his entire life never leaving a fallen comrade behind, he acted in the only way he knew: He risked his life for others.

These are just a few examples of things that do happen in everyday life, and do call on the courage of ourselves, and our friends, to be willing to risk their own lives for the protection of others. John's experience is an example of how few people can be depended on not to sacrifice those around them, but will save themselves the first time they confront real fear. We have had many such adventures in our lives, times when we helped those in need. John and I, and just about every person we know, have happily stepped in to assist women being accosted by inappropriate men, helped exhausted hikers in places like the Grand Canyon, gave first aid or CPR in emergencies, or provided free bodyguard services to battered women looking to leave their abusive husbands.

Keep in mind that the primary criteria for your Life Team members are their character, strength and loyalty. In Special Forces a Team member must be a steady operator first, and a member will be fired from a Team if he cannot be trusted, even if he possesses a critical MOS. It does no good to have a great medic, highly skilled in repairing any type of wound, if that soldier refuses to go into harm's way to help a comrade when he has fallen.

Once established, team members are forever. Over time you will learn that your team does not even have to be people you see every day, nor do they have to be in physical proximity to you. This is a dynamic that exists not only in Special Forces, but throughout the entire military community. As in civilian life, people will serve together for a time, then move on to other duty stations, other units, overseas deployments, or leave military service altogether; just as civilians change jobs or leave their chosen professions to pursue something new. The difference is that in civilian life the depths of many supposed friendships are disproved when such disruptions occur, with few people remaining in touch – much less friends – once the convenience of the relationship disappears.

In SF, once a member of a Team, you will always have those men as your teammates, as lifelong friends. When Green Berets rotate to new duty stations they will always be able to call on their teammates no matter how much time passes. In this way, as Teams disband and members move on to other Teams, forever recreating and expanding the rings of brotherhood that make them special, the Special Forces Command ensures that the bonds of its community are always growing, forever expanding outward.

The same can be true for everyone. One of the great things about the Internet is the ease of regular contact for everyone via email. It is one of the benefits of the computer age of today that friends, teammates and comrades can keep in constant touch, never suffering the atrophy of bonds that time and distance sometimes cause. But even that is not necessary, for true friends will always respond to the call for help, no matter how long they have been out of touch.

FRIENDSHIP

You must be realistic about the friends you are on a Life Team with, however, as no one gets along wonderfully all of the time. We all have occasions when the strength of our personalities and convictions leads to disagreements and sometimes outright disputes. At times I've even gotten into fistfights with good friends over issues that not only *seemed* important at the time, but *were* important. But after cooling down, we always kept things in perspective and the next morning might have been leaping off of Huey helicopters into combat, with only each other for protection.

That is the most important lesson of all when it comes to friends: *Your friends don't come perfect, and neither do you.* We all have a tendency to remember things we do for others, but the wonderful gifts our friends give us, or the sacrifices they make for us, fade with time. Don't ever forget the things your friends have done for you, and when you confront them for not being perfect, be sure to weigh whatever their indiscretions were against all of the things they have done for you over the years. Never let imperfections or natural human failings ruin a friendship. Years ago we developed a simple test for determining the level of commitment we had to each other. If you have a falling out, ask yourself: If my friend suddenly had a crisis, would I come running? Would he do it for me? If the answer to both is "yes," then the disagreement is not worth wrecking your friendship over.

This devotion to friendships is so complete that in the Special Forces world it sometimes results in unlikely bonds. Jim Hetrick was a member of the Green Berets most elite reconnaissance Teams that ran operations deep into the heart of Laos, Cambodia and even North Vietnam during that war. Now the long-standing president of the Special Operations Association (SOA), he continues to work closely with former Green Beret Chuck Berg, despite Jim readily admitting that he got Chuck shot three times in the legs on Valentine's Day 1967 at Khe Sanh, earning Chuck the first of several Purple Hearts. Today, an officer and director of the SOA himself, Chuck now spends much of his time in a wheelchair due to the loss of a leg from another battle, but he and Jim continue to be friends and work closely together in the administration of that fine organization. It is only with warriors like these that you ever see men traveling hundreds, if not thousands, of miles - and sometimes around the world – to see someone who got them shot decades ago.

But in choosing your friends, in selecting those individuals in your life for whom you are prepared to pledge and risk so much, you must first be careful of just who those friends are. Life and history are replete with instances of good people sacrificing much for friends of questionable character, but where no one outside the friendship could understand the level of commitment. Historically, the deep friendship between Wyatt Earp and John "Doc" Holliday was a perfect example of this. Though Holliday was rejected by most in society, Wyatt Earp had developed a profound loyalty to him, one that was fully reciprocated in the cowtown wars that culminated in the gunfight at the OK Corral and subsequent battles over political control for the town of Tombstone. This level of friendship was poignantly articulated in a movie conversation between Holliday, played by Val Kilmer, and another of Earp's U.S. Marshal's deputies when Holliday was suffering greatly from tuberculosis:

Deputy: "Doc, you ought to be in bed, what the hell are you doing
            this for anyway?"
Holliday: "Wyatt Earp is my friend."
Deputy: "Hell, I got lots of friends."
Holliday: *"I don't."* [76]

While dedication and devotion to friends is admirable, and completely necessary if you expect the same from others, it is critical to first ensure that they are worthy of this level of commitment. Just as it is important to make sure you are worthy of their commitment to you. When it comes to taking unsavory characters into your life as friends, do not think that you can dance too close to the fire and not get burned. No one can live vicariously through bad people who do bad things, rejecting responsibility with the pithy remark: "Well, he's

---

[76] *Tombstone*, a Hollywood Pictures film.

never done anything bad *to me*....'" This level of apathy of a friends' behavior and character is morally indefensible.

The Russians have a saying that proves true without exception: "Show me who your friends are, and I'll tell you everything about you." No matter how much you think you can distance yourself from the bursting radius of your friend's character, sooner or later you are going to be splattered by it. If you have a friend who is obsessed with health food, you will find your life influenced in that direction. If he's an alcoholic, you will be presented with many opportunities to drink, often irresponsibly. If he's a criminal, sooner or later bad things will come your way as a result of his behavior. If a successful business-man, investment and other financial opportunities may be laid at your feet. If strong, you will benefit from his strength. If weak, you will suffer when you need him to be strong, and he will forever be leaning on you.

This is the rule of life and human nature. Do not make the mistake of believing that the inherent weaknesses in a person's character will be overcome by their commitment to you when times are the toughest. For it is during those times that people default to the weakest aspects of their natures, just as an overstressed chain will break at the weakest link. The other links, though stronger, will not prevent it. In human terms, no one ever rises to the occasion for another; they descend to the foundations of their character.

Friendship can take on many aspects, and be seen in count-less variations. Those who have worked and traveled extensively together over many years learn to communicate a great deal with hardly a word being spoken. This is necessary in all arms profes-sions and other critical jobs where partners and teams depend on each other for their very survival. Green Berets can operate for days, sometimes weeks, under conditions of total sound control, meaning complete silence. They learn to say all they need with a look, a quick glance in a certain direction, a raised eyebrow or frown, or a subtle hand gesture. They have worked and trained so much together that each knows what every other member of the Team will do when confronting problems or threats. I have seen the same in some of the best SWAT teams in America.

After completing a training program with the Russian Spetsnaz, John and I went to St. Petersburg for a week of R&R with several of the Americans who had taken part, but who had seen nothing of Russia beyond military bases. A lovely young Hungarian lady – a years-long friend of John's – came up from Budapest to meet us. Having just come off of a weeks-long military school, and being responsible for the safety of others now little more than tourists in a strange land, John and I were, perhaps, a little more on edge than we ordinarily might have been. After watching us negotiating our charges through the crowded streets and on excursions outside the city, she observed that she could tell that not only had we worked together for many years, but that we were obviously very close friends. She said that it was clear we were almost never out of each other's sight, that we constantly "checked back in" with each other with quick glances, and that we always knew what each other was doing. She said it was obvious we managed to communicate enormous amounts of information to each other with a single look.

Though few people need to operate at this level, there will be times when your knowledge and understanding of your friends will have to be just as substantial. Few people who are worth being friends with ever want to burden others with their problems. But we will all encounter problems in life that are simply too much for us to handle alone. All too often, it is when we are facing the worst problems that honorable people tend to withdraw. That is the time when a friend needs to be able to tell that you are hurting, without being told.

I have often seen an inverse relationship between the seriousness of a problem, and the degree to which men will talk about that problem. In those instances, a true friend will impose himself on you, whether you say you want him there or not. If necessary, he will move in and refuse to leave until you are better, or at least better able to cope with challenges being faced.

In December 2006 John had his first hip replaced. Recently divorced, he had no one around to help him with the weeks he would be unable to attend to daily chores, or even care for himself. Over his protestations, SWAT and Dive Team Leader Ernie Manerchia and his wife Mare, a career registered nurse, jumped on a plane in Pennsylvania and flew to Colorado.

They stayed with John in his house in the remote mountains, and took care of his every need, which included feeding and watering horses, cleaning stalls and corrals, cooking meals, and helping John through the painful post-operation period. Then Ernie's law enforcement comrade, Capt. Joe Bail, traveled out from Philadelphia to relieve them. But the famous blizzard in Denver that shut down airports throughout the country stranded all of them at John's house. Though they missed Christmas with loved ones, especially their grandchildren, not a single one of them complained. They were being Green Berets, and taking care of their friend and teammate was the most important thing to them. Such friends are rare and to be treasured when found.

This should happen regardless of time or distance. This is an aspect of male friendships that women often do not understand. They don't comprehend how their husbands can get a call from some friend they haven't seen or heard from in a decade, and be ready to fly off at the drop of a hat to help him, or loan him a substantial amount of money. They just don't understand that once a friend, once a member of a team, you are bonded for life.

In paying homage to our cultural weakness of not understanding what friendship is about, we have devised all manner of pop-psychology tests to determine how well we truly know others. Most of these are superficial nonsense. These tests ask such things as whether you know what kind of car your friend drives, what his favorite color is, birth date, major in college and other ridiculous fun facts. Not having ready answers to these, you are forced to admit you are not such a great friend. The tragedy of these modern quantifications of the depth and meaning of friendship, is they convince us that if we learn these things we will be better friends. Nothing could be further from the truth. To be a good and true friend, you need to know the essence of a person, not the superficialities. These silly questions are no more a test of knowledge of a person than knowing the cover photo and chapter titles of a book would mean you knew what was written on the pages, what the plot, themes and sub-themes, and what the lessons were in that book.

To be a good friend is to *know* your friend. But knowing that friend doesn't mean being able to recite daytime television inanities about his life. It means knowing his strengths and weaknesses, how he will react in certain situations. It means knowing when he truly has a problem and when he is exaggerating; and not being afraid to tell him when either is the case. It means knowing when he is hurting, or, just as important, whether he will know when you are hurting. It means knowing that person stripped of the thin veneer of modern-civilized crap that we drape ourselves with, and hide ourselves away in. That is what being a friend is all about.

MARRIED TO A SOLDIER

My husband is a soldier so I must live from day to day,
For tomorrow could bring what he wants most,
A chance to fight for his cause, for his country or for his life.
I could find myself alone and afraid, not knowing where he is or
how he is or if I'll ever see him again.
I live from day to day and give him my love in every way I can.
When he needs me I'm there. When he's restless and anxious to go
and retells stories from "other wars," I smile and agree nothing else could
compare.

I hide my tears when he asks me to be strong and accept his flag
if he should give his life in battle. I silently pray I shall not have to
give him up this way, that a war will never take him from my arms
and my life, but still, I cannot turn away from this reality because
I promised I'd be with him through it all. Stand by and support
him in all he has to do because he was a Soldier long before he
was my husband and for him there is no other way of life.

So I will be strong.
I'll give him everything he needs. I'll love him with all my
heart and soul – every day – every minute that we have
because I'm married to a soldier and tomorrow he may be gone....

Linda McClure-Woodham
(Special Forces Wife)
1980

PART 3

GREEN BERET COMMITMENT

*Women should be proud of their husbands, and husbands
should give them something to be proud of. Wife,
Jody Anderson, pins Sergeant Major rank insignia on
her husband, John, at promotion ceremony, November
1986. To the right of newly-minted SGM Anderson is
Lt. Col. Riley T. Griffin.*

– 6 –

COMMITMENT TO MARRIAGE

I was a commando when she met me.
I have been one my whole life.
That's why she puts up with the way I live
and work, and my constant travel overseas.

Yuri Ferdigalov,
former Russian Spetsnaz soldier, now international bodyguard
working in hot zones throughout the world.

WIVES

If there is one area of life where everyone can learn from the failure of the men in Special Forces, it is marriage. Much of that failure, however, is not the fault of the Green Berets. Many women who are attracted to them learn too late that being a military wife is far more demanding than just strutting around bragging that she's married to a Green Beret. In the work I continue to do with Special Forces, I am shocked at the ridiculously high divorce rate of the young men since the beginning of the War on Terror. Almost to a man, they have received "Dear John" emails while deployed to Iraq or Afghanistan, or have simply come home to empty houses. It is disturbing to see the lack of commitment with which many women enter marriage these days. I have been married to the same woman for more than 30 years. She endured many years of life with me in Special Forces. She stuck by me when I was out of the country more than 250 days a year, often without her knowing where I was, and with no warning that I was about to be deployed.

Through it all my wife, Jody, kept the household running, raised our daughter, and attended to personal and professional duties I was not there to meet. Additionally, she stepped in as the "Wife of the Sergeant Major" and gave needed support to the wives and families of the SF men under me. Being my wife meant that she could not sit around feeling sorry for herself, lamenting the fact that she wasn't out in bars having fun with cool people who had no responsibilities. Being my wife meant that she had to be a Green Beret too, and live her life by trying to be the best, with total commitment to not only our marriage and family, but a commitment to the Special Forces equal to my own. She understood that our family was our team, and that the team was more important than she was.

In a society where fewer and fewer young men are willing to serve someone or something else - something greater than they are - those who choose to wear the beret are ever rarer. Yet those that do cannot seem to find young women with a similar level of commitment, dedication and self-sacrifice. In years past, it was the women who most understood this, who dedicated their lives to husbands and families. Today, we live in the era of women's liberation, where the role of men and fathers has been trivialized, and no one dares contest the politically correct mandate that nothing women do ever be criticized. Our young women have been molded by divorced parents, *Sex and the City, Desperate Housewives*, sexually amoral – if not immoral - female celebrity figures, rampant yet socially acceptable promiscuity, and the influences of others in *Girls Gone Wild* videotapes. They get married because they want a storybook wedding, never giving thought to the work that is involved in making a marriage succeed. And that work is even greater for the wife of an elite soldier.

At first women are attracted by the myth and romanticism of the green beret itself. They are drawn further in when given a glimpse into the world of these elite commandos, the SF parties, and the tight bonds the men have with each other. They become enamored of their own induction into this secretive society. But as soon as it stops being fun, and the hard work of marriage becomes a reality, they are gone. These women are lured away by the superficial relationships and good times to be found outside of their marriages. The frequent travel and long separations prove too much for them, and they are seduced by the party lifestyle they were living before, and immaturely thought would go on forever. It just never occurred to most of them that the men they had chosen were serious professionals, with important jobs to do.

All the while, their husbands are suffering from the loneliness and separation from their loved ones, as well. They miss their wives, and go into battle every day with their pictures taped into Kevlar helmets. They, too, wish that they were home. But they are sacrificing personal needs and pleasures for a greater cause. They are sacrificing everything for freedom and liberty. They are serving their country, and facing death everyday. Despite the level of the men's suffering, their wives do not seem to even be able to handle the separation in the comfort and safety of their own homes.

I see the same social and marital dynamic occurring throughout society. Many women do not understand that their family is their first and most important team in life, just as the A Team is the most important unit to the Special Forces in battle. They do not understand that one of the most important rules of SF is that the Team is always more important than the individual. Following the Green Beret model, everyone in the family must pitch in, which includes children, who should not be paid for doing minor chores that help maintain the household. Which spouse makes how much money is irrelevant, just as it is of no importance how much anyone on an A Detachment earns. Your family is your unit for both everyday tasks, and life. Historically, in most families the wife was the XO or

Executive Officer, the number two in command, who was also in charge of ensuring all aspects of the proper administration of the unit, from timely turn out of the kids each morning, to transportation and logistics, clothing, equipment and food acquisition, and distribution.

Though, today, this model varies from family to family, nothing is different about the importance of the family members supporting each other. Rather than functioning this way, it has become an unfortunate facet of American life for relationships to become incessant power struggles. In any serious relationship, couples should function like a military team. When in a hostile environment, whatever equipment and resources are available get divided among, and used by, the Team as a whole, in the best interest of the Team and its mission. By the same token, the mission of a married couple is to keep the marriage safe and successful. It is to maintain their house and raise their children. Husbands and wives can no more accomplish this mission while fighting each other for dominance than a Team of Green Berets can be effective if they are constantly bickering over what tactics they should employ, or who the Team leader should be. But this is exactly what goes on with couples in our country today.

In social situations, it is increasingly difficult to find couples that do not spend the evening in a never-ending game of one-upmanship. Each tries to outdo the other, correcting minor details of insignificant stories, or relating other stories designed to make the most important person in the storyteller's life look like a fool. This ceaseless competition of who's better, smarter, or has the better memory or family, or who makes more money or contributes more to the household chores, is designed to do one thing: incite hostility and shame into the relationship. The fact that they use friends and strangers as arbiters makes it all the worse and more destructive.

These are battles that should never occur in the first place, but if they do, should never take place in a public venue. When you engage in these tactics, remember the person you have set out to portray as inferior to you is supposed to be the person you have pledged your life to, and would give your life for. How does such a noble commitment become perverted to the extent you would use any opportunity to ridicule and embarrass that person publicly? If any of the issues that spouses so readily trot out to destroy the ego of their life partners for sport are ever that serious, they should be addressed in a serious and respectful discussion, in the privacy of their own homes, and beyond even the knowledge of their children. Rather than vying over the question of who is superior, both spouses should realize that anyone who engages in such a practice has already proven that he – or she – does not deserve a decent, loving person in the first place.

Many people might contend that most of these disputes are minor and that such insignificant slights can't have an adverse effect on a marriage. They see nothing wrong with telling each other to "shut up" in front of others, or calling one another horrible names, giving them the middle finger, or otherwise humiliating them. What they fail to realize is that emotional scarring, like many severe physical injuries, is not usually caused by a single trauma but the accumulation of hundreds of smaller injuries, none of which are ever given the time to heal. This is what causes so many wives to feel that they are the victims of overwhelming emotional abuse, having to bear verbal beatings without respite for years. It is also where men feel that they are nagged to death, reaching a point that they can't take one more complaint. No one of these incidents was ever enough to cause this dramatic effect, but years of accumulated scarring results in one final insult being the proverbial straw that broke the camel's back.

A Zen parable attempts to explain that success in life is not the result of a single great moment, or even a few huge victories, but a lifetime of small positive achievements. This parable says that a great stone wall is not built with a few large boulders, but thousands of little stones. The same, however, is true of a lifetime spent trying to destroy something or someone. Great emotional walls can just as easily be constructed from thousands of small insults and attacks, each having the effect of hurting the person to whom they were directed. And walls in marriages, have only one ultimate consequence.

GREATER AMONG EQUALS

It is fashionable for experts, today, to talk about equal partnerships being necessary in any marriage. They think that both sides should have an equal say in everything. Despite the prevalence of this well-intended advice, however, we are not running out of divorcing couples. The problem with these experts is that they simply are not realistic about human nature. Sure, they may have memorized everything other psychology experts just like them wrote in their books; but if psychologists were doing such a good job, all those books wouldn't need to continually be written.

Human beings are group animals, which is why we naturally fall into comfort in families, tribes, teams, gangs, clubs, cliques and friendships. This is a compelling reason for someone starting a new business venture to want partners, others with whom he can share the adventures and pitfalls of something new and challenging. In order for human groups to function there must be a chain of authority or power, and we all instinctively establish a pecking order. This is true for both men and women, even when functioning in something as casual as a social group of friends. Men and women do it differently, and each likes to poke fun at the manner in which these orders are established among members of the opposite sex. But make no mis-take, it is real for both.

In business ventures two people may be equal partners in terms of ownership, but they cannot be equal partners in terms of operation, function and influence. When there are disagreements as to how the business should be managed, and one is not willing to bow to the superior knowledge, expertise, intensity, plan, instinct or confidence of the other, the "equal" vote on all issues will paralyze the operation. Imagine how disastrous it would be if two surgeons had co-extensive authority during an operation, or two lawyers rep-resenting a single client during a trial were forever trying to override each other.

Marriage is like this. Just as in a business, each partner in the marriage has an equal share of ownership, but they cannot both be the partner-in-charge. There must be one dominant partner, even if that dominance is slight. There is nothing wrong with this, and in fact there is something wondrously right about it. If both spouses are always ready to "vote their stock," as the corporate saying goes, then the marriage will be paralyzed by the lack of any unified decisions being made. Just as happens with the majority of business partnerships, this will result in the dissolution of the organization.

For a marriage to function there must be a dominant partner. But this dominance is not necessarily universal to all aspects of marital life. The best marriages divide dominance among different tasks, just as the military and Special Forces assign different responsibilities to the officers and NCOs in a command. In the event of a disagreement, it may be that the husband is the dominant partner and makes the ultimate decision on what kind of car will be purchased. He may have the final say on investments, or be responsible for preparing their tax returns. He may even make the ultimate decision on when they will buy household appliances. In the same marriage, the wife may be the dominant partner and final decision-maker in what school the kids go to, which house to buy, and where they go for vacation.

How the dominance of issues is divided between the partners will be different for each couple, but over time these things sort themselves out. In this way neither partner is "equal" in a legal sense, and certainly not the therapeutic sense where equal means identical. But they are equivalent, each with varying amounts of influence over the myriad issues and challenges that confront every marriage, but with the sum total of those influences tallying up the same. The most important aspect of recognizing this division of labor with your spouse is to respect the other person's areas of influence and dominance, never belittling or attempting to subordinate them to yourself.

MARRIAGE

Marriage is the bedrock of any family. There is no such thing as a "family" of one parent and kids that is better than a family founded on a strong marriage. Of the marriages I have seen work – my own among them – honesty was always the foundation. That may sound cliché, but the only marriages that could survive the stresses of the life of an SF soldier were always cold-bloodedly honest; which is not to be confused with being maliciously honest. To achieve this, you had to start by being up front about what exactly it was that you did for a living. This had nothing to do with whispered disclosures of secret killings or classified operations. Women were enamored of the men when they had that little green hat on. But they didn't always realize that the soldier might not come home, or would be gone several years at war, or gone 285 days in a single year on different operations, as I was. The same is true in regular society, and much can be learned by the sad experiences of the Green Berets in lost love.

In peacetime civilian society a woman may see a lawyer in his $2,000 suit and alligator briefcase, or a physician with his doctor's coat and stethoscope, and think life with those men would be financially stable and glamorous. Then the reality sets in: 100-hour work weeks; emergency pages in the middle of the night, on weekends and holidays; and mental fatigue and irritability due to stress or constant travel. High demands come with certain professions, and men and women alike need to be realistic about life with those demands.

In the Special Forces, in most instances a woman would be enamored of her husband being a Green Beret. She'd hang in there for about three to four years, but when his re-enlistment came up she would demand that he get out. She had learned to hate the life of an SF wife. "Get out or lose me," was the refrain always heard, "I'll get you a job with my Dad." The usual rationalization for the impossible decision the women were forcing their men to make was, "You have kids now."

For those husbands, soldiering was the best job a man could have. These were men who wanted to live life, not just wander through it admiring what other men did, whose lives seemed better and more exciting than their own. Admittedly, some of these Green Berets were adrenaline junkies, and loved life on the edge. I saw some of those who got out of SF due to the strident demands of their women, get pushed over to the dark side. Even with Green Berets this can sometimes happen. By taking men who are completely dedicated, trained and conditioned to operate under the most stressful and challenging circumstances, then forcing them out of that environment and away from their comrades, they can sometimes be drawn to activities that approximate the extreme conditions they once thrived on, and were so proud to have served in. In the case of most of these men, they did not have college degrees or marketable business skills that would have allowed them to excel in the private sector. In the worst instances, these formerly noble warriors ended up smuggling drugs or guns, and a few became mercenaries. All this would happen over a woman who was too caught up in herself to truly look at her man and see who and what he was, and what he most needed.

The next group of women unsuitable to the lives of men committed to a noble cause and service, were those gold-diggers who were only in the marriage for the money. Of course, the SF soldiers had no significant financial wherewithal of their own, but they did have three things that attracted females looking to exploit a situation for monetary gain: (1) military pensions; (2) life insurance policies; and (3) a high probability of dying. Even these women have to be viewed with some measure of objectivity, however. How different were they, really, than women who married elderly men, or married men solely for their money knowing that if all else failed they would get a divorce and take the poor bastard for everything they could?

This puts a magnifying glass on an inherent weakness in men committed to honorable service, for with men devoted to a profession that requires much personal sacrifice, their love lives always appear as their Achilles' heel. With so much focus on their jobs, they tend not to scrutinize those who come into their personal lives under the guise of love or friendship. Being people of integrity, they don't question the motives of others. For the Green Berets, this naiveté has been a contributing factor in many marriages ending unpleasantly; as they should never have occurred in the first place.

LESSONS FROM THE GREEN BERETS

The men in these failed marriages are not without blame either. While in SF there was a joke that the men frequently told about a young ensign in the Navy who was about to depart on a six month deployment at sea. This young officer's wife was furious that he was going away for so long. Not knowing what else to do, he went to the admiral for advice. The admiral said he always tried not to whistle while he packed.

For years I had a not dissimilar experience that I then got to watch John go through while he was married. Whenever I was to be deployed to a hot zone somewhere in the world, I would begin mentally preparing myself for battle. This was not a conscious thing, but starting about two weeks prior to departure my mind would begin "war gaming" all the possible attacks, ambushes, problems and other dangers that might be encountered. This would go on every minute – even while sleeping – like a movie on a loop that never ends. My mind would continually process these possibilities and my reactions to them.

To my wife, I would just "check out" mentally. As the time for my trip grew near, she was experiencing her own anxiety. She needed me to reassure and comfort her. She was afraid I would not come back and needed me to pay attention to her as she tried to work through those fears. But my mind was already in the combat zone, figuring out how I was going to stay alive. This would go on until about five days before I was to ship out, at which point Jody would start yelling that I should "just get on a plane and go!" She would say that I was already there anyway, so why didn't I "just get out of here?"

Years later, I would get calls from John's wife just before he was to travel to someplace like Sudan, Kosovo, Afghanistan or the Chechen war zone. She would tell me that she had just started a fight because he wasn't paying attention to her, that he was already mentally gone. While I knew this was serious to her, after decades of living this identical marital conundrum, it was hard to keep from laughing. The irony in both our cases – and those of every warrior that has ever prepared to go into a hostile environment – is that the very mental processing we were going through, when our wives needed us to pay attention to them, was the one thing that prepared us for danger and ensured that we came home. Had we given our wives the attention they needed, and taken our minds away from this necessary wargaming process, we would likely have ended up dead.

The lesson to be taken from these experiences is that partners should never start fights, and if they are going to, the fight should be over the real issue. If you are hurt, say that. Sometimes we all just need a reminder that the person we love so adoringly can still be hurt by our unintentional acts. If something is bothering you, say exactly what it is. Only then can you find a resolution, rather than living and reliving the same never ending psycho-drama over hidden issues.

SEPARATION

Before I proposed to my wife, I took her to a *Gabriel Demonstration* and left her in the bleachers. *Gabriel Demonstrations* were named for the first Special Forces soldier to die in Vietnam, and one was exhibited in the opening scenes of the John Wayne movie, *The Green Berets*. They begin with an SF A Team demonstrating to a group of civilians who they are, where they come from, and what their skills and specialties are. The audience is given weapons briefings, parachute demonstrations, and exhibitions in the use of helicopter gunships. To help insure a solid marriage, I knew it was important that I provided a candid and open explanation of what I did and who I was. She examined it objectively, believed she could handle it, and has been true to her word for more than three decades. Over that time she endured many things most women could never. One of those things was the possibility of death.

The ability for a woman to accept that when you go to work you might not come home for six months, or ever, is a rare thing. It takes a woman who can put her own interests aside and think of her husband, his job, and all that he is sacrificing to serve *their* country. It is a service they endure *together*. My wife laughs when she hears civilian women fussing and complaining over their husbands being gone for a night, or several days, or who travel regularly for work. She does not understand how those women can be so insecure in their own marriages, or so selfish as to create problems over something so insignificant, especially when their husbands are eating in restaurants and sleeping in comfortable hotel beds, not foxholes.

HOMECOMING

But if leaving was always difficult, coming home could be worse. This is something that every man who travels needs to be aware of. When men are away, their minds are full of images of returning home to their beautiful wives. For each man, the woman he loves will be adorned in her sexiest lingerie, ready to seduce him into bed as soon as he walks through the door. In the man's mind, once the romantic – or at least sexual – reunion is complete, they will both pick up exactly where they left off before his departure. Women have completely different notions. When a man leaves, his wife establishes her own life, including her own system for maintaining the house and administering to bills. She has her own approach to daily chores and demands, and the rearing and disciplining of the children. Invariably this is different from the method her husband used, or that they had developed together.

After a long separation I can guarantee that within three to four days of him returning, there is going to be a fight. This will be caused by the fact that the man comes back and starts messing up her system. In her mind, once her husband left he tasked her with dealing with all of their life responsibilities on her own. This necessitated changes, and she figured out what worked best for her. In his absence, he lost the right to dictate how things would be done or to re-impose his will on the household and family. For example, if he comes back and disciplines the children, there will be an argument. In her mind, he's been gone too long. He lost that right, and it will take time for him to re-earn it.

Though less of an issue for military servicemen today, another problem would always arise when I returned from missions abroad. Like most families of our era, we only had one car in the family, and I always used it during the day unless Jody needed it for something. While deployed, she got accustomed to always having it available, and would structure her schedule around that convenience. When I got back, I would pop out of bed early the next morning and take the car to work. She would be outraged that I would leave her without transportation.

NO DESPERATE HOUSEWIVES

Once you are dealing with a committed and understanding woman, she must be respected and revered for her dedication and love. Men – whether in SF or civilian society – must respect the women in their lives. In part, this means recognizing that their wives were not virginal angels fallen from the heavens, who never had eyes for another. In Special Forces we had a saying: "Drop a dime and save a marriage." This meant that women should be recognized as human, and you should take steps to deal with the woman in your life as an actual, living, breathing person; one who might be wrestling with loneliness issues of her own.

First, when away you should call. Stay in touch when gone for extended periods. Let her know that she's important. Second, don't surprise her when you come home – EVER. At best, you might have denied her the ability to have dressed up for you, cleaned the house or made you a favorite meal. At worst, you may be confronted with the reality that women are human too. Be a man and recognize that her unsatisfied needs are partially a result of your chosen profession. If she stumbled in her fidelity once, it's best you not know. If it is a regular practice, you will know soon enough.

IN YOUR ABSENCE

The men in Special Forces live with a tactical and operational challenge that does not exist in the private sector. This makes being away from their loved ones all the more difficult. Prior to deploying on an SF mission – whether you were given advance notice or some world emergency imposed an unexpected operation on you – you will first enter something called Isolation. This is a special, secluded part of the base where the Team is locked in with no contact with the outside world. This is where all preparations for the operation are made. It is not unlike the "war rooms" that are developed by a team of lawyers working night and day before a big trial, or a group of businesspeople trying to put everything together for a merger or acquisition.

In many instances, in SF you might go to work on a Friday thinking you only have one day left in the week. You look forward to the end of that day, then a few drinks at the NCO club, a party or dinner with friends, followed by a relaxed weekend with your wife. Then you have the rug jerked right out from under you. As soon as you arrive at work you are shunted into the Isolation unit, and denied even the ability to call your wife. They take care of that for you. From that moment on you exist as a prisoner, inside a building inside a compound that is surrounded by twelve foot high fences, topped with barbed wire, surveillance cameras and armed guards. No one who will be on the mission goes in or out for however long you remain.

As can be imagined, this puts additional stress on both husband and wife. Of course, all SF wives have full power-of-attorney from their husbands with which to conduct any and all personal and financial affairs in their absence. This requires total trust between them. Unfortunately, there have been times when men on my Teams came home to nothing: no house, no car, no wife. What they did come home to were excessive credit card bills, with bankruptcy looming on their horizons.

Over time the wives learn what has become of you when you don't come home. They know you are close, but no matter how great a family crisis might be, you will not be allowed out. They are on their own, with you right next door. They also know that they will not be told how long your deployment will be. America cannot afford to let an enemy figure out how long our Special Forces presence may be in an area. Just knowing, for instance, that a Team will be back in three weeks may give them some indication of the type of operation that is to be run, or the level of our nation's commitment to that region.

The civilian version of this is not too dissimilar. One great advantage is that civilian husbands (or wives) working in the private sector, or in most government jobs, usually know travel will happen beforehand, and can take steps to make things easier for their families. Another is that when in the civilian version of Isolation you do have the ability to call out, or can steal away for a lunch with your wife. But that is what makes it all the harder on her when you don't call or make the effort to see her. For SF wives, it was emotionally ravaging to know their men were so close but could not see or talk to them. For civilian wives it is all the more painful to know you are so close, but won't get in touch.

No matter how important your job, you can't ever ignore your duties to the person most important in your life. While stuck in this military purgatory, the men of SF use the time to write letters to be given to wives and families at designated intervals. For instance, one letter may be written to be sent one month out, telling her that you're fine and that you'll be home as soon as possible. Most important, these letters say that you love her. The next will be delivered two months out and so on. The purpose of writing in Isolation is to comfort your family with words that you are healthy and will be home soon. With many men, a final letter is always drafted to be delivered in the event of their deaths.

For average Americans who travel a great deal, a similar practice will go far to ease some of the anxiety of separation. With the advent of modern communications technology – particularly email, cell phones and Blackberrys – it is much easier to stay in contact. Still, everyone enjoys getting cards, as they show a level of thought and effort beyond the easy immediacy of cell phone messages. Children love getting post cards from places their parents travel, and often they become treasured keepsakes. Always travel with a roll of postage stamps, as it makes the effort easier. While away for prolonged periods of time, send your wife flowers. Have them delivered to her office, where your love and devotion to her is demonstrative to her female friends; something important to women. It also helps keep men at bay who might exploit your absences. If you are going to be too busy on your trip, arrange for the flowers before you leave, just as the SF soldiers pre-write their letters. Finally, when you return home, be sure to bring gifts, however small, for everyone.

This last effort is something John and I have always made when working around the world. Sometimes, when I was running operations in Special Forces, this wasn't so easy, as our presence in a foreign country may not have been authorized by the host government and our departure accomplished not only covertly, but in a hurry. Stopping to shop in such environments was seldom easy, and sometimes the only souvenir opportunities were belt buckles or rank insignia that could be taken from dead enemy soldiers. Needless to say, this was not the type of present my family wanted.

Still, even a small item from the PX of a remote island Air Force base where we might stop for refueling would let our wives and children know we were thinking of them. For men working in the private sector, or even non-military government service, this is much easier, and only takes a few minutes of your time. Much like my SF Teams returning from hot spots, you may have had little time to go shopping while working in some distant city. If so, buy something in the airport shops. This may not allow you to find the most unique gift in the world, but it will be better than showing up with nothing but your insistence that you did think of getting them "something." There is an old saying when you give a present, that it was the thought that counted. But when you should have brought a gift and didn't, the thought alone is not enough.

When you finally get home after an extended trip, take your wife out for a nice evening, or even just a fun lunch and a matinee. Dress your sorry self up and take her someplace nice, somewhere she can show off her best dress and all the jewelry you should have been buying her over the years. No matter how tired you may be from your work and travels remember, if she is the kind of woman who has dedicated herself to you, she's been a good trooper too. While you were away she wasn't partying in bars, but was probably juggling her own job, childcare, grocery shopping, car maintenance, bill paying and family meals, all by herself. When she was not attending to all of that, she was sitting home missing you. She hasn't had a break either, and has more than earned some pleasant, personal time away. This is a mistake we have all made in our lives. I was lucky enough to have a wife who understood, and who would just tell me we were going out when she needed to. Not everyone I've worked and served with over the years was so lucky.

CHAIN OF CONCERN

Due to the long absences and high divorce rate in Special Forces during war and peace time, our community developed a Chain of Concern, separate and apart from our Chain of Command. When away for long periods, the leader of the Chain of Concern was the chaplain. After that, the chain would go from the commanding general's wife down through the military ranks of the husbands.

For women, the Chain of Concern was a device by which they could take care of each other. The wives all knew each other, and covered for each other. Throughout personal, medical and family emergencies, sick children and car accidents, they all stuck together. Necessity drove this: they had no one else. If the husband of one woman in that chain happened not to be deployed, or returned for any reason, if even for a short period such as R&R, she would not hesitate to lend him out to the other women. While on loan, he would perform such husbandly chores as car repair, oil changes, and other household "honey-do" type tasks. Knowing our wives and families were safe and looked after, is what allowed us to commit ourselves to the missions the rest of us were on.

DANCE WITH THE ONE THAT BRUNG YOU

Women can and should bond together for assistance and support. But all too often in regular American society, that support does not come in any meaningful or beneficial way. Rather than provide real assistance to their friends, too many women see their role as one in which they tell a friend how much her husband takes advantage of her, how she shouldn't have to "put up with that," or that the answer is a girls' night out at some bar, or a trip out of town together. Rather than be a real friend to a woman in need, it has become socially acceptable for other women to do everything possible to incite conflict in the relationships and marriages of others. This has been one of my wife's biggest complaints about civilian women for years.

All too often, this behavior leads to wives violating a prime directive of building and maintaining a secure and lasting marriage: Never complain about your spouse to others. This is part of an SF doctrine that says never take anything outside the Team. Within the Special Forces, an inviolable law was always, "What happens in the field, stays in the field." This was not an axiom that allowed errant soldiers to misbehave while away from home, secure in the knowledge their teammates wouldn't rat them out. It was a commitment that whatever happened on a mission would never be disclosed outside of those who were actually there, who were under fire, and who were forced to do things and make decisions that – with the benefit of hindsight and time to critique their actions – might not be so palatable to others. Today, this honorable standard of team unity and integrity has been completely perverted by the "What Happens In Vegas, Stays In Vegas," campaign that allows Americans to fool themselves into believing that one magical place exists where they can do anything they want without violating a sacred duty to their spouses.

TEAM INTEGRITY

In engineering terms, integrity means strength, and that is what integrity in marriage is all about. On the Teams, this means the people who have made a sacred pact to each other do nothing to jeopardize that relationship, or the fulfillment of the duties they have to one another. The very foundation of this doctrine is that no one outside the Team is as important as those on the Team. Nothing negative about, or destructive to, the Team or its members is ever shared with outsiders.

In America today, however, it has become fashionable among women to constantly gripe about their husbands, to take the most intimate of matters between a husband and wife out for public airing. Loyalty of women to their husbands seems to have become a quaint, if not antiquated, notion. I know for a fact that my wife has never once complained about me to anyone else, nor has any human being ever heard me complain about Jody. Her refusal to partake in the female sport of getting together and whining about their husbands lost her many such friends over the years.

Whenever someone else has complained about me to her – even if it has been a friend of mine acting in my own best interest by talking to her – Jody has steadfastly refused to go along. I think the worst thing she has ever said in such situations is, "Well, you know how that boy can be." This does not mean that she won't tell me in no uncertain terms when she is displeased with me. But that is exactly the point: when she is unhappy with her husband, she tells her husband and no one else. She never takes it outside of the marriage. Years after my honorable discharge from the service, she continues to live as a Green Beret.

Women and men alike need to understand that the three pillars of any marriage are honesty, loyalty and fidelity. People hear these words all the time, but never stop to comprehend their meanings. Too many married people believe that "honesty" means they should not tell an affirmative lie and that they aren't being dishonest so long as a direct falsehood is not uttered. If questioned, they play the "witness on the stand" game and carefully answer only what is asked, much like then-President Bill Clinton splitting hairs in answering under oath whether he actually had sex with Monica Lewinsky. If a husband asks his wife is she's been having an affair with some guy at work, and she says "no" with full knowledge that they've gone dancing, gotten drunk together, or kissed and fondled each other in the copy room, her answer is still a breach of her duty of honesty. A duty of honesty to someone is an affirmative duty to disclose anything that would be important or relevant to that person.

The duty of loyalty is greater still. People do not understand that long before the duty of sexual fidelity is violated in a marriage, the duties of honesty and loyalty have been trampled into the ground. Loyalty to another is a pledge of complete and undivided commitment to that person, and that person alone. An employee of a corporation does not work for a competitor or pass secrets to other companies. A lawyer does not allow his duty to his client to conflict with duties to others. As the cowboys used to say: "When you ride, you ride only for the brand."

In modern society, divorce is so common that people have long since lost respect for the sanctity of marriage. They don't hold their own marriages in such high regard; therefore, they cannot expect others to respect their marriage either, unless they make absolutely clear how devoted they are to it. People attracted to married friends, co-workers and classmates, see wedding vows as merely a low hurdle in their efforts at seduction. Opportunities outside of marriage seem to abound and married men and women see the lines of their duties to their spouses blur. A company in Los Angeles acting as a dating service for married people looking for relationships outside of their spouses, has an enormous billboard that proudly proclaims, "Life Is Short, Have An Affair." This the point we've reached in America. A simple test of a spouse's duty of loyalty is easy to remember, and I have always tried to live by this standard: If you are anywhere with members of the opposite sex, and all are acting or talking in a way that would stop instantly if a spouse walked into the room, then the duty of loyalty has been breached.

We are all human and susceptible to human urges. Being an adult, however, means you do not have to act on those urges. Through most of my years in SF, when we deployed we would be in some remote jungle or desert alone, or otherwise sequestered on some secret base by the host government. We were on duty and working hard every waking hour; and those hours spent sleeping were few indeed. The ability to even see females was rare, and contact with them impossible. This alone kept the men focused and marriages intact. But there were also times when we were around women. Being around them might have made everyone hornier, but did not make dalliances permissible.

Long after I left the military, John and I, and a team from Archangel, spent time in the war zone of southern Sudan. We went straight from there to the Chechen War Theater in Russia. After weeks in Africa watching bare breasted young women, followed by our proximity to dozens of attractive young Chechen, Ingush and Russian women in IDP camps,[77] I just couldn't take it anymore. Fifteen minutes later I walked out of the WC[78] in the small lodging we had secured and announced to the guys on our team in my best British accent: "I finally just had to have a wank." Despite their gri-

---

77 Internally Displaced Persons or refugee camps.
78 Water closet or small toilet room found in most countries outside the U.S.

macing faces and expressed disgust at my admission, I could tell they were all on the verge themselves, if they hadn't already been at it.

The important point is that despite human urges, you shouldn't cheat on your spouse. This alone is not enough to ensure a successful marriage, but it is an important component of all of those marriages that are happy, and do succeed. Being a man is not about seducing as many women as possible. Being a man is about finding a good and decent woman, and then pledging your life to her. Being a man is about not violating that trust.

CHILDREN

In many ways children are the most wonderful additions to your life. But their injection into the delicate balance of any marriage is usually a sticky wicket that few spouses are ever prepared for. Over the six decades of my life, I have seen a shift from women realizing they are wives and lovers first, to allowing their motherhood to completely dominate and overwhelm their relationships with – and duties to – their husbands.

Children are, and should be, priorities. However, no one can ever allow their presence to take precedence over their relationship with their spouse. This is usually more of a problem with women than men. When men have children they are happy to enter into fatherhood, but that in no way diminishes their desires for their wives sexually, nor the need for their partners in every other aspect of their lives. Men see childrearing as something they will get through with their wives, together. But too many new mothers allow that status to become their complete identity. No longer are they wives and lovers, with a man who still needs them. It is as though in their minds the act of giving birth has been an act of total consumption, completing them as women, and they no longer need or want anything else, reducing their husbands to little more than a means by which that motherhood is financially subsidized.

All spouses must remember that the person they are married to is the person they are supposed to be with the rest of their lives. That person was there long before the first kid came along, and should be there long after the last kid is gone. That is the person you share your innermost thoughts with, the person you turn to when afraid, or in doubt or confused. That is the person you climb into bed with every night and [should] make love to; the person you cuddle with and whisper to late into the dark nights. That is the person you can depend on to stand with you against all others, and all threats and problems in your life. But you cannot disappear for 18 or 20 years of your children's lives, and expect to find a spouse still waiting for you at the end.

Never allow your children to invade that important and sacred part of your life. Never forget that you are a wife or a husband first. The day will come when the children will be grown. They will move away, marry and have kids of their own. At that point it would be tragic to find that you long ago sacrificed the most important person and relationship you had. Do not wake up one morning and realize that you had years ago destroyed the love and trust of your dearest friend, who had dedicated his life to you. I have seen too many marriages that did not end in divorce, but still had not really existed. With them, the husband and wife had long before moved on, and were involved in entirely separate lives with new interests, even though they both came back to the same house at night. That is no way to live, and would not be necessary if everyone remembered who they had pledged their lives to, and who it was that pledged their lives to them. Marriage is, after all, a holy sacrament. Childbearing is not.

Future Green Beret John Anderson, age 9, carrying an enormous rock while clearing land on the family farm in northern California. The hard work would serve him well in the years to come.

– 7 –

COMMITMENT TO FAMILY

Nothing counts so much as blood.
Everyone else is just strangers.

Kevin Costner in "Wyatt Earp"

EMERGENCY RESPONSE PLANS FOR THE GREEN BERET FAMILY

Like an ODA, all aspects of family organization and survival must be followed. The first goal, every single day of your life, is to make sure that everyone on the team – every member of your family - comes home safely at the end of the day. The second rule is to make sure you get home safely. As a husband you can, and should, violate the second rule to ensure the safety of your wife. As parents, you will both sacrifice your own safety for your children. This is nature's way, and the Code of the Green Beret.

Thus, it is every parent's responsibility to develop emergency safety plans for the entire family. What dangers a family faces are partly dependent on geography and partly on the likelihood of external threats such as hurricanes, earthquakes, forest fires, floods, leaking gas lines, breached dams or nuclear power plants. Emergency response plans must be developed and all members of the family trained in them. As with Green Berets preparing to survive combat, when it comes to life threatening situations for your family, there is no such thing as too much training.

As part of your family survival plan, you should post important emergency numbers near every phone in the house. Other than 911, there must be emergency numbers for your plumber, electrician, power company, water company or public service. Doctors, ambulance services, hospitals, veterinarians, neighbors, friends and other family members must be included. If you have a dog that could pose a threat to paramedics, put a plan in place to have someone secure the animal in the event you have a heart attack or are stricken by some other ailment or injury while home alone, and have to call 911 for yourself. Paramedics and police will not usually attempt to enter if they might be bitten. Or they may shoot your dog.

Have you established a Chain of Contacts so that you would know in what order your children would call others, and where they would flee in an emergency? In addition to these contacts a series of ERVs – Emergency Rendezvous or rally points - should be known by everyone. Each of these should be secure and protected places easily accessible by all family members, especially those who can't drive. Fire extinguishers must be put in critical locations throughout the house, and must be functioning.

All family members should know the location of the gas main, water valves and the breaker box, and how to both turn them on and off. You should create a safe room or closet – a hard defensive position – for your family to flee in the event of a human threat or other natural disaster like a tornado. This should be some place they can all fit, and lock themselves in, that cannot be breached. You must create a means by which family members can escape second or third story windows without having to jump, in the event of a fire blocking the stairs.

These are all things you should consider and put into your family emergency plan. Lt. Col. Grossman points out the inability of anyone to perform under duress if they have not trained. He explains that even something as simple as dialing 911 has often proven impossible for panicked people. To ensure they can do it when in the midst of a crisis, they need to practice calling on their cell phones and then hitting "Send." In an emergency, too many people keep re-dialing without initiating the call. If the home phone – or a work phone – has different lines, everyone needs to train to punch the button to get a line first. If they have to dial 9 to get an outside line before dialing 911, that must be practiced. When it comes to the lives of your family, no detail is too small. Training like this is how the Special Forces stay alive in dangerous environments.

One of the best sources of information in the creation of a family emergency response plan can be found in *Disaster Ready People For A Disaster Ready America* by James W. Satterfield and Harry W. Rhulen.[79] Just as the Special Forces do, you must avail yourself of the intelligence that exists to prepare your team for the worst possible threats.

PREPARE TO REPEL INVADERS

Ensuring the safety of your family does not end at protecting them from unexpected home hazards, accidents, or their own poor judgment. You must be realistic in recognizing threats that exist to the safety and lives of your loved ones from criminal behavior. Far too many people seem to wander through their lives, oblivious to the very real threats surrounding them. Women pay no attention to where they park their cars in the mall lot, and then can't find them in the dark when they come out. Wives and mothers leave front doors unlocked when home alone in the middle of the day. Men blunder down dark streets and alleys with no sense of who is lurking about them.

Every 2.5 minutes a woman or girl is raped in America. Home invaders simply walk through unlocked front doors of people's houses every night, taking whole families hostage, torturing, beating and raping, before robbing them. In the Vietnam War America lost

---

[79] Firestorm Solutions, LLC (Golden, Colorado: 2006), and can be found at www.firestorm.com.

a little over 58,000 troops. During those same years approximately 150,000 American citizens were murdered on our streets and in their homes. Where was the war? Where is it today, with an average annual murder rate close to 20,000? How many of those murder victims were prepared for the life and death situations that confronted them? With the incidence of violent crime in America, we must all be prepared to defend ourselves, just as soldiers prepare to survive combat.

For these reasons, all citizens must realistically understand that every one of us is a potential victim of serious crime, every single day of our lives. Our children are in danger of being attacked and beaten by gangs of kids, of drug dealers, of speeding cars, as well as being kidnapped by child molesters. Our women are in danger of being raped and murdered. I do not understand how anyone can be so naïve as to reiterate the inanity I have heard from civilians for years: "I can take care of myself, I've been doing things this way for years and nothing has ever happened to me." What such people obviously don't understand is that they have not been victimized *in spite of* how they behaved, *not because of it.* The only women who never insist that they are perfectly capable of taking care of themselves, and don't need help or advice, are those who were raped. Once a 100 pound woman stated to me that she saw no reason to ever own or carry a gun. My immediate response was, "If I stopped being a gentleman right now and attacked you, there is no way you could stop me from doing whatever I wanted. Unless you had a gun." Without that gun she had absolutely no way of equalizing the situation between us.

This attitude makes no more sense than allowing someone to go to war, blunder around and luckily make it home, then think because he didn't die that he's ready to deal with the worst that war can throw at him. What I've just described isn't a soldier, it's a fool. We have all known people who drive dangerously fast, risking their own lives and the lives of everyone else on the road. Yet, when we attempt to tell them they need to change their behavior, all we hear is that they've always driven that way. This often turns out to be the epitaph for their own headstones, if not those of innocent people they kill. When they protest that they've been driving like maniacs all their lives and have never been in an accident, we always ask, "But how many accidents have you caused that you drove away from, and didn't even know about?"

People rarely realize the stupidity of their own decision-making until they see their kids get older, and make the same dumb choices. Women who would go out alone and get drunk with strange men, but with no back up, or who went on dates with men they barely knew, see the dangers of this conduct when their own daughters do it. Then they wonder where their children got such ideas.

It is not only the duty of every parent to help the family prevent threats, but to be able to respond to them. Many people do not believe in guns. But these are people who have never been attacked or threatened. The men who think this way never had three or four or five men in their homes raping their wives, while they stood by unable to protect them. John and I are Special Forces hand-to-hand combat instructors. Both of us are experts at dealing with multiple attackers, even when those attackers are heavily armed. Both of us are large, muscular men with weightlifting championships under our belts. But the problem in such instances for even us is that while you can usually successfully defend and extricate *yourself*, you are incapable of protecting *another*. No matter our skills, neither of us could protect a woman in a situation like that unarmed. If we can't, how can the average untrained husband think he will be able to? The reality is that a gun is a tool, like any other. Most of the time it will just sit there, hurting no one. But when the time comes that you need a gun, then *you really need a gun*, and there is no substitute. It makes no sense that anyone could hold personal opinions so dearly that he would risk his family members' lives over them.

Parents – especially fathers – must understand that the safety of the family is their ultimate responsibility. In the old days, men grew up fighting. They fought to protect that which was precious to them because no one else was going to do it for them. We are a more passive society now. Today, even a fistfight between children in a school yard results in suspension if not expulsion, police calls and criminal charges, lawyers and lawsuits. Today courts routinely hear cases of burglars and rapists breaking into houses, while husbands cower behind beds with their wives, begging the police over the phone to save them.

We have created generations of completely feminized – what Ann Coulter calls *pussified* - males who have neither the physical skills nor the courage to do the tough thing, to protect their women. Too many young males today care more about shaving their legs, arms and chests, - more things than women shave - styling their hair and getting body jewelry, than they care about being men. This is a loss to women, children, and society as a whole.

A CALL TO ARMS -
FOR THE SAKE OF YOUR FAMILY

All men in America should aspire to be like Green Berets, they should have at least utilitarian levels of ability at hand-to-hand combat, including the use of weapons. They may choose not to use guns, knives or clubs, but they had better have some comfort with disarming them. Every man should push himself to his physical limits. Able-bodied husbands and fathers shouldn't spend all of their free time on a golf course, or in a bowling alley, or sitting on their fat asses watching football, baseball, basketball and hockey; watching complete strangers living *their* lives. And don't be one of the thousands who claim some debilitating injury either. Find a martial art and get into the dojo. With what free time is left, get into the gym to lift weights and do some cardiovascular work. Periodically get on a shooting range and work on firearms skills. If you need help, you should take a class. This is what Green Berets do, and it keeps them and their Team members alive, both at home and abroad.

There are dozens of different styles of martial arts, and there is one for everybody. With a fraction of the time wasted in these other zero intensity pastimes, every husband and father in

America could have a black belt. Just by throwing the television out the window, everyone would find they had more than enough time to better themselves. Martial arts training alone would put them in much better physical condition, fix injuries, give them longer lives, more discipline, more tranquil minds and healthier bodies, than all the golf courses and couches in the world. Getting yourself into an exercise gym will not only add to those benefits, but enhance your formidability in the event of an actual threat to you or your family.

Combat is exhausting. That's why elite soldiers maintain such high levels of conditioning. Running – should you ever need to escape a threat - is exhausting, too. So are long days at difficult jobs. There is nothing in your life that won't benefit from superior physical fitness. By engaging in these efforts, you are not only benefiting yourself and your loved ones, you are living your life. As a parent, you have a duty to develop sufficient survival skills to keep your family safe. You have no such duty to sit on a sofa, swilling light beer watching TV. Stop living vicariously through the lives of conscienceless celebrity strangers and sports heroes you don't know, and probably wouldn't like if you had to spend time with them.

A number of years ago John had a business client ask him what his plans were for the weekend. This man asked, "So, are you going to watch the Broncos on Sunday?" John said, "No." The man went on to inquire what football teams John followed, what other professional sports he watched, whether he was into watching the college teams, and so forth. To each of these questions, John responded that he didn't watch any of it. The man then asked, "So, if you don't watch any sports on TV, and you aren't going to any of the games, what do you do with your weekends?"

John answered this question by saying, "Saturdays, I go skydiving in the mornings if the weather's clear, then I go to the gym to lift weights; at the end of the day I'll go to the range for either some pistol or archery practice. Sundays, I get up early and hike in the mountains or lift weights, then I teach martial arts at a local school for several hours. I spend a couple of hours on my own training when that's done. Sometimes I'll go to the gym and swim a mile or so. Then I go home, clean the house, do laundry and get ready for the work week." With a look of utter disdain, this man replied, "Man, you really need to get a life." This simple statement by someone confronted, for the first time, with another human being who didn't waste his life watching others live theirs, is sadly representative of how most Americans exist today. Stop and think of the impact you would have on your children if they grew up watching you truly live your life, compared to the example you may be setting today.

A PLACE FOR WARRIORS

No man can establish himself as the archetype of warriorship for his sons and family, nor can he live his life as a Green Beret, when he is shamefully shunted into the garage by a wife intent on turning "his castle" into a bastion of feminine haute couture. Across America, the fact that countless men have surrendered any input or influence in the arrangement and decoration of their own homes has become an almost comedic parody of domestic life. I rarely walk into a civilian home that contains any indication of the presence of a man. Sports trophies, military mementos and photos from years-ago service, hunting trophies, personal and professional awards, certificates, diplomas, sculptures and paintings that reflect anything masculine are at best sentenced to solitary confinement in a tiny room in the basement, away from prying eyes. More typically, they are reduced to serving out their existences in cobweb shrouded boxes on garage shelves; the only place the man is permitted to call his own.

Yet the house is replete with feminine design. The living, dining and family rooms reflect the gender-specific tastes of a woman. The kitchen has been remodeled at great cost, more for ostentatious appearance than function, as many of these women do not even cook. Paintings throughout the house demonstrate the magniloquent tastes of their owner – the lady of the house – and are chosen to bring out the highlights of both furniture and carpets. The walls are painted gentle pastels, or covered with delicate print wallpaper. Frilly curtains, lacy bedspreads, ruffled canopies over color-coordinated comforters are what the man retires to at night. But he cannot get undressed there, as his clothes are not permitted in a closet overcrowded with designer dresses and high heeled shoes. It is as though he doesn't even live there.

The women of these homes get together and mock the brutish Philistinism of their husbands' tastes, and breathe collective sighs of relief at the malleability of their men acquiescing to wives' demands. As a result, every single day of their lives these men come home from work to houses that are, in no way, their own. They walk through doors into buildings that reflect nothing of who they are, of what they like, or what is comfortable to them. Years later, they wonder what happened to the men they used to be. Mostly they wonder what happened to the men they always planned to become.

Decades of marital emasculation see these men surreptitiously buying copies of *Soldier of Fortune* magazine, or any number of hunting, martial arts or wilderness survival publications in distant drug stores, where no one will recognize them. They steal off to secret places where they riffle through the pages, drinking in the photographs of real men off in the world doing real men things; and they dream. They keep this a secret, hiding the object of their fantasies in the only place their wives will not go: the garage. Or they are cached beneath file folders of mind-numbing paper in bottom desk drawers at work. Paper screaming silently at them that they are little more than the gelded versions of the stallions they were born to be. They feel the same shame and guilt they did when mere teenagers, masturbating in secret to pornographic magazines they stole from the store, hiding their secret desires from their families, then, too. If these men thought they could get away with it, they would shoplift these magazines as well. Anything to not bear the shame of being seen buying them.

This is the sad state of many men in our society. Yet walk into the home of any Green Beret – or any top level military man – and you will instantly recognize a completely different set of priorities in décor. For these are warriors' homes. These are the castles of elite soldiers, and every nook and cranny bears testimony to their presence. It is not as though every inch of vertical and horizontal surface is a monument to their soldiery, but the proof is there.

There is always a large den, set right off the main areas of the house; especially in the homes of officers and senior NCOs. This den is, most definitely, his place, with little in the way of empty wall space. It is a shrine, the lair of a warrior, and it is adorned with framed photographs of him in full battle regalia together with his friends, his Teams. Among the pictures are awards; certificates; diplomas, from both academic and military schools; commendations and citations. The framed insignia of the units he has served with are there. In Special Forces, he may have been given numerous plaques from Teams he commanded or served on, and sometimes one will see a framed map of the world with pins stuck in all of the countries he served, defending America and her freedom. The map will be bordered by the flashes of all the Groups he served with. This will have been a gift from his brothers-in-arms, and will never be taken down.

But that one room is not the limit of his presence in his own home. The rooms are always tastefully decorated, evidence of a woman's touch and tastes. But they are festooned with paintings and wall hangings he has drug home from around the world. The floors are covered in Persian and Afghan rugs he brought his wife, coming home from combat tours in those faraway places. Vases and other decorations reflect the overseas tours they spent together, with all of this melding into a well appointed home that reflects the presence, personalities, and tastes of both man and wife. These are the homes of Green Berets. When walking into them, you do not mistake them for the *Better Homes and Gardens* ornaments of women, nor do they look like seedy bachelor pads. But you would never pause to wonder how an elite soldier could come home to such a place. You will feel the nobility of what he does for a living; for she is proud too, and not afraid to have his warriorship accent their castle.

There are some men out there in the civilian world who have insisted that certain things of their own remain, that they not be relegated to those dark and musty corners where, after awhile, the wife thinks he will not notice if she throws them away. But all too often, these men endure wives whose humiliation at his additions find them apologizing to catty friends. Friends who raise eyebrows at the proof of his presence, as though some disease-ridden spoor moved through the home, leaving evidence of its passage. These women simply do not "get it." They neither appreciate, nor understand, the value of having a real man in their lives.

This is part of the emasculation process that goes on in many marriages. According to John Eldredge, "Women are often attracted to the wilder side of a man, but once having caught him they settle down to the task of domesticating him. Ironically, if he gives in he'll resent her for it, and she in turn will wonder where the passion has gone. Most marriages wind up here."[80] But the warrior men who successfully reject this taming process are not to be apologized for, nor are they ever to be embarrassed over. Just as with those Green Beret wives who support their husbands in all they do, these women should be proud of who and what their men are. They should puff up with pride when any guest in their home points out the symbols of his accomplishments and his life, and says, "So, this is what your husband is all about."

My own home is much as I have described. The mementos, plaques, pictures of harrowing operations and dangerous adventures, can be found. Full size paintings and drawings attesting to our service – and to the Special Forces in general – hang framed in the main hallway. Decorating a large cabinet in our dining room are such headgear as an Arab headdress from tours in Saudia Arabia and Jordan, my treasured cowboy hat, and the beret I proudly wore up to my retirement. Beneath these rests an enormous Scottish Claymore[81] a gift from John, attesting to my Scotch heritage, and which I strap to my back every year at the Scottish-Celtic festival in Estes Park, Colorado.

[80] Eldredge, 82.
[81] Original, large Celtic battle sword.

But among all this is a framed picture of me, in dress uniform and beret, placed there *by my wife* who has never once been ashamed of who I was, and who I am. This is the home not so much of an elite soldier, but of a man. As such, it is the home of a warrior, and no man can be such a thing without a place where he can go to rest, and in the process be reminded of the duties, struggles and responsibilities of that warriorship - of manhood. That place can never be the garage, but must be his own home, his own castle. For without castles, there would never have been knights.

THE FAMILY THAT SAVES TOGETHER....

Warriorship is not just about dealing with physical threats, or physical demands and overt duties. Warriorship is about being the best person you can be, and shouldering the responsibility of helping others who depend on you to do the same. One of the aspects of warriorship in maintaining your family in a stable, happy environment is living within your means. Few rules are violated more often and more casually, with more devastating results, than this. Americans - especially younger generation Americans - have lost all understanding of the concept of deferred gratification. In years past, if a couple wanted to buy something like a house or a car, they saved the money for it, and most people wouldn't purchase a house that cost more than the husband made in one year. These same people survived the Depression, which only reinforced such careful and conservative personal financial practices. Then, America was a nation of savers. Today, most adults don't have enough money saved to last a month if they lost their jobs. Despite our high standard of living we rate at the bottom of all developed nations in money saved per household. The ready accessibility of financing is partially responsible for this. But the people who choose to become indebted for ridiculous purchases not only bear the financial responsibility for those decisions, but the moral responsibility for what those decisions can do to their families.

In order to support your family as the Special Forces men do, you cannot allow your family to become slaves to material possessions. If so, your integrity and character will be slaves to the financial demands on you. Make sure you always have the ability to tell a superior, a partner or client, to go to hell and still be able to survive. After living for a quarter century on a miniscule Army salary, I finally retired. The money I was being paid for my second career was more than four times what our family was used to. Still, I was not about to get caught in the trap of overspending, not knowing how long that good fortune would last.

Even while earning a six figure salary at a nuclear weapons plant, I would not allow us to spend beyond what was affordable on my previous military pay. I was always concerned about what my family would do if I died, lost my job or could no longer work. Living within the means we were accustomed to gave us tremendous freedom. To live your life with self-respect, and without compromising yourself, you have to know that you can survive no matter what happens to you. If you are smart, literate, and willing to work hard – and you do not allow yourself to become strangled by unnecessary credit card bills and monthly financial payments – you and your family will always be all right.

Sadly, we have reached a point in our country where everyone feels that he and she is entitled to anything they want. Men waste fortunes on expensive toys, giving birth to the female complaint that little boys don't grow up, their toys just get more expensive. Women insist on enormous houses, expensive vehicles they could never afford if single, expensive jewelry, costly weddings and dozens of pairs of new shoes to go with more clothes than they could possibly wear in a year. When both parents end up with all the junk they think they need, they find their monthly credit card bills exceed their gross income. The loss of a salary, for even a couple of weeks, is devastating. This compulsion to live like we're all rich is so great that I have been in several people's million dollar homes, only to find that they are virtually devoid of furnishings. These couples just had to have big expensive mansions to impress others, but are such slaves to the mortgages that they can't afford anything else.

This is also seen in the demands of our children for fashionable and expensive clothes, costly toys and music systems, specialized or private schools and the hiring of coaches for anything they show a fleeting interest in. Somewhere along the way, middle class Americans became convinced that it is every parent's duty to give their offspring the childhood of someone born into the Kennedy or Trump dynasties. In years past, one of the most frequently heard refrains was, "We can't afford it." If a kid wanted something, he went out and worked for it. Today, that is never heard, and parents act as though they are guilty of criminal abuse if they ever tell their children that something is too expensive.

You do not have to have a lot of money to produce good citizens. In fact, you cannot buy your children's good citizenship for any amount, and that level of overindulgence often has the opposite affect. Overindulgence of any kind is not healthy for children; all it does is create the feelings of entitlement that are a weakness in many Americans today. Too many parents have forgotten that children do not come with rights, they have to earn them. The only true gifts you can give to your kids are the qualities of honesty, self-respect, respect for others, having their own minds and a measure of independence that keeps them from being influenced by outside forces, a strong work ethic, discipline, and the knowledge that they can handle any problem or challenge life throws at them. Ironically, these are the very qualities found in America's Green Berets.

Randy Pratt is one of Archangel's top firearms instructors. Tall and lanky, Randy is a kind, generous and polite man who also serves his community as a firefighter. Randy mixes well with the Green Berets we train, and quickly earns their respect, for he was raised by a Green Beret father. Though he never served in the military, Randy appreciates the level of dedication and skill of these men, and works hard to see that they become all the better. Randy is, thus, the personification of the good, hard working and committed people

SF parents produce, and what all parents can impart to their own children. When children see their parents as honest, hard working, financially and personally disciplined, and individuals who accept responsibility for their own actions, they are most likely to turn out the same way. Our kids will become who we are, never what we tell them to be. This is your legacy to your children and even your grandchildren, which is the best thing you could ever leave them.

To be sure, parents are under siege by TV ads, friends' and co-workers' demonstrative material wealth and conspicuous consumption, as well as the gross indulgence of their own kids' friends by their parents. Despite this bombardment of pressure to act the way all of these other people do, parents have to say "No." Green Berets are so secure in themselves, and in their knowledge of what is right for them, that they cannot be induced to deviate from that path. All Americans must look at their own lives and their family members. They must decide what is right, and absolutely necessary, for them. They then have to act on that realization, and not be dissuaded. The discipline and limitations on your life will be good for you, and make your children much better people than the overindulged, spoiled brats America is now generating in mass numbers.

BASIC NECESSITIES

A simple rule that many in the military follow is that you should never finance anything other than one vehicle for each spouse, and the mortgage for your home. And none of these should be more expensive than necessary. Nothing should ever be put on a credit card that cannot be paid off the next month when the bill comes. This keeps you from buying expensive toys like snowmobiles, ATVs, motorcycles and speed boats. It keeps you from going on clothes shopping sprees. If you don't have the money to pay for something right then that means you can't afford it. As Americans, we are all inordinately spoiled, especially relative to other nations' citizens. What we think we cannot possibly do without typically falls far short of the necessities of life.

If you have a roof over your head, enough food to feed the kids, the ability to get to work (public transportation is always cheap), required medicine for anyone in the family, one good pair of shoes, and at least some clothes, there is nothing else you really need. People who are truly destitute do not have even that much. Back in 1992, shortly after the dissolution of the Soviet Union a Russian lawyer was visiting John here in the U.S. Having heard Communist propaganda for years about all the poor and homeless in America, he asked John to show him some. Walking along a downtown street, John pointed out several homeless men. The lawyer responded, "You call that poor? Look, that man has a decent, warm coat for the winter. He has a quality pair of boots with no holes, some blankets and food in his cart. You people don't know what poor is."

An easy rule to follow that helps you avoid the pitfall of American excess is to never buy anything you see advertised on television or owned by someone else, that you hadn't long before wanted or needed to purchase. This keeps you from falling prey to all of the expensive trends that pervade America; like the recent rage of Harley Davidson motorcycles, that no man can be a man without. In this way, the only times you may violate these rules of fiscal responsibility will be for those rare things you have dreamed of having all your life. For some people that may be a boat, for others it may be a motorcycle; or maybe a horse. For women it might be a fur coat, or a diamond wedding ring after years of waiting to be able to afford one. But if you are susceptible to impulse purchases of expensive items, you will be forever extending yourself financially to purchase things that never held that much meaning for you and may ultimately ruin your life and jeopardize the security of your family. Whenever you are drawn to spend money on something, ask yourself, "Am I being one of those pathetic, weak people advertising agencies target with their commercials, thinking they can brainwash me into buying their junk?" If you are honest with yourself, you might be surprised at the answer.

John and I have both spent a good deal of our lives around Italian immigrant families, and they were perfect models for how to maintain your family. Though most had a large number of kids, they weren't rich. Children wore hand-me-down clothes whether they liked it or not. The houses were small and you would see two or three kids sharing a bedroom, and sometimes more. Though they never had much in material possessions, the cupboards were always well stocked with good, fresh food. Meals were an integral part of the family and the good times it spent together. The only thing in greater abundance than food, was love. I have never known anyone who came from that environment to complain about his upbringing.

CHAIN OF COMMAND

A family is much like the military in terms of Chain of Command (CoC). In the military there is an established Chain of Command, a succession of superiors from the President of the United States down to each individual soldier. Within each Special Forces Team the command hierarchy is well known, too. Each soldier knows the chain and follows it, without exception. Families have a similar Chain of Command, and it must be respected and followed by all members. In American families today, however, the Chain has been disrupted.

Rather than all family members respecting the CoC between father and mother, the focus is on the kids. Past generations did a much better job at this than we do today. Certain aspects of running the family and rearing the children were the province of the mother, and this was respected. Other parts of childrearing fell to the father; often including discipline. The fathers often thought the mothers coddled the kids too much, but never interfered. The mothers sometimes thought the fathers were too harsh, but never let the children know. This resulted in an established CoC that was always respected, and both families and children were the better for it. Certainly, more families survived intact than do today.

One situation where my choice of discipline for our daughter conflicted with my wife's perspective, without adversely affecting our marriage, is illustrative of this. When our daughter was five years old, she wrote all over the walls of her bedroom. When I returned from deployment she was spoken to, and made to understand she was never to do such things again. I had to buy several gallons of paint to repair the damage. No sooner had I finished, when she took a chop stick and carved gouges in the freshly painted walls. She was old enough to understand the seriousness of this, as well as other things she had decided to disobey.

When I saw her most recent decorative masterpiece, I swept her up in one arm, holding her facedown across my hand and arm, and spanked her with the other hand. I had not realized how close to the wall I was standing, and with each thwack on her butt her head tapped the wall. Thinking this was a little excessive, my wife quickly grabbed a pillow and held it between her head and the wall. While this may not have earned either of us parent-of-the-year awards, it demonstrates support between parents that is important for the rearing of children. Our daughter was not emotionally destroyed by this event, nor was she physically injured. In fact, today she regales many by reciting this adventure in her childhood with much humor, and I expect her own daughter will hear it as well. But she did learn her lesson.

DON'T LET THE PRIVATES RUN THE ARMY

When I was a child, parents understood that children were manipulative creatures who would do anything to get their way, and that they would try to work one parent against the other. That is natural for children. It was the parents' job not to allow this to happen. A standard response from any father to a request for permission to do anything was: "It's alright with me, if it's alright with your mother," and vice versa. One parent might think the other was too harsh, or too lenient with the kids, but this was never expressed in front of the kids. Children only ever saw each parent supporting the other. While parents might have a disagreement later, beyond earshot of the children, the kids never saw that they had succeeded in driving a wedge between them.

Today it is just the opposite. Female notions of the proper way to raise children have come to be the dominating force in the household. Gone is the influence of fathers. The role of men has become totally subordinated to the nurturing aspects of motherhood, resulting in increasing generations of impolite, spoiled, undisciplined kids and young adults, who have no respect for others and no work ethic. The desires of the children dictate everything that goes on in the home, and each parent's first priority is giving them what they want. In generations past, the parents were the priority of the entire family, and each parent met its duty to the other, first and foremost. The children knew that they came a distant second to their parents' love and duty to each other. Then, it was all about the parents. Today, it's all about the children.

Today, the focus is far too much on the kids and the privates are running the unit. Parents bounce back and forth between over-coddling the children and allowing them freedom to the point of endangering them. In our efforts to protect our kids from any pain of loss or failure, we only ensure they do not have necessary life experiences, like being hurt and getting over it. We keep them from experiencing rejection until they are adults, when it is far more difficult to deal with. Then as our children get a little older – when they still need adult supervision and guidance – we're too busy trying to be their friends and make them like us.

A parent's job is to parent, which usually means exercising mature judgment and telling them they are not permitted to do the fun things they have concocted. If you are just going to let your kids do what they want, what do they need you for? Unfortunately, most of the time the parent's job is to say "No." It is to make decisions that will result in their children being mad at them, and sometimes hating them. I am frequently confused by ridiculously over-protective parents that won't let little Billy walk out of the house without a helmet, elbow and knee pads, so fearful are they that their little boy might experience some pain in life. But, as soon as Billy reaches an age where he starts thinking for himself, they allow him to engage in all manner of activities that could have horrible and destructive consequences. They buy him an expensive sports car for his sixteenth birthday. They let him stay out too late, tolerate his drinking and drug use without severe sanctions, and actually participate, financially, in sending him away on trips with others of his maturity level, without adult supervision.

Parenting is no different from the role of officers and senior NCOs in the Special Forces. But if fully grown, mature, highly-trained soldiers need their own version of military mothers and fathers to keep them behaving properly and safely, how is it children can afford to have less? For years I've heard John's stories about his father, each one of which struck a chord as they sounded exactly like my own experiences growing up. During his youth, John's father was forever telling his sons, in response to their pining over the inequities of their young lives: "I'm not here to be fair, and I'm not here for you to like me. I'm here to be your father." Nothing sums it up better. Nothing could be closer to the words that I used with my men when serving as Team sergeant.

DON'T GIVE AWAY THE FARM

Overindulgence is also seen in parents frequently attempting to keep their little boys and girls from ever having the slightest negative experience in life. God forbid the kids experience rejection, failure, loss, being ignored, physical pain or injury, delayed gratification or not getting their way in everything. This tectonic shift in society's conditioning of children has resulted in many adverse changes in the development of our young:

- schools that don't want to give grades for fear that students with lesser performances won't feel as smart or accomplished as others (they're not);
- the elimination of competitive sports so kids that aren't as athletically inclined feel that they are the equal of the kids that are (you're allowing them to become deluded about their own abilities);
- the awarding of huge trophies any time children merely show up for any recreational activity (you destroy any true feelings of accomplishment for something that is really worked for);
- parents' refusal to let their kids walk outside without protective equipment for fear of injury (learning that actions have consequences, and experiencing and mastering pain is an important part of life, and much easier learned as a child); and,
- the elimination of traditional childhood activities like recess, gym class and tag (denying children the ability to socialize, and learn to deal with low-level competition, develop strong bodies, and maybe even learn to love a sport).

Even bullying, as unpleasant as it is, is an important and beneficial aspect of life. The lessons children learn when dealing with bullies teach them to deal with aggressors throughout their adult lives. And don't delude yourself into believing bullies, in all their forms, won't always be around.

People today seem to believe that shielding their children from learning from these experiences while young is good for them. Yet, if you ensure that they do not experience life's unpleasantness while young, how do you expect them to react the first time they are encountered as adults, with none of the coping skills developed in childhood? If the first time a male experiences rejection from a female, or competes for, but does not get, a job or promotion at age 25, his ability to deal with that rejection is non-existent. His options then are run to a therapist, or walk into work with a gun. The woman who didn't want him will become the victim of a stalker.

Nature gives us childhood experiences so we can learn at a low level – at a baby level taking baby steps - some of the worst aspects of life. They are there so we can learn to cope with them while they are relatively minor and insignificant. We learn to deal with little external traumas at a time when our whole orientation is our parents, who we run home to with these crises. It seems, today, parents are really looking to avoid having to deal with these tough events in their kids' lives themselves, merely to make their own jobs easier. If we do not experience all the dramas until later in life, they will be devastating to us when they finally come. This is nature's rule, and the further humans move away from that which is natural for us, the more extreme and grotesque our own behavior will become.

Along these same lines, I have seen an increasing number of parents who will not even take their dream job, or a wonderful promotion, because doing so would mean relocating to another state or city and they don't want to disrupt their babies' lives. They will actually deny themselves the best opportunity they ever had, because they think having to make new friends and start at a new school will be irretrievably detrimental to little Johnny or Suzie.

I cannot think of anything more ridiculous than denying yourself – and your family – a great life opportunity because your child might have to make some adjustments, none of which would be harmful or even all that difficult. Having raised my own daughter in a military environment, with the many changes of duty stations and relocations, and having seen hundreds, if not thousands, of other families and children survive the same lifestyles, I can say unequivocally that there is nothing the slightest bit harmful about moving the family. Just the opposite occurs. Children learn to socialize better and faster. They learn to stick up for themselves, and to be good judges of character, assessing and picking good friends quickly. They learn that many people may come and go in their lives, but family is a constant.

Their own family will be making the move with them, and will always be there.

Children who undergo these experiences tend to be much closer to their brothers and sisters. They learn that no matter how many people come and go in their lives, the rest of their family – grandparents, cousins, uncles and aunts – always remain the same and are there for them. They learn that many "friendships" are just relationships of convenience. They understand what real friendships are all about, and how much you sometimes have to work to maintain them. Just as importantly, they learn that they are not the single most important member of the family, and that decisions will be made in the best interests of the family as a whole. They come to understand that the team is always more important than the individual. These are all good experiences, and important life lessons.

CHILDREARING.

Many of these issues can be avoided by understanding how simple children really are. In many ways, raising children isn't much different from buying a puppy. As with puppies, if children are fed, watered, given love and attention, praised when they do good, disciplined when they do bad, and taught important function skills like language, commands, how to walk with you and not wander away, not to go into the street without you, and to find their way home, they'll be fine.

Child rearing just does not have to be that complicated. Babies are going to fall a lot, that's why they're made of human rubber. It's difficult for them to hurt themselves. Love and praise should be freely given, but not to the point where it ceases to have meaning to either your dog or your child, nor should either think that they will be entitled to such treatment regardless of how they behave. Unconditional love may be a reality of bringing a life into the world; however, your kids shouldn't believe you will defend them, or not punish them, no matter what they do. Discipline should start with gentle reprimands and increase with repeated misbehavior, matching the degree of transgression committed by your son or daughter. Or your dog. It should be meaningful, and attention getting, but should never injure. This is why smacking your dog with a rolled up newspaper is so effective. It makes a loud noise and gets his attention, but doesn't injure.

Timeouts are a waste of time. Neither John nor I had fathers who were afraid to be heavy-handed when the situation warranted. In his book *Uneasy Warriors: The Perilous Journey of the Green Berets,* Vincent Coppola examined the typical background from which the majority of Green Berets were spawned. He found the way they were raised to be exactly the way John and I were, and that they all felt the same as us growing up.

> *"[To Hell with] love!"* says Green Beret Joe Argentieri when asked about his childhood in New Jersey. "I wanted my father's respect. ... He was the son of an immigrant, a warrior, wounded in World War II. I was his oldest boy. ... But after I got off that plane coming home from Vietnam, Dad treated me like his equal. My brothers stayed kids for the rest of their lives.[82]

This is exactly the experience I had with my own siblings, as did so many of my fellow SF soldiers. Today, America is producing more and more adults that stay kids the rest of their lives, and fewer warriors.

Looking back John and I marvel that we got hit as little as we did. Even as youngsters, had timeouts been our punishment we would have never had any reason to behave, and would've probably ended up in prison. Timeout was the respite you got when the punishment was over. As teenagers, we knew we had to be bonked on the head just to make sure we were paying attention. Despite such *horrors* in our childhoods, neither of us feel that we had anything but good parents who did great jobs at parenting. We don't want to go on *Oprah*

82 Vincent Coppola, *Uneasy Warriors: The Perilous Journey of the Green Berets*, (Longstreet Press, Inc., Atlanta, Georgia, 1995), 27.

and whine about the lack of love in our homes, or that we weren't nurtured or understood. Neither of us has spent any time with therapists, selling our psyches for a little attention, whining about how our parents were too harsh, or didn't buy some stupid thing that seemed so important to us back then, or that we weren't hugged enough.

As adults we realize that our parents – like the overwhelming majority of parents – were good people, in often tough circumstances, trying to do the best job they could in raising their children and hold their marriages together. If you are one of those people who bemoans how imperfect your childhood was, yet whose parents could be described as I just described mine, then you are an oxygen thief stealing the air from more productive members of society. If I have just described you, you should seriously consider wising up, as you're not doing yourself, your own parents, or even your own children any good.

For all of those nuevo-Dr. Spocks who think that any physical punishment or corporal reinforcement of behavior standards with children is a horror, pull your head out of your fourth point of contact[83] and take a good look around. We are physical creatures existing in a physical world. That means that physicality is a critical component of every aspect of our lives. We eat, defecate and urinate. We exercise our bodies, hold hands, hug each other in greeting, touch, have sex and fight. To travel, we have to physically transport our bodies. When our bodies get sick or injured, we have to do physical things to them to make them better. Often the remedies – as with discipline – hurt more than the problem being remedied.

Thus, physical contact, in all its forms, is a reality of life. That includes physical remonstrations. Children are the most physical creatures of all, completely immersed in the material and food desires they have, and often committing physical transgressions that they expect will have physical ramifications. Children continually ignore parental instructions not to run out into the street, or put their heads

---

83 SF-speak for your *derriere*.

in plastic bags, or run through the house with scissors in their hands or pens in their mouths. If your precious principles against the slightest physical correction keep you from giving your child a disincentive to ignoring your commands, he just may be severely injured or killed. The timeouts didn't work. You wouldn't give him a reason to listen to you, and now your child has suffered a physical fate far worse than any smack on the butt would have caused. If you're a parent and I just described you, then you need to grow up yourself.

This behavioral reality of childhood only gets worse as kids grow into their adolescent and teenage years. If you think kids at those ages respect you, you're fooling yourself. Even through their teens, kids lack the intellectual sophistication to truly comprehend the notion of respect. The closest you can get with anyone that age – especially boys - is fear. Your children should know that when their behavior exceeds certain bounds, there is a reason to fear you. At some point, that fear may be the only thing that keeps them alive, or out of jail.

RAISING YOUR GREEN BERET

I will be the first to admit that, just as with millions of other men over thousands of years, *I do not understand women*. Women are wonderful, but complex and often emotion-based creatures that typically have a perspective on any situation I can neither wrap my mind around, nor ever predict. I only know that their view will be different from my own, and from that of most men. This is nothing new, as through the history of civilized society untold amounts of time and attention have been devoted in theater, drama, art, poetry, songs and novels, to men trying to understand women. Even modern science has taken up the mantle, and made great strides in recent years to analyze and dissect both the psychological and physiological – mostly in terms of brain function – aspects of women that make them act as they do.

For fathers, these differences, and our general lack of understanding of female thought and behavior, are most profound in raising our daughters. It does not take long for any father to admit that he has little clue about all of the dramas, crises, problems and priorities of his daughter, and what is going on in her world. Recognizing this, he comes to rely on his wife to understand these things for both of them, and to be able to relate to their little girl on the level she needs. Like any soldier, he stands ready, willing and able to jump in and defend them, transport them, talk to them, protect them or assist them in any way he can, if they would only tell him what it is they need him to do. If they would only give him his marching orders.

But for all of the dedication of men attempting to understand women, the fact remains that women do not understand men at all, and this finds its way into differences between male and female approaches to the rearing of boys. Author and speaker John Eldredge, makes the point that most of the disagreements between men and women in the rearing of their male children come down to one basic issue: *Fathers are trying to raise men, whereas mothers are raising little boys.*

When confronted with errant behavior from their sons, fathers immediately make the connection to the type of man that child will become if he keeps acting that way throughout his life. Making that causal connection, the father corrects the problem right away. Mothers look at their little boys, and see little boys. As those little boys grow into adolescents, then teenagers, then adults, they still see the same little boys. So mothers respond in a manner that reflects the perennial role of that child as a little boy.

Boys cannot ever be raised this way. While I readily confess to not understanding the female mind, I do understand the male mind and have a good grasp on what is necessary in the raising of boys, especially if you want them to turn into decent men someday. Boyhood is training ground for manhood, and if you ever really pay attention to the way boys behave, you will see that it is dramatically different from that of girls. This is something that humans have always recognized. Despite that, we have now endured almost a half century of women's liberation, and failed educational and social alterations in the *treatment* of the sexes. We have seen disastrous school efforts to indulge only the female way of learning, while completely abandoning the needs of boys in the hopes they would turn out like girls. In recent years, even more research has been done into the utter failure of all of this, to get the "experts" to finally acknowledge that boys are, in fact, different from girls. Imagine the shock of our grandparents and great-grandparents upon hearing of that discovery.

In his book, *Wild At Heart*, John Eldredge explains the dynamic between mothers and sons:

> A boy is brought into the world by his mother, and she is the center of his universe in those first tender months and years. She suckles him, nurtures him, protects him; she sings to him, reads to him, watches over him, as the old saying goes, "like a mother hen." She often names him as well, tender names like "my little lamb," or "Mama's little sweetheart," or even "my little boyfriend." But a boy cannot grow to manhood with a name like that… and there comes a time for the shift when he begins to seek out his father's affection and attention. He wants to play catch with Dad, and wrestle with him, spend time outside together, or in his workshop. If Dad works outside the home … his return in the evening becomes the biggest event of the boy's day. [T]his is a very hard time in a mother's life, when the father replaces her as the sun of the boy's universe. … Few mothers do it willingly; very few do it well. Many women ask their sons to fill a void in their soul that their husband has left. But the boy has a question that needs an answer, and he cannot get the answer from his mother. Femininity can never bestow masculinity. [84]

---

[84] Eldredge, 63-64.

Even through this period – and often well into adulthood – a boy will still turn to his mother for comfort. After all, who does a boy run to when his knee is scraped? But he must turn to his father "for adventure, for the chance to test his strength, and most of all, to get the answer to his question."[85] Eldredge provides an excellent example of the differences between a father, whom a boy sees as the archetype of manhood and warriorship, and a mother whose focus is much different: "We were driving down the road and the boys were talking about the kind of car they want to get when it comes time for their first set of wheels. 'I was thinking about a Humvee, or a motorcycle, maybe even a tank. What do you think, Dad?' 'I'd go with the Humvee. We could mount a machine gun on top.' 'What about you, Mom – what kind of car do you want me to have?' You know what she said … 'A safe one.'"[86]

At its most extreme form, this manifests itself in something I experience all the time with mothers. Since 9-11, and U.S. military efforts in Iraq, Afghanistan and elsewhere, I have met many women who recognize the necessity of our military operations, and support the U.S. hunting our enemies down throughout the world, lest they come back here and attack us in our own homes again. Yet virtually every one of those women concludes her statement of patriotic support for our nation with: "But I don't want my son to go, and I have told him that he should never enlist in the military, and I would never allow him to." I guess being female means it's alright to send someone else's son, while continuing to coddle your own, keeping him from growing up and becoming a man. It is not as though it is ever difficult to identify men who were raised this way. My first experience with men raised exclusively by women was Basic Training in the Army. Every one of them was a whining baby and none of them had the slightest bit of physical ability, strength, dedication or discipline. The drill instructors definitely had their work cut out trying to turn those eunuchs into soldiers. This is not true of all men raised without male

[85] Eldredge, 64.
[86] Ibid.

influences, but it takes a special man to tear off the bonds of such female cloistering, and not many manage to do it.

In tracking my own early experiences in the military, Eldredge offers further examples of daily disparities between male and female rearing of sons: "If a mother will not allow her son to become dangerous, if she does not let the father take him away, she will emasculate him. I just read a story of a mother, divorced from her husband, who was furious that he wanted to take the boy hunting. She tried to get a restraining order to prevent him from teaching the boy about guns. That is emasculation."[87] Sadly, these stories are becoming all too commonplace in American society, where the female version of life and exposure to life experiences is seen as holding some moral high ground that cannot be contested. "My mom wouldn't let me play with GI Joe," a young man said. Another complained, "We lived near an amusement park, and it had a roller coaster. But my mom would never let me go." "That is emasculation, and the boy needs to be rescued from it by the active intervention of the father, of another man."[88]

This is not to say that all women are like this. But with the immersion into a culture increasingly reflective of female beliefs and perspectives, women who understand and appreciate the differences in men and women, and who embrace those differences, are ever fewer. Such women can be found in abundance in a few places, however. Many Christian churches are based on an old fashioned pedagogy, seeing women of a more traditional bent drawn to its teachings and its people. The sporting arena is another place to find women who understand the importance of seeing boys grow into men. Certainly, ice hockey and wrestling mothers rank high among such women, urging their young sons to victory in sports which fall just short of demanding super-human effort and discipline, whose competitions are little more than organized contests of pain tolerance and aggression. This is what boys need. It's what they thrive on, and these are the favored few mothers who "get it." These are the women

[87] Eldredge, 65.
[88] Ibid.

raising men who will succeed and act as men, not cower behind beds begging the police to come save them from dealing with a threat to their own children.

YOUR BODY IS TO USE

There are few things more important than making certain your children are physically active, and learn as many of life's important lessons through their activities as possible. But this isn't exclusive to kids, as these lessons can still be learned by adults, well into marriage and careers. Nothing delivers this, along with immeasurable other benefits, as well as involvement in sports. Sports teach children that it is better to actually go out and do the things they admire than to watch others do them on TV, or engage in some "virtual" experience while sitting on their butts in front of a videogame player. Kids involved in sports do not fall into our nation's runaway obesity rate, and are the last to get involved in drugs and criminal behavior. They do not join gangs, and are not afraid to fight those who attempt to push them in that direction if that becomes necessary. They are respectful to adults, often have the best grades, and learn to achieve all of that on little free time as the demands of school, athletics, family, and even jobs, are great. In most places, it is only the young athletes who ever call someone "sir" or "ma'am."

Col. Grossman always points out in his lectures that there are some commonalities among all of America's children that have committed armed assaults on students and teachers in our schools: none of them were involved in competitive, adult supervised athletics; they weren't certified hunters or formally trained by adults in the proper use of firearms; and none of them were involved in martial arts. This tells us that not only do sports provide great benefits, but perhaps many of those who do not receive those benefits find themselves drifting, lost and alone, with little structured adult supervision and no role models. Perhaps sports, at any level, would have kept them from going over to the dark side. Certainly violent video games and television are not keeping that from happening. This is not to say that sports are a panacea, and that young athletes never get into any kind of trouble. Doing stupid things, and making bad decisions, is part of growing up. That's why it's called "growing up," and we have adults as parents to help guide us through it. This is most often seen during the adolescent and teenage years.

After many years of coaching a kids' wrestling team, with children from ages four to fourteen, John came to realize something about that difficult time in childhood. Whatever a boy was like before he hit the troubled years, was the same adult his parents would eventually get back. If he had been a good, kind, caring and decent little boy, he would be the same person as a man. If, during the in-between turbulent years, he was getting into serious trouble, the only thing the parents could do was keep on top of him, continue to instruct and discipline him, and hope that he didn't do something that would affect the rest of his life, or cause him irretrievable harm.

Over the years, and many opportunities to observe my own and other peoples' children, I came to realize the truth of this. Keeping your kids in sports through these years will continue to imprint the important benefits and lessons on them, even though it may not seem so at the time. Have confidence that your children are continuing to be influenced by the good aspects of athletics and coaching through it all. If you do these things, your children will grow to be good, honest, hard-working adults. They will be people you can respect and be proud of.

COMBAT FOR KIDS

Just as there is a sport for everyone, every kid should also be involved in a martial art. This does not have to be one of the recognized Asian karate styles with formalized belt systems, though many are very good. It need only be some type of unarmed combative sport or discipline. Training in these should begin at a young age for both boys and girls, as even the level of violence among America's girls has been escalating in recent years. Gone is the time when girls never fought, and rape remains a real and constant threat to all of our ladies. Whether karate, jujitsu, kung fu, judo, boxing, Russian Sambo, Israeli Krav Maga, or sport wrestling, every child – just like every adult – needs the ability to defend himself and herself against aggressors. And it is never too late to start. Each of these can, and should, become a lifelong discipline, from which you can continue to learn and grow throughout every period of your life.

For young boys, it is my belief that they all need to spend some time on a wrestling team or in a wrestling clinic, or in some other form of grappling martial art like jujitsu, judo or Russian Sambo. No matter how much parents may wish things were different, the reality is that kids pick on other kids, especially those smaller and weaker. Sooner or later every child will be bullied. When it happens to your son, you can either allow him to go to school each day, in gut-wrenching fear of being physically abused or verbally taunted and humiliated, or you can make sure that he can protect himself.

The rule of one-on-one human fights – and this is true for virtually all kid fights – is that they go to the ground. Just ask any cop how all of his tussles with criminals end up. As with every animal species, humans have an instinctual way of combating each other. It is natural for us to grab a hold of each other and roll around on the ground. Basic wrestling skills are usually all a young boy needs to be able to successfully deal with any attack. Recognizing the increasing threat of sexual assault to our girls and young women, experience in this medium of combat is just as beneficial, and could be life saving. Even in the Special Forces, I was always telling the hand-to-hand tough guys that you never mess with a wrestler. Over the years I have just seen too many instances where a big strong aggressor was taken to the ground and tied up in knots by a wrestler half his size.

BABY GREEN BERETS

Perhaps this is why so many "experts" simply do not get the reality of warriorship, as they never had the benefit of these experiences and the wonderful gifts they bestow. Christina Hoff Sommers is one of the few that points out, "American boys do not need to be 'rescued' from their masculinity."[89] "Capes and swords, camouflage, bandannas and six-shooters – these are the uniforms of boyhood. Little boys yearn to know they are powerful, they are dangerous, they are someone to be reckoned with. How many parents have tried in vain to prevent little Timmy from playing with guns? Give it up. If you do not supply a boy with weapons, he will make them from whatever materials are at hand. My boys chew their graham crackers into the shape of handguns at the breakfast table."[90] Interestingly, for decades my Green Berets would do the same thing. For boys, "every stick or fallen branch is a spear, or better, a bazooka. Despite what many modern educators would say, this is not a psychological disturbance brought on by violent television or chemical imbalance. Aggression is part of the masculine *design*, we are hardwired for it. If we believe that man is made in the image of God, then we would do well to remember that 'the LORD is a warrior.'"[91]

Consider the similarities between the instinctive behavior of boys, and the training of elite soldiers. Boys will forever fashion weapons from natural materials in the woods. Not only are these the same materials that gave the world some of the greatest warrior tribes in history, but they are the same weapons-making materials that all Special Operators are taught to exploit when surviving in hostile wilderness. When turned loose into fields or woods, both boys and Green Berets will first make spears and knives from sharpened sticks. Next come efforts at bows and arrows, followed by snares, pits and other traps, to capture animals for meat and as defenses against enemies. As Eldredge explains, all males are hardwired for this type of behavior, for "the boy is a warrior, and those are not boyish antics he is doing,"[92] no more than they are boyish when done by elite soldiers. "When boys play at war they are just rehearsing their part

89 Christina Hoff Sommers, *The War Against Boys: How Misguided Feminism is Harming Our Young Men*, (Simon & Schuster, New York, 2000), 15.
90 Eldredge, 10.
91 Ibid., citing Ex. 15:3.
92 Eldredge, 11.

in a much bigger drama. One day, you just might need that boy to defend you."[93]

Unfortunately, it has become fashionable to attribute some type of pathology to this kind of behavior, and therefore to millions of healthy male children. "It is a story of how we are turning against boys and forgetting the simple truth: that the energy, competitiveness, and corporal daring of normal, decent males is responsible for much of what is right in the world."[94] All of this begins with the natural tendencies of boys. In her book, *Boys and Girls: Superheroes in the Doll Corner*, career kindergarten teacher Vivian Gussin Paley analyzes children's play. In describing the natural play of even nursery school-age children in a tumbling room full of mats, climbing apparati, and slides, Ms. Paley observes: "The boys run and climb the entire time they are in the room, resting momentarily when they fall down *dead*. The girls, after several minutes of arranging one another's shoes, concentrate on somersaults … after a few somersaults, they stretch out on the mats and watch the boys."[95]

"When the girls are left alone in the room without the boys, they run, climb, and become much more active; but then, after a few minutes, they suddenly lose interest and move on to other, quieter activities, saying 'Let's paint' or "Let's play in the doll corner.' Boys, on the other hand, never lose interest in the tumbling room. They leave only when forced to. They run because they prefer to run, and their tempo appears to increase in direct proportion to crowded conditions, noise levels, and time spent running, all of which have the opposite effect on the girls." [96]

Taken together, both Paley's and Sommers' observations – as well as those of anyone who has spent time with children – dictate the undeniable conclusion that boys are genetically created to serve as warriors. Consider the never-ending activities of boys: open hand striking, play fighting, wrestling, running, jumping, and climbing, all

[93] Ibid.
[94] Sommers, 14.
[95] Vivian Gussin Paley, *Boys and Girls: Superheroes in the Doll Corner* (University of Chicago Press, Chicago, 1984), 65, also cited by Sommers, 96.
[96] Paley, 67.

of which increases in tempo in direct proportion to crowded conditions and noise levels.

Consider the similarity of circumstances boys create for themselves to the training of soldiers for battle. Military training - that is the preparation of young men to not only withstand, but to thrive in, the harsh environment of combat - is largely comprised of running, climbing, jumping, shooting guns, hand-to-hand combat which includes striking (and in the case of the Russian Spetsnaz, open-hand striking), and wrestling (as is taught in U.S. Army Ranger training, as well as in the Marines and SEALs). All of these occur within an environment in which each young man's combat intensity is expected to increase in direct relation to the noise and chaos of battle. At its worst, combat is unbelievably loud, with large crowds of enemy all around you. If you aren't naturally increasing the intensity of your own participation in direct relation, you will not survive.

Add to this, the desire boys have to engage in such play using weapons of any type, whether manufactured toy weapons or imagined, and you have the complete training regimen of elite soldiers. Thus, nature has created for boys an inherent and irrepressible desire to engage in play that develops the very skills society requires of them for protection. How different is a boy's love of jumping from great heights from the ultimate conclusion of that love: soldiers in the Airborne, SEALs and Special Forces stepping out of the doors of airplanes thousands of feet up? How many boys didn't at some point jump off the garage roof with an umbrella, imagining this very thing? How truly different is the rough and tumble wrestling and slap fighting, from the body movement and hand-eye coordination required to deal with an enemy at close quarters?

Practicing good shooting skills, whether with real bullets or "dry firing,"[97] is an important part of combat firearms training. And what of nature's inbred drive to climb trees, cliffs and other structures, or to run quickly or for long distances? It is an ancient axiom in the military that soldiers run *to* battle, and run *from* battle; resulting in

---

[97] Shooting an unloaded gun for technique practice.

conditioning for running still being one of the most important assets of soldiers. Climbing allows soldiers to attack from points they are never expected, or to escape pursuers, and they strive mightily to develop that skill. Boys' play, like war, is all about winners and losers. It is about survivors and the dead. This is why "from the earliest age, boys show a distinct preference for active outdoor play, with a strong predilection for games with body contact, conflict and clearly defined winners and losers."[98] How could nature have designed any better training ground for the protectors of our society, than boyhood?

UNISEX WARRIORS

But warriorship is not the exclusive province of males. As American society moves toward complete co-extensive opportunities for females, it becomes clear that warriorship is alive and well in the female spirit. Today, we have female soldiers, sailors and Marines. We have women skydivers, scuba divers and hunters, shooting champions, martial artists, mountain climbers, extreme skiers, weightlifters, mixed martial artists and racecar drivers. Despite what might be a greater male proclivity for such behavior, ladies have proven themselves more than equal to the task of living as warriors.

Sommers insists that the recognition and application of typical boyhood activities to the military and the protection of our society, is not a bad thing. Indeed, the inculcation of the spirit and discipline of these activities is beneficial to both boys and girls. Despite detractors who believe that, "the military man is one of the potent and deplorable stereotypes that 'the culture of manhood' holds up to boys as a male ideal,"[99] Ms. Sommers believes that any such criticism of the military itself for both sexes, is completely unfounded:

> The American military and its culture are nothing to
> be ashamed of. Indeed, if you want to cite an American

98 Sommers, 94, citing A.D. Pelligrini and Peter K. Smith, "Physical Activity Play: The Nature and Function of a Neglected Aspect of Play," *Child Development* 69, no. 3 (June 1998), 577-98.
99 Sommers, 134.

institution that inculcates high levels of human concern, cooperation, and sacrifice, you could aptly choose
the military.

Anyone who has firsthand knowledge of American
military personnel knows that most are highly competent, self-disciplined, honorable, and moral young men
and women ready to risk their lives for their country....
Yes, the military 'valorizes' honor, competition, and winning.... To suggest that the military ethic promotes
callousness and heedlessness is a travesty of the facts.
To accuse the military of being uncaring is to ignore
the selflessness and camaraderie that make the martial
ethos so attractive to those who intensely desire to live
lives of high purpose and service.[99]

NURTURING YOUNG WARRIORS

Whether male or female, the world that our children face is much
more violent than what we dealt with. Today, increasing numbers of
criminal assaults are staggering, topping more than 720,000 attacks,
and 134,000 aggravated attacks, per year in our schools. These are
just the ones being reported. The number of school shootings continues to rise, as does the number of children planning such horrors,
and our children are aware of it, every single day. Even our young
females often engage in physical confrontation, and sometimes at
rates greater than the males. When I was growing up, girls did not
have to worry about being beaten up. By the time my daughter was a
teenager that had completely changed, making me glad I had taught
her the lessons I had when she was young; making me proud I had
raised her to be a Green Beret in her own right.

Thirty years ago, many experts with a lot of degrees adorning
their office walls, but seemingly little common sense or life experience,

---

[99] Sommers, 135.

thought the root of the problems we faced was excessive violence, aggression and competition in our schools, mostly among boys. As their answers to society's ills were introduced, but violence and kids' inability to cope with the stresses of childhood grew, these same experts reacted by saying, "Isn't it good we came along when we did? If we hadn't, the situation would be so much worse." The answers in their minds, and as being implemented throughout both schools and society, are ever more efforts at turning our children into passive, competition-phobic, *Stepford* children, stoned en mass on Ritalin for exhibiting nothing more than normal childish behavior. They have refused to admit that they were wrong in the 1960s and 70s, when social rearing of boys changed in the first place, resulting in the catastrophic situation they now claim exists. These detractors of boys and their physicality now must recognize that we need to return to the proper channeling of aggression and the formal teaching of boys to treat all females as ladies, which is the proper and healthy channeling of their "maleness."

Back when these experts started all this, there were relatively few criminal assaults in schools and no school shootings, even though firearms were much more accessible to children. Problems between rival gangs were dealt with by rumbling, and only rarely saw the introduction of knives or chains at the worst. The gangs, themselves, were little more than collections of kids following an instinctual need to bond together, which sometimes led to misdemeanor level trouble, rather than the sophisticated and exceedingly violent felony versions we have today. At the lowest level, fistfights were dealt with largely by making the two combatants shake hands, often resulting in them becoming friends, a natural male bonding dynamic.

To correct the "horrible" social problem we faced back then, sanctions for simple fistfights between kids became ever more severe, until we now see many of them almost literally being made into "federal cases." The rights of children to defend themselves were stripped away, and a movement begun to eliminate psychologically devastating competitive sports, corporal punishment and even grades. This eventually found its way into the current prohibitions against many games during recess, including the game of tag which is now under siege as destructive to children's psyches. Even recess has been eliminated in some schools as inciting aggression and competition among children. "The movement to eliminate competitive rankings in American schools has made great headway in recent years.... Throughout the country, battles are raging. Typically, school officials are seeking to eliminate competitive practices, and parents and school board members are fighting to reinstate them."[101]

"The root problem in our schools is poor discipline and too many children acting maliciously with impunity," according to Ms. Sommers.[102] This is made all the worse by the fact that if the victims – often victims because they are rules-followers – fight back they are punished, too. For the same reasons, other kids can't stand up to protect victims from their tormentors. Whole generations have thus lost the compelling example of a duty to go to the rescue of others, to be warriors by protecting the weak and the innocent. We have effectively stripped ourselves of future heroes. A society without its heroes, without its warriors, is a society of sheep. And there is only one consequence of being a sheep.

It is true that no matter how boys are raised, a small percentage of them are destined to become batterers and rapists, and boys with severe conduct disorders are at high risk of becoming criminal predators.[103] Even this small percentage makes the redirection or re-channeling of male energies, all the more crucial. But, these boys are not going to be successfully re-channeled through feminist-version re-gender brainwashing, by forcing them to be more expressive and nurturing. What these boys need is a natural and healthy "male" outlet for their aggression, to be instilled through discipline. They need to be taught how to be the warriors they yearn to be. Finally, for those who are not successfully "intervened," we need well prepared male

101 Sommers, 50.
102 Ibid., 70.
103 Sommers, 50.

and female warriors, ready to confront them, rather than a nation of timid souls.

Recently there has been a growing movement to compel Congress to pass legislation against "Bully-cide." This is suicide committed by children and teenagers who can't take the bullying they receive at school. Many parents are now advocating for this to be made a federal issue, forcing schools to protect children from any and all types of aggressive behavior or suffer federal sanction. While I can certainly sympathize with the pain felt by these parents, it is hard to hear of fathers rationalizing that their own failure to teach their sons to fight back, should take up the time of our federal government in an effort to eliminate even more of life's lessons from the training and proving ground that is childhood.

With a broad social indoctrination into the Warrior Code, there would be less bullying. There would also be an increased incidence of others standing up to stop bullying; as well as increased capability of the targets of bullying to stand up for themselves. Bullies, much like adult rapists, are not looking for a fight, they are looking for a victim. With bullies, even in losing a fight, the victim will inflict some injury. This would send a clear message to other bullies that if they are looking for someone who will passively tolerate their aggression, they have the wrong person. Even if sporting a black eye after such an incident, the bully's target must see himself – or herself – as a combatant, never a victim. When asked, "Who gave you the black eye?," their only answer must be: "No one gave it to me, I had to *fight for it.*"

Growing up in a remote area, when I was about to start ninth grade I had to go to the nearby Indian reservation, as it was the only high school within a hundred miles. Being only one of a very few white boys on a reservation made me an obvious target for bullies. I had been warned by the older brothers of some friends that they were going to attack me, that I would have to fight them, and fight some of them everyday. One graduate of this gauntlet told me, "When one of them crosses you, you've got to fight him. And even if you lose,

every single time you see him, you make *him* fight *you*. Even if you
lose each time, he will be hit and he will be hurt. You make him start
avoiding you, just so he won't have to fight you over and over. That's
how you make a bully respect you and leave you alone."

His advice proved prophetic, as I did have to fight some of
them over and over, sometimes several times in the same day. But
I made them respect, and even fear, me. John's father provided him
the identical advice when, as a little boy, he was confronted with a
bully tormenting everyone in his class. Yet how many young men
have had the benefit of such warrior advice from the recent generations of passive fathers, who themselves have been conditioned by
school, society and fear of legal consequences to never do the hard
thing? Who, themselves, live lives of quiet desperation, fearful of
their wives, their bosses, their co-workers; who have been taught
to keep their heads below the trench line by a culture that has long
since ceased to appreciate acts of manhood? And these are the men
raising the next generation of males, each more passive and fearful
than its predecessor.

It is a guaranteed formula that if you do not, (A) teach your
child to fight to protect himself; and (B) tell him he needs to do so
when attacked or bullied; then (C) you are going to have a child who
will inevitably become a victim of aggressive behavior. If you, as a
parent, have failed to do this for your child, then there is no value
in him coming to you for help when he encounters it! If that is the
case, then you had your chance, but chose to not accept the realities
of life or take advantage of the opportunity to teach your child how to
deal with those realities. If you made that decision, it is your problem,
not that of the federal government. And what type of a man do you
think your little boy will become? As John Eldredge recognizes, boys
"grow bored of games that have no element of danger, or competition
or bloodshed."[104] If it was you, as a parent, who sucked that natural
desire for battle and warriorship out of your child, or who failed to
inculcate it into a child who was naturally passive for his (or her) own

[104]   Eldredge, 11.

survival, then the problems your child will have growing up – and even into adulthood – will be your fault.

FIXING THE PASSIVITY PROBLEM

The problem with children, and even adults, isn't violence per se, it's violence in a certain context. Despite the oft-heard phrase that "violence never solves anything," the reality of human existence is that there is no such thing as a problem that violence can't solve. It's just that violence, in either causing problems or fixing them, is unpleasant. World Wars I and II, the Super Bowl, Stanley Cup championship, heavyweight boxing titles, and every instance of criminals or terrorists attacking innocent victims are resolved by violence. The problem today is that we fail to explain to our children that violence is sometimes a necessary aspect of life, one that should always be accompanied by a moral imperative. In decades past, violence in mass media – movies, books and television – was always attended by a moral lesson. Bad guys were evil, wore black hats, and used violence for heinous purposes. Good guys, in white hats, only used violence when there was no other way to stop the bad guys from hurting innocent people, often women. These were good messages, and continually reinforced both the necessary and appropriate use of violence.

Things are different today. Through contemporary television, cinema, video games and media, children are being conditioned to be criminals, murderers, cop killers and rapists. Nothing makes this point stronger than Col. Grossman's books *On Killing, On Combat* and *Stop Teaching Our Kids To Kill*. As Col. Grossman analogizes, we need to start producing more sheepdogs, rather than wolves and rabid dogs among our society. We can only accomplish that by channeling violent, aggressive or competitive behavior, back into tolerable violence; fistfights with honor. In that way, the sheep population will decrease as well.

How bad would it be if media violence was, once again, limited to fistfights, or the hero always tried to shoot the gun out of the evildoer's hand? Would our social structure collapse if such conditioning supplanted the imagery of indiscriminate shootings among our population? Among our children? There are those in society who argue that all violence is horrid, that to even tolerate non-serious force is to aid and abet something that is immoral in a civilized society. These well-meaning folks do not understand violence, or the aspects of human nature that cause it. Who among them would say it would have been just as reprehensible if Kleibold and Harris had walked through Columbine High School, punching people they despised in the eye? Or if gunman Seung-Hui Cho did the same at Virginia Tech? And if you do not agree, just ask the families of all those dead and wounded children, young adults and teachers, which they would have preferred.

Archangel Team with freed slaves in Sudan, 2003.
From left to right: Attorney and international security
expert Michael S. Rich; former Russian Spetsnaz commando
Yuri Ferdigalov; John Anderson; British special operator,
Darren Nardone; and John Giduck. Serving others less
fortunate is what everyone should strive for in life.

– 8 –

COMMITMENT TO CAREER

"I mighta went to the University of Scranton
and did well.
But look at what I woulda missed.
These friendships. Son Tay.
We all know we'll never be millionaires.
... how many millionaires have had a taste of this life?"

Green Beret Joe Lupyak
"Uneasy Warriors"

JOB VS. CAREER

There is a large difference between a job and a career. A job is just something you do to sustain yourself, anything you're willing to take to pay the bills. College students, for instance, take jobs. Whether summer life guards, construction workers, jackhammer operators, or fast food cooks, they take the "job" that pays them the most, almost no matter how demoralizing, demeaning or difficult. They have no intention of these positions becoming actual careers, but are willing to pay those dues to keep themselves in school so that they can have a career. For some people, something originally taken as a job turns into a career. Kids who start off working at a fast food chain may find themselves, years later, a regional manager in charge of hundreds of stores, distribution centers, and countless employees. During the Vietnam War, some reluctant, if not outright resistant, draftees found a home in the military and made very successful careers of it.

Whether a job or career position, however, when it comes to work you are doing for which someone is paying you money, you must think of yourself as a professional. You should do this no matter what the job. That means you show up at least ten minutes early, appropriately attired, work the entire time you're there, and give your employer your best effort. In many organizations this effort may not be appreciated by your co-workers, and sometimes not even by your own supervisors. In others, it may be appreciated, but union restrictions, or the existence of an egalitarian atmosphere that panders to laziness and a lack of work ethic, may mean it is not compensated. That's fine, as you don't do your best in every undertaking for others; you do it for yourself.

Do your best to be your best. Sure, there will be times when the boss's son, or someone with better political connections in the company, or someone who went to a more prestigious school than you, or who schmoozes the boss, may get some of the early breaks. But over time that will not last, and performance will be rewarded. But even if it isn't, you will know you lived your life as a person of purity in effort and spirit, a person of integrity in action and word. There is no greater reward. If your measure of yourself as a human being is based on the inequities, then you have problems far beyond simple job perks.

BE TRUE TO YOURSELF

On the Teams we often had experienced NCOs who were – by all military standards – discipline problems. Some would get drunk and get in fights. Sometimes this was so bad it would take ten MPs[105] to bring down a single Green Beret, motivated by alcohol and a zest for

105 Military Police.

battle. Others were disrespectful to officers, often punctuating their point with a fist. Military protocol demanded these men be punished, and they would lose stripes as fast as they earned them. But these men were never thrown out of Special Forces as they would have been in other units, because despite the lack of stripes on their sleeves, they also had chests full of medals for valor. These men did not care about the form of leadership, evidenced by rank insignia. They cared about the substance of being an elite combat soldier. This is why they were kept. No matter how troublesome they were when sitting at a base back home, they were great when the *merde* hit the fan, and we had a small team being overrun in enemy controlled territory. This is where these men were at their best. Under such threats everyone knew who to turn to, regardless of rank. In such circumstances even the officers would do what this man, who perhaps had been busted back down to E-4, told them they needed to do to survive.

I've seen the counterparts of these men in many professions, but most often where lives hang in the balance of the job someone does. From firemen and police, to pilots, doctors, nurses and bounty hunters, you find these people. Some men just don't handle the burdens of interpersonal diplomacy well. But they are the ones running to the sounds of battle, when all others are fleeing in the opposite direction. Of the many police, fire and military men we lost trying to rescue others on 9-11, do you think those in fear for their lives stopped to care for a single moment what the rank was of the person trying to save them, or whether they had ever been written up for insubordination? When you are wheeled into an emergency room dying from your injuries, do you care one whit whether your doctor thinks the hospital administrator is an incompetent, or that your nurse can't stand the ridiculous administrative rules that keep getting piled up on her? When everything is on the line, we all have a tendency to strip ourselves of our concerns over the form of things, and care only for the substance.

I am not advocating insubordinate behavior. What I am emphasizing is that, first, you do your job the best that you can. If you have done that, you will be able to carry yourself with pride no matter what you do, or what else might happen. Of the people I have known who lived as I have described, most accepted the foreseeable consequences of their own refusal to bow to power in an existentially Sisyphean way. They realized that author and philosopher Richard Bach was right: all of the problems in our lives, we have drawn to us. We create problems because we need their lessons.[105]

It is axiomatic that in life we all will continue to keep making the same mistake – creating the same problems – over and over until we learn the lesson from that problem we needed to learn. Once we learn it, we stop creating the problem. We all make decisions for whatever reasons we have; but no one should ever sit around crying when the all-too-predictable consequences of their actions find them. If you refuse to treat your superiors with respect because you think it's sucking up, don't complain when others receive perquisites that are denied you, or that you don't get promoted. Don't feel sorry for yourself when someone else gets chosen for a team leader position, when you are the most expert at the tasks of that team, and its members look up to you more than anyone else.

We are all different people with different sets of qualities, strengths and weaknesses that are as unique to us as fingerprints. That's what makes the human race so damn fun, and keeps us from getting bored with each other. John, for instance, is someone who very well falls into the group of people I have been discussing. Highly educated, and a hard worker, he is the type of professional who has to be left alone to do his job. Under those conditions he will be the best performer anyone ever had. But bureaucracies have a difficult time leaving people alone, and bureaucrats have an insecure need to bring everyone under their pedantic and micro-managing control. Not everyone tolerates it well. When he was teaching college, the school had an attendance policy mandating students be penalized for not attending class. John only cared about a student's level of knowledge. He didn't care where or how a student got his learning; if he did "A"

---

106   Richard Bach, *Illusions: Adventures of A Reluctant Messiah*, (Dell Publishing, New York, 1977), 71.

quality work, he got an "A." One of the department chairs told him he was a great teacher, but that he was a management nightmare.

John learned early on in his career that he could, and did, work very well for organizations, but that he sometimes – depending on the company - worked horribly in them. As a corporate attorney, he could be of great benefit as outside counsel. In that role he was paid to give his best advice, lead the company through the minefield that is complex litigation, and win for them; so long as they listened to him. As an in-house general legal counsel, when the company big-wigs thought they had some ability to control him, rather than recognizing that his role demanded he be independent from their regular and nepotistic hierarchy, there were problems. The same is true of his training of law enforcement departments, military units and government agencies. From the outside, he is the consummate professional, and is of great assistance to them, giving them his very best effort in anything he is asked to do. But if he had to actually function within some of those organizations as a long term employee, it would likely end in disaster.

I am a different person, and had a completely different career history. For 25 years, starting from my 20th birthday, I was a soldier in the U.S. Army. For ten years after that, I was an employee of the Department of Energy, bringing all of my Special Forces skills and experiences to bear training and supervising others who were responsible for the safekeeping of nuclear weapons. What that meant was that for 35 years of my life I had a government job, guaranteed salary, benefits and job security with none of the concerns of people that worked in the private sector. What that also meant was that I was at my best inside an organization. When the nuclear weapons facility I was working at started closing, jobs began disappearing. Though I was kept long beyond most, I was ultimately offered a good severance package and knew it was time to move on. But moving on, after having spent my entire adult life in the secure environs of federal employment, was frightening.

During the same ten years I worked for DOE, I maintained a side business as a gunsmith. I had worked with firearms my entire life, and had been trained to be a gunsmith by some of the very best. Without ever doing any advertising – not even having a phone number listed in the Yellow Pages – my business had grown and I had more work than I could handle. Still, abandoning a guaranteed income was difficult, and it was intimidating to think I was going to be relying on my own ability to generate business and money, for the first time in my life. But, as the British SAS motto says, "Who Dares Wins." I went into this new phase of my life with commitment and zeal. As it turned out, I could have moved on from my DOE job years before and made a perfectly fine living.

This is one of the consistencies I have seen with the men of Special Forces after they retire or choose to separate from the service. They often do not fare well in the corporate environment. Most of this is due to their refusal to compromise their values and integrity. They will not be obsequious, dishonest or even diplomatic. They continue to mean just what they say, and say just what they think. This does not always go over well in a culture where bosses want to be lied to and told what they want to hear, not the truth. These men continue to live according to the Code of the Green Beret, but find out just how few other Green Berets there are out in the world.

But they do prove themselves to be quite adept at most types of entrepreneurial enterprise. They are self-starters, and independent operators. They are innovative thinkers, and disciplined in everything they take on. Working for themselves allows them to bring all of these qualities to bear, without wilting under the oppressive rules and pedantry of politically correct corporate America. They just won't tolerate such insanity, and those who do are miserable.

DRESS CODE

Whether your organization imposes a dress code on its members, every single person should decide what his personal, individual, dress code is going to be, and then take steps to adhere to it. For firms with official dress codes, that standard represents the minimum attire or formality that must be met. No matter what you ultimately select as your standard, that clothing becomes your uniform, no different than being in the military. Whether that uniform is extremely formal, or quite casual, it must be clean, unwrinkled, properly arranged and worn with a sense of pride.

In the U.S. military, there is no question that the Marines always had the best looking uniforms. Because of the intense pride they took in their uniforms, which signified who and what they were, every retired Marine I've ever seen continues to dress and carry himself as though he were still in that uniform. This makes it easy to pick them out in a crowd. Even if wearing nothing more than jeans and a polo shirt, their clothes are so clean and crisp, the shirt so perfectly bloused into the pants, and the shoes shined to perfection, that no one would mistake the pride they take in their appearance. These Marines set the standard for personal attire that we can all learn from and incorporate.

No matter what clothing you choose to wear, that selection communicates a tremendous amount of information about you to everyone who sees you. People understand this intuitively, and so make their clothing selections accordingly. Unfortunately, in too many cases this results in people pandering to the worst of their insecurities or other character weaknesses. It is not as though you need a Ph.D. in psychology to recognize what their issues are, and everyone who sees them realizes those insecurities, except themselves.

We've all seen large bodybuilders walking around in spaghetti strap tank tops or tight t-shirts when it's twenty degrees out, complaining loudly about how hot it is, as though that would dissuade anyone from believing that person was terrified some stranger might not think he lifted weights. Or the woman with D-plus breast implants going around in nothing more than a jogging bra, or unbuttoned blouse in locales where this might not be appropriate. We see people constantly checking to make sure their expensive Mont Blanc pens are visible, or their Gucci bags, or their diamond bejeweled Rolex watches. These are all examples of people who make self-promoting selections in their personal uniforms, rather than taking advantage of communicating to all that they are responsible, mature and professional.

It does not matter if your regular uniform is a business suit, business-casual Dockers and button down or golf shirt, workout clothes, a mechanic's or other trade craftsman's uniform, or cowboy boots, jeans and hat with a big belt buckle. So long as it is always clean, pressed, neat, your shirt tucked in and your shoes shined, you will always be communicating the best things possible about yourself, and developing a sense of pride in who you are and what you do. I well recognize that there are jobs where people just get dirty. So be it. But that fact doesn't mean that they still cannot look as good as possible, or show up to work looking like they have pride in who they are and the career they have chosen.

If you're a plumber, pull your damn pants up so no one has to look at your ass. If you're a construction worker, dust your pants off and put on a clean t-shirt to stop at the store, or just to be seen walking into your home by your neighbors. At the very least it will leave your car much cleaner after you get out. If you are stopping at a bar with friends at the end of the day, strive to not bring down the class of the place just by walking in, by bringing a change of shirt. Rick Parks is a custom home builder in the Colorado Rocky Mountains. Despite the intensely physical and dusty nature of his job, he always manages to look like a consummate professional while working down in the dirt on construction sites, and others should emulate him. With regard to the pathetically slovenly "look" affected by so many young adults today, at military and firearms tradeshows there is a popular t-shirt that suggests: "Turn your hat around, pull your pants up, and tuck your damn shirt in." It is a reality of human nature that books are judged by their covers, and for companies, the appearance of their employees is the very cover by which they will be judged, and given or not given work that pays everyone's salary.

BUILDING YOUR COMPANY TEAM

Your Professional Team will not be the same, nor constituted of the same people, as your Life Team. Your Professional Team, by organizational necessity, will be populated by people with whom you work, and in most instances will have no duty to you outside the workplace. If you are in a position of authority and the pool from which you must select the team is inadequate, it is your duty to recruit superior people. You may ultimately become so close to certain members of your work team, that you include them in your Life Team, as they will include you in theirs. This can only work if all members are people of integrity, discipline and honor.

In both the civilian and military worlds, leaders often put their egos ahead of their organizations, their missions and their teams. They think the model for leadership is *self* first, then *mission* and *men*.[107] These are the people who have no business occupying positions of leadership and authority, and who likely got there by manipulating and exploiting those around them and every opportunity that arose. These are the careerists, not the professionals. Just as their every action as subordinates was driven by their own self-interest, so, too, will be their efforts at the top. People like this will never have any loyalty from those under them. For this reason, such a leader's teams will never be committed to success. People who find themselves in organizations like that are merely committed to their own survival, because their leader is the greatest threat to that survival, instead of being their protector and motivator.

In the Special Forces, the people you put on your Team, and try to nurture toward their own positions of leadership and responsibility – your very own position – have to be good if you are to survive. No one selects inferior men to a Team, when the capability of those men is the only thing that is going to keep them alive. To achieve this – and to meet your ongoing duty of leadership to that Team – you

---

107 As opposed to the SF rule of: *Mission, Men* then *Self*

want only men who are better than you. If a Team leader violates this rule and chooses only those less capable or skilled than himself, and each successor-leader does the same, eventually the Team will wither through an attrition of incompetence; assuming they don't get killed by a superior enemy first. In the corporate world, this will be seen in superior competitors driving you into bankruptcy.

When leaders seek out those superior to themselves, they not only give the team the greatest possible chance of survival in a hostile environment, they assure the longevity of that team, as well as all other teams that its members might ever serve on. This is true whether the hostile environment is the jungle of Wall Street or Vietnam. By continuing to improve the quality of the men on your current team, you ensure that it will be better than the team you just came from. This is how all of Special Forces continues to improve. This is the Green Berets' Law of Natural Selection, of Combat Darwinism. If the best only select those better, Special Forces will field the optimal combat force possible. Those forces survive, and their people come home at the end of the day. The combat experiences they have make them even better, and in turn they teach those lessons and skills to others. Those who don't make the grade are forced out, or into support, staff or logistical positions, where they can do less harm.

BONA FIDES

When you first make it onto a Special Forces A Detachment or Team, you know you have all of the qualifications to be there. But you can't force your way into that group of tight-knit men. The Team has to accept you. Until that happens, the Team is an impenetrable rock and will remain so until it chooses to open up. If you try to force it, you're seen as an individualist, an egotist and a prima donna. It is like a tight fist, and you're the lone index finger sticking up; connected with them at one point but not a part of them. You're already *on* the Team, but to actually get *into* it, you must do whatever you're told. You do it to the best of your ability and then you come back and ask if they want anything else done. Even after being accepted, if you are the junior member of the Team you should always be the one who shows up to work first, anticipates EVERYTHING, and works the hardest.

Don't make the mistake of thinking you are the equal of any of those more veteran than you, even if you happen to have the same rank. This is a problem with many entering the workplace from Generation X, and worse now with Generation Y. Police departments we work with confront the problem of young cops who have graduated the police academy and finished their FTO period[108] refusing to listen to the veteran officers on the force. The attitude of these immature neophytes is: "I am a certified police officer just like you, I don't have to listen to a thing you say." It is the ignorance of their youth and inexperience that keeps them from recognizing that, maybe, these older officers stayed alive through decades of police work because they learned something along the way, and because they were smart enough to listen to the veterans when they were young cops.

This is the generation that grew up completely indulged by parents, never punished (other than pathetic and ineffectual time-outs), and who received a three-foot high trophy just for showing up at any quasi-athletic event. At no point in their lives have they ever used unnecessary appellations like, "sir" or "ma'am." They have called every adult by their first names since they were old enough to talk, and have never used the titles Mr., Mrs., Miss or Ms. They have always been aware of their rights, and have never hesitated to threaten litigation for any sanction their schools tried to impose on them, or criminal charges if their own parents attempted to provide the very discipline they needed.

Commonly referred to as "The Most Praised Generation," these young folks are now in the workforce, with ever more entering each year, and their well-cultivated attitude is causing tremendous problems. In a *Wall Street Journal* article analyzing this very problem in corporate America, one recent MBA graduate was reported as showing up on the first day of her first job with a food producer. She

---

108 Field Training Officer phase is a probationary period where the new officer is always under the supervision of a veteran.

placed a recipe for a new cereal that she had developed on the desk of a top corporate officer. She was shocked when the company was not ready to immediately start making her product. This is an attitude – and operational dynamic – that cannot continue in any organization if it is to survive. My message to them is: No matter who you are, or who you think you are, swallow your ego and recognize that there are many people you work with who may have something to teach you. That is a message we can all stand to remember, no matter what point we are in our lives or careers.

No matter how many times you've been through it, when you start with a new group of co-workers, you'll always go back through the same process. You will re-earn your place on every team you are ever put on. Each time, your reputation will precede you; but even if it's good, it only tells your new teammates that you can perform your job as an individual. It will remain to be seen whether you can fit into *their* team, or whether you will insist on remaining outside the group, functioning as a loner. You will have to earn that same reputation every time, and can never rest on your laurels, medals or diplomas.

DEFENDING YOUR HONOR

Once you've worked hard to establish your reputation, you may need to work even harder to preserve it. While you cannot go through life racing to and fro, frantically attempting to correct any statement besmirching your good name, there will be times when you can and should defend the truth about yourself. It is a sad reality of life in America, particularly with an unregulated and unaccountable press, that the greater and better your reputation, the bigger the target you become. As the saying goes: "Big symbols make big targets."

The greater the magnitude of who and what you are, the more others will see destroying you as a way of furthering themselves. Clearly, these are not the Green Berets within their professions. The advent and rise of the Internet has seen this problem worsen exponentially. With the proliferation of websites, blogs and chatrooms, people feel that they have a license to publish any scandalous remark that strikes them, with a reckless disregard of the truth or falsity of their statements. People forget that they are legally and morally responsible for the harm they do to others' hard-earned reputations through their irresponsible remarks and writings.

As with most who attempt to accomplish greater things than just eking out an existence in a dead end job, we have confronted our share of this type of behavior. We have had reporters and respected international publications simply make up quotes that were attributed to us, and invent "facts" that were not only untrue, but for which they had no single bit of evidence or even the basis for allegation. We have had legislators and frightened elected officials do the same. At Archangel, we have been called mercenaries, trainers of mercenaries and military advisers to rogue armies. None of this is true, and no one working with Archangel performs any services for any government or group other than the United States of America. Whenever we have traveled overseas, relevant U.S. agencies have been advised of our every action.

Yet we have seen reporters manufacture supposed statements by us – ones that were never made – just so they could expose the "truth." On other occasions we have had reporters warn us that if we didn't talk to them, and answer all of their questions, they would just write a smear piece about us. We told them to take a hike. Some of these statements about us have gone ignored. But others demanded responses, and when forced into that type of confrontation we fought, and we fought hard. Though we generally eschew legal action, where necessary we have not hesitated to demand retractions or corrections under threat of litigation. Other times we have taken out full page ads in larger rival papers, these in the form of open letters to the malfeasant newspaper and reporter, trumpeting to the world what they had done and what the truth really was. On one occasion we wrote an Op Ed editorial dismembering a self-serving and dissembling reporter's piece which contained little in the way of factual accuracy. When the editor began dragging his heels in having our piece published in a timely fashion, local police commanders quietly informed him that if it was not printed immediately the paper would receive no future cooperation from their department.

Green Berets do not go through life picking fights, or attempting to harm others for no reason, especially not for their own gratification as these people are wont to do. However, there will always be people who are going to do this to you. The more peacefully you try to comport your life, the more you will magnetize this type of behavior. It is a rule of human nature that niceness is seen as weakness, and weakness draws aggression. In some cases these aggressors are so intent upon their victimization of others that they fail to evaluate those they assail. I cannot understand how anyone who has ever met me, or John, or any of the people we work with, could be such a poor judge of character as to think that we would take an attack lying down. In today's culture, any statements that go unchallenged in either the media or on the Internet, seem to take on the imprimatur of absolute truth.

Attacks to your good name will not be found exclusively in mass media. As both the Internet and reality shows have proven, gossip – once a socially deplorable practice – has taken on the mantle of respectable and even entertaining behavior. This has its affect on day-to-day behavior of everyone in society, and I have witnessed the incidence of vicious gossiping rise to epidemic proportions. People see no reason anymore to not denigrate others, particularly in the workplace. In your personal life, you may be able to withstand the odd errant statement without recourse, relying on your friends to know the truth of your character. But as the breadth of dissemination of false statements increases - or they are published among a group that can have a destructive impact on your career – you must take corrective action. Anytime you are forced into a fight in life, there is only one rule: fight and fight hard, and don't stop fighting until you have achieved victory.

Music legend Willie Nelson understands this well. In writing about his own philosophy of dealing with the challenges life throws at everyone, he made his adoption of the Green Beret Code clear: "I believe that you can't lose if you don't give up. Even if you die, you'll die fighting."[108] In his book *The Facts of Life and Other Dirty Jokes,* he tells a story from his early childhood about a family in the small town in which he was raised by his grandparents. An altercation at a basketball game resulted in one of the boys from that family jumping up in the middle of the gym and yelling, "My mama didn't raise nothin' but fighting kids!" Willie Nelson thought, "What a nice family!"[109]

Sometimes, depending on the circumstances, Willie is right and problems cannot be handled with the printed word, diplomacy or litigation. Though I wish it were not so, sometimes physical recourse is the only answer. Though many believe that violence never solves anything, there are many times when other people's behavior warrants – indeed justifies – them getting a punch in the mouth. The real tragedy is that these cretins have learned to exploit the legal system to their own advantage, and to further harm those they have already wronged when they seek redress by confronting them like men. Keep in mind that the famous Spanish saying "mano a mano," used to describe dealing with a problem in a direct manner doesn't mean "man to man," as many think. It means, "hand to hand;" as in hand-to-hand combat.

Years ago I was sitting in the Green Beret Sport Parachute Club on Ft. Bragg. One loudmouth was vocally proclaiming to all who would listen that a well known Green Beret, who had a reputation for being a brave soldier and hard fighter, wasn't so tough after all. This detractor was telling all who would listen that the victim of his slander wouldn't even fight, and that one time he had made this individual back down from him, "take water," and scurry away a coward. I don't know what this guy was thinking, but the SF community is a small one with a well developed grapevine. The man who was being defamed had been in his bunk, sound asleep, but it didn't take long for this attack on his character to reach his ears. Within an hour this soldier walked proudly into the bar, clad only in his bathrobe

109   Willie Nelson, *The Facts of Life and Other Dirty Jokes,* (Random House Trade Paperbacks, New York, 2002), 41.
110   Ibid.

and slippers. He walked straight up to the offender and said, "I under-stand you're telling people you backed me down, you made me take water." Those were the only words this man said. When he was done, he walked out and went back to bed. After last call, some of the rest of us got around to carrying the other guy to the infirmary.

In civilized, peacetime civilian society I do not advocate resolving all of these issues – or any of them – with fists, and certainly not with weapons, driveby shootings or engaging in your own smear campaigns. But I do advocate dealing with such people directly, and to their faces. Most instances of this type of behavior are not so great that they cannot be handled in private. When you must confront such antagonists, make them understand that news of what they were saying or doing against you reached your ears, and that you are not going to tolerate it. Such detractors are just childhood bullies in grown up form, and like all bullies, they will crumble when con-fronted directly by someone not afraid to fight them.

Other times, their actions may rise to a level of real harm to you. The answer for those instances is the same, only they may warrant the defamer being exposed in front of those he used as his audience against you. Follow the Green Beret model and confront such antagonists directly with their lies, but arrange to do it in front of at least a few of those he used as a conduit for his lies. Be aware, however, that people like that never acknowledge they were wrong, and in calling them on the carpet you will have just created a more committed enemy than you had before. But such is life, and warriors don't fret over these things.

CONFRONTATION

No one likes confrontation. Anyone who does has a psychological disorder. It's just that some people, by the nature of their character make-up, are quicker to it, or better at it, than others. Don't make the mistake of thinking that these people are not intimidated by interper-sonal conflict too; like any fight, they just learn to confront others in spite of their anxiety. Such encounters are very difficult for anyone, but you have to *Cowboy Up* and do what is necessary. Human aggression expert, Lt. Col. Dave Grossman tells us that "the average citizen resists engaging in aggressive and assertive activities and dreads facing the irrational aggression and hatred of others."[111] Sometimes it helps to know that you are not the only one who has a hard time confronting others, no matter how wrong their behavior, as everyone gets nervous when they are forced into confrontations. That is natural, so accept it and do what is necessary and right. Remember, courage is not the absence of fear, but what you do in spite of that fear.

Many react to situations confrontationally because they are afraid, as it becomes a defense mechanism. Others become adept at conflict through training and professional necessity, like lawyers. In most cases even they do not enjoy it; they simply learn to be good at that type of combat. In reality, though, no one works harder to avoid the confrontation of a legal trial than lawyers. Being able to deal with conflict, however, is like the transference of conditioning from any other type of training or experience: it is never total. Lawyers with reputations for being ruthless and aggressive typically wilt the moment someone takes a single aggressive step into their personal space with clenched fists and a readiness to resolve the conflict on a different level than the legal procedures that allow them to snipe at others. In such instances, they have been taken outside the comfortable confines of the rules in which they get to be vicious and disrespectful, where they have power and no one can harm them.

The same is true of others who are conflict-oriented in different contexts. Professional boxers and football players become intimidated when forced to participate in hostile contract negotiations, or when called to testify in court. Soldiers who are great at using hi-tech weaponry with which to wage war from great distances, become panicky as the distances shorten, and almost everyone fears hand-to-hand combat. World champion karate fighters are often afraid of a fight going to the ground, and may piss their pants when someone

[111] Grossman, 77.

pulls a gun on them. Even lawyers can get nervous when suddenly finding themselves on the opposite side of the podium, and have to take the witness stand themselves. Once they are no longer in control, but subject to the whim and antagonism of an accuser, the tables turn quickly.

No matter what the medium of confrontation a situation demands, there is only one way to go about dealing with it: The Green Beret Way. Do not resort to manipulation, conspiracy or subterfuge. Those are the tools of the fearful; the tools of your enemies. Deal with them in a forthright manner. Whether through a fistfight or argument, the more you deal with the battle in an emotionless, calm and detached manner – the manner of an elite soldier – the easier it will be, and the less you will fear it.

The other rule of having to confront any difficulty is to do it right away. At the moment you realize you have it to do, do it and get it over with. If you have to have an unpleasant conversation with a boss, co-worker or subordinate, walk into that person's office first thing in the morning and have at it. Then it's over and you can get on with your day, confident that you just ruined his. John and I have always shared a belief that the same holds true when you realize you were wrong about something. Whether it's a fight or an apology, the moment you realize it is a conversation you have to have, address it then. If you wake up at three in the morning with the sudden realization that someone screwed you over – or that you did the same to another – pick up the phone and tell them. But, if it's an apology you want accepted, you might actually want to wait until a more reasonable hour to extend it.

MEDIOCRITY RISING

In Special Forces, changing MOS's is extremely hard; as difficult as changing any career. Despite SF's extreme efforts to only take the absolute elite of all male personnel in our country, the laws of human nature still abound. Some Green Berets will not become fluent in the other four MOS's, which is necessary to Team function and survival. Just as you find people like this in the civilian world, these men are just too lazy to be the best at their jobs. These second-rate performers lack the decency to surrender their berets. Instead, they seek out different types of jobs, off the Teams, often in staff positions. Sometimes this enables them to do even more damage to the Teams they just left.

This is exactly like the kind of promotion-of-the-incompetent witnessed throughout corporations and government agencies. All too often, if you are a liability at your current position, management will promote you rather than endure the political or legal fallout of firing you. That's why in the military we always said that fecal matter and mediocrity rose to the top. This occurs in both the private and public sectors: someone gets moved into management – into a position of authority and increased power – without ever having been that good at his original job. This results in his former co-workers becoming his subordinates, or otherwise being subjected to his new influence, and working under even worse conditions.

In the Special Forces, this can have deadly consequences. The same is true in many professions. Firefighters that go into burning buildings with male co-workers who have let themselves get fat and out of shape - or with females whose inability to meet minimum standards resulted in the reduction of qualifications - will die if they fall in the blaze and need to be carried out. Police who go into dangerous situations with other cops who believe they're in civil service positions, like mailmen, are in danger, or those same cops are held back by a fearful commander while innocent people are dying. The same is true for high rise window washers, sailors, commercial divers, construction workers, steelworkers, bouncers, bounty hunters, plane and helicopter pilots, rescue team members, miners, ski patrol, hunters, mountain climbers, cowboys, ambulance drivers and paramedics, and those in countless other vocations and avocations. With each, the life of one person can depend on the skill, training, discipline and commitment of another in an instant.

THE WRONG STUFF

It is, perhaps, human nature to want to be respected or admired by one's peers. In critical professions this can have profound consequences. Just as scores of men – young and old – will lie to women and others about having been a member of the vaunted Green Berets, so, too, do we see a good number actually undergoing Special Forces training for no real goal other than to win the beret. They have neither the desire, nor the intention, to serve in Special Forces, and if forced to will not make any effort to do it well. They merely want to be able to say, "I was a Green Beret." This is no different from people who become lawyers and doctors, or who pay money to do modeling, become reserve police officers, or attend a bodyguard school, just to claim some tenuous connection to these vocations, yet who never had any love for the profession. Like the SF dilettantes, they were never any good at those jobs and got out as soon as they could, if they ever really worked in them in the first place.

Once out, these also-rans spend the rest of their lives telling stories about their time in that profession, draping themselves in the accoutrements of a noble calling; a calling they never felt. In SF they'd get out quickly, racing back to the safety and lowered expectations of the regular leg Army. Once they made good on their escape, however, those green berets would sit like trophies on the corners of their desks, every day, for the rest of their careers, majestically perched below walls jammed with Special Forces memorabilia. No matter what the profession is, this is no way to work, or to live. You would be far more respected by others if you took some of that stuff down and openly admitted that you did make it through SF selection, but that life on a Team just wasn't for you.

INTEGRITY IN YOUR PROFESSION

Much like the trinity of duties one has to a spouse,[112] so, too, do we labor under similar duties to our employers. America is now living in an age where employee rights are ever-expanding, while companies cower in dark corners of litigation paranoia. This cannot ever lead to better, more efficient, or more successful businesses or government agencies. I am nonplussed by employees who insist on weakening their employers, by forcing conditions on them that make them spend more money to generate less revenue. These workers somehow do not understand that the only long term consequence will be a bankrupt company. It is little wonder that corporations across the country are fleeing our litigation-ridden and overtaxed shores, for cheaper and harder-working labor forces in other countries.

For both professional pride and job stability, employees must willingly assume the legal duties of agents to their principals. In the law, being an agent is a special relationship with a high level of duty to one's principal. The duties include full disclosure; giving their best effort; and full accounting of all expenditures, time spent and money owed, for their work. Another old Western adage wryly depicted the duty of someone to commit his best efforts solely for the one person to whom he owed that duty: You only dance with the one who brung you.

Just as in SF, employers should be able to rely on the complete and unfettered truth from those whose salaries they pay. As an employee, when a report is demanded or you owe your boss a SitRep[113] on a problem, you need to give it to him straight. As a supervisor, you need to make sure your employees know that not only is the truth expected, but that they will not be penalized for their honesty. Be certain that they understand they will be respected for their integrity, candor and courage, and that you will not shoot the messenger. As a

---

112 Chapter 6, Commitment to Marriage.
113 Situation Report

boss, you cannot hope to cultivate Green Berets on your team – men and women who will mean just what they say, and say it straight – if they get ambushed every time that they do.

TRUSTING THE PROS

From regular Army three-star generals at the Pentagon, all the way down to your SF command staff, your officers trust you to be a professional at all times. In so trusting you, they expect you to deserve that trust, to earn that respect. And you expect the same from them. Civilian life is no different. This rule applies to everyone, and his treatment of those below him. If you are in a management position – one where you are commanding troops – set the standard, and lead from the front. You cannot expect the people under you to want your respect, if you have not proven yourself worthy of theirs.

Before you are of any value to your team, you must first prove that you are a man who can function alone, stand alone, and succeed alone. This is why Ranger, Special Forces, and Navy SEAL BUD/S schools first ensure you can succeed without help, otherwise you will forever be a burden to others. This represents one of the fundamental differences between Special Forces and regular Army units. Remember, you cannot push that rope.

Whether or not you find yourself in the company of top level professionals, each one of whom can and will function successfully on his own if need be, you still never stop striving to be the best. Yet, you should never find yourself analyzing the respective talents of your co-workers and then trying to undermine them out of jealousy. Analyze your own abilities, and try to improve each of them, focusing on being a better operator than you are today. Over time, not only will you become that better operator, but your co-workers will begin to see you as the Green Beret of your company: the elite.

Not that competition among members of a team is a bad thing, and depending on the type of work being done and dynamics of the team, it can be highly beneficial. As between the different

Special Forces Groups[114] there is intense competition. Each Group wants to be the best. The Groups are broken down into three battalions each,[115] and each battalion is broken down into three companies.[116] Every company is authorized six, twelve-man A Detachments or Teams, plus a thirteen-man B Team at company headquarters. There is a great deal of competition among the Teams, and even some competition among Team members. This atmosphere of rivalry continually drives every Green Beret to be the best; not only for himself but for his Team, company, battalion and Group.

But it is an atmosphere of friendly competition, one of competitive rivalry among respected professionals, and they will all fall together quickly against any outside threat or attack. Whether that threat is an enemy force, or some administrative puke from Washington jeopardizing training, equipment or ROEs, or even antagonists from other units or branches of the service, they will support each other against all foes. Their behavior is much like a family, where the bitterest dispute among relatives will be quickly forgotten in the face of detractors from outside the clan.

But to be of value to the team, or your corporation, you must be dedicated to that group. In any job, such dedication mandates that you don't just do the jobs you know well, or the ones you like to do. Nor does it apply to only the jobs you were actually hired to do. No one gets to enjoy the luxury of job specialization, nor should they. The ability to do a job you've never done before – whether it is packing parachutes for those who jump, or just sweeping the street – is important. When work needs to be done, rank is irrelevant. All must pull together for the good of the outfit. Remember, *One for all and all for one!*

John's first law firm job was with a boutique litigation outfit whose founding partner was a distinguished elder attorney. The firm had purchased its own small building in an upscale section of Denver, fronting the main street of a beautifully restored area. After

---

114 Each Group is comprised of approximately 1,200 men.
115 Plus headquarters and support battalions.
116 A, B, and C companies.

one particularly large snow storm, John returned to the office to find this elder gentleman the only one out front shoveling the sidewalks. He hadn't asked others to do it, as they were all busy with important tasks. Here was a lawyer, running his business as a Green Beret officer would. Remember, no matter what work you are doing, if you are a salaried or hourly employee, it all pays the same. Staying busy and taking on any task that needs doing not only helps the company, but helps the workday go faster and allows you to walk out feeling that you did something worthy, no matter how minor the task.

We have all done the same in our offices, no one of us hesitating to be the one to empty trashcans or run the vacuum cleaner. Such simple efforts help develop the team – the family – in greater ways than all the ridiculous pretend-bonding teambuilding crap corporations artificially develop in a vain attempt to duplicate the success of the military. It is yet another example of civilian America being satisfied with form over substance. Remember, if it's not unpleasant or life-threatening, you aren't building shit. Or, shit is all that you are building.

You can also be a leader from any position in the company, no matter how low your rank. Regardless of the position you hold, never allow special breaks to be cut for you. Never take the easy out, as others are always watching. Even if your superiors give you a great opportunity you know you haven't earned or can't handle, do not take it. This may cause them a small, short term problem in filling a position, but they will respect you all the more for it. On my very first day of Special Forces training I, like everyone else, was facing many long months of arduous training, wondering if I would be good enough to make the grade. Nothing was less pleasing – or more intimidating – than dwelling on the countless hundreds of miles I would have to run, thousands of miles I would have to ruck, dozens of sleepless nights, and days spent outside training in the rain and snow with little food. All this, without even addressing the academic overload we would be expected to bear on our young shoulders. And that would just be to get through the essentials of SF training. On that same day

I was offered an opportunity to forego all of this, and go straight to an already operating A Team in Vietnam.

When I had arrived at the Q Course I was already an accomplished Morse Code operator, and could do 18/18,[117] which was a near perfect performance, akin to typing 100 words a minute from dictation with no errors. At the time, all of the SF Teams in Nam needed commo guys[118] desperately, and were suffering a shortage they didn't seem to be able to fill. The SF sergeant responsible for filling this quota, and getting anyone he could find on a plane to Vietnam right away, told me that I would get all of the Q Course training on-the-job over there with guys who were highly experienced operators. I was being handed an opportunity to forego more than another full year of daily torture and get right into the game, doing what I most wanted to do.

I was not inclined to accept this offer, but still I asked him what he thought I should do. This man, an experienced and decorated combat veteran Green Beret, charged with the duty of finding men to fill vacancies in front line, and behind-the-lines, units, said that he would recommend getting some training and survival skills first. He was telling me to stick with the Q Course. Despite the fact that this likely meant he would fail to meet the quota he had been given, this NCO proved to me that he was a professional and demonstrated his leadership by proving he cared more about other people than himself; even people he didn't even know. I took his advice, and never regretted it. I used his behavior as a model for myself throughout my career.

This one, lone Green Beret had set a standard of fairness, decency and professionalism that was to see me through the next 24 and a-half years in Special Forces. It set the standard of behavior for "men" that I would follow and attempt to emulate, and try to instill in others. Looking back, I realize today just how young that benevolent sergeant must have been, and do not even remember his name. I can

---

117 Morse messages are sent in five letter groups. To do 18/18 means that you are capable of both copying, and sending, 18 of those groups per minute with virtually no mistakes.
118 Communications specialists.

only hope that I have been worthy of the example he set, and the service that he did me.

This was only the first experience with "mentoring" I was to have from the SF veterans I would come in contact with, even before I knew the word or understood the concept. Throughout my career in SF, I had the privilege of working with many such men, professionals who truly cared more about those in their care and under their command, than they did about promotions, decorations or money. They cared more about their reputations for decency and professionalism, and the legacies they left for their families and loved ones, and their beloved SF, than anything else. I cannot think of a better example of proper living and professional behavior than this, nor have I ever seen one. As I watch the TV news, I often ponder how great the elevation in ethics, performance and pride society would see in all professions if people would only adopt the same attitude and prioritization in their careers. How much improved would the public's opinion of lawyers, judges, politicians, doctors, insurance companies, car salesmen, construction contractors, police, and virtually everyone else be, if we all committed ourselves to the code of conduct and concern of these Green Berets?

This is a standard our own business community can follow to its benefit. Despite the fact that capitalism is based on a free market - and that system is based on everyone acting in his own self-interest - much can be gained by concerning yourself with others. Like Special Operations, no one gets through a business career, or makes a lot of money, by operating alone. It just isn't possible. In every undertaking from your college degree, your MBA, and your first job, to commanding whole departments or corporations, you are benefiting from others' work. The better they are, the more you benefit. The more concerned you are with supporting them in their efforts, ultimately the better will be your career. If successful, you will have accomplished that success without exploiting co-workers, scheming, manipulating, or back-stabbing anyone. Sure, you will suffer some minor, short-term setbacks when you are focused on helping others before acting in your own best interest. But these will be small, and in the end you will have far surpassed others of a different mindset, whose abuse, or exploitation of their co-workers provided them merely short term gains.

SOMETIMES YOU HAVE TO DIG DEEP

Being a worker in any organization does not mean that you will only contribute your time and effort, or that you will be paid for all you do and be reimbursed for everything you spend. If you truly want to be the best, sometimes you will have to contribute more than just your time. Until 1983, Special Forces represented less than one-tenth of one percent of the entire U.S. military budget, yet managed to be the best trained, most skilled, competent and professional of every unit in the military. It was, however, the worst equipped. As a small group, we had little lobbying power, and back then no one was ever permitted to rise through the Special Force ranks to become even a one-star general, so we never had anyone at high levels of command to watch out for us. As an elite and unconventional unit, the conventional military looked at us through jaded eyes. They might have been stuck with us and our seemingly-impossible successes in the field, but no way were they going to let us get a foothold in the political arena.

Don't think that being SF meant we wore silk stockings under our jump boots, ate from silver spoons in mess kits, or that our status had been handed to us. Every Green Beret headed downrange[119] spent his own money to modify his military-issued gear. Exterior pockets were removed and sewn onto more useful parts of his uniform, or were slanted so as to guarantee faster access to important equipment under fire. Each man's heavyweight gear was purchased out of his own pocket for winter survival, and top-of-the-line sleeping bags were ordered from extreme camping and hunting outfitters. Extra magazines were purchased, as were canteen holders in which

[119] SF-speak for traveling overseas to conduct operations usually in a hostile environment.

they could best be carried for fast access when the shooting started. All of this was done by these men on their own dime just so that they could then go out and do the job America asked of them.

Keep this in mind when you find yourself whining about why you haven't accomplished what you should in your company. A few SF operators actually quit the unit just because they weren't willing to spend some of their own money on equipment, and sometimes on extra training from outside instructors. But most were consummate professionals, totally committed to their jobs, willing to do anything necessary to accomplish the mission. We couldn't understand any-one who thought differently: if we were willing to sacrifice our lives for our country, why not three or four hundred dollars? If you care about your profession, you are a professional. It's not always about money.

John Giduck during practice at the Olympic Training Center,
Colorado Springs, Colorado, 1988

– 9 –

COMMITMENT TO SPORTS

Character is that which reveals moral purpose,
exposing the class of things a man
chooses or avoids.

Aristotle

SPORTS AS LIFE'S BATTLEFIELDS

By definition, sports are athletic activities, not necessarily competitive ones. Things like scuba diving, hiking, mountain climbing, rappelling, and hunting are all sports, even though there really isn't a competitive outlet for them. That is not to say that competitive sports are not good - quite the opposite – and they are of particular importance to children. But the first and most important thing to accomplish as an SF instructor-trainer in engineering the physical component in your children's lives, is to see that they receive the benefits of sports. But they are just as important for you as an adult, and you will continue to reap the benefits of lifelong involvement in athletics.

Sports, unlike any other activity, can develop the physical qualities of: coordination; strength; flexibility; improved cardiovascular functioning; reduced fat and cholesterol levels; speed; and endurance. Among the superior character attributes that come from participation in athletics are: discipline; dedication; sacrifice; team-work; individual accomplishment; proper diet and lifetime eating habits; respect; patience; the ability to function within an established system of rules; knowledge of one's place in a hierarchy; ability to deal with loss; modesty in victory; and the most important of all, the perseverance to continue to succeed against all odds.

Much like life in Special Forces, sports are a microcosm of life in America. In both, we find teammates and competitors; ene-mies; work; training and practice; sacrifice; and dedication. There is a mighty striving to make the cut to belong to an elite group, capable of performing to both physical and mental levels beyond that of normal people. It is about having parents who guide and direct you, and those "parents" come in many different people: mothers and fathers in life, coaches and trainers in sports, and superior officers, instruc-tors and NCOs in SF. It is all ultimately tested on the field of battle, in whatever form that battle may take.

It is no big surprise that the Japanese people believe that one of the reasons their country became a highly developed world power after World War II, was the rebirth in popularity of their vari-ous martial arts by the end of the 1940s. The competitive spirit and pride developed in those athletic disciplines helped them survive the psychological and moral shock they had experienced at the end of the war. Master Morihei Uyeshiba, the founder of Aikido, was even presented with a national governmental award for the improvement of morality of the nation as a result of the massive expansion of martial arts.

John and I have both spent our lives involved in sports; some more competitive, and more successful, than others. Most of the people in Special Forces are the same, as are most truly suc-cessful people in life. In the military, it is recognized that sports develop important skills for combat. Indeed, the original Greek sports and Olympic Games were designed to train and test soldiers for battle. Little has changed to this day. Lee James was a young 101st Airborne paratrooper training for weightlifting competition at the 1976 Olympic Games in Montreal, Canada. Blonde, hand-some, and modest in manner, with a pleasant southern accent, he was an early role model for John who was then an up and coming teenage weightlifter.

As an almost unheard of upstart lifter, Lee James went to Montreal with one goal in mind: to defeat the best the Communist Bloc could muster. Not a highly popular sport in the U.S., our weight-lifting teams tended to place low in the world standings, and it had been years since anyone had won an Olympic medal. Then, as now, the Soviet Union[120] and many Warsaw Pact countries dominated this sport. Still, nothing dissuaded Lee from his mission. His own athletic background, together with his elite military experiences, gave him the focus and drive to achieve his ends. Competing at the height of the Cold War, he was often heard to say that international athletics were merely a peaceful war between nations, and it was the duty of every American to do his best to defeat all of our country's enemies.

For this reason he had no tolerance for members of any U.S. sports team whose hair was unkempt, shirt untucked, or who other-wise behaved in a manner not suited to representing our nation. As it turned out, this young man came from nowhere, beating the best the Communist nations had assembled, with the sole exception of the U.S.S.R.'s famed, multiple world champion David Rigert. In win-ning two silver medals, Lee James pushed Russia's best to new records in order to barely win the gold medal. Despite this phenomenal performance, Lee was not satisfied. "I didn't do what I went there to do," he would later tell John while both were training at the York Barbell Club Gym in York, Pennsylvania.

Though he may not have achieved his immediate goals, Lee James set a standard for the rest of our nation to follow. He may not have been a Green Beret at the time, but he certainly lived like one. This is the type of young man – and woman – that athletics produces. They give people the discipline to strive mightily to achieve their

120 Now Russian Federation and Former Soviet Republics.

goals, whatever those goals are in life. All of the lessons taken from sports are directly applicable to other aspects of life.

Athletes will strive harder than others, and not allow defeat to deter them. They will come back again and again, just as they have to in the arena to win. They do not fear. Most importantly they do not fear work, as they know the only way to achieve success at anything is by working hard. They will do this in school, and in their careers, their entire lives. To understand the importance sports has played in just a few of our nation's top people, including government and business leaders, read Brian Kilmeade's bestseller, *The Games Do Count: America's Best and Brightest on the Power of Sports.*[121] In it such notables as Tony Danza, Tony Robbins, Oliver North, Gerald Ford, Henry Kissinger, Ronald Reagan, Tom Ridge, Burt Reynolds, Senator and former SEAL Bob Kerrey, Col. David Hunt, Joan Lunden, John McCain, Condoleeza Rice, Kurt Russell, and Donald Trump detail the tremendous role the lessons and discipline they learned in sports played in their success in later life. Even Secretary of Defense Donald Rumsfeld was a collegiate wrestling champion, and often accurately analogized America's war efforts to the tactics found in wrestling matches.

As a kid, I was a wrestling champion and state championship contender. At age 50, I set a state benchpress record. John was a wrestler and national weightlifting champion. We both boxed non-competitively, did martial arts, and were scuba divers. We both became dive masters, and John became an instructor, ultimately spending many years of his life teaching both recreational and tactical diving. I was a Green Beret hand-to-hand combat, and law enforcement defensive tactics, instructor. John held these same titles, along with several black belts and is a four-time inductee into international martial arts halls of fame. We've both been skydivers, hikers, hunters, outdoor survivalists, swimmers and rappellers. But any of my friends would tell you that I am not a natural athlete. However, I am someone who dedicates himself to a goal and then trains hard to meet that goal. Just

121 *The Games Do Count: America's Best and Brightest on the Power of Sports* (Regan Books, New York: 2004).

as anyone can do. Could anyone doubt that these experiences didn't help me through the torturous tryouts that were the Special Forces Qualifications Course, or the many years of combat and overseas operations I would not only survive, but thrive in? Could anyone doubt that these experiences didn't give John – not a naturally gifted athlete either - the foundation of work, discipline and sacrifice necessary to get through law school in record time while training for the national championships, finish a master's degree while juggling both a law practice and his own heavy teaching schedule, or succeed at so many other endeavors? On the other hand, I shudder to think who we would be, and what we would have accomplished in life, without all of the gifts we received from our years in sports.

SOMETHING FOR EVERYONE

I well recognize that intensely competitive athletics are not for everyone. But that doesn't mean that everyone can't benefit from sports, no matter the level of their participation. Sports are like military service: everyone comes out a better person than they were when they went in. If you are someone who got nothing from sports, it was only because you were trying very hard not to, but were giving everything you had to remain the same worthless, undisciplined and lazy creature you started out.

Fundamentally, sports can be broken into three levels of involvement:

1. Intensely Competitive, such as youth or high school wrestling, hockey, baseball, football, track and field, or gymnastics; or, college and beyond wrestling leagues, professional boxing, kickboxing or mixed martial arts;

2. Recreationally Competitive sports, such as intramural sports or sport clinics, which teach skills and discipline without the pressure of an intensely competitive schedule. This can be seen in adult

basketball and softball leagues, the popularity of health club boxing programs for businessmen, and karate; and,

3. Non-Competitive or Personal Growth physical activities and disciplines.

Some sports can be found in all three groups, such as weightlifting which can be done at a high level of competition; at a lower level of competition, as often happens within a gym, or among members of an athletic team, or in trying to set school or gym records in the weight room; but can also just be an excellent recreational physical discipline and form of exercise for anyone throughout his entire life. This applies to martial arts, baseball, basketball, tennis, running, swimming, cross country bicycling, skiing and so many other activities. There is a sport out there for everyone, something every single person can fall in love with and keep as a constant source of exercise, devotion, pride, motivation, discipline and health throughout his entire life.

ADDING WARRIORSHIP TO YOUR LIFE

By virtue of anyone's dedication and discipline in sports – by each person's commitment to always strive to be the best and continually improve himself through the crucible of physical training – he is living as a Green Beret. However, some sports are certainly more daunting than others, and demand a stronger, more disciplined and dedicated person. What warrior doesn't scratch his head at the fact that synchronized swimmers receive the same gold medals at the Olympics as the top wrestlers, boxers, weightlifters, marathon runners and gymnasts?

Though most sports at a high competitive level are difficult and demand a great deal of personal sacrifice, and a certain amount of courage, those sports that could be classified as the Special

Operations of athletics are what the Russians call the "heavy sports" or "heavy athletics." They include some of the very sports I mentioned above, in addition to such intense tests of courage and physicality as weightlifting, judo, the decathlon, and many others. However, the Green Berets of all athletes are, without doubt, the wrestlers. When it comes to the mettle that is forged upon the anvil of the sports arena, nothing is more difficult than facing another man in simulated hand-to-hand combat. And despite the absence of actual striking - seen in karate and boxing - nothing is more difficult, more demanding, or requires a greater repertoire of skills and conditioning than wrestling. Those who willingly enter this gauntlet do it all on a fraction of the calories that most other athletes enjoy.

In wrestling, a competitor is stripped of virtually all of his clothing, reduced to a shred of material called a singlet. There he stands, virtually naked before his opponent and a crowd of onlookers, devoid of all the affectations we use to impress and intimidate. He is alone, without the posturing and threatening appearance of uniforms, pads, helmets, gloves, or sticks and bats. Mostly, he is alone. As he stands there he hopes the thousands of miles he has run, the hundreds of meals he has foregone (or thrown up to keep from gaining weight, but the ingestion of which relieves his intense hunger pangs for a little while), the relentless eight-hour training days, hours spent running after training, gut wrenching drills and exercises, will be enough to defeat an enemy who he must assume has been training at least as hard. He is terrified of being humiliated on the mats before the crowd, of being turned onto his back in that one posture of total domination and submission consistent with all animals: the exposure of the soft underbelly. It is a fear that touches us to our deepest roots.

The matches themselves are grueling: physically, mentally and emotionally. Dan Gable is the most famous wrestler who ever lived, and in two decades of competition lost only one match. He was a world champion, an Olympic gold medalist and a several time national champion. He always taught, "that only the merciless can succeed on the mat."[122] For any wrestler to experience that success, he can allow himself no quarter, no mercy and no self-pity in his preparations for combat. He must not have mercy on his opponent, but mostly, he can never show himself any mercy in training for battle. "In wrestling, superior conditioning is a survival tactic. A conditioned wrestler, if he can get to the third period, has the edge over the opponent who might have a few more slick mat moves but is rapidly depleting his oxygen supply and beginning to burn in the legs and arms and shoulders. Wrestlers deal with enough pain on a good day. That pain is compounded and magnified if they're not in shape enough to go full speed for six minutes of a match – plus one minute of overtime."[123] On gym walls around the world Green Berets have written that, "Weakness makes cowards of us all." In sports, no one lives this more than wrestlers.

I have had a lot of tough jobs in my life. The toughest of all was combat, and wrestling was the only other thing that came close. This is why the simple rules exists, even in Special Forces, that *you never mess with a wrestler*. I have been saying it for years, but all too often others, with an arrogance born of pride in whatever other combative sport they did, didn't listen; always to their detriment. A number of years ago the Special Forces Reunion was in Colorado Springs. At the end I had a large group of men – both former and current SF soldiers – up to my house for a party. It was a pleasant summer day, and everyone was hanging out in the backyard while I was grilling hamburgers and steaks. John was standing next to me, and we were chatting and sharing a drink. One of the men – a tough and well trained Green Beret I had worked with for years – walked up behind John. He had obviously been explaining to someone the finer art of taking out a sentry from behind, and as he instructed, "First you grab him by the chin and pull it to the side, while you kick a knee out from under him…," without warning he did those very things to John. In about a half second, John had spun behind this commando and

122   Mark Kreidler, *Four Days To Glory:Wrestling With the Soul of the American Heartland,* (HarperCollins Publishers, New York, 2007), 10.
123   Ibid., 77.

thrown him into the lava rocks that served as landscaping around the patio. With his full weight on my friend, John drove the poor guys' face and shoulder into the sharp blades of those stones. Without slowing down the flipping of the hamburgers, I turned to the group and said, "I keep telling you guys: Never mess with a wrestler."

On another occasion a friend of ours was being recruited by both the football and wrestling teams of a university with a championship sports program. During his visit on campus, he was taken by the football strength coach to the weightroom. "No one is allowed to use this weightroom but the football players," this man proudly proclaimed. Our friend pointed out a student who couldn't have weighed more than 145 lbs., doing benchpresses. "Well that guy doesn't look like he plays on your football team," he said. With his head low, and in a shamed voice, the coach acknowledged that ever since a 280 lb. football player had picked on a 132 lb. wrestler he found in the weightroom, and ended up with his kneecap torn out when the wrestler shot low for a single leg takedown after being pushed by the behemoth, that the football team did tolerate the wrestlers' presence. Stories like this are legion.

According to wrestling chronicler Mark Kreidler, the wrestling room is not a place for the meek. For those who happen to be a tad queasy of stomach, the choices are pretty much limited to the following: (1) get over it; or (2) get out. Mothers are usually the first people in a boy's life who attempt to turn him away from anything truly difficult, and certainly anything dangerous. Make no mistake, at wrestling tournaments and matches there are hundreds of mothers in the stands, but they're not like other mothers. "Whether they wear it anywhere else in their lives, upon entering this place they don a mask of toughness that will enable them to get through a day of competition that, while it doesn't always deliver something horrifying or graphic, holds out at least the promise of such dark wonders with astonishing regularity. And these mothers – the parents, that is – understand about wrestling. There isn't a mother of a wrestler who is going to confuse a weekend tournament with summer camp at Boy

Scouts. The parents know the score. But they also recognize that wrestling matters, and will be accepted, glory and gore alike."[124]

It is true that wrestlers deal with awful stuff all the time, far beyond that experienced by most competitive athletes. It is part of what makes them so worthy, that they simply *deal with things*.[125] "Surely it is part of the reason why wrestling has such a hold on people, and why they believe that it is a sport that reveals character as much as shapes it. It's the good part. They come to see heroes, no matter the circumstances."[126] In this intense pressure cooker, wrestling exacerbates whatever problem one may happen to have, be it small or large.[127] The same is true of both SF training and combat, again, raising the grueling crucible of wrestling to the level of elite combat training ground.

A popular t-shirt proudly declares that wrestling is *Basic Training Without the Green*. While there is some accuracy in this, wrestling is really much more than even that. To compare wrestling to regular military Basic Training, would be to compare Special Forces to the Cub Scouts. More accurately, wrestling is like one long, never ending Navy SEAL Hell Week or Green Beret Assessment and Selection phase. In the five months that constitutes most wrestling seasons, they do more, train longer hours and harder, endure cold and rain and winter, drive themselves to insane and inhuman levels, and manage to do it all on a fraction of the calories we give our Special Ops warriors at the toughest points of their training. Make no mistake, wrestlers are the Green Berets of the sports world.

"Hard work solves everything," is a slogan often attributed to Dan Gable, who also once remarked, "After wrestling, everything else in life is easy."[128] The same can be said for time spent in Special Forces, and it is no small coincidence that often the toughest Green Berets are ex-wrestlers. Certainly, they are the ones that never fear hand-to-hand combat. This is why, in 2006, the Navy SEALs began

124 Kreidler, 127.
125 Ibid., 217-218.
126 Ibid.
127 Ibid. at 180.
128 Kreidler, 123.

a program of recruiting their elite commandos directly from college wrestling teams, and they did it in the best way possible: by challenging wrestlers to stack themselves physically up against the Navy's best in a series of athletic challenges that mirrored the physical screening given to anyone undergoing the SEAL training program. After a long period of a too-high washout rate in BUD/S Training, the Navy may have just found the answer we've tried to tell the Army about for years.

John and I have always believed that if any country wanted to put together the most elite soldiers drawn from the civilian world, that would require the least amount of training, they could do no better than recruiting wrestlers. We said that if you could find wrestlers who were hunters, and especially bow hunters, they would need even less preparation for operating in a combat environment. Any wrestler would already be a top conditioned athlete, possessing not only incredible endurance, muscle conditioning and strength, but the ability to go for long periods under the most demanding physical conditions. He could run for miles, race up steep hills, and explode at high speed for short distances. He could not only do this for an entire day, but well into the night as well. And he could do it all on less than a thousand calories a day.

Most wrestlers perform well academically, so he would be possessed of a brain that could think in the most dire of circumstances, and fulfill the SF role as a teacher. As a wrestler he would be the last soldier to become terrified of close quarters hand-to-hand combat, for that is the wrestler's realm, the briar patch he hopes his enemy will throw him into. It is where he is at his best and most comfortable, so he will not suffer the increasing fear of battle as distance closes, as virtually all other soldiers do. If a hunter, he would know firearms.

But if also a bowhunter, he would already know basic principles of camouflage and concealment, he would be a silent stalker for prey possessed of sight, smell and hearing many times that of any human enemy he would ever face. He would have experience at setting up ambushes and tracking animals, and thus would already possess the almost inhuman patience Special Forces teach its men. He will already be an expert at wilderness survival and land navigation. He will be well used to humping long miles in the dark with heavy loads in a rucksack. Mostly, he will already be familiar with death and blood, and the feelings attendant with the taking of any life that hunters know so well. Most importantly, however, the wrestler-hunter would know what it would be like to drive himself to exhaustion, knowing that is the point at which his work would only begin. Such is the physical and mental state in which Green Berets function in combat; and in which wrestlers function everyday of their lives.

The comparison of wrestling to Special Forces and combat is inescapable. The men of SF are never given the option of being fresh, or "ready" in the sense that they are fully rested and can enter the dim and deadly corridors of combat full of needed energy. It's about being ready for the murky threat of a lurking enemy despite the fact that they are not rested, but because they are trained and mentally prepared. They are ready because of the thousands of hours that came before, where they drove themselves to reckless limits and beyond; conditioning that is there waiting to be drawn on. They are ready and walk bravely into the dying places[129] at times and under circumstances that would see lesser men and units crying to be pulled off the line. Like their wrestler brothers, the Green Berets are forever ready, despite the fact that they are always exhausted.

But if you are an adult, and did not have the benefits of a youth spent in wrestling, all is not lost. Due to such Pay-Per-View sporting events as the UFC (Ultimate Fighting Championship), Pride, and other MMA (mixed martial arts) events, grappling martial arts gyms have exploded across the country. Sign up at a judo, Brazilian or Japanese Jujitsu, or Russian Sambo, school and become the Green Beret of all athletes.

---

129 See *The Dying Place,* by David Maurer (Real War Stories: 1986, 2001).

UNITED WE STAND, DIVIDED WE STAND
ON OUR OWN

All Special Operations units like SF, Rangers, SEALs, PJs and Marine Force Recon need people who can and do function as members of a team. But first they need people who can stand on their own two feet, operate alone, and succeed when they have no one else to fall back on. These are the people who become the strongest team members. Corporations are no different, nor are any other aspects of life. As a husband, you need to be self-sufficient as a man, before you can be of value to your wife in a partnership. Throughout your marriage there will be times when each of you is at your limit and falling back on the strength of the other. To give your kids the skills necessary to function like this in later life, it is best and easiest to use team sports as their training and proving ground.

But to get the most from team experiences, however, everyone would benefit from the test that is individual sports. Nothing builds character, inner strength and confidence more than having to face an opponent or apparatus completely alone, knowing you must summon up the drive to push yourself beyond your known limits with no help from anyone else. Sports like boxing, judo, wrestling, jujitsu, tae kwon do, and karate, throw even young practitioners into a modified version of hand-to-hand combat, though under controlled circumstances and with the advantage of adult supervision and safety rules and equipment.

Facing an opponent in such disciplines is a fearsome undertaking, and you should applaud any child (and yourself if you are up to it) who is willing to even step into that arena. But even one-on-one combative sports do not always push the human psyche to its greatest levels. Famed Russian weightlifter, David Rigert, once said, "Many men are brave when they are with other men, but few are brave when they are alone. Even boxers and wrestlers have another human being in the arena with them, whose mistakes they can capitalize on. But when you are by yourself, facing a great weight, you know what it is like to be truly alone, and have your courage tested to its limits." These are not faint words, coming from a man who once set a record clean and jerk to win the World Weightlifting Championships, on a broken ankle. It took him three tries to do this, and he had to shove the bones in his leg into alignment just before pulling the ponderous weight from the floor.

But the same extreme inner challenges can be found in such activities as long distance running, mountain climbing and bicycling, long distance ocean swimming, free diving and skydiving. Whether combative sports or extreme personal tests, this type of sculpting of your character is exactly what the Special Forces go through, and what they look for in recruits. As already discussed, there are few things more intimidating to human beings than direct, one-on-one, inter-personal confrontation. Just having to have an unpleasant conversation with someone causes your internal systems to start their natural anxiety responses, preparing you for survival. In combat, no matter how elite or well trained, everyone fears close quarters, hand-to-hand combat. Even in Vietnam, where most Green Berets outweighed the average Vietnamese enemy soldier by 40 pounds, we would do anything possible to avoid going hand-to-hand. The people who are comfortable with the everyday, civilian version of this – a fistfight – are those who have developed skill and expertise at these disciplines. If your child spends his fun personal time in the gym wrestling others on the mats, or boxing or sparring in the karate dojo, he will be far more capable of handling not only an unwanted confrontation, but will have the strength and ability to be a stalwart member of any team throughout his life.

This is the ultimate goal of every parent: to give to your children that inner strength and confidence, and the skills to know they can function as an important member of any team, while also having the confidence to handle any problem or challenge that life throws at them on their own. It is far more important than spoiling them with money, or fashionable clothes or expensive toys. By giving your children the tools to be strong and confident, there is nothing your children cannot accomplish in their own lives, and they will have you to thank, just as the Green Berets thank their own instructors when things are at the worst for them in later operations. It is only upon confronting the horrible reality of those times, that they are suddenly thankful for all the cruel training sessions they were put through. As the saying goes: The more you sweat in training, the less you bleed in battle. The rearing of children is little different.

LUXURY IS NOT A LUXURY YOU CAN AFFORD

It is endemic to American culture to think that the nicer a place is, the more extensive and elaborate the facilities, that the harder people work and the better the product generated. This is false. Again, one need only look to the example set by the Special Forces and all of the other elite combat units in America and the world. No one produces the best, toughest, most exquisitely conditioned, hardest working and most disciplined troops by allowing them to train in splendor. Rather, you produce the best by making people function in the most Spartan of conditions. And at their highest level, sports are, as Olympic weightlifting medalist Lee James said, nothing more than a peaceful war.

There is an inverse relationship between the luxury of training conditions and how hard people work. No one sees the best athletes coming out of the most palatial and ritzy health clubs; just the opposite. That's where you find the wannabe bodybuilders who strut about in spaghetti strap tank tops, or who strategically tear the necklines out of their sweat shirts to make it look like they have trap and shoulder muscles, or who always wear long pants to hide the fact they don't squat heavy. That is where you find the mirror monkeys; the men who work desperately to develop their chest and arm muscles – the ones they see in the mirror in the morning – but neglect to move heavy weight in leg and back training. These are not the places that produce champions. You are no more likely to see a top level body-builder or weightlifter in these places, than you are to see an Olympic or professional level boxer in one of those high class health clubs that offer basic boxing training to the white collar class. Though the men who voluntarily engage in this type of training are to be lauded far beyond most in society looking for real physical outlets, these are not the gyms where champions are manufactured.

The real training takes place in the dingiest, darkest and most basic of gyms. Like the best restaurants, the best athletes are found in the holes-in-the-wall of society. In *Rocky III*, the American public was treated to a taste of this very reality. Rocky, having trained for his last fight against Clubber Lang - played by a brutish Mr. T. - in a posh hotel, surrounded by colorful banners, an orchestra, beautiful models and souvenir sales, suffered a horrible defeat. He was only able to beat his nemesis by getting back to the basics of the hardcore, inner-city Los Angeles boxing hall that Apollo Creed had come up in. Then, in *Rocky IV*, he repeated this success by insisting on going to Siberia and training in the freezing wilderness with no single piece of equipment with which to hone his skills. The fiction in that movie, however, was America's desire to believe that the almost indomitable Soviet sports machine was the product of the most advanced training, using the most advanced technology and equipment. This was - and is - a fallacy.

During all the Cold War years, when our amateur athletes would complain that the Russians were so successful because the state subsidized their training, or because they had the most advanced facilities, we were fooling ourselves. Even our weightlifters - who consistently ranked toward the bottom of the world - trained in much nicer, better equipped facilities. The Russians trained in conditions that were nothing short of depressing. They trained in poorly heated, and completely un-airconditioned halls. The walls peeled old, lead based paint, and the floors hadn't been cleaned, waxed or treated in decades. The lights were dim - due to their light bulb shortage - and there was no music. The equipment was comprised of a lot of weights lying about, with the seven foot Olympic bars amidst them. There was little to nothing of the weightlifting machines we are all familiar with. Often, the gyms didn't have squat racks. When a lifter was going to do squats, his teammates would lift the weight up – sometimes 1,000 pounds - and put it on his shoulders. All of their athletes, including their Olympic teams, fought to the top of the world in these conditions.

Years ago, when John was training for both the U.S. Open and American Weightlifting Championships, he was a member of the Gold's Gym weightlifting team. The Gold's Gym he was associated with paid for all of his training expenses and for his travel to competitions. He had free access to one of the biggest, best appointed weightlifting gyms in the country, if not the entire world. This gave Gold's bragging rights over the champions it produced, but that is not where John trained. Six days-a-week, twice-a-day, he found himself in the basement of his friend John Schiechl, himself a national super heavyweight champion. Down in that small, dark room, with only a couple of Olympic bars, a lot of bumper plates,[130] a wooden lifting platform and some dumbbells, they sweated, toiled, worked and strove to be the best: all alone. They knew the splendor of Gold's Gym and attention from everyone there would do nothing to drive them further, to exceed their own physical and mental limits. To be the best, they had to work and suffer in all the ways they could arrange for themselves. And that did not include working out in a beautiful facility, full of shiny chrome machines and pretty girls in spandex outfits.

Far earlier than that, when in college, John and his lifelong friend, Larry Pascale, would savage themselves lifting weights in a makeshift gym set up in John's parents' tiny one-car garage. Through sweltering summers and freezing winters, with neither heat nor air conditioning, they trained for hours a day, often after finishing work at construction sites. It is little wonder that not only would John go on to become a national weightlifting champion, but Larry Pascale would win the national bodybuilding championships.

---

130 The rubber-coated weights Olympic style weightlifters use so they can drop them from overhead without having the weights go through the floor.

America's elite, domestic warriors do the same every day. Among the many training groups and facilities I have seen among our law enforcement heroes, none touched my heart so much as the dedication to hardcore training seen with Alabama's Elbert County Sheriff's Department and SWAT Team. Led by former career Marine and SWAT commander Chris Ziegler, every morning at 4:30 you will find a group of the toughest male, and female, cops (and even dispatchers) moving heavy, rusted iron in one of the dingiest weight-rooms John and I have ever seen. And they do it every day, driven to ever greater performance by Sgt. Ziegler, who is forever loading the menacing seven foot long Olympic bars to the point where the bends in them become permanent.

When I was turning 50, I decided I wanted to take all those years of hard – albeit non-competitive – weight training and try to set a state benchpress record. I already worked out daily in a nicely appointed YMCA, not far from my house. However, to push myself to new limits I knew I had to focus, and get the best training I could. I ended up training three to six days-a-week in the garage of my friend Bob Allen, himself a lightweight powerlifting champion. Each day, often in the freezing Denver winter, we worked tirelessly to push my benchpress power to its absolute limit. I couldn't have accomplished what I did in a nicer environment.

The same is true of Arnold Schwarzenegger and all of the champion bodybuilders in the movie *Pumping Iron*. At that time Gold's Gym wasn't a multi-billion dollar franchise operation, but a bare, Spartan place with a lot of weights. If that gym had a spirit, it wouldn't recognize what passes for a Gold's Gym today. Beyond even that, Mr. Universe contender Mike Katz trained day after day, year after year, in an old garage full of handmade weight machines in Connecticut. But these men were the best, and created amazing bodies on either no steroids, or a fraction of the muscle enhancing drugs used by their counterparts today.

Not only does the military understand this concept, but I have seen it applied in many ways. Mountain climbers don't get good by simply climbing up the prefab walls in alpine sporting stores. Marathoners don't win championships by only running on rubberized, indoor tracks in climate controlled gyms, nor do they get there by only running outside in nice weather. Warriors train for such endurance races as the Iditarod in Alaska by savaging their bodies, and building the stamina and tolerance to survive the most extreme weather. They don't get there by sleeping in warm beds every night. The best boxers, wrestlers, weighlifters, karatekas, judo players and mixed martial artists work everyday in the most basic of conditions. As Apollo Creed told Rocky after his tragic defeat in *Rocky III*: "You lost the eye of the tiger, man." To be the best at your sport, you need to be that tiger. And tigers are found only in the jungle. Along with Green Berets.

BE ALL YOU CAN BE

Athletics are not only a microcosm of your own life, but they bring out all of your individual weaknesses and insecurities. They force you to confront the lesser angels of your being, and to not only be honest about their existence inside of you, but to make you overcome them. Sports can enhance both your character and your performance in everything you do. It is important, however, to not make the mistake of so many professional and national level amateur athletes, by measuring your worth as a human being by your performance in the sports arena. Too many people who are top athletes assume that because they have shelves full of trophies, that they are worthwhile and decent people. These are often the spoiled, pampered millionaire professional athletes who treat members of the general public – the very fans who made them celebrities – horribly. Conversely, others who do not achieve their athletic goals, reason that they are inadequate and failures in life.

Neither of these is true. Sports, in whatever form they take, are individual journeys. Each has a unique path, with twists and turns and lessons to be learned every step of the way. There are many people out there every single day, running to the very limit of their physical and spiritual capacity, facing weights that terrify them, or jumping onto the mat with a black belt, certain only of the beating they are about to take. These warriors know themselves better, and have developed themselves to their utmost, often far beyond any personal ascendancy realized by those genetically blessed athletes, for whom championships came easy.

To get the greatest benefit possible from your athletic endeavors – as with all of life's endeavors – you must train with complete investment of your mind, spirit and body. This means committing yourself completely in every training session. Such commitment does not mean that you should – or even can – attempt maximum performances in every exercise of every training session. All top athletes must cycle their training, as no body can function at 100 percent of its capacity every day. Your body needs 50 percent training days, rehab and flexibility days, and other workout sessions demanding less than top performances. It is the hope that as you move through each cycle your top performance will be better than it was the last cycle, but that will not always occur. Trust me: age happens.

For those who are not elite level, competitive athletes, your body will find its own natural cycle. Listen to your body, pay attention to its energy and strength levels, and do not get discouraged when going through the down phases of your body's cycle. It is part of the natural rhythm, and is no more cause for disappointment than needing to sleep each night. The important thing to remember is that whatever level of training you are doing on a particular day, to do it with total focus and both mental and spiritual immersion in those tasks. In the book *Pumping Iron,* such bodybuilding greats as Arnold Schwarzenegger and Franco Columbu were known for their ability to completely subsume themselves into their training, seeing the world disappear as their minds were lost in the muscle they were working. If doing nothing more than stretching, concentrate and lose yourself in the muscles being pulled to their limits. If doing nothing more than light technique work, recognize that developing and retaining those sensory motor neuron pathways is as important as everything else.

When John and I train, we do it with complete investment. In fact, we have to discipline ourselves to back off sometimes, to be a little easy on ancient injuries lurking beneath the skin, ready to put us out of training altogether. We have to be sensitive to our ages and infirmities. A few years ago I broke my neck and endure problems from that, in addition to countless muscle tears accumulated over the years. John has broken over a dozen bones, has had no hip joints for years and recently had both replaced, not to mention other surgeries that impose limitations on his performance.

Neither of us is going to exceed past performances lifting heavy weights, but with modifications for our current condition in life, we can still push ourselves to the limit, and often exceed former personal records of weights lifted for high repetitions. Though we can't squat heavy anymore, when we do leg presses we occasionally still work up to 1,000 pound sets for fairly high reps, each one done with our heels to our butts. We tolerate no partial repetitions in any exercise, and scoff at others that do half and quarter range movements, then brag about the weights they lift. On a typical day, I'll do 20 sets for each body part, pushing myself to failure. Though I have had to adjust to physical changes by increasing my repetitions in most exercises, and dropping my weights correspondingly, I still work myself to maximum capacity.

Due to torn rotator cuffs in his shoulders, John cannot do straight bar benchpresses. But he will do full range repetitions with more than 100 pound dumbbells in each hand, and straight leg deadlifts with over 400 pounds for reps. In the martial arts gym, he does striking all out with thinly padded grappling gloves, or bare hands (most of his front teeth are replacements from years of training in Russia). Kicking is done with shoes on and no pads: combat conditions. No one "pulls" their kicks. Grappling is done all out to choke or submission. He knows that he cannot teach hand-to-hand combat unless his own skills are kept up, unless he keeps a feel for the reality of it and tries to improve himself.

A WARRIOR'S JOURNEY

No one, not even a Green Beret, is called upon to be a warrior in the real tests of life every day, or even very often. To be ready for those tests when they come, however, we must be preparing every single day. At the same time, we must be realistic about the fact that we exist in physical bodies, and then only for a short period of time, before we are called to the next life. Nothing both prepares you for those greatest life challenges and offers the benefits of internal, and external, health and conditioning, like sports. This is why all elite military operators train every day. This training is not just done at work on the shooting range or the obstacle course, but in gyms outside of work.

These top soldiers understand the value of the presence of sports in their lives, and in their preparation for the lives they lead in the service of our country. If those men see how sports make them better, how can any citizen not see the importance of introducing athletics to his own life? So, be like a Green Beret and stop watching other athletes live their lives. Get off the sofa and take some of that time to be something in your life, instead of being a spectator in others' lives. Set a goal and start today, as each day you've wasted is one less day you will ever get to really live your life.

*John Anderson carrying newly freed slave boy in the
Sudan war, 2003. We should all be able to give someone
at least a single day free from threat.*

– 10 –

COMMITMENT TO LIFE

Life is not a problem to be solved;
It is an adventure to be lived.

John Eldredge
"Wild At Heart"

VIEWING LIFE

Despite the fact that I have committed the vast majority of my life to preparing to use, and sometimes using, violence to protect my nation and her innocent citizens, I am not a violent person. Neither is anyone who is a true Green Beret. We are sometimes required to do the worst things imaginable, but only because aggressors and destroyers force us to. If we waited until those possessed of such evil attacked before we prepared to defeat them, it would be too late. We are the rough men who stand ready in the dark of night, to do harm to those who would harm others, those who cannot defend themselves. This is why our agency, Archangel, adopted as its official motto *De Indefenso Defenser*, To Defend the Defenseless. This is what allows our nation to sleep. We do not seek death and destruction. We do not enjoy violence, but we understand there are others who do. And so we are ready, as "Special Forces soldiers are adept warriors when appropriate, but they are also builders and healers; their most effective weapons are sometimes compassion and concern."[131]

Facing the possibility of our own deaths, and the taking of the lives of others by our own hands, everyday, we understand the value of life; perhaps, more than any other. We understand that you must live as though this is your one chance at life. This is why every Green Beret lives as though each day is his last. We know that life and the physical universe is a balanced system; therefore, the energy that you put out into it, you will eventually get back. If you are a murderer, an abuser, a bully or a destroyer - if you put negative energy and hate out into the life force - it will be revisited upon you. All people, ultimately, get what they deserve. As the old saying goes: *What goes around comes around.* Recognizing this, we try to live good lives, and when we are forced to do the unpleasant things – the rough things – we first make certain we are of pure heart and noble intentions.

BE NICE

Green Berets strive never to be conceited or arrogant, and recognize that the world is a much greater place when you aren't so impressed with yourself. We strive for kindness and compassion whenever and wherever we can extend it. I am often outraged at how men will brag about their efforts to run cats over whenever they see one in the street. I never hesitate to ask them just who the hell they think they are, and what that poor cat did to them? I am not above threatening to drag them out into the street at that moment, so I can jump in my car and let them see what it is like. Never be cruel, even when you must do violence. Brake for cats, kids, old people, and all animals. Brake for drunks and idiots, too. There is no positive energy to be gained in life by inflicting gratuitous pain and suffering on any living creature.

Never stop examining your own life, your own motivations, and your own weaknesses. Don't always assume that you're right, and when in an argument give some consideration to the possibility that

---

[131] Halberstadt, 25.

you just may be wrong. When we feel ourselves getting angry at any friend, the first thing we ask is what we wanted that person to do *for us,* that he's unwilling to do? In most instances you will realize that is exactly the source of your anger, and upon reflection, come to recognize that the person you're angry at had no duty to do the thing you are demanding. When you feel anger, recognize that all anger is fear, and all fear is fear of loss. Examine and identify what loss it is you are fearing; what loss is driving your anger. Then deal with your fear, not what some other person did or didn't do.

IN OUR NATURAL STATE

In life you must acknowledge that you have this one body. Take care of it. The more you sit and do nothing, the faster it will degenerate, just like a car left sitting. The Russians have a saying, that "movement is life." It is true as a tactic of hand-to-hand combat and gunfights, but as a principle of life, as a stationary target is a dead target. To remain stationary is the worst thing possible for your body: it was meant to be used, so *Use It!* It is also the worst thing for your mind and your spirit to be stagnant. Move, experience, wonder, and never stop doing these things, none of which can be done flat on your back on your sofa.

To get the most out of life, you need to truly understand not only life, but life for us as human beings. Despite the advances of modern medicine and almost unbelievable quality of life for most Americans, we are seeing record numbers of people suffering mental illness and personality disorders, autism in children, stress related ailments in adults, drug and alcohol abuse, and cancers of mysterious causes. Murder and suicide are rampant. As human beings, we are clearly not dealing with our life circumstances very well. To get through life with any measure of balance, peace of mind, sense of purpose and belonging, and physical health, you cannot stray too far from that which is most natural for us as a species. The rule for a good life is atavism, which demands a return to things that are the most natural for us, to act as medicine for all the ills modern, urban society infects us with.

The further from the natural state of humans, the more unnatural life will be, and therefore the more stressful. The further from a natural state, the more important it is to carve out time for what is natural. Everyone needs to spend time alone on the ground, camping or hiking, hunting or fishing. You need to view life from the lowly perspective of your own two feet or the back of a horse, with plants and animals in the woods or fields. If you are not enjoying these gifts, then what you are doing *is existing* in an unnatural environment, *not living*.

Consider the life so many Americans are living today, then ask yourself how healthy it sounds:

> Living in a high rise condo with only concrete under your feet when you go outside, skyscraper canyons, choking on exhaust with no fresh air, the cacophony of car horns, shouts and mind-numbing music, rather than silence. Being in cars, trains and buses, as your only means of mobility, wearing artificial and restrictive business clothing and hard shoes, spending long days in a windowless cubicle, hunched over a computer screen. You break up this drudgery with frequent trips to the coffee machine, and eat fried food lunches with only the company of other drones.

No one, even those who profess to believe that life in a big city is the only way to live, believes such an existence is a good one. As human beings, we thrive in natural environments. That is why we have plants in our homes and offices, and enjoy the company of pets. There is nothing that tugs at our deepest racial memory as a species than the domestication and comfort that early wolves, and even predatory cats, provided. We respond to fire in the same way, which is why we all are drawn to fireplaces in our homes, and relish time spent around a campfire in the wilderness, or even a backyard grill.

No one draws comfort from sitting around a microwave oven, watching food being "nuked." We all come alive when we're in the woods, or even if we just get to see a horse walking down the street in a neighborhood where such sights are rare. This is even why we have zoos: we need time in a natural state. We need both darkness and silence, and modern life allows us neither of these – ever. This is why our national parks are overwhelmed with city-dwelling visitors every year.

Author and philosopher, John Eldredge, understands this: "The way a man's life unfolds nowadays tends to drive his heart into remote regions of the soul. Endless hours at a computer screen; selling shoes at the mall; meetings, memos, phone calls. The business world – where the majority of American men live and die – requires a man to be efficient and punctual. Corporate policies and procedures are designed with one aim: to harness a man to the plow and make him produce…. A man needs to feel the rhythms of the earth; he needs to have in hand something real – the tiller of a boat, a set of reins, the roughness of rope, or simply a shovel. Can a man live all his days to keep his fingernails clean and trim? Is that what a boy dreams of?" [132] Indeed, that is not life. Quite simply, as John Eldredge points out, "It is fear that keeps a man home where things are neat and orderly."[133]

No matter how much you may think you love the city, never lose sight of the little things in life, the beautiful wonderments that nature offers you. They cannot be found readily in an urban environment, though they can be if you look hard enough. You just have to recognize their value to your life and your spirit, and make the time to find them. Don't just drive your Lexus SUV into work, shutting yourself off from the world. There's a whole planet out there that you can appreciate at the same time. When I'm asked what the greatest thing I ever saw in all my world travels was, I don't say it was a mile-plus sniper shot, a great bomb detonated or an enormous building. I say it was a bird's nest. Long before abandoned when I came across it, I still have that nest. It sits on a hutch in my dining room, and is truly a work of nature, God and wildlife architectural genius.

---

[132] Eldredge, 6.
[133] Ibid., 5.

ON CODES AND PHILOSOPHIES

Since the 1960s, "experts" in all disciplines that encourage excuse-making have kept saying, "Admit your limits and your weaknesses, what you do isn't really your fault." What they don't understand is that being human means you can accomplish anything you put your mind to. That includes changing yourself. You may have to work for it, however. Unfortunately, accepting responsibility for their own behavior and working for a goal, are the two things many people – many men – aren't willing to do anymore.

This is why so many of our citizens wind up in never-ending programs of psychotherapy and counseling. I have heard so many people say that everyone needs a therapist, that it makes me want to puke. The vast majority of these people do not need *psychological* or psychiatric counselors, they don't require medical doctors and drugs. What all of these people need, if anything, are *philosophical* counselors. How many people have a philosophy, whether personal or adopted from another? How many have a code by which they live and comport their lives, and upon which they depend for guidance in times of trouble? A philosophy is not the same as a religious belief, in many instances, but religion can (if it's a worthwhile religion) provide an external code by which its adherents live. Unfortunately, all too often religions, like laws, become outside sets of standards, artificially and seemingly nonsensically created by others, and imposed on and against the will of the individual. Like laws, religious dictates become something to get around, to violate without getting caught. How many people would you ask:

> "What is the philosophy of your life, or how you live your life?"

134 Bach, *Illusions,* 120.

> "What is the code, based on that philosophy, by which
> you live, the tenets of which you never violate because
> you believe in them so deeply?"

How many people, yourself included, would have an answer for such questions? This is what is lacking in people. This is something that needs to be instilled in children from the time they are young, and which could help them navigate the turbulent adolescent years; the years in which so many atrocities have been committed by disaffected youth in the past two decades in America. Not that all children commit atrocities; few of them do. But all of them could and would benefit from the development of their own personal philosophy as a foundation to their lives. Our friend Bob Evans always believed he could help with any adolescent or teenage boy's behavior problems just by making him read Louis L'Amour western novels, so rich in a code of personal honor and behavior for men were they.

In these times of a modernistic, objective and positivist America, where science and logical reason dictate all, and where all religiously imposed rules of morality are under assault by notions of relativism and secularism, philosophy is all too often viewed askance. But it is the development of such codes that must take root. In recent decades it has become fashionable in the corporate world for every business – no matter how small or new – to have a mission statement. Businesspeople fret mightily over exactly how to express what the business will stand for, and how its people will comport themselves. That is each business's code. If the value of that exercise is obvious for a lifeless profit-generating entity, how can so many people have missed its benefits for themselves? Much would be known by the codes people created for themselves. In ages past, family crests communicated this; all that the family or clan stood for. Perhaps we have something to gain by resurrecting that practice.

Though there are an infinite number of admirable codes people could devise to live by, there is no greater, more honorable, or more noble, a philosophy than that of a warrior. America could only be improved by a population of warriors. Certainly America was a better place when populated by warriors. For each person, the Warrior Code might be different in degree and emphasis, but for all the Code of the Warrior would ensure a nation of people dedicated to something great; something greater than themselves. It would ensure a population of citizens ready to serve others, to sacrifice for the greater good, in whatever way that individual might define it. For some, this might demand acts of environmental protest in an effort to save a forest; for others it might dictate the protection of any person from an act of terrorism. Yet, no matter how one feels about such issues, no one could discount the moral imperative each felt in meeting his own established duty to the world, to act for the benefit of others in his life, no matter the sacrifice.

Whose code would say, "Drive as recklessly as you can," or "Abuse children," "Rob banks," or even, "Beat up people weaker than you?" This is not tolerated by any philosophy, and certainly not by the Code of the Warrior. So much pain, abuse and predatory behavior could be reduced by encouraging people to honestly examine their lives, their behavior, what it is that they believe in, and how true they are to those beliefs.

SELF-RESPONSIBILITY

Between the overuse of therapists, daytime talk shows, and courts that encourage people to make excuses for their own behavior, people who face some of life's problems seem to think that these experiences make them somehow special. Anyone who has endured an unpleasant experience seems to want to hang the label of "survivor" on themselves. This has gotten to the point where everyone seems to believe that claiming the title of survivor, casts some type of celebrity status on them.

There are war survivors, alcoholism survivors, survivors of alcoholic parents, car accident survivors, Hurricane Katrina survivors, depression survivors, divorce survivors, and on and on. What all of these people refuse to recognize, however, is that you can't be a survivor if you weren't, first, a victim. If you're willing to think of yourself as a victim, you're already headed down the path of self-pity, self-indulgence and refusing to simply accept that bad things do happen in life. If you're ready to consider yourself a victim of any experience *in life,* then you already think of yourself as a victim *of life.*

It is this very mentality that has led to an America overwrought with litigation and safety procedures, practices and regulations, liability waivers, and federal regulatory agencies controlling our lives. We're so busy trying to keep everyone from ever "suffering" a bad experience, that we never get to "have" any. We don't get to benefit from the wonderful gifts life's toughest and worst experiences have to offer. All too often, when life is at its best, we still see this same mentality manifest itself in constant excuse-making for our failure to live our lives the way we want to – or at least the way we say we want to live them. This is something that we tell our children they can never do, but then show them just the opposite. For instance, we have far too many friends who lament that no matter how hard they exercise that they just can't lose any weight. But, when you're with them, you see that their workouts are pathetic and last less than an hour, and half of that time is spent talking or watching television. Afterward, they eat fried foods at lunch, wash them down with wine or beer or hard liquor, then go home and eat another large meal capped off with fattening deserts. When not drinking calorie-laden alcohol, they quench their thirst with sugar-laden soft drinks. They can't even drink a cup of coffee without loading it with cream and sugar. Then we hear how lucky we are because we have naturally high metabolisms and aren't as fat as them.

This is a bunch of rubbish. Neither John nor I have even average metabolisms, and we always laugh that we burn fewer calories running than most people do sleeping. Neither of us is ever happy with how we look, and so we train and restrict ourselves far more than people think. It's just that we realize that you can't eat like an Italian and hope to look like an Ethiopian. If we don't look the way we'd like, we accept that is only due to our refusal to discipline ourselves to get there. When we care enough we will. What we won't do is fool ourselves, make excuses, or tell others how lucky they are.

This is seen in all aspects of life. When John was in law school, he started in a four year evening program. He quickly began picking up additional classes, overload credits, juggling it all with a full time job at a law firm, and two-a-day, six-days-per-week training sessions for the national weightlifting championships. Needless to say, he had no personal life, and juggling all this meant that his grades were not as good as they might have been. While undergoing this grueling regimen his law school friends kept telling him how stupid he was, that his grades would suffer and he wouldn't ever get any kind of a job. John's attitude was that, first, he had to work to support himself, so time spent at work was essential. Second, his ability to win a national championship and make an Olympic Team would come and go in a very short time. Third, that law was something he could do until his 70s or 80s if he wanted, so he could delay complete devotion to it for a short time and still have a long and successful career if he chose.

Then, after graduating in only two years, when he was a successful practicing lawyer, trying high level cases even as a young attorney, those same friends who were still stuck in school discounted all that he had accomplished and sacrificed, by lamenting: "You're so lucky to already be out of school and practicing law." In Special Forces, we all had similar experiences. People we encountered all said we were so lucky to wear the beret of our nation's most elite unit; yet no one of them would have ever committed himself to the torture and sacrifice necessary to earn it.

PREPARING FOR BATTLE

America doesn't need more feminized and excuse-making males, who are mere pretenders to manhood. Nor do we need the therapized and excuse-making culture that produces them. Eldredge says, "We don't need accountability groups [groups of men who get together through church or what have you, who act as support, like life coaches to tell us we're ok, too]; we need fellow warriors, someone to fight alongside, someone to watch your back."[135] Just like in the Special Forces. Eldredge recounts a story from his own experience: "A young man stopped me on the street to say, 'I feel surrounded by enemies and I'm all alone.' The whole crisis in masculinity today has come because we no longer have a warrior culture, a place for men to learn to fight like men. We don't need a meeting of Really Nice Guys; we need a gathering of Really Dangerous Men. That's what we need."[136]

This is what America needs, not more experts, counselors, teachers, judges or stock market speculators who never dared greatly or performed a courageous act in their lives. Who are they to evaluate or pass judgment on the lives and acts and sacrifices of America's warriors, or to say that having such men is a bad thing? Col. Grossman assures us that there is not anything wrong with such men: there is something wondrously, nobly right about them, and anyone who cannot count himself among them, holds his manhood cheap.

In Special Forces, when we would confront a situation that we were not sure we were prepared for, we would remind ourselves that the entire universe had conspired to get us the training we had, to prepare us and put us there at that moment, confronting that challenge, and that we, thus, were ready to confront it. Winston Churchill recognized this when, during World War II, he said, "I felt as if I were walking with destiny, and that all my past life had been but a preparation for this hour and for this trial." This is true of everyone and everyone's life. It is no small coincidence that you find yourself reading this book, right now, at this moment in your life.

Recognizing all of this, you must live your life to its utmost, beyond any limits imposed by a timid society constituted of fearful men. "The most dangerous man on earth is the man who has reckoned with his own death. All men die; few men ever really live. Sure, you can create a safe life for yourself, and end your days in a rest home babbling on about some forgotten misfortune. I'd rather go down swinging."[137] This is the reason that John and I – and everyone

135 Eldredge, 175.
136 Ibid.
137 Eldredge, 169.

who has ever lived his life as a Green Beret – want to die with our bodies beat to hell. We want to have broken each bone at least once. After all, what good is dying with a wonderful body that you took such great care of, when you could have experienced so many grand adventures, and the dangers that made them grand? While working on this book, John received an email from retired Delta Force Command Sergeant Major Mel Wick, one of the greatest warriors the world has ever seen. CSM Wick's email ended with a quote he had found during his travels: "Life is not a journey to the grave with the intention of arriving in a pretty and well preserved body, but rather to skid in broadside, totally worn out, and loudly proclaiming WOW... What a ride!" Nothing could say it better.

HOW WE LIVE

People in many, if not most, other countries in the world would literally give a limb to live our lives, and have a future in America. Yet, we spend most of our time feeling sorry for ourselves, and daily invent new reasons to indulge our self-pity. Instead of pandering to the recognition that life could always be better – no matter how good it already is – we need to realize just how lucky we are. Anytime we find ourselves starting to think about how bad things are, we need to stop and remind ourselves that we're healthy, free and live in America. It doesn't get any better, and in the entire history of the world no one has ever had it better than us.

In Special Forces, the conditions in which we are often made to survive are so bad that anytime we are out of them, we are happy. Anytime we can say, "I'm warm and dry, I have food in my belly, and no one is trying to kill me," we can't imagine how life could be any better. In the award-winning HBO Series *Band of Brothers*, each episode would show recent interviews of the men depicted 60 years ago. One of the soldiers from that famous unit, Easy Company of the 101st Airborne, more than half a century after being surrounded and shelled relentlessly in the Ardennes Forest outside the town of Bastogne during the Battle of the Bulge, said, "Ask my wife, to this day, no matter how cold it is when we go to bed, I always say how grateful I am that I'm not in Bastogne."

HELPING OTHERS

I encounter people all of the time who have some moral objection to how I've lived my life, to what I've done or trained to do should my country and her citizens have ever needed it. But even if some of those things were less than pleasant, I can also say that I have done far more decent, life saving, charitable and humanitarian things than any of those detractors. Several years ago while in Sudan with John and a small team from Archangel, we were present for the repatriation – i.e., the purchase of the freedom – of several thousand women who had been taken and sold into sex and labor slavery by the Arab Muslim government in the north.

Among one group of a thousand such women there was quite a number of babies and toddlers, the products of the rapes these women regularly endured. One tiny boy of about three, walked right up and stood staring up at me. I was probably, both, the only white man he had ever seen, and the biggest person he had ever laid eyes on. I picked him up and held him in my arms. He wrapped his tiny arms around my neck, and there he stayed for the rest of the day as we helped sort these women out and return them to their families. At first his mother was anxious about her waif of a child being carried about by this strange white man, but quickly realized he was safer than at any time in his young life, and gave me her permission with a smile. I want everyone to be able to pick up a snotty-nosed little tyke in horrible circumstances, and give him a day – or just an hour - of relief and comfort, of freedom from fear or threat. It may be the only good day he ever has. Never forget your humanity, never forget what living the life of a warrior – of a Green Beret – is all about.

THE GIFTS OF AMERICA

Despite all that we have, today our nation is in one of the most politically divisive periods it has ever seen. Between vicious disputes and finger-pointing over the War on Terror, phone and email monitoring by the federal government, abortion, stem cell research, the death penalty, tax rates, the price of oil and gas, the environment, social benefits and the cost of medical insurance, it seems that our country is filled with people who hate much of how our nation is run. Many people believe that we can just ignore a world filled with powerful despots, military aggressors and terrorists, and live perfectly happy and safe lives. Such people are foolish.

Compared to people in many places in the world, all Americans live wonderful lives that are only possible due to the sacrifices of millions who came before them – and the many today – who provided that luxury with guns. They seem to not understand that every civilization died when school programs became more important than both liberty and soldiers. A recent email by an unknown author was making the rounds on computers all over America. The writer stated that a *Newsweek* poll had reported that 67 percent of Americans were unhappy with the direction the country was headed, and 69 percent were unhappy with the performance of the president. "In essence, 2/3s of the citizenry just ain't happy and want a change." The author went on to ask what was everyone so unhappy about:

> Is it that we have electricity and running water 24 hours a day, 7 days a week? Is our unhappiness the result of having air conditioning in the summer and heating in the winter? Could it be that 95.4 percent of these unhappy folks have a job? Maybe it is the ability to walk into a grocery store at any time and see more food in moments than Darfur has seen in the last year?

Maybe it is the ability to drive from the Pacific Ocean to the Atlantic Ocean without having to present identification papers as we move through each state? Or possibly the hundreds of clean and safe motels we would find along the way that can provide temporary shelter? I guess having thousands of restaurants with varying cuisines from around the world is just not good enough. Or could it be that when we wreck our car, emergency workers show up and provide services to help all involved whether you are rich or poor, they treat your wounds and even, if necessary, send a helicopter to take you to the hospital.

Perhaps you are one of the 70 percent of Americans who owns a home. You may be upset with knowing that in the unfortunate case of having a fire, a group of trained firefighters will appear in moments and use top notch equipment to extinguish the flames, thus saving you, your family and your belongings. Or if, while at home watching one of your many flat screen TVs, a burglar or prowler intrudes; an officer equipped with a gun and a bulletproof vest will come to defend you and your family against attack or loss. This all in the backdrop of a neighborhood free of bombs or militias raping and pillaging the residents. Neighborhoods where 90 percent of teenagers own cell phones and computers.

How about the complete religious, social and political freedoms we enjoy that are the envy of everyone in the world? Maybe that is what has 67 percent of you folks unhappy. Fact is, we are the largest group of ungrateful, spoiled brats the world has ever seen. No wonder the world loves the U.S., yet has a great disdain for its citizens. They see us for what we are: The most blessed people in the world who do nothing but complain about what we don't have, and what we hate about the country instead of thanking the good Lord we live here.

No words could say it better.

GETTING INTO THE GAME - OF LIFE

Look at how we all live today. During the times of our parents and grandparents, America was still a country closely connected to its agrarian roots. Even people in the cities were a short step away from that agricultural foundation. There were no supermarkets, and even after there were, most people still had to get their meat from a butcher. If you wanted chicken for dinner, the women either went out back and wrung its neck or chopped its head off. They then bled it out, cleaned and dressed it, plucked its feathers and made dinner. Even going to the butcher was no different. The chickens got their heads cut off in front of you, then turned upside down in a bucket until bled to death. "Running around like a chicken with its head cut off," was not just a saying, but something everyone had seen.

Death was a regular part of life, and children understood that death was a part of the life cycle from the time they were very young. When people died they were laid out in the parlor for a couple of days before being buried. Knowledge and understanding of the reproductive process – of sex – was no different. Back then, no parent had to wring his or her hands over when to have "the talk" with their children, or how to answer the inevitable question of "where do babies come from?" The kids had all grown up watching the farm animals "do it." There was no mystery and no confusion. This is the natural state of things.[138]

138   For a complete analysis of this cultural evolution, read Dave Grossman's *On Killing*.

LIFE – AND DEATH

Today, we have no tolerance for any of this. If women – or even men – had to go out back to kill and dress a chicken, a pig or cow for the family to eat, we'd be a nation of vegetarians. We express our opinions against hunting and protest anyone who wears fur, yet never stop to look down over our own bellies at the leather belts and shoes we're wearing, or briefcases or purses we're holding while doing so. Where do we think that leather comes from? We are wearing the skins of what were once living, breathing creatures; ones that died in a slaughterhouse terrified by all the blood and the scent of death that permeated the room they were herded into. We decry the brutality of anyone taking life, then go to the store and buy a nice steak, sitting pink and perfect under cellophane. We are so far removed that most American kids up to the age of six don't even understand that the meat they're eating is animal flesh, and that some animal had to die in order for him to fill his belly.

Years ago, while engaged in a conversation with a woman who expressed exactly these attitudes, I was struck by something John said in response to her assault on our "way of life," and what she perceived to be our comfort with death. I had witnessed John assailed by others as someone who didn't respect life, who trained with guns, knives and his bare hands with the only purpose being to take life, just as I – and every Green Beret - had also been attacked countless times. As our debate over the issue of hunting proceeded, John told this lady that no one could truly appreciate life who had not taken life. He asked her if she had ever experienced the soul-wrenching regret over taking the life of another living creature so that she might ensure her own existence, her own life. He asked if she had ever wrestled with all of those emotions against the reality that for our own survival we sometimes need to kill? For it is not until you have taken the life of another that the weight of the responsibility of life is actually felt. Just as the Native Americans would chant, and sing and dance in both sadness and appreciation of the lives of the animals they had slain in order for their tribe to live. No one can understand what weight a life bears down on his shoulders until he knows he is responsible for its loss.

This is part of what has become our overall cultural need to hide ourselves from the life cycle. Most people don't seriously stop to contemplate their lives, or their own mortality, until the day they are diagnosed with a terminal illness. Living life, also means living with death. Don't put your head in the sand and pretend that it will never happen to you. Never delude yourself into thinking that it is so far away, that you'll have lots of time to live, and then to get ready for death later. You don't, and won't. One of the ways in which you can become a warrior in facing the toughest aspects of life is to start facing them head on, now, today. And then remember to face them every single day for the rest of your life.

MAKING THE MOST OF THE TIME YOU HAVE

Everyone can be the type of person others can depend on in the worst possible circumstances, in the horrors that life sometimes throws at us. For some, their professional jobs require them to handle difficult things, but then they chose that profession with the knowledge – or hope – that they could handle it. People decry any lawyer who defends someone the media has already convicted of murder; but stop for a moment and think how difficult it is to be that lawyer. He knows that if he isn't at his best his client will get the death penalty and a human life will be lost, and it will be his fault. Stop and realize that if some lawyer doesn't defend that person – who is constitutionally entitled to effective assistance of counsel and a zealous defense – that he goes free. Those are not the lawyers hiding inside plush offices and behind multi-billion dollar corporate mergers. They are down there in the trenches, where the most important principles of our legal system are at war, every single day. On the other side of that war are the police officers, daily risking their own lives to protect the innocent of society. Both are noble groups of people, doing important and necessary work for the survival and freedom of the rest of us.

Stop and think of all those medical professionals who take on the impossible job of never turning away from a human being no matter how badly damaged; of never giving up trying to save a life, even when it is clear there is nothing to be done. Then going home and living with it. Even those citizens out there who volunteer to be trained in first aid and CPR are being like Green Berets, in accepting that these tough situations will come up. When they do, they will not be the ones standing on the sidelines, or gawking at the bloody tangle of wreckage on the side of the road as they drive slowly past, using their own decision to not get trained as a justification not to help.

In Special Forces, the most intellectually difficult of the MOS's – that also required the longest training – was the 18D medic. The medic school is one of the most difficult in our military, and once graduated these men are capable of performing extensive surgery under the most difficult and deadly of conditions; while bullets are flying and the enemy is advancing on them. To prepare these soldiers to function in this environment, they not only have to learn medicine, but learn death. They are forced to inflict all manner of wounds on animals, and then do anything to save them. Once saved, they are made to kill them. Sometimes they are made to kill them with nothing more than a knife. This is not done to be cruel to either the soldiers or the animals, but is necessary for the Green Beret medic to become inoculated psychologically and emotionally against blood, guts, pain and death. To be of any use to their wounded brothers, they have to be able to ignore the pain and pleas, and just function.

These men take this job on, and in doing so become the one person on the Team all others can depend upon to deal with the worst circumstances. Everyone in America can become this same type of person. You all know what the worst jobs are at your company or in your government service. Volunteer to do them. Set a standard for others: let the junior members of your group see that you're not afraid to roll your sleeves up, and lead from the front. As a citizen, don't hesitate to stop and help when someone is in danger, whether you know that person or not. If you have life saving skills, don't sit quietly in your airplane seat while the flight attendants frantically ask for anyone who is medically trained.

Whether you have skills or not, don't drive by an accident that has just occurred. Even if you don't know CPR or first aid – which you should if you're living as a Green Beret - you can put pressure on a bleeding wound, call 911, talk to the victims and keep them calm, still, and alert, until professional help arrives. If nothing else, you can reach in and turn the ignition off before the car catches fire. You can always do something, even if that something is just holding their hand and keeping them company while they die.

A WARRIOR'S LIFE

You do not have to have been in Special Forces to decide to live your life in a special way, and perhaps set a standard for, and be an inspiration to, others. Nor do you have to have been shot, blown up or taken prisoner. You need only look deep into your heart and realize that this is the life that you've been given, and the only real sin is for you not to do as much with it as possible. Once you make this decision, it will show in every action you take, every word that comes out of your mouth, and how you view and interact with others.

Your decision to truly live will resound in the sports and hobbies you choose, and how you approach your participation in them. Whether guns, art or music, you will approach each with complete investment of yourself. It will be obvious to all in the pride you take in doing your job, and the commitment with which you go forward in your career. It will be so resonant in your life, you will wonder how you ever lived differently. Having lived my life as a Green Beret I cannot imagine anything else. I cannot imagine calling your time on earth "living," if you have not lived this way, or started to live this way once you came to understand it.

When you live this way, you will have a dramatic and positive impact on the lives of many others, though in most cases you will never know the inspiration you gave to someone else. When the Ranger School was reconstituted for training early on in Vietnam, the Army didn't want any more elite units. They tried to send as many regular soldiers to it as possible, and then sent them back to their "leg" units. There they were to act as leavening for their entire platoon or company. It was the Army's theory that if you took one man out of a hundred and gave him special training, he would go back to his unit and teach them what he learned, thereby raising the overall level of performance and skill of everyone. This is much the same as the use of Green Berets as force multipliers, by sending them into remote areas with indigenous people, where they will then train many times their number to be soldiers. If you have chosen to live your life as a Green Beret, others will benefit. They will see the advantages of the life you have chosen, and emulate you.

LESSONS LEARNED IN THE SPECIAL FORCES

The uninitiated – the people who do not understand Green Berets – will always wonder just what all those combat and training experiences could have really taught the men of Special Forces. Just what do they know, that others don't? We know that life will throw some difficult, and sometimes terrible, experiences at you. It doesn't make life any less wondrous, it just forces us to learn the lessons we were meant to learn. For each, those lessons are different, thus we each walk a different path. Yet, there are principles of combat that will see everyone through the worst times, and help them make the best of the best times.

Green Berets understand the value of a principle from the Russian Special Forces. When confronting a committed, powerful enemy or threat, "Don't beg, don't trust, don't fear." When life comes at you hard and cruelly, you may feel compelled to crumble and do these things. You just have to discipline yourself not to. Don't ever show weakness to an enemy, whether that enemy be a terrorist on a plane, an enemy soldier in combat, a business competitor, a backstabbing co-worker, or an envious and gossiping neighbor or family member. Never beg; never show those people that they have that amount of control over you. And once you've identified your enemies, never trust them. Remember, people like that don't change. Those who are untrustworthy should never be trusted. You don't have to hate or try to hurt them, simply never allow them to hurt you. Finally, never fear anything in life. Ultimately, we are all ending up the same: dead. Once you've come to grips with that, there is nothing left to be afraid of.

As Green Berets we know that when you identify a threat – and this is particularly true of violent threats to your life and safety – that passive resistance equals death. Do not harbor the illusion that if you do nothing in the face of aggression that everything will be alright. It won't, and you will end up a victim, and sometimes victims die. Sometimes worse.

SAFETY FIRST

If you aren't ensuring your safety in your daily activities, you may not have a life to live. In Special Forces, and many of the arms and security professions, you learn a fundamental rule of daily survival: Always vary your routes going to work, to home, and anywhere else you travel on a regular basis. When running patrols and recon missions, you never return to base along the same route you went out. This is because the enemy will observe how you moved out, and will set up ambushes for your return. Even when at home in the States we always have to be wary of enemy agents, including terrorists looking to identify us and our families, so they can attack us at home. Police officers and their families live with this identical threat, and follow this rule.

Even in the civilian world, this is an important rule of safety. Increasingly, people have enemies. There are stalkers, and women are forever being surveilled by would-be rapists. Not only will this simple practice help keep you safe, but the varying of otherwise daily routines helps the brain engage, provides you with the benefit of increased creativity in problem solving, and allows you to enjoy many of the views and scenery you otherwise become oblivious to if you simply travel down the same ruts at the same times, day after day.

When you do confront a real threat, you will feel your bodily systems coming up. Just as with the instruments on a combat aircraft, you, as the pilot, must go through your check list to make sure your fighting machine – your body – is ready. When you feel fear, recognize that it is a good thing. Do not fear being afraid. Fear is how you, both, know your body has prepared its defenses for maximum effectiveness in a confrontation, as well as telling you the most important thing of all: you are not dead. When you're afraid, it's your body and mind's way of telling you that you are still alive, that you are still in the fight. So long as you are alive, you are not defeated. Not ever!

When you are forced to respond to that threat – especially a physical one – and you feel that overwhelming fear, understand that it is nothing more than adrenaline flowing into your body. That is what gives you superior power and energy. Your body will start to constrict blood flow from the surface areas of your skin. Blood is being channeled into your muscles and organs, where you will need it most to fight. By moving blood from your skin into internal regions, your body is ensuring that if you are wounded there will be little blood loss and you will not die. As Col. Grossman explains, your skin is being turned into a suit of armor.

When confronting a threat, discipline your mind to run through your combat aircraft checklist of your preparedness for the violence that is about to come. This will not only increase your confidence, but allow you to deal objectively with the fear that you are experiencing. Keep in mind that fear is necessary for an appropriate response, both physiologically and tactically; but it can also paralyze.

In the instant you recognize a threat, make the following assessment:

1. *My systems are up – I feel fear;*
2. *I'm in battle position;*
3. *Target is acquired;*
4. *Target is in range; and,*
5. *GO!*

Remember that most social anthropologists and other scientists and educators are wrong: the responses to a threat are not only fight or flight. Those are the two best. The third and most common fear response is paralysis, making your fear responses *fight, flight* or *freeze*. If allowed to proceed unchecked, fear freezes both the mind and the body. The vast majority of animals have a "prey response" hardwired into them. This is the response that allows their systems, including their minds and pain receptors, to shut down. This is what is happening when you see a gazelle being eaten alive by a lion, as it lies there with its eyes glazed over. This is also what allows a human being to have his head cut completely off with a knife, while he lies there, not even struggling; a scene which the American public has only recently come to confront as one of the realities of life outside the safe confines of our country.

This prey response is strong in humans as well. We were never the strongest or fastest animal in the woods. We lacked strong claws and teeth designed for slashing, were poor swimmers and climbers, and possessed skin of low pressure and impact tolerance. Resultantly, we are well designed to be prey for meat-eating predators. Thus, the "prey response" is a reflex that wells up within us when we are confronted by aggressors that we immediately perceive as stronger and more ferocious. At its most basic, its most feral, this is why the human species always needed – and still needs – the ethos of the warrior. For we are not a species suited to unarmed violent conflict with any other animal, with any expectation of survival. Even the bite of a mouse or rabbit to our unprotected skin is extreme. This is also why a 200 lb. man against a 10 lb. monkey is a near-even fight. Using only what nature gave our bodies, we are poorly designed to overcome any animal in a battle. Thus, we are always instinctively ready to submit, and fear is what gives us the ability to first run from a threat, and, second, shut down our systems while we are killed.

These are the responses that must be harnessed, channeling the increased blood pressure to organs, adrenaline to muscles, and reduced pain receptor function, as our bodies prepare for battle. The most effective way to harness our fear responses is through martial arts training. Whether this means karate or Tae Kwon Do classes at the neighborhood dojo, or engaging in any of the combative sports such as wrestling, boxing or judo, conditioning the mind to accept the onslaught of superior aggressors and respond in an appropriate fashion, by harnessing that fear, is the most important aspect of training. Training is crucial to preparing to survive in the world we live in. This is what Green Berets do, and what sees them through the worst combat situations, as well as the worst circumstances of their personal lives.

ON FORTITUDE

There is another fundamental rule of Special Forces that applies to all challenges and endeavors in life: Never Quit. This is such a commonly known article of faith to Green Berets, that it was even part of the tattoo that Mel Gibson displayed in the original *Lethal Weapon* movie, when he was identifying himself and the bad guys as Green Berets. Most people lost in the woods, or in combat, quit when they are 90 percent of the way to victory. People lost in the wilderness will be 90 percent of the way to salvation, when they give up and go back, often dying for that decision. No matter how far you are into a horrible situation or problem in your life, when you start thinking about giving up tell yourself that you are 90 percent of the way to victory, and Charlie Mike – Continue the Mission! Lock it in your head: I may live or I may die, but I will never quit!

That is what got me through Special Forces training and countless battles. It's how everyone survives life and its challenges. Never quit anything that has value in your life; not school, projects, marriage, or business. Many of the men who turned out to be the best Green Berets got recycled through SF training, after failing to complete it the first time. Most of the "overnight" billionaires in the world had two or three failed businesses – and even some bankruptcies – before finally making their ideas work. Many of the nation's best trial lawyers – like Wyoming's famous Jerry Spence – failed the bar exam the first time. This rule is simple: Never quit on anything.

ON RESPONSIBILITY

When confronted with the tough decisions in life, whether to step up and take responsibility or not, never be afraid to do the thing you know is not only right, but necessary. Do not think someone else will do it. If Green Berets decided not to take on the nation's toughest missions would other Army units do it? Likely not. The same is true of the SEALs, Rangers, Air Commandos, PJs and Force Recon Marines: if the nation's elite won't do it, no one will, and people will die. If you confront a crisis, but decide not to shoulder the responsibility of dealing with it, don't expect anyone else to. And people will suffer for your decision.

Years ago, while running operations, we came across a young man from the Air Force who had a horribly shattered leg, a 104 degree fever, and was in extreme pain. His team leader – and even the Air Force medic – were with him. The medic had Keflax and morphine, a powerful drug combination that would have alleviated the excruciating pain he was suffering and helped the injury. There were potential side effects from these drugs, and neither the medic nor the team leader was willing to put his neck out and give the injections. They weren't concerned with this young airman, only their own careers. They were on the radio, attempting to pass the responsibility of the situation onto others, hoping someone else would authorize the medication.

I couldn't stand it, so I said, "I'm the goddamn doctor now, right here on site, and I am ordering you to do it, give him the shot!" Though I didn't outrank them, and was certainly not in their Chain of Command, the automatic weapon I held loosely in their general direction, and glint in my eyes, provided all the persuasion necessary. From that point forward the team leader was ineffectual, emasculated and without respect from anyone else under his command. From then on he was merely a straphanger until he managed to get transferred out of the unit. Don't ever hesitate to step up and be the Green Beret, be the doctor – even if you're not one, as I wasn't – and do the right thing.

ON COMPASSION

Being a warrior is ultimately about showing compassion wherever and whenever you can. No one benefits from gratuitous cruelty to anyone, and it is not a resumé you want to go into the next life with. Remember, what you put out into the universe – into the life force – you will get back. Know that you are a good person, possessed of noble motives, in all that you do. It will pay you back many times over.

In 1978 we were running a training operation in Greece. The men that were under my command were some of the toughest, combat-hardened commandos I ever had the honor of working with. We were prepping to board an aircraft to exfiltrate when two busloads of handicapped people showed up. The few helpers they had were struggling to get these crippled folks out of the bus. Without a word from me, my men – these rough and tough killers – jumped up and started helping them down, assisting them into wheelchairs and restrooms.

It took but minutes for these Green Berets to embrace these people completely, and within a few more minutes these hardcore soldiers were dancing with crippled and legless women, holding them up while they swayed to music coming from a cheap radio. My men were flirting with them, telling them how beautiful they were. In short, they were treating them like women, like people. When our respite with these folks was over, my men quickly boarded our plane and forgot the encounter. To my soldiers there had been nothing unique about how they had behaved. But I, with tears in my eyes over the beauty of what they had done for people less fortunate than they, knew that it had been a great moment for those folks. I knew they would remember it for the rest of their lives, as I have done.

Like the little boy I held all day in the baking desert of Sudan, who had just been freed from a life of horrible slavery, everyone can both feel and demonstrate compassion for our fellow man and woman. To live life completely, you must serve someone else. Green Berets find that in the military; that is why military duty is called being "in the service." We must never stop serving others. It is the highest calling, and the most fulfilling use of our lives. And just being able to say you are a parent or a spouse, and serve your family, isn't enough. That's a cop-out. Admittedly, they are your primary responsibility, and an important one. But you, and they, need to understand the necessity of a higher calling than even that.

This doesn't mean you have to join a religious order, give all of your money to a charity, or donate your worldly possessions to the church. What it means is that you live your life – every single day – ready, willing and able, to take a moment to help someone less fortunate than you. Sooner or later, in one way or another, we will all be that less fortunate person, relying on the kindness of strangers. Do not lose sight of the fact that there are real people out there, with real problems. A lesson we learned from our friend, Bruce Hamon, has always stuck with me: If all you need is money to solve your problems, you don't have any problems. There are many people who have real problems, whose difficulties could not be improved one bit with money. When you encounter them, do what you can. It is better than dwelling on your own money-oriented perception of problems in your own life. This is why John and I spend time and money going to places like Sudan, or provide free bodyguard services to battered women. This is why he has, in the past, handled all of the legal work associated with both suing and having criminal charges filed against abusive men, without accepting a single penny. To us, these efforts were little enough. I am sure, however, that to the people we aided, they were monumental.

You do not always get to do the good things from a position of safety. Sometimes you simply have to be willing to fall on your sword for another. It is always easy to pick a safe and conventional life, to take no risks. The mark of a warrior is to be willing to sacrifice yourself, or at least act, knowing there is a risk. A hero is someone who would give up his life to save another, realizing that no one would ever know the sacrifice he made. The ancient Russian Cossacks had a code that said, in part: "Your life is not yours alone; it belongs to your friends, your family and your community. You can die yourself, but rescue another." It is a certainty that you will suffer for doing the right things in life; but that is what makes doing them so noble. Pay the price, and pay it happily; for the penalty is evidence you are an honorable and courageous person.

ON SACRIFICE

The last, but most important realization that everyone must come to about life, is the rule of sacrifice. Many people do not realize that, not only is all the universe and its life forces in balance, but each and every one of our individual lives is also in complete balance. People want to believe that there is a metaphoric free lunch, that some people get all the breaks, or that they can win the lottery and have a perfect life without having to work for anything. Desiring to be an instant celebrity with what we believe is a perfect life is particularly prevalent in American society. What these folks do not comprehend is that life demands sacrifice, and it will not be denied. We may get to initially decide when we sacrifice, but life decides and ensures that not only will we sacrifice, but to what degree.

Over the years John and I, and all of our friends, colleagues and teammates, who have accomplished anything, have come to recognize this axiom. Just look at each person's life and the choices that got made; then look at the consequences of those choices. When you are young and going through mandatory education, you have the choice of working hard, studying and learning, or blowing your schooling off. Those who make the most of this opportunity – who sacrifice, put the work in, and learn all they can – reap the benefits later in life. They get into college, and may even earn a scholarship. If not going to college, their obvious intellectual development will see them excel at any job they take on, or rise in the ranks in the military, but only if they continue to sacrifice. These early sacrifices will get a foot in the door, and give them the skills to do the job well, but will neither keep that foot in the door, nor see them advance.

For those who do not take advantage of education when they're young, and it is not only free but coming along at the point in their lives when going to school is at its easiest, they will sacrifice later, and often for the rest of their lives. People who enter the work force without a high school diploma will make close to a half million dollars less than those with diplomas. If you enter your working life butchering the English language by habitually using such phrases as: "I ain't got no...," "I seen that," and "I says....," you will always be branded exactly what you are: a barely functioning, and possibly functionally illiterate person. If, in your business writing, you don't know the difference between *there, their* and *they're*, or the differences between *to, too* and *two*, or even the spelling of nouns and adjectives like, *weak* and *week*, you cannot hope for much success in the business world. That lack of success will translate into a lifetime of earning very little money, with neither the ability to give yourself the kind of life you want, nor the ability to give your children opportunities to have more than you had. Sadly, you will brand your kids with the same deficiencies. They will have fewer options throughout their lives; all because you didn't want to sacrifice.

If you make the decision, later in life, to get the education you rejected at first, you can still make sacrifices and achieve your career and life goals. But the sacrifices will be greater. That is another element of the sacrifice formula: you don't just get to make up lost ground if things didn't work out the way you hoped. You always pay a bigger price later on. If you decide to get your GED in your twenties, you have to put a lot of time aside and pay to attend an intensive exam preparation course, while juggling a job and maybe family responsibilities.

After that, you may decide to go on to college. Now you must do it when you have other life responsibilities. You'll likely have to balance night school, a mortgage, a car payment, a spouse and children with both financial and time demands. You didn't want to sacrifice a little when you were young and could have gone to college, so you ended up sacrificing a lot later in life to get to where you wanted to be. Even then, you will continue to sacrifice, as you will always be behind others your age that were willing to make those sacrifices early on.

Just as it is at work in every other aspect of life, the sacrifice rule applies to conducting your own financial affairs. Years ago people lived by the notion of deferred gratification. They worked hard and saved money - i.e., sacrificed - to be able to buy something they wanted; maybe a car, a house, or a refrigerator. Financing didn't exist, and so people handled these aspects of life in the best way possible. Today, the availability of financing anything we want means we think we can have any luxury item we desire, without sacrificing.

Some things have become necessary in life – like having a house or a car – but most people live luxury-ridden lives by financing things they don't need. Expensive clothes, jewelry, luxury cars and Caribbean vacations, boats, motorcycles, ATVs, and even washers and dryers, are all things people do not need, but somehow believe they cannot live without. Having reached that conclusion, they put them on credit cards. Since they have chosen not to sacrifice by working and saving to get these things, they sacrifice all the more in the future by having ridiculously expensive monthly credit card bills at outrageous interest rates. If they don't sacrifice and make sure they keep their payments current, they sacrifice even more by paying three times the original interest rate when the account becomes delinquent.

Just going to college, however, isn't necessarily a sufficient sacrifice. Some people manage to get through college without sacrificing, by letting their parents pay for everything. They cruise through their classes, doing the minimum amount of work, taking the easiest and most useless degree programs, never working to contribute to their own lives or educations - or futures - and then find themselves lost and adrift in adult life after they graduate. Suddenly, they're expected to work, but they've never done that before. In these instances, both parents and kids were unwilling to sacrifice, and both paid a bigger price in the years to come. If on a football scholarship to a top school, a young man refuses to take advantage of the opportunity and get an education, he will make a bigger sacrifice later. In some instances we have seen promising college superstars sustain career-ending injuries, and never get to play pro ball. Or maybe they couldn't make the cut in the pros. Even if successful in the NFL, NHL or major leagues, young professional players suffer a lack of education, business acumen, and maturity, which sees them blowing all of their money on fast lives and stupid investments.

Even with long and successful careers, most players are still retired by their mid-thirties, leaving them a lifetime of business investments and opportunities, which they will not likely be able to manage due to their own refusal to learn some basic business survival skills while in college. If they can't do those things for themselves, they'll end up paying a fortune to a staff of professional advisors - lawyers, CPAs, investment bankers and the like - none of whom they should ever completely trust. In SF, if you didn't learn the survival skills you were being taught in the Q Course, the penalty you paid later on was your own life, or the lives of those around you. You didn't just get to hire someone else to come help you live while being shot at.

No one gets through life without sacrificing, and if you give it some thought, you will quickly realize that no one gets through life without a substantial amount of sacrifice. Even lottery winners sacrifice. A majority of people buy lottery tickets because they never sacrificed to get an education and work hard at a career. When they win the lottery they have no business foundation to bring to bear in the administration of their own money. They stupidly quit their jobs, - another sacrifice abandoned - pay outrageous amounts in taxes, buy hugely expensive luxury items, go on round-the-world trips, and then suddenly are without any money. Many file bankruptcy within a few years.

But this isn't only true with finances, education and careers. In raising children, the same incontrovertible rule of sacrifice applies. If you refuse to do the tough thing as a parent and discipline your children, you will end up later with undisciplined children and young adults, causing problems you will not be able to ignore. If you do not impart a work ethic in your kids, they will grow up refusing to work and expecting you to continue to support them. Being a good parent means often doing the most difficult and unpleasant things; it means doing things that sometimes make your children hate you.

This rule trickles down to every tiny aspect of your life. If you refuse to take the time, and make the effort, to know where your spare tire is – and how to change a tire – you will eventually pay a bigger price some dark night. If you fail to ensure that spare tire has air, the price may be greater still. If you refuse to get up on time, you will forever be racing about, risking speeding tickets and car accidents that could injure or kill someone. At the very least you will eventually suffer for always being late to work. If you have a couple of weeds in your lawn, but won't make the effort to dig them up, you will eventually end up with a yard full of weeds, and a bigger and more expensive problem on your hands. We all have people who are little more than weeds pop up in our lives, from time to time. If we aren't willing to do the tough thing, and eliminate those weeds right away, they will eventually make you suffer for having done the easy thing.

The same is true in the Green Berets. We – and our brothers in the SEALs, Rangers, Force Recon, Air Commandos, and others – sacrifice much more than anyone else in the regular military. We suffer mightily in selection and training. We continue to work tirelessly to always improve, to be better at our jobs. We "eat snakes," jump out of airplanes at ridiculous heights, live in the mud and filth outside, suffer in the deserts, swim the oceans, live on nothing, and go for days without sleep. Yet all this sacrifice gives us the capability to not only survive, but prevail in the very combat that sees those who sacrificed less than us die.

Taking this very example of sacrifice to its logical conclusion, I ask the question: if someone went into horrible combat conditions with no training, - who refused to sacrifice by training - how would he fare? Someone who sacrificed more than that sad and ill-prepared soldier would do better in combat, or at least have a much better chance of surviving. Thus, those who sacrifice mightily, driving themselves through almost inhuman preparation for combat, will overcome all that combat can throw at them. Despite all this, members of the regular Army, and even the citizenry, tell us that we are just lucky to get to be Green Berets. They don't know the level of sacrifice that goes into earning the right to wear such a symbol. The Russian Spetsnaz understand this all too well. Their training is so grueling, so terribly dangerous and almost impossible to survive, that they believe one Spetsnaz commando is the equivalent of one hundred of the enemy. They sacrifice so much in preparing themselves for combat that they believe 100 to 1 odds are an even fight. That is sacrifice.

The relationships between sacrifice and benefit, and of non sacrifice and penalty, are infinite. Yet one does not have to comprehend all of the inter-connectivity of life; he merely needs to clearly see the one law of life that draws it all together: Life is a process of constant sacrifice and benefit. At each phase of your life, you get to choose whether to sacrifice early on. For each sacrifice you reject, you will sacrifice more later on.

THE SPECIAL FORCES CREED

I am an American Special Forces Soldier. A professional!
I will do all that my nation requires of me.
I am a volunteer, knowing well the hazards of my profession.
I serve with the memory of those who have gone before me:
Roger's Rangers, Francis Marion, Mosby's Rangers,
the first Special Service Forces and Ranger Battalions of World War II,
the Airborne Ranger Companies of Korea.
I pledge to uphold the honor and integrity of all I am – in all I do.
I am a professional soldier.
I will teach and fight wherever my nation requires.
I will strive always to excel in every art and artifice of war.
I know that I will be called upon to perform tasks in isolation, far from
familiar faces and voices, with the help and guidance of my God.
I will keep my mind and body clean, alert and strong, for this is my debt to
those who depend on me.
I will not fail those with whom I serve.
I will not bring shame upon myself or the forces.
I will maintain myself, my arms, and my equipment in an immaculate
state as befits a Special Forces Soldier.
I will never surrender though I be the last.
If I am taken, I pray that I may have the strength to spit upon my enemy.
My goal is to succeed in any mission and live to succeed again.
I am a member of my nation's chosen soldiery.
God grant that I may not be found wanting, that I will not fail
this sacred trust.

– PART 4 –
GREEN BERET RULES FOR EVERYDAY LIFE

BlueSky Thai-American Special Forces Combined Training
and Operations Unit, HALO instruction Team, 1984.
Master Sergeant John Anderson is standing in back, far right.
In front of him, kneeling is Staff Sergeant Mitch Conway.
Kneeling, front row, second from left, is Sergeant First Class
Ronnie McCann. Being able to work with people from
other nations is a critical component of the Special Forces
skill set.

– 11 –

RULES OF SPECIAL OPERATIONS

For those who have fought for it,
life has a special flavor the protected shall never taste.
You have never lived, until you have almost died.

Special Operations Association motto

Special Operations and Special Forces developed a series of rules for life, combat preparation, survival and existence within the Special Operations community, that not only has tremendous benefit for those in that life, but for anyone trying to live the best life that he can. The Rules of Special Operations are below, with explanations on their application to the lives of everyone who chooses to live the Green Beret Lifestyle.

1. Humans are more important than hardware.

In Special Operations, this rule articulates the reality that not only is human life precious, but the life of a qualified and experienced Special Operator is far more valuable than any piece of military machinery. The military spends millions of dollars producing an elite soldier, one who can perform beyond the expectations of most mortal men. While that dollar value alone is significant, it pales in comparison to the financial value of what such soldiers can accomplish, and the incredible profit or savings that the United States benefits from as a result of his accomplishments. For this reason, in Special Forces we would never sacrifice any single man for a tank, a plane, or even a billion dollar ship. You can build more hardware, but you can't replace the person. If the best soldiers saw that the government was willing to sacrifice their lives based on some actuarial formula vis-à-vis the depreciation schedule of a tank or plane, there would, simply, cease to be Special Forces. And that, the nation could not afford.

In regular, everyday life, this rule is all the more important. Nothing is more important than the people in your life. Each one of those lives is more important than your cars, house, boat, motorcycle, and all of the other inanimate objects you might think you love. Family and friends are the single most important thing you will ever have, and none of them can ever be replaced. If your wife survived a car accident, get down on your knees and thank God that she came out alive. To hell with the car: you have insurance. Even if you don't, its value pales in comparison to that of the person who loves you enough that she married you, and has stayed married to you.

The same is true of your teenagers. They may have been driving recklessly, and you will have to address that issue. But it should only be addressed to ensure their safety and that it doesn't happen again. Just be happy they came out of it alright. If they were at fault, make them pay for it, but never forget that a car is only four tires, some seats and an engine with a steering wheel to move you about while you sit on your butt. No human being can be reduced to such terms. This is true of all of your possessions. None are more important than family and friends.

2. Quality is more important than quantity.

In this case, the term "quantity" includes both numbers and size. In the military, it is always better to have a few - even if too few - guns, bullets, armored vests, Humvees, helicopters, and grenades that work the way they're supposed to, than many times that number in combat equipment that doesn't function. At the beginning of World War II, the Navy learned the hard way that during the lull since the previous war, it had allowed pork barrel politics to reduce quality to such a degree that almost 50 percent of its torpedoes didn't work.

The military has seen this time and again: bullets that are duds, guns that don't function, radios with no range, body armor that gets penetrated. The list is endless. Just as important is the quality of people. This coincides with Rule Number 3, below, but never lose sight of the fact that when the bullets are flying a few high quality soldiers are much more important than ten times that number in mediocre performers.

In civilian life, this is no different. No one needs huge collections of expensive toys, when one good quality item would suffice, allowing you to spend that extra money on the things and people that should be important to you. As the saying goes, "How many boats can someone ski behind?" The same is true of the accoutrements of success, like clothes, shoes and jewelry. It is much better, for instance, to have a small diamond of good quality, than a large rock of poor quality and bad color, just so someone can show off its size.

This rule applies equally to people in our lives. It is far better to have a few good, true friends, than a large number of people of far less quality, and far less value to our lives. People we could never trust or who would never sacrifice for us, are of no value, even if they are famous or rich. Men need to learn this lesson about women, as well. No one who juggles a lot of women is ever happy. Whether you want to get married or not, spend your time with someone of quality. It will be time far better spent.

3. Special Operations Forces can't be mass produced.

Today, the demands on America's military in the various fronts the War on Terror is forcing us to fight, are enormous. This is, perhaps, the first war that is being fought with Special Forces and Special

Operations Forces taking the foremost role. In short, it is a Special Forces' or unconventional war. The solution for many politicians has been to allocate a lot of money to greatly increase the number of Special Operations soldiers, sailors, airmen and marines. They fail to realize that you cannot mass produce anything of value, especially elite soldiers. In this regard, they can apply a lesson learned by governments with regard to inflation and valuation of currency. If our government needs money, and decides to meet that need by simply producing more, the only result is the complete devaluation of the dollar and gross inflation.

The same is true of our military's best. Prior to America's War on Terror, none of the Special Operations units were able to maintain their teams at full complement. The young men of today's generation were not willing to make the sacrifices necessary to make the cut, to endure selection and join elite units. Then along came a war, and all of the politicians believed that we could just "add more" people to the Teams. John Kerry, in his campaign for the presidency prior to the 2004 election, said that when he became president he would triple the size of Special Operations Forces. That was idiotic.

If America couldn't find enough young men willing to undergo the training necessary to earn the right to fill all of the then-available slots on Teams, what would it take to increase that number by three? The answer is always the same: lower the standards. Just as with currency being overproduced, the only by-product of lowering standards just to say you have more Green Berets, is that you end up with people who have no business wearing that beret, or taking on the nation's toughest assignments. In short, you have just "de-valued" those soldiers, and endangered the lives of the true professionals.

The same is found in the civilian sector. We are lowering quality in everything, and then lamenting the fact that the product we're generating isn't as good as it used to be. In some instances, this loss of quality is critical. In high schools and universities, grade inflation is rampant. When John graduated from Penn State in 1981, out of a class of 10,000 students there was only one with a 4.0 GPA. Today, every school has hundreds, and with some, thousands, with perfect grade point averages.

Twenty years ago, a 3.10 GPA would guarantee admission into a law school somewhere. Today, if you have even a 3.75 GPA, the chances of you getting into law or medical school are not great. Is this because, today, there are so many young students whose performance is perfect? No, of course not. Professors complain that they can barely find an undergraduate student that can spell or form a grammatical sentence, yet they are pressured into giving A's for mediocre performance. In America, we are finding the same problem in every sector of society. From FBI and local police departments, to accountants, lawyers, doctors, carpenters, architects and engineers. There is hardly a profession that isn't suffering the violation of this rule. People have lost sight of the fact that you can't mass produce top quality people. If you are mass producing more and more people, you are only producing one thing: poor quality people. As a society we will suffer, and continue to suffer, for this failure.

4. Competent Special Operations Forces can't be created after an emergency occurs.

If you wait until after you need something desperately, before you start thinking about acquiring it, you are going to have a very difficult time dealing with that emergency. The greater the training, the more skills needed, and higher the quality of people you require to deal with the crisis, the longer it takes to produce them. Sometimes, you just can't produce them fast enough. Consider it from this example: if you don't take the time or trouble to teach your family to learn to swim, and suddenly one of you falls in the river and is drowning, can you learn to swim in time to save your loved one? This is the position America often puts itself in with regard to its Special Operations Forces. As soon as the last war is over, their budgets are slashed, their men released from service, and they run at 50 percent strength. Until they are needed again! Then it's too late.

The direct application of this rule to any critical aspect of civilian society is obvious: You can't create anyone of any competence or give people important skills in life, after the need arises. If you wait until they're needed to think about creating them, you waited too long. This is true of many things. If you are waiting (why, I don't know) to put fire extinguishers in your house, then you're a fool. If you're waiting for it to be convenient to buy a gun and learn to shoot so you can keep your family safe, then you should just go borrow a gun and shoot yourself with it. If you wait until the moment you need it, it's too late.

Are you waiting to put an emergency plan together for your family? Are you waiting before getting your wife and daughter sex-assault defense training? Are they only willing to take that important course if it doesn't interfere with their shopping and are you letting them get away with that? Are you waiting until your wife is stranded on the side of a dark road before changing the oil, tuning up the car, checking the tires, or making sure the spare has air, or get her Triple A insurance? Life is full of opportunities to do things, now, that may save us and the ones we love, later.

5. The team is MUCH more important than the individual.

This is one of the most important rules for all of us to live by. Never forget that your friends and family are the most important people in your life. Your colleagues and co-workers are the most important people you will ever have in your professional life. In both cases, if you take care of them and place them above you, you will succeed. If they are doing the same with regard to you, you will all succeed.

6. History always repeats itself.

This is an old saying, and certainly an axiom with regard to geopolitical affairs If people do not learn the lessons of history, that history will be repeated. Sadly, it seems the human race insists on learning and relearning lessons. However, with regard to both Special Forces and everyone's personal lives, it has a consistent and meaningful resonance. Special Forces has a long history of being called upon to do the most difficult things. After proving their worth – and the worth of the money the government spends on them – they are asked to do ever more things, take on ever more difficult operations. But then, when the war is over and the sacrifices and risks are no longer necessary, the politically-minded stand them down.

After each war – after Special Forces has sacrificed so many, and saved so many others – they are reduced in numbers until their units are mere skeletons of their former combat selves. Training budgets are eliminated. Their equipment allocation is returned to being the throwaways of the conventional military; the military that refused to take on any of their operations, calling them suicide missions. They are forced to limp along, doing the best they can. That is, until America goes to war again, and the Green Berets are once again called upon to do the things no one else wants to do. This is something America's best has learned to live with, and survive, in spite of the impossibility of the circumstances imposed on them. Just like combat.

For the rest of America, this rule is no less valid. It is a rule that all people can recognize in their own lives, in their own families, and either come to some level of acceptance of reality, or learn what is necessary to change history, lest it repeat itself again. When it comes to individuals, it is important to realize that, by and large, people are who they are, and, after about age eighteen they do not change. Their personal history will keep repeating itself. Lazy people will always be lazy, and hard working people will always push themselves. Those who feel sorry for themselves will wallow in a quagmire of self-pity their entire lives, no matter how good their circumstances.

If a man beats his wife, he will continue to do so. All she can do is recognize that history does repeat itself, and create a new future for herself. Addicts are addicts, and will always be. Do you think hypochondriacs ever stop inventing illnesses and ailments, just to get attention? It's interesting, how people are always so ready to believe others will suddenly overcome the worst of their characteristics, but would never consider that those with good qualities would ever stop behaving well.

The only exception to this rule – both with people and nations – is an epiphany to be reached, and for a tremendous effort to be made to completely correct something that they realize is a horrible characteristic. America once enslaved Negroes, people it had brought over from Africa and elsewhere. To overcome that behavior took a war and hundreds of thousands of lives. For more than 100 years after that tremendous effort America still discriminated against those same people, and it took the turbulent period of the 1960s and '70s, along with federal legislation and the virtual invasion of federal troops on American soil, to right that wrong.

If you are an addict, it takes the realization of that addiction and a commitment to counseling, but most of all a personal conviction, to change that behavior; though the addiction itself will never go away. The same is true for bullies, wife beaters, child molesters, compulsive gamblers, and, today, both television and technology junkies. If you aren't ready, willing and able to admit your flaws, acknowledge your addiction, get help and demand of yourself that you cease such unacceptable behavior, you will forever live a life defined by the worst aspects of your character. Alcoholics Anonymous has an axiom that says the definition of madness is making the same decision over and over, but expecting different results. If this is how you are living, you are allowing the worst of your personal history to continue to repeat itself.

7. You don't fight other SF guys.

Whatever branch of the military you're in, you will always be in competition with all of the other units in that branch. Mostly, this competition is positive, and keeps every soldier in every unit striving to be the best. No one wants to admit that another MOS, brigade, regiment, battalion, company or platoon is better, and they all strive to keep that from happening. When you're in "Special" Forces, you *are* special, but more importantly, you are expected to *be special.* A rule of military Darwinism is that you never violate your duty to those in your own unit. They are your brothers – or your sisters – and you never do anything to breach the trust, commitment and loyalty that goes along with that membership. When you are in an elite unit, it is all the more true. You are truly a band of brothers, and you fall together to fight all others, for anyone outside of your unit, your Team, or your family, may be the enemy.

The same is true among non-military citizens. Be more loyal to your Professional Team than others in the company you work for. But be loyal to all your co-workers relative to others outside your organization. Be loyal to your employer. Remember, when you ride, you ride for the brand. Never take things outside of your company to a competitor, or to the news media, just because you didn't get your way about something. The company and its mission must always come first. In your personal life, your friends and family are your Special Forces Team. Never take things outside of the family or marriage just because you don't think something is fair, or it fails to meet your expectations. Be loyal to those on your Life Team. The people you have put in intimate positions in your life are special, and they should be treated that way.

8. You don't steal SF women.

Though in SF Rule Number 7, above, is one that may be violated on occasion, this rule is one that can never be abrogated, under any circumstances. Any true warrior can overlook a small fight with a brother. John and I, and others on our teams over the years, have certainly had our share of spats. But they were just that, minor altercations that we would never allow to destroy a friendship, even if it did end up in a fistfight.

　　　　But the one act that can never be forgiven is to place your sexual desires above your duty to another warrior, to another member of your Team. This is inexcusable. In the military, violation of this duty would mean a court martial for conduct unbecoming an officer or NCO. It could mean prison time, and a dishonorable discharge from the military. In Special Forces no such charges were ever brought. In Special Forces, violation of this duty – the law of the pack – meant that you did not survive your transgression. Though I would never condone or advocate such extreme measures, I do believe all of American society could benefit from the same devotion to honorable behavior. No friend in your life should ever have a reason to worry about what might happen if you and his wife were left alone together.

9. You don't lie to the Sergeant Major.

In Special Operations units the sergeant major (or master chief in the Navy) is the single most important person in the unit. He is the top ranking NCO, which means he is everyone's immediate, most superior ranking officer, every hour of every day. The buck stops at the Sergeant Major. Whatever goes wrong in the unit is his responsibility. Whatever goes right, he passes on to the troops and the NCOs under him. He is every man's commander, leader, friend, advisor, father and confessor. He is the person who can – and usually does – put himself out on a limb to protect his men. For that reason, he is never to be lied to. He is the one person you owe an absolute duty of loyalty and honesty to. If you tell him the truth, he will protect you from those even above him in rank. If you lie to him, he still won't betray you to those other, higher ranking types. But by the time he is done with you, you might wish he had.

　　　　In civilian life, the same duty of absolute honesty must be given to a number of people. As a small child, the sergeant major in your life is usually your mother. She does everything for you. She loves you, but is also the person immediately responsible for ensuring you perform and meet your day-to-day obligations, both at school and home. She comes to your aid, but will also make sure you toe the line. And, if anyone is going to protect you to some degree from your father, it's your mother.

But you have other sergeants major and "mothers" in your life. You may have a boss at work that does the same for you. If so, you owe him the same duty of absolute loyalty and honesty, and maximum performance that a Green Beret owes his sergeant major. For many athletes, this same person can be found in their coaches. John and I have both had many men from whom we derived much about life, manhood and sports. Not that as kids we always met our duties under this rule, but we learned the shame that rightfully came with us violating them; a lesson that stood us well as we worked our way through similar relationships in our adult lives. Everyone should find at least one person who he would never want to be ashamed of anything he did. Having found these people, live your life to make them proud. John and I both had a large number of relatives, coaches and adult role models we felt that way about. I feel sorry for anyone who never took the time to find – or never earned having - such people in his life.

10. If you ain't cheating, you ain't trying.

This is an important rule to the Special Forces, but it is a rule of limited application in life. This is a rule designed exclusively for survival; for instance, for survival in combat, complete self defense, or in fighting to ensure the survival of your wife and family. Only in these circumstances are you permitted, legally and morally, to do whatever it takes. And you must have the discipline to know when those circumstances arise and the strength to both employ those extreme survival skills when warranted, and the strength to deny them to yourself, no matter how tempting that may be in lesser circumstances.

Young SF candidates first encounter this doctrine in the Q Course, as it is intentionally set up to be impossible to successfully negotiate if they do everything they are told, exactly as they are told to do it. SF doesn't want rules-following pedants, it wants creative thinkers, imaginative tacticians; men who improvise, adapt and overcome otherwise impossible circumstances. But, the complete rule is: If you ain't cheating, you ain't trying, but never get caught cheating! The lesson from the Q Course is that you may have to do whatever it takes to succeed, but the price for getting caught is extreme. Just as in combat, and life. The reasoning is that, if you're not good enough to cheat when absolutely necessary and get away with it in training, how can you be relied on to do whatever is necessary to survive combat, or accomplish a delicate mission for your country? But in all instances the penalty for cheating is so great that it should only be done when absolutely necessary.

Thus, Rule No. 10 is actually a rule of limits. Green Berets, for all their great qualities, must live in a realistic world. For them, that reality is deadly. They acknowledge that there are times when rules must be broken, orders ignored, policies viewed merely as guidelines, and protocols circumvented. They make these decisions when necessity demands it, and when they are in the moral right. For instance, if someone is dying and they have to drive 110 mph, or drive drunk, to get them to a hospital they will do so unhesitatingly. They will try to do it in a manner that doesn't get them caught – and doesn't endanger other lives – but they will do it just the same. After all, if they are stopped by the police or cause an accident, they have already failed in the primary mission.

If an SF wife is suffering a stalker and that person has proven himself to be a likely rapist or other physical threat but her husband is in Iraq, his friends may not follow the rules of a passive society. Knowing that they cannot wait and hope to be there in the one moment this predator chooses to strike, they will go on the offensive: they will go hunting for him. "Rough justice" is a concept they are well familiar with, and will only implement when it is both necessary and morally justified. If they get caught, so be it. They will have made the sacrifice happily, and in terms of tactics will have still eliminated the threat. For these men it is far better to pay a price in terms of their own lives or freedom, than have to explain to a friend how his wife was raped or killed because they did nothing. This is a model of duty and responsibility all men can learn from.

Thus, Rule 10 is not a rule that allows you to cheat on your wife, or cheat at school, or lie to your boss, clients or patients. It is arule for survival first and foremost, and one that should, in most instances, only ever be implemented for the safety and protection of others.

Secret Agent Man. *Master Sergeant John Anderson*
performing shooting demo while training Thailand C.I.A.
operatives, 1985.

SPECIAL FORCES CODE

De Oppresso Liber
"To Free the Oppressed"

Official motto of the U.S. Army Special Forces

The Code of the Green Beret is so voluminous, steeped in history and exhaustive, addressing every possible aspect of Special Forces service, that to attempt to recite it *in toto* would result in another book. However, the basic rules by which all Green Berets live form a short list that is applicable to marriage, family, work and friendship. It acts as a reminder of how best to live an honorable and noble life, every day you are alive.

I. Commit yourself totally to your Team and care more about them than you do yourself, and they will do the same.

II. Be unconventional, creative and imaginative in devising ways to complete your mission.

III. Never lie to a member of your Team or your superiors.

IV. Never steal from anyone in Special Forces.

V. Never bring dishonor on your Team, your Group or the Special Forces.

VI. Do your best to be your best.

VII. Never stop training.

VIII. Never complain.

IX. Never take anything outside the Team.

X. Never violate the trust your Team puts in you – be certain to complete all tasks so that they may rely on you without doubt or confirmation.

Archangel Group training today's Green Berets for combat in Iraq and Afghanistan, 2006. Standing from left to right is, Randy Pratt, Special Forces Sergeant First Class Jesse Campbell, John Anderson, John Giduck, and Walter Chi. Note the low, inverted prone handgun shooting position of the Green Beret in the foreground. Special Forces train to be combat effective in all mediums of battle and all situations.

CONCLUSION

We Kill For Peace

Vietnam era Special Forces Recon Motto

The men of the Special Forces are, indeed, special. Just as the men of such other elite units as the Rangers, SEALs, Force Recon Marines, Air Commandos and PJs, and others, are special. What makes them so unique and rare, is not that they were born with some genetic predisposition for greatness, but that they were – and remain – just average, everyday American citizens who made the conscious decision to be the best. These are men who chose to live a life of dedication, discipline and complete investment in all that they undertook. They have committed themselves to living with honor, and a code of nobility in both their professional and personal lives. This is what makes them so very special. This is what makes the men of the Special Forces icons, setting a standard by which all Americans can benefit by following.

But such people are not found exclusively in the U.S. Army Special Forces, and other crack units of Special Operations Command. They can be, and are, found in every walk of life. One does not have to have survived the daunting Q Course or wear a green beret to work to live as the Green Berets live. You simply have to have decided to be honest, hard working, and committed to your family, friends, sports and career. In living with that commitment, you cannot help but be committed to your own life as well. For what are you worth to others, if you are not worth something to yourself first? This is what the Q Course is all about: to first ensure that the men who join the unit of "America's best" are worth something to themselves. The Army recognizes that if you can't trust yourself, stand alone and push yourself to your absolute limits, you will never do it for others, and living to serve others is the ultimate calling of us all.

Anyone can choose to be such a person. Many have already made that choice and are living their lives in such a fashion. But, you cannot do it by shirking duties at work, lying to your boss, friends and spouse. If you are not showing up at work giving your very best for your employer, you are far from being a Green Beret. Just as your employer should be devoting himself to, both, the employees and stockholders of the company. For far too many years, America has watched self-serving corporate managers take ten million dollar bonuses for their running of companies that lost hundreds of millions of dollars that year. These people are not Green Berets. Lee Iacocca set an example for all businessmen when, in the 1970s, he took over a failing auto manufacturer that was losing incomprehensible amounts of money. On the verge of having to shut down and layoff thousands of workers, leaving entire towns of people destitute, he refused to even take a salary unless – and until – he was able to turn the company around and return it to profitability. Lee Iacocca was leading, running his company and living, as a Green Beret.

Anyone can live this way. It merely takes the decision to change your life, right now... this minute. Then developing the discipline to stick to that decision, to not make excuses when you fail. That is the one thing Green Berets never do. Living with honesty and integrity may see you making a little less money, or not profiting from opportunities that a code of honor would never allow. But you will be repaid many times over for each sacrifice that you make for the good of others. The Green Berets believe this; otherwise, there would be no reason for those men to almost kill themselves in training, to get to join a unit that will always draw the most dangerous missions.

It is a sad commentary on our society that we seem to find fewer and fewer people willing to live this way. This is such a problem that I am often asked whether the young men of the Special Forces today are anywhere near as good as the Green Berets of years past. Though I retired some years ago, I have the honor of continuing to train our young elite soldiers. Though they may have grown up with technology that didn't exist when I was young, and are used to email, Internet, text messaging, IPods, video games, virtual reality and Blackberrys, they are as good as any men America has ever produced.

The men of Special Forces today are strong, fit, tough and hardworking. They are honest to, and respectful of, anyone they meet. They have been through far more training than my generation of Green Berets, all crammed into too short a period of time. They are made to apply all those combat skills in dangerous environments, and at an operational tempo that the Teams of my day never experienced; and they keep volunteering to go back and do this job, over and over. Despite this, they are probably more humble than any group of elite soldiers the world has ever seen. They have truly earned the name the Quiet Professionals.

Yes, I can honestly say that the nation is in good hands. I am fortified by the fact that, although we may not be generating as many of the nation's best as we should – and certainly not as many as we need - that those we are producing are as good as, if not better than, the best we managed to field at any time in our past, and in any war we have ever fought. These soldiers continue to set an example by which all of America can not only take pride, but benefit by emulating.

Special Forces chronicler Robin Moore found himself running around Afghanistan in 2001 and 2002 with SF Teams. Though then in his 70s, he was still traveling into places others would not go, with his beloved Green Berets. When asked much the same question, whether the young men of Special Forces today could possibly be on a par with those from the Vietnam era who had set the original standard for elite soldiers, he had this to say: "I had traveled from Green Beret base camp to base camp, living with the men, sharing the fight, the honor, glory, and sorrow. ... I found that the uniform had changed from tiger-striped fatigues, and that the fight was in high deserts and mountains instead of jungles and mangrove swamps, yet the men were the same great chaps as their fathers. American soldiers had remained American soldiers, and those of the Greatest Generation would be proud."

No greater words could be spoken for our elite soldiers. No greater words could ever be spoken about any of America's citizens. I commend to everyone to live your life so that someday someone can write about you, that you were as good as the Greatest Generation America ever produced. For that is the legacy of all Americans.

Today, America is a nation at war. That is not political rhetoric, for we are engaged in a war unlike any we have ever seen. It is a war that will go on far longer than any throughout our history, and some of the battles in that war will be fought on American soil, in the midst of our cities, homes and loved ones. It is not a war that we can ignore by simply bringing our servicemen and women home from distant lands. Our enemy declared war on us decades ago, and we have only recently come to that realization. For now that enemy is satisfied to battle us thousands of miles from our homes, and our men and women – living and serving as Green Berets no matter their service or unit – are fighting and sacrificing mightily. But this will not continue.

Within the lifetimes of every man and woman in America our enemy will find us here, yet again. When that happens, we will be forced to abandon the luxury in which we have existed for so long. When that happens America will need every one of her citizens to be prepared to serve her, to defend and protect our way of life. For this war shall not be fought merely by those who have already heeded the call, who daily shrug weary shoulders through the straining straps of an overloaded rucksack and pick up an assault rifle. For we are all living the American dream, and it is every one of us the enemy is intent on destroying. We are all, quite literally, in a fight for our lives, and for the existence of our nation and our culture. In the years to come America will need every one of her citizens to be the best they can be. She will need them to be honest, disciplined, hardworking and ready to serve something greater than they are alone. She will need her people to be ready to both stand alone, and with others, against daunting odds and a committed enemy. She will need all Americans to be Green Berets.

ACKNOWLEDGEMENTS
— BY —
JOHN GIDUCK

There are always a great number of people any writer wants to thank for their contributions to not only a new book, but for so much help, assistance, advice and influence they have given in other areas. Many of the benefits we have enjoyed from others in our lives have ended up in our words in this book, but it is always impossible to list every single person who was of such importance to us. We can only hope that you all realize who you are, and know that both Andy and I are grateful for all you have done for us.

Andy would first like to thank his wife, **Jody**, who is mentioned on a number of occasions in this book. In all honesty, she should have been mentioned far more than she even was, as she has always been of paramount importance to his ability to live an entire lifetime as a Green Beret. Andy would also like to thank the following Special Forces soldiers, each of whom was of tremendous influence to him either as a young Green Beret, or as he worked his way through his career: Col. **Bo Baker**; Master Sergeant **Joe Alderman**, a true legend in his own time, was the single greatest motivator in his career; Sergeant Major **Jake Jakovenko**, who explained to Andy what soldiers were; Sergeant Major **Richmond Nail**, who with only one eye, one lung and one kidney was the best trainer ever; Sergeant First Class **Gilbert Woods** and Staff Sergeant **Mike Burleson**, who together taught him how to stay alive; Captain **John Bartlett**; Congressional Medal of Honor recipient Major **Drew Dix**; Sergeant Major **Eddie Gleason**; Command Sergeant Major **Ronnie "Beaver" McCann**; and Sergeant First Class **Paul Michaud**. He would like to give special thanks to every Team sergeant he ever had, as well as all of those truly professional officers and NCOs in SF who led him, including Major **Moore** and Colonel **Plummer,** for they were the ones who created and carried forward the Code of the Green Beret.

As for me, I remain ever grateful to all of the members of my family, men and women alike, who taught me so many of the principles presented in this book. To all those sports coaches who took the time to try and turn me into an athlete in my youth, I give you special thanks; the lessons you taught have served me well throughout my life. Later, in my weightlifting career I received the tremendous benefit of such Olympic, world and national champions as **Lee James;** my dear friends and American record holders **Bob Ross** and **Pete Cline;** the late **Dr. Dave Martin,** an Olympic team member; Olympic medalist, the late **Guy Carlton;** and my good friend, national champion **John Schiechl.** I would like to thank my years-long friend, business partner, teammate and advisor, **John "Andy" Anderson,** without whom my ideas for this book could never have become reality. As well, I have had the benefit of having a friend since I was five years old - more than 40 years – and am grateful for the friendship, loyalty and decency that **Larry Pascale** has always shown me. Daily I am blessed with the help and friendship of **Melissa Yerxa,** without whom I likely couldn't function professionally at all.

I am ever proud of my affiliation with the Special Operations Association, and thank all of the men who have opened their arms to me. Special thanks to all of the officers and directors of the SOA, but especially to former Green Berets and special operators **Clyde Sincere; James Hetrick; Earl "Curly" Trabue; John "Tilt" Meyer; Jake Jacobson; Clete "Babysan" Sinyard; Rick Grabianowski; Charles Berg;** and **Ty Furbish.** Many of these men are famous Green Berets and depicted in many books on the Vietnam War. Thank you to **Patrick Hephner** and **Dan Junevicus.** I would like to extend special thanks for all of the assistance and education given me by Delta plankowner and Command Sergeant Major **Mel Wick,** and Delta Command Sergeant Major **Luke Ver Heul,** as well as SEAL Team Six and Red Cell plankowner **John Mason.**

Together, Andy and I would like to thank Special Forces Command Sergeant Major **Charles "Mitch" Conway**; Master Sergeant **Tom Flaherty**; Master Sergeant **Kevin "OC" O'Connor**; and Master Sergeant **Jesse Campbell**, who was the model for the Green Beret described in the opening paragraphs of the Introduction to this book. Andy and I are both grateful to Command Sergeant Major **Mel Wick** for being willing to lend his own words and experiences by writing the Foreword, and for gifting so much credibility to us in attempting to do justice to this topic. Always special thanks go to Ranger Lt. Col. (ret.) **Dave Grossman**, who continues to be an inspiration to warriors throughout America. Thanks to bestselling author **Brad Thor** for your support and your service to America.

Finally, Andy and I would like to thank all of those people who devoted many hours editing our original manuscript, trying to help us turn more than 400 pages of errant ideas and poorly articulated thoughts into readable text with a message of some value. If this book failed to meet that goal, it is solely the fault of the authors and not any of the people who worked so hard to help us. Thank you to **Walter** and **Rena Chi**; **Joseph** and **Dr. Jean Bail**; our good friend and teammate from faraway wars, and another lawyer who found a better life outside of the courtroom, **Michael S. Rich**; former Marine sniper and current SWAT operator **Chris "Hollywood" Hays**; **Rick** and **Madge Parks**, two civilians who live their lives as Green Berets every day; Archangel president, CPA and our great friend **Shawn Gregory**; the lovely **Lisa Tongren**; **Jody Anderson**; **Dr. Walt Copley**; and **Pat** and **Melissa Yerxa**. Thanks to **Pat Yerxa** for coming up with the title to the book. To **Connie Bond**, chief editor of *The Police Marksman* magazine, you contributed a level of professional editing we could not have done without. To **Michel Hogan**, thank you for all of your great work formatting and designing the cover and text, and handling the printing side of its production, especially since you had to do it all from the other side of the world. Thanks, as always, to our long time teammate **Simon Luciow** for doing the artwork for the cover. Last – but in no way least – we want to thank my mother, **Ruth**, and her lifelong friend, **Mrs. Joanie Wimble**, who jumped in like true Green Berets at the last minute to do a final proofread in far less time than was reasonable to ask of anyone.

ABOUT THE AUTHORS
JOHN GIDUCK

John Giduck has a Bachelor's Degree from Penn State and a law degree from the University of Denver. He also earned a Master's Degree, specializing in Russian studies, from the University of Colorado, which included completion of the Russian Culture and Language Program at St. Petersburg State University in Russia. He has traveled extensively throughout Russia and the former Soviet Union for more than 15 years, including training with several of Russia's special forces units.

He has trained state and federal law enforcement officers and SWAT teams throughout the US. He has served as a consultant on various international and terrorism subjects, as well as a law enforcement defensive tactics and Russian Organized Crime instructor. He currently devotes his professional time to the Archangel Group, which provides anti-terrorism consulting and training to U.S. law enforcement, government and military, part of which includes John serving as a U.S. Army Special Forces hand-to-hand combat and firearms instructor. He has been inducted into several martial arts halls of fame, and is a former U.S. national weightlifting champion.

John earned the highest level expert certification in Homeland Security through the American College of Forensic Examiners International, and is a former member of the Executive Advisory Board of the American College of Homeland Security, and is a current member of the executive advisory board of Police Marksman magazine. In addition to other published materials and articles on terrorism, Russian organized crime and close quarters tactics, he authored the book, Terror at Beslan: A Russian Tragedy With Lessons for America's Schools.

As part of his work with Archangel, John Giduck is also a scuba, tactical diving instructor, and teaches terrorist-hostage negotiations, terrorism and global organized crime, and Russian organized crime courses.

JOHN ANDERSON

John Anderson spent 25 years in the U.S. Army Special Forces, retiring at the rank of Sergeant Major. During that time he completed all special forces and special operations training, was a demolitions expert and instructor, an instructor at the Special Forces John F. Kennedy Special Warfare School, hand-to-hand combat instructor, military freefall instructor, and taught weapons and tactics. He served two tours in Vietnam, working with such elite units as CCN (Command and Control North) and the Mike Force (Mobile Strike Force) as part of MACV/SOG.

Upon leaving the military he spent ten years with the U.S. Department of Energy as a lieutenant, training and supervising the nuclear weapons security teams at the Rocky Flats Nuclear Arsenal, and then serving as the tactical commander of the high security area, responsible for the security of all fissile material.

After 9-11 he, along with Green Beret and Medal of Honor recipient Drew Dix, founded the Archangel Anti-Terror Group, a non-profit agency that provides counter-terrorism training, consulting and related services to U.S. law enforcement, military and government agencies. He continues to serve Archangel as chairman of the board of directors, and as a tactical diving, close quarter combat firearms, counter-terrorism tactics and hand-to-hand combat instructor. He continues to this day to provide tactical training to the U.S. Army Special Forces.

In addition, Sergeant Major Anderson owns and operates Andy's Custom Guns and Training, Inc., is a former world combat pistol champion and benchpress record holder. He has operated in more than 50 countries.

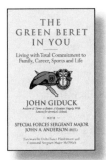

DONATIONS
SAVE THE MONTAGNARD PEOPLE, INC

By way of introducing a group of old "special warriors" who have not faded away, the following information is provided to our readers.

"Save the Montagnard People, Inc." (STMP) is a group founded by, and primarily composed of, US Special Forces veterans who worked with the Montagnards (tribal people of Vietnam) during the Vietnam War. Since the first group of Montagnard refugees arrived in this country in 1986 this small band of Green Beret Vets has assisted the resettlement of thousands of Montagnards in the US. The organization, assisted by members of the Special Forces Association and the Special Operations Association have purchased a one hundred acre farm near Asheboro, NC that serves as a cultural preservation site, farm, graveyard, meeting site and a beautiful natural recreation site on the Uwharrie River. STMP has provided scholarships to almost a thousand students with eighty-eight currently enrolled as this book goes to press. STMP is a unique organization that spends every dollar it takes in on direct assistance to the Montagnards. No organizational funds are used for salaries or administration. Should you like to help, you can send tax deductible donations that can be earmarked for: scholarships, the cultural center, or for refugee support. Donations should be sent to the Treasurer, Arch Gammons.

Arch Gammons
1033 S. 17th St.
Arlington, VA 22202
Phone: (703) 909 8849
Treasurer@montagnards.org

Questions on the scholarship program can be addressed to Carl Regan who directs that program. carljregan@bellsouth.net

Questions on refugee support, the farm and the cultural center may be addressed to the STMP President George Clark. President@montagnards.org

Please also visit the website at montagnards.org

ACTES NOIRS
série dirigée par Manuel Tric

MESSE NOIRE

DU MÊME AUTEUR

LES ADIEUX À L'EMPIRE, France-Empire, 2006.
LE DÉTECTIVE DE FREUD, éditions De Borée, 2010.
CASANOVA ET LA FEMME SANS VISAGE. UNE ENQUÊTE DU COMMISSAIRE AUX MORTS ÉTRANGES,
Actes Sud, 2012 ; Babel noir n° 82.

OLIVIER BARDE-CABUÇON

Messe noire

Une enquête du commissaire aux morts étranges

ACTES SUD

À ma mère qui m'a donné le goût de l'histoire.

La nuit tombe, mais les taches ne partent pas.

ILSE AICHINGER

I

FEUX FOLLETS ET AUTRES DIABLERIES

Une cloche sonna dans le lointain. Le crépuscule avait enveloppé le cimetière d'un fin voile noir, estompant les formes des pierres tombales et des stèles. Une pluie fine et glacée murmurait doucement, détrempant le sol des allées. Le moine effleura le visage de l'homme du bout des doigts et se releva lentement.

— On dirait qu'il est mort de peur…

— Il y a de quoi, murmura le sergent du guet en tendant le bras pour désigner les feux multicolores qui semblaient flotter en l'air dans le lointain.

En ce mois de décembre 1759, le Paris de la mort s'étalait sous leurs yeux. Plus qu'un regroupement de tombes, le cimetière était un immense parc au relief tourmenté et à la végétation abondante. Une large allée bordée d'arbres dépareillés menait jusqu'à une petite colline dévorée par la mousse et peuplée d'ombres spectrales. Là-bas, des flammèches jaunâtres ou vermillon tourbillonnaient au-dessus des tombes. Le son de la cloche expira. Un vent lourd grondait rageusement. Près de là, on entendit un chien hurler à la mort.

— Il faut aller voir, dit le moine d'une voix basse.

— Ce sont là diableries, protesta l'autre. Moi et les archers du guet, nous ne bougerons pas de là !

— J'irai seul alors. Faites-moi donner une lanterne.

Le sergent du guet le considéra avec attention. Sous la capuche de son interlocuteur, on discernait des yeux noirs et vifs, brillants d'intelligence et d'humanité. Son regard reflétait une curiosité attentive pour le monde qui l'entourait. Le moine devait avoir une cinquantaine d'années. Un faisceau de minces rides sillonnait son front comme autant de signes de perplexité ou de curiosité intellectuelle. Les traits de son visage étaient fins et un mince filet de barbe, à peine argentée par endroits, soulignait la courbe aristocratique de son menton.

— Ne devriez-vous pas attendre le commissaire aux morts étranges ? demanda avec nervosité le sergent du guet. On peut affronter seul les hommes mais pas les esprits malins ou les âmes en peine…

— Cela suffit, répondit fermement le moine, j'y vais. Je ne crains rien en ce bas monde, moi !

Il s'empara de la lanterne tendue par un archer du guet et ajouta comme pour lui-même :

— Ni dans l'autre d'ailleurs !

Ses hommes tremblants regroupés autour de lui, le sergent du guet regarda l'énigmatique moine s'éloigner dans la nuit noire. Il avait entendu au sujet du collaborateur du commissaire aux morts étranges, chargé d'élucider les meurtres les plus mystérieux de Paris, autant de choses détestables que merveilleuses : hérésie, duel, dépeçage de cadavres mais aussi une science infinie puisant dans les textes les plus anciens… Silencieusement, il se signa.

Le pauvre halo de lumière de sa lanterne tremblotait devant le moine, dérobant au passage des impressions fugitives de désolation. Autour de lui, lierre, ronces et mauvaises herbes tapissaient les tombes aux pieds d'anges brisés. Une poignante impression de solitude et d'abandon émanait de ces lieux. Le froid se faisait plus mordant à mesure que la nuit tombait. Il gravit d'un pas prudent des escaliers rongés par la moisissure et arriva au sommet d'un monticule. Les flammèches colorées étaient autant de feuilles au vent. Certaines d'entre elles s'éteignaient au bout de quelques secondes seulement mais il en naissait aussitôt d'autres, bleu pâle, rouges ou jaunes… Le moine les contempla avec ravissement.

— C'est magnifique, chuchota-t-il.

Il fit quelques pas afin de poser sa lanterne sur une tombe et mieux jouir du spectacle.

— Ah ! dit-il en se figeant.

Une rigole de sang s'était formée au pied de la stèle et un coq égorgé gisait sur la pierre tombale.

— Cette escapade nocturne commence à devenir intéressante, dit-il en se parlant à lui-même comme il en avait pris l'habitude en prison par le passé. Ainsi, on sacrifie au diable! Pour ma part, je préférerais sacrifier à Bacchus, dieu de l'ivresse, ou à Vénus, déesse de l'amour. Enfin, chacun ses goûts!

En s'accroupissant, il découvrit un cierge de cire noire à moitié consumé.

— Messe noire et évocation satanique, fit une voix grave derrière lui.

Le moine se retourna. Tout absorbé par sa découverte, il n'avait pas entendu arriver Volnay, le commissaire aux morts étranges, vêtu d'une veste à col à revers et enveloppé dans un long frac anglais. Âgé de vingt-cinq ans environ, grand, mince de hanches et carré d'épaules, il avait une figure agréable, encadrée de cheveux noirs longs retenus en arrière par un ruban de taffetas noir plié en forme de fleur. Son nez était court et droit, sa mâchoire bien dessinée mais son maintien restait sombre et sévère. La lueur de sa lanterne s'accrochait à son visage, jetant des reflets dorés sur la cicatrice qui courait au coin de son œil droit jusqu'à la tempe.

— Messe noire et feux follets, mon fils, compléta gaiement le moine en désignant les tourbillons colorés qui s'agitaient autour d'eux. Newton en a parlé dans un de ses traités et les compare à des vapeurs s'élevant des eaux putréfiées, *ignis mentes*, les esprits du feu…

Son père, le moine, aimait à étaler sa science. Stoïque, Volnay attendit la suite.

— Dans notre cas, je dirai que la décomposition des cadavres libère parfois des gaz qui s'enflamment spontanément au contact de l'air. Lorsqu'il y a du vent comme ce soir, le commun des mortels croit voir Jack à la lanterne en personne!

Il eut un ricanement légèrement condescendant.

— Les paysans ont un certain sens pratique. Ils plantent une aiguille par terre pour forcer les feux follets à passer à travers le chas, leur laissant ainsi le temps de s'enfuir. Tout le monde sait en effet qu'il est aussi difficile pour un feu follet de passer par le chas d'une aiguille que pour un riche d'entrer au paradis!

— Laissons les feux follets pour l'instant, décréta froidement le commissaire aux morts étranges, même si le gardien du cimetière en est mort de peur.

Il s'éloigna, sa lanterne à la main comme une âme perdue. Dans la terre humide, ses bottes émettaient un chuintement mouillé. Le vent faisait battre les pans de son frac derrière lui.

— Mon fils, rétorqua le moine en haussant la voix, je doute qu'un gardien de cimetière meure pour quelques feux follets ou coq noir. Il a dû se passer autre chose…

— Quoi?

— Je l'ignore pour l'instant. Je ne suis pas un policier, moi! Je suis un chercheur de sens!

Volnay promena sa lanterne à travers les tombes, évitant soigneusement les flammèches.

— Elles ne brûlent pas, mon fils! s'exclama le moine. Que cherches-tu?

— Des tombes profanées par les célébrants de cette messe noire. Le contact à l'air libre des cadavres expliquerait l'apparition de ce phénomène… Non, je ne vois rien à part quelques croix renversées. Peut-être que l'apparition des feux follets a mis en fuite nos célébrants avant qu'ils n'aient le temps d'achever…

Au loin, les hurlements lugubres du chien reprirent. Dans ceux-ci s'exprimait quelque chose de primitif mais d'incroyablement humain qui glaçait le sang comme s'ils révélaient une véritable souffrance. Le moine tapa du pied par terre pour se réchauffer. L'humidité commençait à le saisir. Il leva la tête vers le ciel et écarta théâtralement les bras.

— Oh vous Seigneur qui faites si peu pour nous d'ordinaire, aidez-nous à comprendre ce mystère!

— Ne blasphème pas! cria sèchement le policier qui s'était éloigné à portée de voix.

Le moine rit, les yeux fermés sous la caresse de la pluie.

— Quel dommage que tout soit détrempé, remarqua-t-il. Nous aurions pu lire quelques traces sur cette tombe. D'habitude, c'est une jeune vierge qui s'étend nue sur la pierre, un crucifix au milieu des seins, tête en bas, et une hostie consacrée entre les cuisses…

— Elle est là, fit une voix basse.

Le moine sursauta avant de reconnaître l'intonation déformée de Volnay. Celui-ci s'était immobilisé sous un arbre, face à une croix brisée. Pataugeant dans la terre humide, le moine s'empressa de le rejoindre.

— Comme tu viens de la décrire, ajouta le policier du même ton rauque. À un détail près : la malheureuse enfant a été étranglée.

La victime se trouvait étendue sur la tombe, les bras en croix, offerte à la pluie. Elle était très belle et très jeune, sa peau pâle et glacée et ses lèvres bleues de froid. Le moine se pencha sur elle et, d'un geste doux, lui ferma les yeux.

— On a tué un ange, murmura-t-il accablé.

Il serra les poings, la rage crispait ses traits.

— On nous rabâche que le bien est à l'origine et le but de chaque être ? On nous trompe : l'homme n'a aucune mesure pour infliger du mal à autrui !

Sa colère enfla encore.

— Siècle de fous, de malades et de pervers où l'ignorance crasse le dispute à l'infamie ! Elle ne doit pas avoir treize ans !

Le commissaire aux morts étranges balaya les environs du regard. Il ne portait pas de chapeau et le vent jouait avec ses cheveux d'un noir de corbeau, portés longs et sans poudre. Il concentra de nouveau son attention sur le moine. Plus son père vieillissait et plus il devenait sensible à la mort ou à la perte d'un être plus jeune que lui.

— Remets-toi de ton émotion, lui dit-il doucement, nous avons à trouver les coupables de cette folie.

Le moine acquiesça.

— Je n'ai après tout rien contre Jésus-Christ, chuchota-t-il. S'il existe, qu'il reçoive près de lui cette pauvre âme désemparée.

Il se releva.

— Ne bouge pas ! ordonna le commissaire aux morts étranges. Nous sommes sur la scène d'un crime. Ici se concentrent tous les indices dont nous avons besoin. Si nous n'y prenons garde l'enquête sera compromise avant même d'avoir commencé.

Il parlait avec sévérité et sur un ton sans appel.

— Commençons par protéger nos indices. La pluie ne nous aide pas mais au moins sommes-nous seuls sur les lieux et personne ne viendra piétiner et tout gâcher. Convenons d'abord de repérer les traces de nos pas pour les neutraliser et d'emprunter de nouveau celles-ci dans tous nos déplacements.

Dans le ciel, les étoiles semblaient figées par le froid. Sous cette pâle lumière, ils établirent de concert leurs repères puis le commissaire aux morts étranges reprit :

— Les indices sont là, sous nos yeux : un cadavre, une hostie, un crucifix, des empreintes de pas. Il nous faut faire parler tout cela! J'ai besoin d'en savoir plus sur le rituel de la messe noire.

Le moine lui jeta un regard vide puis un éclair de lucidité éclaira la prunelle de ses yeux alors que son cerveau recommençait à fonctionner normalement.

— Comme tu le sais, expliqua-t-il d'une voix lasse, la messe noire est un culte rendu à Satan en parodiant la messe. Tout y est donc inversé : le corps d'une femme nue sert d'autel, les cierges sont noirs au lieu d'être blancs. Il ne s'agit pas d'une célébration mais d'un simulacre dénaturé, une profanation… Il existe beaucoup de rituels de messe noire. Un prêtre défroqué ou renégat, des hosties consacrées, une vierge et une prostituée, un crucifix ou un calice rempli de vin ou de l'eau d'un puits où l'on a jeté le corps d'un enfant non baptisé…

Il s'interrompit un instant, le regard dans le vague.

— Au premier coup de onze heures, la messe est dite à l'envers et se termine au douzième coup de minuit.

— Il n'est pas minuit, remarqua Volnay, ils ont dû être interrompus…

— Il faut dire que, pour plus de résultat, la messe est souvent dite trois fois.

— Diable!

— Normalement, continua le moine d'un ton morne, le prêtre dit la messe et la prostituée la sert. Des fragments de messe sont récités à l'envers et le mot *mal* remplace le mot *bien*, *Satan* celui de *Dieu*. La prostituée donne la communion, aspergeant de vin la poitrine de la jeune vierge et plaçant l'hostie pour la souiller dans le… euh… dans l'antre sacré de la jeune fille.

Il se tut.

— Bien, dit pensivement le commissaire aux morts étranges. Cela me permet de comprendre la configuration de la scène. C'est curieux, on a tracé comme une croix dans le sol.

Le moine hocha la tête.

— Celui qui dit la messe fait le signe de croix du pied gauche sur le sol. Je te l'ai dit : tout est inversé.

— Cela signifie donc que l'officiant se tenait ici. À côté de lui, une femme car la terre est nettement moins tassée et l'empreinte plus petite. Les autres sont en face… Je dirais deux… non, trois personnes. Je vais en prendre la mesure.

Il déplia une ficelle et prit les mesures en faisant un nœud pour le début et la fin de chaque empreinte.

— Encore une empreinte de femme, fit-il d'un ton glacial. Trois hommes et deux femmes…

Il fronça les sourcils.

— Avant de savoir, il faut supposer. Nous aurions donc deux célébrants de la messe, trois spectateurs et… une victime à sacrifier.

Le moine se mit à genoux près du corps sans vie. Un instant, bizarrement, le commissaire aux morts étranges crut qu'il allait prier mais déjà les doigts fins et déliés du moine couraient le long du cadavre, soulevant bras et avant-bras, examinant les coudes.

— Des traces d'étranglement peu marquées autour du cou, pas de geste de défense occasionnant des blessures, pas de contusion sur les avant-bras, dit-il, mais je dois l'examiner à la lumière et sans cette maudite pluie glacée.

— Abrite-moi, fit Volnay. J'ai besoin de dessiner la scène du crime sans être trempé.

Le moine s'exécuta et, d'un pan de sa soutane, abrita le papier et le fusain de son fils qui se mit à dessiner avec habileté sur son genou.

— Voilà, fit le commissaire aux morts étranges au bout d'un moment. Je ferai le portrait de la jeune morte une fois son corps à l'abri.

Avec précaution, il fit quelques pas vers les feux follets qui semblaient maintenant s'évanouir dans la nuit et s'arrêta près de la tombe où il avait au départ rejoint le moine. Il reporta son attention sur le coq égorgé.

— Pourquoi avoir sacrifié ce coq sur une tombe éloignée?

Il se tourna vers le moine mais celui-ci semblait ne pas avoir entendu.

— Père?! insista Volnay.

Le moine tressaillit car rares étaient les moments où son fils prononçait ce mot qui remuait son cœur. "Père", c'était un peu comme si son cœur était un instrument de musique et que l'on en pinçait une corde.

Je vieillis et je deviens sensible, se dit-il.

Mais il n'en pensait pas un mot.

— Oui, mon fils?

— As-tu entendu ma question?

— Non, mon fils.

Volnay la répéta et le moine haussa les épaules.

— Je n'en ai pas la moindre idée.

Le commissaire aux morts étranges le considéra d'un air intrigué. Jamais, il n'avait vu son père aussi peu concentré sur la scène d'un crime.

— Y a-t-il quelque chose que tu veuilles me dire?

— Oui, dit le moine.

Ses pupilles semblèrent se remplir d'une eau trouble.

— Lorsque nous trouverons ces meurtriers, faisons en sorte qu'ils soient longuement torturés avant d'être brûlés et dépecés.

Le commissaire aux morts étranges fronça les sourcils. Tout cela ne ressemblait pas à son père, farouche opposant de la peine de mort comme de la torture. Il regarda à nouveau la jeune victime à qui le moine avait fermé les yeux avec tant de douceur et demanda :

— La connais-tu?

Le moine résidait tout comme son fils sur la rive gauche de la Seine, dans une petite impasse discrète, à quelques pas de la rue Saint-Jacques.

Lui et Volnay descendirent le corps de la carriole qu'un archer du guet reconduisit à l'écurie d'une auberge non loin de là. Le policier proposa son aide au moine mais celui-ci tint à porter seul la jeune fille dans ses bras. Il le fit comme s'il s'agissait d'une gamine endormie qu'il ne souhaitait surtout pas réveiller. À un moment, la tête enfantine roula sur sa poitrine. Le cœur du moine se serra et il cligna brièvement les yeux. La pluie avait dessiné comme des larmes sur son visage. Il réajusta brièvement sa prise, sous le regard inquiet de son fils. Un grand froid envahit ce dernier lorsque son père déclara :

— Il nous faut vite l'amener chez moi pour qu'elle puisse se réchauffer.

Sans répondre, Volnay lui ouvrit la porte. Après avoir descendu un escalier raide, ils longèrent avec leur fardeau un long couloir sombre pour se retrouver face à une double porte en fer. Ils déposèrent le corps par terre et le moine tourna une clé dans la serrure. Le policier entra à sa suite dans une profonde cave voûtée aux murs de pierre. Celle-ci recelait un incroyable laboratoire regorgeant de creusets, d'alambics, de cornues et de fourneaux, froids ou ronflants. Il était bientôt minuit. Les deux hommes s'appliquèrent à allumer minutieusement les torches accrochées au mur avant de s'occuper du lustre couronné de bougies. Ensuite, sans un mot, ils soulevèrent à nouveau la jeune fille pour la déposer avec respect sur une table en pierre que le moine recouvrit préalablement d'une couverture. Le cœur du commissaire aux morts étranges se serra lorsque le moine parla doucement au cadavre.

— Ah ma jeune amie, cela me soulève le cœur que d'avoir à procéder ainsi mais il faut me pardonner : c'est pour trouver ceux qui vous ont causé tant de mal.

Il se pencha pour examiner l'hymen de la jeune fille. Le commissaire aux morts étranges s'agita, mal à l'aise. C'était la première fois qu'il entendait le moine parler à un cadavre qu'il examinait. La connaissait-il ? Pourtant, à la question posée, son père avait répondu négativement.

— Elle est vierge, dit froidement le moine en se relevant. Au moins ces chacals ne l'ont pas souillée !

Encore une fois, ce ton rageur éveilla la curiosité de Volnay. Jamais il n'avait vu son père trahir une émotion en examinant un cadavre.

— Une enfant d'une douzaine d'années, répéta doucement le policier comme pour lui-même. Une vierge, une prostituée et un prêtre renégat…

Une mèche de cheveux blonds et soyeux barrait le front de la jeune fille, le moine la remit doucement en place.

— On dirait de l'or filé, s'émerveilla-t-il.

Il ouvrit les doigts et laissa glisser ses cheveux entre ses doigts.

— Peux-tu poursuivre? demanda doucement son fils.

Tout en marmonnant, le moine entreprit avec une loupe l'examen du corps, étudiant avec attention les genoux, les coudes, les bras et avant-bras. Puis, il souleva avec prudence la nuque, écartant les cheveux à la recherche de contusions ou d'une bosse.

Finalement, il se tourna vers Volnay.

— La pluie gâte les indices tandis que le froid pétrifie le corps et nous prive de précieux renseignements, notamment sur l'heure de sa mort. C'est pour cela que j'étais pressé de la ramener au chaud. Je ne relève ni plaie, ni bosse, ni ecchymose sur le corps. Elle n'a pas lutté pour se défendre et ne s'est pas débattue. Même un mouton se démène et bêle devant l'autel où on l'immole. Pourquoi n'a-t-elle pas réagi?

— Elle était consentante à cette mascarade et ne se doutait pas de la suite? hasarda le commissaire aux morts étranges.

Perplexe, le moine se gratta la barbe.

— Quand même, nous sommes en décembre et le froid est mordant. Qui supporterait de se coucher ainsi nue sur une dalle glacée?

Il poursuivit son examen du corps.

— Peux-tu avancer ta lanterne? Là! C'est étrange, les marques autour de son cou sont à peine visibles, pas suffisantes pour la priver d'air. Elle est peut-être morte de peur ou de froid…

— Tu me diras cela après l'autopsie, fit Volnay conciliant.

Son père lui jeta un regard sec.

— Il n'est pas question que j'ouvre cette pauvre enfant!

Le policier prit un air soucieux que l'autre ignora. Le moine recula d'un pas et contempla songeusement le corps.

— Instinctivement, dit-il, elle aurait dû tenter de se protéger et on devrait trouver des entailles sur ses mains ou ses avant-bras. Mais non, il n'y a même pas de marque autour de la bouche pour l'empêcher de crier.

— Ses dents sont bien soignées, remarqua le commissaire aux morts étranges en lui écartant légèrement les lèvres. Il en va de même pour ses mains. Elle n'est pas du peuple…

— Que connais-tu du peuple? grogna le moine.

Le policier ne répondit pas. Il contemplait la jeune morte. Séchés par une serviette, ses cheveux blonds apparaissaient lisses et clairs. D'une main tranquille, il ébouriffa la chevelure sous l'œil agacé du moine.

— On dirait qu'on lui a coupé plusieurs mèches.

— Foutre du pape! jura son père. Je ne l'avais pas remarqué!

Pour se rattraper, il entreprit de comparer chaque mèche l'une après l'autre.

— Tu as raison et je doute qu'elle se soit taillé cela elle-même.

Le moine plissa les yeux comme pour mieux réfléchir.

— Elle s'allonge nue, les bras en croix, en plein mois de décembre sur une dalle glacée et humide puis présente son cou au bourreau!

Il secoua la tête.

— À moins que…

Le moine commença à s'agiter.

— Mais oui, sacrebleu, c'est bien sûr! Que n'y ai-je pensé plus tôt?

— Penser à quoi? s'impatienta le commissaire aux morts étranges.

— J'ai mon idée mais il est trop tôt pour en parler, maugréa son père. Et j'ai besoin de ne pas être dérangé tout le temps…

— Tu es d'une humeur détestable, fit Volnay. Je te laisse et je rentre me coucher!

— Bonne idée, la nuit porte conseil à qui sait l'entendre!

Après avoir raccompagné son fils et fermé soigneusement la porte derrière lui, le moine redescendit dans son laboratoire. Il entreprit alors d'examiner la bouche de la petite victime. À l'aide d'un mouchoir, il récolta sous sa langue un peu de jus laiteux et collant. Il le renifla avec suspicion.

— C'était donc cela, murmura-t-il satisfait. On l'a droguée…

Volnay sortit de l'impasse, goûtant à la beauté silencieuse des rues enneigées la nuit. À peu de pas de là, il se retrouva face à un chien au pelage tout crasseux. Ses yeux noirs, étrangement humains, brillaient d'intelligence. L'animal geignit, ouvrit la bouche en rejetant la tête en arrière comme pour hurler mais, au lieu de cela, poussa une plainte triste, presque un gémissement. Volnay s'approcha lentement de lui et, s'assurant qu'il ne montrait pas les crocs, le flatta un instant.

— Nous sommes-nous déjà rencontrés quelque part mon ami à quatre pattes ? lui demanda-t-il gravement.

Puis il sourit, gratta une dernière fois le chien derrière les oreilles avant de regagner son domicile à peu de distance de là. Ses bottes battaient le pavé avec assurance mais, le regard aux aguets, il scrutait les zones d'ombre, la main sur la poignée de son épée.

Pour le commissaire aux morts étranges, la nuit n'était pas plus une tranquille parenthèse qu'un instant de repos. Les crimes les plus abominables se commettaient aux heures les plus noires et, au petit matin, les décrotteurs de Paris ramassaient les cadavres. La nuit semblait placer Paris hors de tout droit et de toute morale.

Des rires joyeux fusèrent de l'obscurité. Volnay dressa l'oreille puis hocha lentement la tête. Du jour de l'Épiphanie à la veille du mercredi des Cendres, régnait le temps de Carnaval. Avant que ne lui succèdent l'austérité du Carême et Pâques, symbole de renouveau, qui anéantirait les péchés et les ténèbres de l'hiver, Carnaval permettait à tous de renier sa spiritualité et de laisser libre cours à ses instincts bassement matériels. Déguisements et masques gommaient les classes sociales et les différences entre êtres humains, donnant à ceux-ci l'occasion de s'oublier dans une identité précaire qui laissait débrider les instincts et parler les sens.

La police du royaume n'appréciait guère cette période où l'ordre royal même était remis en question. Elle donnait lieu à de nombreuses rixes, violences et paillardises. Les valets volaient leurs maîtres et débauchaient leurs maîtresses. Les archers du guet et le clergé étaient insultés. La farce tournait parfois au drame. Aussi, une ordonnance de police de 1746 interdisait désormais aux personnes masquées de porter bâtons et épées ou d'en faire porter par leurs laquais. Une autre ordonnance, de 1742, défendait d'entrer de force dans les lieux où se jouait de la musique, de violenter les traiteurs, leurs femmes et enfants et de contraindre les violons à jouer toute la nuit. C'était un moyen sûr pour lutter contre le tapage nocturne en temps de Carnaval.

Seulement voilà, ce n'était pas le temps de Carnaval ! Malgré tout, il rencontrait souvent, depuis le début de décembre, ce genre de groupes. Une fois le soleil couché, à l'approche de Noël, une étrange exaltation semblait saisir la ville.

Bientôt, le commissaire aux morts étranges aperçut la lueur d'un flambeau porté par un jeune homme avec un masque en papier au nez démesurément allongé. Il annonçait un groupe joyeux d'une douzaine de jeunes gens. Les filles dansaient une sorte de farandole tandis que les garçons chantaient des couplets obscènes. En découvrant Volnay seul, ils eurent une exclamation collective d'heureuse surprise puis, satisfaits, se dirigèrent vers lui pour le tourmenter ou le détrousser. Le commissaire aux morts étranges eut un sourire froid et dégaina à moitié son épée. Le groupe marqua un temps d'arrêt puis reprit sa direction initiale. Manifestement, on trouvait plus facile d'humilier un bourgeois esseulé qu'un homme armé et décidé. Volnay se recula pour les laisser passer à deux mètres de lui. Des quolibets fusèrent et certaines jeunes filles lui tendirent leur croupe de manière suggestive en chantant :

Enfile, enfile, enfile, l'aiguille de Paris !

L'une d'elles, à la silhouette grande et élancée, quitta alors le groupe et vint s'accrocher à son bras. Elle portait le masque de la mort.

— Viens danser avec la mort et goûter à ses baisers!

Elle joignit la parole à l'acte et l'embrassa à pleine bouche avant de s'enfuir en riant pour rejoindre les autres. Volnay resta un moment immobile, le cœur battant dans le noir. Puis, il reprit sa marche comme si de rien n'était. Derrière lui, le chien, qui s'était immobilisé, reprit une marche prudente à sa suite.

II

AFFAIRE D'ÉTAT ET AUTRES DIABLERIES

Une lueur pâle filtrait à travers les tentures, s'aventurant jusqu'aux reliures dorées des livres qui ornaient tout un pan de mur.

— Debout! Debout!

Volnay ouvrit un œil et puis un autre. Son regard tomba sur la pie qui tournait et retournait dans sa cage dans un grand bruissement d'ailes. Parée d'une longue queue étagée, elle arborait avec fierté un plumage noir aux reflets violacés sur la poitrine et la tête, blanc au niveau du ventre, des flancs et à la base des ailes, verdâtre sur la queue.

— Debout! répéta-t-elle.

Encore tout ensommeillé, Volnay la fixa stupidement. Il s'était endormi à sa table de travail en tentant de récapituler les maigres indices en sa possession : un prêtre renégat, une prostituée, une jeune vierge étranglée et trois spectateurs. Ah oui, il y avait aussi un gardien de cimetière mort de peur et des feux follets!

Ses pensées le ramenèrent à son père. Il se frotta le visage avec la paume de ses mains et, faute d'interlocuteur à qui se confier, dit à la pie :

— Je ne l'ai jamais vu comme cela. Voici bientôt trois ans que je travaille avec lui sans qu'il laisse transparaître la moindre émotion devant un cadavre. De la compassion certes mais pas d'émotion…

Il secoua la tête, continuant son monologue comme pour se convaincre.

— C'est avant tout un homme de science et de raison, je le sais depuis l'enfance même s'il a peu passé de temps avec moi pendant celle-ci…

Il eut un sourire amer.

— Mon père préférait la compagnie des philosophes ou des alchimistes à la mienne. Un enfant, ça n'est pas assez intelligent pour soutenir une conversation sur les systèmes politiques à travers le temps ou les théories de M. Newton sur les corps en mouvement…

La pie resta silencieuse mais son regard noir semblait lire en lui. Volnay continua, comme encouragé de ne pas être interrompu.

— Et voilà qu'aujourd'hui, c'est un peu comme si, en tuant cette pauvre enfant, on venait de lui briser le cœur. Je ne comprends pas…

— Comprends pas, répéta la pie bavarde. Comprends pas!

Il était tombé sur Paris un froid à rompre les os. La ville semblait se recroqueviller sur elle-même comme une vieille femme transie. Pourtant, des artisans travaillaient bien avant l'aube à la porte de leur boutique. Ils se retournèrent avec curiosité à la vue de la carriole conduite par le moine, escortée de deux exempts de police. Il avait neigé peu avant l'aube. Le cheval allait au pas, posant avec précaution ses sabots dans cette neige fraîche.

Une fois arrivé dans son impasse, le moine sauta de la carriole avec agilité.

— Allez, dépêchez-vous de m'amener ce cadavre à l'intérieur! D'habitude on me les apporte de nuit. Mes voisins vont encore dire du mal de moi!

Les deux exempts obtempérèrent sans un mot. Ils craignaient presque autant le moine que son supérieur, le taciturne commissaire aux morts étranges. Le premier posa le pied sur une plaque de verglas et chuta lourdement. Le second descendit plus prudemment. Ensemble, ils se penchèrent pour saisir le cadavre enveloppé dans une couverture et, d'une démarche pataude, encombrés par leur pesant fardeau, ils suivirent le moine.

Une fois les exempts congédiés, le moine contempla le corps du gardien du cimetière en se frottant les mains de plaisir.

— À nous deux, mon gaillard! déclara-t-il. Je sens que tu as beaucoup de choses à me dire! J'en donnerais la queue de mon chat à couper, quoique je n'aie pas de chat…

Une mince couche de givre étincelait dans la cour sous le soleil du matin. En sortant de chez lui, Volnay cligna des yeux, ébloui. L'acacia dressé face à sa maison était recouvert de cristaux de glace. Le commissaire aux morts étranges inspira à pleins poumons l'air froid et de minces filets de vapeur s'exhalèrent de ses lèvres. Un bref jappement le fit sursauter. C'était le chien de la veille.

— Tu es encore là, toi?

L'animal l'observa avec une expression d'intelligence quasi humaine avant d'agiter joyeusement la queue comme s'il le reconnaissait. Volnay chercha dans sa poche le quignon de pain qu'il y avait glissé avant de sortir et le lui lança. L'animal s'en saisit et se hâta de déguerpir avec son butin.

Le policier quitta la cour minuscule devant sa maison pour en gagner une seconde un peu plus grande puis une troisième, de brique et de pierre, avec en son centre un puits à margelle. Celle-ci donnait sur le passage pavé, bordé de bornes chasse-roues par lequel la rue de la Porte-de-l'Arbalète menait à la rue Saint-Jacques.

Les ruelles, les allées et les portes cochères tenant de lieux d'aisances pour une grande partie de la population, la neige était par endroits souillée d'excréments. Heureusement, la pureté de l'air glacé chassait la puanteur qui habitait nombre de quartiers aux beaux jours. C'était l'avantage de l'hiver, l'été la ville puait plus fort qu'une porcherie.

Volnay se dirigea vers l'auberge dans laquelle il laissait habituellement son cheval. Ensuite, au pas prudent de sa monture, il prit la direction du cimetière de la veille, croisant les garçons limonadiers qui se répandaient dans les rues pour apporter cafés ou bavaroises dans les garnis. Arrivé au cimetière, le commissaire aux morts étranges gravit le monticule habillé d'un blanc manteau immaculé. La neige recouvrait désormais d'un voile de pureté ces lieux blasphémés dans la nuit. L'air lui piquait les poumons de mille aiguilles glacées. Une gaze légère semblait s'étirer pour envelopper les tombes d'un voile laiteux. Un début de brume sans doute. Il fallait faire vite. Il hâta le pas.

Conformément à ses instructions, un archer du guet se trouvait en faction sur une pierre tombale, à distance du lieu du crime afin de ne pas piétiner les éventuels indices. Il avait relayé deux heures auparavant un de ses compagnons d'infortune et battait de la semelle pour se réchauffer, les lèvres bleuies par le froid. Personne n'était venu, assura-t-il, et il avait évité de marcher ailleurs que sur la plate-bande qu'on avait assignée à la première sentinelle. Les empreintes de pas sur la glace pouvaient d'ailleurs en attester.

Le commissaire aux morts étranges le remercia et l'autorisa à rentrer à sa caserne. Ce qui devait être préservé l'avait été et, pour le reste, il préférait rester seul.

Avec méthode, il quadrilla les rangées de tombes à la recherche de traces suspectes mais la neige tombée dans la nuit avait tout recouvert si quelque chose lui avait échappé la veille. Le commissaire aux morts étranges s'arrêta pour réfléchir. Il pensa au gardien du cimetière. Si la venue de l'homme avait dérangé la cérémonie, acteurs et spectateurs de la messe noire se seraient empressés de quitter les lieux. Mais par où ? L'entrée du cimetière risquait d'être surveillée alors…

Il chercha des yeux un escalier qui redescendrait de la colline de l'autre côté. Il le trouva et suivit ensuite une allée qui le mena jusqu'à une porte couverte de rouille et protégée par des broussailles. Il lui sembla que certaines avaient été foulées aux pieds. Il déblaya doucement la neige près de la porte et découvrit ce qu'il cherchait : l'empreinte d'un pied enfoncé. Ce devait être la personne qui s'était arc-boutée pour tirer la porte à elle. Il sortit d'une de ses poches son rouleau à ficelle et compara l'empreinte avec ses mesures. Elle correspondait parfaitement à celle d'un des spectateurs de la messe noire !

Il entreprit de déblayer toute la neige alentour mais ne trouva pas d'autres empreintes. Alors, il examina minutieusement les broussailles. Au bout d'une longue recherche, son obstination fut récompensée par la découverte d'un fil de laine rouge accroché à des ronces. Il le récupéra soigneusement et s'empressa de le ranger à l'abri dans sa bourse à indices.

Lorsqu'il revint à l'entrée du cimetière, le sergent du guet l'attendait comme on le lui avait ordonné la veille. Son teint était blême et il respirait à grand-peine. Face à lui, l'œil sévère et les joues pâles, le commissaire aux morts étranges le toisa d'un air ni aimable, ni affable.

— Sachez tout d'abord que je n'ai pas apprécié que vous ayez laissé mon assistant s'aventurer seul dans ce cimetière en pleine nuit. Maintenant, répondez à mes questions. Qui vous a appelé ?

Le commissaire aux morts étranges avait beau ne pas avoir plus de vingt-cinq ans, il en imposait tant par son autorité personnelle que par celle de sa fonction. Aussi, l'autre se hâta de lui répondre.

— Les assistants du gardien du cimetière. Ce sont eux qui ont trouvé celui-ci mort de saisissement.

— Où cela ? Soyez précis, je vous prie !

— En haut du monticule. Ils se sont empressés de le ramener à l'entrée du cimetière et de nous alerter. Ils étaient de plus terrifiés par les feux…

— Ils ne sont donc restés là-bas que quelques instants ?

— Oui, ils me l'ont confirmé.

— Cela a donc laissé tout le temps aux participants de la messe noire, si ce sont eux que le gardien a surpris, pour s'enfuir.

— Et jamais nous ne les retrouverons, soupira le sergent du guet.

— Détrompez-vous, le reprit sèchement Volnay, ils ont laissé derrière eux assez d'indices pour que je leur remette un jour la main dessus !

Les rayons du soleil au zénith se réfléchissaient sur la neige dans un scintillement aveuglant lorsque le moine pénétra dans la ruelle de l'Or. C'était une longue voie étroite bordée de maisons à un ou deux étages. Une population mystérieuse et discrète la peuplait : marchands d'onguents, spirites, exorcistes, alchimistes, astrologues, sorcières ou nécromanciens…

Non moins fugace était le passage des personnes qui leur rendaient visite, de la mégère qui souhaitait nouer l'aiguillette de son bourgeois au grand seigneur de la cour en quête d'un peu plus de pouvoir et d'argent. On pénétrait dans ces maisons selon des codes établis. Leurs caves profondes recelaient maints instruments de laboratoire ou symboles d'autres temps. Des cérémonies secrètes s'y déroulaient parfois pour évoquer des esprits disparus. On se pressait chez un tel pour y bénéficier de philtres favorisant l'amour ou chez un autre pour s'y faire lire l'avenir à travers la fumée d'une tête d'âne en train de brûler. Ici, les chercheurs de trésor évoquaient les âmes du purgatoire pour les aider à localiser l'or enterré, là on vendait des flûtes enchantées ou des runes. À l'inverse des rues de Paris, personne ne criait ou parlait fort, tout se déroulait de manière silencieuse et furtive.

Derrière les carreaux recouverts de givre, le moine sentit le poids des regards des curieux habitants de la ruelle de l'Or. Un homme le bouscula, son manteau déformé par des objets qu'il dissimulait dessous, contre sa poitrine.

— Formules magiques, philtres, amulettes, matériel pour envoûtement et talismans de protection, lui glissa-t-il, êtes-vous intéressé ?

— Non.

— Poudre magique pour vous soutenir dans l'effort de faire plaisir aux femmes ? insista l'autre.

Le moine secoua la tête en souriant.

— Merci, pour cela j'ai déjà tout ce qu'il faut sur moi !

Sans hésiter, il se dirigea vers une maison qui semblait rentrer sous terre et, après avoir frappé un rythme convenu, entra. Dans la semi-pénombre, il cligna des yeux pour accommoder. Il se trouvait au-dessus d'un escalier qui le conduisit par deux révolutions symétriques dans une cave voûtée au sol jonché de tapis épais et de coussins colorés. Au fond de celle-ci, près d'une cheminée où crépitait une belle flambée, se dressait une silhouette frêle couverte de la tête aux pieds d'un voile blanc, les bras croisés sur la poitrine. Ses cheveux semblaient de fil d'argent et ses yeux verts ornés de longs cils rappelaient la couleur des fonds marins.

— Vous revoilà, fit une voix féminine. Il y a bien longtemps que je n'ai eu l'honneur de votre visite.

— Un mois et une semaine, précisa le moine. Je le sais car lorsque vous m'honorez d'un sourire, je suis le plus heureux des hommes, ma belle Dame de l'Eau.

— Incorrigible flatteur! Allons approchez près du feu et dites-moi ce que vous avez en tête. Il y a des années, vous me visitiez pour des raisons personnelles mais aujourd'hui je sais bien qu'il n'en est plus de même. Cette bure a quelque peu éteint votre sensibilité!

Il s'approcha d'elle, les yeux pétillants.

— Vous vouliez sans doute parler de ma sensualité? Rassurez-vous, elle n'est pas complètement étouffée!

La Dame de l'Eau eut un haussement d'épaules impuissant et son rire frais emplit la pièce.

— Ces galanteries ne sont hélas plus de mon âge, vous avez trop tardé à vous déclarer!

Le moine hocha gravement la tête.

— C'est bien moi : je fais tout à contretemps! Effectivement, je suis ici pour une raison précise. Avez-vous entendu parler de résurgence du culte satanique?

Elle lui jeta un doux regard de reproche.

— Pourquoi parler de résurgence? Ce culte a existé de tout temps. Le diable est le grand négateur de la puissance divine et il se trouvera toujours des gens pour dénier celle-ci.

Le moine approuva et déclama d'un ton sentencieux :

— "Ils donnent au diable leur âme immortelle puis le baisent au cul tenant des chandelles ardentes en leurs mains. Ils crachent sur la croix, en dépit de Jésus-Christ et de la Sainte-Trinité avant de tourner leur cul vers le ciel, en dépit de Dieu."

La Dame de l'Eau eut un rire indulgent.

— À qui pensez-vous, mon ami?

— Ma chère, je pense à des gens qui n'hésitent pas à tuer…

— Des nourrissons comme du temps de la Voisin?

— Non, de jeunes vierges.

Le regard de la dame s'assombrit.

— Voilà qui est bien nouveau quoique je ne sois pas surprise.

Elle eut un moment d'hésitation et ajouta d'une voix basse :

— En fait, rien de ce qui est mauvais dans la nature humaine ne me surprend plus aujourd'hui.

Le moine approuva sombrement avant de reprendre ses questions.

— Avez-vous remarqué dans la ruelle de l'Or des gens cherchant cierges noirs, coqs à sacrifier ou hosties consacrées ?

La Dame de l'Eau réfléchit.

— Comme vous le savez, répondit-elle prudemment, il existe deux types de magie : la noire et la blanche. La magie blanche a vocation à soulager les maux de l'humanité et la magie noire à contenter des intérêts personnels. Dans nos campagnes, on trouve encore nombre de mages capables d'influer sur l'ordre de la nature pour faire pourrir les moissons sur pied, tarir les vaches ou empêcher les fruits de mûrir. Dans la ruelle de l'Or, nous comptons autant de personnes qui vendent les articles nécessaires à la magie blanche qu'à la magie noire. Cependant, aucun n'est assez fou ou démoniaque pour commercer des hosties consacrées. Nous évitons ici toute magie qui a recours aux démons et tout pacte diabolique même si quelques nécromanciens évoquent les morts.

D'un geste circulaire, la Dame de l'Eau désigna tout ce qui se trouvait à l'extérieur.

— Voyez-vous, nous formons ici une sorte de communauté avec, comme partout, de bons et de mauvais éléments. Cependant, même ces derniers ne supporteraient pas d'être exposés au danger de ce type de cérémonie. C'est la roue assurée et toute la ruelle de l'Or rasée et brûlée. Non, jamais notre communauté n'accepterait que de telles pratiques se développent ici.

— Et les envoûteurs ?

— Asservir la volonté d'autrui ou la détruire est le propre de l'homme, qu'il soit envoûteur ou pas.

— C'est vrai qu'on peut être roi de France et envoûteur, approuva le moine. Mais, sans nous lancer dans des considérations politiques, certains ont-ils ici pignon sur rue ?

— Oh, la demande d'envoûtement a toujours été très forte, c'est un marché d'avenir ! Élixirs, charmes et philtres d'amour, poupées ensorcelées pour réduire ses ennemis, nouage d'aiguillette pour maris infidèles, potions pour modérer le trop grand désir de l'action de Vénus chez la femme… ce sont là pratiques courantes et, à vrai dire, le principal fonds de commerce de la ruelle de l'Or avec la divination et la lecture de l'avenir. De plus le commerce de l'envoûtement alimente celui des leveurs de maléfices et génère un autre marché : celui de la protection contre l'envoûtement : amulettes, talismans… On vend de quoi se protéger contre les maléfices que l'on a vendus, ainsi l'équilibre est préservé !

— Un peu comme des marchands d'armes qui en vendraient à chaque camp qui s'affronte. C'est la loi de l'équilibre revue et corrigée par les charlatans !

— Oui, cependant, attention ! Parfois, fausse est la magie, vrai est le magicien !

Elle contempla songeusement le feu.

— Tout ce que désirent les gens est d'avoir ce qu'ils ne possèdent pas. De manière extravagante, c'est toujours ceux qui ont le plus qui souhaitent en posséder plus encore. Si l'on veut définir le rôle de la ruelle de l'Or, il est simple : leur faire croire que cela est possible.

Le moine soupira.

— Magie d'appropriation…

Il se campa près du feu, tendant ses mains à réchauffer aux flammes.

— Notre commissaire aux morts étranges est expert et savant en beaucoup de choses mais pas en magie noire, confia-t-il. Je n'aime pas notre mission. Elle va nous mener dans des lieux ignobles et je ne sais même pas vers quoi orienter notre enquête.

La Dame de l'Eau se joignit à lui auprès de l'âtre pour contempler d'un air pensif les bûches enflammées.

— Tout comme vous, votre fils s'adapte aux situations les plus complexes.

C'était une des très rares personnes à connaître leur lien de parenté mais le moine avait foi en elle comme en lui-même.

— Mon fils est trop rigide, maugréa le moine. Je crois qu'il s'est construit en opposition à moi.

— C'est souvent le cas avec les enfants, dit-elle doucement, mais parfois cela leur passe…

Le moine hocha la tête. Ses pensées semblaient affleurer jusque dans ses yeux. On y lisait une douleur muette.

— Il est tout ce que j'ai sur cette maudite terre mais le sait-il?

— Le lui avez-vous dit?

— Il ne m'en offre pas l'occasion…

— Provoquez celle-ci!

Face au silence épais de son compagnon, la Dame de l'Eau fit diversion.

— Pour en revenir à notre premier sujet, sabbat, messes noires ou rituels d'envoûtement, vous trouverez toujours un point commun entre eux : l'acte de copulation!

Un éclair joyeux traversa le regard du moine.

— Je vois très bien ce que vous voulez dire!

Elle le gronda gentiment.

— Vous êtes insupportable!

S'approchant d'un bassin de marbre au milieu de la pièce, elle effleura de la paume la surface de l'eau et dit :

— Mon art à moi est véritable, vous le savez. Ma magie est celle de la nature. Tout ce qui est en haut est comme ce qui est en bas pour faire miracle d'une seule chose…

Le moine se pencha et plissa les yeux devant les rides qui parcouraient le bassin.

— L'eau est un miroir, continua la Dame de l'Eau. Et qui sait en interroger la surface trouvera un signe ou une réponse à ses questions…

L'autre resta immobile avant de soupirer :

— Le charme de l'eau n'opère plus sur moi. J'ai vieilli et perdu la clé des rêves. Je vais avoir besoin d'autre chose…

Sa compagne arqua délicatement un sourcil.

— Mon ami, vous faites trop de cas des plantes.

— Sans elles, je ne dormirai plus depuis longtemps! J'ai accumulé tant de cauchemars en moi!

Il battit l'air des mains comme pour chasser cette dernière remarque et reprit :

— À propos, avez-vous entendu parler de certaines drogues qui plongent les gens dans une sorte de léthargie bienheureuse?

— C'est-à-dire?

— Je cherche quelqu'un qui vend des plantes hallucinantes, celles qui rendent fou ou donnent des visions merveilleuses, procurant félicité et grande satisfaction…

— De quel genre?

— Du genre qui ne donne pas envie de revenir car l'illusion de la réalité est bien plus plaisante que la réalité elle-même.

— Il suffit de dormir pour cela, remarqua-t-elle.

— Certes, certes mais tous les savetiers ne rêvent pas qu'ils sont roi. Il est des va-nu-pieds qui rêvent chaque nuit qu'ils sont va-nu-pieds!

Elle sourit.

— Vous avez raison, comme d'habitude! Enfin, pour en revenir à votre question, je vais vous indiquer deux maisons dans la ruelle où vous trouverez de telles choses. La première est celle d'une rebouteuse et guérisseuse. C'est plutôt une bonne créature et les plantes n'ont pas de secret pour elle. Vous y trouverez des fleurs de pavot…

— *Papaver somniferum*, approuva le moine. J'y ai pensé un moment.

— Il existe aussi l'herbe-aux-sommes, la jusquiame noire.

— *Hyoscyamus niger*, elle est très toxique mais soulage les maux de dents. Toutefois, l'utilisation combinée de certaines plantes peut conduire à une transe ou un sommeil léthargique.

La Dame de l'Eau approuva de la tête.

— La seconde personne est un Grec, marchand de potions. On dit qu'il a commerce avec l'Orient.

— Oh, s'exclama le moine, c'est lui que j'irai visiter le premier.

— Attention car il est fier et ombrageux. Ne vous présentez pas à lui comme policier mais plutôt comme acheteur.

— Je vais suivre vos conseils de ce pas, ils m'ont toujours clairement montré la voie!

— J'aime votre esprit et la gaieté de celui-ci, dit-elle.

— Vous avez toujours été très indulgente avec moi, ma chère amie…

Il prit congé de la dame, baisa galamment sa main et sortit.

Dans les couloirs du Châtelet, le commissaire aux morts étranges croisa procureurs, huissiers et greffiers tout de noir vêtus, sinistres corbeaux le jaugeant du regard avant de mieux le condamner. Un maroquin sous le bras, jouant les importants, ils le bousculèrent sans un mot d'excuse. Tous participaient d'une manière ou d'une autre à tisser cet écheveau inextricable de lois, coutumes et jurisprudence édictées selon les caprices des gouvernants et de leurs serviteurs en noir. Ici on vous réprimandait pour le vol d'une grappe de raisin, là on vous envoyait aux galères pour le même délit.

S'il ne travaillait plus au Châtelet depuis sa nomination comme lieutenant général de police, Sartine y conservait un bureau. Sa nouvelle fonction était complexe car, outre la police au sens strict, il avait également en charge les bonnes mœurs, la santé, la religion, l'approvisionnement des vivres, la voirie, la réglementation des domestiques et des manœuvres. La surveillance du prix du pain lui causait le plus de soucis car à celui-ci pouvaient être attachées bien des révoltes du peuple par le passé. Il gérait également les sciences et les arts mais cette dernière fonction se contractait surtout dans la police du livre! Quant à la gestion de la pauvreté qui relevait de ses services, elle se résumait principalement à envoyer les mendiants en prison.

Volnay entra donc dans une grande pièce au sol froid jonché de tapis précieux et aux murs recouverts de tapisserie de prix. Malgré l'heure matinale, des flambeaux éclairaient les lieux. Le lieutenant général de police aimait à scruter les traits de ses visiteurs. Sous les mèches bouclées de sa perruque blanchie de poudre de riz et son front haut et dégarni, son regard était autoritaire et incisif. Il portait un habit de velours jaune tissé de motifs floraux avec des boutons revêtus de fil d'argent et des volants de manche en dentelle aux fuseaux.

— Ah, chevalier de Volnay! Vous arrivez bien! Au rapport, vite!

Habitué à la sécheresse de son supérieur, Volnay obtempéra.

— Cinq personnes se trouvaient sur les lieux du crime, expliqua-t-il d'un ton neutre. D'après les empreintes, je déduis que trois hommes et deux femmes étaient présents en plus de la victime.

— Ah oui, vos méthodes nouvelles… maugréa Sartine.

Il pianota nerveusement des doigts sur son bureau, un meuble au bois précieux, décoré d'appliques en bronze doré.

— Deux de ces personnes semblaient officier, reprit Volnay impassible. Vous savez ce que l'on dit pour la célébration des messes noires…

— Oui, l'interrompit Sartine avec brusquerie. Un prêtre renégat et une prostituée donnent la communion sous les deux espèces. Le célébrant abaisse l'hostie noire, au lieu de l'élever, avant de la souiller en la plaçant dans le sexe de la jeune vierge. Ensuite il la déchiquette pour faire souffrir le Christ dans sa propre chair. Quant au vin, je n'ose vous dire ce qu'il est réellement !

Le commissaire aux morts étranges hocha la tête. Il n'avait jamais douté que Sartine connaisse ses classiques.

— La sixième personne est la victime, ajouta le commissaire aux morts étranges. Une jeune fille d'une douzaine d'années. Je vous en ai apporté un croquis.

Sartine le prit du bout des doigts comme s'il s'attendait à trouver quelque chose d'horrible et regarda le croquis avec attention. Une lueur de surprise sembla traverser son regard.

— Une bien jolie enfant, murmura-t-il.

Une seconde, Volnay crut qu'un sourire attendri venait d'adoucir la physionomie froide de son interlocuteur mais, l'instant d'après, il ne retrouva plus que le masque impassible du lieutenant général de police. Celui-ci lui rendit le dessin, avec regret semblait-il, puis se ravisa.

— Je le garde, vous en avez d'autres, j'imagine.

— Certes…

Volnay savait que Sartine, comme tant de personnes puissantes, dirigeait de loin. Le simple fait qu'il conservât le portrait de la victime d'un meurtre était en soi une chose étonnante. Que se passait-il ?

— Chevalier de Volnay, reprit son supérieur d'un ton compassé, vous n'êtes pas sans vous rappeler l'affaire des messes noires pendant le règne du prédécesseur de notre bon roi ?

— Oui, la favorite de Louis XIV, la Montespan, employait la femme la Voisin dans de misérables cérémonies pour conserver les faveurs du roi…

— Comme vous y allez ! Il n'a jamais rien été prouvé à l'encontre de Mme de Montespan ! s'exclama le lieutenant général de police.

— Et pour cause ! Le roi brûla personnellement les documents du procès et vous seul devez être dépositaire des notes du lieutenant de police de l'époque, M. de La Reynie.

Le teint de Sartine, d'habitude vieil ivoire, passa au cramoisi.

— Esprit frondeur ! Votre insolence n'a donc pas de limites, prenez garde !

Le commissaire aux morts étranges ne broncha point. Son supérieur savait se montrer cassant et le rabaisser si besoin. Il tenait de temps à autre à rappeler l'importance de ses fonctions et la distance qui le séparait du commun des mortels. Ce genre de manifestation d'autorité glissait sur Volnay comme la pluie sur la montagne.

M. de Sartine fit quelques pas dans la pièce pour se calmer et entreprit de réajuster sa perruque.

— Reprenons les faits, fit-il en plissant les yeux, car il y a bien deux affaires distinctes : celle de la marquise de Brinvilliers et celle de la femme la Voisin. En 1672, Godin de Sainte-Croix, un officier en demi-solde perclus de dettes, meurt. Lors de l'inventaire après décès, on découvre un coffret plein de fioles remplies d'arsenic et une cassette de documents édifiants. Sa maîtresse, la marquise de Brinvilliers, y reconnaît avoir empoisonné à l'arsenic son propre père et ses deux frères, manquant de peu son mari légitime, tout cela pour s'approprier leur héritage. La cassette découverte, la marquise de Brinvilliers se réfugie à Londres puis à Liège dans un couvent. En 1673, La Chaussée, le valet de Godin de Sainte-Croix, est reconnu coupable de crimes et condamné à être rompu vif.

Sartine sortit une blague à tabac de sa poche et cala une prise dans le creux de son pouce écarté avant de renifler profondément. La reniflade terminée, il éternua, se moucha et poursuivit d'un ton satisfait.

— Au mois de mars de l'année 1676, François Desgrez, le plus fin limier du lieutenant général de police, La Reynie, se déguise en prêtre pour pénétrer dans ce couvent, arrêter la marquise et la ramener en France pour la faire écrouer à la Conciergerie.

Une grimace crispa le bas de son visage.

— L'enquête se poursuit pendant plusieurs années et La Reynie remonte patiemment le réseau des deux amants, s'épouvantant de ce qu'il découvre. Après un long procès, la marquise de Brinvilliers est exécutée. La police arrête de nombreuses personnes, dont la femme la Voisin, fournisseuse de poisons et jeteuse de maléfices. L'identité de certains de ses clients est tout bonnement stupéfiante…

Mme de Montespan, ancienne favorite du roi et mère de ses enfants, le maréchal de Luxembourg, Racine, des nièces de Mazarin, la duchesse de Bouillon, la comtesse de Polignac, la comtesse de Soissons, Mme de Vivonne, belle-sœur de Mme de Montespan, et les femmes de chambre de celles-ci… compléta en silence Volnay.

— Les révélations des accusés mettant en cause des personnes de haute naissance, un tribunal spécial est créé : la Chambre ardente, acheva Sartine d'une voix sourde. La Reynie fait arrêter trois cent soixante personnes dont cent dix sont jugées. On en pend ou brûle trente-six et les autres finissent leurs jours en prison ou aux galères. La Voisin est brûlée vive en place de Grève le 22 février de l'année 1680. La cour de Louis XIV est éclaboussée par cette affaire.

Surtout la cour, se dit Volnay qui, cette fois, évita d'exprimer sa pensée. S'il provoquait souvent ses supérieurs, il savait toutefois s'arrêter à temps. La liberté de pensée n'était guère prisée par les autorités.

— Il y a autre chose, reprit Sartine soudain très grave. À toutes les accusations d'empoisonnement, s'ajoutent celles de meurtres d'enfants par des prêtres débauchés lors de ces messes noires.

Il déglutit.

— Volnay, dit-il d'un pressant, il ne faut pas que cela se reproduise !

— Peut-être serait-il intéressant que je relise les notes du lieutenant de La Reynie, risqua le jeune homme.

— Pourquoi donc?

Le commissaire aux morts étranges haussa légèrement les épaules.

— Pour comprendre ce qui peut pousser des gens à ce type de cérémonies, à savoir comment tout cela arrive, par quels réseaux on passe…

Sartine secoua la tête, catégorique.

— Après avoir relu toutes les pièces de l'affaire des Poisons, Louis XIV décida que celle-ci devait rester dans un *éternel oubli*. Il fit brûler en 1709 tous les registres, procès-verbaux et rapports de police. Il ne reste plus rien.

— Si! La mémoire, la mémoire collective. Celle-là, rien ne peut l'effacer.

Sartine haussa un sourcil.

— C'est pour cela qu'il nous faut très rapidement résoudre cette affaire. Je ne tiens pas à passer les dix prochaines années de ma vie à instruire une nouvelle affaire des Poisons!

— Nous n'en sommes pas là, remarqua calmement le commissaire aux morts étranges. Il n'y a aucun poison dans cette affaire. J'ai simplement à retrouver cinq meurtriers qui ont étranglé une jeune fille après un simulacre de messe chrétienne.

— Une seule de ces personnes l'a étranglée, non? fit remarquer Sartine.

Il arpentait la pièce d'une démarche nerveuse. De temps en temps, ses doigts trituraient sa perruque comme pour se rassurer.

— Et les autres sont ses complices, termina Volnay d'un ton glacial. Elles ne valent pas mieux que lui.

— Oui, sans doute. Enfin peut-être… L'affaire est plus grave que vous ne le pensez. Les archers du guet n'ont pas tenu leur langue, ils seront punis mais le mal est fait. Déjà la rumeur se répand dans tout Paris et vous savez à ce que l'on pense…

— L'affaire Montespan…

— L'affaire la Voisin! le corrigea vivement Sartine. Mais tout ceci est du passé, un passé terrible qu'il faut oublier. Depuis que j'ai acheté ma charge dans la police au service du roi, je n'ai jamais été confronté à ce type d'affaire. Aucun rapport quelconque de police ne m'informe de tels actes. Il convient de clore rapidement cette enquête avant que la rumeur ne s'étende à toute l'Europe que Paris voit une résurgence du culte satanique. Je compte sur vous et votre père pour mener cette affaire à bien et avec la plus grande discrétion possible.

Il sortit sa blague à tabac puis, semblant se rappeler qu'il venait déjà de priser, se ravisa.

— La rumeur, Volnay, la rumeur… Elle est légère au départ, elle s'envole puis elle devient une opinion : l'opinion publique.

Il fit une pause.

— Nous ne demandons pas au peuple d'avoir une opinion, vous en êtes conscient, Volnay ?

— De plus en plus, monsieur !

Néanmoins, pensa Volnay, *Versailles décline et c'est désormais à Paris que naît l'opinion. Un jour, nous vous pendrons vous et les vôtres !*

Sartine réajusta sa perruque.

— Je suis au courant de tout ce qui se dit dans la capitale du royaume. Des officiers de police en tenue civile fréquentent les auberges, les tavernes, les marchés ou les parvis des églises après la messe. Ils écoutent et notent tout ce qu'ils entendent. Je lis avec attention tous leurs rapports dont je rends compte au roi une fois par semaine.

Volnay hocha sombrement la tête. Il savait que, chaque mardi matin, Sartine racontait au roi tous les mauvais propos qui se tenaient dans Paris contre lui, sa cour, le pape ou simplement l'autorité. On appelait cela le mardi des grenouilles et le roi s'amusait surtout à entendre les ragots sur les gens de sa cour ou de son Église ; apprendre qu'un tel commettait le péché de Sodome et de bougrerie ou que telle marquise couchait avec ses domestiques le mettait en joie.

— Eh bien, reprit Sartine en haussant le ton, vous serez heureux d'apprendre que l'on parle de messes noires ! C'est même devenu le sujet préféré de conversation des Parisiens !

Il alla à son bureau, ouvrit un tiroir et s'empara d'une bourse qu'il lança à Volnay.

— Alors faites vite! Voici pour délier les langues si besoin et couvrir vos frais. Tenez-moi au courant personnellement et directement. Pas de papier qui traîne ou de rapport. Vous viendrez me voir régulièrement.

D'un geste sec, il congédia le commissaire aux morts étranges. Avant de sortir, Volnay se retourna. Sartine lui avait déjà tourné le dos et, debout devant son bureau, contemplait pensivement le portrait de Sophia.

Après son rendez-vous avec Sartine, Volnay demeura quelques heures au Châtelet pour lire les rapports du guet pour les nuits précédentes. Il s'intéressa également aux violations de sépultures. Après une après-midi ainsi passée à la lumière des chandelles, il rentra chez lui, les yeux rougis par la lecture. La nuit tombait et les artisans commençaient à fermer leurs échoppes. Des lumières brillaient derrière les carreaux des cafés. Ouvriers et manœuvres quittaient chantiers et ateliers pour regagner leur pauvre grabat. D'autres se glissaient dans les cabarets pour y fumer une dernière pipe et s'abrutir d'alcool. Lorsque Volnay poussa la porte de sa demeure, ce fut pour découvrir le moine s'entretenant en latin avec la pie.

— *A bove ante, ab asino retro, a morionem undique caveto.* "Prends garde au bœuf par-devant, à l'âne par-derrière, à l'imbécile par tous les côtés!"

— C'est un conseil que je suivrais!

— J'aimerais que ton oiseau parle plusieurs langues, expliqua son père en se retournant.

— Cela lui servira certainement beaucoup dans la vie! répondit sans rire son fils.

Le policier remarqua que le moine était passé de l'affliction à une gaieté surfaite. Cela ne le rassura pas.

— J'espère que tu as quelque chose de décent à boire, fit le moine, car j'ai à te parler.

— Toi, tu as découvert quelque chose, fit Volnay en souriant.

Le moine eut une petite mimique victorieuse.

— Diable, je n'en suis pas très fier mais hier nous avons oublié un cadavre.

— Quoi ?! Une seconde victime ?

— Le gardien du cimetière…

— Oh, c'est vrai, reconnut le policier. De ce point de vue-là…

Le moine balaya l'objection d'un revers de main.

— Pas d'excuse. Nous étions sur une scène de crime et nous nous sommes préoccupés d'une seule victime, éliminant d'emblée l'autre de l'acte criminel. Nous avons sauté aux conclusions en ce qui la concerne. On nous dit qu'elle est morte de peur. Comme un âne je répète qu'elle doit être morte de peur et au total on n'examine pas son corps ! *Errare humanum est ! Perseverare diabolicum !*

Le moine s'amusa à lancer quelques graines à la pie en murmurant doucement :

— Vilain roi, vilain roi…

— Vilain roi, répéta la pie d'une voix aux intonations vaguement humaines.

— On te pendra… On te pendra…

— Vas-tu m'expliquer ? s'agaça le commissaire aux morts étranges.

Son père se retourna vivement, un sourire radieux aux lèvres.

— Mon cher fils, j'ai l'honneur de t'annoncer que le sieur Fontaine, ci-devant gardien de cimetière, n'est pas mort de saisissement. On l'a tout simplement étouffé sans laisser de traces extérieures.

Il s'approcha du feu qui flambait joyeusement pour s'y chauffer les mains. L'hiver restait froid et la température dans la maison basse.

— J'ai noté des signes d'hémorragie à la tête et à la poitrine, reprit-il. Des bleus sur sa poitrine semblent démontrer qu'un homme de forte corpulence, voire plusieurs, s'est assis sur lui. On lui a maintenu les poignets contre le sol. Le dos de ceux-ci en est presque ensanglanté. Je relève également une bosse derrière la tête qu'il a dû se faire en se cognant tandis qu'on le suffoquait en appuyant sans doute un manteau ou une couverture sur sa bouche et ses narines. On a bien évité de l'étrangler afin de ne pas laisser de marques autour de son cou.

Il prit un air modeste et s'empara du tisonnier pour retourner une bûche trop grosse.

— Ce n'est pas tout! fit-il triomphalement en se redressant. Son fils soupira.

— Eh bien?

— Tu te rappelles que je ne m'expliquais pas que cette jeune fille se soit laissé étendre nue sur une tombe glacée sans un geste de défense. J'ai retrouvé dans sa bouche les restes d'un jus laiteux et collant. Il s'agit à ma connaissance d'une drogue qui provoque une espèce d'heureuse somnolence, un sentiment profond de bien-être et de satisfaction. Voilà pourquoi elle s'est laissé mener comme un mouton au sacrifice. Cette drogue est coûteuse car elle provient d'une plante qui se cultive dans des contrées d'Asie. Le vendeur en est un Grec de la ruelle de l'Or que j'ai visité ce matin et qui m'en a très obligeamment vendu une fiole. L'homme est peu bavard. J'y retournerai avec toi pour le persuader de nous parler de ses clients!

Il conclut modestement :

— Tu vois que j'ai progressé en peu de temps de manière spectaculaire! Et toi, de ton côté? s'enquit-il innocemment.

Volnay le rejoignit près du feu et leva ses mains. Même protégés par des gants de laine, ses doigts étaient gourds et raides.

— Notre bon M. de Sartine m'a fait tout un couplet sur l'affaire des Poisons, dit-il d'un ton détaché.

— Gens peureux, gens puissants! Sartine a peur, tout simplement. Autant la sorcellerie est campagnarde, autant les messes noires se sont développées dans des milieux très aisés quand ce n'est pas au sein même de la cour comme dans l'affaire de la Brinvilliers.

— Tu n'étais pas né, remarqua sans rire le commissaire aux morts étranges.

Le moine se retourna vivement vers lui.

— Oh, cela remonte peut-être à Louis XIV mais nous continuons encore à en parler dans le cercle des philosophes. Les lumières de notre siècle sont loin d'avoir chassé toutes les ombres. Nous aimons à prendre en exemple cette affaire comme de tout ce qui nous fait le plus horreur.

Il sautilla sur place, ravi de pouvoir commencer son exposé.

— La marquise de Brinvilliers, par ailleurs jolie et intelligente femme, est arrêtée après la découverte chez son amant d'une cassette remplie de documents compromettants. Ces documents, dont l'amant se sert pour faire chanter sa maîtresse, démontrent que la belle marquise a aidé son père et ses frères à avaler leur langue afin de s'approprier leurs biens. Son mari a réchappé de justesse au poison mais quelques servantes qui en savaient trop n'ont pas eu cette chance!

— Père, nous en avons déjà parlé avec Sartine!

Le moine se planta devant la cage à oiseau et entreprit de lisser d'un doigt le plumage noir aux reflets métalliques de la pie.

— Et ce n'est pas tout! continua-t-il comme s'il n'avait rien entendu. La très charitable marquise de Brinvilliers apporte vins et confitures aux malades dans les hôpitaux. Malheureusement, après ses passages le taux de mortalité croît à une vitesse stupéfiante. C'est que notre belle empoisonneuse teste ses produits sur les malades avant de les utiliser sur les bien portants! Ah! L'expérimentation des potions médicinales, voilà un sujet intéressant...

Une fois lancé, le moine était intarissable. Volnay s'assit donc en silence pour écouter la suite.

— L'exécution de la Brinvilliers en 1676 n'est que le prélude à quelque chose de bien plus grave. Travaillée par le bourreau, la marquise révèle beaucoup de choses. Le lieutenant de police de l'époque, La Reynie, dispose alors d'assez d'informations pour remonter les filières. Il se rend compte avec effarement que des milliers de personnes de toute condition s'adonnent dans Paris au poison ou aux messes noires et à l'envoûtement. Même le roi est effrayé de découvrir autant de noirceur sous son règne.

Le moine s'interrompit pour caresser amoureusement les plumes de la pie et lui murmurer qu'elle était le plus bel oiseau du monde.

— En 1679, reprend-il, l'enquête rebondit avec l'arrestation d'une certaine Marie Bosse qui aurait fourni des poisons à certaines épouses de membres du Parlement souhaitant se débarrasser de leur mari.

— Et voilà que Marie Bosse dénonce la femme d'un mercier-joaillier, dame Catherine Monvoisin, dite la Voisin, intervint

Volnay toujours pressé d'arriver aux faits plutôt que de supporter les interminables digressions de son père.

Le policier ajouta une bûche dans le feu, ce qui provoqua une gerbe d'étincelles.

— Et La Reynie continue avec zèle son enquête qui l'amène dans le milieu des messes noires...

Son père fit mine de se boucher le nez et se hâta de reprendre l'histoire à son compte.

— Cela sent mauvais à la cour! La marquise de Brinvilliers avait prévenu : *S'il pleut sur moi, il dégouttera sur beaucoup de monde!* Or, un proche de Colbert a été mis en cause par la Brinvilliers et d'autres sont accusés par la Voisin. Louvois, ministre de la Guerre et attaché à la perte d'un Colbert successivement affaibli par cette affaire, la faillite de la Compagnie des Indes occidentales et par la liaison du roi avec la marquise de Maintenon, mène de son côté une enquête secrète pour le compte du roi.

Il plissa le front et le frotta du plat de la main comme s'il voulait stimuler sa mémoire.

— Après l'exécution de sa mère, reprit-il, la fille de la Voisin met en cause la favorite du roi en disgrâce, Mme de Montespan. On raconte qu'elle commerce avec la Voisin pour obtenir des poudres lui permettant de lui ramener les faveurs du roi mais aussi pour empoisonner des rivales.

À cet instant du récit, le moine se plaignit de la soif et, lui connaissant cette manie, Volnay déboucha prestement une bouteille d'un vin de Bourgogne.

— Ah, du vin de Givry! Le préféré de feu le bon roi Henri IV si tant est qu'un roi puisse être bon ce qui n'est pas dans la nature de cette fonction!

Il s'interrompit pour boire une rasade et claqua des doigts pour ramener à lui une attention pourtant déjà tout acquise.

— Dans le bel hôtel particulier de la Voisin, on découvre une drôle de sacristie et, dans sa cave, des milliers d'ossements d'enfants. Soumise à la question, la Voisin va tout avouer. Elle fabrique et vend des poisons à base d'arsenic et de bave de crapaud! On surnomme ce mélange, pilé dans un mortier et saupoudré dans les plats, *la poudre de succession* tant on l'emploie pour hâter le trépas de ses proches! Tu veux hériter d'un parent en trop bonne santé? Un peu de poudre et hop l'argent est dans le sac!

À ce moment on cogna brutalement contre la porte. Le commissaire aux morts étranges sursauta légèrement. Les visites étaient rares sinon inexistantes depuis le départ de Casanova et Chiara de Paris au printemps. Le policier alla ouvrir. Un souffle glacé se rua à l'intérieur. Volnay cligna des yeux car la lumière du jour était faible dans la petite cour. Il se trouvait devant deux personnages qui portaient un loup sur le visage et faillit leur refermer la porte au nez tant l'avait agacé l'incident de la nuit dernière avec la jeune femme au masque de mort. La perruque sur la tête de l'homme retint toutefois son attention et il s'effaça devant eux.

— Vous ici?

Sartine eut un bref ricanement et ôta son masque.

— Allez savoir pourquoi, cette année, tout le monde se masque à l'approche de Noël. C'est étrange mais bien pratique pour se déplacer discrètement. Me voilà donc!

— Lorsque l'on parle du diable, marmonna le moine en se levant machinalement.

Le lieutenant général de police lui jeta un regard peu amène mais l'autre ne s'en soucia guère. Il venait d'apercevoir une forme délicieusement féminine sur le pas de la porte et guettait le moment où l'inconnue allait tomber le masque. Elle le fit d'un geste charmant, révélant un visage à la beauté sauvage et au regard assuré. Elle était presque aussi grande que le commissaire aux morts étranges et de longs cheveux fins, d'un brun aux reflets roux, ruisselaient dans son dos. Elle portait des boucles d'oreilles en forme de croissant et à ses poignets des bracelets d'or tintaient à chacun de ses gestes. Sous des cils longs et fournis, d'immenses yeux verts, mouchetés de jaune, brillaient d'une lueur surnaturelle.

Son regard balaya la pièce qui servait à la fois de salon, bureau et salle à manger, s'attardant au passage sur les étagères de livres reliés, aux couvertures cloutées et aux reliures gaufrées, qui s'élançaient à l'assaut des murs.

— Laissez-moi vous présenter Mlle Hélène de Troie, fit Sartine.

Hélène de Troie? Le commissaire aux morts étranges et son père échangèrent sans mot dire un regard entendu. Sartine avait décidé de se moquer d'eux ouvertement. Le moine s'inclina toutefois avec la galanterie d'un grand seigneur devant la jeune femme. Même le lieutenant général de police semblait enchanté d'être aussi bien accompagné. Seul le commissaire aux morts étranges ne marqua ni surprise ni intérêt. Son visage s'était figé en un masque de pierre, indéchiffrable. À l'intérieur, ses pensées prenaient toutefois une tournure vertigineuse. Jamais encore Sartine n'avait mis un pied en sa demeure et il fallait un événement exceptionnel pour que cela arrivât. Qui plus est, tout s'était décidé très vite puisque Sartine, rencontré vers midi le jour même, ne lui avait pas fait part de sa prochaine visite.

Le moine s'empressa de débarrasser la visiteuse de son manteau et l'invita à s'asseoir près du feu. Elle portait une robe de velours rouge à l'anglaise, fermée sur le devant, la jupe montée par fronçage et couturée selon une ligne remontant sur les hanches vers la taille, les pans relevés dans les poches latérales de la robe et drapés dans le dos. Un habit pour quelqu'un intéressé par plus de liberté de mouvement.

— Votre enquête sur la messe noire devrait être difficile, vous allez avoir besoin d'aide, décréta solennellement Sartine.

Son visage vint s'orner d'un méchant sourire. Aussitôt Volnay redouta la suite.

— Et j'ai décidé de vous en procurer!

Il fit un vaste geste en direction d'Hélène de Troie.

— Mademoiselle vous accompagnera dans vos recherches et vous sera d'un précieux secours. Vous n'imaginez pas tout ce dont elle est capable!

Le moine se leva et s'inclina de nouveau devant elle, lui baisant cette fois la main avec ravissement.

— Monsieur de Sartine, vous vous trompez, je ne l'imagine que trop bien!

La jeune femme le remercia du compliment, si c'en était un, d'un sourire distant.

— Cela signifie-t-il que mademoiselle va nous accompagner durant toute notre enquête? demanda le commissaire aux morts étranges toujours impassible.

Sartine prit un air réjoui.

— Vous avez tout à fait saisi ma pensée!

— Il n'en est pas question, décréta Volnay d'un ton égal. Je mène seul mes enquêtes avec mon... avec mon assistant.

En dehors de Sartine qui savait tout, comme il se doit, le commissaire aux morts étranges évitait en public de révéler que ce savant, jadis condamné au bûcher et qui pour y échapper portait désormais la bure, était son père. Le lieutenant général de police jeta un bref coup d'œil au moine qui contemplait le plafond avec insistance comme s'il souhaitait se faire oublier. De fait, l'entrée de Sartine semblait l'avoir plongé dans de graves tourments, certes tempérés par l'entrée de sa charmante escorte féminine.

— Vous ne menez pas une enquête ordinaire, fit le lieutenant général de police qui n'aimait pas qu'on remette en question ses décisions. Une messe noire s'est déroulée dans un lieu public, un cimetière! Et cela s'est terminé par deux meurtres!

— Il n'y a pas de meurtre que nous ne sachions élucider seuls, répliqua Volnay d'une voix tranchante. Et je ne vois pas ce qu'une personne comme mademoiselle pourrait bien nous apporter.

Il s'inclina sèchement vers cette dernière et ajouta :

— Cela dit sans vouloir vous offenser, mademoiselle.

Machinalement, les deux hommes en face d'elle s'étaient approchés tandis que Sartine se reculait. Le plus jeune semblait soupçonneux, le plus âgé admiratif. Sous ses longs cils noirs, la jeune femme observa le commissaire aux morts étranges à la dérobée. Sa mise sobre était impeccable, ses bottes noires rutilaient et son gilet entrouvert sur le haut laissait blouser une écharpe de batiste. La minceur de Volnay, la force tranquille qui se dégageait de lui et la finesse des traits de son visage attiraient le regard des femmes. Toutefois, il était aussitôt arrêté par la froideur qui lui servait de bouclier pour se protéger des autres. Au contraire, le moine adoptait une attitude ouverte et ses yeux reflétaient une sagesse infinie.

— Vous ne m'offensez pas, dit-elle, j'ai déjà entendu bien pire.

Elle allongea négligemment une jambe et l'on devina aussitôt sous le tissu la courbure parfaite de celle-ci.

— Maintenant, je crois en Dieu, murmura le moine extasié.

Sans s'émouvoir de la remarque, Hélène lui adressa un léger sourire. À la couleur des flammes, la couleur de ses yeux avait encore changé et évoquait maintenant celle d'une prairie brûlée par l'été.

— Heureux d'entendre ça! marmonna Sartine. Mieux vaux tard que jamais!

Il considéra le moine avec un brin d'hostilité.

— Je vous aurais plutôt cru tenté par le culte du diable!

Volnay tressaillit, l'allusion était claire. La jeune femme resta impassible mais toute son attention était concentrée sur la réponse à venir du moine. Celui-ci ne déçut pas son public.

— Contrairement aux courtisans de Versailles, fit-il froidement, je n'ai aucune attirance pour un culte qui me forcerait à baiser le cul d'autrui!

Sartine sembla prêt à exploser mais le rire frais d'Hélène s'éleva dans la pièce, dissipant toutes les tensions.

— Vous êtes tel que je l'imaginais, conclut-elle.

— Et pire encore, conclut sèchement Sartine en revêtant de nouveau son masque.

Il fit quelques pas vers la porte.

— Je vous laisse, mademoiselle. Quant à vous, messieurs, vous devrez l'écouter, répondre à toutes ses questions et la laisser vous accompagner partout où elle le désirera. Si vous ne le faites pas, je vous dessaisirai de cette enquête! Suis-je clair?

Il les considéra d'un air hautain. Le moine ne dit rien mais un éclair brilla dans ses yeux calmes. Volnay s'empressa d'acquiescer pour éviter un esclandre.

— Nous ferons comme vous le désirez.

Sartine parut surpris de cette reddition soudaine. Il considéra un instant le commissaire aux morts étranges d'un air soupçonneux puis tourna les talons, non sans avoir galamment salué la jeune femme. Une bourrasque glacée accompagna sa sortie. Le moine poussa un juron. Dans sa morgue, Sartine n'avait pas refermé la porte. Le commissaire aux morts étranges alla s'appuyer au battant puis se retourna et marcha lentement vers Hélène. La jeune femme le considérait, une expression énigmatique sur le visage.

— Si jeune et déjà la confiance du lieutenant général de police, murmura-t-il songeusement. Est-il possible de vous demander en quoi consistent vos fonctions auprès de M. de Sartine?

Il se tenait parfaitement droit devant Hélène qui ne le quittait pas du regard. Ils se jaugèrent en silence.

La jeune femme eut une moue amusée.

— Bien sûr que non!

Volnay fronça les sourcils.

— Peut-être pourriez-vous alors nous aider en remettant la main sur les notes de M. de La Reynie lors de l'affaire la Voisin?

— Pourquoi donc? La Chambre ardente qui jugea de ces affaires fut dissoute il y a bien longtemps…

— Certes, insista le commissaire aux morts étranges, mais il est intéressant pour nous de bien connaître le sujet et savoir comment s'organisaient ces messes noires, qui elles réunissaient, comment elles se déroulaient…

Hélène hocha lentement la tête. Une mèche de ses cheveux fins tomba sur ses yeux sans qu'elle prenne la peine de l'ôter.

— Je comprends. Ce qui vous intéresse est surtout le mode opératoire. On dit que la Voisin n'était pas seulement empoisonneuse mais faiseuse d'anges. Elle utilisait le petit corps des nourrissons pour en extraire le sang, le foie et le cœur pour ses mixtures…

Le moine la contempla avec curiosité.

— Vous savez bien des choses pour une personne de votre âge.

— J'ai passé ma journée à parcourir les notes du lieutenant La Reynie, répondit-elle très naturellement!

Le moine échangea avec le commissaire un nouveau regard entendu. Qui donc dans le royaume pouvait se targuer d'avoir lu les notes de La Reynie? Cela confirmait également que Sartine redoutait bien une nouvelle affaire…

— Ceux qui servent la messe, reprit Hélène en dardant sur eux son regard, le font pour l'argent. Ceux qui y assistent sont souvent en disgrâce et recherchent un retour de faveur de leur monarque. Vous savez comment sont les courtisans : ils ne vivent et respirent que pour être vus du roi. Seule sa lumière les éclaire. Seul son soleil les réchauffe.

— Les courtisans sont des ignares, marmonna le moine, ils ne savent que deux choses : l'heure du lever du roi et l'heure de son coucher !

Hélène le gratifia d'un sourire charmeur.

— Dites-moi, mademoiselle, demanda froidement Volnay. Êtes-vous informée de choses que M. de Sartine n'ait pas daigné porter à notre connaissance ?

La jeune femme arqua délicatement un sourcil, semblant peser sa réponse à l'aide d'une toile d'araignée.

— À ma connaissance, non, répondit-elle enfin d'un ton neutre. Ceci dit, il est tout à fait possible que le lieutenant général de police ait omis de me faire part de certaines données du problème s'il les juge confidentielles...

Le commissaire aux morts étranges daigna enfin lui accorder un hochement de tête approbateur.

— Et peut-on savoir quelles sont les compétences que le lieutenant général de police Sartine vous prête ?

— Eh bien...

Elle s'interrompit pour réfléchir.

— Je sais monter à cheval, tirer au pistolet, me battre à l'épée et à la dague. Je m'intéresse aux mathématiques, je connais le nom de toutes les étoiles dans le ciel. Je parle également anglais, italien, allemand, latin, grec et araméen...

Le moine haussa un sourcil intéressé et la complimenta.

— C'est très bien, mademoiselle.

— Ce n'est pas tout...

— Oui ? fit-il.

— Je suis un peu sorcière !

Il y eut un silence stupéfait puis le moine partit d'un grand éclat de rire.

— J'adore, j'adore !

Volnay fit un pas en avant.

— Où avez-vous appris tout cela ? On n'apprend guère ces choses-là aux jeunes filles.

Le moine intervint.

— Étiez-vous au couvent pour apprendre ces langues ? À celui de la Madeleine de Traisnel par exemple ?

Hélène eut un rire moqueur.

— C'est un couvent à la mode mais on n'y forme que des coquettes. Est-ce que je leur ressemble donc? Danser, chanter et jouer de l'épinette, voilà ce que l'on apprend à ces charmantes cervelles d'oiseau, soit dit, monsieur, sans vouloir offenser votre pie!

La jeune femme fit une pause songeuse.

— On ne veut pas que les femmes apprennent, on leur enseigne simplement comment avoir l'air de tout savoir sans rien connaître. Des serins, voilà ce qu'on en fait, des serins dans une cage.

Elle se tourna vers Volnay pour ajouter du même ton :

— Soit dit, monsieur, toujours sans vouloir offenser votre oiseau en cage!

Et, comme pour se faire pardonner, elle se leva pour aller lisser les plumes de la pie qui se mit à jacasser bruyamment. Le père et le fils s'entreregardèrent. En quelques minutes, Hélène venait de faire exploser la condition féminine soumise de leur siècle et reculer les limites de la pensée.

Elle ressemble à Chiara, faillit dire le moine mais il se retint justement pour ne pas raviver le chagrin d'amour de son fils. Chiara avait regagné ses terres de Toscane depuis six mois et, si son fils en recevait des nouvelles, il ne lui en parlait pas.

— Si l'on en revient à l'affaire des Poisons, poursuivit Hélène d'un ton soigneusement neutre, il est clair que Louis XIV ne pouvait se permettre de voir sa favorite, la Montespan, accusée de tels crimes. La crainte du scandale était trop forte. Et puis, il lui aurait été humiliant de reconnaître ainsi s'être autant trompé sur le compte de sa maîtresse. Par orgueil, il ne l'a même pas disgraciée et se comporta comme si elle était innocente de tout, continuant à lui rendre visite chaque jour pour donner le change.

— J'ignore si au cours de ces entrevues, ce bon Roi-Soleil lui parlait des nourrissons égorgés pendant les messes noires, grommela le moine.

Le commissaire aux morts étranges jeta un bref coup d'œil à la jeune femme, elle ne semblait pas désarçonnée ni surprise de la tournure de cette conversation. Le policier jugea toutefois bon de clore cette discussion qui pouvait s'avérer dangereuse devant une inconnue.

— Louis XIV comprit le danger de toutes ces révélations et se hâta d'ordonner la clôture de la procédure, dit-il. Grâce à cela, la majorité des suspects ou accusés s'en sortit à bon compte.

— Les rois sont sans morale et sans viscères, conclut le moine.

Hélène le considéra longuement et avec intérêt. Le commissaire aux morts étranges frémit. Le moine parlait trop et disait à n'importe qui ce qu'il pensait. Certains allaient en prison pour de telles paroles et il ne se passait pas une semaine sans que Volnay ne tremble pour son père. Comme si elle avait compris l'inquiétude du commissaire aux morts étranges, la jeune femme se tourna vers lui.

— Rassurez-vous, je ne suis pas ici pour vous espionner et rapporter vos paroles à M. de Sartine. Je suis là pour vous aider.

Elle se pencha vers le moine.

— Je suppose que le cadavre de la jeune morte est dans votre cave?

Il hocha lentement la tête sans la quitter des yeux.

— Je voudrais la voir.

— J'ai fait des dessins d'elle, ils sont très ressemblants, intervint le commissaire aux morts étranges.

Hélène ne releva même pas.

— Rien ne remplace un visage que l'on voit en face et il ne faut pas trop attendre, non?

Le moine pâlit légèrement.

— Est-ce bien utile?

Elle se raidit.

— Je pense que ma requête n'a rien d'exagéré. Vous m'avez accepté dans votre enquête devant M. de Sartine. Respectez-en les conditions et tout ira bien. Écartez-vous-en d'un pas et il vous en cuira!

III

LE MOINE, LA FEMME
ET AUTRES DIABLERIES

Les derniers lambeaux de jour disparaissaient lorsque le moine et la jeune femme arrivèrent rue de la Lanterne, pataugeant dans une bouillasse froide qui macula de traces grises les jolies bottes couleur crème d'Hélène. La bise transformait l'air en mille aiguilles acérées. Ils s'engouffrèrent en toute hâte dans l'impasse du Loup-Pendu.

— J'ai emménagé là récemment, expliqua le moine, pour me rapprocher de mon… du commissaire aux morts étranges. Cela facilite la vie et puis je dispose ici d'une double cave très fraîche et servie par deux escaliers dont l'un donne directement dans ma chambre. C'est d'un pratique! Enfin, je peux conserver plusieurs jours dans ces caves les cadavres dans de bonnes conditions.

Sortant son trousseau de clés, il introduisit la plus grosse dans la serrure de la porte. Celle-ci était en chêne, épaisse et cloutée, renforcée d'acier. Une porte difficile à enfoncer, jugea Hélène. Le propriétaire des lieux était de toute évidence soit prudent, soit méfiant, l'un n'empêchant d'ailleurs pas l'autre.

Les restes d'un feu agonisaient dans une vaste cheminée de marbre rouge du Languedoc. Le moine raviva les flammes et alluma suffisamment de chandelles pour chasser la pénombre de la pièce. Les rideaux de serge cramoisie étaient tirés. Près du feu, une belle table à écrire en palissandre, recouverte de papiers, trahissait le goût du propriétaire des lieux pour la plume. Au mur, des tableaux sur toile ou des estampes sous verre reproduisaient des sujets galants plaisamment exécutés. Bergers et bergères s'y livraient au délicieux jeu de l'aveu des sentiments mais, parfois, des personnages aux allures de courtisans affichaient plus nettement leurs désirs en semblant réclamer leur dû à leurs compagnes. Une tapisserie en chiné flambé couvrait le mur au nord et une bordure de bois doré surmontait la porte d'une pièce attenante, qui devait être la chambre. Au sud, se trouvait une cuisine où les plantes aromatiques grimpaient jusqu'aux casseroles de cuivre.

Tout indiquait l'aisance, un goût pour le beau et une certaine légèreté. Les yeux d'Hélène glissèrent sur un tableau représentant un groupe de jeunes gens égarés dans un parc boisé. Selon l'humeur de celui qui le contemplait, il invitait soit à la gaieté, soit à la mélancolie. Un couple d'amoureux s'en allait au hasard d'une allée, bras dessus, bras dessous, gracieux et fragile à la fois. Le regard dur et attentif d'un homme tout de noir vêtu les suivait. D'autres personnes venaient peupler le tableau de leur jeunesse et de leur insouciance. Mais, à bien y regarder, les têtes penchées, les regards en biais et les corps tendus semblaient signaler les tensions exacerbées de relations amoureuses complexes. Hélène remarqua alors que, dans ce tableau, tout était fait pour cacher le véritable sujet de celui-ci. Sur un tapis d'herbe verte, un jeune homme s'emparait de la main d'une adolescente à la nuque exquise. La posture du buste de celle-ci dénotait un mouvement de recul mais il se pouvait bien que ce retrait ne fût que feint car la main de son compagnon n'enserrait guère sa taille élancée. Un instant, elle crut saisir dans le profil du jeune homme qui guidait sa compagne les traits du moine moins âgé.

La jeune femme s'attarda devant le tableau mais le moine ne semblait pas désireux de commenter cette peinture. Il entraîna la visiteuse à sa suite jusque dans la seconde cave et souleva la lourde couverture qui la recouvrait.

— Voici donc notre jeune morte, fit Hélène d'un ton détaché une fois devant le cadavre. C'est étrange, on dirait qu'elle dort…

Elle l'examina avec curiosité mais sans s'en approcher et se retourna vers le moine.

— Que faites-vous avec les corps que l'on vous amène ?

Le moine haussa un sourcil.

— Que voulez-vous donc que j'en fasse? J'examine la température et la couleur du corps, la rigidité ou la flexibilité des membres, l'état des yeux et de la mâchoire, l'enflure, la bouffissure, l'engorgement des voies, l'état des sphincters, les taches, les ecchymoses, les plaies, les ulcères, les fractures, luxations, hernies, chutes, écoulement du sang et autres liquides de la bouche du nez ou des oreilles, voire de l'anus et du vagin...

Il avait une voix chaude aux accents calmes et cultivés, un ton aux nuances élégantes. Devant elle, il débordait d'une vie insolente. Elle l'écoutait avec attention, une lueur d'admiration dans le regard. Le moine s'en aperçut et conclut modestement mais théâtralement :

— En bref, je regarde tout ce qui peut paraître s'éloigner d'un état normal et régulier.

Inclinant la tête, elle le récompensa d'un sourire éclatant.

— J'admire votre science nouvelle, fit-elle.

Le moine se rengorgea.

— Ce n'est rien, j'ai toujours été en avance sur mon époque mais je n'ai guère de mérite à cela car elle est en retard sur tout!

Un rire cristallin jaillit de la gorge d'Hélène. Elle balaya la pièce du regard et s'approcha d'une table d'expérience dans la première cave.

— Oh, qu'est-ce que ceci? Quel étrange appareil!

— Il s'agit d'un microscope composé, il a été inventé en 1590 par Zacharias Jansen. La version que vous voyez est plus évoluée et doit beaucoup aux travaux de Robert Hooke au siècle dernier. Ces combinaisons complexes de lentilles, soigneusement polies, permettent un agrandissement jusqu'à trois cents fois la taille initiale mais je pense que l'on peut faire mieux!

— Trois cents fois! Comment est-ce possible?

— Grâce à la science... Cela me permet d'étudier tous les indices trouvés sur une scène de crime.

— Et qu'examinez-vous aujourd'hui?

Le moine se mordit les lèvres. Il s'agissait du fil de laine découvert ce matin même par son fils sur les lieux du crime.

— Une expérience que je mène sur les tissus, répondit-il avec aplomb. Mais ceci est peu de chose. Donnez-moi votre main!

Elle le regarda droit dans les yeux puis se déganta avec lenteur. Le moine frissonna intérieurement. En ôtant son gant, Hélène donnait l'impression de retirer un vêtement. Enfin, elle lui tendit une main souple et tiède, aux doigts longs et déliés. Le moine retira le fil de laine et attira l'index de la jeune femme à sa place.

— Mettez votre œil à cette extrémité. Vous voyez les sillons imprimés sur le bout de vos doigts. Voilà, c'est encore mieux qu'une empreinte de pas! Je travaille à produire une substance qui permette de relever les empreintes laissées par les doigts sur les lieux du crime. Une fois un suspect arrêté, je pourrai ainsi lui prendre une empreinte en mettant son doigt dans de l'encre puis sur un papier ou simplement sur une plaque de verre comme celle-ci. Ensuite, je comparerai les deux empreintes.

— Admirable! Encore faut-il que vous attrapiez le bon suspect!

— Pas forcément, songez que je peux aussi innocenter celui-ci! Tenez, regardez!

Il s'empara d'une petite plaque en verre et y posa son index qu'il pressa fortement.

— Faites de même.

Hélène s'exécuta non sans hésitation.

— Parfait!

Il plaça la plaquette de verre à la place du morceau d'étoffe.

— Maintenant regardez…

Elle colla l'œil à la lunette et poussa une brève exclamation de surprise.

— Oh, comme c'est intéressant! Elles sont très différentes et donc…

— Vous avez bien deviné. L'empreinte de nos doigts révèle nos identités. Un jour, sur les lieux de crime, on relèvera ces empreintes pour les comparer à toutes celles des criminels que l'on possède déjà!

— Vous êtes décidément très savant, fit-elle.

Le moine dissimula sa satisfaction derrière un grognement modeste.

— Une seule chose m'inquiète : il faudra beaucoup de plaquettes de verre et bien les étiqueter!

La jeune femme lui décocha un regard irrésistible.

— Vous trouverez bien un moyen…

Il hocha la tête.

— Sûrement, mais dans une prochaine vie! Les chats en ont bien sept. Pourquoi le moine n'en aurait-il pas deux ou trois?

À nouveau, Hélène reprit sa marche dans le laboratoire. Du fait de la présence des cadavres, le moine avait éteint la plupart des fourneaux mais certains recélaient encore bien des merveilles en train de cuire.

— M. de Sartine prétend que vous recherchez le secret de l'immortelle jeunesse…

— Comme tout le monde, mademoiselle, comme tout le monde…

— Si vous le trouvez, faites-moi signe, cela m'intéresse!

— Je vous ferai un prix d'ami!

Hélène s'immobilisa devant une masse qui révélait les contours d'un corps humain. Le moine fronça les sourcils. Sous la toile qui le recouvrait, se trouvait le cadavre du gardien de cimetière.

— Qui avez-vous donc là? demanda-t-elle négligemment.

— Oh, un de mes paroissiens de passage, répondit-il sans rire. Je fais chambre d'hôte parfois…

Tout sourire s'effaça du visage de la jeune femme.

— Ne serait-ce pas plutôt le corps du gardien de cimetière que vous avez fait enlever à l'aube en sa demeure, l'arrachant à sa veuve éplorée, avec deux exempts du Châtelet?

Ah diable, pensa le moine, *il faut que j'arrête de sous-estimer cette jeune dame sous prétexte qu'elle est jolie!*

— Si fait, mademoiselle, si fait…

— Et qu'avez-vous découvert?

Elle s'était approchée du corps et sa main effleurait le drap qui le recouvrait.

— Mort de peur, dit rapidement le moine.

D'un coup sec, elle arracha le drap et se pencha sur l'homme.

— Moi, je dirais plutôt mort congestionné, fit-elle calmement.

— Vraiment?

Le moine s'était approché.

— Oh, vous avez raison, fit-il en se penchant à son tour, j'ai dû mal regarder dans la pénombre !

Le visage attentif d'Hélène se trouvait à quelques centimètres du sien, au-dessus du cadavre. D'un coup son parfum l'envahit. Il exhalait les senteurs de bien des choses oubliées comme la sensualité de l'ambre, la mélancolie de la rose, la fraîcheur de la fougère… Sans modifier sa position, la jeune femme se tourna lentement vers lui.

— Et si nous faisions la paix pour vraiment travailler ensemble ? fit-elle en articulant chaque syllabe.

Il la considéra, fasciné par les paillettes dorées qui s'agitaient dans ses prunelles.

— J'en serais ravi, répondit-il rapidement. Cet homme a été étouffé.

Elle hocha la tête.

— Il a dû surprendre les célébrants de la messe noire…

— Sans doute et ceux-ci ont pensé à l'étouffer plutôt que l'étrangler afin de ne pas laisser de marques ! Surprenant, non ?!

— Ils ont beaucoup de sang-froid.

— Il en faut pour tuer une enfant !

Un courant d'air glacé entra par une lucarne et balaya la pièce. Il sentit la jeune femme frissonner.

— Vous allez prendre la mort ici, dit le moine d'un ton paternel. Montons, je vais vous préparer une boisson chaude. Nous deviserons ensuite plus confortablement.

Un sourire mutin passa sur les traits d'Hélène.

— Et de quoi allons-nous parler, monsieur l'érudit ?

Le moine rabattit d'un geste sec le drap.

— De vous, voyons !

Quelques instants plus tard, il s'effaça pour la laisser entrer dans la pièce qui lui servait à la fois de salon et de cuisine. Elle passa devant lui en l'effleurant. Le même parfum chaud d'herbes et de fleurs sauvages émanait d'elle, rehaussé par l'ambre gris. Sans fébrilité, le moine en huma l'arôme avec reconnaissance comme on respire un bouquet fraîchement cueilli.

Hélène fit le tour de la pièce, s'attardant au passage devant le clavecin dont ses doigts effleurèrent les touches.

— Savez-vous jouer ? demanda-t-elle.

Le visage du moine se ferma.

— Non, il appartenait à ma femme avant sa mort.

— Oh, je vous demande pardon.

— Elle jouait divinement, continua-t-il comme s'il n'avait pas entendu. Elle chantait aussi. Un ange n'aurait pas chanté mieux qu'elle.

Il y eut un silence profond que le moine rompit le premier.

— On gèle ici, je vais rallumer le feu.

Habilement, il raviva le foyer jusqu'à ce qu'une langue de flamme vînt lécher les bûches sèches rajoutées. Puis il approcha de la cheminée un grand fauteuil aux coussins rembourrés et moelleux.

— Prenez place, je vous en prie.

Elle s'assit avec un soupir d'aise puis contempla ses pieds d'un air désolé.

— J'ai marché dans la neige et mes pieds sont trempés, se plaignit-elle. Mes bottes étaient trop fines. Voulez-vous bien m'aider à les retirer?

Le moine acquiesça gravement et mit un genou à terre. Sans hésiter, elle lui tendit un pied botté en le regardant droit dans les yeux. Les doigts du moine flânèrent un instant, caressant le cuir mouillé.

— Il faudrait les huiler, remarqua-t-il d'un ton neutre.

Il tira lentement, surpris par la douceur inattendue du cuir et la facilité avec laquelle le pied glissa hors de la botte. Une cheville gainée de soie apparut. Le moine la tint un instant entre ses mains avant de poser délicatement le pied à terre.

La jeune femme lui tendit alors de manière très naturelle son autre pied botté. Le moine cilla brièvement et renouvela l'opération mais cette fois il garda quelques secondes de plus la cheville légère de la jeune femme comme pour mieux en examiner les contours fragiles.

Hélène resta immobile et silencieuse mais un frisson la parcourut. Le moine se releva et fit un pas en arrière. S'il était troublé, il se gardait de le montrer.

— Il vous faut ingurgiter quelque chose de chaud et de consistant tout à la fois car je suppose que vous n'avez pas soupé.

— Vous supposez bien.

— Je vais d'abord vous chercher une couverture.

Il revint bientôt avec une étoffe de laine. La jeune femme se pelotonna sur les coussins réchauffés par les flammes et s'enroula sans mot dire dans la couverture, ne laissant dépasser que ses pieds posés près de l'âtre de la cheminée. Le moine s'émut devant ce tableau mais n'en oublia pas pour autant de poser les interrogations qui l'agitaient.

— Je me pose beaucoup de questions depuis la venue de Sartine. Que le lieutenant général de police s'intéresse assez à cette affaire pour nous dépêcher un de ses plus précieux agents révèle qu'il est effrayé.

— C'est bien essayé mais qui vous dit que je suis un de ses plus précieux agents ? rétorqua-t-elle. Enfin, toujours est-il que Sartine craint une résurgence du culte satanique.

— Sartine raisonne juste et carré comme une flûte, se moqua le moine, et il n'ose éternuer de peur de péter !

— Que voulez-vous dire par là ?

— Sartine est prudent, dans cette affaire, il n'y va que d'une fesse…

— Il m'a prévenue contre vous…

— Vous m'en direz tant !

Un silence puis le moine demanda avec un brin de dureté dans la voix :

— Mais pourquoi me le dites-vous ?

La jeune femme se leva et, ses pieds chaussés de bas, glissa sans bruit vers le feu.

— M. de Sartine dit ce qu'il veut et moi je me fais mon opinion par moi-même. Comme vous, monsieur, je n'ai ni dieu, ni maître, ni tribun.

Un sourire éclaira son visage et elle poursuivit :

— "Faute de savoir ce qui est écrit là-haut, on ne sait ni ce qu'on veut, ni ce qu'on fait et on suit sa fantaisie qu'on appelle raison ou sa raison qui n'est souvent qu'une dangereuse fantaisie qui tourne tantôt bien, tantôt mal…"

Le moine applaudit chaleureusement.

— Diderot ! Vous choisissez bien vos auteurs !

Il se dirigea vers un coin de la cuisine garni de plantes séchées : feuilles de laurier, bouquets de thym ou de persil, sauge, cerfeuil ou ciboule. Rangés en colonnes conquérantes sur les étagères, les bocaux recélaient des trésors aromatiques : poivre, mélisse, clous de girofle, cannelle ou coriandre. D'un panier d'osier dépassaient quelques légumes un peu ratatinés. Il en choisit quelques-uns avec soin puis décrocha du mur une casserole de cuivre

— Voyez, fit-il en versant délicatement le vin de Bourgogne, c'est un plat simple, mais délicieux. Après avoir fait revenir ces choux rouges avec du bouillon, deux quartiers de pomme de reinette séchée et un oignon, je rajoute un verre de vin rouge par chou.

Avec un sourire un peu forcé, il ajouta :

— C'est un plat de pauvre mais je l'ai moi-même été trop souvent et ma soif de liberté fait que je terminerai certainement ma vie dans cette condition.

— Vous êtes pourtant d'une haute lignée, remarqua-t-elle négligemment.

Le moine tressaillit légèrement.

— Vous êtes décidément bien renseignée et bien surprenante car vous ne me cachez rien de ce que vous savez.

— Pourquoi en serait-il autrement ?

— Parce que vous travaillez pour Sartine et que c'est un fourbe.

— Vous ne devriez pas toujours dire ce que vous pensez, lui reprocha-t-elle d'un ton doux. Cela a déjà causé votre malheur par le passé…

— Ce n'est pas ma façon de penser qui a fait mon malheur, rétorqua-t-il, mais la façon de penser des autres.

— Certes.

— Tenez, par exemple, un jour j'écrivis dans un de mes livres : *Je crois en moi, le reste, je vérifie.* Cela parut comme une attaque contre Dieu et l'Église. J'aurais dû écrire pour être tranquille : *Je crois en Dieu, le reste, je vérifie !*

Pendant qu'ils parlaient, le moine s'affairait comme à son habitude et un parfum délicieux se répandit dans la maison. Il avait rajouté deux bûches dans la cheminée et un feu d'enfer crépitait mais le froid était tel dehors que la température était encore très basse dans la maison.

— Voilà, c'est prêt. Je vous l'apporte.

Silencieusement, ils savourèrent le met puis la jeune femme soupira.

— Il est tard, il me faut rentrer dormir si je veux vous accompagner demain dans votre enquête.

— C'est la pleine nuit, protesta le moine. Les rues ne sont pas sûres. Nous passerons chez le chevalier de Volnay et nous vous escorterons jusque chez vous.

— C'est bien aimable à vous mais je ne crains pas les rues de Paris la nuit.

— Je n'aime guère cette mode actuelle des masques, remarqua le moine, une jolie femme comme vous, seule de surcroît, sera immanquablement importunée par de jeunes gens ivres. Je refuse de vous laisser aller seule.

Elle le fixa un long instant.

— Eh bien soit, j'attendrai le jour ici. Ce fauteuil et cette étoffe sont très confortables. Remettez quelques bûches dans l'âtre et je passerai une nuit merveilleuse.

— Je peux vous proposer un lit dans ma chambre, je prendrai le fauteuil.

— Le fauteuil me convient, fit-elle d'un ton définitif.

Le moine sembla réfléchir.

— Je vais vous préparer une tisane pour vous délasser, fit-il enfin. Je possède le secret des herbes qui détendent les nerfs.

Des guirlandes d'herbes aromatiques et odorantes pendaient du plafond comme les tresses de la chevelure d'une fée. Il en sélectionna quelques-unes avec précaution et les mit à infuser.

Étrangement, quelques minutes après l'avoir bue, la voix d'Hélène se fit plus faible puis elle ferma les yeux. Le moine la contempla à la lumière vacillante de l'âtre. Une douce lassitude semblait la saisir à la chaleur des flammes. Le moine attendit encore quelques instants avant qu'elle ne s'endorme puis se leva.

— Allons, au travail ! murmura-t-il pour lui-même.

Et il se mit à la fouiller.

Assis en silence sur un tabouret, le moine contemplait Hélène endormie. Son air oscillait entre le doute et l'attendrissement, admirant les traits purs du visage, les longs cils noirs et sa chevelure qui alternait d'une mèche à l'autre entre le brun et le roux. La jeune femme ne dormait pas paisiblement. Son sommeil était agité et ses lèvres s'entrouvraient parfois pour laisser échapper des mots inaudibles mais qui semblaient exprimer la peur et le désarroi. Intrigué, le moine se penchait alors pour écouter mais n'y entendait rien comme si elle parlait en dormant dans une langue qui lui était inconnue même si les consonances appartenaient sans doute aux pays d'au-delà de la mer.

À cet instant, un souffle glacé glissa entre ses chevilles et la réveilla. Elle ouvrit un œil. Le commissaire aux morts étranges refermait la porte derrière lui.

— Que se passe-t-il ? demanda-t-elle d'une voix ensommeillée.

— C'est le petit matin, dit calmement Volnay.

Il dissimulait sa surprise. Pourquoi la jeune femme avait-elle passé la nuit ici ?

Comme le froid avait envahi la pièce, il s'accroupit près de la cheminée. Les braises luisaient faiblement, quelqu'un avait manifestement alimenté le feu pendant la nuit. Il jeta un regard soupçonneux au moine immobile sur son tabouret et entreprit de tisonner avant de rajouter une bûche. Lorsque les flammes claires s'élevèrent, il se redressa et tendit ses mains au-dessus de l'âtre pour se réchauffer.

— Avez-vous un peu d'eau pour ma toilette ? demanda Hélène en quittant son fauteuil.

Elle réajusta autour d'elle les plis froissés de sa robe.

— Je vais vous en apporter dans ma chambre après l'avoir tiédie, répondit galamment le moine en se levant.

La cheminée était garnie de crochets et d'une crémaillère. Il versa dans celle-ci un broc d'eau.

— Cela sera bientôt prêt, lança-t-il avec enthousiasme.

Son fils leva les yeux au ciel avant de se plonger dans la contemplation des flammes. Il ne s'en tira que lorsque l'eau fut chaude et la porte de la chambre refermée derrière Hélène. Alors, le moine se glissa près de lui.

— Hier soir, chuchota-t-il, je lui ai donné une tisane de mon invention. Elle s'est endormie comme un bébé et j'ai pu la fouiller sans la réveiller.

— Oh !

À l'évidence, le procédé choquait le commissaire aux morts étranges.

— Ne t'inquiète pas, précisa le moine en se méprenant, c'était en tout bien tout honneur. Je n'ai pas l'intention de lui montrer mon goupillon !

— Je l'espère bien, fit sèchement son fils, quoique je ne comprenne pas le pourquoi de cet acte.

Son père se permit un sourire amusé.

— Une jeune femme d'une beauté sauvage est introduite par Sartine dans notre duo d'enquêteurs. Te jugeant imperméable à sa séduction, elle s'en prend à moi. Tu aurais vu la manière dont elle m'a demandé de la déchausser !

— Elle t'a demandé de la déchausser ?! s'exclama Volnay.

— Oui, sous prétexte d'avoir les pieds mouillés. Bref, des regards de braise, des compliments… j'ai beau avoir ma vanité, j'ai l'âge que j'ai et je sais pertinemment que cette jeune beauté veut avant tout assujettir son pouvoir sur moi. Pourquoi ? Eh bien je pensais le découvrir en fouillant ses affaires.

— Et tu n'as rien trouvé, conclut froidement Volnay.

— Rien à part une amulette qu'elle porte au cou et une dague bien aiguisée ! L'amulette est une pierre de bénédiction, appelée *abraxas*, très prisée en Égypte ou en Perse. Tout cela n'est pas normal ! Et que dire de ce pied mignon qu'elle m'a fourré dans les mains…

— Calme-toi, dit froidement son fils. Elle n'a pas la moitié de ton âge.

— Mais elle n'est pas moitié moins savante que moi ! Elle a dit à un moment qu'elle parlait araméen.

— Et alors ? fit son fils qui ne voyait pas le rapport.

— L'araméen était une langue apparentée à l'hébreu, celle des tribus nomades de la Chaldée, avant de s'imposer comme la langue administrative de l'Empire babylonien puis de l'Empire perse jusqu'en Égypte. Elle avait supplanté l'hébreu en Israël avant Jésus-Christ, lequel Jésus prêchait également en araméen.

Il se tut un instant et chuchota comme pour lui-même :

— Mais qui parle encore l'araméen de nos jours?

Ses épaules se voûtèrent légèrement. Il se pencha en avant comme pour prêcher mais en fait il se parlait à lui-même. Longtemps seul en prison, le moine avait pris cette habitude de confronter ses opinions à haute voix avec quelque double de lui-même qu'il se créait. Il sembla ainsi avoir oublié la présence de son fils pourtant attentif.

— En dormant, elle parlait dans une langue qui m'est inconnue mais dont les racines me semblent familières. Or seul notre non-conscient s'exprime lorsque l'on dort. Cela signifierait-il qu'elle parlait dans sa langue natale?

— Quel est ce non-conscient dont tu parles? demanda Volnay.

Les yeux du moine pétillèrent de malice.

— Oh, c'est une théorie à moi qui m'écarte quelque peu de mon cher Aristote! Lorsque nous sommes éveillés, notre conscience l'est également, tu es d'accord? Et lorsque nous dormons elle ne l'est plus. Or nos rêves sont toujours riches de sens. Conclusion : nous possédons une conscience non éveillée en nous!

Le commissaire aux morts étranges haussa légèrement les épaules.

— C'est une théorie intéressante mais ce n'est pas dans le sommeil que je mène mes enquêtes.

— Tu as tort, l'activité de veille de l'esprit alors que notre corps est inerte pourrait te surprendre! Et qui pourrait diriger cette veille, sinon notre cerveau? Un cerveau alors débarrassé de toutes nos petites limites et du pitoyable carcan de nos règles… Rends-toi compte que le sommeil est le seul moment de notre vie où nous n'avons de compte à rendre ni à notre conscience, ni à notre raison. Le rêve est alors comme un enfant que ses parents ne surveillent plus!

Ses yeux étincelaient et il en sautillait sur place d'excitation.

— Bref, reprit le moine en voyant le désintérêt de son fils, je pense que la nuit, l'esprit d'Hélène la ramène à une époque de son enfance. Cela ne t'arrive jamais?

Volnay pâlit imperceptiblement.

— Je n'ai pas le temps de rêver, moi! répondit-il sévèrement. Et je n'en ai pas plus pour découvrir qui est cette femme. C'est une espionne de Sartine et nous n'avons pas d'autre choix que de l'associer à notre enquête puisque telle est la volonté du lieutenant général de police! De toute façon, si elle n'était pas là, Sartine nous ferait suivre et espionner par ses mouches. Au moins, nous aurons moins de monde sur nos talons!

Il s'interrompit car la porte de la chambre venait de s'ouvrir et la jeune femme réapparut. Si elle avait entendu leur conversation, elle n'en laissait rien paraître.

— Avez-vous du nouveau? s'enquit-elle.

— Oui, répondit froidement le commissaire aux morts étranges. J'ai demandé que les procureurs et les commissaires de quartier me signalent toutes les disparitions de jeunes filles dans la semaine qui a précédé le meurtre. J'ai ainsi appris à l'aube qu'il y avait eu trois disparitions. Couvrez-vous chaudement, nous sortons! Notre victime est peut-être l'une d'elles!

IV

JEUNES FILLES DISPARUES
ET AUTRES DIABLERIES

Dehors, le froid les saisit de plein fouet. Le moine battit des bras pour se réchauffer et tomba en arrêt devant le chien.

— Bonjour toi!

Volnay le rejoignit.

— Ce chien me suit depuis hier. Il est vrai que je lui ai donné à manger…

Hélène lui jeta un regard surpris. Le moine s'en aperçut et rit.

— Eh oui, fit-il, notre commissaire aux morts étranges n'est pas aussi insensible qu'il veut bien le laisser paraître!

La ville ne se déclinait plus qu'aux couleurs blanches et grises de l'hiver. Dans le ciel bas, les fumées des cheminées se tordaient au-dessus des toits comme de gigantesques serpents cherchant à étrangler leurs proies. Ils commencèrent par l'adresse la plus proche et remontèrent la rue de Saint-Yon pour gagner la rue Saint-Jacques peuplée d'échoppes de libraires, de graveurs et de marchands d'estampes. La proximité de la Sorbonne avait conduit ces professions ainsi que de nombreux imprimeurs à s'y installer.

La neige semblait avoir enveloppé les rues d'une ouate feutrée. Seuls résonnaient dans l'air froid le carillon des cloches des églises environnantes et les jurons des voituriers. Ils passèrent devant l'échoppe d'un écrivain public qui tenta de leur vendre une lettre d'amour pour cinq sous puis devant l'étal odorant d'une marchande de beignets.

— Gare dessous! cria une voix au-dessus d'eux.

Ils évitèrent de justesse le contenu du seau d'excréments destiné à évacuer les besoins de toute une maisonnée. Bientôt, Volnay désigna la devanture d'une librairie.

— Ce doit être celle-ci car il est indiqué dans le rapport de police qu'elle se trouve entre deux échoppes de graveur.

Le commissaire aux morts étranges poussa la porte. Il régnait dans la boutique une ambiance studieuse, presque austère. Les rayons étaient garnis de livres soigneusement rangés. Même le comptoir en était encombré. Une paire de bésicles sur le nez, un homme vint à leur rencontre. Son regard se porta sur le moine qui, pour lutter contre le froid, avait passé sur ses épaules une peau de loup. Cela lui donnait avec sa bure un air étrange, presque sauvage, même s'il gardait aux lèvres un sourire aimable.

Le libraire s'exprimait dans un langage très châtié et avec un brin de suffisance. La communauté des libraires et des imprimeurs se réduisait à quelques centaines de membres. Pour y entrer, on devait suivre des études classiques, certifiées par le recteur, et réussir un examen professionnel devant un jury de la chambre royale et syndicale, rue du Foin-Saint-Jacques. Attachées à l'université, ces professions en étaient d'autant plus considérées. Le commissaire aux morts étranges lui présenta sans succès le portrait de la jeune fille morte dans le cimetière et ils quittèrent le pauvre père désemparé.

Hiver comme été, toute une foule d'oisifs, de rentiers ou de domestiques se pressait en course dans tout Paris. La ville regroupait six cent mille âmes et amenait de France ou d'Europe tous ceux attirés par ce qui brillait. Dans les rues commerçantes, le parcours devenait éprouvant au milieu de la foule et sur le sol gelé. Un jeune voiturier avec une charrette à bras leur proposa de prendre la jeune femme. Volnay et son père se mirent donc à marcher de part et d'autre du véhicule qui creusait deux sillons noirs dans la neige fraîche.

Un monde équivoque et bigarré se pressait autour d'eux. Les voix aigres des crieurs perçaient parfois le brouhaha de la foule. À travers celle-ci, des porteurs d'eau se faufilaient avec adresse sans perdre une goutte de leur précieux liquide. Les vinettiers vendaient leur piquette à la pinte et les coupeurs de bourse les frôlaient dangereusement. Le moine en attrapa un, la main dans la poche de son fils.

— Le cou te démange à ce point que tu veux être pendu, grommela-t-il au mécréant, ou bien as-tu simplement besoin de te faire allonger la colonne?

Il le repoussa brutalement et l'autre s'empressa de déguerpir. De sa voiture, Hélène avait suivi la scène avec attention.

— Quel curieux policier que celui qui laisse s'enfuir les voleurs, se moqua-t-elle.

— Je ne suis pas chargé de serrer ceux qui volent pour manger, répondit froidement le commissaire aux morts étranges.

Le moine intervint avec philosophie.

— Voyez-vous, jeune dame, le problème de ce royaume est que ses ressources sont grandes mais ses bénéficiaires peu nombreux!

Et il ajouta sans rire :

— Nous en tenons compte dans nos interventions!

Ils poursuivirent leur chemin en se protégeant des jets de déjection sous les étages en saillie de maisons biscornues. Le nom de certains endroits témoignait à lui seul de l'état de saleté dans lequel ceux-ci se trouvaient : rue Merdière, Pipi, Merderon… En chemin, le moine tira plusieurs fois sa bourse pour des enfants ou des femmes, gueux comme des rats d'église, qui mendiaient. Hélène lui en fit compliment.

— Ce n'est rien, répondit-il modestement, c'est l'argent de Sartine!

— Il est bien employé mais il ne suffira pas.

Le moine s'arrêta de marcher.

— Peu importe, mademoiselle. Je porte un amour fraternel à toutes les classes de la société et plus particulièrement à celles qui souffrent.

Ils se rangèrent pour laisser passer un convoi funèbre au corbillard timbré aux armes d'une grande maison. Les chevaux caparaçonnés de noir et de moire d'argent marchaient d'un pas lourd et pesant, suivi de carrosses drapés de voiles sombres. Les passants se signèrent. Une femme cria parce qu'on lui écrasait les pieds. On crut qu'il s'agissait d'un vol à la tire et il y eut de dangereux mouvements de foule car, instinctivement, celle-ci se pressait alors aux trousses du voleur jusqu'à l'attraper. On appelait cela les arrestations *à la clameur publique*.

Le voiturier les tira de cet embarras en empruntant une petite rue moins fréquentée, seulement peuplée de badauds frileux ou de poissonniers qui hurlaient pour avertir les gens de l'arrivée de leur marchandise. Sur les marches gelées des églises dormaient ou mouraient de pauvres hères.

Dans une pierre dure incorporée à la façade de la première et dernière maison de chaque rue étaient gravés le nom de celle-ci et le numéro du quartier. Mais aucune maison ne possédait de numéro propre et le commissaire aux morts étranges questionnait les passants et se guidait par rapport aux indications soigneusement notées par le greffier : enseignes de commerçants ou d'auberges, églises, fresque, statue... Volnay connaissait un huissier qui avait ainsi erré une journée entière avant de trouver sa destination.

Arrivés devant la menuiserie recherchée, ils congédièrent le voiturier après rétribution et entrèrent dans une cour de terre battue entourée de maisons hautes qui la privait presque entièrement de lumière. Des monceaux de planches de bois l'encombraient. Quelques enfants sales et dépenaillés jouaient avec des clous à même la terre gelée. Sabots aux pieds, une femme au visage grêlé s'employait à faire sa lessive dans une auge, les doigts gourds de froid. Sourcils et barbe gris, vêtu d'un habit râpé et de bas rapetassés, le menuisier vint leur parler mais le croquis le laissa indifférent.

— Ce n'est pas elle, fit-il d'un ton bourru. Je ne risque d'ailleurs pas de la revoir si elle a rejoint son coquin de Pierre que je lui défendais de fréquenter. Si elle revient, elle recevra du bâton comme elle n'en a encore jamais reçu !

Le moine et son fils échangèrent un regard entendu puis tournèrent les talons, suivi de la jeune femme. Dans leur dos ils entendirent un compagnon jurer et le menuisier s'écrier :

— Tu es à l'amende de vingt sols !

Toujours attentionné, le moine offrit galamment son bras à Hélène pour l'aider à marcher sur le sol glissant même si ses assises semblaient aussi sûres que les siennes.

— Le père de la troisième disparue est un astrologue, déclara le commissaire aux morts étranges. Il loge rue des Canettes, paroisse Saint-Sulpice.

— Alors, nous n'avons qu'à nous fier à notre bonne étoile pour parvenir chez lui! remarqua malicieusement le moine.

— Pas vraiment, selon mes indications, sa maison se situe entre une boutique de perruquier et celle d'un marchand chapelier.

Le ciel virait au noir et les maisons en encorbellement, avec un étage supérieur débordant sur l'étage inférieur, obscurcissaient encore plus la rue. Il leur fallut s'en remettre aux indications bourrues des riverains jusqu'à ce qu'ils pensent être arrivés à destination.

C'était une maison aux murs de pierre noircis par le temps, avec un étage et une curieuse tourelle accolée qui la surplombait. Ils montèrent une demi-douzaine de marches pour accéder à l'entrée. Après qu'ils eurent frappé à une lourde porte cloutée, une grosse servante au visage revêche vint leur ouvrir. Le commissaire aux morts étranges se présenta et on les introduisit dans un hall mal éclairé par une étroite fenêtre. À leur gauche on devinait la cuisine et à droite un salon de réception. La servante bâilla puis se signa quatre fois avec son pouce devant la bouche pour empêcher que le diable n'y entre.

— Il est dans son maudit cabinet, en haut de la tourelle comme à son habitude, maugréa-t-elle. Je vous laisse y monter car mon genou me fait mal!

Lorsqu'elle eut le dos tourné, le moine remarqua gaiement qu'elle avait les hanches et le derrière si large qu'ils semblaient renforcés sur la culasse.

L'escalier était raide et les marches rendues glissantes par l'humidité qui imprégnait les lieux. À plusieurs reprises, Hélène trébucha et, chacun à leur tour, le père et le fils qui l'encadraient la retinrent de justesse, l'un avec empressement, l'autre avec agacement. Ils se retrouvèrent devant une porte en fer, fermée à clé. Le commissaire aux morts étranges frappa vigoureusement.

— Monsieur, ouvrez-nous, je vous prie! Je suis le chevalier de Volnay, commissaire du Châtelet!

Ils tendirent l'oreille mais n'entendirent rien. Le policier allait cogner de nouveau lorsque le bruit d'une clé dans la serrure l'arrêta. Un visage tout chiffonné apparut à hauteur de son épaule. Le crâne entièrement chauve ressemblait à un œuf trop longtemps couvé. Les yeux de l'homme étaient profondément enfoncés dans leur orbite et une poche gonflée comme une pêche ornait chaque dessous de paupière. Il leur jeta un regard hagard.

— Monsieur! Vous venez pour ma fille? Je suis si inquiet…

Ils entrèrent prudemment. La pièce était ronde et éclairée par une grande fenêtre dans le toit. Une tenture défraîchie mettait en scène des personnages mythologiques et réchauffait quelque peu les murs de pierre. Volnay la considéra attentivement. La scène représentait Héraclès bébé tétant la déesse Héra avec tant de force qu'elle en avait mal et le repoussait. Un jet de lait venait alors éclabousser le ciel, formant la Voie lactée.

Le feu qui brûlait dans une petite cheminée ne parvenait pas à assainir la pièce glaciale si bien qu'un nuage de vapeur se formait à leurs lèvres lorsqu'ils respiraient.

— Est-ce votre fille que j'ai représentée sur ce croquis? questionna le commissaire aux morts étranges en sortant celui-ci de sa besacc.

Un hurlement de douleur lui répondit.

— Elle est morte, c'est cela? Ma pauvre Sophia est morte?

— C'est bien elle, murmura lugubrement le moine.

L'astrologue était tombé à genoux et se labourait le visage de désespoir. Hélène le prit doucement par les épaules et, aidé par le policier, le releva. Ils le firent asseoir devant son bureau, attendant que l'homme se calme. Alors, chose étrange à voir, Hélène le saisit dans ses bras et le tint longuement serré contre elle alors qu'il pleurait. Lorsque cela fut terminé, elle s'écarta doucement de lui. L'homme ravala ses sanglots et hoqueta :

— Les astres me l'avaient annoncé mais je ne voulais pas le croire.

— Les astres? demanda le moine soudain curieux.

— Le jour de sa disparition, son thème était désastreux. J'ai tout de suite compris qu'un grand malheur allait arriver.

Volnay parla enfin et le son de sa voix était si grave que tout le monde l'écouta attentivement.

— Quand a-t-elle disparu?

L'astrologue renifla.

— Hier, en début d'après-midi. Nous l'avons attendue jusqu'au soir puis je suis allé prévenir le guet.

— Quelqu'un a-t-il vu quelque chose?

— Non, personne. Elle était assise sur l'escalier comme elle aimait le faire et puis, l'instant d'après, elle n'y était plus…

Le visage du commissaire aux morts étranges était fermé mais son regard brillait d'une détermination farouche.

— Monsieur, je vous assure que je n'aurai pas de repos avant de retrouver le meurtrier de votre fille.

L'autre ne répondit rien. Il contemplait ses chaussures avec le plus profond désespoir. Pendant ce temps, Hélène s'était approchée du bureau sur lequel, à côté d'un livre sur l'Apocalypse, s'étalait une carte colorée. Elle se pencha pour la regarder.

— Monsieur, ne serait-ce pas la carte de la constellation du Crabe?

L'astrologue renifla encore et leva la tête.

— Oui… oui!

Il se releva et la rejoignit d'un pas mal assuré. De ses longues mains maigres et jaunâtres, il balaya la carte.

— À l'ouest, vous trouvez la constellation du Lion et à l'est celle des Gémeaux. Dans les récits des Grecs anciens, on raconte qu'Hercule écrasa du talon le crabe qui osait lui pincer l'orteil alors qu'il combattait l'Hydre!

— Dans les civilisations mésopotamiennes, remarqua la jeune femme, on dit que le Crabe représente la porte que traversent les âmes ayant séjourné dans les étoiles afin de renaître sous la forme humaine.

— C'est juste, madame, c'est juste, murmura l'astrologue étonné par sa science.

Les yeux du moine s'étrécirent. Si les connaissances exprimées par Hélène le ravissaient, elles ne l'en intriguaient que plus encore.

— En quoi consiste votre travail? demanda Volnay.

L'autre frotta vigoureusement ses yeux rougis. Le commissaire aux morts étranges remarqua à un de ses doigts une chevalière sertie d'un énorme et magnifique rubis.

— Les étoiles nous parlent, fit l'astrologue. Les planètes influencent nos actes, nos rêves même…

Les yeux du moine brillèrent de curiosité.

— Comment cela?

L'astrologue le considéra avec attention, dérangé par la bure de son interlocuteur, vêtement qui ne prédisposait pas à l'écoute de son sujet.

— La lune, les planètes et leurs conjonctions exercent une fascination sur nos vies tout comme sur nos rêves. Ainsi Mercure nous poursuit dans la recherche de nos plaisirs matériels tandis que Saturne engendre des rêves de mort…

Il considéra d'un œil soudain terne la tapisserie en face de lui.

— Oui, sombres sont les rêves de Saturne qui nous entraînent dans les recoins les plus obscurs et au bord de profonds précipices pour écouter les chants de la mort…

— Les étoiles prédisposent, remarqua le moine. Elles ne déterminent pas. L'homme conserve son libre arbitre!

— Vous vous trompez, s'écria l'astrologue, les astres influencent nos pensées comme nos actes.

— Pas du tout, rétorqua le moine, l'homme sage commande à ses étoiles. Le fou leur obéit.

Son regard tomba sur un papier couvert de signes et de chiffres.

— Qu'est-ce que ceci? demanda le moine. À qui appartient ce thème astral?

L'astrologue se troubla.

— À quelqu'un du quartier, répondit-il d'une voix tendue.

Sous le regard insondable du commissaire aux morts étranges, il fit disparaître le thème sous un monceau d'autres papiers.

— D'où observez-vous les étoiles? s'enquit le moine avec curiosité.

— Je vais vous montrer.

L'astrologue emprunta une échelle qui donnait sur une petite plate-forme éclairée par une grande lucarne. Sur celle-ci était fixée une lunette.

— Voici un bel engin, apprécia le moine.

Après avoir jeté un dernier regard au bureau de l'astrologue, son fils les rejoignit sans bruit mais demeura sur le dernier barreau de l'échelle car la plate-forme était trop étroite pour les accueillir tous les trois. M. Marly caressa amoureusement la lunette. Il semblait avoir oublié la mort de sa fille.

— "En tant que mortel, je sais que je suis né un jour, mais quand mon regard suit la course circulaire des innombrables étoiles, mes pieds ne touchent plus terre ; j'implore Zeus de me régaler d'ambroisie, la nourriture des dieux."

— Ptolémée… murmura le moine en reconnaissant l'auteur.

Perché sur son échelle, Volnay se sentit ridicule et entreprit de redescendre à reculons en prenant garde de ne pas se rompre le cou. Il fut accueilli au sol par le regard ironique d'Hélène. Sans se soucier d'elle, il gagna à pas rapides la table de l'astrologue et souleva les papiers pour examiner le thème astral que leur hôte s'était trop vite empressé de dissimuler. Ceci effectué, il remit soigneusement tout en ordre. Un instant, ses doigts hésitèrent au-dessus du livre de l'Apocalypse comme si quelque chose l'y attirait. Et puis, sa main retomba à ses côtés et, sans répondre à l'interrogation muette d'Hélène, il retourna au pied de l'échelle. Là-haut, son père discutait à bâtons rompus avec l'astrologue, citant Platon pour qui la contemplation de la voûte étoilée amenait l'homme à mettre son âme en harmonie avec l'ordre divin.

— Pourriez-vous redescendre? demanda sèchement le policier.

Au-dessus de lui, les deux hommes se turent et puis le moine commença à descendre avec agilité.

— Sais-tu que ce sont les Babyloniens qui ont inventé l'astrologie? demanda-t-il à son fils en touchant terre.

— Ce sont eux qui ont eu l'idée les premiers d'une table d'interprétation des qualités données à chacun des astres, s'empressa d'ajouter l'astrologue à mi-chemin sur l'échelle.

Il mit pied à terre avec une grâce pataude et continua :

— Car il faut comprendre à un instant précis la correspondance entre la position des astres et les événements qui se déroulent sur terre.

À cet instant, le commissaire aux morts étranges reprit la parole pour questionner l'astrologue sur les habitudes de sa fille et ses connaissances. Lorsqu'il eut terminé, il dit :

— Monsieur, nous repasserons dans une heure. Il faudra nous suivre pour reconnaître formellement le corps de votre fille. En attendant, pouvons-nous examiner sa chambre pour les besoins de notre enquête?

Le pauvre père les contempla d'un air vide puis un éclair de compréhension traversa son regard et il hocha finalement la tête.

— Ma servante va vous y conduire.

Le commissaire aux morts étranges fit un signe discret à ses compagnons et ils se retirèrent. Au bas de l'escalier, ils trouvèrent la femme qui semblait les attendre.

— Quelque chose ne va pas? demanda-t-elle d'un air méfiant.

— Veuillez nous montrer la chambre de Sophia, s'il vous plaît, fit le commissaire aux morts étranges d'un ton sans appel.

La chambre était étroite, meublée d'un lit bas, d'une table qui servait à la fois pour le travail et pour la toilette et d'un grand coffre pour ses effets personnels. Près du lit, sur un chevet, se trouvait une chandelle à moitié consumée. Le commissaire aux morts étranges l'alluma car la pièce était très faiblement éclairée par une minuscule fenêtre sans rideau qui donnait sur une cour murée au-dessus de laquelle le ciel semblait peser comme un couvercle gris.

Le policier fit un tour rapide mais professionnel du lieu, promenant un doigt sur une étagère pour remarquer :

— Pas un brin de poussière…

Il se mit à genoux pour examiner dessous le lit puis se releva et, soulevant le matelas de laine, le palpa d'une main experte.

— Le lit est propre et bien aéré. On ne peut rien dire de l'hygiène de cette jeune fille, ou de sa servante.

De son côté, le moine examinait des livres soigneusement rangés sur l'étagère, quelques-uns à reliure pleine de veau, la tranche marbrée à l'éponge mais la plupart de la Bibliothèque bleue, ces livres imprimés à peu de frais, seulement protégés d'une couverture de papier bleu et racontant contes et légendes ou aventures épiques.

— Au vu de leur état, constata-t-il, elle les a lus et relus des dizaines ou des centaines de fois pour s'évader de ces quatre murs gris…

Il en feuilleta quelques-uns et eut un imperceptible mouvement de surprise avant de reposer le livre qu'il tenait en main comme si de rien n'était. Hélène observait de son côté les deux hommes sans rien dire. Le commissaire aux morts étranges examina la table. Il y avait là un broc d'eau pour la toilette, un peigne, une plume avec son encrier et quelques papiers.

— Des pages d'écriture en latin… des exercices de conjugaison. Rien de signifiant mais c'était quelqu'un d'instruit.

Lui et le moine fouillèrent ensuite le coffre, y trouvant quelques effets simples et sans coquetterie. La fouille exécutée, le policier appela la servante.

— Regardez le coffre puis la chambre et dites-moi s'il manque quelque chose en dehors des vêtements que votre jeune maîtresse portait.

— Il lui est arrivé quelque chose? demanda la femme d'un ton revêche.

Elle ne paraissait guère émue.

— Étiez-vous attachée à cet enfant?

L'autre haussa les épaules.

— Je sers ici depuis trois ans, je me suis habituée à elle mais elle est toujours dans la lune.

— À quoi passait-elle ses journées?

— Quand elle était plus jeune, elle jouait dans la cour avec des petits cailloux ou avec sa poupée mais, le plus souvent, elle restait des heures entières à rêver devant la tapisserie du salon. Ah oui elle aimait aussi moucher les chandelles et m'accompagner au marché.

— Ma foi, sortir de cette maison lugubre devait être effectivement un vrai plaisir, maugréa le moine.

— Elle en avait peu l'occasion. Son père sortait peu et, lorsqu'il le faisait c'était seul. Sa fille ne pouvait donc que m'accompagner au marché ou pour quelques menues courses mais parfois, elle se faufilait dehors sans qu'on la voie. Elle est morte, c'est ça?

— Oui, répondit le commissaire aux morts étranges en observant ses réactions.

Il en fut pour ses frais. Cette femme était d'une rare insensibilité.

— Si c'est pas malheureux, maugréa-t-elle. Et de quoi est-elle morte que vous êtes donc tous ici?

— Vous le saurez le moment venu, répondit froidement le policier. Ne quittez pas cette maison, nous aurons à vous interroger.

— Et où voulez-vous donc que j'aille, marmonna-t-elle. Je n'ai que ce toit sur ma tête même si je dors sur un mauvais grabat. Mieux vaut ça que rien du tout…

Et elle sortit tout en continuant à ronchonner. Le moine prit la parole en s'adressant à Hélène et à Volnay.

— En sortant, sur votre gauche et de l'autre côté de la rue, il y a une auberge. Vous n'avez pas faim?

— Mais…

— Partez devant, fit le moine à voix basse, je vous rejoindrai.

Le commissaire aux morts étranges réprima sa surprise. Il jeta un coup d'œil incisif à son père puis se saisit du bras d'Hélène.

— Venez, lui fit-il d'une voix grave.

Resté seul, le moine reprit en main le livre qui avait retenu son attention et s'assit lourdement sur le lit. Était-ce un problème d'impression, le verso de chaque page était blanc mais la jeune fille y avait consigné son journal en une écriture serrée. Il fronça les sourcils et entreprit de lire.

C'était le journal d'une enfant qui n'avait personne à qui se confier et qui racontait là sa vie, ses tristesses et ses espérances. Ses journées étaient longues et grises, ses jeux pensifs. Le moine parcourut quelques pages, se laissant gagner par la mélancolie profonde qui s'en dégageait.

Quand elle était petite, une nourrice faisait déjeuner Sophia à la cuisine, lui portant la cuillère à la bouche. Le moine l'imagina, absorbant avec gravité les mets et surveillant du coin de l'œil la nourrice attentive. Plus tard, Sophia apprit à se nourrir toute seule mais même encore la nourrice restait à la surveiller pour vérifier qu'elle mange tout. La nourrice sembla s'attacher à elle et lui parla du reste du monde : les bois, les lacs, les montagnes, les animaux… À l'âge de six ans, Sophia se mit alors à retranscrire d'une écriture maladroite tout ce qu'elle entendait dans un livre qu'on lui avait offert mais qui comportait des pages blanches. Elle n'y parla jamais de son père.

Parfois, le soir, sa nourrice lui lisait la Bibliothèque bleue et Sophia émerveillée écoutait sans broncher des contes peuplés de voleurs et de revenants qui tourmentaient la nuit les vivants. Elle aimait aussi les histoires d'ogres qui mangent les enfants et frissonnait jusqu'à ce que le héros échappe à son terrible destin.

Le moine l'imagina, les yeux écarquillés, se mordillant les lèvres à l'approche du dénouement. Le soir de l'Avent, sa nourrice la régalait de deux histoires au lieu d'une. Elle les écoutait en grignotant des friandises avant d'aller se coucher et prolonger dans ses rêves les naïves aventures entendues à la veillée.

Le moine plissa son front, se souvenant de soirs où il lisait à son fils des contes remplis de nains, de gnomes et d'esprits malins. Un jour, lorsqu'il revint après un séjour de quelques mois en prison, son fils lisait désormais seul. Un frisson nostalgique le secoua. Le temps passait si vite, filant entre les doigts. Il soupira et reprit sa lecture.

À sept ans, l'âge de raison pour les enfants, son père décida que Sophia n'avait plus besoin de nourrice. Sept ans! Elle n'était pas une demoiselle, rien qu'une enfant à qui on retirait le seul être cher. Sept ans! Le moine savait qu'à cet âge on troublait l'âme des enfants en leur annonçant avec gravité qu'ils se trouvaient désormais en âge de pécher et de perdre leur innocence.

De la paume de sa main, le moine se frotta le front, geste habituel lorsque quelque chose le tourmentait. Qu'avait-il dit lui-même à son fils à l'âge de sept ans? Rien qu'un baiser sur le front et une pensée fugitive : *comme le temps passe vite!*

À sept ans, donc, on congédia la nourrice de Sophia. Peut-être s'attachait-elle trop à l'enfant. Désormais, Sophia déjeuna seule à la cuisine. Elle le nota dans son journal, avec gravité mais sans révolte car elle semblait douce et docile. Mais désormais, plus personne ne s'occuperait d'elle jusqu'à sa mort.

Le livre en main, le moine se releva et d'un pas fut à la fenêtre, scrutant le pauvre horizon offert à l'enfant. La cour ressemblait plus à la cellule d'une prison qu'à un espace de jeux et de liberté. Il appuya son front contre la vitre froide et s'amusa, comme elle avait dû le faire, à laisser se dessiner sous son souffle une buée fantomatique. Son jeu terminé, il retourna s'allonger sur le lit et contempla le plafond. Sophia passait-elle ainsi son temps lorsqu'elle ne lisait pas? Imaginait-elle sur ce plafond des personnages de conte de fées qui viendrait la tirer de sa morne vie? Comment trompait-elle son ennui dans ces journées interminables où personne ne lui adressait la parole?

Il ferma les yeux et réfléchit. Sophia n'était pas une enfant maltraitée. Elle avait eu un toit et de quoi se nourrir. Son corps ne portait aucune trace de coups. C'était seulement une enfant ignorée.

Mais qui était-il pour juger les autres et qu'avait pensé de lui son fils lorsque, sous couvert de répandre les lumières de l'esprit dans son siècle, il avait laissé filer tous ces précieux instants que rien ne pourrait jamais faire revivre?

Une pesante tristesse l'envahissait. Il aurait voulu rattraper le temps perdu mais n'y parvenait pas.

Il était plus de midi et tout un peuple d'artisans, ouvriers et maçons, portefaix ou journaliers cherchait sa pitance. De la table des plus riches parvenaient sur celles des bourgeois les restes des soupers. Et ce que ne mangeaient pas les bourgeois finissait dans les étals, pour les plus pauvres, en compagnie des fruits gâtés, des viandes décomposées et des poissons puants. Les deux jeunes gens n'avaient rien avalé depuis la veille. Une enseigne en fer forgé signalait la présence de l'auberge. Le givre avait tissé autour des guirlandes glacées. Ils poussèrent la porte avec soulagement, soulevant les récriminations des convives qu'un vent froid balaya. Ils découvrirent alors qu'ils se trouvaient dans un cabaret à bière empli d'une faune bruyante qui fumait de longues pipes en terre ou buvait un vin aux relents aigres. Quelques filles de petite vertu s'y pressaient. Le commissaire aux morts étranges insista pour choisir une table près d'une fenêtre et, sans souci d'Hélène, s'empara de la chaise qu'il souhaitait occuper. Ensuite, il regarda dans la rue et parut satisfait car il apercevait de là la maison de l'astrologue.

Hélène jeta un coup d'œil aux autres tables. On servait un ragoût noirâtre d'où émergeaient des os et des petits paquets de chair compacte. D'un commun accord, les deux convives jugèrent préférable de s'en tenir à une soupe et une omelette.

— Voulez-vous boire un peu de vin ? demanda Volnay avec une politesse forcée.

— Pourquoi pas mais votre moine tarde à venir, remarqua la jeune femme. Que fait-il exactement ?

Le policier haussa légèrement les épaules.

— Il s'imprègne des lieux.

— Pas vous ?

— Moi, j'ai vu tout ce que j'avais à voir.

— Pas votre moine ?

Le commissaire aux morts étranges eut un rire bref.

— Oh, lui, il voit les choses derrière les choses…

Elle le considéra attentivement. Le commissaire aux morts étranges soutint tranquillement son regard, dissimulant son trouble car il remarquait pour la première fois que les yeux d'Hélène semblaient recéler un fragment de nuit étoilée. Ses souvenirs le renvoyèrent à une autre femme, Chiara, qu'il avait connue l'année précédente et qui s'en était allée. Les femmes ne lui portaient pas chance.

— Comment en êtes-vous arrivée à travailler pour Sartine ? demanda-t-il abruptement.

Elle ne parut pas s'offusquer d'une question aussi directe mais répondit par une autre question :

— En dehors du mariage, que laisse-t-on comme choix à la femme sinon le couvent ou le bordel ? J'ai pour ma part emprunté une autre voie !

Elle a le même caractère que Chiara, pensa fugitivement Volnay, *mais en moins innocent et bien plus dangereux… Chiara a vécu dans un écrin de velours mais Hélène porte une dague sur elle !*

Il n'eut pas le temps de s'appesantir sur ses souvenirs. La porte du cabaret s'ouvrit et le moine apparut.

— Eh bien, fit-il gaiement, comment est le vin ?

Son fils lui jeta un regard inquiet. Le faux entrain de son père ne le trompait pas et Dieu seul savait pourquoi il s'était attardé dans la chambre de cette enfant. Le moine s'assit et jeta autour d'eux un coup d'œil méfiant. Les mouches de Sartine pullulaient dans les tavernes, observant et écoutant tout.

Volnay intercepta son regard et, d'un imperceptible signe du menton, lui désigna Hélène. Cela signifiait clairement :

Fais donc attention à tes propos devant elle!

Le moine resta imperturbable. Si la jeune femme demeurait pour lui un mystère, il ne pensait pas qu'elle était une mouche et rapporterait leurs conversations.

Le silence s'établit et l'on entendit le vent siffler à travers les carreaux. Une serveuse vint leur apporter leurs bols et une grosse miche de pain. Avec ses flancs étroits, elle ressemblait à un petit chat maigre mais son minois était piquant et son regard plein d'assurance.

— Voici la soupe de Ses Seigneuries, fit-elle.

Elle ne devait certes pas avoir souvent l'occasion de servir des gens de condition. Le commissaire aux morts étranges la questionna.

— Connaissez-vous les occupants de la maison à deux étages avec une tourelle que nous apercevons par cette fenêtre?

Elle se pencha légèrement pour regarder, lui dévoilant un peu d'une poitrine manifestement peu fournie.

— L'homme qui regarde les étoiles?

— C'est bien cela, fit le jeune homme en détournant les yeux et en lui glissant une pièce.

— Que voulez-vous savoir? demanda-t-elle en l'empochant prestement.

— Tout ce que vous savez d'eux.

Elle se renfrogna.

— Je n'en sais pas trop.

— Allons, allons, fit le commissaire aux morts étranges en dardant sur elle un regard pénétrant. Dans chaque quartier, tout le monde observe tout le monde, c'est même la principale occupation de chacun!

— C'est que leur servante passe sans s'arrêter devant l'auberge et elle est aussi peu bavarde qu'une pie.

Le moine intervint.

— Les pies sont très bavardes, jeune fille. En fait, elles peuvent parler comme vous et moi si on les éduque…

Hélène lui posa la main sur le bras pour l'empêcher de continuer. Déçu, le moine se concentra sur sa soupe, un bouillon dans lequel on avait ajouté des pois, des fèves et des morceaux de pain d'orge.

— La jeune enfant? demanda Volnay.

— Oh, elle est bien mignonne et bien aimable même si elle paraît toujours triste. Mais elle sort peu, sinon accompagnée par la servante.

— Connaissez-vous la mère qui l'a couvée? demanda le moine.

— Non, elle est morte alors qu'elle avait trois ou quatre ans je crois.

— Hum… et qui voit-elle?

— Elle n'a pas d'amis dans le quartier, à part un chien.

— Un chien?

— Oui, elle lui donne à manger quand elle sort, alors il la suit.

Elle darda sur Volnay un œil effronté en se campant en arrière pour tenter de faire ressortir sa poitrine.

— C'est comme cela la vie, non? On suit celui qui vous fait du bien!

Le commissaire aux morts étranges jeta un regard bref à son père. Ils venaient tous deux de penser au chien qui hurlait à la mort devant le cimetière.

— À quoi ressemble ce chien?

— Oh, il me va à la cuisse, plein de poils blancs quand il est propre avec des taches marron. Parfois, quand son père n'est pas là et la servante sortie, elle l'emmène chez elle pour le laver!

— Quelle gentille enfant, murmura le moine attendri.

Le policier se mordit les lèvres. Cela ressemblait bien au chien rencontré devant la maison de son père la nuit de la mort de Sophia puis de la sienne le lendemain matin. L'intelligent et fidèle animal avait pu suivre la carriole qui transportait le corps de sa petite maîtresse. Il soupira tristement et la servante lui jeta un regard curieux. Sentant son flottement, Hélène prit alors le relais.

— Parlez-nous du père. Sort-il parfois ou vient-on le visiter?

La serveuse haussa les épaules.

— On ne le voit pas trop traîner dans le quartier et il ne vient jamais ici. On dit qu'il est si avare qu'il n'ose cracher de peur d'avoir soif. S'il sort parfois, c'est à la nuit tombée. Il reçoit aussi quelques visiteurs, plutôt entre chien et loup.

— À quoi ressemblent ces visiteurs?

La servante fit une petite moue.

— Comment voulez-vous que je le sache? Je suis moi-même plus souvent à servir les clients qu'à rôder dehors ou à regarder par la fenêtre. D'ailleurs, j'ai encore de la marmite à remuer. Je n'ai guère de temps naguère!

Volnay lui glissa une autre pièce.

— Vraiment pas une idée?

Elle s'empara de la pièce qu'elle glissa dans son corsage, pointa en avant son petit nez retroussé et répondit insolemment :

— Vraiment pas!

Le commissaire aux morts étranges lui retint le poignet mais Hélène laissa fuser un rire amusé.

— Laissez voyons…

La serveuse lui jeta un regard complice et s'en fut prestement.

— M. Marly, notre astrologue, est un cul de plomb, commenta le moine, il ne bouge guère de son cabinet…

— Sauf la nuit, remarqua Volnay. Étrange pour un astrologue qui devrait la passer à observer les étoiles! Je vais placer une mouche près de la maison pour observer les allées et venues…

Tous méditèrent quelques instants cette réflexion en nettoyant leur bol puis le commissaire aux morts étranges reprit, en s'adressant au moine :

— Nous devons dessiner le profil des personnes qui ont assisté à cette messe noire.

— Dessiner le profil? répéta Hélène surprise.

— L'action de la police de Sartine se fonde sur l'espionnage et la délation, expliqua pompeusement le moine. Mon fils et moi développons des théories nouvelles et plus subtiles en matière de crime. La vérité ne doit pas être simplement le résultat d'une intuition mais les conclusions de la raison par l'esprit d'observation, d'analyse et la déduction logique. Les certitudes sont toujours des obstacles à son apparition.

Il agita le doigt avec un sourire malicieux.

— Je suis un sceptique, je doute. Et mon esprit critique me permet de me remettre sans cesse en cause et de me préserver de l'erreur !

— C'est de la simple logique, le coupa le commissaire aux morts étranges peu porté sur l'emphase. Nous avons remarqué que chaque crime a sa propre signature, pas seulement sur un plan matériel. Les motivations et comportements des meurtriers diffèrent d'un individu à l'autre.

— L'étude des cas, renchérit le moine déterminé à briller aux yeux d'Hélène, démontre que la victime connaît en général son meurtrier et que celui-ci est souvent un proche. Je m'efforce de tenir les comptes. Sur dix affaires résolues par nos soins, huit des criminels connaissaient bien leur victime. Toujours sur dix affaires, trois sont le fruit d'adultères ou de rivalités amoureuses. Les autres relèvent d'intérêts pécuniaires ou d'hostilité de longue date. Quant à l'infanticide, nul ne risque plus d'être assassiné qu'un enfant !

Il nettoya du doigt le bord de son bol et reprit :

— Les enfants risquent avant tout d'être assassinés le jour de leur naissance ou dans le premier mois. Plus âgés, de mauvais traitements répétés peuvent également les tuer.

Un éclair de pitié traversa son regard.

— Nul n'est plus sans défense qu'un enfant et certains adultes en profitent. Ceux-là mêmes qui n'ont que le courage d'abuser des plus faibles qu'eux…

Il se pencha sur son verre qu'il vida d'un trait.

— Mais Sophia n'était pas une enfant maltraitée, murmura-t-il, simplement une enfant ignorée…

Un silence lourd sembla couler entre eux une chape de plomb. Volnay réagit le premier :

— Le meurtrier n'est pas forcément un gueux brutal, un vicieux borné ou un vicieux intelligent. Nous pouvons nous trouver face à des individus, qui, fous ou non, commettent leur crime dans un schéma de pensées ou de convictions bien précis. Dans notre affaire, le profil s'esquisse déjà car le crime s'est produit lors du rituel très particulier d'une messe noire.

Il marqua une pause et jeta un coup d'œil circulaire pour vérifier que personne ne les écoutait.

— Qui trouve-t-on dans les messes noires? Des gens qué-mandant des faveurs terrestres de la part de Satan. Risquer son salut éternel en invoquant *le Très Bas* dénote généralement un goût avide du pouvoir et des biens matériels.

— Cela peut être aussi une certaine forme de désespérance, hasarda Hélène.

— Ou de la simple perversité, murmura lugubrement le moine. Et Dieu sait comme la nature humaine peut être per-verse!

— Ne sois pas trop catégorique, conseilla Volnay. Nous vivons dans un siècle où beaucoup de gens contestent l'ordre établi quel qu'il soit. Ils assimilent à tort le sacrilège à une forme de liberté.

— Dire non à Dieu pour dire oui à Satan, c'est seulement changer de maître, remarqua le moine sarcastique.

On revint pour les débarrasser de leurs bols. Les convives se turent et observèrent avec amusement la jeune servante se déhancher devant le commissaire aux morts étranges pour atti-rer en vain son attention.

— Quand je parle de perversité, reprit plus tard le moine, c'est que les messes noires peuvent se terminer aussi bien par les plus honteuses débauches que par des sacrifices de nourrissons!

— Oui, et comme l'Église proscrit le meurtre et le péché de chair, on s'y livre! conclut le commissaire aux morts étranges. Le satanisme se construit uniquement en opposition et dans le déni de toute dignité humaine.

Hélène intervint.

— Si vous voulez insinuer par là que les participants à des messes noires sont des libertins, des pervers ou encore des oppo-sants à l'ordre social, nous avons affaire à beaucoup de monde!

— Certes, en convint le policier, mais toutes les formes de sacrilège sont systématiquement observées pendant les messes noires. Derrière cela, il y a l'horreur, l'horreur absolue. Nous affinerons progressivement le profil de ces êtres pervers avec chaque élément glané.

La serveuse revint avec une omelette baveuse à souhait et l'on se tut, le temps de lui faire honneur. Cela fut rapide car les portions n'étaient pas copieuses.

— Ma foi, ils nous font chier petite crotte, remarqua le moine dépité.

Il continua néanmoins à manger en racontant avec entrain des anecdotes amusantes sur sa vie passée, s'évertuant à faire rire Hélène sous le regard impassible de Volnay qui dit finalement :

— Il est temps. Retournez chez l'astrologue et amenez-le reconnaître formellement le cadavre de sa fille. Pour ma part, j'ai à faire au Châtelet puis en un certain lieu.

Et en disant cela, il jeta un regard appuyé à son père qui approuva d'un imperceptible mouvement de tête.

Dehors, le policier suivit longuement du regard son père et Hélène. Malgré leur différence d'âge, ils formaient un duo harmonieux qui s'en allait en devisant gaiement. Volnay pensa que son père suivait une mauvaise pente.

V

LE CHIEN, LE BROUILLARD
ET AUTRES DIABLERIES

Saturé d'humidité, un brouillard épais se formait dans la ruelle de l'Or. L'après-midi était avancée lorsque le commissaire aux morts étranges y pénétra après un tour au Châtelet pour y laisser un rapport à Sartine. Ici, chaque maison semblait bâtie sans tenir compte de la position de la maison suivante et, par moments, la ruelle devenait si étroite que deux personnes s'y croisaient avec peine. Suivant les indications de son père, Volnay se dirigea vers la maison de la dame qui lisait l'avenir dans l'eau. La sensation d'être suivi le saisit de nouveau. C'était une présence furtive, à peine perceptible. Quelque chose qui n'avait rien d'humain et se manifestait par moments avant de se projeter dans une autre dimension. Cette fois-ci pourtant, il surprit ce qui l'avait pris en chasse.

— Ah te voilà, toi! Décidément, tu as tout d'un chien policier! Veux-tu donc entrer au service de M. de Sartine?

Il s'approcha de l'animal qui demeura immobile. Seule sa queue remuait comme s'il venait de retrouver une vieille connaissance. Volnay lui caressa la tête.

— J'ai pensé à toi dans cette auberge et j'ai emporté ce bout de pain au cas où je te retrouverais devant chez moi. Je ne pensais pas que tu me suivrais, mon discret compagnon. Tu es plus doué qu'une mouche pour cela! Il faudra que je te trouve quelque emploi au Châtelet!

— Quel tableau touchant! fit une voix ironique. Notre commissaire aux morts étrange n'est donc pas si insensible que ça!

Volnay releva vivement la tête pour se retrouver face au moine, hilare.

— Que fais-tu là? Tu devais faire reconnaître le corps par le père puis occuper Hélène… euh, l'espionne de Sartine pour éviter qu'elle ne me suive.

— Ne t'inquiète pas! Elle s'est rendue chez le commissaire de quartier pour découvrir s'il est fait mention de notre astrologue dans quelque dossier.

— Elle a accès aux dossiers d'un commissaire du Châtelet? s'étonna le commissaire aux morts étranges.

— Apparemment! Quant à moi, j'avais compris, à ton regard à l'auberge, où tu te rendrais après le Châtelet…

Il s'interrompit et sembla découvrir la présence du chien.

— Oh le bon *chien-chien*!

Il le flatta vigoureusement avant de le gratter derrière les oreilles.

— Mais c'est un bon *chien-chien* ça!

Son fils poussa un soupir exaspéré.

— Pour l'amour de Dieu, parle normalement et arrête d'appeler cette bête *chien-chien*!

Son père prit un air vexé.

— Mais dis-moi, serait-ce donc là le chien de Sophia dont nous a parlé la servante de l'auberge?

— C'est fort possible. Il correspond à la description et il me suit depuis la nuit du drame.

Le moine s'émerveilla.

— Intelligent animal! On raconte qu'il y a trois ou quatre siècles, rue des Marmousets à Paris, un barbier tuait parfois un client de passage puis faisait basculer son corps dans la cave de son voisin pâtissier qui le transformait en excellent pâté! Les aboiements du chien d'une victime, qui resta jour et nuit à hurler à la mort devant la boutique du barbier, attirèrent l'attention et permirent de découvrir les procédés criminels de ces deux mauvais commerçants!

Son fils hocha la tête.

— Il y a dans la fidélité de certains de ces animaux quelque chose de troublant. Allez viens!

Volnay tapa sur sa cuisse et le chien suivit.

— L'astrologue a bien reconnu sa fille?

— Oui, répondit le moine, et ce fut pénible. Nous l'avons ensuite reconduit chez lui. Il voulait emporter le corps mais j'ai refusé. Je ferai d'abord venir un cercueil chez moi.

— Oui, il vaut mieux qu'il ne voie pas le corps de sa fille ouvert.

Le moine baissa la tête comme un enfant pris en faute.

— Je ne l'ai pas autopsiée. À quoi bon? Cela ne nous apprendra rien et j'aurai bien d'autres cadavres pour continuer à me faire la main!

Son fils le considéra comme s'il était devenu fou.

— C'est toi qui décides, dit-il finalement d'un ton neutre.

Décidément, son père ne se comportait en rien comme à l'ordinaire. Le moine releva vivement la tête.

— Eh oui, c'est moi qui décide!

Le policier eut un hochement de tête pensif.

— Je n'ai pas voulu te demander devant Hélène pourquoi tu restais dans cette chambre chez l'astrologue mais, te connaissant, il devait bien exister une raison.

— J'avais remarqué que notre victime tenait un journal dans le livre que je feuilletais. Je voulais le dérober pour le lire plus attentivement mais pas sous les yeux de notre nouvelle amie!

Son fils parut rassuré. Le comportement de son père lui semblait de nouveau logique.

— Qu'as-tu appris dans son journal?

— Rien qu'une enfance grise et solitaire.

Son ton lugubre alerta de nouveau Volnay.

— Eh bien, lança ce dernier pour dérider son père, que penses-tu de notre astrologue et de sa servante revêche?

Le moine ne répondit pas directement mais lui désigna une bâtisse au toit biscornu.

— Ici, tu trouveras un augure qui se livre à l'examen du foie et des entrailles. Les Mésopotamiens se livraient à ce type d'augure ainsi que les Grecs qui en codifièrent l'étude sur des tablettes d'argile. En Mésopotamie encore, on étudiait l'aspect que prenait le mélange de l'eau et de l'huile…

— L'eau? Comme ton amie?

— Oui. Elle étudiait également la fumée en faisant brûler de l'encens mais elle a abandonné cette pratique car cela la faisait tousser !

Il glissa sur le sol verglacé, se rattrapa miraculeusement à la manche de son fils et poursuivit sa savante péroraison comme si de rien n'était :

— En Grèce, on étudiait les bruissements des feuillages d'un chêne. Dans la Rome antique, on interprétait tous les signes comme autant de messages des dieux. Tonnerre, éclairs, tout leur parlait ! Les augures interprétaient le vol des oiseaux, l'appétit des poulets sacrés et déchiffraient également dans leurs entrailles. Certains s'avisèrent même de lire l'avenir dans les viscères humains. Rome s'en émue et condamna ces pratiques en instituant la loi des Douze Tables proscrivant l'usage de la magie.

— Et désormais, on se tourne toujours vers le ciel mais la nuit et pour observer les étoiles !

Le moine lui jeta un regard satisfait.

— Tu as bien compris où je voulais en venir : à notre astrologue ! C'est un augure ! L'astrologie a pris le pas de nos jours sur toutes ces anciennes formes de divination. La connaissance sans cesse approfondie des mouvements cycliques des planètes et des étoiles leur a donné un sentiment de puissance. Sentiment éphémère ! Voici un homme qui lit dans les étoiles le destin des hommes mais n'est même pas capable de prédire la mort dramatique de sa fille ! Quant à sa servante, elle n'a pas paru plus étonnée que ça d'apprendre cette dramatique nouvelle. Voilà une femme sans cœur !

Il claqua des doigts en l'air.

— Au fait, as-tu remarqué le thème astral que notre astrologue s'est empressé de dissimuler lorsque je l'ai remarqué ?

— Oui, répondit nonchalamment Volnay, j'ai jeté un coup d'œil lorsque vous étiez en conversation et j'ai noté la date de naissance du thème.

— Digne fils de ton père ! Puis-je la voir ? Où l'as-tu écrite ?

— Là, fit le commissaire aux morts étranges en pointant son index sur sa tempe.

Son père lui jeta un regard fier et admiratif.

— Et alors ?

— C'est une date de naissance que nombre de personnes connaissent en ce royaume de France puisque c'est celle du roi !

Le moine sautilla avec excitation sur le sol gelé.

— Oh… Je comprends pourquoi il l'a dissimulé. Faire le thème astral du roi est un délit passible de prison. Un crime de lèse-majesté ! L'astrologie est sanctionnée par la mort dès lors qu'elle touche au destin du roi ou de ses enfants.

— Surtout s'il prétend prévoir la date de la fin de leur règne !

Le moine s'arrêta devant une maison dont l'entrée, plus étroite que le reste du bâtiment, laissait penser à la proue d'un bateau fendant le brouillard.

— Ah, c'est là où je me suis rendu suite aux conseils de ma belle amie, maîtresse des eaux. Je t'accompagne. Comme il m'en a vendu hier, il ne pourra nier en posséder. Pour lui faire raconter qui sont ses clients, je compte sur ton pouvoir de persuasion ! D'autant plus qu'il possède dans un vase des fleurs de chanvre et de coquelicots, des racines d'ellébore et des graines de tournesol…

— Et alors ?

— Alors, mêlées à de la mandragore et de la graisse d'humain non baptisé, on en fabrique l'onguent des sorcières !

Le commissaire de quartier était grand et corpulent mais tout son corps semblait disproportionné tant sa tête était petite, ses jambes démesurément longues et ses bras trop courts. D'épaisses paupières voilaient par moments ses yeux mais ses lèvres remontant aux commissures suggéraient une perpétuelle bonne humeur. Il se présenta à Hélène sous le nom de Cornevin et lut avec soin le papier que lui tendit la jeune femme. Lorsqu'il releva la tête, son regard était devenu respectueux.

— Diable, madame, une introduction du lieutenant général de police lui-même ! Je suis bien entendu à votre entière disposition. Que puis-je pour votre service ?

— Je m'intéresse à la rue des Canettes.

— Oh, cette rue est plutôt calme. Il y a bien quelques voleurs de mouchoirs dans les appartements ou des voleurs de boucles de chaussures dans l'église Saint-Sulpice…

— Des voleurs de boucles de chaussures?

— Oui, elles ont un certain prix parfois et lorsque les gens sont agenouillés, il est assez aisé de les leur dérober.

Il marqua une pause.

— Nous connaissons peu de violence dans ce quartier. Bien entendu, quelques maris frappent durement leurs femmes ou des artisans leurs apprentis mais cela ne va jamais bien loin.

La jeune femme pinça délicatement l'arête fine et étroite de son nez.

— Connaissez-vous un astrologue du nom de Marly?

— Marly, dites-vous? Un astrologue…

Le commissaire de quartier se leva pesamment et alla jusqu'à une pile de registres sur une table près de la fenêtre.

— J'ai eu affaire à la fille de l'astrologue, une enfant d'une douzaine d'années, très aimable même si un brin mélancolique. Elle est venue de son propre chef pour se plaindre que quelqu'un frappait un chien. Vous rendez-vous compte?

Il eut un petit rire grinçant.

— Je lui ai demandé si la personne était propriétaire dudit chien et elle m'a répondu que oui mais qu'il ne lui donnait pas à manger et se bornait à le cogner du poing et du pied!

— Et qu'avez-vous fait? demanda Hélène intéressée.

Cornevin se tourna vers elle, un registre dans les mains, l'air désabusé.

— Que voulez-vous que je fisse? Deux jours après un homme est venu se plaindre qu'on avait tenté de lui voler son chien. Il avait appelé un sergent de guet qui l'accompagnait avec la jeune fille en question, la fille de l'astrologue. Comment se nommait-elle déjà?

— Sophia, fit doucement Hélène en jetant un coup d'œil par la fenêtre.

Elle constata que l'ombre commençait à envahir les rues.

— C'est cela, oui. Un bien charmant nom mais qui ne lui correspondait pas trop. Voyons mes registres.

Le policier se mit à tourner des pages, les sourcils froncés.

— Ah, voici! Peut-être ne connaissez-vous pas la procédure. Mon greffier enregistre toutes les plaintes. Je vais vous lire leurs déclarations.

Hélène se pencha, attentive. L'autre commença sa lecture, son doigt soulignant chaque ligne à lire au fur et à mesure.

— "Le 7 mars 1758 à deux heures de l'après-midi, en notre hôtel par-devant moi, conseiller du Roy commissaire au Châtelet, est comparu Legrand, sergent du guet de poste près de l'église Saint-Sulpice, lequel nous dit avoir été requis par un particulier maintenant une jeune fille d'environ treize ans qui l'aurait rudoyé et poussé dans le ruisseau. Pourquoi on les a conduits en notre hôtel. Interrogé, le particulier dénommé Berger-Rabot a dit qu'aujourd'hui, il était occupé à cercler un tonneau dans sa cour lorsque ladite Sophia s'est approchée de lui pour lui crier d'un ton très insolent : Allez-vous finir de frapper votre chien. Il n'est pas méchant mais vous si! A répondu que ce n'était pas son affaire et ordonné de s'en aller. A refusé et entrepris de détacher la corde qui maintenait le chien. Lui a alors arraché ladite corde des mains. En réponse, ladite jeune fille l'a poussé et fait choir lourdement, lui faisant mal au dos. A crié alors : Au guet! À la garde! Que, ayant été entendu, un sergent du guet en poste non loin d'ici est venu le secourir."

Le commissaire porta un doigt à la bouche, le lécha et tourna une page.

— "Ayant examiné la dénommée Sophia et trouvant qu'elle portait des traces de coups au visage, moi, commissaire au Châtelet, lui a demandé s'il ne l'avait pas frappée. Le dénommé Berger-Rabot ayant reconnu l'avoir poussée à son tour, j'ai ordonné l'élargissement de la jeune fille et les ai renvoyés tous deux chez eux après admonestation et remontrance sur leur conduite mutuelle."

Il joignit les mains et adressa à la jeune femme un sourire aimable.

— Voilà toute l'affaire! Vous voyez que c'est bien peu de chose. Pourquoi vous intéressez-vous à cette charmante enfant?

— Parce qu'elle est morte.

Lorsque le moine et le commissaire aux morts étranges sortirent de chez le marchand grec, le brouillard voilait peu à peu les ombres grisées du crépuscule. À leur vue, le chien remua la queue.

99

— Brave *chien-chien*, fit le moine.

Son fils eut un soupir excédé et claqua des doigts à l'intention de l'animal.

— Viens !

Le chien s'exécuta docilement.

— J'ai déjà rencontré des gens peu loquaces mais notre marchand grec vient en tête de ceux-ci, dit Volnay.

— Toujours est-il, rétorqua le moine, qu'une fois la menace de la question agitée, il a parlé *celerius quam asparagi cocuntur*. "En moins de temps qu'il n'en faut pour cuire les asperges !"

— Et il nous a avoué avoir vendu sa potion à une prostituée du faubourg Saint-Marcel, renchérit Volnay, connaissant même le cabaret où elle exerce l'hiver ! Nous nous y rendrons demain.

— Espérons que ces prostituées ne soient pas trop nombreuses, soupira son père, je ne me vois pas toutes les soumettre à confesse !

En quittant la ruelle de l'Or, ils remarquèrent des ombres difformes glisser rapidement sur les pavés glacés. Ces longues silhouettes emmitouflées de noir et coiffés de chapeaux à larges rebords marchaient l'une derrière l'autre dans un ordre parfait. Une brève plainte s'échappa de la gueule du chien.

— Ces gens-là s'en reviennent de la ruelle de l'Or, remarqua le commissaire aux morts étranges. Je me demande ce qu'un tel groupe y fabriquait… Suivons-le !

La nuit envahissait tout. Les artisans se hâtaient d'installer des barres de bois pour bloquer les volets de leurs boutiques. Dans les boutiques, les commis préparaient leurs lits à même les tables sur lesquels ils travaillaient le jour. Lentement la brume s'épaississait. Le moine et le policier suivaient toujours à distance l'étrange procession.

— Il fait un temps à ne pas mettre un assassin dehors ! grommela le moine. Qu'avons-nous donc à suivre ces gens que nous ne connaissons pas ? Sans doute, vont-ils à quelque fête…

Le commissaire aux morts étranges hésita. Son instinct de policier l'avait poussé à emboîter le pas aux hommes en noir. Malgré son peu d'habitude de la ruelle de l'Or, surtout fréquentée par son père, il savait qu'il était rare d'y croiser un groupe de personnes. Des gens seuls et méfiants s'y glissaient discrètement pour y accomplir leurs achats ou acheter quelque prestation inavouable. On se gardait bien d'être accompagné.

— Ces gens-là m'intriguent, s'entêta-t-il, suivons-les un instant et voyons où ils se rendent.

Jugeant que son fils était devenu fou, le moine grommela :

— Toi, tu as bien des chambres à louer dans ta tête!

Mais, comme d'habitude, il s'exécuta, s'assurant discrètement que le chien les accompagnait toujours. Ce lien animal et familier avec la jeune Sophia lui plaisait et, sans trop de raisons, il appréciait de le conserver.

Ils marchèrent en silence à la suite de l'étrange procession, traversant d'étroites rues tortueuses bordées de maisons aux rez-de-chaussée de pierre et aux étages de bois en saillie. Le brouillard et l'obscurité rendaient la filature difficile et les contraignaient à se rapprocher afin de ne pas perdre de vue les hommes en noir. Au fil du temps, la bourre grisâtre qui flottait dans l'air sembla se solidifier, estompant toutes formes. Aussi, au détour d'une rue, le commissaire aux morts étranges ne fut pas trop surpris de constater la disparition des suspects, happés d'un coup par la nuit.

— Nom de Dieu! fit le moine.

— Ne blasphème pas, le gronda Volnay. Il est interdit de jurer le nom de Dieu ou celui du roi. N'oublie pas que cela est puni de mort!

Il ne manquait jamais une occasion de donner la leçon à son père tant, des deux, c'était lui qui semblait parfois faire l'enfant.

— Tiens, remarqua-t-il. Il y a un cimetière là-bas, allons voir.

— Nous ne savons pas qui sont ces gens, protesta le moine. Tu sais comme moi qu'il est recommandé de ne pas traverser les cimetières pendant les heures noires.

— Allons voir quand même!

Ils pénétrèrent sans bruit dans le lieu funèbre et se faufilèrent à travers les tombes. Le brouillard semblait s'exhaler de la terre, l'âme des morts sourdre d'entre les pierres. Peu impressionné par l'atmosphère, le chien errait de droite et de gauche, reniflant et levant la patte par endroits sous le regard désapprobateur de Volnay. Les deux hommes plissèrent les yeux pour scruter les environs. Plus loin, la nuit semblait parcourue de mouvements furtifs et, bientôt, le bruit mat d'une pioche qui mord la terre glacée les aiguilla. Des silhouettes sombres se regroupaient autour d'une tombe fraîchement creusée. Le commissaire aux morts étranges les rejoignit à grands pas. Ses bottes écrasaient la neige fraîche avec un bruit sourd, faisant voler une poudre blanche à chaque enjambée. Il pointait résolument son pistolet et sa main ne tremblait pas. De son côté, le moine avait dégainé sa dague. Les hommes en noir ne bougèrent pas, figés par la surprise.

— Je suis commissaire au Châtelet, s'écria Volnay, et je vous décrète de prise de corps! Savez-vous qu'à la nuit tombée, les peines sont doubles pour les délits? Vous risquez la corde pour cela!

Le grand homme qui semblait commander la petite troupe fit un pas en avant. Il émanait de lui une autorité tranquille.

— Monsieur, je suis un anatomiste. Je ne déterre pas les cadavres comme certains pour en prélever la cervelle en vue de fabriquer des potions magiques mais afin de pousser plus loin les limites de la science.

— Vos buts ne m'intéressent pas, répondit Volnay avec une rectitude glaçante, je ne retiens que les faits!

Le moine lui saisit vivement le bras.

— Tu as perdu une roue ou quoi? Ce sont des scientifiques!

L'anatomiste approuva et désigna du doigt trois jeunes gens échevelés.

— Ceux-là sont mes étudiants. Eux deux…

Il pointa du doigt vers deux hommes à la mine plus farouche.

— Ceux-là sont moins portés vers la science que nous. J'ai bien peur qu'ils ne soient plus intéressés par le profit que par les progrès de la médecine. Il faut dire que les cadavres se paient trente livres pièce. Néanmoins, ils me sont loyaux…

Le moine posa une main sur l'épaule de son fils.

— Mon garçon, il ne nous appartient pas de nous mettre sur le chemin de la science.

L'anatomiste fit un pas hésitant en direction du moine.

— Vous! Seriez-vous qui je pense?

Il s'approcha plus près pour le scruter.

— Mon Dieu, c'est vous! Je vous croyais mort! Alors ce que l'on dit est vrai? Vous travaillez pour la police, messire Guillaume de…

— Pas de nom, mon ami, pas de nom! Je travaille à découvrir les coupables de crimes horribles et j'emploie pour cela toute ma science. Pour le reste, j'estime toujours que le roi et sa cour sont des jean-foutre!

L'anatomiste rit.

— Vous n'avez pas changé, me semble-t-il, et c'est tant mieux!

Il réfléchit un instant puis appela près de lui un homme court et râblé.

— Nous sommes, lui dit-il, dans une situation complexe. Il nous faut donner preuve de notre sincérité envers ce policier sinon il nous mènera en prison. Je sais que tu répugnes à livrer le nom de tes clients mais il le faut, c'est pour notre bien à tous. En dehors bien entendu des médecins ou professeurs comme moi…

L'autre hésita.

— Eh bien, insista l'anatomiste, n'as-tu donc pas livré, en dehors de gens de science comme moi, des clients récemment, ces deux dernières semaines?

— Cela ne se passe pas comme cela, grommela l'homme. On me donne rendez-vous à un endroit et l'on y charge le cadavre dans une voiture. Après, je ne sais pas ce qu'ils en font. On dit que certains mages utilisent le cœur ou la cervelle pour des potions ou des sorts. Mais la plupart du temps, ce sont des étudiants de médecine qui préfèrent s'exercer sur les morts plutôt que sur les vivants! Ils jettent ensuite les restes dans la Seine et gardent la graisse des corps pour se chauffer l'hiver.

— Eh bien, constata l'anatomiste d'un ton égal, vous avez l'information que vous souhaitez. Nous allons prendre congé les uns des autres.

Mais Volnay n'avait pas baissé le canon de son arme.

— Tout doux, monsieur, les réponses me laissent insatisfait. Et il y a toujours entre nous le cadavre d'un gardien de cimetière!

— Quel gardien de cimetière? Oh! Cette histoire-là?

L'anatomiste se tourna de nouveau vers le déterreur de cadavres.

— N'est-ce pas celle que tu nous as racontée tout à l'heure à la taverne ?

L'autre hocha lugubrement la tête.

— C'est que j'aimerais mieux ne pas la répéter !

L'anatomiste soupira.

— Je crains que nous n'ayons guère le choix et puis tu n'es pas obligé de citer les noms !

Le déterreur de cadavres prit un air buté mais, devant le regard résolu du commissaire aux morts étranges, s'exécuta.

— Nous, les déterreurs de cadavres, nous nous retrouvons parfois pour boire quelques pintes ensemble. Hier soir, j'ai vidé des chopines avec un collègue à moi. Je ne savais pas s'il était ivre mais il m'a raconté une drôle d'histoire.

Il fit tourbillonner machinalement sa pioche en l'air.

— Or donc, dans la nuit de dimanche à lundi, il s'est rendu à son travail avec ses aides dans un grand cimetière. Ils déterrent un client sans bruit puis vont plus loin mais ne voilà-t-il pas que lui et ses hommes butent sur un cadavre pas du tout enterré ! Ils veulent rebrousser chemin mais d'autres personnes sont près de là et les ont vus. Croyant avoir affaire à la police, mes collègues se mettent en garde avec leurs pelles et leurs pioches. Mais les autres sont aussi surpris et effrayés qu'eux d'autant plus que des feux multicolores s'échappent de là où ils ont creusé ! Au bout du compte, tout le monde se sauve prestement de son côté !

Le commissaire aux morts étranges réfléchit. L'histoire paraissait vraisemblable et expliquait en tout cas l'interruption de la messe noire et l'abandon des deux cadavres dans le cimetière. Après tout, cette explication payait bien le déplacement ! Il abaissa le canon de son arme.

— Filez, dit-il.

L'anatomiste le salua de son chapeau.

— Monsieur, merci de votre contribution à la science !

Le moine et son fils regardèrent les hommes en noir détaler sans plus de commentaire.

— Ils vont probablement aller ailleurs, fit le moine amusé.

— Probablement, répondit sèchement son fils.

Le chien sur leurs talons, ils sortirent discrètement du cimetière. Plus épais qu'à leur entrée, le brouillard semblait prendre une consistance plus dense, avalant les maisons de la rue les unes après les autres.

— Par où prendrais-tu ? demanda le policier.

— À droite.

— Nous prendrons donc à gauche, fit Volnay qui n'avait qu'une confiance limitée dans le sens de l'orientation de son père.

Le moine marmonna quelque chose d'inintelligible dans sa barbe mais suivit son fils. Il sentit alors comme un souffle chaud sur sa cuisse et s'aperçut que, pour ne pas le perdre, le chien marchait pratiquement sur ses talons.

— De nos jours, reprit le moine pour combler le silence de la nuit, de plus en plus de monde s'intéresse à l'anatomie. Même les femmes s'en passionnent ! La comtesse de Coigny ne voyage jamais sans un cadavre dans son coffre !

— À droite ?

— Non, à gauche.

— À droite !

Ils empruntèrent de sordides venelles, incapables de se repérer dans la ouate épaisse qui les entourait. Une dizaine de minutes plus tard, le commissaire aux morts étranges s'immobilisa, les narines frémissantes.

— Je sens l'odeur des quais, murmura-t-il.

— J'avais dit : à gauche !

Les deux hommes se regardèrent silencieusement. Leurs sens atrophiés par la nuit et le brouillard, ils ignoraient exactement où ils se trouvaient et retrouver leur chemin ne serait pas chose aisée.

— Rentrons vite chez nous, dit le moine en frissonnant. Nous allons attraper la mort.

D'un geste, son fils le fit taire.

— Écoute !

Quelques instants auparavant opaque et silencieuse, la nuit semblait soudain s'éveiller et fourmiller d'une vie inquiétante.

— Il y a du monde derrière nous, chuchota le commissaire aux morts étranges, et je doute qu'il s'agisse d'une patrouille du guet. Prenons rapidement les quais de Seine et mettons de la distance entre eux et nous !

En trébuchant dans la rue non pavée, ils rejoignirent le quai, serrant au plus loin du fleuve. Soudain le bruit d'une course les fit sursauter. Le policier porta la main à son pistolet mais n'eut pas le temps d'achever son mouvement. Une forme noire s'écrasa contre lui dans un soupir inarticulé et, avec un juron qui ne lui était pas habituel, Volnay chuta lourdement.

Avec une vivacité surprenante, le moine se jeta sur l'agresseur et le cloua au sol. Lorsqu'ils se penchèrent sur lui, le policier et son père découvrirent un petit homme replet, aux bajoues tremblotantes, habillé comme un bon bourgeois. Il semblait en nage, comme au terme d'une longue course, et dégageait une forte odeur de singe.

— Non, non ! Ne me tuez pas ! geignit-il.

Le moine et le commissaire aux morts étranges s'entre-regardèrent.

— Je suis commissaire du Châtelet, fit Volnay. Vous n'avez rien à craindre de nous. Qui êtes-vous ?

— Je m'appelle Lefranc, je suis maître rôtisseur rue des Postes.

— Que fuyez-vous ?

L'autre leur jeta un regard hagard.

— Ils m'ont pris en chasse et m'ont forcé à aller sur les quais !

Par-delà le souffle haletant de l'homme, Volnay perçut un nouveau bruit, une sorte de piétinements étouffés et le bruit de bâtons heurtant le sol avec une régularité de métronome.

— Ils sont nombreux, constata le policier. Peut-être une centaine…

On commençait à distinguer des silhouettes fantomatiques qui avançaient en une ligne serrée. D'affreux nez de papier déformés ornaient leurs visages.

— Avec leurs bâtons, ils battent à mort ceux qu'ils trouvent sur leur passage, souffla Lefranc.

— Cela ne se peut, souffla le policier en baissant néanmoins la voix. Ce groupe porte des masques de Carême et des femmes en font partie !

— Existe-t-il encore un quelconque bon sens aujourd'hui ? Ces débordements font gémir toutes les âmes pieuses, se plaignit le bourgeois.

— Je vais leur parler, décréta Volnay en sortant son pistolet. Je suis policier.

À cet instant, un hurlement éclata dans la nuit. Un bruit de coups sourds se fit entendre et une longue plainte s'éleva dans l'air froid avant de s'éteindre dans un dernier râle.

— Policier ou pas, à ta place je ne bougerais pas ! fit le moine.

Son fils hocha sèchement la tête.

— Tu as raison, nous n'avons pas affaire à un groupe d'étudiants qui jouent à effrayer le bourgeois mais à des tueurs !

Il plissa les yeux, essayant de percer nuit et brouillard.

— Ils doivent sortir les nuits de mauvais temps, lorsque les patrouilles des archers du guet se font rares. Ils s'affublent de masques de Carnaval au cas toutefois où ils en rencontreraient une…

— Ils arrivent ! Sauve qui peut ! cria le rôtisseur en prenant ses jambes à son cou.

— Attendez, restons ensemble ! fit le policier.

L'autre ne ralentit même pas. Le bruit de la course du bourgeois se perdit dans la nuit, derrière eux la troupe avançait.

— Ne restons pas là, fit le moine. Imitons notre peu courageux compagnon ! Comme le disait Démosthène : "Tel qui fuit peut combattre encore !"

— Je me demande si c'est vraiment la meilleure solution, rétorqua Volnay.

Il se leva toutefois et suivit son père.

— Ils connaissent l'endroit, ils vont plus vite que nous, remarqua le moine. Ventrebleu ! Le chien n'est plus là !

— Rassure-toi, je pense qu'il est nettement plus malin que nous ! Allons-y !

Ils se mirent à courir en aveugle. Ils n'entendaient plus que le bruit incertain de leur course et leur respiration haletante, trébuchant parfois sur des obstacles inattendus. Il leur semblait toutefois plus logique de risquer de se rompre le cou que de s'offrir aux bâtons de leurs poursuivants. Le moine pesta car il venait de perdre sa peau de loup. Devant eux retentirent un hurlement horrible puis le bruit mat mais distinct de coups étouffés. Ils stoppèrent net. Le moine gratta son collier de barbe.

— Nous venons de perdre notre maître rôtisseur. Il en vient par-devant.

— C'est ce que je craignais, murmura Volnay d'un ton lugubre. Comme à la chasse, on rabat le gibier sur les autres chasseurs. Ils doivent se disposer de part et d'autre des quais pour chasser leurs proies. S'ils n'en trouvent pas, ils démarrent leur battue dans les rues adjacentes.

— Et personne ne survit pour raconter quoi que ce soit, termina le moine. Remontons dans les rues.

— Si des complices y sont embusqués, c'est notre fin assurée.

Des bruits de voix étouffées se firent entendre devant eux. Derrière, les silhouettes fantomatiques se rapprochaient.

— Voilà qui n'est pas bon du tout! constata le policier sans perdre son sang-froid.

— L'eau! Sautons dans le fleuve, c'est le seul endroit où ils ne nous suivront pas.

— Nous n'y survivrons pas! À tout prendre, je préfère essayer de remonter des quais mais la pente est raide et avec la neige cela ne sera pas facile.

— Essayons de trouver un endroit où il y a des anneaux.

Volnay s'appuya dos au mur et joignit ses mains pour que le moine y pose un pied.

— Trouves-tu une prise?

— Non et je n'y vois goutte! Cela glisse trop. Nous aurions dû choisir l'eau.

Le bruit de pas martelés se rapprochait. Une écorce de glace semblait raidir les muscles du moine alors que ses pieds cherchaient une fente où se placer.

— Il est trop tard, père. Trouve quelque chose ou ils vont nous réduire en purée!

— Non, je ne… un anneau! Décale-toi un peu à droite sans me lâcher! Voilà!

— Dépêche-toi!

Les assassins se rapprochaient. Ils avaient amorcé un mouvement d'encerclement en entendant les deux hommes. Déjà, leurs bâtons fouettaient l'air.

— Prends ma main, vite!

Volnay fit quelques pas en arrière. Un bref regard lui permit de voir à quelques mètres de lui les sinistres silhouettes au regard aveugle, affublées de leur horrible masque de papier au nez démesuré.

Le policier se précipita en avant et sauta, la main de son père se referma sur la sienne.

— Saisis l'anneau, vite!

Alors qu'il s'en emparait, un coup porté à sa jambe par un bâton le fit hurler de douleur.

— Je vais me mettre debout sur l'anneau, fit le moine. Si je tombe, je suis mort. Donc, adieu peut-être…

Volnay jura et, de sa main libre, sortit son pistolet.

— Je vais faire un peu d'air en dessous de nous, haleta-t-il. Attention, je tire!

Le coup de feu troua l'air. Un cri d'agonie traversa la nuit. Les bâtons cessèrent de s'agiter et les poursuivants reculèrent. Ils n'avaient pas l'habitude d'une si forte résistance. Volnay lâcha son arme et, les deux mains tenant l'anneau, il tenta de grimper jusqu'à celui-ci. Au-dessus de lui, le moine poussa un cri de triomphe.

— Les pierres dépassent, on peut s'y appuyer. Voilà! Je suis arrivé. À toi. J'enlève ma bure et je te la lance.

À son tour, Volnay se dressa sur l'anneau, s'écorchant les mains sur de mauvaises prises gelées. Il sentit le bout de la bure effleurer sa tête et leva les mains pour l'attraper. Au-dessous de lui, le sifflement des bâtons avait repris.

— Tu tiens bien? demanda-t-il.

— Penses-tu! Je suis vieux et faible!

Tout en pestant, le moine entreprit de le hisser tandis que Volnay s'efforçait de faire reposer le poids de son corps sur l'arête des pierres sous ses pieds. Haletant, il s'effondra enfin près de son père.

— Je suis mort, dit celui-ci en claquant des dents. Mort de froid.

Volnay l'aida à remettre sa bure.

— Quelle folie!

Derrière eux, ils entendirent leurs poursuivants s'efforcer de se hisser à leur tour.

— Filons d'ici, fit le moine, je n'ai pas envie de voir leur sale tronche sous leurs masques de papier !

Après une course éperdue, ils se retrouvèrent devant la porte de la maison du moine. Sur ses épaules, la bure de celui-ci semblait être devenue une armure de glace. À leur grande surprise, la porte n'était pas fermée à clé. Les deux hommes entrèrent prudemment et découvrirent une Hélène souriante, assise près d'un bon feu.

— Que faites-vous là ?

Elle se leva.

— Je vous attendais…

— Comment êtes-vous rentrée ?

— Je vous ai dérobé une clé !

— Vous avez osé ?!

— Vous m'avez bien droguée pour me faire dormir !

— Oh, ça… murmura le moine gêné. Ce n'était qu'une petite décoction…

Une longue toux caverneuse s'échappa de la gorge du moine. Hélène se tourna vers lui, inquiète.

— Stoppons là nos querelles, vous avez pris la mort. Ôtez tous deux vos habits et mettez-vous près du feu, je vais vous apporter des couvertures.

Tremblants et frissonnants, les deux hommes s'exécutèrent piteusement.

— Qu'est-ce que ceci ? demanda Hélène.

On venait de gratter à la porte.

— Incroyable ! s'exclama le moine. Il est revenu.

Volnay se hâta d'ouvrir et le chien se faufila sans gêne entre eux pour se coucher avec un soupir de satisfaction devant l'âtre après s'être ébroué.

— Un compagnon à quatre pattes, commenta le moine, nous vous expliquerons plus tard.

— Ne serait-ce pas le chien que Sophia voulait protéger ? demanda Hélène. Son propriétaire a porté plainte contre elle et j'ai pu entendre toute l'affaire…

— Oui, admit Volnay. C'est sans doute lui qui hurlait à la mort à la porte du cimetière. Il nous suit depuis que nous avons porté le corps de sa maîtresse mais apparemment il a plus un faible pour moi que pour le moine !

— Pas du tout! rétorqua l'autre, c'est juste que…

— Taisez-vous et ne gardez rien sur vous! décréta avec autorité la jeune femme. Je vais chercher des couvertures.

Le moine tourna la tête vers son fils.

— J'ai bien entendu? Elle nous a bien dit de ne rien garder sur nous?

Une minute plus tard, comme si elle connaissait par cœur la maison, Hélène revint et marqua un temps d'arrêt devant les deux hommes qui ne conservaient que leur haut-de-chausses et se frottaient mutuellement à la chaleur des flammes. D'un œil exercé, elle apprécia la carrure de leurs épaules, leur torse musclé et leur ventre plat. S'en apercevant, le moine bomba avantageusement la poitrine. En souriant, Hélène leur tendit à chacun une chaude couverture de laine. Gênés, le moine et le policier s'en couvrirent avant d'enlever leur dernier vêtement. Alors, Hélène se mit à les étriller comme des chevaux, en commençant par le plus âgé. Elle ne tarda toutefois pas à marquer un temps d'arrêt.

— Oh pardon, fit joyeusement le moine, vous réveillez la nature qui est en moi!

Hélène le considéra un instant.

— Trop honorée, terminez donc seul de vous sécher!

Elle se tourna vers le policier.

— À vous!

À sa surprise, Volnay se laissa faire, semblant même prendre plaisir au passage vigoureux des mains sur son corps. Instruite par son expérience, Hélène se borna à lui frotter le dos et les épaules, s'attardant pourtant sur lui peut-être plus que de raison. On décida ensuite que la jeune femme prendrait la chambre et que les deux hommes dormiraient, gorgés de tisanes et enveloppés de couvertures, près du feu qui fut alimenté avec soin.

— Que nul maléfice ou mauvais rêve ne vienne troubler votre sommeil, fit Hélène en les contemplant d'un air doux. Bonne nuit et dormez!

VI

LA VORACE ET AUTRES DIABLERIES

Lorsque Volnay ouvrit un œil, ce fut pour découvrir Hélène s'affairant auprès du feu. Éveillé, le moine la contemplait avec ravissement.

— Je ne me sens pas très bien. J'ai une fièvre de veau ! Jeune fille, voulez-vous bien m'apporter la carafe que vous voyez là-bas ?

Une quinte de toux lui déchira les poumons. Le moine soupira puis reprit :

— L'eau de Paris est putrescible, je ne bois de l'eau de fontaine qu'après l'avoir fait bouillir avec une racine de réglisse et laissée reposer.

Il s'interrompit pour éternuer.

— Je passe ensuite mon eau par un entonnoir bouché avec un bouquet de thym séché.

Une autre série d'éternuements le secoua tout entier.

— J'y ajoute un peu de vinaigre et d'eau-de-vie, ajouta-t-il dans un souffle. Cela donne meilleur goût.

Interdite, Hélène se tourna vers Volnay qui s'était redressé sur son séant.

— Il délire ?

— Je ne crois pas, non. Il fait vraiment tout cela !

— Installons-le dans sa chambre, fit-elle.

Celle-ci était meublée d'un lit bas avec un matelas de plumes recouvert de couvertures de laine blanches, d'un poêle en faïence, d'un secrétaire en noyer et d'un siège de travail. Sur une étagère se côtoyaient des bronzes féminins couchés et des volumes in-folio reliés en veau du *Dictionnaire encyclopédique*.

Une haute fenêtre était occultée par de lourds rideaux de velours rouge qui réchauffaient la pièce.

— Il est très malade, insista Hélène après avoir aidé le moine à se coucher. Il va falloir appeler un médecin.

Le commissaire aux morts étranges leva les yeux au ciel.

— Il n'acceptera jamais d'en voir approcher un de son lit.

— Il n'est pas en état de le rosser ! Dépêchez-vous !

En maugréant, Volnay se hâta de s'habiller et, en milieu de matinée, revint avec un médecin du quartier qui n'avait pas trop mauvaise réputation. Celui-ci, sec comme une trique, vêtu d'une robe longue à grandes manches et le crâne surmonté d'une belle perruque poudrée, se hâta de brosser un tableau d'ensemble de la situation.

— Tout Paris est malade, c'est l'action conjointe des brouillards, de la neige et du mauvais air. Il n'y a guère de maisons dans le quartier où l'on ne saigne ou fasse prendre des lavements.

— Purgez ceux-là, saignez ceux-ci, se moqua le moine entre deux quintes de toux.

— Monsieur mon consultant ferait mieux de garder ses forces. Gardez-vous la nourriture que vous ingurgitez ?

— Ma foi oui, si elle est bonne.

— *Sus ad vomitum !*

Il pointa un doigt accusateur vers le moine.

— J'espère que vous n'êtes pas de ces gens qui s'empiffrent ! Respect au malade innocent mais honte au malade qui sacrifie sa santé à ses vices.

— L'indigestion du riche venge la diète forcée du pauvre, remarqua le moine, mais en l'occurrence, j'ai simplement pris froid.

— Bien, bien… Si l'on en juge par l'état de monsieur mon consultant qui me paraît d'un âge avancé…

Le moine eut un cri de protestation.

— Monsieur mon consultant, reprit le médecin en s'adressant désormais à Volnay qu'il semblait juger seul digne de l'entendre, souffre visiblement d'une forte fièvre et ses poumons sont encombrés comme le démontre suffisamment sa toux. Son sang doit être trop épais, voire acrimonieux. Une bonne saignée le délivrera de ses humeurs âcres. Mais, pour parfaire mon diagnostic, je dois goûter à ses urines…

— Ne vous gênez pas ! dit le moine.

— D'abord, toussez puis crachez dans ce mouchoir, je vous prie. Hum…

Il se tourna vers Volnay, l'air peiné.

— Crachats d'écume sanguinolente, il y a lieu de le saigner abondamment.

— Pas de saignée, cela l'affaiblirait.

Le médecin jeta au policier un regard peu amène.

— Remettre en question la Faculté, c'est dénier la raison ! *Per scientiam ad salutem aegroti* : "Le salut du malade passe par la science !" D'abord, il faut aligner le lit parallèlement aux poutres pour hâter la guérison puis aérer cette chambre à coucher tous les matins afin de la débarrasser du produit de la respiration de la nuit. Faites de même le soir pour évacuer celle de la journée. En effet, il s'agit de deux principes contraires qui s'opposent, exposant l'occupant des lieux à cette lutte malsaine dont il sera la principale victime. Et commençons tout de suite !

Il alla jusqu'à la fenêtre qu'il ouvrit bien grande. Un vent glacé s'engouffra dans la pièce, arrachant un hoquet de stupéfaction à Hélène.

— Le sommeil, s'exclama le docteur avec enthousiasme, le sommeil !

Il leva les bras en l'air pour ânonner :

— *"Lever à cinq, dîner à neuf,*
Souper à cinq, coucher à neuf
Font vivre d'ans nonante et neuf."

— Votre malade sera mort de froid sous peu, dit le commissaire aux morts étranges qui referma la fenêtre d'un geste sec. Monsieur, merci de vos services, je vous reconduis.

L'autre ouvrit la bouche pour protester mais le commissaire aux morts étranges lui saisit le bras avec fermeté pour le conduire à la porte. Avant que celle-ci ne se referme, les deux hommes entendirent clairement le moine crier de sa chambre :

— Dehors le médecin d'eau douce !

Volnay n'attendit pas la prochaine saillie pour pousser le battant de la porte mais le moine hurlait assez fort pour qu'on l'entende de dehors :

— Estropié de la cervelle ! Sot à triple étage !

Restée seule avec le malade, Hélène se pencha sur lui et lui caressa la joue.

— Arrêtez de crier comme cela, vous allez vous briser la voix.

Le moine éternua et répondit :

— J'ai cette engeance en horreur. En France, en dehors des soldats, les médecins sont les seules personnes habilitées à tuer ! Certains d'entre eux ne voient même pas leurs patients et se contentent de répondre en latin à leurs courriers où ils décrivent leurs symptômes ! Il ne viendrait pas à l'esprit de cette bogue de châtaigne qui m'a visité de me prendre le pouls, la température ou de faire la percussion des poumons !

Il s'interrompit pour tousser et reprit d'une voix éraillée :

— Son seul remède est d'ouvrir les fenêtres et saigner son patient. Si j'avais survécu, il m'aurait ensuite prescrit de la purgation suivie de la prise de bouillon et de lait d'ânesse tous les matins. C'est très à la mode…

— Ne vous agitez pas comme cela, lui reprocha Hélène compatissante. Reposez-vous plutôt.

— Allez me chercher mes herbes à la cuisine, répondit faiblement le moine. Je vous expliquerai quoi faire.

Il pointa le menton vers son fils qui se tenait coi sur le pas de la porte et les observait.

— Bourre ce poêle jusqu'à la gueule et ajoute-moi une couverture. Il me faut bien suer. Quand ce sera fait, tu calfeutreras la fenêtre de linge de manière à ce que je ne prenne pas un mauvais courant d'air.

La jeune femme apporta dans un torchon une poignée d'herbes. Le moine se redressa pour les contempler.

— Prenez celle-ci, un brin de celle-là, une feuille ici. Voilà, ajoutez ceci et deux feuilles de celle-là effritées entre vos mains. Tout est là ? Faites bouillir une grande casserole d'eau et plongez-y tout cela quelques instants.

Il toussa puis reprit.

— Vous passerez au tamis d'un linge le liquide et m'apporterez deux bols bien pleins avec du miel. Vous mettrez le reste en carafe que vous poserez près de mon lit. Avant de partir, mettez de grosses bûches dans la cheminée. Il est important que toute la maison soit bien tiède.

— Je vais chercher quelqu'un pour veiller sur toi, décida son fils. À deux pas de là, il y a une ouvrière en linge qui s'occupe de nos vêtements. Elle a peu d'ouvrage actuellement et sera heureuse de passer la journée au chaud et bien rémunérée.

Restée seule avec le moine, Hélène chercha un tissu vierge et se mit à écrire dessus *ABRACADABRA*. Elle répéta ce mot à la ligne d'après en enlevant la dernière lettre et ainsi de suite jusqu'à ce qu'il ne subsiste plus que le "A" initial, formant un triangle inversé, une espèce d'entonnoir par lequel s'écoulerait le mal en se réduisant.

— C'est amusant, dit le moine s'intéressant à l'ouvrage. Savez-vous que cette célèbre formule magique *ABRACADABRA* provient d'une contraction des mots hébreux *abreq ad hâbra*, ce qui signifie…

— Envoie ta foudre jusqu'à la mort.

— Oh…

Le moine lui jeta un regard respectueux.

— J'oublie toujours que vous êtes presque aussi savante que moi ! Qui donc vous a enseigné cela ?

— Ma mère.

Elle n'en dit pas plus mais lui noua le tissu autour du cou.

— Vous serez vite guéri, ajouta-t-elle. C'est un triangle magique !

Volnay revint bientôt avec une femme d'une quarantaine d'années à la nature joviale et au large sourire édenté. Hélène leur apprit que le moine s'était endormi.

— Très bien, fit son fils soulagé.

Il se tourna vers l'ouvrière.

— Veillez-le jusqu'à notre retour.

Il lui tendit quelques pièces.

— Voici pour votre peine, vous aurez le double à notre retour. S'il se réveille, faites tout ce qu'il vous demandera même si cela vous étonne !

Il était plus de midi lorsque le commissaire aux morts étranges et la jeune femme quittèrent le domicile du moine, laissant celui-ci à la garde du chien et de l'ouvrière en linge. La neige s'était mise doucement à tomber et leur piquait les yeux.

— La prostituée que nous recherchons est surnommée la Vorace, expliqua Volnay. Je n'ose imaginer ce que traduit ce terme dans ce métier-là !

Hélène lui jeta un regard amusé. Le ton léger du policier était nouveau pour elle. Était-il capable de drôlerie comme le moine ? Elle jugeait Volnay sévère et rigide mais, aujourd'hui, il semblait se détendre avec elle. Il lui conta d'un ton badin quelques anecdotes pittoresques sur le quartier qu'ils traversaient, allant même jusqu'à la faire rire, et lui tint galamment le bras lors des passages difficiles.

À mi-chemin, le vent se leva pour les cingler. Mordus par le froid, Hélène et Volnay se rapprochèrent instinctivement pour s'en protéger. Forte de cette nouvelle complicité, la jeune femme s'appuya sur son bras plus que de nécessité. Ils empruntèrent des rues étroites et malodorantes, bordées d'immeubles aux façades lépreuses et de petits commerces d'où s'élevaient des clameurs bruyantes. Une population bigarrée s'y pressait, toujours en mouvement. Des portefaix se tuaient à la tâche en portant des colis presque aussi lourds qu'eux. Chiffonniers, crocheteurs, colporteurs et petits ramoneurs savoyards au visage ravagé par la suie des cheminées se bousculaient sur la chaussée glacée. Dans les échoppes, on vendait l'arlequin, une mosaïque des mets dont plus personne ne voulait. Les traiteurs quant à eux proposaient des ragoûts, les tripiers des abats. Même en l'état peu appétissant, tout restait cher pour les habitants des environs.

À un coin de rue, ils croisèrent un fourgon où des archers du guet chargeaient un colosse au regard abruti et un vieillard épouvanté. Des lèvres du colosse hagard s'échappait comme une mélopée.

— Que se passe-t-il ? demanda doucement Hélène qui s'était arrêtée.

Volnay la considéra calmement. Même la neige ne pouvait faire oublier les lueurs mordorées dans ses grands yeux verts.

— On enfourne pêle-mêle, pour l'hôpital de Bicêtre, les fous, les vagabonds, les épileptiques et les vieillards, expliqua-t-il.

— Dans ce mouroir ?

— Remerciez-en le roi et son zélé serviteur, M. de Sartine !

Elle lui jeta un regard triste mais ne répondit pas. Il avait cru la mettre en colère mais, au contraire, elle se rapprocha plus encore, comme cherchant auprès de lui un soutien qu'elle ne pouvait espérer trouver ailleurs.

Lorsqu'ils arrivèrent faubourg Saint-Marcel, la neige avait cessé de tomber et un soleil anémié tentait de réchauffer quelque peu le monde à ses pieds. Ici, la pauvreté se lisait aussi bien sur les visages maigres qu'à travers le mouvement des corps, immensément douloureux, brisés par la fatigue. On y sentait tant le manque de nourriture que la brièveté du sommeil et les mains rendues calleuses par les travaux les plus pénibles. Les gens ne portaient pas de souliers mais des sabots. Leurs vêtements étaient dépareillés, boutons et poches arrachés. La rudesse de leur vie n'empêchait pas le recours au vice. Ils virent deux jeunes hommes qui commettaient sous un porche des indécences avec une prostituée. Malgré le froid, le plaisir se prenait aussi toujours dans la rue, rapidement et brutalement. Hélène jeta un rapide coup d'œil à Volnay qui détourna le regard.

Dans le cabaret décrit par le marchand grec à Volnay, se trouvaient trois grandes tables. L'une d'elles était jonchée de débris de nourriture et, tels des rats affamés, hommes, femmes et enfants aux vêtements rapiécés se chargeaient de la nettoyer, mangeant avidement. Leurs ventres maigres, leur teint blanc et leurs yeux brillants dévoilaient tout de leur misère. Dieu seul savait où ils passeraient ensuite la nuit.

À une autre table, des ouvriers tentaient d'oublier leur fatigue à coups de vin servis dans des vases de grès et la fumée de leur pipe ajoutait une note boisée à l'odeur rance de leur boisson.

À la dernière table, l'atmosphère était plus tendue. On jouait aux cartes en buvant et en s'apostrophant. Auprès des joueurs chanceux s'agglutinaient des femmes qui se voulaient agui-cheuses. Parfois des éclats de voix jaillissaient et des chopes ou des poings cognaient lourdement la table. On sentait qu'il suffisait d'un geste ou d'une parole pour que tout s'embrase et qu'une rixe éclate.

Volnay prit le bras de la jeune femme et l'entraîna dans un coin où un demi-tonneau servait de table.

— Sacrée garce, dit bruyamment un joueur en lorgnant effrontément Hélène.

Le commissaire aux morts étranges coula vers lui un regard glacial et s'assit en soulevant son manteau, laissant dépasser la pointe de son épée. Les rires se turent et l'on se mit à chuchoter tout en les observant de biais. Leurs vêtements trahissaient leur condition et seuls les gentilshommes ou les militaires étaient autorisés à porter l'épée. On se demandait bien ce qu'un tel couple fabriquait par ici. Le policier commanda et on leur servit pour huit sols deux pintes de vin et pour vingt sols un morceau de salé.

Pendant qu'il mangeait, Volnay observa du coin de l'œil les personnes à la table de jeu. Plusieurs prostituées se trouvaient manifestement parmi elles et lui adressaient des œillades coquines. Aucune d'elles ne semblait assez âgée pour être la Vorace que le marchand grec dépeignait comme une femme d'une quarantaine d'années. Le policier repéra une fille aux manières plus soignées que celles de ses collègues. Son visage, parsemé de taches de rousseur sur le nez et les pommettes, était encadré d'une courte chevelure rousse. Sa vivacité, ses yeux noisette, deux jolies fossettes et un ravissant petit menton en pointe faisaient penser à un écureuil. D'un geste discret, le commissaire aux morts étranges l'invita à sa table.

La prostituée eut un imperceptible mouvement de surprise et, après un court moment d'hésitation, les rejoignit sous les quolibets des joueurs. Les mots de *putain* et de *coquine* revenaient maintenant dans les conversations sur le couple. La fille se tint devant eux, les mains dans le dos, en se mordillant les lèvres. Volnay la considéra. De près, elle semblait très jeune, presque fragile, dans ses vêtements de mauvaise qualité : un casaquin de toile violette, des jupons à raies rouges et des bas de laine grise. Des bijoux de pacotille tintaient faiblement à ses poignets. Ses yeux laissaient filtrer une lueur inquiète que n'arrivait pas à atténuer son sourire engageant.

— Asseyez-vous, dit gentiment Hélène. Quel est votre nom ?

— Ici, on m'appelle l'Écureuil, répondit-elle en froissant nerveusement ses jupons aux couleurs défraîchies.

— Asseyez-vous, fit Volnay. Nous ne vous voulons aucun mal. Je cherche une de vos compagnes, une dénommée la Vorace. La connaissez-vous ?

L'autre prit une expression rusée.

— Pourquoi la voulez-vous elle plus qu'une autre ? Elle n'est pas de première jeunesse !

— Mais elle a bien d'autres qualités, répondit Volnay en clignant de l'œil.

L'Écureuil le considéra avec méfiance.

— C'est pour vous deux ?

Cela ne semblait guère avoir de sens pour elle qu'un couple aussi distingué soit à la recherche de cette femme. Volnay sentit la faiblesse de son argument sans trouver pour autant la bonne répartie. Ce fut Hélène qui vint à son secours.

— Mon mari a l'aiguillette nouée et n'est donc plus en mesure de me faire du bien au lit.

Si l'aiguillette était le lacet ferré à ses extrémités qui permettait de fermer les vêtements, c'était aussi le surnom du sexe des hommes. L'Écureuil prit un air soucieux.

— Oh ! Est-ce qu'on lui a jeté un sort ?

— Je l'ignore mais il m'a avoué que la Vorace est la dernière femme avec qui il a pu mener à bien son affaire.

Elle jeta un coup d'œil espiègle à Volnay.

— Mon mari a l'air sérieux comme cela mais en vérité c'est un homme à femmes !

Le policier ne broncha pas.

— Nous espérons tous deux, reprit Hélène, qu'en retrouvant la Vorace, elle puisse lui dénouer l'aiguillette.

La compréhension se fit jour sur le visage de la jeune fille.

— Mais, dit-elle encore méfiante, il n'a pas besoin de vous pour cela.

— C'est que, avoua Hélène en baissant les yeux d'un air gêné, j'aimerais bien voir comment elle s'y prend avec lui. Je pourrais reproduire ce qu'elle lui fait…

La prostituée hocha la tête. L'explication lui paraissait claire maintenant. Elle côtoyait le vice depuis assez longtemps pour ne plus être étonnée de rien.

— Je peux vous conduire jusqu'à elle mais cela vous coûtera quelques pièces car pendant ce temps c'est autant de clients que je ne prends pas.

— Vous serez bien rétribuée, intervint Volnay, mais dehors car je ne tiens pas à attirer l'attention sur ma bourse dans ce cabaret.

— Vous êtes un homme avisé, approuva-t-elle en le contemplant songeusement. Si madame votre épouse le permet, après que vous serez passé sur la Vorace, je pourrai lui montrer comment on ranime la flamme d'un homme avant de la moucher à nouveau.

Son regard s'attarda sur le beau visage du commissaire aux morts étranges.

— Vous seriez surpris de ce que je peux lui apprendre, ajouta-t-elle en se passant la langue sur les lèvres.

Le policier se leva, imité par Hélène.

— J'en suis persuadé! Allez chercher votre manteau et sortons retrouver la Vorace.

Le temps s'était gâté mais, sous la clarté de la lune, les flocons de neige semblaient de la poudre d'argent. Volnay regarda Hélène et la trouva belle. À côté d'elle, la prostituée vacillait légèrement comme si la boisson et le froid la saisissaient soudain. Le policier leur prit le bras à toutes deux pour les aider à marcher sur le sol glacé. Étonnée par tant de délicatesse, l'Écureuil lui jeta un regard surpris.

L'immeuble sale et délabré dans lequel ils pénétrèrent exhalait des odeurs de fange fortes et prenantes. Des immondices formaient un tas puant à son entrée. Au rez-de-chaussée, se trouvait un atelier de menuiserie bruissant de vie.

— Garce à soldats! marmonna un apprenti en les bousculant, une serpette à la main.

— Je ne connais pas cet homme, murmura l'Écureuil la tête baissée.

Derrière une porte, ils entendirent la querelle d'un couple suivi de quelques claques bien senties et des hurlements. Sans mot dire, ils empruntèrent un escalier aussi raide qu'une échelle, se tenant aux murs tant les marches craquaient, menaçant de se rompre à tout moment sous leur poids. Hélène lui prit naturellement la main et, un instant, le policier sentit son parfum l'envahir. Au second étage, à peine essoufflée, l'Écureuil désigna une porte sous laquelle filtrait une faible lueur. Tout à son rôle, Hélène se blottit contre Volnay. Tendant l'oreille, le policier distingua des bruits sourds et des halètements significatifs.

— Ah, fit la jeune prostituée, elle est en affaire. Il va falloir attendre. Avec les hommes, ce n'est jamais très long!

Volnay haussa légèrement les épaules. Hélène sourit, s'écarta de lui et croisa les bras sur sa poitrine, les yeux fixés sur le plancher. Soudain on entendit des cris :

— Garce! Savate de tripière!

— Il ne la ménage pas, commenta sobrement l'Écureuil.

Des coups sourds se mirent à pleuvoir suivis d'exclamations :

— Gueuse! Puante! Prends ça!

Hélène tressaillit violemment comme si c'était elle qu'on venait de frapper. D'un geste instinctif, Volnay porta la main à son épée.

— Laissez, fit l'Écureuil d'un ton neutre, les hommes aiment à battre les femmes. Cela les aide à se croire plus forts que nous.

La porte ne tarda pas à s'ouvrir sur une face de rat d'un âge indéterminé. Surpris de trouver tant de monde sur le palier, l'homme les examina en écarquillant les yeux.

— Quelle foutue drôlesse! dit-il dans un souffle avant de s'élancer dans l'escalier en se cognant l'épaule contre le mur.

— Au suivant! cria une voix aigre. Et fermez la porte ou je vais attraper la mort!

Le commissaire aux morts étranges entra, suivi des deux femmes.

— Êtes-vous la Vorace?

Celle-ci les fixa un instant. Elle avait dû être belle avant que la dureté des temps n'altère et ne durcisse ses traits. Ses paupières à demi baissées laissaient filtrer une lueur rusée, presque sournoise.

— À qui dois-je frotter le cul? demanda-t-elle finalement.

Volnay réprima un sourire. À ses côtés, Hélène prit un air détaché. Le policier tira la pièce promise de sa bourse et la tendit à l'Écureuil.

— Merci, fit celle-ci en singeant une révérence. Si vous avez encore besoin de mes services, vous savez où me trouver quand je ne suis pas occupée.

— Je m'en souviendrai, répondit poliment Volnay.

Il la poussa doucement dehors et ferma la porte derrière elle.

— À nous deux, fit-il en se tournant vers la Vorace.

— À nous trois plutôt, remarqua la prostituée.

— Ce n'est pas ce que vous croyez. Je suis commissaire au Châtelet et je viens vous interroger sur votre participation à une messe noire qui a conduit au meurtre d'une enfant dans un cimetière.

Son ton était assuré, le policier préférant commencer par la conclusion plutôt que par la question. Le coup porta. Le visage fripé de la Vorace devint tout blanc comme si on venait de la vider de tout son sang. Elle ouvrit la bouche, la referma comiquement puis coassa dans un murmure :

— Quoi? Que dites-vous? Non, non! Jamais je n'ai fait ça!

Volnay planta durement son regard dans le sien.

— Allons, je sais tout! Comment vous avez acheté ce produit au marchand grec dans la ruelle de l'Or et comment vous avez administré la communion dans ce cimetière! Vos complices ont parlé. Si vous ne voulez pas être accusée de meurtre, il faut tout me dire.

— Ce n'est pas moi! Pas moi! C'est ce damné curé!

— Comment se nomme-t-il?

— Je ne sais pas! On l'appelle le curé dansant. C'est un diable, il ne tient pas en place!

— Et les autres? demanda Hélène. Il y avait trois hommes et deux femmes en plus de la victime dans ce cimetière…

— Je ne les avais jamais vus!

Le ton de sa voix était désespéré.

— Cela suffit! fit Volnay en saisissant le coude de la femme. Vous allez me suivre au Châtelet.

Il la traîna jusqu'à la porte mais, arrivée là, elle cessa toute résistance et se projeta soudain en avant, déséquilibrant le policier. Avec l'énergie du désespoir, elle s'engouffra dans l'escalier. On entendit soudain un cri suivi du bruit sourd d'un corps qui roule. Volnay et Hélène se précipitèrent. La Vorace gisait sur le palier du premier, le corps désarticulé comme un pantin. Le policier s'agenouilla auprès de la prostituée.

— Elle s'est brisé la nuque, murmura-t-il lugubrement.

La jeune femme s'accroupit près de lui. Derrière eux, des portes s'entrouvraient et des visages hagards apparaissaient, contemplant le spectacle d'un air effaré. Volnay fixa curieusement Hélène.

— Le prêtre récite la messe à l'envers, la prostituée donne l'eucharistie et nous avons retrouvé les autres traces des pieds de deux hommes et d'une femme qui assistaient à cette messe. Cela dit, comment le saviez-vous puisque nous ne vous en avons jamais parlé ?

— Sartine me l'a indiqué, vous lui avez fait un rapport, souvenez-vous...

Cette fois, Volnay ne détourna pas les yeux, plongeant dans ses immenses yeux verts aux reflets mouchetés de doré. Silencieusement, ils s'affrontèrent, aucun d'eux ne voulant céder le premier.

— C'est juste, dit enfin le policier d'un ton neutre.

Il lui prit la main et l'aida à se relever.

— Venez, nous allons prévenir le guet. Ensuite, nous rentrerons. La nuit tombe et je n'aime guère laisser mon père seul et malade.

Baignés par la lueur grisâtre d'un crépuscule précoce, les deux jeunes gens quittèrent le quartier populeux du faubourg Saint-Marcel et regagnèrent la demeure du moine.

— Il a dormi quelques heures, expliqua l'ouvrière en linge lorsqu'ils prirent des nouvelles du malade. Lorsqu'il s'est réveillé, il m'a demandé de lui préparer de nouveau une tisane et de lui appliquer sur les tempes un onguent pour faire tomber la fièvre. Ensuite, il s'est rendormi. J'ai dû le réveiller toutefois lorsque les messieurs sont venus pour le corps.

— Le corps ?

Volnay se souvint tout à coup des embaumeurs qui devaient venir faire la toilette de Sophia et la mettre en bière.

— Ah oui, ceux-là… je les avais oubliés.

— Après, il a dormi de nouveau, continua l'ouvrière en linge.

Elle se mordilla les lèvres.

— Il faut que je vous dise, pendant qu'il dormait, j'entendais comme le bruit d'une conversation mais, lorsque je suis entrée dans la chambre, elle avait cessé et votre père se trouvait seul, l'air extasié…

— La fièvre devait le faire délirer, risqua Hélène.

La brave femme se tourna vers elle.

— C'est étrange pourtant, on aurait dit deux voix, la sienne et une voix féminine. À la porte, je l'ai entendu l'appeler Sophia. Le chien est devenu comme fou. J'ai été obligée de le sortir dans la cour. Mais même là, il continuait à gratter contre la porte…

Le commissaire aux morts étranges prit un air soucieux et tira de sa bourse quelques pièces.

— Je vous remercie. Peut-être aurai-je encore besoin de vos services demain.

— Vous savez où me trouver!

Elle empocha l'argent en remerciant et sortit. Une toux déchirante s'éleva de la chambre. Hélène se précipita et, lorsque Volnay la rejoignit, la jeune femme était assise sur le lit, caressant la main du moine.

— Voilà exactement le genre de soins que mon père adore! commenta sans réfléchir le policier.

— Votre père?!

Hélène le contemplait, les yeux écarquillés de surprise. Volnay se rembrunit. Cela lui avait échappé.

— Je ne pensais pas Sartine aussi discret, murmura le moine.

— Il l'est, fulmina Volnay. C'est moi qui suis un âne bâté!

Un sourire illumina le visage d'Hélène.

— Votre père?! répéta-t-elle.

Elle rit.

— Cela explique bien des choses!

— Sartine est seul au courant de notre parenté, fit sèchement Volnay. Je compte sur vous pour conserver ce secret.

— Mais pourquoi? demanda Hélène.

— Cela vaut mieux pour nous deux, intervint le moine. Dans ma jeunesse, j'ai dit et fait bien des bêtises!

— Si c'était seulement dans ta jeunesse! soupira son fils.

À nouveau, le rire clair d'Hélène emplit la pièce, résonnant joyeusement entre les murs froids. La jeune femme se leva, rejeta sa splendide chevelure en arrière et les contempla d'un air amusé.

— Jamais le proverbe tel père tel fils ne s'est révélé aussi faux! commenta-t-elle avant de sortir de la pièce. En tout cas, vous vous êtes bien joué de moi, endormeurs de mulots! Bon, je vais vous chercher à manger.

Elle sortit. Le moine l'accompagna du regard jusqu'à la porte. Volnay agacé secoua la tête mais son père sourit.

— Cette jeune femme est admirable, j'aimerais l'avoir pour fille!

— Il est vrai que tu n'as cure de ton fils, marmonna Volnay.

Le moine le considéra avec effarement.

— Mais pourquoi donc dis-tu ça?

— T'es-tu jamais soucié de moi quand j'étais enfant?

Le moine étouffa une quinte de toux sèche.

— C'est faux!

— Tu me disais que tu allais venir jouer avec moi et moi je te croyais bêtement, attendant des heures que tu lèves la tête de tes maudits bouquins.

— Mais je venais! Et puis je t'ai appris à écrire et à lire…

— Tu ne m'as appris à lire que pour te débarrasser de moi en me mettant dans les mains un de tes foutus bouquins!

Son père prit une expression attristée.

— Tu me fais de la peine, mon fils!

Il s'interrompit car Hélène revenait, une miche dans les mains.

— Nous avons acheté cela sur le chemin du retour, expliqua-t-elle. C'est un bon pain blanc à la farine de froment. Il vous faut reprendre des forces.

— Il me reste des noix, dit faiblement le moine. J'en mangerais bien quelques-unes trempées dans du bon sel blanc.

— Je vous les apporte tout de suite!

Le moine cligna de l'œil en direction de son fils.

— Je découvre tous les plaisirs d'être malade avec une jeune et jolie femme pour s'occuper de moi…

— N'en abuse pas! Et maintenant raconte-moi en détail ton rêve…

— Mon rêve? Mais est-ce bien un rêve?

VII

LE RÊVE DU MOINE
ET AUTRES DIABLERIES

Ce fut d'abord comme une présence invisible mais insistante qui lui fit ouvrir les yeux. Il s'efforça de garder son calme pour distinguer l'imaginaire du réel. Au bord du lit, fragile et pâle, les mains sagement posées sur ses genoux, Sophia assise le contemplait d'un air grave. Il nota qu'elle avait un petit air perdu mais rien de sa beauté subtile n'en était occulté et ses cheveux blonds lui ceignaient la tête comme un casque doré. Ses yeux bleus avaient la pureté des glaciers. Si, à son âge, il avait été son camarade de jeux, le moine pensa qu'il en serait tombé follement amoureux.

— Vous êtes bien malade et vous avez de la fièvre, dit-elle.

Le moine ne bougea pas comme si la jeune fille était un oiseau qu'un seul mouvement, même furtif, pouvait faire s'envoler.

— Dormez-vous? demanda-t-elle.

— Non, je ne dors pas. Je ferme simplement les yeux pour me reposer de la vie.

— Vous devriez dormir, reprit-elle d'un ton très sérieux. Vous n'avez pas l'air bien du tout…

— Ce siècle est trop dur pour me permettre de dormir, répondit le moine.

Un gémissement se fit entendre derrière la porte.

— Qu'est-ce que c'est?

— Votre chien. Il nous a adoptés moi et votre fils.

Elle battit des mains, ravie.

— Oh que je suis contente. Je peux lui ouvrir?

— Il ne vaut mieux pas, il y a une dame dans l'autre pièce. Il ne faut pas qu'elle vous voie!

Il se redressa sur son séant. Sophia était habillée d'une robe de velours bleu pâle qui lui allait bien malgré la pâleur de sa mine. Un manteau couvrait ses épaules.

— N'avez-vous pas froid?

— J'ai trouvé ces vêtements dans votre armoire. Ils étaient bien pliés, j'espère que cela ne vous contrarie pas.

— Ils appartenaient à ma femme, personne ne les porte plus aujourd'hui.

— Oh, j'en suis désolée.

— C'est ainsi.

— Enfin, ils sont un peu grands pour moi mais ils me tiennent chauds, surtout le manteau. J'ai eu si froid dans votre cave.

— J'en suis navré, je vous croyais morte.

— Mais vous avez posé cette grosse couverture sur moi, remarqua-t-elle. C'était gentil. Je vous entendais, vous savez? Vous paraissiez tellement triste de me voir morte. Qui êtes-vous donc?

Le moine plissa les yeux pour réfléchir.

— Disons que je suis une sorte de philosophe en avance sur son temps et de savant un peu fou. J'aide mon fils qui est policier. Il est chargé d'enquêter sur votre mort.

— Oh! Alors, je suis morte? Vraiment morte?

Elle avait pris un air désemparé, presque apeurée.

— Que va-t-il m'arriver?

Le moine tenta de la rassurer.

— J'imagine que vous allez gagner la lumière. C'est notre but à tous.

Sans un mot, Sophia se leva et alla à la fenêtre.

— Le ciel est si gris, murmura-t-elle. Serai-je encore là demain? Passerai-je l'hiver et sentirai-je de nouveau les lilas et la rose?

— Vous serez toujours en moi, répondit gravement le moine. *Macte animo! Generose puer, sic itur ad astra.*

Et il traduisit pour être certain qu'elle comprenne:

— "Courage noble enfant! C'est ainsi qu'on s'élève vers les étoiles."

Elle se tourna vers lui, son sourire flottait dans l'air, teinté de mélancolie.

— Je n'ai rien eu le temps d'apprendre, murmura-t-elle, et j'avais tant de choses à donner...

Pensive, elle se mordilla les lèvres avant de revenir vers lui à pas lents, les mains dans le dos.

— Avez-vous d'autres enfants que votre fils?

Le moine se troubla.

— Non mais c'est la fierté de mes vieux jours même s'il l'ignore.

— L'important est qu'il sache que vous l'aimez!

À cet instant, le soleil sembla la frapper d'un de ses rayons anémiés. Le moine lui trouva une pâleur qui lui rappela la nuit au cimetière.

— Qui donc vous a tuée? demanda-t-il.

Sophia se troubla.

— Tant de gens, chuchota-t-elle. Si vous saviez... À cet instant on entendit un bruit de pas puis une voix inquiète :

— Monsieur? Tout va bien?

Sophia posa un doigt sur ses lèvres pour lui intimer de se taire.

— Il faut que je disparaisse. Rendormez-vous! Non, en fait, vous dormez déjà et moi je suis morte!

VIII

LE CURÉ DANSANT
ET AUTRES DIABLERIES

Le moine termina ainsi son récit, trônant comme un roi dans son fauteuil près de l'âtre. Il portait une magnifique robe de chambre d'indienne aux couleurs vives et aux motifs orientaux qui lui donnait l'apparence d'un monarque d'un pays exotique. Hélène et son fils l'écoutaient à ses pieds comme de fidèles sujets.

— Et c'est tout? demanda Volnay.

— Diable, fit le moine, oui. Je me suis rendormi mais sa présence était bien réelle, je te l'assure. Tiens, regarde, même le chien en a encore le poil tout hérissé!

Le policier jeta un coup d'œil à l'intelligent animal. Celui-ci haleta brièvement, la langue pendante avant de jeter un bref aboiement.

— Que veux-tu me dire? demanda le commissaire aux morts étranges avec un grand sérieux.

Les oreilles du chien bougèrent dans sa direction.

— Je vois, ma pie est plus explicite que toi…

Il contempla de nouveau le chien. Son poil était blanc mais parsemé par endroits de touffes rousses.

— Cet animal n'était-il pas d'une autre couleur lorsque je t'ai quitté?

— La bonne dame qui m'a gardé l'a jugé trop sale et l'a frotté. Cela l'a mis dans un état proche de la folie!

Volnay grogna quelque chose et s'approcha du feu, prenant plaisir à réchauffer ses doigts gourds au-dessus des flammes.

— Tout ceci est bien mystérieux mais je ne suis pas certain d'être le mieux placé pour interpréter tes rêves!

— Les rêves viennent à l'homme par des voies bien étranges, remarqua Hélène, et je ne pense pas que ceux-ci doivent quelque chose à la disposition des étoiles. Il me semble que c'est plutôt une voix extérieure, mais pourtant pas étrangère à nous-mêmes, qui nous parle sans que nous voulions l'entendre.

— Je tiens pour très intéressante votre approche des rêves, ma chère, fit le moine. Moi-même, il y a peu, j'ai rêvé d'abeilles. Vous savez ce que cela signifie ? Profit pour les pauvres, rien pour les riches ! Mais attention, si elle vous pique dans votre rêve, cela révèle un prochain échec !

Il étouffa une toux sèche.

— Enfin, pour en revenir à notre sujet, je ne suis pas certain que l'apparition de cette enfant puisse être qualifiée de rêve. J'ai plutôt l'impression que Sophia me parlait depuis l'au-delà.

Volnay et Hélène se jetèrent un coup d'œil entendu.

— Cette petite me hante, reprit le moine sans paraître remarquer leur inquiétude. J'ignore pourquoi mais elle m'a parlé, j'en suis certain !

— C'est sans doute parce qu'on l'enterre demain, hasarda Hélène, tout cela vous trouble.

Le commissaire aux morts étranges soupira puis tenta de changer de sujet de conversation.

— Il est bien de s'intéresser à la victime d'un meurtre mais il est plus important de porter son attention sur ses assassins. Tu es tellement fasciné par cette petite Sophia que tu ne nous as même pas interrogés sur notre enquête !

Il lui raconta alors l'épisode de la Vorace et le moine, les yeux brillants, poussa des exclamations.

— Eh bien, conclut-il, la justice a frappé. La prostituée a payé sa participation à cette sinistre messe noire, au tour de ce curé dansant !

Volnay se rembrunit. Il ne parvenait pas à s'habituer au comportement inhabituel de son père, d'habitude si posé, logique et réfléchi dans une enquête.

— Nous nous en occuperons plus tard, la nuit tombe tôt et je suis fatigué. J'aurais d'ailleurs peut-être besoin de quelques mouches pour m'occuper du curé dansant. Et puis demain matin, c'est l'enterrement de Sophia. Son père nous en a finalement laissé la charge. Il ne s'en occupe pas plus dans la mort que dans la vie! On viendra chercher le cercueil dans la cave demain vers dix heures.

Il jeta un coup d'œil à Hélène.

— Je vais rester veiller mon père. Si vous le souhaitez, vous pouvez passer la nuit chez moi puisque c'est à deux pas de là.

Il réalisa soudain qu'il ignorait où logeait la jeune femme, celle-ci ayant toujours couché chez son père jusqu'à présent!

— Je préfère rester là, un fauteuil me suffira. Allez prendre du repos, vous êtes fatigué, je le veillerai.

Volnay se figea.

— Ce n'est pas la peine, il n'est pas à l'article de la mort.

— Il est malade et encore faible, il faut que quelqu'un reste près de lui.

— Certes et je resterai.

Ils se défièrent du regard.

— C'est mon père, articula doucement Volnay avec une nuance dangereuse dans le ton. Je demeurerai près de lui.

Le moine intervint doucement.

— Non mon fils, rentre chez toi. Tu as besoin de repos car tu as beaucoup de sommeil en retard. Hélène restera près de moi. Et puis, ta pie a besoin de ta présence!

Le jeune homme se raidit.

— Père, je ne pense pas…

— Au contraire, tu penses trop. Rentre vite te reposer et dis bonsoir à la pie pour moi!

D'habitude impassible, le visage de Volnay sembla exprimer toute une série d'émotions contraires puis, comme sonné par un coup porté trop violemment, il se dirigea vers la porte en titubant légèrement. Avant de sortir, il se retourna comme s'il venait de se souvenir de quelque chose.

— Viens ici, toi! ordonna-t-il au chien.

Celui-ci le regarda puis se retourna pour fixer le moine. Il semblait perplexe. Finalement, il choisit de se coucher aux pieds du propriétaire des lieux. Volnay sortit en claquant sèchement la porte derrière lui.

— Pourquoi avez-vous renvoyé votre fils? demanda Hélène.

Le moine prit un air contrit.

— Quand je suis malade, je préfère la compagnie féminine.

— Vous avez déjà eu Sophia, lui fit-elle remarquer ingénument.

— Oui mais vous, vous êtes bien réelle!

Volnay était sorti furieux de chez son père. Il rentra chez lui, alluma du feu puis ôta la chaude couverture sur la cage de sa pie avec laquelle il engagea sa conversation habituelle.

— Ce vieil égoïste n'en a plus que pour cette Hélène! Ah, j'enrage! Elle est en train de lui mettre la main dessus. Et lui ne se rend compte de rien, trop heureux de pavaner devant elle qui l'écoute étaler sa science!

Cette fois, la pie resta silencieuse.

J'aurais dû tenter de l'embrasser, songea Volnay mais il n'en dit rien à la pie.

Il tourna encore en rond un moment avant de se décider à sortir. Ses pas rageurs le ramenèrent au cabaret où il avait fait la connaissance de l'Écureuil. La Vorace connaissant le curé dansant, peut-être en serait-il de même de la jeune prostituée. L'entrée du commissaire aux morts étranges suscita un regain de curiosité et les réflexions fusèrent. L'Écureuil se trouvait là, agrippée aux épaules d'un joueur chanceux. Le commissaire aux morts étranges commanda à boire et s'efforça d'avaler la piquette sans grimacer. Après un instant d'hésitation, la jeune prostituée le rejoignit et se tint près de lui, les mains dans le dos, se balançant d'un pied sur l'autre.

— On parle beaucoup dans le quartier, chuchota-t-elle. On raconte qu'un policier brutal a rendu visite à la Vorace et qu'elle en est morte.

— Elle s'est précipitée la tête la première dans l'escalier en voulant s'enfuir, se brisant la nuque contre les marches.

L'Écureuil déglutit péniblement.

— N'importe! Je ne veux pas avoir affaire à vous. Je tiens à ma réputation dans le quartier.

Volnay hocha la tête. Il savait que tout le monde connaissait tout le monde dans un quartier et qu'une réputation perdue pouvait dresser contre soi toute une communauté, rendant la vie impossible.

— Si l'on savait que c'est moi qui vous ai conduit à elle… reprit l'Écureuil en frissonnant.

— Que diriez-vous d'un louis d'or? demanda Volnay qui savait toujours trouver les bons arguments.

Une lueur d'envie voila le regard de l'Écureuil.

— Deux! fit-elle précipitamment. Congédiez-moi violemment comme si je vous agaçais puis sortez et rejoignez-moi à ma chambre dans une heure. La seconde rue à votre droite en remontant vers le maître bonnetier. Comptez trois portes et montez au dernier étage. J'ai dessiné un oiseau sur ma porte pour que les clients trouvent plus facilement.

— Un oiseau? Savez-vous que j'ai une pie chez moi? Elle sait parler…

— Vous m'en direz tant! Vous verrez que mon oiseau à moi est des plus ordinaires. Maintenant repoussez-moi, traitez-moi de gueuse et dites-moi de fiche le camp!

Le policier haussa les épaules, lui donna une bourrade et la repoussa brutalement en l'insultant, déclenchant des quolibets et des menaces à la table des joueurs. Volnay jeta ensuite son manteau sur ses épaules et se leva, toisant la tablée d'un air glacial, la main sur la garde de son épée. Cet avertissement muet éviterait qu'on ne le suive dans la rue.

Dehors, la nuit semblait porter tout le poids de la neige. Le vent jouait à projeter dans le ciel des gerbes d'écume blanche. Volnay cligna des yeux et, à travers les bourrasques, s'efforça de trouver l'adresse indiquée qu'il dépassa. Au coin de la rue, il s'embusqua pour vérifier que personne ne le suivait. Puis il revint prudemment sur ses pas, tous ses sens aux aguets. Il entra dans l'immeuble de l'Écureuil et gravit silencieusement les marches jusqu'à la porte de la jeune fille, reconnaissant le dessin grossier annoncé de l'oiseau.

Il s'emmitoufla dans son manteau et s'assit sur la dernière marche de l'escalier, les mains serrées autour de son corps pour se réchauffer, essayant d'oublier les effluves nauséabonds qui emplissaient les lieux. Au bout d'une petite heure qui lui parut interminable, un pas léger lui fit dresser l'oreille. Il se pencha avec précaution au-dessus de la balustrade et aperçut dans la pénombre une ombre menue. Bientôt se précisa la silhouette de l'Écureuil. Elle montait lentement, économisant son souffle en marquant une pause à chaque étage. Personne ne la suivait. Lorsqu'elle fut devant lui, les yeux brillants, Volnay craqua une allumette.

— Vous voilà…

La neige avait laissé son empreinte blanche dans ses cheveux. Volnay se retint de les épousseter même si l'envie lui en prit. L'Écureuil fourragea dans sa poche et en sortit une grosse clé qu'elle introduisit dans la serrure.

— Je vais faire de la lumière, dit-elle en passant devant lui.

Bientôt, la maigre lueur d'une chandelle se refléta contre le mur, révélant un réduit si étroit que Volnay eut la sensation qu'en écartant les deux bras il toucherait les murs de chaque côté. L'unique fenêtre était garnie de papier huilé et un froid atroce régnait dans la pièce. Hormis une paillasse recouverte de deux couvertures de laine, seuls un coffre pour les affaires, une petite table et une chaise meublaient l'appartement. Le commissaire aux morts étranges entra. En souriant, la jeune fille referma à clé derrière lui.

— Est-ce bien utile? demanda Volnay étonné. Je ne compte pas rester.

— Monseigneur sera plus rassuré qu'on ne puisse pénétrer ici, remarqua-t-elle finement.

Le policier hocha la tête pour marquer son approbation mais conserva ses distances lorsque la jeune fille s'assit sur son grabat. Elle était si maigre qu'elle semblait avoir les flancs cousus. Ses jupons relevés laissaient entrevoir une paire de bottines noires et des bas de laine gris rapiécés. Elle tendit la main.

— Mes deux louis, s'il vous plaît.

Volnay lui en glissa un dans la paume et tira la chaise à lui.

— Vous aurez l'autre si vous me renseignez bien.

— Ce n'était pas convenu ainsi, se plaignit-elle.

— C'est ainsi. Je cherche un curé, sans doute défroqué. On le surnomme le curé dansant. Avez-vous entendu parler de lui?

Elle rit.

— C'était un bon ami de la Vorace mais il n'est pas plus curé que vous et moi. Il était bedeau mais on l'a chassé car il buvait trop, surtout le vin de messe! C'est un mauvais homme. Il rôde dans le quartier et l'on raconte qu'il travaille avec les voleurs de cadavres.

— A-t-il des amis?

L'Écureuil eut un bref haussement d'épaules.

— Personne ne peut le supporter. Il vous regarde avec le mauvais œil et vous lance des sorts! Ici, on craint cela. Savez-vous que le démon est déjà passé par la taverne d'où nous venons il y a dix ans de cela?

— Vraiment? fit Volnay sceptique mais amusé.

— Oui, on raconte qu'un soir de grand orage un homme vêtu de noir entra dans la taverne et offrit à boire à tous les clients jusque tard dans la nuit. Sa bourse était bien pleine. Le tavernier alla dormir en cachant celle-ci sous son oreiller. Au matin, lorsqu'il l'ouvrit, elle ne contenait plus que du charbon et du fumier!

— Et il en déduisit que c'était le diable qui l'avait payé!

Volnay songea qu'on avait surtout habilement détroussé le tavernier mais il n'en dit rien.

— Revenons à notre curé dansant, savez-vous où il demeure?

Elle secoua la tête.

— Je n'en ai aucune idée.

— Alors, vous n'aurez pas ce second louis.

— Attendez!

Elle fronça comiquement les sourcils et tordit sa jolie bouche en une moue désabusée.

— Comme vous êtes dur avec moi! Ne vous êtes-vous jamais demandé pourquoi on le nomme le *curé dansant*?

Vexé, Volnay dut reconnaître que non.

— Eh bien, triompha l'Écureuil, parce qu'il danse! Je connais un cabaret où l'on joue de la musique pour danser. Chaque fois que j'y suis allée, je l'ai aperçu. Je peux vous y conduire. Nous y serons une heure avant minuit.

Elle tendit la main.

— Ma pièce!

— Je vous la donnerai lorsque nous verrons notre homme. Vous avez fort bien pu inventer cette histoire de cabaret !

Elle fit semblant de bouder.

— Méchant policier !

Mais Volnay n'était pas d'humeur à plaisanter.

— Allons-y, la pressa-t-il en se levant.

L'Écureuil ne bougea pas. Sa main froissait et défroissait nerveusement les plis de son jupon. Un instant, le bas qui couvrait sa cheville luit faiblement à la clarté de la chandelle.

— D'accord ! fit-elle précipitamment en sautant sur ses pieds.

Et elle trébucha pour tomber dans les bras de Volnay. Le jeune homme la retint instinctivement, les bras autour de sa taille. Elle en profita pour plaquer ses lèvres sur les siennes. Volnay la repoussa doucement, sa bouche encore fraîche du baiser déposé. Son cœur était ailleurs, à soupirer après Chiara qui s'en était allée après le lui avoir brisé.

— Je ne suis pas assez bien pour vous, c'est cela ? regretta l'Écureuil.

— Cela n'a rien à voir, la rassura-t-il.

Et cela était vrai tant Volnay n'éprouvait aucune fierté particulière à tenir son rang et ne portait en lui que des idées d'égalité et de fraternité.

— Mettez votre manteau, reprit-il, nous sortons.

La jeune fille recula d'un pas et, levant la main, effleura du bout des doigts la fine cicatrice qui courait du coin de son œil droit à sa tempe.

— On a été bien méchant avec vous, j'espère que celui qui vous a fait cela subira le feu de la justice divine…

Le commissaire aux morts étranges la considéra soudain avec attention.

— Vous parlez bien pour une fille des rues, remarqua-t-il. Vous avez dû recevoir de l'éducation. D'où venez-vous donc ?

Charmée que le policier s'intéresse enfin à elle, la jeune prostituée se montra bavarde.

— Mon grand-père était fabricant de bas et mon père maître tailleur. Il épousa ma mère qui était étalante au marché Saint-Martin. Mes parents étaient très sévères avec moi, un peu moins avec mes deux frères. Ils nous firent apprendre à lire et à écrire, à compter et quelques petites autres choses qui peuvent servir.

Elle regarda autour d'elle, hésita puis se rassit sur son grabat.

— Pour mon malheur, lorsque j'eus quatorze ans, je rencontrai un beau garçon aux manières très honnêtes et qui me paraissait sincère. Il était garçon parfumeur et me fit la cour avec suffisamment de sentiment et de conviction pour toucher mon cœur. Il vint à bout de toutes mes réticences jusqu'à jouir de moi et prendre mon pucelage. Il s'en vanta ensuite dans le quartier, ce qui fut vite rapporté à mes parents.

Le policier hocha la tête. Dans un quartier tout se savait et la rumeur allait parfois aussi vite qu'un cheval au galop, souillant et dévastant les réputations.

— Je fus jetée à la rue sans procès. Mon amoureux m'installa avec lui dans sa mansarde mais se lassa de moi et prit l'habitude de me partager avec un de ses camarades. Je n'osais dire non, de peur d'être jetée dehors, seule et sans travail, et de finir en prison. Un soir, ce garçon amena deux amis à lui avec un pâté et un tonnelet de vin. On but, on mangea puis on abusa de moi. On me frappa tellement fort que les voisins vinrent s'en plaindre et menacer d'appeler le sergent du guet. Cette fois, on me jeta dehors et je finis la nuit sur le parvis d'une église. À partir de là, je me jurai qu'on ne me prendrait plus mon corps sans m'en payer le prix.

Elle baissa la tête.

— Même s'il n'est pas très élevé…

Un frisson la saisit. L'Écureuil frotta ses mains l'une contre l'autre pour se réchauffer. Volnay ôta son manteau pour lui couvrir les épaules et s'assit à côté d'elle.

— Vous valez plus que tout l'or du monde, dit-il gentiment.

Elle ouvrit grande la bouche et oublia de la refermer, surprise de tant d'attention désintéressée à son égard. Pour sa part, le commissaire aux morts étranges savait qu'en ville une jeune fille sans famille ni protection courait facilement le risque de tomber dans la prostitution. Les plus chanceuses parvenaient à se faire embaucher dans l'industrie où les ouvrières se trouvaient bien payées, même si elles occupaient les plus bas emplois, mais pour cela des connaissances étaient nécessaires.

Les autres, si elles ne vendaient pas leur corps, se retrouvaient dans les petits métiers de rue, à vendre des vêtements usagés sur les marchés, des bottes d'épingles sur les trottoirs ou à colporter du charbon ou du bois. D'autres enfin arrivaient parfois à coudre et repriser lorsqu'elles trouvaient un compagnon qui connaissait suffisamment de monde pour obtenir de l'ouvrage.

— Allons, racontez-moi la suite, l'encouragea Volnay.

— Au petit matin, reprit l'Écureuil enhardie en se serrant contre lui, j'allai mendier un quignon de pain dans une boulangerie. Le boulanger me proposa de me donner chaque jour une miche de pain contre mes faveurs. Dans la nuit, il quittait quelques instants son fourneau pour me promener dans les rues et me prendre rapidement sous un porche ou dans une cour dès qu'il en avait l'occasion. Je fis cela avec plusieurs commerçants du quartier, le temps d'avoir de quoi louer une petite chambre.

Du regard, elle parcourut les tristes lieux.

— Ici, c'est tout petit. Je ne possède presque rien et mon logement sent mauvais mais j'ai un toit pour dormir chaque nuit et j'arrive à manger deux fois par jour. C'est bien mieux que rien !

Elle ouvrit sa paume et contempla avec ravissement le louis d'or qui scintillait faiblement.

— C'est la première fois que j'ai quelques économies. Je vais aller m'acheter des vêtements plus chauds, une bonne couverture et payer quelques mois de loyer d'avance. Peut-être pourrai-je même faire mettre une vraie fenêtre !

Ému malgré lui, Volnay la questionna.

— Quel âge avez-vous ?

— Seize ans. Et vous ?

Ses yeux noisette le fixaient avec curiosité.

— Presque dix de plus !

— Oh ! Vous faites plus vieux que cela !

Un mince sourire éclaira le visage pâle du commissaire aux morts étranges. Embarrassée, elle rougit.

— Ce n'est pas ce que je voulais dire. Vous ne faites pas vieux, c'est juste que vous êtes un peu… sérieux !

Elle s'arrêta stupéfaite. Volnay riait aux éclats, surpris et charmé par tant de fraîcheur. Elle jugea qu'il paraissait bien plus jeune lorsqu'il se laissait ainsi aller et se prit à espérer toucher son cœur car il lui plaisait bien.

Le commissaire aux morts étranges baissa la tête et sembla s'absorber dans la contemplation des bottines de l'Écureuil. La distance qu'il maintenait par rapport aux autres ne le privait ni d'émotions, ni de sentiments. Ému par l'histoire de la jeune fille, il n'en voulait toutefois rien laisser paraître.

— Venez, petit Écureuil, dit-il d'un ton très doux. Il faut nous en aller. Couvrez-vous bien ! Je ne veux pas que vous preniez froid.

Ils sortirent sous la voûte étoilée, silhouettes solitaires dans la nuit glaciale, marchant prudemment côte à côte à travers les rues enneigées. La rue Bordelles se prolongeait au-delà de l'enceinte de Philippe Auguste et des eaux putrides de la Bièvre par la rue Mouffetard traversant le bourg Saint-Médard. L'odeur des tanneurs, écorcheurs et tripiers qui la bordait souleva le cœur de Volnay mais ne sembla pas incommoder sa compagne.

La foule s'amassait dans une sorte de grange auberge au fond de laquelle se dressait une estrade. Des violonistes échevelés y tiraient l'archet, arrachant de leur instrument un son triomphant. Sous les lampions dansait, sautait et hurlait une foule bigarrée. Les danseurs portaient de mauvais habits, souvent rapiécés. Leurs chaussures ou sabots frappaient le sol de terre battue, provoquant un nuage de poussière, dans un rythme sourd qui reproduisait celui d'un cœur battant follement.

— Cela vous prend dès que l'on entre, n'est-ce pas ? fit l'Écureuil.

— Quoi donc ?

— L'envie de danser et de se serrer l'un contre l'autre !

Et elle accompagna cette déclaration d'un regard brûlant. Volnay haussa les épaules. Il ne suffisait pas d'une œillade pour enflammer le cœur du commissaire aux morts étranges.

— Faisons ensemble le tour de la salle pour tenter d'apercevoir notre homme.

— Sans danser ?

— Oui, sans danser.

— Alors, tenez-moi par la main comme si nous étions ensemble et souriez. Vous ressemblez trop à un policier!

Il lui prit donc la main, elle était toute menue dans la sienne. On jouait maintenant une gavotte à deux temps, assez enlevée, et les danseurs formaient une ligne pour suivre le mouvement vif et gai. Il fut alors plus aisé de dévisager les hommes présents et l'Écureuil secoua la tête.

— Il n'est pas là.

— Vous êtes sûre? Regardez encore, s'il vous plaît. Prenez votre temps.

— Il n'est pas là, vous dis-je.

— Et parmi ceux-là?

Il désigna du menton des hommes qui ne dansaient pas. Les yeux assombris de désir, ils fixaient durement les plus mignonnes des filles qui se déhanchaient.

— Non, confirma-t-elle. Et je vous l'ai dit, le curé dansant danse! Nous pouvons peut-être l'attendre en mangeant quelque chose?

Elle désignait dans un coin de la salle une table qui venait de se libérer. Volnay considéra un instant ses flancs maigres et approuva. Pour dix sols chacun, ils eurent droit à une soupe, un bouilli, un petit morceau de fromage et un demi-verre d'un vin aigre à déchausser les dents. L'Écureuil mangea gaiement et avec appétit. Elle semblait satisfaite de sa soirée et glissait de temps à autre un regard langoureux en direction du commissaire aux morts étranges, fort beau garçon au demeurant. Mais lorsqu'une femme aux sourcils peints frôlait son compagnon, elle fronçait les sourcils en guise d'avertissement, indiquant clairement qu'il était sa propriété.

Volnay se détendit et raconta une anecdote qui courait en ville. Un médecin bien connu se pavanait à l'Opéra avant une représentation, accompagné de deux danseuses. Par jeu, l'une d'elles lui ôta sa perruque et l'autre s'exclama :

— Oh, qu'as-tu fait? Tu viens de lui ôter sa réputation!

Un rire irrépressible gagna l'Écureuil et Volnay charmé l'accompagna jusqu'à ce que la main de la jeune fille couvre la sienne. Il tressaillit et la retira avant de jeter un coup d'œil autour de lui.

— Il n'est toujours pas là ?

Dépitée, l'Écureuil secoua la tête.

— Attendons-nous encore ?

— Il se fait tard.

— Vous ne voulez toujours pas danser ?

— Non.

— Je suis sûre que vous n'avez jamais essayé !

Sans répondre, il donna le signal du départ en se levant et en lui tendant la main. Debout face à face, ils se considérèrent en silence. L'Écureuil trouvait difficile de se plonger dans le regard sans fond du commissaire aux morts étranges. Et puis, celui-ci se détourna et leur fraya avec assurance un chemin dans la foule.

En sortant, ils rencontrèrent un groupe masqué qui semblait pris de boisson. Des quolibets fusèrent à l'intention de la jeune fille. D'une main, Volnay saisit le bras de l'Écureuil et de l'autre caressa la poignée de son épée, geste qui ne passa pas inaperçu et refroidit l'ardeur des moqueurs.

— Les rues ne sont pas sûres. Je vais vous raccompagner chez vous.

Elle le considéra songeusement avant de répondre d'un ton neutre :

— Si vous le désirez.

Ils marchèrent l'un contre l'autre dans la rue pour se protéger du froid et de la bise sifflante. Arrivés en bas de l'immeuble de l'Écureuil, Volnay s'arrêta.

— Vous ne montez pas ? demanda la jeune fille.

— Non.

Elle se mordit les lèvres.

— Je ne vous plais pas ?

— Ce n'est pas cela.

— C'est parce que je suis une prostituée alors ?

— À la cour de Versailles, on se prostitue beaucoup plus que dans les rues de Paris !

Il ôta son gant et caressa du bout des doigts la joue rosie par le froid de la jeune fille qui frémit.

— Vous valez beaucoup mieux que vous ne le pensez.

— Alors pourquoi ne pas monter quelques instants avec moi, je prendrai soin de vous, fit-elle d'un ton plein d'espoir.

— Le frottement de deux épidermes l'un contre l'autre ne résout pas tout! Que reste-t-il après cela?

— Il n'y a pas que les corps, fit-elle d'un ton plein d'espoir. Il y a aussi l'amour…

Volnay recula d'un pas, désabusé.

— L'amour est un jeu de dupes, pourquoi y jouerions-nous?

Il se saisit de sa main et y déposa le second louis d'or. Puis, mû par une étrange impulsion, il se recula pour baiser cette main en effleurant le bout des doigts de ses lèvres comme il aurait fait avec une marquise.

— Mais nous n'avons pas trouvé le curé dansant, s'étonna-t-elle en rougissant.

— Vous n'y êtes pour rien.

— Vous reverrai-je? demanda-t-elle d'une voix soudain fluette.

— Oui. Je reviendrai chez vous demain soir, à neuf heures. Nous retenterons notre chance. D'ici là, renseignez-vous mais discrètement. N'éveillez pas l'attention. Si nous trouvons notre curé dansant, vous aurez droit à deux autres louis d'or.

— Oh, s'exclama-t-elle. Je serai riche!

Elle se haussa sur la pointe des pieds et, avant qu'il ne puisse réagir, déposa sur ses lèvres un baiser glacé.

— À demain alors! fit-elle.

Il la contempla s'éloigner et, alors même que la porte de l'immeuble s'était refermée derrière elle, resta un long moment immobile, songeur sous la neige qui tombait et recouvrait toute chose.

IX

SARTINE ET AUTRES DIABLERIES

Au petit matin, Volnay prit le chemin du Châtelet. Il devait signaler les assassins des quais et en profiterait pour visiter Sartine. Le lieutenant général de police était un personnage considérable dans le royaume et il n'était pas de bonne politique de le négliger.

Malgré le froid dans la pièce, Sartine se trouvait en gilet sans manches. Pour une fois, il reçut cordialement son collaborateur et sembla satisfait des premières explications de son commissaire aux morts étranges.

— Alors, vous avez pu identifier la victime. Sophia, vous dites?

À sa grande surprise, Volnay le vit aller à son bureau et se saisir du croquis de la jeune victime qu'il lui avait laissé. Ainsi Sartine le gardait à portée de main?

— Voici donc son nom, murmura le lieutenant général de police en contemplant songeusement le portrait. Sophia...

— Ce n'est pas tout, reprit le commissaire aux morts étranges en cachant son étonnement devant l'attitude inhabituelle de Sartine. J'ai pu retrouver la prostituée qui donnait l'eucharistie au cours de cette messe noire.

Et il raconta toute l'histoire.

— Comment avez-vous fait pour laisser échapper cette femme? tempêta Sartine à la fin du récit. La prochaine fois, prenez avec vous des archers du guet! Cette histoire pourrait déjà être terminée sans votre maladresse!

Le commissaire aux morts étranges encaissa sans broncher ces injustes reproches et parla du second suspect, sans toutefois mentionner la piste de l'Écureuil.

— *Le curé dansant ?* répéta Sartine. Quel drôle de surnom ! Il dansera encore mieux au bout d'une corde ! Je vais mettre mes agents sur ses talons. De votre côté, ne vous en mêlez pas et concentrez tous vos efforts à rechercher l'identité des trois autres participants. Deux hommes et une femme, c'est cela ?

Le commissaire aux morts étranges acquiesça. Sartine s'assit sur son bureau, une jambe balançant dans le vide et le fixant d'un air pensif.

— Dites-moi, cet astrologue traitait-il bien sa fille ?

Volnay haussa un sourcil interrogateur.

— Était-il un bon père ? La battait-il ? insista le lieutenant général de police.

— Je ne pense pas. Il ne s'en occupait pas tout simplement. Comme bien des gens de nos jours.

— Ah oui, je comprends.

Sartine hésita.

— Néanmoins, possédait-elle une chambre à elle, prenait-elle trois repas par jour ?

— Oui, elle avait un toit et de quoi manger, répondit Volnay de plus en plus étonné par l'insistance de son supérieur et l'étrangeté de ses questions.

Le lieutenant général de police lui tourna le dos et alla se planter devant la fenêtre, les mains dans le dos. Volnay l'observa à la dérobée, remarquant que le teint vieil ivoire de Sartine avait fait place à une pâleur extrême. D'habitude vif, une espèce de langueur semblait aujourd'hui accompagner tous ses mouvements.

— J'ai rêvé d'elle.

— Pardon ? fit Volnay abasourdi.

— Cette nuit, j'ai rêvé de Sophia, dit Sartine d'une voix basse. Elle venait me parler.

Il se retourna vers Volnay, l'air gêné, attitude également peu fréquente chez lui.

— Ce n'est qu'un rêve me direz-vous mais elle semblait si réelle. Comment était-elle habillée dans le cimetière ?

— Vous savez bien que nous l'avons retrouvée nue.

Sartine parut embarrassé.

— Certes, certes! C'était curieux, dans mon rêve, elle portait des vêtements qui convenaient plus à une femme qu'à une enfant de son âge.

— Que vous a-t-elle dit? demanda le commissaire aux morts étranges en entrant dans son jeu.

— Elle m'a raconté qu'elle était à la recherche de son chien.

Malgré la fraîcheur de la température dans la pièce, Volnay sentit une sueur glaciale lui couler dans le dos. Sartine ne manqua pas de remarquer qu'il se raidissait.

— Ah, je vois que cette histoire de chien éveille quelque chose en vous! Dites-moi tout! Ne me cachez rien!

Le commissaire aux morts étranges lui rappela alors les plaintes et gémissements du chien devant le cimetière le soir du meurtre.

— Oui, je me souviens, fit Sartine. Vous m'aviez très bien restitué l'ambiance de cette nuit-là.

Et pour cause! Le policier savait que son supérieur allait raconter chaque semaine au roi tout ce qui se passait et qu'il aimait mettre un peu de piquant dans ses récits pour mieux capter l'attention de Louis XV.

— Cet intelligent animal m'a ensuite suivi.

— Quoi?!

Volnay développa toute l'histoire ainsi que les découvertes d'Hélène chez le commissaire de quartier. Sartine parcourait la pièce de long en large, étrangement agité, ne s'arrêtant que pour prendre une prise qu'il s'envoya directement dans les narines avant d'éternuer.

— On me cache des choses!

— Ce n'était qu'un chien! Ce n'est pas lui qui nous conduira aux assassins!

— N'importe!

Sartine froissa nerveusement son mouchoir de dentelle.

— Je veux tout savoir sur cette affaire, vous m'entendez? Tout!

Il réprima un frémissement et s'approcha du feu qui brûlait joyeusement dans la cheminée. Le commissaire aux morts étranges fit de même, tendant avec lui les mains vers les flammes pour les réchauffer. Ainsi côte à côte, Sartine prit le ton de la confidence.

— Ce qui est très curieux, c'est que j'ignorais cette histoire de chien. Je n'ai pas donc pu l'inventer.

— L'esprit nous joue souvent des tours, fit Volnay. Mon père a ses théories là-dessus et affirme qu'une certaine voix, étrangère et familière à la fois, tente de nous parler dans notre sommeil.

— Votre père est un fou! Je ne parle pas de cela, moi!

Il hésita et jeta un coup d'œil derrière son épaule comme s'il avait peur d'être espionné et chuchota d'une voix basse :

— On dit que l'âme des défunts erre quarante jours…

Un instant, la raison de Volnay vacilla, saisie d'une peur subite. Après son père, Sartine…

— Je n'y crois pas, murmura-t-il.

Le lieutenant général de police lui jeta un regard acerbe.

— Vous et votre père ne croyez en rien d'autre que ce que vous pouvez prouver!

Le commissaire aux morts étranges hocha sèchement la tête.

— C'est juste!

Sartine s'abîma dans la contemplation des flammes claires qui jaillissaient de l'âtre.

— C'est votre force, Volnay, mais aussi votre faiblesse. Votre esprit manque de spiritualité. Vous n'êtes pas ouvert comme moi à l'invisible et à l'inattendu!

Le commissaire aux morts étranges se mordilla pensivement les lèvres. La conversation avec son supérieur prenait une tournure surprenante. Elle aurait même pu être dangereuse avec quelqu'un d'autre que lui mais Volnay savait pertinemment que Sartine n'entretenait plus aucun doute sur son impiété et celle de son père. Le lieutenant général de police se tourna brusquement vers lui, l'air effrayé.

— Volnay, et si l'âme de Sophia était revenue pour se venger de ses meurtriers?

X

L'ENTERREMENT ET AUTRES DIABLERIES

La lumière pâle du jour perçait à travers les volets lorsque le moine ouvrit les yeux. Ses médications semblaient lui avoir vidé la poitrine des humeurs mauvaises qui l'habitaient. Le lait chaud et le miel enveloppaient encore son palais d'une gangue douceâtre. Pour apaiser sa soif, il prit un verre de la tisane de sa composition qui ne quittait plus son chevet. Ensuite, il alluma la chandelle et, ne percevant aucun bruit dans la maison, quitta son lit tiède pour alimenter son poêle et rapporter avec lui le livre de Sophia sous les couvertures.

Avec impatience, il tourna les pages. La jeune enfant consignait ses rêves lorsqu'elle s'en rappelait au matin. Connaissant les saintes Écritures, le moine savait qu'elles enseignent que *Dieu se sert des rêves afin que l'homme puisse voir à travers les ténèbres*. Ce n'était pas le cas de Sophia. Les récits de sa nourrice et les histoires dont elle s'était nourrie avaient gravé dans son imaginaire l'ombre effrayante d'ogres qui s'en prenaient aux enfants pour les dévorer ou pire encore. La tombée de la nuit l'effrayait car, selon les récits à la veillée, elle annonçait la sortie des spectres de leurs tombeaux et leur errance jusqu'au chant du coq à l'aube. Le moine fronça les sourcils, attentif à déceler dans ces pages le réel de l'imaginaire afin d'y découvrir des faits qui auraient secrètement imprégné son esprit.

La tour dans laquelle vivait en reclus son père, l'astrologue, lui inspirait les plus vives terreurs. Sans trop savoir pourquoi, Sophia la considérait comme un endroit dangereux, fermé sur d'horribles vérités. Le moine essaya de débrouiller les temps de rêve des temps de réalité. Seule subsistait une pénible impression de peur de l'inconnu et le désagréable sentiment que la tour de son père recélait un danger innommable. Il lui était d'ailleurs formellement interdit d'y pénétrer.

Le passage suivant était plus pénible. Âgée de onze ans, Sophia accompagna son père à la boutique d'un graveur. Pendant que les deux hommes discutaient entre eux sans lui prêter la moindre attention, l'enfant s'aventura jusqu'à l'atelier où travaillait un jeune apprenti. Celui-ci leva les yeux sur elle avant de l'inviter à voir de plus près son ouvrage. Tandis qu'elle admirait la gravure, l'apprenti s'empara de sa main pour la porter jusqu'à son entrecuisse. Sous les doigts de Sophia, quelque chose d'extrêmement dur se contracta et se rétracta comme un monstrueux serpent. Troublée et mal à l'aise, Sophia retira vivement sa main. Malgré son ignorance de la vie, elle sentait confusément que le jeune garçon cherchait à abuser d'elle.

— Oh, ce doit être très mal! chuchota-t-elle.

L'autre eut un rire dur.

— Votre père fait bien de même avec votre mère, se moqua-t-il.

À la pensée de sa pauvre maman, les larmes vinrent aux yeux de Sophia et elle s'enfuit. Plus tard, elle consigna son émoi dans son journal. Cette incursion inattendue dans le monde des adultes n'éveilla en elle aucun désir, simplement une certaine révulsion et une aversion profonde pour les hommes qui abusaient de son jeune âge pour des choses malhonnêtes.

Le moine reposa le livre pour essuyer ses yeux. Dans la promiscuité des immeubles, des boutiques et des ateliers, sans surveillance des parents qui laissaient errer leurs enfants pendant qu'ils travaillaient, ce genre de choses était monnaie courante. Il plissa les narines avec dégoût. Par moments, la nature humaine le révulsait si fortement qu'il en était prêt à oublier sa fraternité pour elle.

Il tourna une page. Heureusement, la très sérieuse Sophia laissait parfois place à la fantaisie, ainsi lorsqu'elle racontait avoir versé une bouteille d'encre dans le bénitier de l'église!

Le moine rit puis subitement la réalité le glaça. C'était ce matin qu'on enterrait la jeune fille. Un coup discret se fit entendre contre la porte qui s'entrebâilla lorsqu'il y répondit. Les beaux yeux mouchetés d'or d'Hélène brillèrent dans la demi-pénombre.

— Vous êtes réveillé ? Je vous ai apporté du pain frais et du lait. Je n'aurai pas le temps de vous le chauffer.

Il laissa son regard traîner nonchalamment sur elle.

— Où allez-vous donc, ma chère ?

Elle hésita.

— À l'enterrement de Sophia.

Le moine rejeta brusquement ses couvertures.

— Je vous accompagne !

La jeune femme le gourmanda.

— Est-ce bien raisonnable ?

Le moine ne prit même pas la peine de répondre et commença à se déshabiller. Hélène émit un petit cri de désapprobation et referma vivement la porte. Une fois chaudement vêtu, le moine tourna en rond dans la maison.

— Je ne retrouve plus ma clé ! Pourtant, je la laisse toujours dans la serrure, c'est le meilleur moyen de ne pas la perdre. Ah, les clés ! Les clés !

Il toucha son trousseau à sa ceinture.

— N'importe, j'en ai une autre. Je chercherai plus tard !

Dehors, ses pieds mordirent dans une couche de neige fraîche. Un vent cinglant le frappa au visage, lui tirant les larmes des yeux. Il s'immobilisa, les narines frémissantes.

— Quel est le jean-foutre qui vient pisser devant ma porte ?

Hélène le rejoignit et passa sur ses épaules un chaud manteau de laine.

— Ce n'est pas moi, je vous l'assure !

Le moine étouffa une toux sèche.

— Diable ! C'est que je ne vous accusais pas mais regardez vous-même cette tache dans la neige.

— Le chien ?

— Non, je suis sorti en même temps que lui et il a directement filé plus loin pour gambader sans même daigner lever la patte ! Bah, n'en parlons plus ! Où sont donc les employés pour emporter le cercueil ? Ah, les voici ! Je crois que je vais aller boire ma potion pour me protéger du froid.

Elle le regarda avec malice.

— Celle à base d'eau-de-vie ?

L'enterrement avait lieu en fin de matinée dans le petit cimetière Saint-Sulpice. Le cercueil était parti de la demeure du moine pour marquer une première étape à la demeure de l'astronome afin qu'il se recueille une dernière fois dans l'intimité devant la dépouille de sa fille. Pour sa part, le commissaire aux morts étranges était venu un peu à l'avance pour mieux observer les gens assistant à l'enterrement et noter leur ordre d'arrivée. On en apprenait parfois plus devant un cercueil que dans une conversation.

Un attroupement se pressait devant la grille et Volnay accéléra le pas pour en connaître la cause. Lorsqu'il en vit la raison, un grand froid l'envahit et les paroles de Sartine à propos de Sophia revinrent à sa mémoire. Sur un panneau était inscrite cette simple phrase : *Interdit à Dieu d'entrer dans ce lieu.*

Volnay sentit une fois de plus sa raison attaquée par l'irrationnel. Les propos de Sartine l'avaient surpris et ébranlé. Et voici qu'une main inconnue venait d'inscrire cet avertissement qui résonnait comme une provocation.

Interdit à Dieu d'entrer dans ce lieu... Les satanistes étant gens discrets, aucun d'eux ne s'amuserait à une telle provocation. Cette interdiction planait plutôt comme une menace insensée et désespérée. Le commissaire aux morts étranges contempla avec attention les visages des badauds attroupés. Leurs expressions étaient outrées et indignées. Personne parmi eux ne souriait. On ne plaisantait pas avec la mort.

Volnay se décida rapidement, fendit la foule et, sortant sa dague, décrocha le panneau. Ceci fait, il se tourna et, sans rien dire, fixa de ses yeux bleu pâle et gris les gens autour de lui. Cela sentait le policier. Les gens baissèrent la tête et s'éparpillèrent en grommelant.

À ce moment-là, une procession approcha et l'on se signa avec respect devant elle. M. Marly et sa servante marchaient en avant, suivis d'une vieille parente et de quelques voisins. Malgré sa faiblesse, le moine avait tenu à venir et Hélène lui tenait le bras. Volnay vit la jeune femme saluer un grand homme au maintien compassé et devina qu'il s'agissait du commissaire de quartier. Ainsi, lui aussi avait-il tenu à rendre hommage à la petite Sophia. Le commissaire aux morts étranges connaissait de réputation cet homme, plus enclin à la conciliation qu'à la répression. Avec intérêt, il nota également la présence de la servante de l'auberge.

Le commissaire aux morts étranges examina tous les participants, les uns après les autres, marquant leurs traits dans sa mémoire. Son attention fut tout à coup attirée par l'attitude étrange d'un homme qui priait devant une tombe à cinquante pas de là. Le commissaire aux morts étranges remarqua qu'en réalité celui-ci semblait suivre la cérémonie du coin de l'œil. L'homme était grand, les épaules larges et un air brutal se lisait sur ses traits marqués par la petite vérole. Une longue épée pendait à ses côtés. Lorsque le prêtre bénit le cercueil, il se signa discrètement.

Un sourire froid illumina le commissaire aux morts étrange. Cela s'était déroulé rapidement mais pas assez pour échapper à l'attention acérée du policier. Le signe de croix catholique allait d'abord vers le ciel puis vers la terre avant de toucher l'épaule gauche puis la droite, celle de *Celui qui bénit du haut de sa croix*. L'homme près de la tombe s'était signé par l'horizontale avant de monter au ciel et de terminer par une plongée en direction de l'enfer. Le signe de croix inversé des satanistes...

Volnay se déplaça lentement dans une allée adjacente, s'appliquant à garder de vue l'homme au visage vérolé. Lorsque celui-ci se détourna afin de quitter le cimetière, le policier le suivit discrètement avant de gagner la rue. Il conserva une distance prudente avec son suspect, jouant avec les piliers des maisons pour esquiver un éventuel regard en arrière.

Au détour d'une rue, il se précipita pour ne pas perdre son homme mais glissa malencontreusement sur une plaque de verglas. Jurant, il se releva prestement et se précipita. La réverbération du soleil sur la neige l'éblouit. Il plissa les yeux et fit quelques pas hésitants avant de se rendre à l'évidence : le sataniste avait disparu !

Le soleil frappait les lieux de rayons gris et ternes.

— *Sit tibi terra levis*, murmura le moine en jetant une poignée de terre dans la tombe. "Que la terre te soit légère."

Avec Hélène, il quitta le cimetière parmi les derniers. Plantée entre deux tombes, la servante du cabaret le regardait à la dérobée. Le moine le remarqua et alla la rejoindre après avoir échangé quelques mots avec Hélène. Celle-ci hésita à les rejoindre avant que Cornevin, le commissaire de quartier, ne lui propose de se réchauffer devant un bon feu à une auberge près de là.

— J'ai à vous parler, ajouta-t-il pour la convaincre.

Ceci décida Hélène. Le commissaire de quartier la conduisit alors à travers un dédale de rues qu'il semblait connaître comme sa poche. La neige piétinée et foulée par les passants, les chevaux et les voitures était devenue une boue noirâtre qui, mélangée aux excréments qu'on continuait à vider dans la rue, crottait les bas. Avec un soupir de soulagement, Cornevin poussa la lourde porte d'une auberge qui se révéla accueillante. D'un œil approbateur, il contempla un gigot de mouton entrelardé d'ail qui tournait à la broche tandis que le rôtisseur l'arrosait régulièrement de son jus.

Une petite femme volubile les conduisit à une table, pas loin de la cheminée où brûlait un feu d'enfer, avant de leur apporter un pichet d'un vin clair et parfumé.

— Cet endroit est bien agréable, fit le commissaire de quartier. On y sert ce petit vin de Suresnes qui chatouille la gorge…

— Vous désiriez me parler, rappela Hélène avec un léger sourire.

L'autre soupira et se frotta le visage avec les mains. Il semblait soudain abattu.

— Eh bien, pour tout vous dire, cette petite Sophia n'arrête pas de me hanter. J'ai même rêvé d'elle…

La jeune femme prêta aussitôt l'oreille. Après le moine, voici donc que Sophia venait d'entrer dans les songes nocturnes d'une autre personne. La jeune fille semblait avoir marqué de son empreinte tous ceux qu'elle avait croisés, vivante ou morte.

— Pourquoi ?

L'autre plissa les yeux et les rides de son front s'accentuèrent.

— Vous vous souvenez de l'affaire du chien qui m'a donné l'occasion par deux fois de la rencontrer. Chaque fois, je l'ai écoutée et traitée avec bienveillance. Je pense donc que, dans une certaine mesure, elle avait confiance en moi, voire même que je lui inspirais quelque sympathie. Ce n'était pas une enfant ordinaire, vous savez…

Hélène se pencha un peu plus vers lui. L'émotion se lisait sur son visage et elle se souvenait à quel point l'annonce de la mort de la jeune fille l'avait bouleversé. Elle posa doucement sa main sur la sienne et, d'un sourire, l'invita à poursuivre.

— Ce que je ne vous ai pas raconté, c'est que je l'ai revue une troisième fois.

Il fit une pause pour s'humecter les lèvres.

— Je ne vous en ai pas parlé car, sur le moment, cela m'a semblé insignifiant.

— Elle est venue vous demander quelque chose?

— Pas exactement. Elle paraissait effrayée et m'a parlé d'un homme qui semblait la suivre ou la surveiller lorsqu'elle sortait.

On les servit et le commissaire de quartier commença à manger sa volaille avec les doigts, rompant les os avec dextérité. Bientôt des taches de graisse ornèrent ses vêtements.

— Que lui avez-vous répondu? demanda Hélène qui ne toucha pas à son assiette.

Cornevin jeta un regard à la broche puis reporta son attention sur la jeune femme, s'attardant un instant sur la courbe de ses lèvres avant de se ressaisir.

— Je lui ai conseillé de ne pas sortir seule. Je suis même allé flâner près de sa maison à l'heure où elle sortait pour aller au marché. Je n'ai pas remarqué cet homme.

Il suça pensivement un os puis scruta attentivement Hélène.

— Ceci peut-il vous aider dans votre enquête?

La jeune femme secoua la tête et sa belle chevelure brune aux reflets roux s'éparpilla sur ses épaules.

— Malheureusement, non.

Le commissaire de quartier jeta son os d'un air dépité.

— Dommage, j'aurais pu vous aider. Je reste néanmoins votre serviteur.

Il la couva d'un regard paternel.

— Prenez garde à vous toutefois, toute cette histoire ne me dit rien qui vaille. Quel dommage! Saint-Sulpice était un quartier si tranquille…

Le moine et la serveuse marchaient lentement dans les allées du cimetière bordées d'herbes figées par le givre. Le moine avait proposé son bras que la jeune femme accepta après quelques instants d'hésitation, peu habituée à la galanterie des hommes.

— Désirez-vous que nous allions boire un verre ou manger quelque chose dans un endroit où il fait plus chaud? proposa le moine en réprimant une quinte de toux.

— Merci mais je n'ai pas le temps. Il faut que je retourne vite à mon travail. Et puis ici, c'est calme et personne ne peut nous voir.

— Vous aviez quelque chose à me dire?

La serveuse hocha la tête.

— Serai-je payée si je vous donne quelques informations intéressantes?

— Comment savez-vous ce qui pourrait m'intéresser ou pas?

Elle prit un air rusé.

— J'ai bien compris que vous travaillez pour la police. Vous recherchez le meurtrier de la petite Sophia, n'est-ce pas?

— C'est vrai, reconnut le moine. Qu'avez-vous à me dire?

La jeune femme frissonna. Ils marchaient à travers les tombes glacées et jamais la mort n'avait trouvé un pareil écrin blanc.

— Hier, j'ai vu Sophia!

Le moine tressaillit.

— Vous dormiez?

— Non, j'allais travailler à l'auberge et, en passant devant la maison de l'astronome, je l'ai vue, assise sur le perron, son chien à ses pieds.

— Son chien?

— Oui, cet animal sale qui la suivait tout le temps. Il était couché devant elle. Sophia a levé la tête et m'a jeté un regard triste.

— Qu'avez-vous fait?

— Je me suis signée avant de m'enfuir. J'ai couru sans me retourner jusqu'à l'auberge. Quand j'ai regardé par la fenêtre, elle n'était plus là.

Elle se mordit les lèvres.

— J'avais peur qu'elle vienne me hanter, mais pourquoi moi?

Le moine ne répondit pas. Il fixait droit devant lui un point imaginaire, le regard sombre. Enfin, comme avec effort, il détourna son attention de ce point et se tourna à demi pour la regarder.

— Peut-être était-ce une jeune fille qui lui ressemblait, hasarda-t-il sans conviction.

— Non, répondit la serveuse dans un souffle, c'était bien elle.

Elle esquissa un rapide signe de croix et chuchota :

— Pauvre enfant ! Le repos éternel lui est refusé et voilà qu'elle erre comme une âme en peine !

— Nous sommes tous des âmes en peine, murmura le moine.

Pensif, le moine rentra à sa demeure. Le chien lui fit fête et lui tendit la patte. Le moine s'en saisit et la secoua gravement puis le caressa et lui gratta la tête derrière les oreilles. Il s'absorba ensuite dans la préparation d'une savante décoction à base d'eau-de-vie, de noix de muscade et de safran. Sa gorge lui faisait encore mal et, parfois, ses poumons le brûlaient. Il cracha pour les vider puis bourra la cheminée de bûches bien sèches et s'assit pour contempler les flammes. De sombres pensées le tourmentaient. Il se prit le front entre les mains. La chaleur dégagée par l'âtre n'était pas sans lui rappeler messes noires et flammes de l'enfer mais la glace qui entourait son cœur et recouvrait les rues l'amenait à penser à Sophia. Il songea à son petit corps frêle et raide dans ce cercueil trop grand et à son âme qui errait maintenant à travers les rues dans une immense solitude.

Un courant d'air glacé courut dans la pièce. Il frissonna mais ne se retourna pas, son oreille désormais habituée au pas léger, presque glissant, d'Hélène.

— Vous voilà, fit-il.

Et son ton n'exprimait rien d'autre que cette simple constatation.

— Comment vous sentez-vous ? demanda-t-elle d'une voix inquiète. Ce n'était pas très raisonnable de sortir même si vous vous sentez mieux.

— La nuit m'a redonné calme et vigueur. Je vais bien.

Il s'obstinait à fixer le feu sans la regarder.

— Que se passe-t-il? demanda-t-elle.

— Ce matin, à mon réveil, le chien était couché près de la cheminée et n'a pas exprimé le besoin de sortir. Je vous ai demandé si vous lui aviez ouvert pour ses besoins et vous m'avez répondu que non.

— Oui, nous l'avons fait sortir dans la cour.

— Et il n'a ni uriné ni déféqué, remarqua le moine. Étrange non, puisqu'il n'était pas sorti depuis la veille au soir?

— Effectivement, car la maison était propre. Il s'est retenu…

— Ou bien, il était déjà sorti mais alors qui lui a ouvert?

Hélène hésita.

— Votre fils est peut-être passé?

Le moine lui jeta un regard froid.

— Je ne vois pas pourquoi…

Il s'enfonça dans une rumination silencieuse.

— N'avez-vous pas faim? lui demanda-t-elle au bout de quelques longues minutes.

Le moine sursauta.

— Diable, maintenant que vous m'en parlez!

Il alla jusqu'à la cuisine.

— Par la queue de Neptune, fit-il, il ne reste déjà plus de ce beau pain blanc?

— Vous aviez faim, c'est bien normal.

Le moine jeta un regard soupçonneux en direction du chien.

— Je n'ai pas souvenir d'en avoir mangé beaucoup.

Hélène rit.

— Après avoir soupçonné le chien, ne me mettez pas en cause s'il vous plaît. Je n'y ai tout simplement pas touché!

— Alors, c'est cet intelligent animal, fit gaiement le moine. Mon fils se vante de sa pie bavarde mais moi j'ai un chien qui sait tourner la clé dans la serrure, ouvrir la porte et trancher le pain!

— J'ai une autre explication, se moqua Hélène. Pendant la nuit, les lutins pillent volontiers les garde-manger des maisons où ils vivent!

— Des lutins?

— Oui mais rassurez-vous, ils ne sont jamais bien méchants! Sortons donc pour acheter de quoi vous sustenter.

Hélène avait acheté un collier de cuivre pour le chien. Elle le lui attacha sans problème mais, étonnamment, l'animal refusa de sortir. Ils durent littéralement le traîner dehors.

— Ce chien a un comportement de plus en plus étrange, constata le moine intrigué. J'espère que sa maîtresse ne vient pas aussi le visiter en rêve.

L'animal eut un bref glapissement puis se mit à hurler. Tout son corps semblait pris de tremblements. Il fallut toute la patience d'Hélène pour le calmer. Enfin, il les suivit docilement, non sans jeter de fréquents regards derrière lui.

Au marché Saint-Jacques, des vendeurs échangeaient des coups de poing avec de petits revendeurs qui usurpaient leur place. Le moine les ignora et entraîna sa compagne devant les étals des commerçants transis jusqu'à la devanture d'un boucher. Celui-ci achetait le regrat, c'est-à-dire le reste des plats des maisons riches de la veille pour en remplir de vastes terrines et revendre le tout le lendemain. Mais il commerçait aussi de beaux quartiers de viande. Hélène choisit un rôti de porc. Rentré dans leur chaude demeure, le moine s'empressa de l'entrelacer adroitement de thym et de feuilles de laurier. Hélène revint de la cuisine avec un plat de fèves.

— Hum, des fèves! fit gaiement le moine. Quelle bonne idée! Pour Pythagore, le poisson est phosphorescent et donc aphrodisiaque, quant aux fèves, elles sont échauffantes!

Elle lui jeta un regard entendu.

— Grand bien nous fasse!

Une fois le rôti et les fèves disposés à cuire, Hélène s'assit et tapa légèrement du talon sur le sol en arquant les sourcils.

— Quelle est la date de naissance de Sophia? demanda-t-elle abruptement.

Il le lui dit. Elle le considéra avec surprise.

— Comment savez-vous cela?

Il le tenait du journal de Sophia qui était tombé dans ses mains. Celui-ci commençait par : "Je m'appelle Sophia et je suis née…"

— Je sais parce que je suis! répondit-il laconiquement.

Hélène arqua délicatement un sourcil.

— Et moi, je sais que vous l'avez lu dans le livre que vous avez subrepticement rapporté chez vous et qui tenait lieu de journal à Sophia.

— Diable, vous possédez le troisième œil!

Elle allongea les jambes près de l'âtre et, nonchalamment, les yeux du moine suivirent ce mouvement, épousant les plis de sa robe. Ils restèrent ainsi sans parler, gagnés par la douce chaleur du feu. Il la regarda feindre ne pas sentir ses regards sur elle. Des pensées sans nom s'agitaient chez le moine. Et le soir n'arrêtait pas de tomber et elle se tenait là, rêveuse au coin du feu, tandis que son âme à lui se troublait. Surpris d'entendre une voix au fond de son cœur, le moine écoutait.

Que se passe-t-il dans mon âme?

Il se leva et vint sans bruit derrière le fauteuil où Hélène rêvassait. Comme hypnotisé par sa nuque blanche, il se pencha vers elle. Une volupté plus chaude encore que l'enfer le fit frissonner des pieds à la tête.

Je suis un fou, pensa-t-il en se redressant. *Me voici à bander comme un carme auprès d'une jeune femme qui a la moitié de mon âge!*

Mais il savait bien qu'il ne s'agissait pas de cela. Un sentiment plus profond mûrissait en lui, le rapprochant inexorablement d'Hélène. Même consciente de l'agitation dans son dos, la jeune femme n'avait pas bougé.

— Qu'avez-vous, mon ami? demanda-t-elle.

Il se corrigea de son affolement en décidant d'affronter l'air glacé de la nuit.

— Rien, j'ai besoin de prendre l'air. Je vais amener le chien avec moi.

— Ce n'est pas très prudent, vous n'êtes pas encore guéri.

— Je vais bien me couvrir...

Dehors, le froid était si vif que le sang lui monta au visage, rosissant ses joues comme une paire de gifles. Il se morigéna.

Quelle vacuité de mes pensées! Je la regarde avec des yeux de jeune fou!

Le vent s'était levé et rabattait les pans de sa bure derrière lui. Près de lui, le chien s'était mis à gronder sourdement.

— Rentrez tout de suite!

La silhouette fine d'Hélène s'était encadrée dans la lumière. Docilement, le moine revint à l'intérieur.

— Quel temps du diable, murmura-t-il avant de se courber en deux pour éternuer.

— Un temps à ne pas mettre un moine hérétique dehors! Elle lui tendit son mouchoir.

— Tenez…

— Grand merci! L'air est si frais!

Il se retourna pour se cacher pendant qu'il se mouchait mais elle perçut son souffle irrégulier et lut la tension qui habitait ses épaules.

— Venez près du feu, insista-t-elle. Voulez-vous que je réchauffe pour vous un peu de cette potion contre la toux? Le rôti sera bientôt cuit.

Elle virevoltait soudain dans l'espace, emplissant la maison de bruits et de mouvements comme pour en chasser les mauvais souvenirs ou les pensées trop étroites.

— Comment êtes-vous devenu moine? lui demanda-t-elle plus tard alors qu'il buvait à petites lampées son remède brûlant, le chien couché à ses pieds.

Les yeux de son interlocuteur brillèrent.

— On a voulu faire de moi un membre du clergé parce que j'étais le second des garçons de ma famille et que, selon l'usage, l'aîné est destiné au métier des armes. Je n'avais à l'égard de la religion qu'une simple curiosité intellectuelle. Lorsque je découvris la diversité des religions dans le monde et le mal qui régnait sur terre, mon scepticisme s'accrut. Certes, je tenais l'homme comme seul responsable de ses propres maux puisque c'est lui qui sciemment crée et entretient l'enfer sur terre. Mais, comme vous l'entendez, j'étais moins sensible au catéchisme enseigné qu'à la hardiesse de pensée de nos philosophes. En fait, je brûlais d'un feu réformateur bien avant l'heure!

Il trépigna sur place et reprit d'un ton plus exalté:

— Mon aîné mourut au combat, le pauvre, lui qui était si doux de nature. Je courus le venger, abandonnant l'habit pour l'uniforme. Vous n'imaginez pas dans quel état de déla-brement se trouvait l'armée! On recrutait les plus pauvres et désespérés de la société par force ou supercherie. Les grades s'achetaient et ce sont les plus sots qui commandaient nos troupes. De fait, rien n'a changé aujourd'hui. Sous Louis XIV, de bons officiers roturiers parvenaient à s'extraire du lot. C'est maintenant chose impossible. À part l'excellent maré-chal de Saxe, tous nos généraux et maréchaux sont des sots et des estropiés de la cervelle. Avec eux, on ne fait jamais retraite mais on recule toujours! Bref, à l'armée, je me las-sai des combats et un médecin m'enseigna. Rentré à Paris, je me passionnai pour l'anatomie, disséquant le plus possible de cadavres pour me former.

Il s'interrompit pour ajouter un peu de miel dans sa tasse.

— Je rejoignis ensuite Padoue où enseignait Giovanni Bat-tista Morgagni qui pratiquait très régulièrement des autopsies. Il est âgé aujourd'hui de soixante-dix-huit ans! Il a découvert que toute maladie que nous observons du vivant des personnes, à travers les signes habituels de celle-ci, laisse des lésions dans les organismes. Dès lors, les lésions cadavériques peuvent nous permettre de connaître les causes de la mort par maladie des personnes. C'est ce que je dis toujours: ouvrez les cadavres et vous en saurez plus!

Les étranges yeux verts d'Hélène étincelèrent joyeusement.

— Comment avez-vous fait pour devenir si savant? demanda-t-elle en caressant affectueusement sa main.

Le moine reposa sa tasse.

— J'ai étudié sans trêve jusqu'à dompter les sciences. C'est à la lueur des lampes que l'on travaille le mieux. Je ne connais plus belle récompense qu'une nouvelle découverte après une âpre nuit sans sommeil!

— Vous avez été une lumière dans ce siècle où demeure tant d'obscurité…

— J'en ai trop fait! Je ne sais pas m'arrêter! Tous mes ennuis sont venus de là!

— Racontez-moi!

— Un jour, je commençai à écrire sur le ridicule des pré-éminences, remettant en cause la distinction des fonctions et la supériorité des uns et des autres. Je partais du principe que ce qui est petit peut être grand. Par prudence, je maniais l'ironie, la seule arme possible face à la monarchie policière. Donner de soi une image plus sotte que celle de l'autre, faire d'une apparente maladresse le comble de l'adresse et paraître louer ce que l'on blâme alors qu'en vérité l'on s'en moque, voilà ce qu'est l'ironie. J'acquis ainsi beaucoup de prestige et d'ennemis. Des femmes m'aimèrent. Elles s'en allèrent aussi, lassées par la vacuité de mes pensées. L'une d'elles resta. Je l'épousai et elle mit bientôt mon fils au monde. Hélas, hélas…

Il fourragea dans sa barbe comme pour y chercher ses mots.

— Elle prit une fluxion de poitrine et mourut alors que notre enfant avait quatre ans. Il me revint la douleur de pleurer ma chère femme et la lourde tâche d'éduquer mon fils.

— Vous avez été très certainement un bon père.

— N'en soyez pas si sûre, regretta-t-il, j'ai éparpillé mon âme aux quatre coins de l'Europe alors que j'avais un fils merveilleux qui m'attendait.

Il baissa la tête.

— J'ai manqué à mes devoirs de père et il m'en veut toujours pour cela.

— Voyons, remarqua Hélène, il est aujourd'hui à vos côtés.

— Oui mais avec lui j'ai l'impression de ne pas pouvoir rattraper le temps perdu. C'est comme si le sable me coulait des doigts.

La jeune femme s'assit sur l'accoudoir de son fauteuil et, à la manière d'une petite fille, entoura son cou de ses longs bras. Son corps était aussi souple que celui d'un chat et, comme cet animal, ses grands yeux le fixaient avec des reflets mordorés dans les prunelles.

— Pourquoi être revenu en France travailler avec lui?

Il soupira.

— J'étais tel Ulysse un voyageur fatigué et je n'avais nulle Ithaque à regagner.

— Et puis vous songiez à vous rapprocher de votre fils…

— Il me manquait tant.

— Et bien sûr, vous ne lui disiez pas!

— Vous me comprenez si bien, ma chère…

Il porta une de ses mains à sa bouche. Ses lèvres esquissèrent une moue clémente et elle le laissa baiser délicatement le bout de ses doigts. À cet instant, une bourrasque s'engouffra en hurlant par la porte. Le commissaire aux morts étranges entra et s'immobilisa en découvrant la scène.

— Je ne vous dérange pas? demanda-t-il sèchement.

Les mains d'Hélène quittèrent le cou du moine.

— Que vous arrive-t-il? demanda tranquillement la jeune femme.

Volnay lui jeta un regard couleur de glace.

— Je trouve votre conduite envers mon père inconvenante.

Hélène se leva tranquillement et lui tourna le dos sans répondre.

— Oh, mon fils, protesta le moine, tu fais erreur. Nous évoquions juste les sentiments filiaux.

— Je ne les avais jamais vus aussi tendrement évoqués! persifla Volnay. Certainement pas avec moi en tout cas!

— Tu es injuste!

— Je suis consterné de te voir jouer les jolis cœurs avec une intrigante qui pourrait être ta fille!

— Mon fils, tu vois Padoue à la place de Pise et tu fais des montagnes d'un rien. Avec toi, autant chie un bœuf que mille moucherons!

De nouveau, la porte s'ouvrit brusquement. Le commissaire aux morts étranges et son père échangèrent un regard surpris. C'était la seconde fois de leur vie que Sartine faisait irruption chez le moine, et cela en l'espace de quelques jours!

— Ah! Je vous trouve tous ensemble, s'écria le lieutenant général de police. C'est bien! Je suis allé chez vous Volnay mais vous n'y étiez pas!

— Que se passe-t-il? s'étonna le commissaire aux morts étranges.

Il était encore tout pâle de son altercation avec son père et Hélène. Un peu surpris, Sartine le jaugea du regard puis eut un sourire sarcastique.

— Nous avons retrouvé votre curé dansant. Il danse toujours mais, comme je l'avais prédit, au bout d'une corde!

XI

UN PROCUREUR ET AUTRES DIABLERIES

Volnay grimpa dans la voiture derrière Sartine. Il y trouva un troisième passager.

— Je vous présente le procureur Siltieri, fit sobrement le lieutenant général de police. C'est lui qui instruit notre affaire avec… euh… toute la discrétion voulue.

Le procureur était un grand homme efflanqué, aux joues creuses, au menton proéminent et au regard brûlant. Il déplut tout de suite au commissaire aux morts étranges par ses manières sèches et hautaines.

— Il était temps de nous rencontrer, dit-il à Volnay d'un ton acerbe. M. de Sartine m'a raconté comment vous avez laissé échapper la prostituée qui participait à cette messe noire.

— Il m'a d'abord fallu la trouver, répondit froidement le commissaire aux morts étranges. Je n'avais au départ pour indice qu'un cadavre dans un cimetière. Cette femme s'est ensuite rompu le cou dans un escalier mais je n'ai pas perdu pour autant le fil de cette enquête puisque je recherchais le curé dansant.

— Malheureusement, il ne vous a pas attendu pour se pendre, ricana Siltieri. Il est grand temps que j'intervienne!

— Nul doute que vous sachiez faire mieux que moi!

Siltieri lui jeta un regard noir.

— J'ai une certaine expérience en la matière, voyez-vous. J'instruis des dossiers de sorcellerie depuis dix ans. J'ai eu affaire à ces maîtres en perversité, pères du mensonge et serviteurs du démon qui prient le diable à la place de Dieu. Ces boucs fornicateurs singent l'eucharistie et rendent un culte fébrile à

Satan. Ils récitent l'introït à rebours pour dénier la virginité et appeler à la débauche. Tout chez eux est grotesque. Leurs flatulences remplacent l'encens. Ils chantent *Gloria in profundis Satani* au lieu de *Gloria in excelsis Deo*. L'*Ite missa est* étant remplacé par un *laus Satani*.

Il se signa fiévreusement.

— Dieu m'est témoin qu'en d'autres temps, la répression aurait été plus sévère avec les tribunaux de l'Inquisition!

Sartine s'agita, mal à l'aise.

— Il appartient à la justice du roi de rendre celle-ci et non aux tribunaux de l'Église.

— Certes mais il fut un temps où ils collaboraient ensemble! Rappelons-nous que feu notre bon roi Louis XIV a sommé sorciers et sorcières de quitter son royaume sans délai et ordonné de punir exemplairement ceux qui ont pratiqué la magie.

— Ma police s'y emploie, rétorqua Sartine d'un ton aigre.

— Pas assez! Pas assez! Ils sont toujours là à tenter de nous faire prendre une paille pour une poutre!

Volnay frémit intérieurement. Chargé par la justice d'instruire l'enquête, Siltieri était un nostalgique des tribunaux de la très sainte Inquisition! Cela le situait certainement dans le camp du parti des dévots contre celui de la marquise de Pompadour, ces deux camps se livrant à une lutte féroce dans les coulisses du pouvoir. Les deux policiers gardèrent le silence durant le reste du trajet, laissant le procureur continuer un monologue fébrile sur la nécessité de purifier l'hérésie par le feu.

Leur voiture suivit un lacis de ruelles ténébreuses dans le faubourg Saint-Marcel avant de s'arrêter dans un cahot devant un immeuble mal entretenu, rue du Puits-de-l'Ermite. Des archers du guet les attendaient et les conduisirent dans un appartement haut de plafond où régnait un froid glacial.

Le curé dansant avait été un grand gaillard dégingandé, long et maigre, sec comme une trique. Vêtu d'un mauvais gilet de serge noir et d'une culotte de peau rapiécée, il se balançait maintenant au bout d'une corde, la langue hors de la bouche. Le commissaire aux morts étranges le contempla un instant en silence puis se mit à arpenter la pièce, notant du regard chaque objet ou meuble qui s'y trouvait : une mauvaise tapisserie, un coffre pour les affaires, une table et quatre chaises...

Le spectacle qui s'offrait à eux dans ce qui semblait être la cuisine était assez édifiant.

— Que pensez-vous de tout cela ? lui demanda Sartine.

Volnay n'eut pas le temps de répondre car le procureur se planta au milieu de la pièce et prit la parole d'une voix forte.

— Mon avis est fait. J'ai déjà vu par le passé tant de signes de ce type ! Voyez par vous-même : hosties noires, cadavre de chat noir, cierges noirs. Quant à la présence de ce crucifix, n'ayez crainte, il sera probablement piétiné au cours de quelque séance. Il n'est pas possible que l'on ne l'ait pas entendu psalmodier ses diableries. Il doit y avoir des complices dans cet immeuble. Que les archers du guet fouillent tout !

Sartine jeta un bref regard à Volnay puis fit un signe au sergent du guet. Des hommes sortirent précipitamment de l'appartement.

— Ah, dit Siltieri en se ruant dans un coin de la pièce, un bâton de sorcier ! "Bâton blanc, bâton noir, mène-moi là où tu dois, de par le diable !"

Le commissaire aux morts étranges s'approcha calmement.

— Il s'agit d'un bâton de marche. Voyez, il est ferré à son extrémité.

— Vous ignorez donc que ces maudits sorciers font poser à leur bâton une ferrure avec la lame d'acier grâce à laquelle ils ont égorgé une victime afin d'en accroître la puissance ?

Volnay préféra ne pas répondre.

— Que quelqu'un dépende cet homme ! ordonna le lieutenant général de police pour tenter d'être utile.

Le commissaire aux morts étranges intervint.

— Un instant ! Cette scène de crime a été assez tourmentée comme cela. Toutes les traces ont été piétinées par le guet. Il faut que je me fasse une idée des assassins, moi !

Il prit une chaise et monta dessus pour examiner le cou de la victime. En bas, le procureur Siltieri haussa les épaules.

— Il n'y a ni empreinte de pas, ni indices qui tiennent. Toutes les preuves sont là sous vos yeux, jusqu'à ces hosties noires et triangulaires ! Les hosties à trois pointes comme ces hérétiques les appellent! Voici les premiers ingrédients pour se livrer à une parodie de messe où tout est inversé et perverti!

— Cela ne me dit pas qui a tué cet homme, remarqua tranquillement Volnay en tirant sur le crochet.

— Il s'est pendu tout seul par repentir ou bien ses acolytes ont probablement jugé qu'il leur fallait un autre sacrifice...

— Je pense surtout que ses complices ou commanditaires ont eu peur, osa le commissaire aux morts étranges. Ils ont dû apprendre que nous avions trouvé la prostituée qui assistait à la cérémonie et que nous étions sur les traces du curé dansant. M. de Sartine, ici présent, ayant mis tous ses agents à sa recherche, je suis certain que cela n'est pas passé inaperçu.

Le lieutenant général de police se rembrunit. Le commissaire aux morts étranges examina la poutre à laquelle était accroché le curé dansant.

— Le crochet est planté ici depuis longtemps, constata le commissaire aux morts étranges. Il ne l'a pas été pour l'occasion.

Il redescendit et se saisit des mains de l'homme.

— Pas de traces de lien. Elles n'ont pas été attachées puis détachées.

— Cela confirme l'hypothèse selon laquelle il s'est donné la mort, intervint Sartine. S'il se savait recherché...

Volnay secoua la tête.

— Pas forcément. Il pouvait être déjà mort étranglé avant la pendaison ou simplement assommé. Le moine nous le dira.

Il examina les ongles du mort.

— Hum, il y a de la peau sous certains ongles. Il a dû griffer ses agresseurs. Voyons pour la longueur de ses souliers.

Il sortit d'une poche une cordelette avec différents nœuds.

— Celle-ci correspond à une empreinte relevée sur les lieux du crime, tout comme celle de la Vorace. Et de deux! Il m'en reste encore trois à trouver...

Redescendant de sa chaise, il jeta un coup d'œil aux souliers du curé dansant qui pendaient dans le vide.

— Tiens, un boiteux, remarqua-t-il machinalement.

— Que dites-vous? s'enquit Siltieri.

— Voyez les talons de ses chaussures, l'un est complètement déformé sur la droite, signe qu'il s'y appuyait plus que sur l'autre.

— Voici encore une preuve! s'exclama le procureur.

— Pardon?

Siltieri eut un reniflement méprisant.

— Vous ignorez donc que ceux marqués par la lettre "B" sont plus prédisposés que les autres à devenir des agents du diable? Bohémiens, boiteux, borgnes, bègues, bossus, bâfreurs ou buveurs!

— Et baveux, compléta Volnay sans rire.

Il se recula.

— Je vais faire un croquis de la scène.

Sortant d'une poche papier et fusain, il se mit à dessiner les lieux. Malgré lui, Sartine s'approcha pour admirer la sûreté et la justesse de la main de son commissaire aux morts étranges. Pendant ce temps, un archer du guet rapporta de la chambre du curé dansant un livre dont Siltieri s'empara avec un rugissement de triomphe.

— Nous sommes dans l'antre du démon! Voyez plutôt!

Sartine s'approcha et jeta au livre un coup d'œil prudent avant de se reculer vivement.

— La liste des principaux démons a été établie il y a mille deux cents ans par l'Église au canon 7 du concile de Braga, expliqua Siltieri avec ferveur. Tous ces noms abjects me sont malheureusement familiers: Adramelech, grand chancelier des Enfers mais aussi dieu du meurtre! Il est ici représenté sous sa forme de paon. Astaroth, démon et trésorier des Enfers qui chevauche un dragon et tient dans sa main une vipère car il aime se changer en serpent. Ayperos qui commande à trente-six légions et connaît le passé et l'avenir. Astarté à la tête de génisse, démon femelle de la débauche. Béhémond, démon, sa force est dans ses reins. Bélial, le meurtre et le vice réunis…

Sartine et les archers du guet se signèrent en frissonnant tandis que Siltieri poursuivait avec frénésie son étrange litanie. Sans lui prêter attention, le commissaire aux morts étranges termina son croquis et demanda qu'on emmène le corps du curé dansant chez le moine. Le cadavre venait d'être descendu et chargé dans une voiture lorsque les archers du guet revinrent de leur fouille dans l'immeuble. Ils poussaient sans ménagement devant eux un couple terrorisé. Des couches de saindoux superposées semblaient tenir lieu de cou et de menton à l'homme, court et mal bâti. Jamais deux personnes n'avaient été aussi mal assorties car la femme était maigre comme une brindille.

— Nous avons trouvé des cierges noirs chez eux, dit le sergent du guet en brandissant triomphalement la pièce à conviction.

— Sacrilège! Hérésie! s'écria le procureur. Qu'on les emmène au Châtelet!

La femme se jeta à ses genoux.

— Pitié monseigneur! Nous n'avons rien fait de mal! Nous sommes d'honnêtes fournisseurs en bougies pour un marchand du Marais.

— Et vous le fournissez aussi en cierges noirs?!

— Non, ce sont des commandes de notre voisin. Il faut bien vivre…

— *Confessionem esse veram, non factam vi tormentorum!* s'écria Siltieri. "Les aveux ont été spontanés et non obtenus sous l'effet de la torture!"

La femme s'accrocha avec désespoir aux genoux du procureur.

— Pitié! Nous ne faisons que fabriquer des cierges et des chandelles!

Le visage de Siltieri se fendit d'un sourire méchant.

— Vous chanterez un autre refrain lorsque l'on vous mettra les brodequins! En attendant, nous visiterons demain cette échoppe que vous fournissez. Je suis curieux de savoir ce que nous allons y trouver! Allons, au Châtelet! Au Châtelet!

Il se tourna vers le commissaire aux morts étranges sans prendre garde aux cris effrayés poussés par le couple qu'on emmenait de force.

— Vous voyez que les choses sont simples : la mauvaise engeance s'assemble! Ces blasphémateurs et agents sacrilèges du mal vont livrer leurs complices sous la question!

— À travers les messes noires, ce n'est pas seulement le goût pervers du sacrilège qui s'exprime, remarqua Volnay, mais toute la cruauté et l'inhumanité d'un monde pour lequel la vie de l'autre n'est rien. Ces gens-là n'en sont pas.

Le procureur haussa les épaules.

— Les choses sont moins complexes que vous ne le supposez : il s'agit d'hérésie.

Il lui tourna le dos, salua Sartine et sortit en ramenant le pan de sa cape derrière lui d'un geste sec. Le commissaire aux morts étranges demanda à monter chez les suspects arrêtés. Ceux-ci devaient dormir dans une grande armoire sans battants, sur un grabat posé sur la planche. L'appartement était sombre et sentait le renfermé. Une lucarne l'éclairait, fermée par une planche à coulisse. Dans les cendres du feu refroidissaient des oignons et des raves. Volnay fit le tour du misérable logis, ne trouvant que de quoi fabriquer des cierges noirs. Peu convaincu de sorcellerie, il rejoignit Sartine. À cet instant, un des archers du guet eut un hoquet de surprise.

— Que font-ils donc tous ceux-là ?!

Le commissaire aux morts étranges alla le rejoindre à la fenêtre et jeta un coup d'œil dans la rue où la population s'assemblait, le visage rouge de colère et l'invective aux lèvres.

— Les nouvelles vont vite dans un quartier, murmura-t-il. Ils ont l'air hostile. Il faut dire que la police embarque sans ménagement des gens qui sont leurs voisins ou leurs amis…

Sartine le rejoignit et jeta un bref coup d'œil avant de s'essuyer nerveusement le front avec son mouchoir de dentelle.

— Regardez-la, Volnay, cette foule canaille. Si nous n'avions pas vingt archers du guet avec nous, elle nous mettrait en charpie. De nos jours, nous ne pouvons plus faire d'exécution publique sans que l'on insulte le bourreau et nos hommes ne parviennent même plus à mettre un gueux au pilori sans qu'on leur jette des pierres !

Le commissaire aux morts étranges demeura silencieux. Il avait senti la peur de Sartine. Ce n'était pas un manque de courage car l'homme possédait un caractère bien trempé mais la crainte de ce que représentait la foule, les grandes masses incontrôlables. Sartine savait pertinemment que la loi du nombre appartenait au peuple. Celui-ci l'ignorait mais un jour il se compterait. Sartine haïssait la foule car il avait prise sur tout sauf sur elle.

La foule, songea Volnay, est comme l'eau. Rien ne l'arrête lorsque la digue cède. Et qu'est-ce que la digue au final? Quelques milliers d'hommes en uniforme, eux-mêmes fils du peuple? La foule n'était ni consciente de sa force, ni dirigée.

Un jour, moi ou quelqu'un d'autre, nous l'enflammerons comme une torche et la lancerons contre la monarchie.

— Ne restons pas là!

La voix sèche et coupante de Sartine ramena Volnay à la réalité. Déjà une pierre venait de briser une vitre et roulait dans la pièce. Le peuple avait aperçu la perruque et le visage poudré et fardé du lieutenant général de police.

Ils descendirent précipitamment les escaliers et s'engouffrèrent dans la voiture sous un jet de pierres. Les archers du guet débordés reculaient en désordre.

— Tenez vos positions! cria le sergent du guet. Tenez vos positions!

Une pierre bien ajustée le fit taire. Ce fut la débandade. Des archers du guet tirèrent.

Volnay jura.

— Allez! Allez! cria Sartine au cocher.

Celui-ci claqua son fouet et, d'une voix brutale, hurla après ses chevaux. Des hurlements de peur et de rage jaillirent de la foule. La voiture eut un soubresaut avant d'être secouée de cahots. Volnay comprit qu'on venait de passer sur un corps humain. Des mains apparurent à la portière du carrosse puis un visage. Sartine frappa dans le front de l'homme qui lâcha prise. À sa portière, Volnay vit un assaillant entrer le buste dans la voiture. À la main, il tenait un couteau. Le commissaire aux morts étranges sortit son pistolet.

— Tirez! cria Sartine.

Le doigt de Volnay se crispa sur la détente.

— Tirez!

L'homme le contemplait stupidement, son couteau toujours pointé dans sa direction. À cet instant, la voiture prit de la vitesse et vira brusquement, l'homme déséquilibré chuta.

— À quoi vous sert de tenir une arme si vous ne vous en servez pas! cria Sartine mécontent.

Volnay rangea calmement son pistolet.

— Je n'en avais pas réellement besoin.

Le lieutenant général de police maugréa puis s'enferma dans un silence maussade dont il ne sortit qu'une fois quitté le quartier.

— Nos hommes vont regagner le Châtelet, espérons que la foule ne les accompagne pas.

Volnay eut un sourire sombre.

Un jour, le peuple ne se contentera pas de les reconduire jusqu'à leur caserne mais il marchera sur Versailles.

— Cela vous amuse, Volnay? gronda Sartine. Vous espérez un jour voir nos corps gigoter à un réverbère! Croyez-vous réellement que je ne connaisse vos convictions?

Le commissaire aux morts étranges ne répondit pas. Sartine savait trop de choses sur son passé pour le berner. Cela lui donnait d'ailleurs prise sur lui. Ceci et son efficacité dans les enquêtes expliquaient qu'un serviteur aussi zélé de l'État que Sartine conservât dans ses services un opposant secret au régime monarchique.

— Je ne souhaite la mort de personne, dit doucement Volnay. Et je voudrais bien résoudre cette enquête. La prostituée, le prêtre renégat… il nous manque encore trois participants et ceux-là j'aimerais les prendre vivants!

— Le procureur Siltieri ne va pas tarder à les identifier parmi tous les mécréants qu'il a fait embarquer.

Volnay secoua la tête.

— Je ne crois pas. Les trois personnes assistant à la messe noire devaient en être les commanditaires. Ce sont des gens d'un autre niveau et d'une autre condition que les malheureux qui vont subir la torture. J'ai parlé avec la Vorace et je peux vous assurer qu'elle n'avait ni l'imagination ni l'intelligence nécessaires à une telle chose. Mais voilà, le procureur Siltieri est un fanatique à l'esprit étroit. Il a déniché quelques pauvres bougres qui se trouvaient au mauvais endroit, au mauvais moment, et pense avoir tiré la fève du gâteau! Il va les mettre à la question et leur faire avouer tous les crimes que l'on souhaite. *Postquam depositus fuit de tormento.* "Aveux déposés après retour de la torture", comme dirait le moine!

Sartine sortit une prise mais les cahots de la voiture sur les pavés l'empêchèrent d'enfourner sans dégât le tabac dans les narines. D'un geste agacé, il brossa ses habits parsemés de brins.

— Si vous étiez plus rapide, nous n'aurions pas Siltieri sur le dos, maugréa le lieutenant général de police. Qu'allons-nous faire maintenant?

— Si nous passions chez le moine? proposa Volnay.

À sa grande surprise, Sartine accepta.

Le moine les contempla d'un œil satisfait. Cabotin, il ne lui déplaisait pas d'avoir pour public une aussi haute autorité que le lieutenant général de police. Hélène absente, la présence inespérée de Sartine le remplissait d'aise.

— J'ai procédé au déshabillage du corps, commença-t-il d'un ton docte, et j'ai relevé la présence d'importantes ecchymoses. L'homme s'est défendu. Cela s'est passé récemment car la couleur des ecchymoses est rouge vif le premier jour.

Il fronça délicatement les sourcils et poursuivit.

— La pendaison produit une pression qui provoque une compression du cou, ce qui empêche les vaisseaux d'amener le sang au cerveau ou à la trachée. Enfin, les muscles du cou sont atteints par la chute mais la hauteur de celle-ci a été faible selon ce que m'ont dit les agents du guet. J'ai observé que les marques de strangulation existent bien mais qu'elles sont situées à un niveau beaucoup plus bas qu'en cas de pendaison. De plus, les marques ne sont pas celles d'une corde car elles sont plus larges, probablement un bas ou quelque chose de ce type... En tout cas, un matériau plus souple que la corde...

— N'a-t-il pas pu être étranglé à mains nues? demanda Sartine.

Le moine se tourna vers lui, les yeux brillants.

— Question intéressante, monsieur le lieutenant général de police! Mais la réponse est négative car l'étranglement par voie manuelle exige plus de pression et donc les marques en seraient beaucoup plus nettes et les dommages musculaires plus importants. Je ne vous parle même pas de l'état de la gorge…

— Cela suffira en effet, s'empressa de dire Sartine. Vous soutenez donc que notre curé dansant a été étranglé par un bas et pendu ensuite à un crochet pour laisser croire à un suicide ?

— Je ne soutiens pas : je prouve ! Tiens, qu'est-ce que ceci ?

Le moine ouvrit avec précaution le sachet que le curé dansant portait autour du cou.

— Du sel… On en porte autour du cou pour se prémunir du malin. Le curé dansant devait craindre que le diable ne l'emporte avec lui après l'invocation…

Le lieutenant général de police se tourna vers Volnay.

— Les participants tueraient leurs complices car ils les savent repérés ?

Le commissaire aux morts étranges haussa légèrement les épaules.

— Peut-être l'auraient-ils fait de toute façon. J'ai la conviction que la prostituée et le curé n'étaient que des pions dans leur jeu, de simples outils pour respecter un rituel. Une fois celui-ci accompli, ils n'en ont plus besoin.

— Pensez-vous que les commanditaires de la messe soient de plus noble condition ?

Volnay décrypta la question muette de Sartine : la cour pouvait-elle être impliquée ? Si c'était le cas, le parti des dévots s'en réjouirait car cela lui permettrait de porter des coups à tous ceux qui n'étaient pas du même bord.

— Je ne vois guère la cour de Versailles mêlée à ce meurtre, dit le commissaire aux morts étranges.

— Tu as tort, intervint le moine au grand désespoir de son fils. Les grands de ce monde courent les devineresses et les tireurs d'horoscopes. Ils achètent des potions magiques ou des runes. Et il est de notoriété publique que la vicomtesse de Polignac recourait à des chercheurs de trésor. Quant au duc de…

— Nous parlons de meurtre, le coupa sans ménagement Volnay. Et il existe suffisamment de chapelles privées dans les châteaux ou les hôtels particuliers pour éviter que les grands de ce monde viennent salir leurs bottes la nuit dans des cimetières glacés !

Il laissa échapper un sourire sarcastique.

— À moins que notre ami Siltieri ne découvre que le marchand de chandelles fournissait en cierges noirs quelque seigneur...

Sartine émit un soupir irrité mais son attention fut attirée par le moine.

— Voyons voir ce que tu as dans les poches, disait ce dernier en s'adressant au cadavre.

Le moine énuméra un à un les objets trouvés sur le corps.

— Un mouchoir, une clé, une tabatière en bois, oh...

Il tenait entre deux doigts un anneau dans lequel était enchâssé un œil.

— Quelle horreur, fit Sartine en plissant le nez de dégoût.

— N'ayez crainte, le rassura le moine, ce doit être un œil de belette. C'est une amulette pour empêcher que l'on vous jette un sort pour vous nouer l'aiguillette. Pour les hommes, c'est toujours gênant!

Il ricana avant de reprendre son énumération :

— Un almanach, une paire de dés, un couteau, un billet de loterie sur l'hôtel de ville et une inscription en latin sur un billet...

— Laissez-moi voir! s'écria Sartine.

Sa mine s'allongea lorsqu'il lut :

— *Cintra me ad incarte cla, a filiia Eniol, Lieber, Bruya, Braguesca...* Qu'est-ce encore que ceci?

— Une formule magique pour gagner aux dés, expliqua le moine. On en vendait déjà quand j'avais vingt ans et je vous confirme que cela ne marche pas du tout!

Une toux qui sembla lui déchirer la poitrine l'interrompit.

— Pardonnez-moi, dit-il au lieutenant général de police, voulez-vous avoir l'amabilité de me passer le verre d'eau derrière vous?

Tandis que l'autre se retournait, le moine dissimula rapidement sous sa bure une feuille de papier pliée. Volnay le fixa intensément mais ne dit rien.

— Il n'y a aucun verre derrière moi, dit sèchement Sartine.

Il lui fit face de nouveau, l'air mécontent.

— Ah pardon, fit le moine, c'est ma maudite fièvre. La carafe est à côté de toi, mon fils. Si tu veux bien avoir la gentillesse…

Volnay lui servit un verre qu'il but goulûment.

— Nous disons donc, continua-t-il après s'être essuyé les lèvres d'un revers de sa manche, un couteau, une quittance de loyer et de l'argent.

Il compta minutieusement.

— Trois livres et douze sols très précisément.

Sartine croisa les bras et les contempla d'un œil sec.

— Tout ceci ne nous avance pas vraiment. De son côté, Siltieri va faire mettre à la question ce couple qui va leur livrer des noms…

— Qu'ils parlent sous la torture, j'en suis bien certain, fit Volnay d'un ton calme, mais je ne pense pas qu'ils sachent grand-chose. Ils fabriquaient des cierges noirs pour le curé dansant mais seul celui-ci savait où les livrer…

Il s'interrompit. Au-dessus de leur tête, un hurlement à glacer le sang se faisait entendre. Sartine frissonna.

— Qui crie ainsi à la mort?

— Oh, ce n'est rien, s'empressa de répondre le moine. J'ai recueilli un chien mais parfois il semble devenir fou…

— C'est de vivre sous le même toit que vous! répliqua Sartine.

Le moine se rembrunit mais, sagement, ne répondit rien.

— Il est vrai que nous sommes tous sur les nerfs, conclut Volnay conciliant.

Sartine regarda avec stupéfaction son commissaire aux morts étranges à l'impassibilité et au calme légendaires.

— Nous n'avons pas connu d'affaire aussi difficile depuis longtemps, ajouta le moine. Et la victime est ici la plus délicieuse des enfants, la plus triste aussi…

— Comment savez-vous cela? demanda le lieutenant général de police.

— Parce qu'elle me l'a dit!

Sartine le considéra comme s'il était devenu fou.

— Cette Sophia vous a tourné la tête!

Le moine lui jeta un coup d'œil complice.

— Cette jeune fille nous hante tous. Elle n'aura de repos avant que l'on ne trouve son assassin!

— Votre fils vous a raconté notre conversation privée, constata Sartine en jetant un méchant regard à Volnay.

— Oh, il n'y a pas de mal à cela, intervint le moine. Pas plus qu'il n'y en a à rêver. Depuis l'Antiquité, les hommes tentent de trouver une explication à leurs rêves. Artémidore d'Éphèse racontait déjà des tas de choses très intéressantes à ce propos. À Babylone, les prêtres révéraient le Soleil, *seigneur de la vision*, et l'on se rendait au temple des songes pour y décrypter ceux-ci.

— Tout ceci n'en fait pas une science, remarqua le lieutenant général de police d'un ton acerbe.

— Détrompez-vous, l'oniromancie est la science de la divination à travers les rêves. Il nous revient à chacun de déchiffrer la révélation ambiguë de ceux-ci et de devenir les interprètes de nos songes.

Sartine le contempla d'un air sarcastique.

— Ne me dites pas qu'un esprit aussi rationnel que le vôtre s'emploie à ces fadaises.

— Mon esprit rationnel, comme vous dites, s'intéresse à tout ce qui est inexpliqué!

Une fois la porte de la maison refermée derrière le lieutenant général de police, Volnay s'empressa auprès de son père.

— Eh bien, qu'as-tu donc dissimulé aux yeux de Sartine?

Le moine sourit finement.

— Tu as remarqué ma présence d'esprit? Le verre d'eau, Sartine tourne la tête et hop!

On aurait dit un enfant se vantant d'une farce réussie. Volnay secoua la tête, atterré par les facéties de son père.

— Tu as pris un risque inconsidéré. Si Sartine s'en était rendu compte, je n'ose imaginer les conséquences… Tu sais qu'il ne nous apprécie guère et qu'avec lui nous sommes toujours sur le fil du rasoir…

— Peut-être mais bon je préfère que cette enquête progresse sans interférence extérieure. Ah oui, il reste du rôti de porc si tu en veux quelques tranches. Hélène et moi ne t'avons pas attendu pour lui faire honneur…

— Je n'ai pas faim.

— Bien, bien…

Le moine déplia soigneusement la feuille et l'approcha près du feu.

— Ma vue n'est plus ce qu'elle était mon fils, peux-tu me donner cette loupe sur la table à écrire ?

Volnay s'exécuta.

— Ah ! fit le moine d'un ton triomphant. Quelques adresses de livraison pour les cierges avec le nom des rues et des dates. J'aime les gens ordonnés !

Son fils s'approcha et lut par-dessus son épaule.

— Trois adresses seulement ces dernières semaines, observat-il. Le commerce n'est plus aussi lucratif qu'autrefois !

— Et le premier nom de rue qui apparaît est la rue des Canettes où réside notre astrologue ! Mon Dieu, le curé dansant livrait en cierges noirs le père de notre victime !

— La coïncidence est troublante mais ne sautons pas à des conclusions hâtives, tempéra Volnay. Des centaines et des centaines de personnes habitent dans cette rue.

— La seconde adresse mentionne un quartier de Versailles. Sartine n'aimerait pas cela ! Sans indication pourtant, autant chercher une aiguille dans une meule de foin. Mais quand même : Versailles !

Il approcha encore son œil de sa loupe.

— La troisième adresse est le Palais-Royal, sans autre mention ! Sans doute un lieu de rendez-vous…

Le commissaire aux morts étranges examina le papier puis le rendit à son père. Il croisa ensuite les bras sur sa poitrine et laissa son esprit s'échapper des lieux. Lorsqu'il parla, son ton était ferme et décidé.

— Demain matin, nous irons interroger sans ménagement l'astrologue. Nous prendrons avec nous des archers du guet pour fouiller toute sa maison. Depuis le début de cette affaire, je ressens la pénible sensation de passer à côté de quelque chose d'évident !

— Cela arrive souvent ! expliqua son père. Une part de ton esprit a découvert une partie de la solution mais ton esprit conscient ne veut pas en entendre parler pour des raisons diverses et variées. Ainsi luttent en nous *ce* qui croit savoir et *ce* qui sait.

L'expression du commissaire aux morts étranges resta indéchiffrable mais un léger mouvement d'épaules marquait son incrédulité face aux thèses osées de son père. Un instant le silence régna puis une bûche en se consumant s'écroula dans l'âtre, ce qui les fit tous les deux sursauter. Le moine se baissa pour tisonner le feu et rajouter du bois. En se relevant, il se saisit du poignet de son fils et baissa furtivement la voix.

— Je n'en ai rien dit à notre supérieur mais un nouveau mystère a surgi.

Il s'humecta nerveusement les lèvres avant de continuer.

— Lorsqu'on a descendu dans la première cave le cadavre du curé dansant, je suis allé dans la seconde cave chercher mes instruments. Or, c'est dans cette seconde cave que j'avais transporté le corps du gardien du cimetière pour le saler afin qu'il ne sente pas. Ma maladie m'a empêché d'accomplir cette corvée. Bref, je vais dans ma seconde cave et là, surprise, plus de cadavre!

Volnay sursauta.

— Hélène sait tout cela?

— Oui, je l'ai envoyée chez le commissaire de quartier déclarer le... euh... vol. Un cadavre cela ne passe pas forcément inaperçu.

Les mains dans le dos, le commissaire aux morts étranges se mit à marcher de long en large comme pour donner de l'ampleur à ses pensées.

— Pourquoi vole-t-on un cadavre? demanda-t-il.

Il s'apprêta à répondre lui-même à sa propre question.

— On le vole pour qu'on ne reconnaisse pas l'identité de la victime ou pour dissimuler la cause de sa mort. Or, toute personne sensée doit penser que ce cadavre dans la cave de l'assistant du commissaire aux morts étranges a été autopsié et identifié!

Le moine approuva.

— Bien entendu, on vole aussi des cadavres pour alimenter les médecins qui veulent progresser en matière d'anatomie. Ceux-là sont prêts à payer cher pour cela. Cependant, il y a des cimetières pour ça! Les déterreurs de cadavres n'oseraient pas s'introduire dans ma cave. Et d'ailleurs comment sauraient-ils que ce cadavre s'y trouve?

— Il y a bien les hommes qui sont venus chercher le cadavre de Sophia, remarqua Volnay. Ils ont pu remarquer l'autre corps mais ils n'auraient pas pu s'en emparer sous tes yeux.

Le moine baissa la tête.

— Tu ne les accompagnais pas? s'étonna son fils.

— Je n'avais pas le cœur de voir le corps de cette petite et puis tu sais bien que j'étais malade et alité. Ils se sont occupés de tout : nettoyage, habillage et mise en bière.

— Et tu les as laissés seuls dans ton laboratoire? Toi!

Son père haussa les épaules.

— Ils travaillent pour moi depuis deux ans. Ils connaissent mon laboratoire et se garderaient bien d'y toucher quoi que ce soit, me connaissant et me craignant!

— Étrange, fit le policier en plissant les yeux. Il doit pourtant exister une explication logique. Quelque chose auquel nous ne pensons pas!

— Peut-être n'a-t-on rien volé, murmura songeusement le moine. Tout cela pourrait être diablerie mais Sophia possédait un cœur pur. Il est possible après tout qu'elle soit devenue un ange et que son corps ait disparu.

Volnay lui jeta un regard soucieux mais se tut. Par habitude, il inspecta les lieux comme s'il s'agissait d'une scène de crime avant de secouer la tête.

— Une messe noire dans un cimetière est déjà inhabituelle en soi. Une enfant nue que l'on retrouve morte sur une dalle et qui hante les esprits des vivants, le gardien du cimetière que l'on assassine et dont le corps disparaît… tout cela sort décidément de l'ordinaire.

Le commissaire aux morts étranges réfléchit avant de reprendre :

— Le gardien du cimetière n'a pas vraiment été étranglé…

— Oui, répondit vivement le moine, comme je l'ai dit, on l'a privé d'air par compressions successives pour ne pas laisser de marques…

Le jeune homme fronça les sourcils.

— On n'a pas tué Sophia de cette façon. Les marques sur son cou étaient peu prononcées. Tu n'as d'ailleurs pas accompli toutes les recherches qu'il fallait en refusant de l'autopsier! On ne sait si elle est morte de froid ou de l'étranglement.

— Certes, fit le moine troublé. Certes…

— Et si l'assassin n'était pas le même? demanda Volnay.

Son père plissa les yeux, tentant de capter les pensées de son fils.

— Tu insinues que deux faits différents se sont produits cette nuit-là dans ce lieu?

— Peut-être. N'oublie pas que la messe noire a probablement été interrompue. Mais par qui? Qui donc peut bien se promener seul la nuit dans un cimetière?

— Mais le gardien de celui-ci, fit le moine.

Volnay s'impatienta.

— Si ce gardien n'a pas été tué par les célébrants de la messe noire, qui, en dehors de tous ces gens-là, peut rôder dans un cimetière pendant les heures sombres?

Le moine se frappa le front.

— Quelle bourrique je fais, moi qui suis si intelligent! Bien sûr! Les déterreurs de cadavres! Mais, de ce que nous avons appris d'eux, ils n'ont tué personne!

— C'est ce qu'ils ont raconté aux hommes de main de ton anatomiste, à moins que ceux-ci n'aient inventé cette histoire afin que je les laisse filer.

Son père demanda :

— Veux-tu retourner de nuit dans le cimetière où nous avons retrouvé Sophia?

— Sartine y a certainement posté des hommes à lui et, après ce qui s'est passé, je pense que l'endroit va être évité pendant quelques années!

Il hésita.

— Je suppose qu'Hélène va passer la nuit ici.

— Mon Dieu, si elle le souhaite…

— N'a-t-elle donc pas de logement? s'agaça Volnay.

Le moine écarta les bras en un geste de désespoir comique.

— Nous ne sommes pas intimes…

— Mais vous n'êtes pas loin de le devenir! Bonne nuit, père!

Volnay sortit. La neige tombait dans un silence magique. Dans l'impasse, il vit soudain Hélène s'avancer vers lui. Le vent semblait lutter avec les plis de sa longue robe, provoquant des frémissements de soie. Une certaine langueur paraissait affecter tous ses gestes. Elle sourit en le voyant.

— Hélène…

Elle s'arrêta, frémissante devant lui.

— Vous ne restez pas?

— Non. Mon père vous racontera les derniers événements de la journée. Il faut que je rentre chez moi pour réfléchir en paix. Il me semble que je ne vois pas les évidences!

Elle le regarda avec curiosité.

— Voilà qui ne vous ressemble pas!

Des flocons de neige s'accrochaient à ses magnifiques cheveux. D'un geste doux, Volnay les cueillit comme autant de fleurs.

— Vous êtes très attentionné, remarqua-t-elle.

— Vous êtes très belle.

Il la saisit à la taille et l'attira à lui. L'haleine d'Hélène vint se briser contre son visage, réveillant en lui des souvenirs oubliés. Sa bouche trouva la sienne. Elle se laissa faire mais ne lui rendit pas son baiser.

— Pardonnez-moi, chuchota-t-elle, mais c'est votre père que je préfère!

Le policier sursauta et recula d'un pas comme s'il venait d'être giflé.

Lorsque Hélène rentra, elle trouva le moine le front appuyé contre la fenêtre qui donnait sur l'impasse.

— Que faites-vous devant votre fenêtre?

— Je guette les âmes esseulées…

Volnay rentra chez lui à pas lents, accablé. Il raviva le feu et sortit son oiseau de la cage.

— Eh oui la pie, le croiras-tu? J'ai essayé d'embrasser Hélène! L'oiseau leva la tête.

— Et ce n'est pas par inclination pour elle, continua le policier. Je me méfie de cette espionne que Sartine m'a mise dans les pattes. Simplement, j'ai pensé que si elle était dans mes bras, elle cesserait ses familiarités avec mon père!

Il s'appliqua à lisser soigneusement le plumage de la pie.

— Eh bien mes craintes étaient fondées, elle en a bien après mon père. Et elle a eu le culot de me le dire!

La lueur des flammes se réfléchissait sur la tranche dorée des livres. Il la contempla un instant puis son attention se reporta sur l'oiseau.

— Toutefois, si cette femme est bien l'aventurière que je soupçonne, pourquoi m'avoir fait cet aveu? Je ne comprends pas.

— Comprends pas, répéta la pie.

XII

LE FEU ET AUTRES DIABLERIES

La lune n'était plus qu'une coulée d'argent sur les toits. Cornevin, le commissaire de quartier, se planta devant Volnay. Il s'était trop approché du feu. Son visage avait pris une teinte de pierre cuite et ses cheveux une couleur de cendre.

— La maison a commencé à brûler après minuit. Je me suis rendu sur les lieux puis j'ai songé à vous prévenir.

— Vous avez bien fait, répondit Volnay.

L'autre se tourna vers les ruines fumantes.

— Les gens ont jeté des boules de neige sur le feu en attendant qu'on tracte par cheval des pompes à bras sur le lieu de l'incendie !

— Comment le feu a-t-il pris ?

— Peut-on savoir ? Il y a bien des incendies dans Paris. Une cheminée mal ramonée, le vent qui attise, les structures en bois de l'immeuble… La neige a empêché que le feu ne se communique aux autres maisons alentour.

Leur attention fut attirée par une carriole qui arrivait au pas prudent d'un cheval au poil gris, creusant de grandes balafres sur le sol enneigé.

— Oh, fit le commissaire de quartier. Il est déjà là…

— Oui, je l'ai prévenu avant de venir, dit Volnay.

Il se souvenait du baiser refusé par Hélène et de son aveu envers son père. Ses traits se durcirent. Le moine descendit tranquillement de sa voiture et avança vers eux en récitant :

— *"Hier, durant la nuit obscure*
Un grand feu s'éprit d'aventure

Mais avec soin et diligence
On amortit sa véhémence!"

— Tu m'en diras tant! fit son fils.

Ils contemplèrent en silence les ruines calcinées. Une douce chaleur s'en échappait.

— Il va me falloir un peu d'aide, dit enfin le moine. Je dois récupérer les corps dans la maison, si corps il y a.

— Pourquoi? s'étonna le commissaire de quartier.

Volnay et son père échangèrent un regard complice.

— Pour identifier les victimes, répondit le commissaire aux morts étranges, et connaître la cause de leur mort.

Le commissaire de quartier les regarda avec effarement.

— Mais s'il y a quelqu'un, il est mort brûlé, voyons!

Le moine eut un petit rire condescendant.

— Ah, si toute chose pouvait être aussi simple!

Et sans un mot de plus, il se dirigea vers les restes de la maison.

— Donnez-lui des hommes, fit le commissaire aux morts étranges, et allons un peu interroger le voisinage pour savoir s'ils ont vu quelque chose.

— Mais pourquoi?

Volnay le considéra d'un œil sévère.

— Mais pour faire notre métier!

À l'aube, Hélène entra dans le bureau de Sartine au Châtelet. Celui-ci se tenait frileusement devant le feu qui éclairait son visage de reflets incendiaires sous sa perruque poudrée et frisée. La jeune femme ôta nonchalamment son manteau de fourrure pour le confier à un domestique. Elle soignait ses apparitions chez le lieutenant général de police, s'étant vêtue pour l'occasion d'une belle robe de velours rouge. La pièce d'estomac triangulaire était décorée d'une échelle de rubans. La coupe et le tissu soulignaient la rondeur des seins moulés dans le corset. Des engageantes de la plus belle dentelle ornaient les poignets de sa robe toute couverte de rubans et de fleurs artificielles.

Une lueur intéressée brilla un instant dans l'œil de Sartine avant qu'il ne retrouve sa froideur habituelle.

— Aucun d'eux ne vous suspecte? demanda-t-il abruptement.

— Le moine est on ne peut plus charmant mais Volnay se méfie de moi.

— Cela ne me surprend guère, rien n'a prise sur mon commissaire aux morts étranges.

Il dit cela avec un mélange de dépit et de fierté.

— Pour le moine, reprit-il avec une grimace, c'est un savant cabotin, toujours prêt à faire la roue comme un paon devant les jolies femmes. Mais ne le sous-estimez pas, son intelligence est remarquable. En revanche, et c'est sa faiblesse, son orgueil en ses capacités est incommensurable. Flattez-le toujours et il vous adorera.

— Je sais comment le manier, ne vous inquiétez pas!

Sartine hocha la tête, satisfait, puis son regard s'assombrit.

— Notre cheval de Troie est dans la place, tout cela est fort bien mais la prostituée et le curé dansant sont morts, le père de Sophia a sans doute brûlé dans sa maison… Que reste-t-il comme piste?

— Un homme au comportement suspect pendant l'enterrement de Sophia…

— Oui, grogna Sartine, encore un que Volnay a laissé filer entre ses pattes. Il épuise une demi-douzaine de mes mouches à le chercher dans le quartier où il l'a perdu! Je me demande s'il ne serait pas plus sensé de jeter mon filet dans la ruelle de l'Or ou dans quelques endroits de ce genre et de mettre à la question tous ces nécromanciens, alchimistes, jeteurs de sorts ou marchands de philtres! Tant pis pour les honnêtes marchands, il se trouvera bien un ou deux coupables dans le lot!

— Le résultat n'est pas certain mais vous pourrez être sûr que tout Paris en parlera. Gardez vos enquêteurs. Ne vendez pas votre cheval pour acheter de l'avoine!

Le lieutenant général de police la considéra un instant en silence.

— Ce n'est pas mon intention, vous l'avez deviné. Hélène, vous n'êtes plus une enfant et vous connaissez les rouages du pouvoir. Le procureur Siltieri m'a été imposé. Il est proche de l'Église mais loin de Dieu! C'est un homme du parti des dévots. Ce parti est soutenu par le Dauphin, fils du roi, et en lutte contre celui de la marquise de Pompadour, proche des encyclopédistes. Pour se conforter auprès du roi, les dévots ne rêvent que de l'effrayer avec un scandale sans précédent qui soit le fait d'hérétiques.

Sartine se tut. La personnalité tourmentée et morbide du roi l'effrayait secrètement. Persuadé d'être monarque de droit divin et ayant ancrée en lui une peur terrible de la mort et de la justice divine, il n'en était pas moins incapable de résister à ses pulsions et ses vices. Seule sa jouissance du moment l'inté-ressait. Une fois celle-ci passée, il devenait à nouveau un pan-tin sans âme aux mains de l'Église. Isolée et occupée à contrer les dévots avec le clan philosophique, la favorite, la marquise de Pompadour, s'éteignait doucement, rongée par la fatigue et la maladie.

— Ma situation est extrêmement compliquée, reprit le policier d'une voix tendue qui lui était inhabituelle. Je me vois dans la double obligation d'étouffer cette affaire et de la résoudre! Le procureur Siltieri n'a, quant à lui, pour seul objectif que de faire le plus de bruit possible et d'envoyer à la potence quiconque sera pris la main dans le sac, coupable ou innocent!

Il s'assit sur le bord de son bureau et soupira.

— J'ai besoin d'une arrestation et Volnay ne me ramène que des corps!

— Il est parti de rien et il a déjà relevé plusieurs pistes, objecta Hélène.

Sartine darda sur elle un regard impérieux.

— N'allez pas succomber à son charme, ce n'est pas ce que je vous demande. Volnay a une conception de la justice bien particulière et le sens de la hiérarchie lui fait cruellement défaut. Vous êtes avec lui et le moine pour me rapporter tout ce qu'ils me dissimulent. Tenez, l'histoire de ce chien... Pour-quoi me cacher cela?

— Ils craignaient peut-être que vous ne le soumettiez à la question!

Devant l'impertinence de sa visiteuse, un rare sourire illumina le visage de Sartine avant de disparaître aussi vite, laissant même douter de son apparition.

— Des résultats, vous m'entendez? Je veux des résultats et ceci par tous les moyens! C'est peut-être le sort politique de la France qui se joue derrière tout cela!

Il alla s'asseoir à son bureau qu'il se mit à tambouriner avec ses doigts. Son œil avait pris une teinte vitreuse.

— Cette affaire est propre comme une écuelle de chats, murmura-t-il. Et dire qu'il faut que cela tombe justement sur Sophia!

La jeune femme le considéra attentivement.

— Savez-vous sur sa naissance quelque chose que j'ignore?

Sartine la fixa sans mot dire. Son regard était dur et impitoyable.

— Ai-je dit quelque chose de tel? Tenez-vous-en aux faits, répondit-il, et non à des hypothèses!

Le moine avait allumé les chandelles dans la cave et frottait ses mains pour les réchauffer. Devant lui, une masse informe noirâtre gisait sur une table.

— Alors? demanda le commissaire aux morts étranges.

— Deux corps. Une femme et un homme. Ils sont complètement calcinés mais le corps féminin pourrait bien être celui de la servante, quant au corps masculin il a la même taille que notre astrologue. Et puis regarde sa main. J'ai remarqué cette énorme bague avec un rubis lors de notre première visite. Il la porte. C'est bien lui car c'est elle!

Volnay fronça les sourcils et contempla fixement le cadavre de l'astronome.

— Que se passe-t-il?

Le commissaire aux morts étranges haussa les épaules.

— Je ne sais pas. J'éprouve une étrange impression mais je ne saurais dire quoi. Cette pierre…

— Elle est de grande valeur assurément. Chaque pierre a ses particularités. On dit que le rubis donne de la persévérance aux indécis…

Le commissaire aux morts étranges fit quelques pas dans la cave, caressant du bout du doigt un alambic, rangeant sans s'en rendre compte ce qu'il jugeait en désordre sur la table.

— Arrête de toucher à mes affaires, dit le moine, tu sais bien que j'ai horreur de ça!

— Toi et tes manies de rangement! grogna son fils.

Il se tourna vers son père, perdu dans ses réflexions.

— Tout se complique, dit-il. Une enfant tuée, le gardien du cimetière étranglé, la prostituée qui se rompt le cou et notre curé dansant qui gigote au bout d'une corde, récapitula-t-il comme si cela était une comptine. Ajoutons deux cadavres brûlés... l'astrologue et sa servante...

— Je n'ai trouvé aucune trace de meurtre sur ces cadavres, dit son père. Enfin, vu l'état...

Il désigna d'un geste dégoûté les restes calcinés.

— J'ai l'habitude qu'ils soient moins... abîmés!

Devant la porte de l'église Saint-Sulpice, un tremblement saisit tout entier le corps d'Hélène. Elle se figea et le laissa passer, fermant les yeux pour calmer les battements désordonnés de son cœur. Une douce plainte la saisit pourtant lorsqu'elle pénétra dans les lieux sacrés. Ceux-ci ne lui étaient ni agréables, ni familiers. Elle n'appréciait pas plus le Christ qui se tortillait sur la croix que les saints des vitraux, agonisant dans d'atroces souffrances.

Ses pas résonnèrent lugubrement sur les dalles froides. À la lueur tremblotante des cierges qui se consumaient, elle se dirigea vers un coin de l'église où étaient placés en vis-à-vis des chaises et des bancs. Au milieu, sur un siège surélevé, trônait le curé qui faisait répéter le catéchisme à des enfants.

Hélène attendit patiemment qu'il termine. De plus en plus intrigué par sa présence, discrète mais attentive, le curé lui jetait des regards curieux. Lorsqu'il la vit se saisir d'une bourse qui semblait remplie de bonne monnaie sonnante et trébuchante, il termina rapidement et renvoya d'un geste les enfants qui l'écoutaient, l'air grave et recueilli. La mine onctueuse, le curé s'approcha d'elle. Il avait atteint cet âge intermédiaire où, faute d'exercice et d'hygiène de vie maîtrisée, les muscles laissent place à l'embonpoint avant de se transformer définitivement en graisse. L'homme était pourtant sagace et avisé. Hélène savait qu'il avait fait établir dans sa paroisse une fabrique de mousseline.

— Madame, je suis le curé de la paroisse, puis-je quelque chose pour vous?

La visiteuse arbora son plus beau sourire, s'efforçant de ne pas le fixer de face car il avait des yeux rapprochés et elle ne savait trop comment porter son regard.

— Vous le pouvez. Puis-je vous entretenir en particulier?

D'un geste, il l'invita à le suivre jusqu'à la sacristie. Là, elle lui montra la lettre de recommandation de Sartine, ce qui l'impressionna fort.

— Je vous remercie, mon père, de me recevoir à l'impromptu, dit-elle en rangeant la lettre.

— Dieu, madame, vous avez des titres de recommandation qui obligent... Pensez donc! M. le lieutenant général de police en personne! Il a beaucoup œuvré dans notre bonne ville pour son approvisionnement et le commerce des grains. Je ne parle même pas de la sécurité publique. Que puis-je pour votre service?

Hélène dissimulait derrière un masque aimable d'étranges pensées. La remarque anodine de Sartine l'avait alertée.

Et dire qu'il faut que cela tombe justement sur Sophia!

L'agressivité du lieutenant général de police lorsqu'elle l'avait questionné sur la naissance de Sophia la confirmait dans son soupçon. On lui cachait quelque chose!

— Je souhaite quelques renseignements sur la famille Marly, fit-elle d'un ton neutre. Vous savez, l'astrologue de la rue des Canettes...

— M. Marly, je vois, oui. On parle un peu de lui dans le quartier...

Le curé eut un reniflement dédaigneux.

— Faire commerce des étoiles pour prédire l'avenir! Vous pensez bien que je ne vois pas un tel homme à la messe!

— Est-il homme de mauvaise vie?

L'autre haussa un sourcil.

— Pas à ma connaissance, il se tient à l'écart autant des récréations mondaines que de la messe! Mais l'astrologie...

Il se signa.

— Voilà bien diablerie que de prétendre connaître le sort des mortels en contemplant les étoiles. Ceci est blasphème! Notre sort est entre les seules mains de Dieu.

Sa bouche marqua un pli sarcastique.

— Mais hélas, nous vivons dans un siècle de superstition, il est encore des parents qui m'apportent leur enfant à baptiser avec un morceau de pain noir autour du cou pour éloigner le mauvais sort!

— C'est surtout à la fille de l'astrologue que je m'intéresse, précisa Hélène.

Elle prit un air enjôleur.

— Je sais combien les archives des paroisses sont admirablement tenues. M. Marly a toujours vécu dans le quartier et je connais la date de naissance de sa fille. Je voudrais vérifier qu'elle a bien été déclarée à votre paroisse à sa naissance ou à son baptême.

— Je ne peux rien vous refuser! dit onctueusement l'ecclésiastique. Quelle est cette date de naissance?

— Le 12 janvier 1747.

— Je vais vous chercher cela dans nos archives des registres paroissiaux.

— Je suis certaine que tout y est consigné.

Un sourire suffisant éclaira le visage du curé.

— Madame, avec les registres des commissariats de police, les archives paroissiales sont ce qu'il y a de mieux tenu en France. Vous verrez que dans trois siècles, on y lira encore toute l'histoire de France!

Le curé revint une vingtaine de minutes plus tard avec un ouvrage relié de cuir noir.

— Pardonnez-moi. Le recueil était parfaitement bien archivé mais difficile d'accès!

D'un revers de la manche, il fit voler la poussière.

— Hum, l'année 1747... Janvier, m'avez-vous dit. Elle n'avait donc pas douze ans lorsqu'elle est morte cette pauvre enfant!

— Comment savez-vous cela?

L'ecclésiastique lui jeta un regard surpris.

— Ignorez-vous que tout se sait dans un quartier?

Il mouilla son index et son pouce avant de tourner les pages.

— Janvier… voilà…

Il lut, avança encore, fronçant les sourcils.

— Non, elle n'y figure pas. Je vais regarder par sécurité le mois de février.

Hélène attendit patiemment, voyant la déception se peindre progressivement sur le visage de son interlocuteur.

— Non décidément mais peut-être a-t-elle été déclarée à une autre paroisse? J'étais là à cette époque mais je n'ai pas souvenir d'elle.

Il se gratta pensivement la joue.

— À l'époque, ce Marly n'était pas astrologue. Étonnamment, il était maître joaillier.

Hélène fronça délicatement les sourcils. Elle se souvenait de l'énorme et inhabituel rubis monté sur bague au doigt de l'astrologue.

— Maître joaillier? répéta-t-elle pour marquer son intérêt et l'inciter à continuer.

— Oui, il épousa une femme qui était la domestique d'une personne de qualité à la cour. Je crois que c'est à la mort de son épouse, deux ans après la venue au monde de leur fille, qu'il vendit son commerce pour se consacrer aux étoiles. Le chagrin probablement et sans doute un brin de folie…

— La petite a donc perdu sa mère très jeune.

— Certes.

— Et elle n'a pas été déclarée et baptisée à votre paroisse?

— Non.

Hélène se pencha légèrement en avant et le regard du curé effleura sa poitrine avant de se réfugier dans ses yeux.

— Dites-moi mon père, savez-vous de quelle personne de qualité la mère de Sophia était la domestique?

Son interlocuteur s'agita nerveusement.

— Dieu tout-puissant! Pensez-vous donc que l'on sache dans les quartiers de Paris ce qui se passe à la cour de Versailles?

La jeune femme haussa négligemment les épaules.

— Ma foi, oui!

Elle posa une bourse sur la table. Les écus tintèrent dans un bruit métallique qui fit sursauter le curé.

— J'aimerais faire un don aux pauvres de votre paroisse.

Mais elle garda ses doigts serrés autour de la bourse. Le curé se racla la gorge, embarrassé.

— Madame, vous me mettez dans une situation délicate…

— Dieu a confiance dans votre jugement!

L'homme se tortilla les mains. Malgré le froid de la pièce, une goutte de sueur coula le long de sa tempe. Hélène contempla le sillon humide qu'elle avait laissé. C'était celui de la peur.

— Tout ceci restera entre nous?

— Je vous le jure sur le Christ, répondit-elle d'une voix égale.

— Ce n'étaient d'ailleurs que des rumeurs…

— Bien entendu.

Il baissa encore la voix et, lorsqu'il parla, celle-ci était devenue presque inaudible.

— C'était une danseuse de l'Opéra, à l'époque tout Paris était à ses pieds. On la surnommait Mlle Belle Ange.

Ils étaient remontés de la cave. Tandis que son fils bourrait la cheminée de grosses bûches, son père dépliait avec précaution une couverture qui recélait ses découvertes de la nuit.

— En fouillant dans les décombres avec le commissaire de quartier, j'ai trouvé ce livre. Il se trouvait dans une niche de pierre, ce qui l'a protégé. Seule la couverture a souffert.

Les yeux du moine brillaient de plaisir en effleurant les pages du bout des doigts.

— Ce livre n'a pas brûlé. Une chance car il propose quelques recettes pour enflammer les sens de sa belle!

Il commença à le feuilleter avec un plaisir évident.

— Cette recette-là est un peu compliquée puisqu'elle nécessite de réchauffer des excréments de crocodile et d'antilope, de la bile de bouc sauvage et je t'en passe. J'aurais un peu de mal à trouver tout cela! Celle-ci me semble plus abordable mais elle nécessite quand même les cheveux d'un mort, des grains d'orge enterrés dans son tombeau, du sang de tique d'un chien noir… Non vraiment… Ah, voilà pour retrouver vigueur : "Frictionne ton membre d'écume de la bouche d'un étalon…"

Il releva la tête pour se retrouver sous l'œil inquisiteur de son fils.

— Naturellement, je n'ai pas besoin de tout ça, s'empressa-t-il d'ajouter. Je suis resté jeune et très vigoureux…

— J'espère que ce n'est pas Hélène qui te met ainsi en émoi, remarqua froidement Volnay.

Le moine cilla brièvement.

— Au cours de nos investigations dans les ruines, poursuivit-il rapidement, le commissaire de quartier a également découvert un second livre. Celui-ci était dans un coffret de fer, sans doute scellé dans un mur. Pour le dissimuler ainsi, il devait posséder une certaine valeur.

— Qu'est-ce que ceci ? demanda son fils en pointant un doigt inquisitorial sur la couverture du livre.

— Des sceaux démoniaques : Lucifer, empereur, Belzébuth, prince, et Astaroth, grand-duc des Enfers… Et ce cavalier portant lance et sceptre se nomme Abigor. Il commande soixante légions de démons et est très prisé des chefs de guerre pour sa science militaire. Et voici Baël, chef de guerre aux trois têtes de chat, d'homme et de crapaud. Ici Ayperos, le lion à la tête et aux pattes d'oie avec une queue de lièvre et enfin là, épervier au poing, Balan, roi des Enfers qui connaît tout du passé comme de l'avenir…

— Tes connaissances de l'occulte me stupéfieront toujours, fit son fils d'un ton aigre-doux.

Gêné, le moine haussa négligemment les épaules.

— Tu sais, je m'intéresse à tout et à n'importe quoi !

Volnay lui jeta un regard impavide.

— Ainsi, notre astrologue s'intéresse aux forces de l'Enfer. Serait-ce lui l'instigateur de la messe noire dans laquelle a péri sa fille ?

— Pas forcément ! s'écria le moine. On peut aussi s'intéresser à Satan par curiosité intellectuelle ou encore pour mieux le combattre…

— Et la servante ? Non, je l'ai vue se signer lorsqu'elle a bâillé à notre arrivée. Or, l'on se signe pour empêcher que le diable entre par votre bouche et s'empare de votre âme. Mais l'astrologue… Il achetait peut-être des cierges noirs à un homme qui a participé au meurtre de sa fille et lisait des livres à la gloire des démons… À propos, que dit donc ce livre?

— Il est en latin. Je le maîtrise bien mais c'est un ouvrage ésotérique et compliqué. J'aurai besoin de temps pour le lire et le comprendre. Tant mieux car, pour achever de me remettre, il me faut rester au chaud et boire des tisanes!

— Avec une jeune et jolie garde-malade! compléta sans rire son fils.

La neige tombait en petits cristaux blancs et froids. Giflée par la bise, Hélène tenait sa tête rentrée dans les épaules. Elle ne releva la tête qu'avant de passer l'angle de la rue Saint-Jacques. Des passants la bousculèrent sans un mot d'excuse car elle s'était immobilisée sans avertissement. Le sentiment d'une présence derrière elle la tenaillait. La jeune femme résista à la tentation de se retourner comme elle l'avait déjà fait à plusieurs reprises sans résultat. La foule se pressait, anonyme, grelottante. Tous les visages se ressemblaient, beaucoup exprimant la même difficulté de vivre. Un instant, elle hésita. Ce n'était pas une personne qui la suivait, plutôt une ombre… quelque chose de fluide qui se faufilait à travers la masse compacte des gens dans la rue.

Hélène s'engagea rue de la Lanterne, retrouvant le calme et le silence ouaté procurés par la neige. Là, elle s'arrêta. Un regard pesait lourdement sur ses épaules. Lentement Hélène se retourna. Son cœur rata un battement. Une lueur laiteuse baignait maintenant la rue, estompant les formes d'une irréelle silhouette frêle. C'était Sophia! Elle avait un petit air perdu dans ses vêtements trop amples et ses grands yeux tristes la fixaient, semblant lire au-dedans d'elle. Un instant le soleil perça les nuages et Hélène ferma les yeux, éblouie par la réverbération sur la neige. Lorsqu'elle les rouvrit, Sophia avait disparu.

Hélène rentra sans frapper. Volnay lui jeta un regard mécontent et allait se livrer à quelques réflexions mais il s'arrêta à la vue de son visage couleur de cendres.

— Qu'avez-vous? On dirait que vous venez de croiser un fantôme!

La jeune femme s'adossa à la porte, la poitrine frémissante.

— J'ai vu Sophia!

Le moine se précipita vers elle.

— Ah vous aussi!

Il se tourna vers son fils.

— Avec moi et la servante de l'auberge, cela fait trois maintenant? Persisteras-tu à me prendre pour un fou?

— Un instant, fit Volnay en saisissant le bras d'Hélène. Où l'avez-vous aperçue?

— Dans la rue, à deux pas de là.

Le policier se précipita dehors. Le moine soupira.

— La réaction de mon fils est parfaitement logique et rationnelle mais je sais qu'elle ne le mènera nulle part. On ne voit Sophia que lorsqu'elle le veut bien!

Une dizaine de minutes plus tard, le retour de Volnay lui donna raison.

— Personne en vue, fit-il. Vous avez rêvé!

Hélène jeta un regard entendu au moine. Elle avait appris à connaître les mécanismes intellectuels du commissaire aux morts étranges basés sur l'observation, la réflexion, l'analyse puis la synthèse. Il n'y avait pas place pour tout ce qui relevait du domaine de l'irréel. Pour lui, un fait irrationnel signifiait simplement que l'explication était plus difficile à trouver!

— Vous avez été longtemps absente, remarqua le policier. Où étiez-vous donc?

— Chez moi, j'avais besoin d'un bon bain!

Volnay renifla l'air comme s'il voulait vérifier et marqua son scepticisme d'un haussement de sourcils.

— Et où résidez-vous?

Une lueur de moquerie traversa le regard d'Hélène.

— Seriez-vous en train de mener un interrogatoire, commissaire? Dans notre cas, mon adresse ne vous regarde en aucune manière à moins que vous n'ayez en tête l'espoir de me rendre quelque visite…

Gêné, Volnay détourna la tête.

— Pas le moins du monde!

Le souvenir du baiser volé à Hélène le tourmentait tout autant que l'attitude de la jeune femme.

— Allons, fit le moine d'un ton conciliant, arrêtez de vous chamailler tous les deux!

On frappa à la porte. Un coup timide d'abord puis renouvelé avec un peu plus d'assurance.

— J'espère que ce n'est pas encore Sartine! se plaignit le moine.

Hélène arbora un sourire figé.

— Pour le savoir, le mieux est d'aller ouvrir! dit sèchement le commissaire aux morts étranges.

Un étrange individu fit son apparition sur le seuil de la maison. Il avait un visage rond et hilare, une bouche pleine de dents gâtées et une haleine à faire tomber par terre. D'un geste ample il salua Volnay et le moine puis se courba presque à terre devant Hélène en l'appelant *Votre Gracieuseté*.

— Ah, voilà une de mes mouches, constata le commissaire aux morts étranges. Venez donc Gaston vous réchauffer devant le feu avant de me conter ce qui vous amène.

L'autre ne se fit pas prier et, après avoir quitté ses gants, promena avec ravissement ses mains au-dessus des flammes.

— Oh, que faites-vous là? demanda-t-il en baissant la tête.

— Des œufs à la braise, répondit le moine. Je vous en donnerai un si vous nous avez rapporté de bonnes nouvelles!

— Avec plaisir, monsieur le moine!

Il sembla alors découvrir la présence de l'animal près du feu.

— Oh, vous avez un chien maintenant! Quelle belle bête!

Il se tourna vers Volnay.

— Je suis d'abord passé chez vous mais ne vous y trouvant point, j'ai couru jusqu'ici. J'ai de la chance que vous ne soyez pas au Châtelet!

— Qu'avez-vous à me dire? demanda le commissaire aux morts étranges en lui servant un petit verre d'eau-de-vie pour se réchauffer.

La mouche vida celui-ci d'une traite, s'essuya la bouche d'un revers de main et remercia aimablement.

— J'ai retrouvé la trace de votre homme, celui avec l'épée au côté. Grand, blond, les cheveux filasse, les épaules carrées, l'air brutal et le visage mangé par la petite vérole… Il se peut qu'il en existe d'autres mais celui-ci répond point par point à votre description.

— Avez-vous trouvé où il habite?

— Ah commissaire, hélas non. J'ai repéré l'homme dans une taverne mais ensuite il est reparti à cheval. J'ai eu beau courir, je l'ai vite perdu!

Le moine soupira.

— Je suis ensuite revenu interroger les gens à la taverne, reprit vivement la mouche. J'ai dû payer quelques tournées pour cela. D'ailleurs, monsieur le chevalier, si vous pouviez faire quelque chose pour mes frais… J'attends toujours des mois avant que l'on me rembourse!

Volnay hocha la tête et sortit sa bourse.

— Voici de la part de M. de Sartine.

— Oh, commissaire, vous êtes généreux. Grand merci!

Il empocha les pièces et reprit son récit.

— J'ai donc appris dans cette taverne que l'homme est un habitué. Il vient boire seul ou, parfois, avec quelque prostituée du quartier. Je me suis donc permis de poster une mouche dans cette taverne jour et nuit. D'ailleurs, si je pouvais avoir une petite avance car là-bas nous sommes obligés de consommer…

— Ce que je vous ai donné ne vous suffit pas?

— Diable, commissaire, pour moi si mais je ne suis pas seul! Nous allons nous relayer à quatre pour ne pas manquer votre homme!

De nouveau, la main de Volnay plongea dans sa bourse.

— Ne buvez pas trop, conseilla-t-il, mes petites mouches doivent garder tous leurs sens en éveil.

— Vos mouches, commissaire, ont leurs yeux et leurs oreilles bien ouverts et rien ne peut leur échapper! s'exclama Gaston.

Il fit mine d'ouvrir ses ailes et de s'envoler.

— Avant de partir, puis-je avoir un de ces œufs à la braise? demanda-t-il plein d'espoir.

XIII

ABBAYE ET AUTRES DIABLERIES

Une fois Gaston parti, ils se partagèrent avec plaisir les derniers œufs à la braise, se brûlant les doigts et les lèvres.

— La mouche s'est envolée mais nous avons encore beaucoup à faire, dit le moine en débouchant une bouteille. Vous allez me goûter celui-ci, c'est du vin de Bordeaux, il vient de mes amis libraires les Madison, à Livourne, des gens plein d'esprit. Que faites-vous cette après-midi, ma chère ?

— Je vais poursuivre mon enquête.

— Très bien, fit le moine d'un ton un peu pincé, nous poursuivrons la nôtre également. Décidément, vous nous délaissez ces temps-ci. Je vais bouder !

En réponse à son caprice, elle lui adressa un sourire charmant.

— Mais pour le moment, rebondit-il gaiement, j'ai à vous soumettre une amusante petite énigme. Vous souvenez-vous qu'hier soir je vous ai raconté nos découvertes dans les poches du curé dansant ?

Il but une lampée de vin et claqua la langue d'un air appréciateur.

— Par acquit de conscience, j'ai depuis fouillé la doublure de la veste du curé dansant, j'y ai trouvé un second papier, soigneusement dissimulé. Deux adresses y figurent : le quai de la Mégisserie, sans plus d'indication, et la seconde certainement un lieu connu de notre curé dansant mais pas de moi ! Voyez par vous-même : *la couche ou la louche de lensser…*

— Jamais entendu parler de ce lieu ! Montrez-moi donc ce papier.

Le moine alla le lui chercher tandis qu'elle portait son verre à ses lèvres. Elle but encore une gorgée en examinant le papier, ses jolis sourcils délicatement froncés.

— Je ne lis pas la même chose que vous, murmura-t-elle enfin. Les lettres sont mal tracées et je ne suis pas certaine que notre curé dansant maîtrise parfaitement l'écriture. Je lirais plutôt *la bouche de l'enfer*!

Le moine jaillit brusquement de son siège.

— La bouche de l'enfer! Mais oui! C'est ainsi qu'on surnomme une abbaye abandonnée à quelques lieues de Paris. Le père abbé était tellement intraitable qu'on raconte que des moines se jetèrent dans le puits par désespoir et revinrent ensuite hanter les vivants. Persécuté par les revenants, le père abbé se pendit. Les derniers moines s'empressèrent de déguerpir et plus personne n'osa reprendre possession des lieux car on entendait la nuit des cris et des gémissements. On imagina bien vite que les diables avaient pris possession de cet endroit et même les bergers des environs n'osèrent plus s'en approcher.

Il jeta à Hélène un regard complice.

— Les diables vous font-ils peur, ma chère?

— Pas le moins du monde, répondit-elle, puisqu'il en existe un dans chaque homme!

Pour gagner l'endroit, ils avaient décidé de prendre la carriole du moine. Au pas prudent mais sûr de leur cheval, ils quittèrent Paris et gagnèrent les hauteurs du Petit-Montrouge. Ils prirent ensuite, en direction de la Beauce, une route environnée de moulins à vent à la toiture en charpente couverte de bardeaux. Enchanté, le moine se fit lyrique et déclama :

— "En ce moment, ils découvrirent trente ou quarante moulins à vent et don Quichotte dit à son écuyer : La fortune conduit nos affaires mieux que ne pourrait y réussir notre désir même. Regarde ami Sancho ; voilà devant nous au moins trente démesurés géants auxquels je vais livrer bataille et ôter la vie à tous tant qu'ils sont. Avec leurs dépouilles, nous commencerons à nous enrichir car c'est prise de bonne guerre et c'est grandement servir Dieu que de faire disparaître si mauvaise engeance de la face de la terre!"

Hélène rit et se blottit près de lui pour échapper à la morsure du froid. Instinctivement, le bras du moine lui enserra les épaules. À une intersection, ils empruntèrent une voie sinueuse dont l'état se dégrada au fur et à mesure de leur avancée. Envahi de broussailles, le chemin qui menait à l'abbaye baignait dans la boue et la neige. Les ronces griffèrent les roues de la voiture et égratignèrent le flanc de leur cheval. Plus loin, couvertes d'une croûte de neige, les branches des arbres formaient une voûte immaculée sous laquelle ils s'engouffrèrent.

Au détour du chemin, ils découvrirent le sommet d'un colombier puis les ruines grises de l'abbaye, dévorées par les mauvaises herbes et recouvertes d'une nappe de lierre. Des fleurs de givre décoraient le bord du toit de l'église surmontée d'un modeste clocheton. Le moine se souleva de son siège pour examiner les environs.

— Eh bien, mon fils, toi non plus tu n'as pas peur des diables?

Volnay haussa les épaules.

— Pas plus que des hommes!

Le moine rit puis fit silence lorsqu'ils franchirent le portail de l'abbaye.

— As-tu remarqué qu'il y a des carrières à côté? demanda le policier à son père. Par temps de grand vent, cela doit faire un bruit impressionnant. De là viennent peut-être les bruits et gémissements que les gens croient entendre.

Le moine se tourna vers Hélène, un large sourire à la bouche.

— Vous voyez, c'est tout mon fils, il a une explication rationnelle à tout!

Volnay sauta à terre et tira son pistolet.

— Soyons prudents, nous pourrions tomber sur un repaire de brigands ou de contrebandiers.

Il lança un regard ironique à son père.

— Cela aussi peut être une explication à la réputation des lieux. Un endroit hanté est un endroit sûr pour qui se cache de l'ordre royal!

Le moine haussa les épaules et descendit à son tour. Il tendit ensuite les bras pour aider Hélène, recevant sans frémir son corps frais contre le sien et le conservant près de lui un instant de trop, les cheveux de la jeune femme au vent lui fouettant le visage.

— Où donc sont vos diables? lui demanda-t-elle gaiement.

— Ils sont probablement allés traire les vaches!

L'abbaye était disposée en trois épis bas et trapus qui s'appuyaient comme un gros animal engourdi contre le flanc sud de l'église. Rongés par la mousse, les vantaux de la porte de l'église tenaient encore bon et leur livrèrent passage dans un geignement criard. Les pas des trois visiteurs résonnèrent lugubrement dans l'austère église au transept flanqué de part et d'autre d'une chapelle. Les vitraux ornant la façade éclairaient faiblement les lieux déserts. La nef voûtée comptait huit travées dont les voûtes reposaient sur des colonnes en faisceaux. Au plafond, des oiseaux avaient fait leurs nids, jonchant le sol de leurs immondices. Ils remontèrent jusqu'au maître-autel surélevé, impressionnés malgré eux par la solitude imposante des lieux.

Deux portes s'ouvraient sur le cloître dont l'une dans le haut de la nef. Ils s'avancèrent en silence, frappés par la froide beauté de la pierre dans la perspective enneigée. Entre les contreforts, deux arcs reposaient gracieusement sur des colonnettes sculptées. Dans une niche creusée, l'abbé des lieux devait pouvoir donner ses lectures publiques avant l'office de complies. La salle du chapitre ne leur révéla rien, aussi se dirigèrent-ils vers le réfectoire, le moine n'oubliant pas de donner la main à Hélène. Le battant de la porte pivota sans bruit comme s'il était bien huilé. Ils clignèrent des yeux, cherchant à accommoder leur vision à la semi-obscurité qui régnait. Le moine se saisit de son briquet et alluma la torche dont il s'était muni.

Ils firent quelques pas. Lorsque la porte se referma derrière eux, la flamme de la torche vacilla et le moine s'immobilisa. Un souffle contraire venait face à eux, du passe-plat creusé dans le mur attenant à la cuisine, et la fumée de la torche leur piquait les yeux, irritant leur gorge. Le moine leva haut sa torche, éclairant la charpente en châtaignier qui surplombait le réfectoire. C'est alors qu'ils aperçurent les peintures.

— Comment a-t-on pu faire des restes d'une abbaye un lieu aussi sacrilège? murmura Volnay choqué.

— En matière de magie noire, rétorqua le moine, on utilise beaucoup de rituels chrétiens en les détournant de leur sens initial. Ici, c'est un lieu sacré que l'on détourne de son objet.

Il brandit sa torche devant lui.

— Pour savoir contre qui vous vous battez, il vous faut connaître votre adversaire car, comme vous le savez, Satan se nomme aussi l'Adversaire.

Satisfait de son jeu de mots, le moine fit une petite pause comme s'il s'attendait à des applaudissements. Déçu, il reprit :

— Comme Zeus contre les Titans, le grand Rê en Égypte contre les dragons et tant d'autres divinités, Dieu aussi dut combattre les siens en révolte. C'étaient des anges rongés d'orgueil ayant à leur tête Satan. Il les combattit avec ses anges restés fidèles et les précipita dans les profondeurs de la fosse, la géhenne.

"Te voilà tombé du ciel
Astre brillant, fils de l'aurore!"

Un long silence régna. Ils contemplaient tous comme hypnotisés les peintures démentes.

— Ce n'est pas tout, fit doucement le moine.

Ses doigts coururent le long des murs pendant qu'il se déplaçait, les amenant à une autre fresque.

— La chute, reprit-il, s'accompagne de la métamorphose. Voyez ces anges si beaux qui se couvrent d'écailles, de cornes et de queues fourchues. Quel châtiment pour ces splendides créatures qui ambitionnaient de s'élever et de siéger au-dessus des montagnes de Dieu.

— Des animaux… murmura Hélène d'une voix étranglée.

— Sept animaux, précisa le moine. Le lion pour son orgueil démesuré, le porc pour sa gloutonnerie, l'âne pour sa paresse, le singe pour son impudeur, le loup pour sa férocité, le rhinocéros pour sa colère et enfin le dragon rouge pour sa cupidité. *Benedicite omnes bestiae et pecore Domino* : "Bêtes sauvages et troupeaux, bénissez tous le Seigneur!"

La jeune femme était blême. Semblant ne pas s'en apercevoir, le moine les conduisit au mur suivant.

— Le diable a tous les vices… comme l'homme! commenta-t-il brièvement.

Hélène exhala une plainte à la vue des images représentant toutes les perversions de l'humanité dans leur horreur la plus crue.

— Voici l'œuvre de l'homme, conclut le moine. Cet enfer qu'on appelle le monde!

Et il ajouta d'un ton sec :

— Il est parfois plus aisé de dire qu'elle est celle du diable!

Il y eut un bruissement d'air et un choc contre terre. Hélène venait de s'évanouir.

Le rat se figea soudain dans le noir. Il tourna la tête. Le sol était rongé par une lueur orangée qui semblait envahir le monde, jetant pêle-mêle contre les murs des ombres monstrueuses. Avec un petit couinement, il s'empressa de disparaître dans un trou.

Portant un flambeau, le moine ouvrait la marche. Le commissaire aux morts étranges le suivait, portant dans ses bras Hélène comme si elle pesait moins qu'une plume. Volnay la déposa à l'entrée de l'église, près de la porte sous laquelle s'infiltrait un vent cinglant. Son manteau avait glissé pendant qu'il la portait, il l'emmitoufla dedans. Le moine l'examina et lui tapota les joues jusqu'à ce qu'elles reprennent un peu de couleur. Hélène ouvrit les yeux et les referma aussitôt. Le moine tendit une fiole à son fils.

— Je vais lui soulever la tête. Tâche de lui glisser quelques gouttes de ceci entre les lèvres. C'est de la liqueur de fleur d'oranger que je fabrique moi-même.

Son fils lui jeta un regard de reproche.

— C'est juste pour lutter contre le froid, ajouta précipitamment le moine.

Il saisit délicatement la nuque de la jeune femme. Hélène ouvrit de nouveau les paupières. Le moine la contempla gravement. Ange inconnu, il y avait dans ses yeux quelques éclats de la splendeur des cieux.

— Buvez, dit Volnay avec une douceur inattendue.

Elle but puis hoqueta et toussa.

— Vous allez mieux? s'enquit le moine. Que vous est-il arrivé?

Il hocha la tête et continua :

— Toutes ces diableries sont impressionnantes!

Du menton, il désigna l'extérieur à son fils.

— Peux-tu aller chercher une couverture dans la carriole? Nous partirons lorsque Hélène sera remise de son malaise.

Il reporta son attention sur la jeune femme, inquiet de son teint diaphane.

— Je ne vous pensais pas si sensible, pardonnez-moi. Qu'est-ce qui vous a donc tant effrayée dans ces peintures?

— Moi, répondit-elle d'une faible voix.

Elle se releva à demi pour lui saisir le poignet.

— Aidez-moi à prier Dieu.

— Je ne peux pas, répondit le moine, je ne crois plus en lui.

XIV

RITUEL ET AUTRES DIABLERIES

Depuis leur dernière venue, une chape blanche s'était abattue sur la maison de la Dame de l'Eau. Désorientés, le commissaire aux morts étranges et le moine contemplèrent les lieux, le chien sur leurs talons. Discrète de nature, la ruelle de l'Or sous la neige s'était enfoncée dans une ouate cotonneuse qui étouffait jusqu'aux respirations des rares passants. Le temps semblait s'être arrêté, figé dans une gangue de glace.

— C'est une bonne chose qu'Hélène n'ait pas manifesté l'intention de nous accompagner, déclara Volnay en s'approchant de l'entrée.

— De toute manière, dit le moine, je n'autorise que toi à rendre visite à ma bonne amie Dame de l'Eau ! *Chien-chien* également, bien entendu !

La première remarque parut rasséréner Volnay. Manifestement, il lui savait gré de conserver quelque méfiance envers la jeune femme, notamment pour ses relations avec Sartine. Son père n'avait pas dû juger nécessaire que le lieutenant général de police apprenne l'existence des étranges et anciennes relations entre lui et la Dame de l'Eau. Satisfait, il poussa la porte.

Le plafond était haut et quelques chandelles sur le lustre jetaient des ombres lugubres sur le sol et contre les murs. La propriétaire des lieux et ses deux visiteurs se pressèrent près du feu pour se réchauffer car la température dans la pièce était glaciale.

— Oh, le joli chien ! s'exclama la Dame de l'Eau en découvrant qui les accompagnait. Je vais lui donner un os à ronger.

— En parlant d'os à ronger, fit le moine, nous avons quelque chose pour vous!

— Des livres magiques et des déterreurs de cadavres? s'exclama leur hôtesse après les avoir écoutés. Que ne m'aurez-vous demandé mon cher moine!

— Tout cela est monnaie courante par ici, plaisanta celui-ci.

Il jeta un regard en coin vers son fils au masque impassible avant de plaider sa cause.

— Nous avons besoin d'aide. Comme je vous l'ai déjà expliqué, nous sommes ici aux lisières de la nuit. Nous avons besoin d'un guide!

— D'un guide ou d'un indicateur? Une mouche, comme vous dites si élégamment...

Le moine lui prit le bras avec empressement.

— Sartine ne patientera pas indéfiniment. Si nous n'avançons pas dans notre enquête, le procureur Siltieri fera mettre à sac la ruelle de l'Or et ses hommes ne feront aucune distinction entre magie blanche et magie noire!

La Dame de l'Eau hésita. Elle jeta une poignée d'herbes sur les charbons ardents et une fumée âcre se dégagea de l'âtre.

— On dit que certains mages déterrent des cadavres pour fabriquer philtres ou potions, murmura-t-elle, mais je pense pour ma part qu'ils sont plus nombreux à s'en vanter pour donner du sérieux à leurs tours qu'à le faire réellement!

Elle jeta un bref regard aux deux livres que le moine avait posés sur une table basse près de là.

— Quant à ces ouvrages, fit-elle mal à l'aise, je ne sais si...

— Jetez donc un coup d'œil à celui-là, proposa le moine, il y a toutes sortes de recettes que les clients de la ruelle de l'Or doivent adorer!

D'un geste prudent, la Dame de l'Eau se saisit du premier livre que le moine lui tendait et le feuilleta avec méfiance. Rapidement, elle se détendit et un rictus ironique vint orner ses lèvres.

— Voyons voir, dit-elle avec indulgence, comment nouer l'aiguillette : "Prendre une verge de loup mort, appelez le nom de celui à qui vous voulez nouer l'aiguillette et liez ladite verge avec un fil blanc. L'homme sera alors aussi impuissant pour accomplir l'acte de Vénus que s'il était châtré!"

Elle jeta un regard aiguisé au moine.

— C'est amusant comme le monde entier semble parfois tourner autour de l'aiguillette des hommes !

Ses doigts longs et fins coururent le long des pages pour s'arrêter au hasard.

— Oh mais voilà comment réparer le pucelage perdu ou paillarder avec vigueur toute la nuit !

Elle leva les yeux au ciel et reprit sa lecture en secouant la tête d'un air consterné.

— Des recettes de grand-mère tout cela, propres à flatter la virilité de l'homme !

Avec un air moqueur, elle rendit l'ouvrage au moine.

— Est-ce là tout ce que vous avez à me montrer ? Des recettes pour déflorer les pucelles ?

Le moine alla reposer le livre en souriant puis lui apporta le second ouvrage.

— Savez-vous qu'il est extrêmement facile de connaître les passages préférés d'un livre de ce genre ? demanda-t-il. En effet, lorsqu'on l'ouvre toujours au même endroit, il en prend la marque. Regardez, je feuillette et il s'ouvre à cet endroit. Je le referme, je recommence et c'est la même page. Essayez…

D'un pas prudent, la Dame de l'Eau s'approcha. Elle tendit une main hésitante au-dessus du livre ouvert et la retira soudainement comme si on venait de la mordre.

— Magie noire ! fit-elle en reculant vivement.

Elle frissonna.

— Une magie très puissante…

Dans un coin de la pièce, les bras croisés sur sa poitrine, Volnay observait la scène en silence. Les traits de son visage restaient indéchiffrables. La Dame de l'Eau s'approcha à nouveau très lentement de l'ouvrage. Un instant, sa main sembla flotter dans l'air comme l'aile d'un ange, pure de toute ombre. Et puis, elle glissa jusqu'au livre et fut envahie par l'obscurité.

— Mon Dieu, chuchota-t-elle, où donc êtes-vous tombé ?

Surmontant sa répugnance, elle tourna les pages jusqu'à celle que lui désignait le moine.

— C'est un rituel d'envoûtement, chuchota-t-elle d'une voix oppressée. Un envoûtement de sang…

— Dites-nous-en plus! la pressa le moine.

— Non! Je ne lis pas ce genre de livres! Pour rien au monde, je n'oserais prononcer ces formules même silencieusement! Je ne sais pas où vous avez mis les pieds mais vous êtes face à…

Elle hésita avant de terminer dans un souffle :

— Satan…

Le moine lui effleura le bras.

— Comment procède-t-on au rituel d'envoûtement?

— Il faut une mèche de cheveux, répondit-elle à contre-cœur, ou une rognure d'ongle de la personne qu'on désire envoûter. Pour les envoûtements de sang, plus puissant, une goutte du sang de la personne ou de celui de sa descendance est nécessaire. Une statuette de cire ou une poupée de chiffon représente l'envoûté. On la baptise et on lui donne parrain et marraine. Ensuite, on la pique avec une aiguille tout en récitant une certaine formule.

La Dame de l'Eau s'écarta du livre et revint au centre de la pièce, les contemplant d'un air soucieux. Elle tenait loin de son corps sa main qui avait touché le livre.

— Y a-t-il moyen de faire cesser l'envoûtement? s'enquit le moine.

— Le maléfice ne peut être levé que par le sorcier lui-même mais celui-ci doit obligatoirement le transférer à une autre personne. C'est une règle essentielle de la magie noire : ce qui a été formé ne peut être détruit, juste transmis. Dans le cas contraire, le maléfice retombera sur lui. C'est ce que l'on appelle le choc en retour.

La Dame de l'Eau se dirigea vers une grande vasque remplie d'une eau claire.

— J'ai besoin de me purifier au contact de l'eau. Venez, je la lirai pour vous.

Elle s'adressait au policier. Celui-ci ne bougea pas d'un pouce. Il se souvenait d'une séance précédente où il avait vu dans cette même eau un crime qui allait se commettre.

— Vous avez peur?

Cela décida à la rejoindre le commissaire aux morts étranges, dont la fierté ne tolérait pas une telle suspicion. Son hôtesse agita l'eau du bout de ses doigts et lui dit :

— Ne prononcez aucune parole inutile et surtout ne vous signez pas.

— Ces deux choses ne sont pas dans mes habitudes ! répondit froidement Volnay.

La cloche du couvent des Bénédictins sonnait quinze coups lorsque Hélène arriva chez l'ancien inspecteur de police qui lui servait à l'occasion d'informateur. Maintenant âgé de soixante ans, il résidait avec sa mère dans un appartement simple mais propre et bien entretenu où elle avait déjà eu l'occasion de se rendre. Si quarante-huit commissaires de police contrôlaient Paris sous l'autorité d'un lieutenant général de police, vingt inspecteurs assuraient des tâches plus spécialisées comme la censure du théâtre ou des livres, la pédérastie, les juifs, la voirie, les étrangers… Il avait été l'un d'eux.

À sa grande surprise, l'occupant des lieux lui ouvrit la porte, ses mains pleines de mousse de savon.

— Je lave les cheveux de ma mère, expliqua-t-il d'un air embarrassé, cela vous ennuie-t-il que je termine ? Elle adore ça. Elle a si peu de plaisir, la pauvre…

Hélène l'accompagna près du feu où, sur une chaise au dossier roide, se tenait une petite femme toute rabougrie qui ne se retourna même pas à son approche. Les yeux clos, elle était si raide et immobile qu'un instant la jeune femme craignit qu'elle ne fût morte. Et puis, elle vit la poitrine se soulever doucement et les lèvres s'entrouvrirent sur un refrain. La chose était douée de respiration et fredonnait une chanson !

— Vous pouvez parler devant elle, dit l'ancien inspecteur. Elle est sourde comme un pot et ne possède plus tous ses esprits.

Il entreprit de lui frotter avec vigueur la tête, faisant poindre le sang jusqu'à la racine des cheveux. Hélène expliqua brièvement son cas à son interlocuteur.

— Vous étiez chargé de la surveillance des prostituées et des mœurs des chanteuses ou danseuses des théâtres royaux…

— Tout comme le contrôle des écrivains, ce qui n'était pas moins passionnant. Mais bon, ce sont les enquêtes sur la vie amoureuse des grands de ce monde qui intéressent le pouvoir, si possible avec des anecdotes bien croustillantes. Notre bon M. de Sartine ne déroge pas à la règle. Il se fait bien voir du roi en le régalant chaque semaine des mœurs déplorables de son temps.

D'un geste, il fit voler des bulles de savon dans l'air. Hélène suivit des yeux l'étrange ballet de celles-ci jusqu'au sol.

— Et tout ça, pour quoi? reprit l'homme. Qu'en font-ils là-haut de tous nos rapports? Savoir que tel fermier général entretient une danseuse ou une comédienne et se rend tous les dimanches après la messe dans une certaine maison de plaisir du Louvre? Entretenir toute une armée d'agents pour cela, c'est jeter les épaules de mouton rôties par la fenêtre!

Il haussa les épaules avec philosophie.

— Seulement, voilà : le pouvoir est fasciné par la chose, toujours!

Hélène jugea bon de reprendre en main le cours de la conversation.

— Vous avez connu la Vorace?

Il fronça les sourcils.

— Oui, une prostituée aux plus bas instincts. Elle se faisait cogner mais cognait aussi durement les hommes qui le lui demandaient à l'occasion! De riches négociants se faisaient ainsi fesser en soirée après avoir rossé leurs employés dans la journée! Mais croyez-moi, les premiers y prenaient plus de plaisir que les derniers!

— Chacun trouve ses plaisirs où il peut! dit la jeune femme d'un ton neutre. Connaissiez-vous ses fréquentations?

L'ancien inspecteur haussa les épaules.

— Toute la racaille et quelques bons bourgeois qui aimaient à s'encanailler. Elle ne possédait pas de protecteur en particulier.

Les bracelets s'entrechoquèrent aux poignets d'Hélène alors qu'elle agitait la main pour stopper la discussion.

— N'en parlons plus. Parlez-moi plutôt de Mlle Belle Ange. Je sais qu'il y a douze ans, elle dansait à l'Opéra et tout Paris se traînait à ses pieds.

— C'est peu de le dire, ricana l'ancien policier. De tous les péchés, la luxure est celui auquel l'homme a le plus de mal à résister. Je ne connais pas un des grands de ce monde qui n'adore entretenir une jeune danseuse du corps de l'Opéra.

Ses yeux brillèrent.

— La beauté de Mlle Belle Ange surpassait sans fioriture celle des autres. On se battait pour déposer sa fortune à ses pieds. À vingt ans, elle roulait déjà en carrosse avec deux laquais à plumet derrière sa voiture.

— Comment se nommaient ses amants?

L'autre eut un rire gras, imité niaisement par sa mère.

— Comment voulez-vous que je me souvienne? Dans ce royaume, tout le monde fornique!

— Fornique! Fornique! braille soudainement sa mère.

Hélène pensa fugitivement à la pie de Volnay qui aimait tant répéter la fin des phrases qu'elle entendait. Cette femme ressemblait à un petit oiseau blessé, faible et dépourvu d'esprit mais, quelque part, toujours à l'écoute du monde qui l'entourait.

— Il y a douze ans qui cela pouvait-il être?

L'autre agita en l'air ses mains trempées.

— Elle les prenait puis les laissait. Vous savez bien comment sont les femmes! Que voulez-vous que je vous réponde?

Hélène hocha la tête. Elle s'était préparée à la réponse.

— Mlle Belle Ange a mis une petite fille au monde douze ans plus tôt. Savez-vous qui est le père?

— Personne ne s'en est vanté à l'époque!

— Si vous ne savez pas, déclara Hélène, je passerai alors par l'accoucheuse. Dans ce milieu-là, il faut des femmes discrètes et compétentes et elles ne sont pas si nombreuses que cela. Donnez-moi des noms.

Devant sa ténacité, l'ancien inspecteur lui jeta un regard admiratif.

— Ah mais ça, c'est tout à fait possible!

Il jeta un coup d'œil à la bourse qu'elle venait de prendre en main.

— Vous avez les petites pièces en or qui ravivent la mémoire?

Le commissaire aux morts étranges fixait sans ciller l'eau claire. Derrière lui, il entendit son hôtesse murmurer :

— Gardez bien les yeux ouverts et surtout ne devenez pas fou !

D'abord, Volnay ne vit rien. Il se pencha plus encore et soudain la terre sembla fuir sous ses pieds et un vertige le prit. Un gigantesque brasier se consumait au milieu d'une clairière et une ronde infernale s'était formée autour. Des crapauds à la bouche énorme s'épuisaient à souffler à contresens dans leurs flûtes, des scarabées boiteux battaient la mesure tandis que des écrevisses faisaient claquer leurs pinces.

Au son de cette musique horrible, chaque danseur entraînait en hurlant derrière lui une danseuse échevelée et débraillée. Puis le feu s'éteignit d'un coup et seule la lune éclaira la clairière enfumée. Les hommes se jetèrent sur le corps énervé des femmes. En un instant, chasubles et soutanes furent arrachées et les membres s'entremêlèrent dans la plus obscène des orgies. Des râles et des gémissements montèrent au ciel. Soudain le feu se ralluma et le silence se fit, craintif et respectueux. Les corps se détachèrent lentement les uns des autres. Les danseurs se relevèrent pour s'attrouper au pied du brasier devant lequel un trône noir était apparu. Sur celui-ci siégeait un prince au visage de bouc. Sur ses genoux se trémoussait l'une des danseuses, livrée à ses caresses lubriques. Lorsqu'il en eut fini avec elle, il la renvoya d'une chiquenaude. Alors la foule sembla se fendre en deux comme si elle venait de recevoir un coup d'épée. Pâle et glacée, une femme la traversa pour aller droit jusqu'au prince noir. Son corps luisait faiblement à la lune et ses yeux étincelaient d'une joie sauvage dans l'obscurité. Volnay la reconnut d'un coup : c'était Hélène !

Hélène déversa sur la table une bourse remplie de pièces et les étala devant elle jusqu'à ce qu'elles forment un éventail doré.

— Il y a douze ans, vous avez accouché une jeune danseuse de l'Opéra, Mlle Belle Ange. Son enfant a été confié à un maître joaillier nommé Marly et à son épouse. Vous souvenez-vous de tout cela ?

La sage-femme contempla l'argent avec effarement.

— Dieu, madame, je suis tenue dans mon métier à la plus grande discrétion. Et croyez-vous qu'en me faisant venir pour accoucher quelqu'un de qualité, on me précise qu'elle était la maîtresse d'un tel ou un tel?

Hélène sourit ironiquement.

— Dans votre milieu, tout se sait! À Versailles tout se sait!

Elle soupira.

— C'en est même étonnant : on ne peut plus garder un seul secret de nos jours!

Et bien entendu, pensa-t-elle fugitivement, *M. de Sartine sait également. Seulement voilà, il sait mais ne veut pas dire, lui!*

— Marly… fit songeusement l'accoucheuse. Mme Marly, oui…

Ses doigts tremblants effleurèrent les pièces.

— Mlle Belle Ange avait dix-sept ans, dit-elle très vite, belle mais pas plus de cervelle qu'un joli oiseau. On m'a fait venir au soir alors que le travail commençait. L'affaire se présentait mal et j'y ai passé toute la nuit. Mais à l'aube…

Son regard se teinta de fierté.

— À l'aube, reprit-elle, je réussis à tirer le bébé de son embarras, une mignonne petite fille.

Elle hocha la tête.

— Mlle Belle Ange n'a pas voulu prendre son enfant dans ses bras. Cela arrive parfois… Elle m'a demandé si je connaissais quelqu'un d'honnête condition qui désirerait l'adopter. Je n'eus pas à répondre car la dame de compagnie de Mlle Belle Ange s'écria qu'elle voulait un enfant de tout son cœur mais que la nature ne lui en laissait pas la possibilité. Cette dame de compagnie s'appelait Mme Marly…

L'accoucheuse ramena d'une main avide les pièces vers elle tout en regardant Hélène avec crainte.

— Par la suite, j'ai ouï dire que Mme Marly avait quitté son travail, sans doute avec l'enfant et une pension. Vous savez comment cela se passe… Plus personne n'a reparlé de cette histoire.

Elle commença à compter les pièces.

— Un mot encore, intervint la jeune femme en plaquant sa main sur la sienne, donnez-moi le nom du père.

L'accoucheuse sursauta au contact de la main d'Hélène. Sous sa paume, elle sentait les pièces marquer leur empreinte dans sa chair. Prise de panique, elle ferma les yeux pour mieux se concentrer.

— Je vous jure que je l'ignore mais en sortant, je croisai deux hommes qui en étaient presque venus aux mains et que l'on tentait de séparer. L'un d'eux était M. de Sartine ! Quant à l'autre, il s'agissait de messire Guillaume de…

Elle dit le nom et Hélène resta sans voix en reconnaissant le nom secret du moine.

La Dame de l'Eau tendit à Volnay un bol fumant.

— Tisane de toile d'araignée ! annonça-t-elle.

Le policier eut un mouvement de recul.

— Je plaisantais, voyons !

Le moine éclata de rire. Le commissaire aux morts étranges prit un air boudeur.

— Très drôle !

Assis à califourchon sur une chaise, près du feu, le moine laissa reposer sa tête sur ses poignets.

— Ainsi tu as assisté à un sabbat et tu y as vu Hélène… fit-il songeusement.

— Comme je te vois !

— Hum, hum, étrange… Hélène avec le prince à tête de bouc…

Le moine leva le doigt en l'air pour réciter doctement :

— "Aimer un bouc puant ardemment, le caresser amoureusement, s'accointer et s'accoupler avec lui horriblement et impudemment !"

Un sourire naquit sur ses lèvres.

— Non, cela ne lui ressemble pas !

— Je me suis toujours méfié d'elle, maugréa Volnay.

— Tu crois maintenant à la divination, s'étonna son père. Lorsque cela t'arrange en fait !

Le moine secoua la tête.

— Il faut savoir interpréter les choses que l'on voit. Hélène est peut-être celle qui nous conduira jusqu'à la résolution de cette énigme. Quant au sabbat…

Il réfléchit.

— S'il y a sabbat, il y a adoration de Satan. Ceci confirme bien que nous sommes face à des satanistes. Dis-moi, tu n'as pas vu de sorcières sur des balais par hasard?

Le commissaire aux morts étranges secoua la tête.

— Ah dommage, regretta le moine, j'aurais bien voulu savoir à quoi elles ressemblaient!

Il se gratta la barbe.

— J'ai lu quelque part que les balais qu'elles chevauchent figurent la verge de Moïse. C'est un puissant symbole phallique!

La Dame de l'Eau secoua la tête en souriant :

— Tout tourne autour de cela!

Le moine approuva vigoureusement et continua :

— Sais-tu que les sorcières n'ont pas besoin de cours pour chevaucher leur balai? Il leur suffit d'accrocher une chandelle à son extrémité et de dire : "Bâton blanc, bâton noir, mène-moi là où tu dois, de par le diable."

— Tu as de drôles de lectures, remarqua sèchement Volnay.

La Dame de l'Eau et le moine échangèrent un fin sourire.

— Plus que tu ne l'imagines mon fils, rit le moine, plus que tu ne l'imagines!

Il eut encore un long rire silencieux, ses épaules se soulevant et s'affaissant. Une fois calmé, il expliqua :

— Dans *L'Âne d'or*, Apulée, un auteur latin du IIe siècle, raconte comment Pamphile se change en hibou pour se rendre au sabbat. Pour cela, elle se sert d'un onguent en s'en couvrant du plus petit orteil à la racine des cheveux! C'est de cette lecture qu'enfant mon goût de l'insolite est né!

Il questionna de nouveau son fils.

— Tu n'as rien vu d'autre?

— Non, la scène s'est brusquement évanouie.

— À l'aube, tout disparaît d'un coup, murmura la Dame de l'Eau.

Volnay ne releva pas. Il porta le bol fumant à ses lèvres et but une gorgée prudente.

— Messe noire ou envoûtement alors? demanda-t-il en reposant le récipient d'un air gêné.

— Les deux, répondit son père.

— Mais nous n'avons retrouvé sur les lieux du crime ni poupée, ni statuette de cire!

— Si, elle était sous tes yeux!

Le commissaire aux morts étranges le considéra avec effarement. Le moine haussa les épaules.

— Non, mon fils, je ne suis ni vieux, ni fou, ni gâteux.

Et il ajouta avec un plaisir évident :

— D'ailleurs, si tu étais un peu plus concentré sur ton sujet et si tu gardais l'esprit plus ouvert, tu aurais déjà deviné de quoi il retourne!

Volnay ouvrit et referma la bouche sans prononcer un mot comme si on venait de lui jeter un sort. Enfin, il réussit à articuler :

— J'ai fouillé toute la scène du crime, en long, en large et en travers. Je te dis qu'il n'y avait nulle statuette de cire et nulle poupée!

Le moine lui jeta un regard triste.

— Ils n'en avaient pas besoin, la poupée c'était Sophia!

XV

NEIGE ET AUTRES DIABLERIES

Il s'était mis à neiger très doucement alors qu'ils remontaient la ruelle de l'Or. Les flocons de neige tombaient avec une grâce aérienne. Le moine releva la tête comme pour humer l'air du soir.

— La sorcellerie, dit-il, est née de l'ignorance et de la misère mais aussi d'une révolte contre l'ordre établi qui en était la cause. La messe noire n'est qu'une rébellion contre le culte de Dieu et son Église. Tout est inversé dans le satanisme et l'inversion, c'est la rébellion!

Il s'amusa à tendre la main pour y recueillir de la neige. Chaque flocon semblait posséder sa propre structure, merveille architecturale plus complexe qu'on ne l'imaginait.

— Une messe noire, chantonna-t-il comme s'il s'agissait d'une ritournelle, un flocon de neige, un rituel d'envoûtement par le sang, un flocon de neige, une vierge que l'on n'a pas profanée, un flocon de neige et autres vilaines diableries...

Le commissaire aux morts étranges haussa les épaules et dit :

— À mon avis, la clé de l'énigme réside dans le choix de Sophia comme poupée d'envoûtement. Lorsque nous en aurons découvert les raisons, nous trouverons les coupables.

— Et qu'est-ce qui pousserait un père à sacrifier sa propre fille? C'est impensable!

Il sursauta soudain.

— Sauf s'il ne s'agissait pas de sa fille mais d'une enfant adultère... Mais comment savoir maintenant que notre astrologue est mort?

Volnay réfléchit une seconde puis se décida.

— Je dois passer au Châtelet pour faire un point sur l'affaire avec Siltieri. Accompagne-moi.

Le moine sursauta.

— Moi ? Au Châtelet ? Tu veux ma mort !

Son fils haussa les épaules.

— Il ne t'est pas interdit d'y entrer et Siltieri ne te connaît pas.

Lorsque les deux hommes arrivèrent au Châtelet, le moine ne put s'empêcher de commenter.

— Les cachots sont abominables et l'air est difficile à respirer car il n'y a point d'ouverture extérieure et descend seulement d'en haut. Tout n'est que ténèbres et contagion.

Si le Châtelet comportait des prisons, il abritait aussi les affaires de police et celles de justice, aussi y croisèrent-ils conseillers, procureurs, notaires, gardes-notes, commis-greffiers ou huissiers à verge que le moine s'amusa à dévisager impudemment. Avant d'entrer chez Siltieri, Volnay confia le chien à un archer du guet de sa connaissance. Il hésita une seconde et jeta un regard en biais à son père.

— Siltieri n'est pas très commode. Certains le considèrent même comme assez buté alors ne va pas le provoquer ou te moquer de lui. Fais attention à ce que tu dis.

Il fit encore un pas et ajouta :

— Ne dis pas de mal du roi, du pape ou de l'Église, ne jure pas et ne parle pas de tes expériences de laboratoire.

Tout à coup, il s'arrêta net et se tourna vers son père.

— En fait, il vaudrait mieux que tu ne dises rien du tout !

On les introduisit dans le cabinet de travail de Siltieri, seulement éclairé par la chiche lumière d'une fenêtre et d'une chandelle. Celui-ci les salua sèchement. Volnay présenta le moine comme son assistant et s'enquit des suites de l'arrestation des voisins du curé dansant. D'un coup, le visage fermé de Siltieri se fit rayonnant.

— J'ai soumis à la question les gens que j'ai fait arrêter hier et ils ont donné le nom d'un boulanger.

— Magnifique ! dit le moine.

Le procureur ne releva pas l'ironie.

— Le maudit hérétique fabriquait des hosties avec de la farine, des herbes et de l'urine !

— J'espère bien que tous les boulangers ne font pas ça, murmura le moine sans se soucier des sourcils froncés de son fils.

Siltieri s'approcha de lui.

— Pardon?

— Non, je disais que cela me rappelle que l'on réduit cette mixture en poudre pour empoisonner les puits.

Triomphant, le procureur se tourna vers le commissaire aux morts étranges.

— Vous entendez!

Volnay jeta un regard noir à son père.

— J'ai mis aussi le boulanger à la question, reprit Siltieri. Il ne parle pas, il chante!

Le procureur exultait.

— Les noms tombent les uns après les autres et vont nous permettre de remonter tout le réseau de ces diables.

Le commissaire aux morts étranges eut une moue dubitative.

— Tout cela est de la piétaille, de pauvres gens qui contribuent à alimenter les commerces de fausse magie des escrocs qui pullulent dans Paris. Vous savez bien que ceux-ci exploitent la crédulité du peuple comme des bourgeois et des nobles. Ils leur promettent l'immortalité ou la fortune, leur vendent des cartes au trésor, des formules ou des carrés magiques…

Siltieri le coupa.

— Faire acte de magie, c'est faire croire au peuple qu'il peut rivaliser avec Dieu et le roi!

Volnay contempla le procureur d'un œil neutre, notant son visage illuminé, brûlé de l'intérieur par une flamme noire. Son âme ardente semblait lui sortir par les yeux.

Un exalté au service de Dieu et du roi. La pire espèce.

— Si vous croyez que tout ceci ne concerne pas votre enquête, reprit Siltieri, vous vous trompez. Les mauvaises gens que vous cherchez sont plus près que vous ne le pensez. Des fabricants de cierges, je remonte au boulanger, du boulanger je vais au meunier puis, curieusement, je bifurque sur des mécréants se livrant à la vente de cadavres…

Son regard accrocha celui du moine.

— Cadavres souvent destinés à des hérétiques qui croient lire dans les corps des réponses qui n'y sont pas!

Impavide, le moine ne cilla pas. Volnay sentit la sueur lui glacer l'échine. Manifestement, il s'était fourvoyé en amenant son père au Châtelet. Siltieri savait parfaitement qui était son père.

— Sorts, maléfices, propos diaboliques, sabbats, gronda le procureur en se plantant devant le moine, je vais passer au fer rouge toute cette ville! Puis je ferai brûler vifs sorciers et sorcières, au bois vert pour prolonger leur agonie. Seuls ceux qui se confesseront pourront être étranglés!

— Nom de Dieu! siffla le moine.

— Attention! gronda le procureur. Jurer le nom de Dieu, de Jésus ou du pape constitue un blasphème inspiré par le diable et en France on vous coupe la langue pour cela! Les blasphèmes sont des indices du crime de sorcellerie et, en ce domaine, je peux poursuivre sur la simple clameur publique!

— Je n'ai voulu sacrifier personne sur une pierre tombale, fit doucement remarquer le moine, je suis ici pour trouver le coupable de ces crimes.

Siltieri resta un instant interdit.

— Certes, fit-il, certes…

Le moine renchérit :

— Nous soupçonnons le père de cette jeune victime d'être peut-être le coupable de ce crime.

— Vraiment? Ce tireur d'horoscopes!

— Nous n'avons pas de preuve, d'autant plus qu'il est mort cette nuit dans l'incendie de sa maison.

— Mort? Tout comme cette prostituée et ce curé dansant? Voilà beaucoup de coïncidences…

Siltieri n'était pas l'idiot à triple étage que l'on pensait.

— Oui, renchérit le moine devant son fils interdit, et nous avons trouvé dans les ruines de sa maison des livres terribles et interdits.

Il les cita et se signa. Siltieri apprécia. Il revint à sa table de travail et trempa sa plume dans l'encre.

— Ainsi ce maudit bougre d'astrologue versait dans le satanisme! Le châtiment de Dieu l'a rejoint, à moins que ses complices…

Avec application, il se mit à tracer des lettres serrées.

— J'ordonne qu'on enquête auprès de son entourage, fit-il.

— Il n'avait pas d'amis et sa servante est morte dans l'incendie, remarqua Volnay.

— Qu'importe! dit Siltieri. Nous trouverons bien quelqu'un à qui brûler la plante des pieds pour l'inciter à parler!

Le commissaire aux morts étranges et son père s'entreregardèrent avec anxiété.

— Eh bien, nous allons vous laisser et continuer l'enquête de notre côté, conclut Volnay. Je ne manquerai pas de vous tenir informé de la suite.

— Faites, faites…

Siltieri ne releva pas la tête lorsqu'ils sortirent. Les deux hommes ne dirent pas un mot avant d'avoir quitté le Châtelet rempli de courants d'air glacé. Le chien trottinait auprès d'eux, tout à sa joie de les avoir retrouvés.

— Ton Siltieri a une tête à boire des infusions de queues de cerises! remarqua gaiement le moine une fois à l'air libre.

— Pourquoi lui as-tu raconté toutes ces choses? grommela Volnay.

— Pour me faire bien voir de lui! Je croyais que c'était ce que tu désirais!

— Je t'avais demandé de te taire.

— C'est difficile pour moi!

Le commissaire aux morts étranges exhala profondément et un halo de brume sembla se dérouler de sa bouche.

— Était-il nécessaire de le mettre au courant pour l'astrologue?

— Sartine le sait bien, lui. Et de toute façon, cela ne mènera Siltieri nulle part car je ne le juge pas plus intelligent que nous et sans doute beaucoup plus obtus. Par ailleurs, s'il ne sait rien sur l'astrologue, c'est qu'il ne dépense guère en espions.

Volnay opina du chef puis fit la moue.

— Quand même, j'aurais préféré que tu te taises. Sais-tu seulement ce qu'est le silence?

— Comme dit M. Pascal, le silence est la pire des persécutions : jamais un saint ne s'est tu!

Son fils leva les yeux au ciel.

— Tu es tout sauf un saint!

Une cohue encombrait le Pont-Neuf. Ils piétinèrent sur place avant de l'emprunter, observant autour d'eux comme à leur habitude. Ils virent un maître joaillier sortir avec son client de la boutique afin de lui montrer l'éclat d'une bague à la lueur du jour. Il la retira ensuite du majeur de sa main gauche pour l'enfiler au doigt de la main droite de son client. Volnay jeta un coup d'œil distrait au manège puis s'immobilisa brusquement comme si une idée venait de le frapper net. Son souffle resta suspendu une seconde alors qu'il comprenait enfin ce qui le tourmentait.

— Oh, mon Dieu! Pourquoi n'y ai-je pas pensé plus tôt! Que c'est bête de ma part!

Et, le regard dans le vague, il répéta encore dans un murmure accablé :

— Que c'est bête!

Hélène avait trouvé refuge dans le faubourg Saint-Jacques où, dans un morne silence, se bousculaient cloîtres, hôpitaux ou couvents. De temps à autre, on entendait une cloche sonner mais, hormis cela, la neige épaisse semblait étouffer tous bruits, venant encore ajouter à l'impression de solitude et de recueillement de l'endroit. La jeune femme n'aimait pas ce quartier mais il avait pour avantage que personne ne songerait à y chercher quelqu'un comme elle.

Alors qu'elle grimpait l'escalier de son immeuble, rue des Marionnettes, Hélène perçut dans son dos un pas léger et jeta un rapide coup d'œil par-delà la rambarde. Derrière elle, un homme montait avec prudence, se gardant de faire du bruit. Un chapeau rabattu sur ses yeux dissimulait son visage. Elle gagna rapidement un coin de son palier et s'immobilisa dans l'ombre. Sa main glissa sous sa robe et en ressortit armée d'une dague. L'homme passa devant elle sans la remarquer et s'arrêta devant sa porte. Hélène fit deux pas rapides et lui mit le fil de sa lame sous la gorge.

— Ce ne sera pas nécessaire, fit alors Sartine.

Le lieutenant général de police l'avait aidée à allumer du feu dans la cheminée et tendait ses mains aux flammes. Son expression était pensive.

— Pourquoi a-t-il fallu que vous alliez là-bas? demanda-t-il.

Il soupira et appuya son front sur le manteau de la cheminée.

— Qui vous a renseigné? demanda-t-elle.

Et elle pensa : *L'accoucheuse ou l'inspecteur?*

Un éclair de fierté traversa l'œil de Sartine qui s'était redressé.

— Ce sont vos sales petites mouches, c'est cela? fit dédaigneusement Hélène. Vous me faisiez suivre parce que vous n'aviez pas plus confiance que ça en moi!

— Ai-je eu tort? demanda-t-il d'un ton tranquille.

Et il ajouta d'une voix neutre, sans regret inutile :

— De toute façon, je n'ai confiance en personne.

Il remit en place une boucle de sa perruque.

— Mes mouches sont effectivement partout!

Et tout à coup, avec ses deux bras, il imita un vol désordonné tandis que sa bouche émettait un bourdonnement bizarre. Hélène frémit. Par moments, cet homme lui faisait peur.

— Vous avez connu cette femme, n'est-ce pas? demanda-t-elle.

— Elle était très belle, répondit-il d'une voix basse et sourde. Nous la voulions tous mais elle n'était à personne…

Et il ajouta dans un soupir :

— Sinon au plus offrant comme il se doit…

Elle attendit.

— Sophia lui ressemblait beaucoup, ajouta-t-il après un silence.

— Volnay m'a dit que vous aviez gardé son portrait, c'est pour cela?

Il lui jeta un regard vide.

— Décidément, mon commissaire aux morts étranges est bien bavard avec vous, à moi il n'en dit pas autant!

— Et pourtant, il est loyal.

Sartine secoua la tête.

— On ne peut rester loyal qu'à un idéal et je ne corresponds pas à celui du chevalier de Volnay.

Il sourit.

— Encore moins à celui du moine d'ailleurs!

Hélène se raidit.

— Il ne faut rien leur dire, reprit Sartine d'une voix basse et pressante. La chose doit rester discrète. Ce n'est pas tant Volnay qui m'inquiète que le moine. Je ne sais pas comment il pourrait réagir.

Il fixa la jeune femme dans les yeux.

— Soyez certaine que, de mes deux enquêteurs, le moine est le plus dangereux. C'est aussi un homme redoutable, les armes à la main. Vous ne devineriez jamais ce dont il est capable!

Hélène cilla brièvement. De découvrir que Sartine craignait le moine la remplissait de surprise et d'effroi.

— Qui de vous deux était le père de Sophia? demanda-t-elle néanmoins.

XVI

LOGIQUE ET AUTRES DIABLERIES

Un vent violent soufflait, le moine repoussa avec difficulté la porte de sa demeure derrière lui.

— *Chien-chien* est content de rentrer chez lui! constata-t-il en voyant l'animal filer vers la cheminée.

— Hum. Descendons à la cave, vite! commanda son fils. Je veux revoir le cadavre de notre astrologue.

Tout en dévalant l'escalier, le commissaire aux morts étranges expliqua à son père :

— Quelque chose m'a troublé la première fois que j'ai vu le corps mais je ne parvenais pas à comprendre quoi. Il y avait, coincée dans mon esprit, comme une évidence, une vérité qui ne voulait pas se faire connaître. Et puis tout à coup, lorsque dans la rue j'ai vu ce joaillier, tout s'est éclairci. Quand je rencontre quelqu'un au cours d'une enquête, je ne me contente pas de le regarder, je l'observe et je m'imprègne de mille détails. Or, l'astrologue portait une chevalière d'un genre très particulier, à la main droite. Cette chevalière nous a permis entre autres d'identifier le cadavre.

Ils étaient arrivés devant le corps calciné. Le commissaire aux morts étranges le considéra un instant, un sourire de satisfaction aux lèvres.

— Voilà! Sur ce corps affreusement brûlé et méconnaissable, la chevalière ne se trouve pas à la bonne main!

Il hocha la tête.

— Lorsque nous répétons sur quelqu'un en face de nous le même geste que pour notre propre personne, la gauche et la droite s'embrouillent. Ce n'est pas l'astrologue qui est mort. Il a voulu nous le faire croire en mettant sa bague à la main d'un cadavre mais il s'est saisi de sa main gauche et non de la droite!

Le moine se figea.

— Mais tu as parfaitement raison, il la portait à l'autre main. Je m'en souviens car c'est de celle-ci qu'il nous a ouvert la porte!

Ses yeux brillèrent d'excitation.

— On a incendié cette maison après y avoir introduit un cadavre de la même taille que l'astrologue. La chevalière à son doigt avait donc pour but de nous permettre de l'identifier comme étant M. Marly, l'astrologue.

— Et d'échapper ainsi à nos soupçons. Avec la découverte de la Vorace, l'astrologue a dû sentir l'étau se resserrer autour de lui et a choisi de disparaître.

Ils regagnèrent pensivement le rez-de-chaussée de la maison, s'épuisant en hypothèses. Soudain, le commissaire aux morts étranges s'immobilisa. Ses yeux s'étrécirent en regardant le sol.

— Des miettes de biscuits par terre… cela vient de la cuisine.

Le moine le rejoignit et s'exclama :

— Mes biscuits secs! On m'a mangé tous mes biscuits secs! Ce doit être Hélène…

— Qu'ai-je fait? demanda une voix enjouée derrière eux.

Hélène s'arc-boutait pour refermer la porte.

— Euh, ce n'est rien ma chère, fit le moine. Nous nous demandions qui a mangé les biscuits secs…

— Ce n'est pas moi, je vous assure, dit-elle tranquillement en époussetant son manteau recouvert de neige.

Le commissaire aux morts étranges la scruta attentivement. Elle avait l'air pâle et fatiguée. Finalement, il se retourna vers son père.

— Tu as normalement quatre clés de cette maison. Tu en portes une sur toi, moi également et…

Il jeta un coup d'œil incisif à la jeune femme qui ne broncha pas.

— Si j'ai bien compris tu en as confié une à Hélène…

— Certes, fit le moine qui avait compris où son fils voulait en venir. Et la quatrième clé est pendue ici…

Il désigna un clou au mur de la cuisine.

— Mon Dieu, elle a disparu!

Volnay se tourna vers Hélène.

— Est-ce vous?

— Non.

— Bien sûr... et pourtant, il existe toujours une explication rationnelle!

Le commissaire aux morts étranges sembla s'absenter en lui-même. Il était immobile mais ses pensées prenaient une tournure vertigineuse. Hélène et le moine virent le bleu de ses yeux se teinter d'un gris aux textures d'acier trempé. Ses paupières se fermèrent et plus rien en lui ne bougea. Le moine retint Hélène de parler car il savait comment procédait son fils. Lorsque celui-ci ouvrit les yeux, le bleu avait de nouveau envahit ses yeux.

— Père, peux-tu prendre le livre de Sophia, là où elle a consigné son journal? Ensuite, suis-moi.

Le moine s'exécuta en silence et, bien qu'elle ne fût pas formellement invitée, Hélène les accompagna jusque chez Volnay. La pie les accueillit dans un torrent de jurons à l'adresse de la jeune femme. Manifestement, l'oiseau tenait Hélène comme responsable des absences répétées de son maître, à moins que celui-ci n'ait prononcé devant la pie des mots qui visaient la jeune femme.

— Calme-toi, gentil oiseau, fit la jeune femme en grattant les barreaux de la cage. Je suis Hélène...

— Hé... lè... ne, fit la pie, gaar... ce...

Hélène se tourna vers Volnay.

— Monsieur, que dit votre pie? demanda-t-elle froidement.

Sans répondre, le commissaire aux morts étranges alla droit à son cabinet de travail et ouvrit un tiroir en bois de rose.

— Vous vous souvenez du panneau qu'on a placé sur la porte du cimetière et sur lequel était inscrit...

— *Interdit à Dieu d'entrer*, compléta le moine.

— Le voici!

Il le posa sèchement devant eux, près de la cage de la pie.

— Et maintenant, père, ouvre le livre dans lequel Sophia a consigné son journal et compare les deux écritures.

Le moine s'exécuta et se figea instantanément sur place. Tout le sang semblait s'être retiré de son visage.

— Mon Dieu, fit-il au bord de la panique, celle qui a écrit ce journal et celle qui a inscrit ces mots sur le panneau à l'entrée du cimetière sont une seule et même personne : Sophia!

Tandis que la pie jacassait, Volnay arpentait rageusement son salon.

— Tout était pourtant logique : toi, Hélène et la servante de l'auberge voyez Sophia après sa mort. Son chien devient fou à certains moments comme s'il sentait sa présence. Le cadavre du gardien de cimetière disparaît. Vous avez tous voulu mettre cela sur le compte des esprits, soit!

Il se planta devant son père.

— Mais ne pouvais-tu pas te rendre compte que quelqu'un vivait dans ta maison? De la nourriture disparaît dans ta cuisine. On urine devant ta porte. On sort le chien pendant que tu dors, on t'emprunte une clé…

Pour la première fois de sa vie, le moine resta muet car son esprit avait du mal à accepter la vérité. Sans pitié, le commissaire aux morts étranges reprit sa diatribe contre son père :

— On vit chez toi et il faut encore que ce soit moi qui aie l'idée de comparer l'écriteau du cimetière au journal de Sophia!

— Mais…

— Pour moi, cela signifie une chose : Sophia n'est pas morte!

— Mais on l'a enterrée! protesta le moine.

— Enterrée? Tu ne l'as ni autopsiée, ni mise en bière!

— Les embaumeurs l'ont mise en cercueil!

— Qu'en sais-tu? explosa son fils. Tu n'y étais pas! Sophia avait quitté la cave quand les embaumeurs sont venus. Tu leur as demandé de s'occuper du cadavre dans la première cave mais sans préciser qu'il s'agissait de celui d'une jeune fille, n'est-ce pas?

Le moine essaya de se souvenir.

— C'est ma foi vrai, murmura-t-il.

— Tu as pour excuse ta maladie, bougonna son fils. Les embaumeurs se sont donc rendus dans la première cave, ne trouvant pas le cadavre, ils ont regardé dans la seconde. Au vu de ton état, ils ont dû penser que tu avais confondu le lieu et se sont donc occupés du corps du gardien du cimetière, le mettant en bière. Comme, pas plus que toi, le père de Sophia n'a voulu la contempler une dernière fois, les embaumeurs ont cloué le cercueil. Ainsi, il est naturel que l'erreur n'ait pas été réparée. Voilà ce que c'est que de devenir gâteux !

Pour la première fois depuis qu'elle les avait suivis, Hélène intervint d'une voix dure.

— Vous ne devriez pas parler ainsi à votre père.

Volnay se figea. Le noir de ses prunelles sembla grandir démesurément, signe d'une intense colère.

— Qui êtes-vous, intrigante, pour vous permettre de me juger ? gronda-t-il d'une voix basse et rauque. Que savez-vous de nous et de quel droit vous mêlez-vous de nos affaires ?

— Vos affaires ? ironisa-t-elle.

Elle balaya la pièce d'un vaste geste de la main.

— Des livres, un oiseau savant et quelques cadavres, voilà à quoi se réduisent et vos affaires et votre vision du monde ! Respectez donc votre père, entendez-le et écoutez-le pour changer.

— Mon père est un vieux fou !

Hélène le gifla. La claque résonna sèchement dans toute la pièce. La joue marbrée de rouge, Volnay la fixa d'un air abasourdi. Le moine ouvrit la bouche et la referma comiquement. Les mains le long du corps, légèrement cambrée en avant, Hélène défia du regard le commissaire aux morts étranges. Puis, elle passa très lentement devant lui et recula jusqu'à la porte, sans le quitter un instant de ses étranges yeux aux reflets dorés. Une bouffée d'air froid coucha les flammes des bougies lorsqu'elle sortit sans prononcer un mot. À son tour, le moine tourna les talons.

— Où vas-tu ? demanda son fils.

— Le vieux fou rentre chez lui.

— Père…

Le moine leva la main pour l'arrêter.

— N'en rajoute pas, tu en as assez dit pour aujourd'hui.

Demeuré seul, Volnay ralluma le feu et resta quelques instants à le contempler sombrement. Puis, comme s'il venait de prendre une résolution, il jeta un manteau sur ses épaules et sortit, ignorant les commentaires dépités de sa pie.

Sans surprise, le moine retrouva Hélène chez lui. Ce n'était pourtant pas la compagnie qu'il souhaitait. Les reproches de son fils l'avaient profondément blessé et il préférait rester seul pour ressasser ses pensées.

— Mais où est donc *chien-chien*? s'étonna-t-il. Je pensais qu'il allait me faire la fête.

C'est alors qu'il s'aperçut de l'émoi d'Hélène.

— Le chien a disparu! dit-elle. Je l'ai cherché dans toute la maison.

— Voyons, cela ne se peut! Nous l'avons laissé ici pour aller chez mon fils et nous avons refermé la porte à clé.

— Certes.

Le moine voulut descendre dans les caves puis gagna le cellier, sa chambre et le séjour, cherchant partout.

— Il n'est plus ici, quelqu'un nous l'a pris!

— C'est une chose certaine. Nous n'avons plus qu'à attendre qu'on nous le ramène.

Elle n'avait osé prononcer le prénom de Sophia. Sans mot dire, le moine gagna son fauteuil favori devant le feu qui flambait joyeusement et s'abandonna silencieusement à la contemplation des flammes.

Hélène hésita un instant. Elle savait que la détermination du commissaire aux morts étranges à mener ses enquêtes cachait une faillite personnelle intime. Son père en souffrait pour lui. Par amour pour son fils, il l'avait rejoint pour l'aider et le conseiller mais celui-ci n'était plus l'enfant qu'il avait connu. De se voir ainsi rejeter devait lui avoir brisé le cœur.

Elle vint près de lui et, très naturellement, s'assit sur ses genoux. Le moine ne réagit pas. Il grattait sa barbe d'un air pensif, évoquant des souvenirs de temps heureux ou en tout cas tels qu'il croyait avoir été.

— Il vous aime, dit Hélène, n'en doutez point.

Le moine hocha la tête sans rien dire. La jeune femme posa la main sur son épaule. Elle n'était pas sans ignorer que, tel le cheval de Troie, son intrusion dans le duo d'enquêteurs suscitait tension, désir et méfiance. Le couple père et fils se trouvait au bord de l'explosion et ce n'était pas ce qu'elle désirait.

— Quelle erreur épouvantable ai-je commise, murmura soudain le moine. Ma fierté intellectuelle ne s'en relèvera pas!

Hélène sourit. C'était tout lui!

— Voilà qui est mieux, chuchota-t-elle à son oreille. Il vous faut raisonner en homme de science. Une succession de faits vous a mené où vous en êtes : la présence d'une drogue inconnue, le corps d'une enfant que vous refusez d'ouvrir parce que tout votre être s'y oppose, votre maladie, la présence de deux corps dans votre cave… et une enquête bien compliquée.

— En verrons-nous jamais le bout?

Les lèvres d'Hélène se pincèrent et elle le considéra avec une certaine sévérité.

— Il le faut! Je termine toujours ce que j'ai commencé et je ne vous sens pas différent de moi.

La main du moine se posa sur son genou.

— Oui, je crois que nous nous ressemblons beaucoup!

Il eut un sourire d'excuse.

— Pour ce qui est de notre caractère, pour le reste, je ne vous ferai pas injure…

Comprenant ce qu'il voulait dire, elle eut un sourire indulgent.

— Vous êtes resté très bel homme et vous avez beaucoup de charme…

— Vous êtes bien aimable!

À cet instant, Volnay entra chez le moine et jeta un rapide regard circulaire dans la pièce, notant au passage la présence d'Hélène sur les genoux de son père, la main de celui-ci sur la jeune femme, et s'abstenant stoïquement de tout commentaire.

— D'où viens-tu, fils? demanda le moine d'un ton neutre.

— Je reviens de chez les embaumeurs, répondit Volnay en lorgnant sur les mains que son père venait de poser sur les hanches d'Hélène comme pour le narguer.

Il détourna le regard.

— Pas de chance, poursuivit-il d'un ton neutre, nos bougres sont partis à cinquante lieues de Paris pour s'occuper de la tante de leur patron qui est morte. Ils ne reviendront pas d'ici trois jours. Avec ce temps affreux, envoyer un archer du guet à cheval

237

leur poser la question ne nous aidera guère. Il nous faut déterrer le cercueil pour en avoir le cœur net.

— Mais…

— J'ai toute autorité par Sartine. Et puis, le père de Sophia étant mort, personne ne s'y opposera. Je vais aller de ce pas voir notre obligeant collègue commissaire de quartier. Il m'a paru assez compréhensif jusque-là.

Ses yeux se posèrent brièvement sur Hélène.

— Inutile pour l'instant d'en informer Sartine. Je peux m'être trompé et il peut y avoir une autre explication à la similitude d'écritures sur le panneau et dans le livre de Sophia.

Son ton n'était guère convaincant. Il hésita encore, contrairement à ses habitudes.

— Eh bien, je crois que je vais vous laisser…

Pour la première fois, Volnay ne semblait pas remettre en cause la présence d'Hélène dans la maison de son père. On ne lui répondit pas.

— Bonne nuit! dit-il en tournant sèchement les talons.

— Bonne nuit, mon fils! fit le moine en relevant la tête.

Lorsque la porte se referma, Hélène se leva pour aller ajouter une bûche dans le feu et resta un instant devant l'âtre, comme hésitant sur l'attitude à adopter. Le regard du moine coula de nouveau vers la jeune femme et il soupira.

— Mon fils me cause bien des soucis, mon amie.

— Ne vous inquiétez pas pour lui, il est allé raconter ses malheurs à sa pie!

Le moine ne dit rien. Il contempla songeusement Hélène et les rides autour de ses yeux s'accentuèrent. C'était un peu comme lorsqu'on découvre qu'un félin n'est pas qu'un bel animal mais aussi un tueur.

— Nous avons oublié de lui parler de la disparition du chien, constata-t-il, mais cela attendra bien demain.

Il fit une pause.

— Je vais me coucher dans mon lit, reprit-il en se levant lentement. Peut-être feriez-vous bien de rentrer chez vous… Il n'est pas tard et les rues sont encore sûres. Si vous le souhaitez, je vous raccompagnerai.

Elle secoua la tête.

— Ce n'est pas nécessaire mais, si vous me le permettez, je boirai une de vos tisanes avant de partir.

Il lui tourna le dos.

— Je vous en prie, faites. Bonne nuit. Fermez bien la porte à clé en partant même si cela n'a guère d'importance. On entre et l'on sort de cette maison comme dans un moulin !

Allongé sur son lit, le moine ferma les yeux, se laissant envahir par le chagrin et la mélancolie. La vie passait trop vite. Il n'avait pas vu son fils grandir et maintenant voilà que celui-ci le rejetait.

Le temps passe et nous emmène comme feuilles au vent.

Le bruit d'un loquet l'arracha à ses pensées. Un bref courant d'air balaya la pièce. Hélène tira la porte de la chambre derrière elle et annonça d'un ton définitif :

— Je viens dormir avec vous.

XVII

CERCUEIL ET AUTRES DIABLERIES

Volnay ne trouvait pas le sommeil. Il retira du tiroir de son secrétaire la lettre de Chiara qu'une fois de plus il lut et relut. La jeune femme lui donnait un an pour la rejoindre en Italie sans toutefois lui en promettre. Le cœur du jeune homme se serra. La trahison de Chiara avait encore valeur de fer rouge.

Il porta la lettre à ses narines pour en humer le parfum qui s'en était évaporé depuis longtemps. Par moments, il lui semblait retrouver quelques notes florales qui, effet de son esprit, lui remontaient en mémoire avec quelques souvenirs en lien comme ce jour où leurs lèvres s'étaient trouvées en un baiser profond et sensuel. Le souffle court, il reposa brutalement la lettre.

— Que croit-elle donc? demanda-t-il à la pie.

Mais l'oiseau resta sage dans sa cage. Volnay se sentit ridicule. Au lieu de rester à raconter sa pauvre vie à sa pie, il se revêtit d'un chaud manteau et, armé de la tête aux pieds, se glissa parmi les ombres de la nuit. Pour quelques liards, il trouva un porteur de falot qui lui dénicha un fiacre qui le conduisit au faubourg Saint-Marcel. Là, il se rendit directement chez l'Écureuil. L'odeur des égouts et des immondices le saisit dès qu'il descendit de voiture. Il inspira l'air glacé et expira bruyamment comme pour nettoyer ses poumons de toute cette pestilence. Le voyant seul et bien de sa mise comme de sa personne, des prostituées s'accrochèrent à lui comme autant de sirènes abandonnées. La pénombre masquait à peine l'épaisse couche de fard rougissant leurs joues. Dans ce quartier, elles ne portaient pas de bas de soie mais de laine grossière et rapiécés recouvrant leurs longues jambes. Volnay écarta doucement de lui ces pathétiques appels à l'amour et poursuivit résolument son chemin vers l'immeuble où résidait la jeune prostituée.

Il trouva l'escalier aussi raide que dans son souvenir. Il le gravit sans faire de bruit, s'arrêtant à mi-chemin pour reprendre sa respiration. Devant la porte, il reconnut l'oiseau gravé d'une main malhabile et cela le fit sourire. Tendant l'oreille, il perçut les halètements d'un homme. Il n'entendit pas l'Écureuil. Volnay imagina son corps se tortillant dans la chambre et son cœur s'assombrit inexplicablement. Pensif, il redescendit l'escalier et affronta de nouveau le froid, se forçant à contourner le pâté de maisons à pas lents avant de revenir à son point de départ et remonter l'escalier. En haut, il colla l'oreille à la porte avant de frapper doucement. Un pas léger puis un verrou qu'on tire et la porte s'ouvrit, accompagnée d'une petite exclamation inquiète :

— Tu as oublié quelque chose ? Oh…

L'Écureuil considéra le commissaire aux morts étranges qui se tenait gêné dans l'embrasure de la porte et s'empourpra.

— Je vous dérange ? demanda-t-il.

Elle rougit violemment.

— Non, j'allais juste me coucher…

Sur la table se trouvaient un broc d'eau et une bassine. Les éclaboussures marquaient l'usage que l'on en avait fait. Le regard de l'Écureuil rattrapa le sien, allant avec lui jusqu'à la bassine puis vers le galetas en désordre. De nouveau, une rougeur envahit la jeune fille.

— Vous…

Elle hésita.

— Vous êtes venu pour…

— Pour parler, dit rapidement Volnay.

— Ah…

Imperceptiblement, elle se détendit et répéta comme pour mieux s'en convaincre :

— Me parler…

Et elle ajouta d'un ton espiègle :

— C'est vrai que vous n'êtes pas comme les autres hommes !

La jeune fille le fit asseoir sur son grabat et le rejoignit, calant son flanc contre le sien comme pour rechercher un peu de sa chaleur.

— Avez-vous toujours besoin de moi pour votre enquête? s'enquit-elle avec curiosité.

Un instant il hésita et puis, sa raison reprenant le dessus, il lui décrivit très précisément l'homme croisé au cimetière.

— Cet homme est dangereux, la prévint-il. Si vous le voyez, suivez-le très discrètement pour connaître ses habitudes : un appartement où il se rend ou un endroit où il aime à se divertir, cabaret ou tripot. Venez ensuite m'en avertir.

Il lui donna son adresse ainsi que celle du moine, lui décrivant comment y aller pour le trouver ou lui laisser un message. Ceci dit, il retomba dans une pesante torpeur car il n'avait nulle idée de la conversation à tenir.

— Qui était la femme qui vous accompagnait? demanda l'Écureuil d'un ton faussement innocent.

— Quelqu'un qu'on m'a imposé pour cette enquête.

— Ah donc, elle n'est pas... enfin... elle n'est pas votre...

— Dieu me garde, elle n'est rien pour moi! dit sans hésitation Volnay.

La jeune fille remua d'aise.

— Et vous n'avez personne pour s'occuper de vous?

Le commissaire aux morts étranges baissa la tête.

— Je suis seul, vous savez. J'ai cru connaître l'amour mais il m'a abandonné. Il me restait mon père mais il s'est perdu dans les jupons d'une aventurière et moi je suis comme un benêt à parler à ma pie qui ne sait que répéter mes dernières paroles...

L'Écureuil se pencha vers lui et son doigt suivit lentement la cicatrice qui courait du coin de son œil à sa tempe.

— Vous avez bien fait de venir, chuchota-t-elle. Je saurai comment chasser vos idées noires.

Il secoua la tête.

— Je ne suis pas venu pour cela, j'avais juste besoin de parler à un être humain, pas à une pie.

Les lèvres de l'Écureuil cherchèrent les siennes et, un moment, Volnay sentit son souffle tiède sur sa bouche. Il se laissa embrasser sans joie ni réaction. La jeune fille se recula comme s'il venait de la frapper.

— Pardonnez-moi, dit-elle.

Désorientée, elle le contempla. Sa connaissance des hommes ne lui était d'aucun secours face à celui-ci. Finalement, elle posa sa main sur son épaule.

— N'avez-vous donc personne chez qui aller?

Il secoua la tête.

— Je n'ai pas d'amis…

Et il ajouta dans un murmure :

— À part vous…

L'Écureuil se pencha encore un peu plus sur lui. Ses doigts glissèrent sur ses joues, y recueillant avec surprise une larme amère qui laissa un sillon argenté sur son passage.

— Vous feriez mieux de rentrer chez vous, fit-elle d'une voix soudain paniquée, ce que vous attendez de moi, je ne puis vous le donner…

Au début, le moine pensait résister à la tentation. Et puis, il s'aperçut que ses mains soudain empressées couraient sur le corps d'Hélène comme prises de folie et voilà que, sur son ventre lisse et poli, il imprimait la marque de dizaines de baisers. Maintenant, la jeune femme se tenait couchée à ses côtés et il goûtait au bonheur de la savoir là, son jeune corps encore vibrant d'énergie auprès de lui. Ses lèvres chaudes et aimées, cette haleine de vie, faisaient frissonner l'âme du moine. Le parfum d'Hélène semblait être passé par son sang qui charriait désormais dans ses veines des parfums d'automne et de printemps mélangés. La jeune femme souffla doucement sur son visage et à ses narines puis dit :

— Par la vertu de mon souffle, je t'enflammerai d'amour.

Le moine rit.

— J'aime toujours à la folie, on s'ennuie quand on aime médiocrement!

Et il ajouta malicieusement :

— J'ai toujours su que vous fréquentiez les sorcières!

— Et moi que vous étiez un homme vigoureux!

Le rire du moine s'amplifia.

— Certes!

Il rejeta la couverture et se leva.

— Où allez-vous?

— Faire de la lumière!

Elle se redressa avec un sursaut et la couverture glissa de ses épaules.

— Non, n'y allez pas!

Son ton était paniqué. Surpris, le moine gratta une allumette et se retourna vivement avant de se figer. Sur l'épaule d'Hélène, il venait d'apercevoir fugitivement une fleur de lys marquée au fer rouge. Elle était donc flétrie! Pas avec un "V" pour voleur mais par l'emblème royal réservé aux crimes les plus graves!

Elle le considéra avec un mélange de haine et d'effroi saisissant avant de recouvrir vivement son épaule.

— Vous avez vu?

Le moine ne répondit pas. La flamme de l'allumette lui brûla soudain les doigts et il la lâcha avec un grognement de douleur.

— Qu'avez-vous fait pour mériter une telle infamie? demanda-t-il d'un ton douloureux.

— J'ai tué un homme, répondit-elle d'un ton tranquille et détaché.

— Oh, fit le moine en reculant d'un pas.

— Ne craignez rien, je ne vais pas recommencer ce soir!

Il revint près d'elle et s'assit au bord du lit, gardant néanmoins une distance prudente avec la forme allongée immobile.

— Vous deviez avoir une bonne raison, lâcha-t-il enfin, prêt à tout lui pardonner.

— Des tas! Si vous saviez…

Dans la pénombre, il sut qu'elle gardait les yeux fixés au plafond.

— Nous vivions à Paris où mon père était apothicaire. Ma mère l'aidait à préparer ses drogues, cuissons et distillations. Elle possédait un réel talent pour cela. Mon père mourut lorsque j'étais très jeune et ma mère, qui avait bonne réputation, parvint à faire survivre son commerce. Mais elle ne se contenta pas de composer. Elle avait l'esprit curieux…

Hélène s'interrompit pour tourner lentement la tête vers lui.

— Comme vous, remarqua-t-elle.

Le moine hocha la tête et vint se recoucher auprès d'elle, humant discrètement le parfum de sa chair tiède.

— Elle cherchait à comprendre la propriété des plantes, les actions entre elles, et les principes chimiques, reprit Hélène d'un ton neutre. Elle se mit en quête d'explications dans des livres anciens, dans l'observation de la nature et en interrogeant les plus savants.

Elle fit une pause.

— Peut-être même vous a-t-elle consulté? ajouta-t-elle.

Le moine perçut un mouvement dans le noir, le bruit de draps froissés et tout à coup la jeune femme posa sa tête sur sa poitrine.

— Comme votre cœur bat vite, remarqua-t-elle.

Il l'enveloppa de ses bras.

— Continuez votre récit, ma chérie.

Un léger soupir s'exhala des lèvres d'Hélène.

— Ma mère se trouvait en butte à la jalousie d'autres apothicaires de son quartier. Le travail en laboratoire est en effet exclusivement réservé aux médecins, aux professeurs de chimie et aux maîtres apothicaires. On lui en contesta le titre et on lui en fit procès mais, comme vous le savez, la justice est lente, aussi continua-t-elle à exercer. Ses recherches l'amenèrent à composer un élixir d'anti-vapeurs crâniennes puis elle composa un philtre de beauté, un philtre d'amour... Au fil du temps, la clientèle changea. Sa réputation grandit mais pas dans les bons milieux. Les gens ne venaient plus seulement pour se faire soigner mais aussi pour espérer. Elle voulut leur faire plaisir et se plongea dans les grimoires de Paracelse ou Agrippa. Elle inventa une potion de répulsion pour faire fuir les indésirables puis un philtre de jeunesse.

La jeune femme s'interrompit et darda sur lui un œil pénétrant.

— D'après les croyances populaires, on est sorcière de mère en fille. Je ne vous fais pas peur?

Le moine secoua la tête en silence.

— Vous avez tort, rétorqua-t-elle. Peut-être puis-je d'un souffle dessécher la moelle de vos os!

246

Sans réaction de son compagnon, Hélène fit une petite moue et reprit son récit.

— La police commença à s'intéresser à ma mère et, de nouveau, ses confrères la dénoncèrent. Les policiers envahirent son laboratoire. On y trouva, comme chez tout apothicaire, des plantes, poudres, pommades, liqueurs et drogues qu'un expert jugea *bonnes ou mauvaises suivant l'utilisation que l'on en fait et la dose utilisée.* Ses grimoires la trahirent toutefois car ils contenaient des formules magiques. Elle se retrouva donc en prison au Châtelet. On la fit croupir dans une cellule infestée de rats avec de l'eau jusqu'aux mollets. Sa santé se détériora rapidement. Elle n'y résista pas un mois.

D'un geste instinctif, le moine la serra contre elle. La chaleur de son jeune corps sembla se joindre à la sienne, l'engourdissant insidieusement.

— Lorsqu'elle mourut, reprit Hélène, elle me laissa seule et sans famille. Les amis de mon père s'étaient depuis longtemps détournés de nous et les nouveaux amis de ma mère me fuirent comme la peste, craignant d'avoir affaire à la police. On me jeta à l'hôpital des Enfants-Perdus, c'était un mouroir. Je crus y devenir folle.

Elle sentit la main du moine lui caresser les épaules et ferma les yeux. C'était une main rassurante, celle d'un homme droit et loyal qui ne faillit jamais.

— Un couple de maraîchers cherchait un enfant à adopter, murmura-t-elle d'une voix altérée par l'émotion. Le mari me choisit. Ce n'était pas par charité mais pour faire de moi leur bonne à tout faire. J'avais quatorze ans. Comme je possédais de l'éducation et qu'eux relevaient d'une ignorance crasse, ils aimaient à m'humilier comme si cela pouvait être une revanche sur leur pauvre vie. Le moindre prétexte était bon, une marmite mal récurée et le mari m'attachait pour me suspendre à la poutre maîtresse de la grande pièce, parfois par les pieds, la tête en bas. Sa femme se contentait de m'appliquer contre les aisselles des œufs à la coque bouillants ou de me planter des aiguilles dans la paume de la main. Leurs enfants contemplaient le spectacle en hurlant de joie.

Le moine se raidit et attendit la suite avec appréhension.

— Un an passa, mon corps se développa et ma poitrine affirma ses rondeurs. Un jour, ce qui était écrit arriva. L'homme m'amena avec lui, soi-disant pour l'aider à vendre les produits de sa ferme au marché. À l'aller, il arrêta sa carriole sur le bord de la route, m'attacha les mains dans le dos et me viola. Comme je me débattis, pour me punir, je fis le reste du chemin à pied jusqu'au marché au bout d'une corde. Pendant la foire, je lui dérobai un couteau. De nouveau, au retour, il décida de me violer. Je comprenais désormais pourquoi son choix s'était porté sur moi à l'hôpital des Enfants-Perdus.

Elle jeta un regard farouche au moine. Dans la pénombre, celui-ci vit ses yeux briller comme ceux d'un chat en colère.

— Il ne revit plus jamais sa maison, fit-elle d'un ton glacial. Je le persuadai de me laisser faire pour qu'il ait plus de plaisir. Tout émoustillé, il accepta et je m'assis à califourchon sur lui avant de lui planter mon couteau dans le cœur. Je visai mal et il me fallut m'y reprendre à plusieurs reprises. Il criait plus fort que les cochons qu'il saignait à la ferme. Je l'ai frappé et frappé, ensuite, j'ai attendu qu'il se vide de son sang. Cela a été le plus heureux moment de ma vie.

Le moine sursauta. Il sentit plus qu'il ne vit Hélène poser sur lui un regard moqueur.

— Vous avez cru à mon histoire ?

— Oui, fit-il doucement.

— Il ne faut pas, fit-elle sur un ton de doux reproche. Mais je vais quand même vous raconter la suite.

De nouveau, elle appuya la tête sur sa poitrine. Cette fois, le moine caressa ses cheveux comme pour l'apaiser.

— Je retournai à la maison où l'on m'avait tant maltraitée et j'y mis le feu. Je regardais la femme et ses enfants s'éparpiller dans les champs en hurlant, m'assurant qu'il n'en restait plus un dans la maison. Ma vengeance terminée, je marchai jusqu'à Paris en mendiant. Là-bas, je fus arrêtée pour vol et on m'amena devant le commissaire de quartier. Je sentis que je le troublais. Je lui lançai quelques œillades engageantes et il me proposa d'arranger mon affaire et de me prendre pour servante. Il vivait seul avec une cuisinière qui lui servait de bonne à tout faire. Il l'envoya dehors sous prétexte de courses et me prit, à moitié habillée, sur la table de la cuisine. Cela dut lui plaire car il me conserva avec lui.

— Quel porc ! lança le moine d'un ton dégoûté. Un commissaire du Châtelet.

— Un homme, Guillaume, le reprit-elle d'un ton las. Seulement un homme…

Elle semblait fatiguée.

— Il n'était pas vraiment méchant d'ailleurs. Il ne me battait presque jamais et ses besoins étaient vite satisfaits. J'eus droit à une chambre sous les combles et à des livres. Il m'apprit à tirer au pistolet et à manier l'épée. Un jour, je proposai qu'il m'emploie pour une enquête. Je me fis marquer au fer rouge des criminels pour m'introduire dans une bande de voleurs et d'assassins que je lui permis d'arrêter. Tout cela l'impressionna fort. Dès lors, je lui devins indispensable et un jour, peu avant sa mort, il me présenta à Sartine… Vous pouvez deviner la suite…

Le silence tomba brutalement entre eux.

— Pour la fleur de lys, lui glissa-t-elle au bout d'un instant, ne dites rien à votre fils !

— M'avez-vous vraiment menti pour votre histoire ?

— Bien sûr que je vous ai menti ! Pourquoi irais-je donc raconter ma vie au premier venu ?

À sa grande surprise, le moine approuva.

— Je comprends, moi-même je ferais de même ! Néanmoins, votre histoire est en partie vraie pour ce que j'en sais.

Étonnée, elle le regarda.

— Votre mère m'a effectivement consulté à un moment de ma vie, expliqua le moine avec une douceur infinie. Je n'étais pas en France à l'époque où elle fut jetée en prison. Ce n'est qu'un an plus tard que j'appris cette affreuse nouvelle. Son corps avait été jeté à la fosse commune et je n'avais pas un endroit où me recueillir. Je savais qu'elle avait une fille et la recherchai pour m'assurer qu'elle allait bien mais personne ne put me renseigner sur votre sort.

Il soupira et ajouta d'un ton las :

— Je suis désolé.

Hélène se souleva sur un coude et le contempla songeusement.

— Ce n'est pas votre faute, dit-elle enfin. Je sais que si vous m'aviez retrouvée, vous vous seriez bien occupé de moi.

La main de la jeune femme se promena impudemment sur le corps fin, noueux et musculeux du moine, suivant les nombreuses cicatrices qui marquaient sa peau de l'empreinte indélébile d'une jeunesse tumultueuse.

— Mais peut-être pourrez-vous me renseigner? chuchota-t-elle.

— Quoi donc?

Elle lui mordilla légèrement le lobe de l'oreille et demanda d'un ton provocant :

— Est-ce que je fais l'amour mieux que ma mère?

XVIII

LEVÉE DE CORPS ET AUTRES DIABLERIES

L'aube se levait à peine, baignant d'une faible lueur croix et angelots aux pieds glacés. Les rafales de vent faisaient tourbillonner la neige poudreuse entre les tombes. Telle la statue du commandeur, la haute et rigide silhouette du commissaire aux morts étranges se découpait comme une ombre spectrale. À ses pieds s'entassaient des pelletées de terre. Le soleil n'avait pas encore percé lorsqu'on ôta le couvercle du cercueil de Sophia. Volnay s'approcha d'une démarche raide et baissa les yeux. Impassible, il se retourna ensuite vers son père.

— Regarde par toi-même!

Le moine vint à pas lents, presque malgré lui. Il jeta un coup d'œil prudent au cercueil et son teint vira au gris.

— Je suis un âne bâté.

Il venait de constater qu'il s'agissait bien du cadavre du gardien du cimetière.

— C'est peu de le dire! renchérit son fils.

Le commissaire de quartier, Cornevin, s'approcha à son tour. Volnay devait à son obligeance l'ouverture de la tombe.

— Mon Dieu, fit-il en blêmissant, ce n'est pas la petite Sophia.

Volnay se tourna vivement vers lui.

— Gardez cela secret! Rien de tout ceci ne doit être révélé.

L'autre déglutit péniblement et acquiesça.

— D'accord mais m'expliquerez-vous enfin ce que signifie cette diablerie?

— Plus tard, plus tard…

Volnay se saisit du bras de son père et l'entraîna loin de la tombe au bord de laquelle le commissaire de quartier et les fossoyeurs les observaient avec curiosité. Il jeta un coup d'œil pour s'assurer qu'ils se trouvaient assez éloignés du petit groupe.

— Père, il y a une chose que je ne m'explique pas, c'est que tu aies considéré cette enfant comme morte alors qu'elle ne l'était pas ! Comment as-tu pu ?

Le moine se tordit les mains de désespoir.

— C'est sans doute la propriété de la substance qu'elle a ingurgitée malgré elle. Avec une dose importante, celle-ci doit ralentir toutes les fonctions vitales, les battements du cœur et donc tout signe de vie. D'ailleurs, bien des personnes ne doivent pas s'en réveiller dans de telles circonstances car seule la dose fait le poison…

— Oui, et comme tu ne t'es pas livré sur elle à une autopsie…

— Dieu du ciel, heureusement que je n'ai pas eu envie de charcuter cette pauvre enfant !

Le moine se signa ce qui surprit fort son fils.

— Sophia était plongée dans un sommeil aux portes de la mort mais elle était bien vivante, déclara Volnay les yeux mi-clos. La cérémonie devait l'exiger. La mise à mort n'intervenait qu'à son terme. Mais le gardien du cimetière est arrivé. Il a fallu le tuer. On l'a étouffé avec beaucoup de sang-froid pour ne pas laisser de traces. Et puis les participants ont dû vouloir reprendre la cérémonie. Seulement, ce n'était pas leur jour : des déterreurs de cadavres sont arrivés ! Nos participants de la messe noire ont cédé à la panique et se sont enfuis en laissant Sophia sur la pierre tombale. La suite, tu la connais. Les assistants du gardien sont allés voir les feux follets, ont trouvé le cadavre de leur maître et alerté le guet.

Le moine respira un grand coup.

— J'étais très troublé ce soir-là, avoua-t-il. Le corps de Sophia était glacé et elle portait des marques à son cou. Cela, ajouté à la substance qui la mettait en état d'hibernation, m'a complètement trompé. Dans ma cave aussi il faisait froid. Et puis, je suis tombé malade.

Une vapeur s'exhala de ses poumons en même temps qu'une longue plainte. Celle-ci n'émut pas Volnay qui considéra son père avec colère.

— J'ai mis du temps mais je suis arrivé à comprendre que Sophia n'était pas morte, moi! Toi-même serais arrivé aussi vite, sinon plus, à la même conclusion en temps normal. Seulement voilà tu n'es pas dans ton état normal. Cette jeune femme, Hélène, t'a fait tourner la tête!

Pour la première fois depuis longtemps, le moine se mit en colère.

— Mon fils, tu commences à me baver dans la cornemuse!

Surpris, Volnay ouvrit toute grande la bouche et la referma stupidement. Il contempla un instant son père et puis son attention fut attirée par l'irruption intempestive d'un homme dans son champ de vision. La perruque aux rouleaux de pigeon de Sartine semblait voler d'une tombe à l'autre. Le lieutenant général de police marchait à grands pas dans l'allée, le visage fermé. Avec appréhension, Volnay le regarda se diriger vers eux d'un air décidé, écrasant la neige fraîche sous ses talons.

— Qu'est-ce que ceci? murmura le moine.

— Ça, fit son fils, ce sont les ennuis!

De loin, ils entendirent les imprécations de leur supérieur qui venait de les apercevoir.

— Tambour et cymbales, soupira le moine. Cet homme remplit le monde de bruit!

En arrivant devant eux, Sartine ne les salua même pas.

— Alors, est-ce vrai?

— Oui, monsieur, fit Volnay d'un ton neutre. C'est le gardien du cimetière qui a été enterré à sa place. À mon avis, Sophia est bien vivante. Nous avons également découvert que M. Marly, son père, n'est pas mort et sans doute à l'origine de toute cette affaire…

Et le commissaire aux morts étranges raconta pourquoi il en était arrivé à cette évidence. Sartine le coupa sans ménagement.

— Décidément, vous êtes en dessous de tout! Non seulement, vous laissez cette prostituée vous échapper mais vous perdez aussi le cadavre de la victime qui par ailleurs n'est même pas morte! Pas plus que son père d'ailleurs, d'après vous! En

253

fait, dans cette affaire, personne n'est mort à part le gardien du cimetière ! Mais qu'est-ce que c'est que cette histoire abracadabrante ? De qui se moque-t-on ? De la police du roi ?

Il se tourna vers le moine et, se haussant sur la pointe des pieds, vint coller son visage à un fil du sien.

— Et vous, vous n'êtes même pas capable de voir qu'une personne est vivante ? Vieux fou !

— Je ne suis pas vieux, rétorqua le moine.

Puis il se retourna vers son fils :

— Décidément, c'est l'évangile en cours : je suis vieux !

Sartine recula et siffla entre ses dents comme un serpent. Jamais, Volnay ne l'avait vu dans cet état.

— Mes policiers, dit-il d'une voix où perçait une sourde menace, doivent être de bonnes vie et mœurs et de confession catholique lorsqu'ils me prêtent serment. Ce n'est pas votre cas, je le sais parfaitement. Je vous tolérais jusqu'à présent comme un élément étranger au sein d'un corps parfaitement sain pour votre efficacité mais force est de constater que celle-ci a disparu.

Il contempla un instant ses bottes souillées par la neige puis releva la tête.

— Je vous retire cette enquête et vous suspends de vos fonctions !

— Qui mènera l'enquête à votre place ? protesta Volnay. Ce sot de Siltieri ?

Sartine l'écrasa de son dédain.

— Vous me connaissez mal ! Ai-je la réputation de mettre tous mes œufs dans le même panier ?

— C'est Hélène qui va poursuivre l'enquête, constata le commissaire aux morts étranges avec amertume.

Le lieutenant général de police eut un geste agacé.

— Votre moine me l'a convertie ! Elle ne me servira plus à rien dans cette affaire. Non, j'ai un autre atout dans ma manche et il est temps pour moi de le jouer !

Dans un grand bruissement, il tourna les talons et s'éloigna. Soudain il s'arrêta et se retourna.

— Bien entendu, vous ne serez plus rémunéré et vous devrez me faire parvenir au Châtelet le solde de mes avances pour vos frais en me justifiant ceux-ci !

— Ça, c'est très mesquin, murmura le moine lorsque Sartine eut de nouveau tourné le dos. Il veut rogner notre écuelle pour étrangler l'affaire!

Et il ajouta pour lui-même :

— Heureusement que j'en mets un peu de côté à chaque enquête pour assurer nos arrières. Il n'est pas encore venu le temps où nous ne pourrons plus faire frire!

Volnay le considéra avec effarement.

— Quoi?

Son père haussa les épaules avec fatalisme.

— Tu es trop honnête alors je suis prévoyant pour deux! Sans le savoir, Sartine finance nos vieux jours!

Pour la première fois depuis longtemps, Volnay rit. Son rire s'éleva au-dessus des pierres, léger dans l'air immobile. C'était le rire clair d'un enfant qui retrouve son père. Il semblait soudain débarrassé d'une chape de glace. Sous les yeux des fossoyeurs, les deux hommes se livrèrent alors à un étrange manège en se tapant dans les mains, paumes retournées avant de se congratuler. Puis, leur gaieté exprimée, ils retournèrent à l'entrée du cimetière sous un soleil qui ne réchauffait rien.

— Père, qu'a voulu dire Sartine en disant que tu avais converti Hélène?

Le moine eut l'air gêné.

— Je n'en ai pas la moindre idée, au fil du temps, Sartine devient de plus en plus difficile à comprendre!

— Toi et Hélène, vous n'avez pas… euh… tu vois ce que je veux dire?

— Oh, mon fils, elle a vingt ans de moins que moi!

— Un peu plus, père, un peu plus…

Ils marchèrent en silence entre les tombes glacées, heureux de leur complicité retrouvée jusqu'à ce que le moine questionne Volnay.

— Mon fils, puis-je te poser une question?

— Oui, père.

Le moine humecta ses lèvres gercées par le froid. Sa mâchoire tremblait légèrement.

— Ai-je tant vieilli que ça que tout le monde me traite de vieux gâteux?

Sa voix était si tremblante que le cœur de Volnay se serra. Dans un geste instinctif, il s'arrêta et prit son père dans ses bras.

— Sartine et moi ne sommes que des imbéciles. Bien sûr que non, papa!

Le moine tressaillit, Volnay venait de prononcer le plus beau mot du monde pour son oreille. Naturellement, sa main prit celle de son fils et celui-ci qui, adolescent, avait horreur de cela, se laissa faire sans résistance. Ce fut ainsi qu'ils sortirent du cimetière.

XIX

SOPHIA ET AUTRES DIABLERIES

D'abord Sophia n'avait rien vu, rien entendu. Ce fut une voix grave et cuivrée qui la sortit de sa léthargie. De plus en plus réceptive, elle s'efforça de capter des sons, au début inaudibles, puis elle entrouvrit les yeux, s'efforçant d'accommoder sa vision. Une présence s'affairait dans la pièce froide. Elle guetta du coin de l'œil une ombre dans son champ de vision ou un changement de forme, s'efforçant de distinguer les couleurs mais le monde restait gris. Elle se rendormit.

Les heures passèrent et, lorsque Sophia s'éveilla véritablement le matin du second jour, ce fut pour constater qu'elle se trouvait dans une cave glaciale. Seule une lugubre lumière mouillée filtrait d'un lointain soupirail. Heureusement une épaisse couverture la recouvrait tout entière et, délicatesse suprême, on lui en avait étendu une autre sous elle. Dans sa compassion, le moine avait même glissé en cette occasion un coussin sous sa nuque.

Sophia essaya de bouger ses membres mais sans vraiment y parvenir. Évitant de céder à la panique, elle se concentra sur une de ses mains jusqu'à faire fonctionner ses doigts l'un après l'autre. Lorsqu'elle glissa un mollet hors de la couverture, le froid la mordit. Tous ses mouvements semblaient se ralentir. Frissonnante, elle réussit au bout d'une heure à s'asseoir, enveloppée dans la chaude couverture.

Si l'enfer était un gigantesque laboratoire rempli de fourneaux, de fioles et de cornues, Sophia devait donc s'y trouver mais, en y réfléchissant, elle ne se souvint pas d'avoir commis quelque chose pour le mériter. Elle pensa alors au purgatoire car elle n'estimait pas avoir vécu suffisamment pour avoir mérité son paradis. Mais pourquoi personne n'était-il là pour l'accueillir? Perplexe, elle réfléchit. Il y avait bien eu une personne près d'elle. Il lui semblait se souvenir d'une bure comme celle d'un moine. Il lui parlait gentiment. Il fallait qu'elle retrouve cet homme ou cet esprit.

Sophia se laissa glisser à terre, étouffant un gémissement lorsque ses pieds nus prirent contact avec le sol glacé. Resserrant la couverture autour de son corps, elle entreprit d'explorer les lieux. Jamais, elle n'avait observé un tel endroit. On aurait dit qu'un savant fou avait entrepris de mettre le monde en éprouvettes ou en alambics. D'un pas mal assuré, elle tenta d'échapper à ces lieux étranges mais la porte de la cave était fermée à clé.

C'est donc bien le purgatoire, se dit-elle. *On ne peut en sortir avant l'heure mais où donc sont les autres âmes en peine?*

Elle remarqua alors qu'on avait laissé un morceau de pain blanc sur une table ainsi qu'une carafe d'eau. Elle avait faim et mangea donc le pain, s'étonnant que dans la mort on dût ainsi continuer à s'alimenter. Ensuite, elle eut soif et but. Ainsi rassasiée et désaltérée, elle fit de nouveau le tour du laboratoire et découvrit une seconde cave. Un frisson la secoua tout entière. Le cadavre d'un homme gisait là et nulle couverture ou drap ne le recouvrait.

Fébrilement, Sophia fit le tour des lieux, secouant en vain la lourde porte. Le cœur battant, elle revint ensuite dans la deuxième cave. Là, elle découvrit une autre porte, plus petite et plus basse. Elle tendit la main vers le loquet et découvrit qu'il jouait. Un escalier très raide la mena jusqu'à une chambre. Dans celle-ci, sur un lit à bas piliers, dormait un homme. Elle le contempla avec surprise puis pensa qu'il ressemblait à l'inconnu qui parlait souvent au-dessus d'elle pendant qu'elle dormait. Une certaine tiédeur régnait dans la pièce et elle se sentit mieux, s'enhardissant à ouvrir un coffre et y découvrant avec plaisir des robes et mantelets, des manchettes et coiffes ornées de dentelles, des bas et une paire de mules et des bottines. Elle se vêtit, choisissant la robe la plus chaude même si elle était trop grande pour elle, des bas de laine. Les bottines étaient en revanche à peu près à sa taille.

Une fois vêtue, Sophia regarda autour d'elle. Ses besoins primaires assouvis, boire et ne plus avoir froid, elle se sentait vide et inutile. Son attention fut alors attirée au chevet du dormeur par une belle couverture au cuir vieilli et marbré sur laquelle elle déchiffra un titre : *Éloge de la folie* d'Érasme. Elle le prit en main pour le feuilleter puis le reposa, le trouvant trop compliqué.

Ne sachant que faire, elle s'assit au bord du lit, savourant le confort de celui-ci, le plaisir de ses nouveaux vêtements et la douce quiétude de la pièce. Au bout d'un moment, l'homme ouvrit les yeux. Ils étaient remplis d'humanité. Il lui parla et elle lui répondit même si la conversation n'avait pas grand sens pour elle. Saisie d'une brusque impulsion, elle lui déclara avec beaucoup d'assurance qu'il rêvait. Elle en venait en effet à penser qu'elle était un ange et que nulle personne sur terre ne devait connaître sa présence. L'homme ferma les yeux et, légère et silencieuse, elle se glissa de nouveau par la porte.

Sophia ne redescendit pas dans la cave. À mi-chemin de l'escalier, une porte donnait sur un minuscule cellier. En refermant la porte, elle avait tout juste la place pour y étendre ses deux couvertures et s'y enrouler. Il faisait moins froid ici que dans la cave. Après avoir vidé un pot de confiture, elle s'endormit, enroulée dans sa couverture, un goût de framboise dans la bouche.

Elle se réveilla d'un sommeil sans rêve qui parut lui avoir duré des années et gagna la chambre où elle avait rencontré le moine malade. Elle n'y trouva personne. La maison qu'elle traversa était vide et silencieuse mais soudain une masse de poil se précipita sur elle en glapissant de joie. Elle tomba à terre et une langue râpeuse courut sur son visage. Éperdue de joie, elle serra son chien dans ses bras.

— C'est donc vrai que tu es là ?

Un long moment, elle le tint contre elle, réchauffant son corps à sa chaleur. Puis elle eut faim et trouva un reste de beau pain blanc qu'elle partagea avec le chien. Ainsi ragaillardie, elle s'enhardit et résolut de sortir pour voir à quoi ressemblait le monde après la mort.

La porte était fermée. Elle explora les lieux et trouva une clé suspendue à un clou dans la cuisine. Elle s'en saisit, la tourna dans la serrure et sortit. Ensuite, très naturellement, elle referma à clé derrière elle. Le monde était le même que dans la vraie vie. Dans la rue, elle fut assaillie par le bruit. Les commerçants vantaient leurs produits et, par moments, lui parvenait aux oreilles la voix reconnaissable des cochers, le timbre cassé d'avoir trop crié.

Elle avançait à pas lents dans la ville avec une liberté nouvellement acquise. La jeune enfant éprouvait désormais un sentiment de paix même si des souvenirs mélancoliques frémissaient encore en elle. Sophia entreprit de retourner à la maison qui l'avait vue grandir. Elle ne s'y sentait rattaché en rien. La vie y avait été des plus mornes et des plus ennuyeuses. Néanmoins, elle constituait un repère dans une existence, ou plutôt une non-existence, qui en manquait. Sans émotion, elle revit les pierres noires et la tour qui se dressait dans le ciel. Elle s'assit un instant sur les marches, perdue dans ses réflexions. Des souvenirs contraires la firent alors frissonner et elle se hâta de s'éloigner. Elle croisa la servante, lui jetant un regard vide qui parut la terroriser car elle se signa comme pour conjurer un mauvais sort. Sophia comprit alors qu'elle était morte et devenue une de ces revenantes dont sa nourrice lui parlait à la veillée.

Témoin fidèle de ses pèlerinages, le chien l'accompagnait, la queue frétillante. Son séjour chez le moine lui avait profité. On l'avait lavé et frotté, coupé le poil en trop, flatté et donné sans compter une nourriture abondante. De retrouver ensuite sa petite maîtresse, ou celle qu'il s'était choisie comme telle, semblait lui conférer une énergie débordante.

Ne sachant où se diriger, Sophia décida de suivre le chien qui semblait parfaitement savoir où aller. Il la conduisit non loin de la maison du moine, dans un curieux dédale de cours, chacune plus petite que l'autre au fur et à mesure qu'elle avançait. Dans la troisième de ces cours, se dressait un arbre. Elle s'amusa à en secouer les branches et la neige retomba en poudre sur elle. Le chien alla jusqu'à la porte de la maison sur laquelle donnait la cour et leva la patte pour uriner. Elle rit puis le gronda avant de l'imiter.

Lorsqu'elle jugea qu'il était temps de rentrer, Sophia s'age-nouilla près de son chien et lui demanda de la ramener à ce qu'elle considérait désormais comme sa maison ou son lieu de transit vers une autre vie. Le chien haleta doucement entre les paumes de ses mains puis la conduisit non loin de là. Sophia sortit la clé de sa poche et ouvrit. Elle alla jusqu'à la cuisine et partagea un biscuit avec son ami à quatre pattes, près des cendres de l'âtre. Se sentant fatiguée, elle embrassa son animal et gagna la chambre du moine. Le chien geignit et gratta à la porte puis se tut. Sophia descendit jusqu'à la cave. Horrifiée, elle y découvrit un corps calciné et regagna vivement le cellier. Encore frissonnante, elle s'y réfugia. L'endroit était rassurant avec ses jambons pendus, ses pots de confitures, ses herbes odorantes et ses bouteilles cachetées soigneusement rangées. Elle trouva un panneau et un fusain près des bouteilles. Un autre panneau récapitulait les noms des vins et leurs années. Elle s'amusa à écrire sur celui qui était vierge : *Interdit à Dieu d'entrer* et songea à l'apposer sur la porte de son repaire avant de renoncer. Elle trouverait bien une autre manière de l'employer. Comme elle y songeait, la fatigue la gagna soudain. Elle ferma les yeux et sentit son esprit dériver avant de s'endormir au milieu de parfums de thym et de laurier.

XX

DANS LA TÊTE D'UN CHIEN ET AUTRES DIABLERIES

Un blanc laiteux flottait dans les rues. Comme à leur habitude, au petit matin, les employés de la voirie ramassaient crottes et cadavres dans Paris. Les boulangers de Gonesse envahissaient les rues avec leurs petits pains. Par centaines, les porteurs d'eau se faufilaient dans les immeubles pour vendre l'eau de la Seine, désinfectée au vinaigre blanc. Dans l'aube glacée, les deux enquêteurs regagnèrent à grands pas le domicile du moine. Celui-ci ressassait toute l'affaire dans sa tête avant de la régurgiter en phrases hachées.

— Sophia entendait nos paroles dans son demi-sommeil ou sa demi-mort et puis elle s'est réveillée. Par chance pour elle, j'avais posé une chaude couverture sur son corps. Cela l'a empêchée de mourir définitivement de froid dans ma cave !

— Elle aurait pu mourir de froid dans le cimetière.

— Nous sommes venus très vite et l'avons apportée. De plus, la substance avait ralenti son métabolisme pour la faire entrer dans une sorte d'hibernation tout comme un ours.

— Mais quand elle s'est réveillée ?

— Elle s'est crue morte ! C'est une pauvre enfant de douze ans à qui on a parlé de l'enfer, du paradis et du purgatoire ! Elle est venue me visiter dans ma chambre car j'ai un accès direct à ma seconde cave. Elle s'est habillée dans un coffre des vêtements de ta pauvre mère et elle m'a parlé. Fiévreux et croyant avoir affaire à un spectre, je ne l'ai pas détrompée sur son état. Plus tard, elle a navigué entre la cave et ma chambre, allant dans la cuisine pour se nourrir.

— Et c'est probablement ce faisant qu'elle a compris qu'elle n'était pas morte…

— C'est vraisemblable. Aussi s'est-elle rendue chez elle en amenant le chien mais elle s'est contentée de s'asseoir sur le perron de sa maison. Quelque chose l'a empêchée de rentrer.

— Est-ce elle qui a mis le feu à la maison de son père?

Le moine fronça les sourcils.

— Tu m'en demandes trop!

Une fois arrivés, ils fouillèrent minutieusement toute la maison du moine, découvrant dans le petit cellier l'endroit où Sophia avait dormi et le pot de confiture vide.

— Où peut-elle bien être? se lamenta le moine.

— Elle entre et elle sort à sa guise, remarqua Volnay. Toutefois cette nuit elle n'est pas rentrée puisque tu m'as raconté avoir mis une clochette à ta porte, côté intérieur pour te prévenir de son éventuel retour après la disparition du chien.

— Par un tel froid, elle est peut-être morte cette fois-ci.

— À moins que…

— À quoi penses-tu?

— Le chien l'accompagne. Si elle ne sait où aller, elle peut suivre cet intelligent animal.

Le commissaire aux morts étranges croisa les bras, appuyant son poing sous son menton et fermant à demi les yeux, dans l'attitude qu'il adoptait parfois pour mieux réfléchir.

— Je ne sais pas entrer dans la tête de Sophia, avoua-t-il au bout d'un instant, aussi vais-je tenter de pénétrer dans celle de son chien!

— Tu as parfaitement raison, mon fils. Platon remarque que le chien sait distinguer un ennemi d'un ami, l'ennemi étant celui qu'il ne connaît pas, ce qui suppose, sinon un certain savoir, une certaine mémoire. Quant à Aristote, dans *De anima*, il attribue quelques qualités intellectuelles aux espèces animales, spécialement à celles qui ne se contentent pas de procréer mais nourrissent et élèvent leurs petits, allant même jusqu'à développer une forme de collaboration sociale. Note d'ailleurs que dans l'espèce humaine, certains ne vont pas si loin et, après avoir procréé, abandonnent femme et progéniture!

Les parenthèses du moine pouvant être interminables, Volnay le coupa gentiment.

— Le chien ne la conduira donc pas chez son ancien maître où il ne prenait que des coups.

— Quoique la fidélité de ces animaux soit parfois touchante, ils sont comme ces enfants que leurs pères frappent mais qui tentent désespérément de leur manifester de l'amour.

— Oui, bien. Le chien connaît son quartier. Il y a peut-être des endroits où il trouve plus facilement à se nourrir, dans les cours des auberges par exemple… Il a suivi aussi Sophia au cimetière où on l'avait entraînée pour la messe noire mais pourquoi y retournerait-il ? Il t'a enfin suivi chez toi mais aussi chez moi puis dans la ruelle de l'Or… Oui ! Il est entré avec nous chez la Dame de l'Eau et y a trouvé un bon feu ! Elle lui a même donné à manger !

— Tu crois donc que son estomac gouverne *chien-chien* ? s'exclama son père outré.

— Arrête de l'appeler ainsi et trouve-lui plutôt un nom !

Le moine plissa les yeux.

— Bonne idée, je vais l'appeler Aristote !

Volnay leva les yeux au ciel puis se décida rapidement.

— Couvre-toi, nous allons aller chez moi puis, si nous ne trouvons rien, nous nous rendrons à la ruelle de l'Or.

— Bien, je vais laisser un mot à l'intention d'Hélène pour qu'elle nous attende ici. Je ne sais pas où elle est passée après… euh… cette nuit.

Son fils lui jeta un bref coup d'œil mais se tut. Dehors, un ciel vitrifié les accueillit. Ils se rendirent chez Volnay puis gagnèrent ensuite la rue Saint-Jacques. Là, le commissaire aux morts étranges s'immobilisa. Face à eux, une silhouette sombre se découpait dans la blancheur immaculée. Les yeux du commissaire aux morts étranges s'étrécirent.

— Attends-moi, fit-il au moine.

Il traversa rapidement la rue et rejoignit la silhouette encapuchonnée. Les têtes des deux hommes s'inclinèrent l'une vers l'autre. Le moine observa attentivement. L'inconnu semblait murmurer à l'oreille de son fils. Celui-ci l'interrompit à plusieurs reprises pour le questionner. À la dernière réponse, le commissaire aux morts étranges leva la tête en l'air, son regard semblant se perdre dans les tourbillons frisés des fumées de cheminée. Puis il tira quelques pièces de sa bourse et les glissa dans la main de l'autre avant de rejoindre le moine.

— C'est une des mouches qui surveillent le quartier où a disparu l'homme à l'épée croisé au cimetière lors de l'enterrement de Sophia, expliqua Volnay. Les recherches n'ont rien donné mais je leur ai demandé de persévérer.

— Vraiment? fit le moine avec méfiance. Sartine nous a retiré l'enquête et donc tout pouvoir sur ses mouches.

Il s'arrêta devant une vieille femme qui, pour deux sols, vendait du café au lait dans un gobelet. Le visage rouge, l'œil sanglant et la respiration saccadée, elle portait sur le dos une fontaine en fer-blanc qui devait peser bien lourd.

— Les ordres du lieutenant général de police vont mettre un peu de temps à parvenir aux mouches, dit Volnay tandis que son père sirotait son café. Ce ne sont que des pions, des ombres dans la rue…

Son père acquiesça. Il prit une nouvelle tasse de café, autant pour soulager un peu la femme de son fardeau que pour doubler son obole. Ceci fait, ils reprirent leur route.

— Dans la *Métaphysique*, reprit gaiement le moine, Aristote écrit que les chiens sont pourvus de sensations, celles-ci générant la mémoire. Or la mémoire permet d'apprendre et donc de développer une forme d'intelligence. Il est plus aisé d'ailleurs de la développer lorsque l'on est doté de l'ouïe, ce qui n'est pas le cas de tous les animaux, les abeilles étant par exemple sourdes comme un pot!

Le commissaire aux morts étranges continua sa marche sans répondre, entièrement concentré sur les paroles de la mouche qui résonnaient encore à ses oreilles, ouvrant un abîme sous ses pieds. Sans s'apercevoir de ce manque d'attention, son père gazouillait tout en battant l'air des bras.

— Un philosophe stoïcien, Sextus Empiricus, démontre qu'un chien poursuivant un gibier qui peut avoir pris trois voies différentes, s'il renifle et ne sent rien pour les deux premières, ne reniflera pas la troisième car il en déduit qu'il l'a prise!

Le moine agita triomphalement un doigt en l'air.

— Il manifeste donc une capacité de réflexion!

Le moine pouvait être intarissable. Volnay subit en chemin, sans broncher, l'étude du philosophe Héraclite d'Éphèse, son père concluant par sa citation préférée de ce dernier : "Je gémis sur l'instabilité des choses ; tout y flotte comme dans un breuvage en mixture ; amalgame de plaisir et de peine, de science et d'ignorance, de grandeur et de petitesse : le haut et le bas s'y confondent et alternent dans le jeu du siècle."

Les deux hommes pénétrèrent enfin dans la ruelle de l'Or. L'étrangeté de l'endroit qu'ils connaissaient pourtant bien leur fit adopter spontanément l'attitude furtive et silencieuse des gens qui s'y glissaient. Le moine baissa sa capuche sur ses yeux et le commissaire aux morts étranges rentra le menton dans le col de son manteau. Ensemble, ils frappèrent à la porte de la Dame de l'Eau.

On leur ouvrit très rapidement et ils entrèrent avec reconnaissance dans la maison, découvrant du même coup le chien et un bon feu flambant dans la cheminée. L'animal se leva en glapissant et se jeta sur le moine, les deux pattes avant levées, cherchant à lui passer sa langue râpeuse sur le visage.

— Voilà *chien-chien*… euh… Aristote! s'exclama le moine en lui ébouriffant le crâne. Remarque comme il a le sens du juste puisqu'il remue la queue de contentement en nous voyant! Ce qu'il fallait démontrer!

La Dame de l'Eau le regarda avec stupéfaction. Volnay haussa les épaules.

— Une démonstration de l'intelligence animale, expliqua-t-il brièvement. Sophia est-elle là?

— Oui. J'ai entendu gratter à la porte cette nuit. C'était le chien et je l'ai tout de suite reconnu. Il était accompagné de cette jeune fille. Elle semblait épuisée et transie. Je l'ai fait entrer puis lui ai donné à manger. Elle a répondu à mes questions par des réponses sans queue ni tête et s'est endormie à table. Il a fallu que je la réveille pour l'amener à ma chambre. Cela fait bien douze heures qu'elle dort! Je pensais l'accompagner chez vous une fois debout.

Elle les conduisit à sa chambre où dormait Sophia. À leur entrée, le chien agita joyeusement la queue, fit le tour du lit, renifla les draps puis se coucha pesamment en poussant un profond soupir.

Les deux hommes contemplèrent Sophia dans un silence émerveillé. Bien que pâle, son visage n'avait plus la teinte livide de la nuit dans le cimetière. Sur l'oreiller, il était auréolé d'un casque de cheveux d'or filé. Les deux hommes admirèrent la finesse de ses traits, la moue charmante de ses lèvres abandonnées au sommeil et ses petits poings crispés sur les draps.

Le moine sembla en tomber amoureux à l'instant même. Aussi son fils crut-il plus prudent de le raisonner d'emblée.

— Nous ne pouvons pas la ramener chez nous, dit-il. Sartine nous a retiré l'affaire et il serait immédiatement informé par ses mouches de l'arrivée de Sophia.

Il s'interrompit et fronça les sourcils, l'air tendu.

— Je pense également que Sartine nous cache bien des choses dans cette affaire.

Couché au pied du lit, le chien releva la tête avant de la reposer sur ses deux pattes avant, l'air désolé. À cet instant, Sophia ouvrit les yeux et les fixa. Son regard semblait être le miroir de son âme. Le moine la contempla, extasié.

— Sophia!

Un long frémissement saisit l'enfant.

— Suis-je morte? demanda-t-elle angoissée.

— Non, ma jeune amie, vous êtes bien vivante!

Elle coula vers lui un doux regard de reproche.

— Alors pourquoi ne pas m'avoir détrompée lorsque nous avons parlé?

Le moine soupira.

— J'étais dévoré par la fièvre et je croyais rêver…

Il baissa la tête et murmura :

— Où donc peut-on rencontrer des êtres tels que vous sinon dans nos rêves?

Elle ne sembla pas comprendre. Aussi le commissaire aux morts étranges intervint avec peu de ménagement.

— Qui donc a voulu vous tuer?

Sophia se troubla.

— Je ne sais pas, je ne sais plus… tant de monde…

Le policier se pencha vers elle.

— Avez-vous rencontré des gens effrayants ou des inconnus qui n'auraient pas dû s'intéresser à vous?

Elle ferma les yeux comme pour mieux réfléchir avant de les ouvrir tout grands, la mine effrayée.

— L'an dernier, je crois, un jour où je jouais aux cailloux sur les marches de ma maison, un carrosse s'est brusquement arrêté devant moi. Un homme a passé la tête par la portière. Il portait une très jolie perruque et de beaux habits. Il m'a demandé si je me nommais Sophia. Quand je lui ai répondu que oui, il m'a souri et m'a tendu une pièce en or pour que j'aille m'acheter une belle poupée.

— Cet homme a-t-il dit comment il s'appelait? la questionna Volnay.

— Non mais lorsqu'il a ordonné au cocher d'aller de l'avant, celui-ci lui a répondu : Où désirez-vous aller monsieur le lieutenant général de police?

Le moine laissa échapper un terrible blasphème.

— Enfer et damnation! Ce fils de chien de Sartine!

La Dame de l'Eau et l'enfant le regardèrent avec effarement. Sophia semblait sur le point de pleurer.

— Où est mon père? demanda-t-elle d'une voix faible.

Le moine lui prit alors la main et lui apprit prudemment que son père était mort. Cela ne sembla pas chagriner outre mesure Sophia mais le moine savait que les enfants n'associaient pas à la mort la même peur que les adultes. Mourir, c'était simplement partir. Parfois d'ailleurs, après avoir appris la mort d'un proche ou d'un parent, ils demandaient quand il allait revenir…

Avec beaucoup de délicatesse, le moine ne la détrompa pas.

Mal à l'aise, le commissaire aux morts étranges écoutait son père sans mot dire et son regard ne quittait pas la pointe de ses bottes. Il releva pourtant la tête lorsque le moine demanda à Sophia si elle se souvenait de qui l'avait enlevé.

Les souvenirs de l'enfant semblaient brouillons, ses impressions se chevauchaient. Elle avait échappé à la surveillance de la servante pour se glisser dans la rue afin de retrouver le chien. Une voiture, noire comme un corbillard, s'était arrêtée près d'elle. Une main gantée, tenant une fiole, sortit de la portière.

— Mon enfant, fit une voix masculine bien timbrée, bois cette potion et tu t'échapperas enfin de ce monde qui te tient prisonnière.

Sophia était restée immobile, à la fois fascinée et terrifiée. Soudain, un bras puissant avait emprisonné les siens tandis qu'un mouchoir humide s'écrasait sur ses narines. Ses muscles étaient devenus tout mous tandis qu'elle flageolait sur ses jambes et que sa vue se brouillait.

Le commissaire aux morts étranges hocha la tête, comprenant toute l'affaire. Tandis qu'un homme accaparait l'attention de l'enfant, un autre se glissait derrière elle pour l'endormir et la jeter dans la voiture.

Sophia pleurait maintenant, revivant ses peurs.

— Que me voulait cet homme qui m'appelait mon enfant ? sanglota-t-elle.

La Dame de l'Eau jeta un regard inquiet au moine mais celui-ci n'avait aucunement l'intention de lui raconter la messe noire dans le cimetière.

— Sophia, nous t'avons retrouvée inconsciente et comme morte. C'est pour cette raison que nous t'avons conduite dans ma cave. Tu t'es ensuite éveillée et tu as commencé à aller et venir dans ma maison. Tout cela est du passé. Aujourd'hui, tu es en sécurité ici. Néanmoins…

Il fit une pause et jeta un bref regard à son fils.

— Néanmoins, il nous paraît plus prudent que tu demeures ici jusqu'au moment où nous arrêterons les deux hommes qui t'ont enlevée.

— Vont-ils revenir ?

— Non, car ils ne savent pas où tu te trouves.

Sophia le regarda avec de grands yeux innocents.

— Pourquoi les adultes font-ils ainsi du mal aux enfants ?

Le moine secoua sombrement la tête.

— C'est une question que je n'ai pas fini de me poser…

Dans cette matinée laiteuse, les deux hommes se pressaient au milieu de la foule des portefaix, des colporteurs et des domestiques. Une armée de jeunes gens s'employait à décrotter bas et chaussures. À un coin de rue, malgré ses doigts gourds de froid, un escamoteur divertissait le public de ses tours de passe-passe. Le moine et son fils lui accordèrent un regard entendu.

— Voici Sartine! gronda Volnay. Il agite une main vide devant nous et tiens la pleine dans son dos! Depuis le début, il nous mène en bateau. Cet homme est d'une duplicité sans égale!

Il retrouva son calme, le temps que des pensées cohérentes s'ordonnent dans son esprit. Sartine l'avait intrigué en gardant pour lui son croquis de Sophia. Il s'était même enquis avec une espèce d'émotion de ses conditions de vie avant qu'elle ne trouve la mort. Il avait ensuite rêvé d'elle...

— Cela explique l'intérêt qu'il a toujours manifesté pour cette petite à partir du moment où il a vu le dessin, dit-il.

— Mais pourquoi ne rien nous dire tout en nous confiant cette enquête? objecta le moine.

— À qui pouvait-il la confier à part nous? rétorqua Volnay. Tout le monde aurait été étonné que le commissaire aux morts étranges ne soit pas en charge du plus mystérieux des crimes de Paris depuis...

— Depuis la femme sans visage, compléta le moine.

Le commissaire aux morts étranges ne répondit pas. Parler de cette affaire le ramenait à Chiara.

— Père, dit-il brusquement, promets-moi de ne dire à personne où se trouve Sophia.

— Bien entendu.

— Ni à Hélène... surtout pas à Hélène!

Songeuse auprès du feu, Hélène les attendait chez le moine. Elle releva la tête à leur entrée dans une interrogation muette.

— Nous avons retrouvé Sophia, lui apprit le moine d'un ton réjoui.

— Quoi? Comment?

— Grâce à Aristote!

Le commissaire aux morts étranges intervint.

— Ce serait un peu long à expliquer et cette information doit rester secrète. N'avez-vous rien à nous apprendre de votre côté?

— Non. Où se trouve Sophia ?

— Cela ne vous regarde pas, décréta froidement le commissaire aux morts étranges. Je répète ma question : n'avez-vous rien à nous apprendre ?

Hélène demeura impassible. Ses beaux yeux verts mouchetés d'étoiles étaient aussi peu expressifs qu'une pierre précieuse.

— Rien, répondit-elle.

Volnay se tourna théâtralement vers le moine.

— Père, la preuve en est donnée que nous ne pouvons faire confiance à Hélène puisqu'elle nous cache des informations de la plus haute importance.

La jeune femme ne broncha pas.

— Que voulez-vous dire ?

Volnay se planta devant elle, irradiant d'une satisfaction mauvaise.

— Vous ne nous racontez pas vos visites à un ancien inspecteur de police à Paris ou à une accoucheuse ? Ni celle de Sartine, ensuite, à votre domicile ?

Hélène le contempla avec des yeux ronds. La surprise semblait l'avoir figée sur place.

— Comment savez-vous ? murmura-t-elle.

Puis un éclair de colère traversa brutalement son regard.

— Les mouches ! s'exclama-t-elle horrifiée. Vous m'avez fait suivre par des mouches !

Le commissaire aux morts étranges eut un imperceptible haussement d'épaules.

— Pas exactement, c'est Sartine qui vous fait suivre par ses mouches. Moi, je me suis contenté d'acheter l'une d'elles !

Il se tourna vers son père et lâcha avec bonne humeur.

— Tu vois qu'il n'y a pas que toi qui utilises l'argent de Sartine à des fins qu'il ne soupçonne pas !

Un rare sourire illumina son visage et ses yeux pétillèrent de gaieté. Tout à coup, Hélène eut l'impression de voir en lui son père le moine tel qu'il avait pu être plus jeune.

— En l'occurrence, reprit Volnay, j'achète une mouche de Sartine avec l'argent de Sartine !

Cette fois, il rit comme si la chose le ravissait. Le moine et Hélène le contemplèrent avec effarement.

— J'oubliais de vous dire, précisa le commissaire aux morts étranges en reprenant son sérieux, que la mouche en question a cuisiné l'accoucheuse. Il lui a fait très peur, aussi lui a-t-elle avoué ce qu'elle vous avait confié. Pour la mouche, cela ne signifiait pas grand-chose, ces gens-là se contentent d'espionner, de faire parler puis de rapporter sans toujours comprendre.

Hélène chercha en vain à sonder le regard de Volnay pour savoir s'il mentait. Peine perdue. Qui donc pouvait se vanter de lire dans ce puits sans fond? Elle se décida et dit très rapidement à l'attention du moine :

— Sartine m'a fait suivre par ses mouches. Il a su le résultat de mes découvertes et m'a interdit d'en parler à quiconque.

Aiguillonné par le serpent du doute, le moine fixa Hélène d'un œil étincelant.

— Je comprends. Néanmoins, fit-il d'un ton où perçait le regret, entre nous et Sartine, il vous faut choisir votre camp!

Impressionné par la fermeté de son ton, Volnay jeta un regard approbateur à son père.

— Cette accoucheuse, reprit Hélène d'un ton égal, a mis au monde le bébé d'une danseuse de l'Opéra il y a douze ans. La mère ne voulait pas de l'enfant qui a été confiée à sa dame de compagnie de l'époque : Mme Marly. Celle-ci a quitté son emploi contre sans doute une rente. Son mari était alors joaillier. À sa mort, deux ans plus tard, il a vendu son commerce pour se livrer à sa passion : l'astrologie.

Impavide, le moine acquiesça sans mot dire.

— Et comment se nommait cette jeune danseuse de l'Opéra? s'enquit son fils.

C'était reconnaître qu'il l'ignorait. Hélène eut le sentiment d'avoir été jouée. La mouche de Volnay n'avait pas questionné l'accoucheuse. Cela dit, rien n'empêchait le redoutable commissaire aux morts étranges de le faire plus tard. Aussi, répondit-elle de bonne grâce, son regard accrochant au passage celui du moine dont elle guetta la réaction.

— Mlle Belle Ange.

Un frisson sembla ébranler tout entier le moine. Volnay s'en étonna.

— C'est le froid, je n'arrive pas à me réchauffer, expliqua son père.

Son expression restait indéchiffrable mais ses sentiments remontaient à fleur de peau.

— Intéressant, fit-il en se levant. Je te laisse réfléchir là-dessus, mon fils. Moi, je vais visiter mes pauvres, cela me changera les idées.

— Tu me laisses pour tes bonnes œuvres alors que nous venons de découvrir que Sophia n'est pas morte et que nous avons un nouvel indice ? s'étonna le commissaire aux morts étranges.

— Tu n'es pas seul, répondit son père d'un ton sarcastique. Hélène est là. J'ai toute confiance en sa sagacité et en ton esprit logique !

Quittant la rue de l'Arbalète, il emprunta la rue des Postes puis la rue Sainte-Geneviève. Là, il entra chez une fripière qui, le reconnaissant, le conduisit sans mot dire à l'arrière de sa boutique. Elle lui porta des vêtements dignes d'un gentilhomme et l'aida à enfiler une chemise de soie, un gilet brodé et à nouer son jabot. Une culotte à pont d'un bleu éclatant souligna sa taille mince et une veste à velours de soie sa belle prestance. Ainsi paré, et après s'être complaisamment admiré dans une glace, le moine lui glissa quelques pièces dans la main et elle lui ouvrit une porte qui donnait sur une cour. Il s'inclina pour lui baiser galamment la main et l'appela *princesse des étoffes*, ce qui la fit rougir de plaisir.

— Attention, le prévint-elle, le sol est très glissant jusqu'à l'immeuble d'en face.

Il sortit donc d'un pas prudent en murmurant :

— Eh bien, je souhaite beaucoup de plaisir à la mouche qui m'attend devant cette friperie !

Une patache survint. Il se gara prudemment pour éviter d'être renversé ou de salir ses beaux vêtements contre les essieux de la voiture.

Restés seuls, Volnay et Hélène se regardèrent en chiens de faïence.

— Vous vous valez bien vous et Sartine, grogna enfin le policier. Dire qu'il nous lance sur une enquête sans nous apprendre ce qu'il sait, nous adjoint les services d'une femme pour nous aider et lui interdit de nous révéler ce qu'elle a trouvé !

La jeune femme soutint son regard avec une expression d'audace sur le visage.

— Vous avez raison sur un point : Sartine ne veut pas que cela se sache. Il était très fâché de ma découverte.

Elle réfléchit rapidement. Ce n'était pas à elle de révéler à Volnay que son père pouvait être aussi celui de Sophia.

— Votre père ne semblait pas intéressé à connaître le nom du géniteur de Sophia mais vous peut-être…

— J'allais vous poser la question, la coupa Volnay.

— L'accoucheuse ne connaissait pas le nom du père, dit-elle rapidement, mais le jour de l'enterrement, elle a aperçu dans le corridor M. de Sartine.

Le commissaire aux morts étranges se figea.

— Sartine encore… murmura-t-il.

Voici pourquoi le carrosse de Sartine s'était arrêté devant Sophia et que le lieutenant général de police lui avait demandé son nom, souri et tendu une pièce. Sophia était sa fille ! Volnay exhala profondément comme pour se vider d'une trop grande colère.

— Ce maudit bougre savait tout cela depuis le départ mais il n'en a rien dit !

Toute sa rancune envers son supérieur trouvait à s'exprimer en cette occasion.

— Je vais aller le voir !

Hélène se jeta à son bras, l'épouvante se lisait sur son visage.

— Non, il saura que j'ai parlé et sa rancune sera terrible envers moi ! À moins que vous ne lui racontiez que vous le faites espionner par une de ses propres mouches et alors sa vengeance s'abattra sur vous !

Volnay la dévisagea avec étonnement.

— Vous avez peur de lui ?

— Terriblement !

Son visage était d'une pâleur diaphane.

— Pas vous ? demanda-t-elle d'une petite voix.

— Mais… non…

Volnay réfléchit.

— Mais parfois pour mon père, oui…

— Et l'inverse doit être vrai, remarqua Hélène.

Le commissaire aux morts étranges la contempla pensivement puis alla prendre son manteau.

— Rassurez-vous, je vais simplement le voir pour le convaincre de nous confier de nouveau l'enquête. Je lui dirai que je suis sur les traces de Sophia et que je me fais fort de la retrouver sous deux jours.

— Vous allez lui livrer cette petite?

— Lui livrer?

Il s'était planté devant elle et l'affrontait.

— Lui livrer? répéta-t-il d'un ton offusqué. Vous oubliez que cet homme, si impitoyable qu'il paraisse, pense être son père. Et de toute façon, nous ne pourrons lui cacher bien longtemps Sophia. Que voulez-vous donc que nous fassions d'elle? La dissimuler et l'élever dans la clandestinité?

Il se dirigea vers la porte et, lorsqu'il l'ouvrit, se retourna une dernière fois.

— Je ne le crains pas mais j'ai appris une chose ces dernières années, c'est que l'on ne peut pas avoir sur terre pire ennemi que Sartine!

L'hiver aidant, de grands braseros brûlaient dans les cours des hôtels particuliers de la rue Saint-Honoré, délicate attention pour les invités lorsqu'ils descendaient de leurs carrosses. Pendant ce temps, dans les rues, on mourait de froid.

Sans hésiter, le moine se dirigea vers l'entrée et se fit annoncer sous son nom. Il savait que Mlle Belle Ange était devenue Mme de Morange. À l'époque, les mauvaises langues insinuèrent qu'elle avait conservé ainsi son ange. Son mari était riche mais réputé pour être fort bête. Pour se moquer de lui, des amis de la nouvelle Mme de Morange lui prêtèrent un livre, chose fort nouvelle pour lui, puis un second du même auteur qui était en fait le même. "Tout ceci est très intéressant, avait dit le mari, mais l'auteur se répète un peu…"

Dans l'antichambre, un valet somnolent se redressa en sursaut. Il portait une livrée rouge garnie de galons tissés aux couleurs et armoiries de sa maîtresse.

Mme de Morange était encore à sa toilette du matin, la toilette légère, et, comme toutes les dames de la bonne société, elle y recevait. Celle plus sérieuse du soir s'y accompagnait d'un bain de modestie. Il s'agissait d'un bain moussant qui préservait l'intimité de l'hôtesse à ses visiteurs.

La maîtresse des lieux se trouvait entre les mains de son coiffeur. Autour d'elle trônaient dans un joyeux désordre des boîtes à poudre, des boîtes à mouches, des pots à pommade et des flacons de parfum. De jolis bronzes et d'exquises porcelaines décoraient des consoles et des tables de marbre. Deux petits marquis occupaient des fauteuils de noyer sculpté, ornés de tapisseries de soie au petit point. Le moine dissimula sa contrariété et, d'un regard, jaugea les importuns. De jeunes prétentieux à la langue bien pendue qui savaient tout sans avoir jamais rien fait, s'étant donné comme seul labeur celui de naître.

Le moine fut accueilli dans ce lieu exquis par la maîtresse de maison avec une surprise ravie. Du moins, c'est ce qu'elle laissa paraître. Mme de Morange dardait sur le monde des yeux de poupée de faïence. Son visage était fin, sa bouche vermeille se découpait en un arc gracieux et elle présentait une gorge bien blanche. Elle possédait les mille et une manières de plaire de ces femmes éduquées pour cela ou ayant tout compris de la vanité des hommes.

Malgré lui, le moine ressentit un frisson nostalgique. Il se souvenait d'une époque où les baisers coulaient de ses lèvres. Il observa les plis rouges de celles-ci tandis qu'elle parlait d'une voix fraîche et sucrée. Son regard glissa ensuite le long de son corps, admirant la robe en fil de soie bleu, aux broderies au point de chaînette et aux boutons recouverts de taffetas doré. À la naissance de ses seins, sa poitrine semblait jaillir en globes de l'échancrure de sa robe. Sagement posées sur ses genoux, il lui trouva également les plus belles mains du monde, blanches et délicates, perdues dans un flot de dentelles, et le lui dit. Cela fit rire les petits courtisans.

— Monsieur est d'une galanterie d'une autre époque, remarqua l'un d'eux.

Le sourire du moine vacilla.

— Vous avez l'esprit en écharpe, leur répondit-il, je ne vous comprends guère !

Le coiffeur frisa les cheveux de Mme de Morange avec des papillotes et des fers chauds. Pendant ce temps, la conversation allait bon train. On faisait assaut d'esprit tout en se moquant des absents. Le moine jouait son rôle avec une indifférence étudiée, l'air vaguement ennuyé par la conversation des deux petits marquis. L'acuité de son regard démentait toutefois cette fausse nonchalance. Il était prompt à relever leurs erreurs, à redresser un propos ou se moquer d'eux sans y paraître. Comme leurs habits étaient surchargés de dorure, il leur dit humblement :

— Je fais pâle figure à côté de vous qui êtes dorés comme un calice !

Ils froncèrent les sourcils et décidèrent de se liguer contre lui, faisant allusion à son âge avancé et l'appelant grand-père des sages.

— Décidément, marmonna le moine, c'est l'évangile du jour !

— Madame, fit soudain le plus jeune des petits marquis à la maîtresse de maison. On ne voit plus à vos dîners ce monsieur toujours assis en bout de table, qui ne parle jamais et a l'air un peu bête…

— Il s'agit de mon mari, répondit-elle aimablement, et il est mort l'année dernière.

Cette fois, le moine éclata et dit aux jeunes marquis :

— Vous avez la bouche trop près des oreilles, vous vous écoutez parler comme de jeunes sots que vous êtes ! Sortez donc avant que je ne vous embroche sur mon épée !

Ils sortirent en se bousculant comme des gazelles et l'on entendit nettement l'un d'eux dire à l'autre d'un ton offusqué :

— Cet homme est grossier et sans industrie !

Le sourire du moine s'accentua et il se tourna vers la maîtresse de maison.

— Vos petits marquis ont des cervelles de colibri.

— Ne me les abîmez pas, ils sont de très bonne famille!

— Oh, ne vous inquiétez pas, la rassura le moine, je ne sors désormais mon épée que pour les affaires sérieuses.

Et il ajouta après réflexion :

— Je suis désolé d'apprendre la mort de votre mari…

Mme de Morange haussa les épaules d'un air indifférent.

— Ne le soyez pas, c'est vrai qu'il était bête et son seul mérite est d'avoir fait de moi une veuve très convenable.

— Je qualifierais en d'autres termes que *convenable* une veuve de trente-deux ans, si je ne m'abuse, aussi fraîche et belle que vous!

Flattée, elle hocha modestement la tête.

— Quel beau parleur!

— Oh, la langue est une des rares choses qui ne rouille pas avec l'âge!

Elle sourit.

— Mais que me vaut le plaisir de vous voir après tant d'années? Comment se fait-il que vous ayez tout à coup trouvé le chemin de ma demeure?

Le front du moine se plissa de rides profondes.

— Une fâcheuse affaire, madame, très fâcheuse.

— Mon Dieu, vous m'effrayez…

Il posa sur elle un regard triste.

— Madame, pardonnez-moi de raviver peut-être de mauvais souvenirs mais il y a douze ans, vous avez donné naissance à une enfant que vous abandonnâtes le jour d'après.

Mme de Morange chancela et porta la main à son cœur.

— Mon Dieu, pourquoi me parler de cela? Pourquoi remuer ainsi le passé? Que vous prend-il?

— Cette jeune fille est aujourd'hui au cœur d'une enquête policière. Vous ne le savez peut-être pas mais j'assiste le commissaire aux morts étranges de Paris.

Mme de Morange agita frénétiquement son éventail.

— Lui est-il arrivé quelque chose?

Le moine la contempla un instant sans rien dire puis secoua doucement la tête.

— Non madame, n'ayez crainte.

— Alors, je ne comprends pas.

— Il n'y a rien à comprendre, fit-il, une enquête de police a lieu sur ses parents adoptifs. J'ai besoin de renseignements sur Sophia.

— La vérité est que je n'en ai malheureusement aucun à vous donner, regretta-t-elle.

— La vérité est que vous n'avez rien à faire de cette enfant, corrigea le moine.

— Que voulez-vous, mon cher, répondit-elle négligemment, je n'ai pas l'instinct maternel. D'autres l'ont pour moi!

Le moine la considéra gravement.

— Vous pouvez, certes, ne pas me répondre. C'est votre droit le plus strict, comme est mon droit d'aller poser la question à mon supérieur, M. de Sartine.

Mme de Morange se troubla.

— Que vient faire là M. de Sartine?

— C'est un homme que j'apprécie beaucoup, dit sans rire le moine. Et sans doute, le personnage le mieux renseigné de tout notre royaume.

Son hôtesse prit un ton enjôleur :

— Déranger le lieutenant général de police pour cela alors que je pourrais tout vous révéler…

— Me direz-vous enfin qui est le père de cet enfant?

Le moine perdait patience mais sans hausser le ton et il accompagna cette question d'une gracieuse révérence comme pour s'excuser d'insister. Mme de Morange cilla nerveusement.

— Soit, je vous le dirai mais ce soir, après le souper que je donne et à la condition que vous l'animiez suffisamment de votre brillant esprit.

Devant ce caprice de femme du monde, le moine conserva son sang-froid. Mme de Morange était charmante mais son cerveau ne pesait pas plus lourd que celui d'un moineau. Il s'inclina devant elle.

— Il en sera fait selon vos désirs…

Dans son bureau du Châtelet, Sartine se retourna vivement et s'empressa de réajuster sa perruque. Un valet était en train de la poudrer à l'aide d'une grosse houppe emplie d'un mélange de farine et de racine réduite. Pour se protéger de la poudre qui volait, le lieutenant général de police portait un cône sur le visage qui lui donnait l'apparence d'un grand échassier. Il l'ôta brusquement et toussa. Volnay réprima un sourire. Lorsque Sartine se poudrait, il devait y en avoir pour une journée de pain!

— Pour qui donc vous prenez-vous à forcer ainsi ma porte? gronda ce dernier.

— Je suis sur le point de retrouver Sophia!

Avec satisfaction, Volnay vit Sartine se troubler. D'un geste sec, il congédia son laquais.

— Sophia? s'écria-t-il. Elle est donc toujours en vie?

— Toujours, oui.

Sartine ferma les yeux un bref instant.

— Ramenez-la-moi et il vous sera beaucoup pardonné, dit-il très rapidement.

— Je n'avais pas le sentiment d'avoir trop de choses à me faire pardonner, remarqua froidement le commissaire aux morts étranges. Mais n'êtes-vous pas désireux que je vous ramène également le criminel derrière tout cela?

Le regard du lieutenant général de police se fit calculateur.

— Son père, l'astrologue? Peut-être auriez-vous meilleur marché de me le ramener avec une balle entre les deux yeux! Cela éviterait beaucoup d'explications...

— Évidemment!

— Oh, ne prenez pas vos airs supérieurs, Volnay! Je m'efforce de maintenir l'ordre royal et il est menacé. La messe noire, la mort du curé dansant et les arrestations de Siltieri ne sont pas passées inaperçues et c'était sans doute l'intention de ce dernier. L'imagination fait le reste! J'ai ici un rapport selon lequel, dans un cabaret où l'on s'ivrognait, une femme de mauvaise vie prise de boisson a évoqué le diable. Aussitôt, au dire des témoins, celui-ci est apparu, l'a soulevée dans les airs avant de la projeter contre un mur, comme un fétu de paille, lui brisant le crâne!

— Ce sont les autres convives qui ont dû la tuer.

— Sans doute mais j'ai encore trois rapports de police où le guet a dû s'introduire dans des maisons car l'esprit malin frappait dans les murs ou détruisait tout sur son passage. Un gendre a même été tué par son beau-père qui l'avait pris dans la nuit pour Satan en personne alors qu'il se rendait à la cuisine pour calmer une petite faim !

— Quelqu'un alimente ces rumeurs et colporte des ragots !

— Et qui donc croyez-vous que ce soit, sinon le parti des dévots ? hurla Sartine.

Il se calma et réajusta sa perruque.

— Vous les connaissez pourtant et les conclusions de Siltieri vont dans leur sens. Plus on craint le diable, plus on craint Dieu et plus ils ont d'influence !

Volnay hocha la tête, toutes ces considérations politiques ne lui avaient pas échappé mais son affaire à lui était simplement de trouver des meurtriers. À chacun ses préoccupations !

— Puis-je reprendre mon enquête et vous ramener Sophia ? demanda-t-il tranquillement.

Le lieutenant général de police le considéra attentivement, cherchant sans succès à percer le masque impénétrable de son collaborateur.

— Quarante-huit heures à partir de maintenant, siffla-t-il. Pas une minute de plus. À vous et vous seul !

— J'ai besoin de mon père pour réussir !

— Votre père décline. Il croit qu'il a toujours vingt ans mais ce n'est pas le cas.

— Où voulez-vous en venir ?

Sartine lui jeta un regard glacé.

— À ceci : votre père a jugé morte Sophia lors qu'elle était vivante. Il est dépassé. Je ne peux plus l'employer dans ma police.

Il leva la main en l'air pour interrompre les protestations du commissaire aux morts étranges.

— Il y a pire ! Votre père se livre à l'exercice de la chimie qui conduit inévitablement à des agissements plus dangereux comme la transmutation des métaux en or. Des arrêts ont été rendus par le Parlement de Paris en matière de sortilèges et de maléfices. L'enrichissement par l'alchimie ou la recherche de trésors par conjuration d'esprits sont interdits et punissables !

Volnay l'arrêta d'un geste.

— Vous savez bien que mon père est un scientifique et que seule le pousse sa curiosité intellectuelle.

Sartine coupa court à sa défense.

— Votre père est un danger pour moi comme pour vous. Oh, je ne suis pas un ingrat. En récompense de ses bons services, je lui ferai attribuer une jolie pension et il pourra se retirer à la campagne. Pourquoi pas en Bourgogne? C'est une terre si riante...

Il se campa devant son subordonné, les pieds écartés et les mains dans le dos, adoptant un ton d'une rondeur enjouée.

— Là-bas, il pourra se livrer à toutes les expériences qu'il souhaite dans un beau laboratoire que nous lui ferons installer...

Un sourire rusé s'afficha sur ses lèvres.

— Qui sait, peut-être qu'une fois le poids de ses enquêtes enlevé de ses épaules il trouvera le secret de l'élixir de longue vie et nous enterrera tous!

La fausse bonne humeur de Sartine inquiéta Volnay.

— Et si mon père trouvait la solution de notre énigme, le réintégreriez-vous dans votre police?

— Cela n'arrivera pas! répondit Sartine. Cela ne peut arriver!

On frappa. D'un ton impatient, le lieutenant général de police ordonna d'entrer. Un valet lui remit un pli après moult courbettes. Sartine fronça les sourcils en voyant le sceau et le déplia d'une main fébrile. Sans qu'il sût pourquoi, Volnay vit la figure de son supérieur devenir mortellement pâle. Finalement, le lieutenant général de police congédia le laquais et se tourna vers Volnay.

— Le roi, dit-il. Il veut nous voir tous les deux.

Dire que Sartine parut contrarié aurait été un euphémisme. Jamais, le commissaire aux morts étranges n'avait observé son supérieur dans un tel état d'agitation. Comme s'il en était conscient, Sartine expira doucement, ferma brièvement les yeux et les rouvrit pour les poser sur Volnay.

— Nous allons nous mettre d'accord sur l'histoire à raconter au roi, dit-il.

Le moine se dirigea vers l'Observatoire. Lui et son fils avaient déjà discuté de la nécessité de cette visite mais les événements qui se succédaient à un rythme frénétique l'avaient toujours repoussée à demain.

Construit au siècle dernier sous Louis XIV, l'Observatoire royal était une construction rectangulaire flanquée de deux tours octogonales à ses angles méridionaux. Une troisième tour carrée servait d'entrée au nord. Haut de vingt-six mètres, le bâtiment était imposant et l'atmosphère à l'intérieur confortait l'impression que ceux qui y demeuraient se sentaient investis d'une mission suprême. Le moine avait bien connu l'un des astronomes qui y travaillait, un certain Jean de Foy. Il s'enquit de lui et bientôt un homme au profil énergique et aux yeux de charbon le rejoignit. Sous sa veste, il portait un gilet de taffetas agrémenté de broderies de soie. Le moine le salua comme s'ils s'étaient quittés la veille. L'autre le considéra avec attention, ses yeux pleins d'une prudence visible, avant de le reconnaître.

— Messire Guillaume de…

— Pas de nom, pas de nom ! le coupa vivement le moine. Ma situation n'est pas officielle même si j'aide à mener des enquêtes qui le sont !

Jean de Foy approuva d'un mouvement sec du menton.

— Je comprends, dit-il.

Il tira de sa poche une longue bouffarde de terre blanche puis, sortant sa tabatière, entreprit de découper une carotte de tabac.

— *Nicotiana tabacum*, murmura le moine en plissant les yeux.

— Je préfère la pipe à la prise, précisa l'astronome comme s'il fallait s'en excuser.

— Éternuer est réservé aux gens de la bonne société, dit gaiement le moine en pensant à Sartine.

L'autre, décontenancé, haussa un sourcil.

— Que puis-je pour vous ?

— Je m'intéresse à M. Marly. Il a trouvé la mort dans l'incendie de sa maison, le saviez-vous ?

— Oui, les nouvelles circulent vite à Paris !

— L'avez-vous connu ? questionna le moine.

Jean de Foy jeta un regard circulaire autour de lui.

— Ne préférez-vous pas faire quelques pas dans le jardin?

— Certes, dit le moine en souriant.

— Je vais chercher mon manteau.

Leurs pas crissèrent bientôt sur la neige tassée qui recouvrait l'allée.

— M. Marly, n'est-ce pas? fit l'astronome en soufflant la fumée entre ses dents serrées sur le tuyau de sa bouffarde. Oui, il venait parfois lorsqu'il se posait des questions et comme sa connaissance des étoiles était extrêmement pointue et précise, nous avions toujours plaisir à discuter avec lui, même s'il n'était pas des nôtres.

— Que savez-vous de lui?

Jean de Foy se gratta la tête.

— Je crois que son père était officier de marine.

Il baissa le ton pour qu'on ne l'entende pas.

— Il s'est fait tuer loin des siens au cours d'une guerre inutile, laissant seule sa femme élever son fils…

— Parlez-moi de lui. Il s'intéressait à des choses bien étranges…

— Vous parlez des étoiles?

— Des étoiles et de ce que l'on peut en faire…

Jean de Foy réfléchit une seconde et hocha la tête.

— Il est vrai que M. Marly développait des idées peu conformes à celles du pouvoir royal. À vous je peux le dire. Même si la science d'aujourd'hui nous fait tout passer au crible de la raison, il n'en reste pas moins que les sciences humaines ont observé maintes choses merveilleuses et inexplicables.

Il posa une main fraternelle sur l'épaule du moine.

— Mais nous sommes des scientifiques, vous comprenez cela? Aux yeux de la police, la limite est floue entre astrologie et magie. Nous autres, astronomes, nous observons les étoiles. Les astrologues, eux, les font parler.

— Que croyait Marly?

L'autre soupira.

— Que tout était écrit dans la voûte étoilée. La géomancie astronomique pour connaître les choses passées, présentes et celles futures.

Il fit une pause, regardant autour de lui et formant sans en être vraiment conscient un globe de ses mains.

— Vous savez, l'astronomie a pour but l'observation et la découverte des étoiles, nous ne tirons pas de conclusion autre que scientifique dans cet Observatoire. L'astrologie, elle, s'est développée à partir de croyances puisant dans des civilisations aussi riches que variées, en Perse, à Babylone ou en Égypte, le tout saupoudré de philosophie grecque. Aujourd'hui, les astrologues observent le mouvement des planètes et, à partir d'une date de naissance, révèlent le caractère et le destin de cette personne. Mais d'autres s'intéressent à quelque chose de plus grand.

— La divination, suggéra le moine.

— Oui. En Chine comme dans les Amériques, on dresse depuis longtemps des calendriers prophétiques. Cela fascinait Marly. Que ce ne soit pas que les destins individuels qui soient prédéterminés mais aussi le sort des civilisations.

Il marqua une pause et ajouta :

— Et aussi que l'on puisse influencer la destinée sur terre en s'appuyant sur le secret des étoiles.

— Le secret?

Jean de Foy haussa les épaules.

— Dieu me garde de le connaître, je serais le plus savant des hommes! Mais Marly estimait que si l'on accomplissait telle chose, avec la bonne conjonction des étoiles, on possédait plus de chance pour que tout se passe parfaitement.

Le moine hocha la tête.

— C'est le principe même de l'astrologie! Mais dites-moi, je me souviens d'avoir vu sur son bureau un livre sur l'Apocalypse. Bien étrange lecture pour un admirateur des étoiles.

Jean de Foy se troubla.

— Dites-moi tout mon ami, fit doucement le moine, vous savez bien que nous sommes du même bord.

L'astronome écarta la bouffarde de ses lèvres et se racla la gorge.

— Il existe une tradition selon laquelle le Christ serait descendu trois jours aux Enfers après sa mort et avant sa résurrection. Nul ne sait ce qui s'est passé durant ce séjour mais l'on dit qu'aux Enfers le Christ aurait remis à Lucifer une étoile à cinq branches. Pourquoi? Cette question tourmentait bizarrement Marly.

— Je comprends, murmura le moine. Selon l'Apocalypse, le mal doit être racheté à la fin des temps. Lucifer donnera alors aux justes l'*Étoile du matin* et recouvrera son état angélique.

Il inspira profondément.

— Serait-ce l'Étoile du matin que le Christ a remise à Lucifer?

Jean de Foy s'arrêta de marcher et toussota. Une écharde de brume semblait plantée dans sa gorge.

— Ce n'est pas quelque chose dont on peut discuter avec tout le monde car cela signifierait que Lucifer est en fait le serviteur du Christ.

Les yeux du moine s'étrécirent.

— Étoile tombée du ciel, il aurait volontairement accepté de tomber dans le mal pour servir les desseins de Dieu, tout comme Judas, la rage au cœur, trahit Jésus pour accomplir sa mission et achever l'œuvre…

Il se tourna vers Jean de Foy.

— Savez-vous ce qu'il avait en tête?

— Je l'ignore mais…

L'astronome s'arrêta net, sous le coup d'une pensée.

— Il citait souvent Shakespeare, un auteur anglais.

— Je connais. Que disait-il?

Jean de Foy plissa les yeux puis, les mains théâtralement levées, récita :

— *"Lorsque les mendiants meurent, on ne voit aucune comète ; Mais les cieux s'enflamment d'eux-mêmes à la mort des princes!"*

XXI

VERSAILLES ET AUTRES DIABLERIES

Figés sous le givre, les jardins de Versailles dégageaient une impression féerique. Volnay ne leur accorda pourtant qu'un regard éteint. Tous ces carrés de verdure glacés, ces allées rectilignes et ces angles droits ne reflétaient pour lui qu'une société trop surveillée et en coupe réglée. Son esprit aspirait à plus de courbes, de souplesse et de liberté.

Un nuage de poudre annonça le passage d'un courtisan aussi immaculé que le mont Blanc tellement il s'était poudré à la toilette. La rencontre des dames de la cour, transies dans leurs beaux atours au milieu de leurs promenades, le laissa de marbre. Les perruques des hommes lui semblaient trop poudrées, les coiffures des femmes de véritables pièces montées et leurs joues trop colorées par les rouges pour rehausser le teint. La mine superbe et la gorge blanche, ces femmes ne le faisaient pas rêver. Elles nourrissaient à leur façon l'atmosphère de fin de partie d'une cour décadente, arc-boutée sur son arrogance et ses privilèges.

Volnay regarda du coin de l'œil les courtisans regroupés dans les couloirs glacés du château. Si son expression demeurait indéchiffrable, répulsion et dégoût s'agitaient en lui. Non contents de posséder la majorité des terres de France, tous les courtisans grouillant autour du monarque s'accaparaient encore rentes et pensions. Du matin au soir, ces inutiles gravitaient autour d'un seul point fixe : le roi. Dès l'aube, gagnés par l'unique obsession d'être vus de celui-ci, ils s'affolaient dans les escaliers et les corridors pour se trouver sur son passage. Leur journée se passait ainsi dans une course éperdue après leur astre pour parvenir peut-être à assister à son coucher. Un duc racontait que le plus beau jour de sa vie était celui où il avait porté la lumière pour le coucher du roi!

La vie des courtisans était une vie d'esclaves. Il leur fallait faire des grâces pour être admis à dîner par quelqu'un en vue qui leur permettrait de rencontrer un proche du roi. Ensuite, ils devraient manœuvrer auprès de celui-ci pour être conviés à un des soupers royaux. Les plus chanceux parviendraient à se faire inviter à la chasse du roi qui forçait le cerf trois à quatre fois par semaine pour oublier ses idées noires. La récompense de cette interminable partie de chasse se manifestait parfois sous la forme d'une invitation à l'un de ces petits voyages qu'affectionnait le roi à Choisy, La Celle ou Marly. Arrivés dans un de ces châteaux, les courtisans se retrouvaient soit dans le camp des "Polissons" qui repartaient au soir dans de grandes voitures inconfortables, soit dans celui des "Logeasses" qui restaient coucher. Le cœur battant, ces derniers se regroupaient alors en bas d'un escalier, attendant qu'un huissier vienne lire la liste des participants au souper.

Telle était la vie à la cour de Versailles.

Volnay jeta un coup d'œil à la dérobée à Sartine. Celui-ci dénotait assurément dans le lot : plus intelligent que la moyenne, plus dangereux… Il accomplissait un dur labeur au service de son roi et en était raisonnablement récompensé. Mais, comme les autres, pour conserver l'estime du monarque, il devait en permanence éviter les pièges de ses concurrents, les chausse-trapes des envieux, flatter la favorite pour rester dans ses bonnes grâces, soigner ses relations avec le Dauphin, se méfier du parti des dévots et se garder des jésuites… toute une vie d'équilibre.

Pour conserver ses privilèges, Volnay savait Sartine prêt à tout. Serviteur sans état d'âme, il avait fait persécuter M. de Tiercelin, qui tentait de préserver la vertu de sa fille des faveurs royales. Celle-ci finit dans une maison du roi, avenue Saint-Cloud. Une fois lassé par la jeune fille, comme par toutes les autres, le monarque se rendit à Saint-Cloud pour jouer une dernière fois son rôle d'amant attentionné avant de les faire embastiller le lendemain, elle et son père. Il la fit libérer plusieurs années plus tard pour qu'elle finisse sa vie au couvent.

Si Volnay avait la patience des chats, Sartine, lui, n'aimait pas attendre. Il soupirait bruyamment, pianotait sur l'accoudoir de son fauteuil et fixait d'un œil courroucé l'huissier impassible comme s'il le rendait responsable de son attente.

Enfin, on les introduisit dans le cabinet de travail du roi qui donnait sur la magnifique cour de Marbre. Le monarque revenait de la chasse et avait offert le pied du cerf tué à une marquise dont il convoitait les faveurs. Maintenant, il tournait en rond car, une fois l'animal tué, il lui fallait un autre gibier.

Louis XV, qui approchait de la cinquantaine, conservait une belle prestance et il portait fort majestueusement son habit et son gilet richement brodés de fils d'or et d'argent. Cependant, tous les excès de sa vie dissolue lui donnaient un teint de plomb et une bouche aux commissures crapuleuses. Cet écart entre majesté et canaillerie devenait frappant selon les sujets qu'il abordait dans la conversation.

— Sire, fit cérémonieusement Sartine en s'inclinant, voici le chevalier de Volnay que vous avez demandé à voir. Notre fameux commissaire aux morts étranges…

Un instant, le roi sembla s'évader du sombre cachot de ses pensées et regarda Volnay avec curiosité.

— J'ai appris que vous retourniez les tombes ?

Le jeune homme cilla brièvement. Il connaissait le caractère morbide du monarque. Celui-ci aimait à s'enquérir de qui était mort ou qui allait bientôt l'être. Une histoire de tombe ouverte devait le fasciner. Mais cela suffisait-il pour le recevoir en particulier ?

— Votre Majesté est bien informée.

— Je suis au courant de tout ce qui se passe dans mon royaume, répondit le roi d'un ton condescendant.

Et il ajouta avec un brin d'ironie :

— Quand ce n'est pas mon bon Sartine qui me le raconte, c'est quelqu'un d'autre qui le fait…

Du coin de l'œil, Volnay vit le lieutenant général de police pâlir imperceptiblement. Il savait qu'avec ce roi la disgrâce frappait sans prévenir. Un soir, il vous parlait aimablement et vous félicitait, le lendemain, vous étiez démis de vos fonctions sans rien comprendre.

— Alors, cette tombe? s'impatienta Louis XV.

Le commissaire aux morts étranges sentit tout le poids du regard de Sartine sur lui et répondit comme convenu :

— Sire, j'ai pris sur moi de faire ouvrir une tombe car je soupçonnais que la bonne personne ne s'y trouvait pas.

Une lueur d'intérêt traversa l'œil du roi.

— Racontez-moi ça.

Volnay jeta un coup d'œil de côté. Sartine fixait un point du mur devant lui avec une indifférence affectée.

— Sire, expliqua le commissaire aux morts étranges, par un incroyable concours de circonstances les cadavres de deux victimes d'un meurtre ont été inversés.

— Voyez-vous donc! Mais comment est-ce possible?

Sartine jugea opportun d'intervenir.

— Sire, lui rappela-t-il, il s'agit de cette affaire de messe noire dans un cimetière.

Le roi pâlit.

— Messe noire, murmura-t-il d'un ton atone. Il n'y a jamais rien eu de tel sous mon règne.

Sartine s'agita à côté de Volnay.

— Monsieur le lieutenant général de police, lui dit le roi, il est important que vous disiez à vos policiers de ma part tout ce que des gens de bien comme eux doivent faire pour déconcerter ceux qui, de quelque qualité qu'ils soient, sont mêlés à un si vilain commerce.

Il avait parlé d'un ton ferme, inhabituel. Tout ce qu'il y avait d'adulte et de responsable en lui s'était concentré dans cette phrase. Un instant, Volnay le vit comme il aurait pu être s'il avait pris son devoir de roi au sérieux et considéré l'étendue des obligations de sa charge envers ses sujets. Puis sa curiosité malsaine reprit le dessus et l'impression passa :

— Dans quel état se trouvait le cadavre lorsque vous avez fait ouvrir le cercueil?

Sartine lui avait soufflé préalablement sa réponse, aussi Volnay fit comme son supérieur attendait de lui. Pour amuser le roi, Sartine prit le relais, racontant que les embaumeurs devaient être saouls pour avoir inversé les deux cadavres et qu'il était très difficile de creuser la terre dans les cimetières par ce froid avec la couche de neige qui recouvrait la terre.

Le roi se lassa vite. C'était Louis XV. Trop éphémère, tout plaisir le laissait sans joie une fois l'instant passé. L'anecdote l'avait amusé quelques secondes avant qu'il ne retombe dans son mortel ennui.

— Cette enquête avance-t-elle ? demanda-t-il soudain.

Son regard glacé pesait lourdement sur eux. Sartine se raidit.

— Oui, sauf erreur de sa part, le chevalier de Volnay est en passe de remonter une piste jusqu'au commanditaire.

C'était là faire peser sur le commissaire aux morts étranges tout le poids de l'échec si l'enquête échouait. Volnay comprit en un quart de seconde l'habileté du lieutenant général de police. L'attention du roi attirée sur cette affaire, il se devait de fournir un coupable. Cela dit, Sartine se montrait rusé en évitant de parler des soupçons pesant sur l'astrologue mort. Cela pouvait constituer une porte de sortie honorable. Trois coupables : la prostituée, le curé renégat et le père de Sophia. Une bonne histoire pour régaler le roi.

Volnay se détendit légèrement. Louis XV se pencha vers son lieutenant général de police.

— Pensez-vous que des gens de ma cour se livrent à de telles choses ?

Le ton était coupant.

— Non, sire, s'empressa de le rassurer Sartine. L'enquête du chevalier de Volnay démontre bien qu'il s'agit de gens du peuple, de petits-bourgeois.

Le roi se rejeta en arrière, arborant une moue satisfaite.

— Tant mieux, tant mieux… je ne supporterais pas que des gens de haute naissance sacrifient des êtres humains pour acquérir gloire, richesse et puissance.

C'est pourtant ce que vous faites à longueur d'années, pensa Volnay. *Sacrifier des gens sans autre raison et résultat que satisfaire à votre grandeur et votre gloire… Quant à vos gens de haute naissance, qu'ont-ils de plus que les autres, à part d'être nés dans un berceau doré ?*

— Votre Majesté, fit Sartine en aiguillant de nouveau la conversation dans la direction qu'il souhaitait, dans ce type de messe noire, il est plus souvent question de débauches que de sacrifices.

— Vraiment? fit Louis XV de nouveau intéressé.

— Sire, généralement la cérémonie sacrilège a lieu dans une cave. On étend un matelas sur des sièges avec des tabourets à chaque bout. Une jeune fille nue s'y couche. Elle est vierge mais ne le demeure pas longtemps!

Le roi s'esclaffa malgré lui.

— Son corps sert d'autel vivant au célébrant, continua Sartine impavide. Il place un calice entre les seins de la vierge et, sur son ventre blanc, un crucifix posé à l'envers. Après avoir chanté la messe à rebours, au moment de l'Offertoire, lorsque les fumées d'encens contenant des parfums capiteux envahissent la pièce, l'assistance arrache ses vêtements et se livre à des luxures éperdues. Le célébrant, quant à lui, s'occupe de son autel...

Volnay jeta un coup d'œil étonné au lieutenant général de police. Celui-ci semblait bien renseigné sur ces pratiques. Le roi, convenablement émoustillé, attendait la suite avec intérêt.

— Ainsi, continua Sartine d'un ton ennuyeux pour bien montrer que le sujet ne l'excitait pas, l'acte accompli, les hommes s'échangent... que dis-je, s'arrachent leurs partenaires et se livrent avec elles à tous les transports possibles, y compris ceux que Dieu comme la Nature réprouvent...

Volnay songea avec tendresse à son père. Celui-ci aurait simplement dit que, le péché de chair se trouvant au centre des préoccupations du monde chrétien, le culte de Satan permettait bien évidemment de s'en libérer dans le délire de la débauche.

— Je peux néanmoins affirmer, reprit le lieutenant général de police, que ces pratiques, existant depuis des siècles, sont fort rares sous le règne de Votre Majesté. L'affaire de cette messe noire dans un cimetière nous a conduits d'ailleurs à nous livrer à des arrestations qui permettront, dans la plus grande discrétion, de mettre totalement fin à ce type de pratiques exécrables.

— Je n'en attendais pas moins de vous. Dites-moi mon bon Sartine, est-il vrai que la duchesse de...

Il jeta un bref regard à Volnay et reporta son attention sur son lieutenant général de police.

— Vous voyez qui je veux dire ?

Sartine hocha la tête.

— Est-il vrai, reprit le roi, qu'elle paillarde avec un garçon d'écurie et ceci aux pieds de ses chevaux ?

— Certes, fit Sartine vaguement gêné par la présence du commissaire aux morts étranges.

— Et est-il exact qu'elle se fasse également monter par les chevaux ?

S'enfermant dans son monde, Volnay n'écouta plus la conversation entre les deux hommes. Le roi y révélait une fois de plus que le seul intérêt qu'il portait aux autres était d'ordre nauséeux. Isolé dans son château glacé de Versailles, à des lieues de l'humanité, il n'aimait personne, pas plus lui que ses proches. Personne.

Le jeune homme se mit à le considérer d'un œil perçant, l'imaginant courir nu autour du lit auprès de toutes jeunes filles. Dans cette nudité, dépouillé de son faste, le roi devait apparaître comme un homme comme les autres.

Sa naissance a placé son destin plus haut que tous, son comportement le fait redescendre plus bas que nous tous, songea-t-il.

Il dut supporter encore quelques minutes le croassement du roi et de son lieutenant général de police. Quand l'audience fut terminée, il suivit Sartine, familier des lieux, pour sortir au plus vite de cet endroit.

Ils empruntèrent la galerie des Glaces et Volnay se questionna à propos de ce détour inutile. Mais sans doute le lieutenant général de police aimait-il à se montrer lorsqu'il revenait de visiter le roi. Peut-être, plus subtilement, désirait-il rappeler à son insolent collaborateur toute la majesté du roi dans le miroir de sa splendeur.

Les miroirs… Reflet des vanités, trois cent cinquante-sept miroirs au mercure apportaient une transparence et une luminosité un peu trouble. Mais l'essentiel se trouvait ailleurs. Quand on parcourait la galerie des Glaces sur ses soixante-treize mètres de longueur, il était inévitable de porter les yeux au plafond pour se perdre dans des cieux d'un bleu unique traversés par mille mètres carrés d'histoire en allégories ou trompe-l'œil.

Se reprenant pour ne pas céder à l'admiration, il baissa la tête et remarqua alors la femme de loin, reconnaissant son port altier mais fatigué. Son beau visage intelligent affichait une grâce tranquille et le charme particulier de ses yeux subjuguait ceux qui croisaient son regard. Une dame de compagnie et plusieurs courtisans marchaient derrière elle. À son passage, on s'empressait de lui faire place et de la saluer avec déférence.

C'était la marquise de Pompadour. Souriant, Volnay s'apprêta à la saluer mais elle détourna la tête en passant près de lui.

— Eh oui, ricana Sartine ravi de sa déconvenue, les amitiés tournent vite avec les grands de ce monde. Vous leur servez un jour, ils vous en récompensent parfois. Et lorsque vous les croisez de nouveau, ils ne vous reconnaissent même pas ou font semblant de ne pas vous remettre!

Comme si une idée nouvelle venait de lui traverser l'esprit, il jeta un regard froid au jeune policier.

— Il me semble tout à coup, chevalier de Volnay, que vous n'avez plus de protecteur en ce beau royaume de France!

Le commissaire aux morts étranges rentra directement de Versailles jusque chez lui, ruminant sombrement l'inexplicable comportement de la marquise de Pompadour. Elle lui devait pourtant beaucoup pour avoir résolu au printemps dernier une affaire dans laquelle elle était impliquée. À sa grande surprise, il trouva son père chez lui, s'adonnant à la conversation avec son amie la pie. Un grand feu flambait dans la cheminée et réchauffait quelque peu la pièce sans que la température atteigne toutefois une quelconque tiédeur.

— Toi ici et seul! voulut plaisanter Volnay.

Le moine ne releva pas l'allusion à Hélène.

— Je ne suis pas seul puisque j'instruis ta jolie pie! Elle s'ennuie, tu sais? Tu la délaisses…

— Et Hélène?

— J'ignore où elle se trouve depuis ce matin puisque je suis passé à l'Observatoire après avoir rendu visite à Mme de Morange.

— Mme de Morange?

Le moine fit signe à son fils de s'asseoir près de lui.

— Mlle Belle Ange, jeune danseuse de l'Opéra il y a encore douze ans, a trouvé un riche benêt pour l'épouser il y a une dizaine d'années et est devenue Mme de Morange. Tu devrais un peu plus t'intéresser aux commentaires des gazettes!

Volnay haussa les épaules.

— Et tu ne m'as rien dit!

Le moine eut une moue d'excuse.

— Je ne tenais pas à en parler avec Hélène. Sans les révélations de ta mouche, elle ne nous aurait rien dit de ce qu'elle venait d'apprendre. En conséquence, j'ai revu ma position. Jusqu'à ce que j'aie la preuve qu'elle soit fiable, je me considérerai en droit de lui dissimuler certaines informations. Qui plus est si ce froid au cul de Sartine rôde dans les parages!

Rien ne pouvait faire plus plaisir à son fils.

— D'autant plus, renchérit celui-ci, qu'Hélène nous a été imposée par Sartine lui-même!

— Oui, fit le moine dubitatif.

Il marqua un temps et plissa les yeux. Les rides de curiosité de son front se creusèrent.

— Néanmoins, fit-il, cela ne ressemble pas à Sartine d'employer des femmes, encore moins de nous en lancer dans les pattes.

— Tu sais, remarqua Volnay soucieux, je me suis moi aussi demandé pourquoi Sartine avait introduit Hélène dans notre enquête et notre intimité. J'ai pensé à Hélène de Troie et au cheval de Troie. Le but de Sartine, par l'intermédiaire d'Hélène, n'était-il pas de nous séparer? Tout ce jeu de la séduction qu'elle a joué avec toi…

Le moine resta impavide. Le souvenir de la jeune femme lorsqu'elle était venue s'allonger près de lui, tout son corps rayonnant d'énergie, le poursuivait encore.

— "Elle a terriblement l'air, quand on l'a devant soi, des déesses immortelles", dit-il en récitant un vers d'Homère sur la vraie Hélène de Troie.

— Celle-là a aidé à déclencher la guerre de Troie, remarqua Volnay, mais j'ai aussi pensé à Hélène de Tyr…

Son père lui jeta un regard noir.

— La prostituée?

— La compagne de Simon le Magicien, le concurrent de Jésus à l'époque! Était-elle un ange déchu dans un bordel de Tyr?

Le regard du moine sembla s'éparpiller autour d'une nuit passée, d'une fleur de lys gravée comme un joyau brûlant sur une épaule lisse.

— Les anges déchus… murmura-t-il. "Elle fut la lune, l'accord parfait, puis un jour, les anges, ses fils, se révoltant contre elle, de son empire la chassèrent et, dans un corps de femme, l'enfermèrent."

Il se tut. Ses regrets étaient autant d'éclats de verre plantés dans son cœur. Son fils l'examina avec curiosité.

— Père, es-tu attaché à cette jeune femme?

Le moine hésita. À nouveau, son cœur s'affolait mais il n'en montrait rien.

Plus que je ne saurais le dire…

— Je l'apprécie certes beaucoup mais elle a semé le doute dans mon esprit en nous dissimulant des démarches et des informations cruciales.

— Ses relations avec Sartine sont fort troubles, renchérit son fils, elle me paraît assez le craindre pour bien le servir.

Le moine ferma un instant les yeux, lorsqu'il les rouvrit, son regard était de nouveau serein.

— Ne la condamnons pas trop vite comme d'autres l'ont fait pour nous car je la tiens en haute estime. Revenons plutôt au cœur de notre affaire. Après toutes nos découvertes, il semble certain que notre astrologue a voulu sacrifier au diable la fille qu'il avait adoptée, en échange de quelque chose. Le portrait que l'on me fit de M. Marly à l'Observatoire est révélateur. C'est celui d'un illuminé, un illuminé qui s'intéresse autant à l'Apocalypse qu'au roi dont il a tiré l'horoscope, souviens-toi.

— Mais quelle est la raison qui l'a poussé à sacrifier Sophia?

Le moine réfléchit.

— Tu te souviens de l'affaire des Poisons ? Nous en avons suffisamment discuté. Lors de son arrestation, on a retrouvé dans les papiers de la marquise de Brinvilliers des lettres de confession dans lesquelles elle s'accusait de ses crimes commis. Elle y racontait aussi son viol, à l'âge de sept ans, par un de ses frères. Le passé n'excuse rien mais explique tout !

— C'est-à-dire ?

— Cet homme en veut beaucoup au roi parce que celui-ci a envoyé son père officier se faire tuer sur les mers, laissant sa mère élever seul son fils.

Il s'interrompit et leva les bras d'un geste ample pour réciter :

— *"Lorsque les mendiants meurent, on ne voit aucune comète ; Mais les cieux s'enflamment d'eux-mêmes à la mort des princes !"*

— Qu'est-ce ? demanda Volnay.

— Shakespeare ! Et lorsque M. Marly le récite, ce n'est à mon avis pas anodin. Il en veut au roi pour avoir bridé les libertés de son peuple et assez peut-être pour le tuer.

— Et ceci en assassinant Sophia…

— Envoûtement de sang. Je te l'ai dit, Sophia est la poupée que l'on sacrifie !

Un silence pensif s'ensuivit, seulement rompu par les jacassements de la pie qui s'affolait en tourbillonnant dans la cage, son plumage reflétant des lueurs métalliques. L'évocation du diable et de ses anges déchus semblait imprégner l'atmosphère de la maison d'une menace impalpable.

— Où étais-tu de ton côté ? s'enquit enfin le moine.

— Au Châtelet, faire la paix avec Sartine. Et de là à Versailles…

— Versailles !

Le commissaire aux morts étranges lui narra sa rencontre avec le roi tandis que son père secouait doucement la tête, un sourire ironique aux lèvres.

— Pour Sartine, conclut le policier, la situation n'est pas aussi désespérée que je le pensais mais elle est néanmoins préoccupante.

Volnay considéra son père d'un œil attentif.

— Sartine ne nous aime pas mais toi il te craint.

Un silence.

— Aurais-tu une quelconque prise sur lui?

— Non.

— Attention, l'avertit son fils. Tu sais qu'on peut vite se faire égorger au coin d'une rue.

Le moine eut une moue indulgente.

— Un homme menacé peut avoir mis en sécurité certains papiers qui, à sa mort ou sa disparition, peuvent être remis à la bonne personne au bon moment. C'est pour cela que cet homme ne craint pas de se faire égorger au coin d'une rue.

— Tu disposes de moyens de pression sur Sartine? s'étonna Volnay.

— Je ne dis ni oui ni non. Reste à l'écart de tout ça! Moins tu en sauras, mieux cela sera!

Le commissaire aux morts étranges considéra longuement son père. Il le savait homme ouvert mais rempli de secrets accumulés tout au long de son existence.

— Sartine veut t'écarter de moi et donc de son chemin, avoua Volnay mal à l'aise. Il te verrait bien couler de vieux jours paisibles en Bourgogne devant les fourneaux de ton laboratoire.

— Pour que je puisse couler *de vieux jours*, répliqua avec humeur le moine, il faudrait d'abord que je sois vieux et ce n'est pas le cas!

Il se leva vivement et ajouta d'un ton rageur :

— Quant à mes fourneaux, Sartine peut toujours aller se cuire un œuf dessus!

Un coup discret à la porte interrompit le moine.

— Si c'est Sartine, fit-il, son cul va lui en cuire!

Il bondit à la porte.

— Mais ce peut être Hélène, ajouta-t-il en s'apaisant. Ah non, elle ne frappe pas, elle!

Il ouvrit la porte et baissa la tête, surpris de l'apparition d'une frêle jeune fille de seize ans aux vêtements rapiécés et au visage couvert de taches de rousseur.

— Mademoiselle? Vous cherchez quelqu'un?

Elle parut intimidée à sa vue et une légère rougeur envahit son visage. Le moine lui sourit pour la rassurer.

— Ne vous êtes-vous pas trompée de porte?

Prenant son courage à deux mains, elle releva la tête avec plus d'assurance.

— Monsieur, pardonnez-moi mais je cherche M. le commissaire aux morts étranges…

— Oh…

Volnay avait rejoint son père et découvert la visiteuse.

— Entrez, fit-il précipitamment, il fait si froid dehors…

Elle pénétra dans la pièce comme à contrecœur, regardant timidement autour d'elle. Son regard trahit son admiration pour la belle bibliothèque qui regorgeait de livres aux belles enluminures. Elle eut un petit cri de surprise en découvrant la pie.

— Oh, le bel oiseau! s'exclama-t-elle.

— Elle parle plusieurs langues, intervint le moine avec orgueil. C'est moi qui les lui enseigne!

— Elle est à moi, intervint le commissaire aux morts étranges, en bousculant légèrement son père pour arriver à la cage avant lui. Tenez, ajouta-t-il en se saisissant d'une main de la jeune fille, vous pouvez la caresser, elle y est habituée…

L'Écureuil se laissa faire, partagée entre la crainte et le ravissement, enchantée de la présence de la main de Volnay autour de la sienne. Le moine s'émerveilla de voir son fils sourire et rire en présentant sa maison, fier des rangées bien alignées de ses livres et de sa merveilleuse pie parlante. De son côté, la jeune fille semblait consciente que derrière la sécheresse feinte du commissaire aux morts étranges se dissimulait une sensibilité exacerbée, et les regards qu'elle lui lançait dénotaient plus qu'un simple calcul.

Son tendre intérêt pour le beau commissaire aux morts étranges l'avait conduite à un achat dont elle n'était pas coutumière. Dans son quartier, on parlait d'une vieille femme qui vendait des philtres d'amour à base de sang de mouton noir mêlé à du sang menstruel. Le garçon qui l'absorbait tombait inévitablement sous votre charme. Seule une infusion de nénuphar pouvait rompre le sortilège. Néanmoins, la composition du philtre lui déplaisant, elle avait opté pour un sachet de poudre de chauve-souris.

Vous en jetez une pincée par-dessus l'épaule du jeune homme et il ne pourra plus se détacher de vous.

Encore fallait-il en avoir l'occasion sous le regard d'un témoin et alors que l'œil de son commissaire aux morts étranges semblait toujours aux aguets.

La visite de sa demeure accomplie, Volnay fit asseoir la jeune fille dans son meilleur fauteuil et ajouta deux bûches dans le feu, lui proposant ensuite une boisson qu'elle déclina. Surpris de tant de sociabilité de la part de son fils, le moine hochait la tête d'un air approbateur. Enfin, lorsqu'ils furent tous assis près de l'âtre, gagnés par une douce tiédeur, Volnay s'enquit des raisons de la visite de l'Écureuil.

— J'ai retrouvé l'homme dont vous m'avez parlé dans une taverne, expliqua-t-elle. J'ai fait en sorte qu'il me remarque et très vite je...

Elle baissa les yeux gênés.

— Je lui ai plu... Il voulait... enfin... je lui ai dit que ce n'était pas possible car j'avais un autre rendez-vous. Il n'était pas très content de ce contretemps mais je lui ai proposé de le revoir le lendemain. Il m'a donné rendez-vous devant le jardin des Tuileries demain matin, dimanche, à neuf heures.

— Vous êtes très habile, apprécia le moine.

— Merci, dit Volnay. Merci !

Il alla à son cabinet de travail et en sortit une bourse. L'Écureuil le rejoignit vivement et posa la main sur son poignet.

— Je ne veux pas d'argent pour cela.

Elle hésita.

— Ce que j'ai accompli, c'est pour vous...

Dans un coin de la pièce, le moine eut un sourire entendu.

— Je serai chez vous demain à huit heures, dit-elle doucement.

— Plutôt sept, si vous le permettez, j'aime arriver à l'avance.

— Comme vous le désirez...

Elle se haussa sur la pointe des pieds pour lui donner un baiser sur la joue. Alors il se passa une chose étonnante, loin de la repousser, Volnay se pencha sur elle pour chercher ses lèvres et accompagna tendrement son baiser tout en la serrant contre lui.

Oh, se dit le moine, *mon fils s'humanise !*

Oh, pensa l'Écureuil, *je n'ai même pas eu à jeter ma poudre de chauve-souris!*

Hélène avait parcouru la ruelle de l'Or dans la journée, observant et posant des questions, la bourse à la main pour délier les langues. Finalement, elle s'arrêta devant la maison de la Dame de l'Eau. La neige recouvrait tout mais des traces fraîches ornaient celle-ci. Un animal était sorti de la maison pour se soulager et avait gaiement gambadé sur l'étendue blanche. Hélène observa un instant les empreintes, cligna des yeux sous la luminosité trop forte puis se détourna et reprit le chemin de sa maison.

Entrée dans son appartement du faubourg Saint-Jacques, Hélène fit le tour de la pièce après avoir allumé les bougies. La clarté de celles-ci jeta des lueurs incendiaires sur le cercle qu'elle traçait en disposant autour d'elle les chandeliers. Les lueurs dorées dans ses beaux yeux verts semblèrent lutter contre le noir des prunelles. Une plainte sourde, presque un gémissement, s'exhala de la poitrine de la jeune femme.

Lorsqu'elle était enfant, le soir, Hélène rejoignait sa mère apothicaire dans la salle de préparation où elle la trouvait devant ses balances, une balance avec scrupule et une balance à trébuchet. Elle y pesait minutieusement ses préparations car si une dose guérissait, une infime proportion supplémentaire pouvait aussi tuer. Hélène se promenait alors au milieu des bassines et des chaudrons, admirant au passage les moules à pilules ou les alambics dans lesquels sa mère préparait les eaux distillées.

Sa mère lui racontait parfois des légendes d'un autre temps. L'homme est un dieu fourvoyé qui ne se souvient plus des cieux car son œil a mesuré tout l'abîme de la nuit. Mais, si l'homme est tombé, la rassurait-elle, il conserve sans le savoir certaines des facultés que Dieu lui a données. Ce pouvoir endormi, pour d'obscures raisons, quelques-uns encore savent le réveiller...

Quelques-uns...

Assise en tailleur, les mains reposant sur ses genoux, paumes ouvertes, Hélène cligna des paupières. Ses yeux semblèrent alors

se révulser et elle se mit à psalmodier d'une voix caverneuse et dans une langue qui ne ressemblait à nulle autre sur cette terre :
— *Atha Gabor Leonam Adonaï!*

XXII

DÎNER D'ESPRIT ET AUTRES DIABLERIES

Dans les bureaux d'esprit des salons de la bourgeoisie, régnait une légèreté qui n'existait pas à Versailles. La cour fascinait encore mais n'attirait plus. Beaucoup de grands de ce monde qui n'avaient plus rien à obtenir du roi préféraient habiter à Paris et s'y divertir. La capitale dictait désormais le ton en matière de bon goût et d'art de vivre.

À une cour rigidifiée par l'étiquette, se substituait ici la plaisante réunion d'une bonne société. Le snobisme n'en était pas absent mais sans affectation outrée et le ton de la conversation restait badin. L'hôtesse y recevait toutes les attentions galantes propres à la contenter et un public divers s'y pressait : poètes ou hommes d'affaires, comédiens ou négociants, gens de lettres, danseuses et demi-mondaines. La seule obligation était de laisser tous ses soucis à l'entrée du salon. On ne tolérait ni les gens frustes, ni les esprits chagrins. La vie se résumait au jeu, à l'art de la conversation, au rire et au plaisir de faire la cour et d'aimer.

À son époque, et sous son propre nom, le moine avait fait fureur dans ce type de soirées, dispensant bons mots et saillies drolatiques, inventant des charades et poussant le couplet en chantant fort juste. Parmi les plus anciens, on l'accueillit donc avec curiosité mais le vrai centre d'intérêt restait Mme de Morange, mélange fascinant de jeunesse à demi éteinte et de grâce espiègle.

Elle portait une robe de soie bleue rayée d'argent avec des motifs de ruban floral et des manches pagodes à double volant. Un collier de perles fines ornait sa gorge. Le haut du corset replié à la naissance des seins laissait apercevoir deux globes d'un blanc laiteux. Sa main agitait nonchalamment un éventail brodé.

Le souper était un ambigu. Tous les mets se trouvaient sur la table de manière à exciter l'appétit par la vue et le sentiment du beau. La salle se parait de lumières qui se réfléchissaient dans la porcelaine délicatement ouvragée et jusqu'à la pointe des couverts. Dans leurs flacons du cristal le plus pur, vins et liqueurs brillaient de mille éclats. Pâtisseries et confitures sèches ornaient le milieu du jour de table. Les colonnades de sucre des gâteaux miroitaient de couleurs roses ou jaunes sous les girandoles de lumière. Viandes, poissons, tourtes et chartreuses entouraient les desserts en cercles concentriques, entremêlés de sauces ou de crèmes de toutes les couleurs. Les corbeilles débordaient de pain blanc en forme de cygne ou de tourterelle. L'image de ces mets se projetait en même temps que les flammes des chandelles dans une succession de miroirs vénitiens des plus exquis.

L'hiver étant là, d'exquises guirlandes de fleurs en papier remplaçaient les plantes. Elles ornaient vases et urnes, serpentant auprès des chandeliers tandis que des lierres se trémoussaient autour des lustres de Murano. On avait même poussé la délicatesse à figer dans de la gelée des herbes et des piments de couleur.

On passa bientôt à table et le moine nota la ronde parfaite des valets débarrassant par la droite, dans un seul mouvement semi-circulaire, l'assiette usagée tout en introduisant la nouvelle par la droite.

De nos jours, apprécia-t-il, *le bon service se perd. Voilà une maison où l'on sait tenir son rang!*

Après le bon dîner de quatorze heures, il se contenta des plats les plus proches de lui, à savoir des écrevisses cuites à l'eau et farcies de laitance de carpe avant d'être rôties au beurre et panées à la mie de pain. Il goûta aussi par distraction à un saucisson royal à base de chair de perdrix et de chapon crue, assaisonnée d'épices, de champignons et de truffes. Il ne s'en soucia pas plus que cela car il mangeait maigre le premier jour de la semaine et soumettait son corps au jeune le second.

La conversation ne l'intéressa guère car sa venue avait pour seul but de questionner Mme de Morange. Néanmoins, il lui fallait justifier sa place et le moine n'était pas homme à passer pour un cul pincé ou un sot d'esprit même si l'assemblée cherchait surtout le bon mot qui ferait rire l'hôtesse ou la flèche qui percerait le cœur d'un rival. Les convives prenaient des airs fins et entendus, adressant à leur interlocuteur de fades sourires. On développait, dans ce qui se prenait pour la bonne société, la raillerie au rang d'un art. Avec une politesse extrême, on amenait sournoisement la victime dans le ridicule en approuvant tout ce qu'elle disait, en l'exagérant même à l'extrême.

— Dieu a décidé qui naîtrait pauvre ou riche, il n'y a rien à redire là-dessus, lançait justement un nobliau qui, de notoriété publique, devait son titre à l'enrichissement de son père dans le commerce des esclaves.

— Dieu a très certainement pourvu aux quartiers de noblesse de chacun et décidé quelles familles participeraient ou non aux saintes croisades, répliqua vertement le moine.

L'autre rougit. C'était lui faire subtilement remarquer sa position de parvenu.

— Les croisades n'ont pas été la seule façon de servir Dieu, remarqua-t-il.

— Certes, il n'y a pas de sots métiers, admit le moine. Les petits Savoyards sont bien utiles pour ramoner les cheminées et permettre à la fumée de celles-ci de grimper haut vers le ciel.

— Je ne vous parle pas des petites gens! s'emporta le nobliau.

Le moine se rafraîchit avec une douce plombières avant de répliquer :

— Il n'y a pas de petites gens, simplement des petites personnes! Tenez, prenez les marchands d'esclaves…

Des rires moqueurs fusèrent autour de la table. Les regards se portèrent vers le fils du marchand d'esclaves. Sans bonne répartie, son sort était scellé dans la bonne société.

— Et moi, je vous réponds que petites gens et petits métiers sont une seule et même chose car Dieu l'a ainsi décidé! lança le parvenu.

— Vous prêtez sans savoir à Dieu beaucoup d'intentions, répondit le moine d'un ton mordant. A-t-il voulu que des enfants meurent de faim ou de froid tandis que vous vous gorgez de carpes bien grasses ou de cochon de lait?

— Dieu pourvoira au bien-être des méritants dans l'au-delà! Je doute que vous en soyez avec votre esprit hérétique et séditieux.

Le moine lui jeta un regard glacial.

— On dit que les choses qui mènent l'homme en enfer sont au nombre de trois : la calomnie, l'endurcissement et la haine. Ce chiffre de trois vous désignera-t-il pour les flammes éternelles?

Le nobliau se leva écarlate, jeta sa serviette par terre et sortit après avoir salué la maîtresse de maison. Un silence gêné tomba dans la pièce. Le moine fut le premier à le rompre.

— Cette plombières, dit-il en agitant nonchalamment sa cuillère, est à damner le saint que je ne suis pas.

Des rires coururent le long de la table et la conversation reprit son cours. Le souper terminé, on passa dans un salon pour organiser des parties de pharaon. Les invités s'éparpillèrent autour des tables, sortant leur bourse pour miser. Un joueur représentait la banque et possédait les cinquante-deux cartes, les deux autres, nommés *les pontes*, misaient sur une nappe de velours de soie.

Le moine rejoignit Mme de Morange dans son boudoir, une ravissante pièce aux lambris imprimés d'un rose tendre. La pièce sentait le jasmin comme si l'on venait d'y brûler un parfum. Dans une niche peinte couleur lilas, une ottomane reposait sur un parquet de marqueterie. La maîtresse de maison s'y allongea voluptueusement et darda sur lui un regard flamboyant.

— Vous avez manqué ruiner ma soirée, lui reprocha-t-elle vertement.

— Ce grand singe n'a eu que ce qu'il méritait!

— Quand même, vous êtes bien prompt à offusquer mes invités, ces petits marquis ce matin et ce soir…

— Un fils de marchand de viande humaine.

— Sont-ce vraiment des hommes que l'on envoie travailler dans les îles?

— Oui, madame, je vous l'assure, répondit gravement le moine, et ils ont une âme et des sentiments comme vous et moi.

Enfin, surtout moi, pensa-t-il fugitivement, en contemplant Mme de Morange.

Il la jugeait désormais sans plus de cœur que les hommes et les femmes de son époque, sa seule conscience, légère, semblant née de la jambe gauche.

— Vos idées nous amèneraient tout droit à… à une révolution ! s'exclama-t-elle. Et d'abord, pourquoi s'appesantir sur une idée ? On peut bien disserter sans raisonner !

— Parler pour ne rien dire me fatigue !

— Allons, mon bon Guillaume, lui dit-elle en lui pressant affectueusement la main, laissez tomber vos bonnes causes et parlons plutôt de vous.

Le moine ne se laissa pas enrober par son sourire sucré.

— Madame, je me suis plié à toutes vos exigences. J'ai participé à votre souper, j'ai donné la réplique à vos caniches, j'ai aboyé avec eux contre les gens qu'on peut se permettre de moquer mais il est tard et je suis fatigué. J'ai une enquête à mener et besoin de réponses. Mon ami Sartine n'apprécierait pas de me voir perdre mon temps dans les soupers.

— Oh, Sartine…

Elle semblait soudain en avoir moins peur. Le moine lui jeta un regard aigu et ajouta :

— Le procureur Siltieri s'occupe également de cette question et il n'est pas homme facile !

À la mention de Siltieri, Mme de Morange s'agita, mal à l'aise.

— Que venez-vous me menacer ? gémit-elle. J'étais si tranquille dans mon hôtel à recevoir mes amis et à jouir de la vie. J'en avais même oublié jusqu'à…

— Jusqu'à l'existence de votre fille, termina sèchement le moine. J'avais bien compris !

Il la considéra d'un œil neuf, conscient d'avoir devant lui les restes d'une enfant gâtée, une poupée de porcelaine dans une maison de marbre, une femme qui se nourrissait du regard que les autres portaient sur elle, une personne qui recevait mais ne donnait rien.

On est parfois bien surpris de retrouver plus tard qui l'on a aimé, pensa tristement le moine.

— Ma question est simple, reprit-il d'une voix glaçante, à l'époque vous fréquentiez plusieurs hommes à la fois. J'en étais. Sartine, de même. Peut-être d'autres… Et puis, le roi vous avait remarquée… Qui est le père de Sophia?

Mme de Morange froissa nerveusement les plis de sa robe et releva la tête, les larmes aux yeux.

— Vous me pressez de questions sur mon enfant, que se passe-t-il donc? Lui est-il arrivé quelque malheur?

Le moine secoua la tête d'un air désapprobateur.

— Madame, vous n'avez pas vu votre enfant depuis sa naissance. Me trompé-je? Non! Alors, ne parlons pas de sentiment ou d'émotion et gardez au sec vos jolis yeux.

Elle ravala ses larmes.

— Que savez-vous donc de l'instinct maternel, moine du diable? J'avais dix-sept ans lorsque je la mis au monde. Dix-sept ans!

Il lui renvoya un sourire dur.

— Madame, vos remords et vos regrets sont tardifs et je ne peux qu'y compatir mais, encore une fois, j'ai à faire. Je mène une enquête pour laquelle je dois trouver des réponses. Je vous repose donc une dernière fois ma question : qui est le père de Sophia?

Mme de Morange le fixa, le regard vide.

— Après tout… dit-elle simplement.

Malgré lui, le moine contempla ses lèvres pleines et rouges, suspendu à celles-ci comme si le reste de sa vie en dépendait.

— Le père de Sophia… commença-t-elle.

Il se pencha en avant, son cœur cognant durement contre sa poitrine.

— C'est le roi, termina-t-elle.

Comme frappé d'apoplexie, le moine chancela.

— Le roi, répéta-t-il. Bien sûr, que je suis bête…

Le moine fit quelques pas dans la rue déserte et, frissonnant, ramena son manteau au plus près de son corps. Le vin cognait trop dans son crâne, il trébucha sur le sol glacé. Dans la rue de lourdes masses d'ombre semblaient se précipiter sur lui. Il se releva et fit quelques pas en expirant doucement, laissant la brise caresser ses tempes et rafraîchir son front, abandonnant au vent ses idées noires. Ardemment, il avait souhaité que Sophia fût de lui mais il n'en était rien. C'était l'enfant d'une crapule royale. Sur terre, le mal régnait et la justice n'existait pas. Seules subsistaient quelques âmes de bonne volonté.

Peut-être que les satanistes ont raison : le diable tient Dieu prisonnier de son ciel!

En faisant le tour de l'hôtel particulier, il surprit le manège du cuisinier et de l'intendant, revendant déjà à quelques traiteurs les restes du dîner dont les invités s'étaient régalés.

Sophia… Accablé de chagrin, le moine prit le chemin du retour et bientôt la nuit l'avala. Les rues obscures de Paris semblaient étrangement calmes par rapport au brouhaha de la journée. Il passa devant le Palais-Royal. On y jouait ou on soupait en caressant les filles. Il obliqua rue du Coq en direction du Vieux Louvre. Des cabarets italiens s'échappaient déjà des mélopées avinées et il se mit à chantonner à l'unisson. Alors la nuit fut trouée d'éclats métalliques et l'enfer se rua sur lui.

— Tue! Tue!

C'était le cri des assassins qu'ils poussaient autant pour se donner de l'audace et de la rage que pour impressionner leur victime. Brutalement dégrisé, le moine dégaina son épée et se mit souplement en garde. Une lueur froide et affûtée brillait maintenant dans son regard. Tirant sa dague de la main gauche, il para les coups d'épée de chacun de ses assaillants. Le moine en compta quatre, armés de lourdes rapières et conduits par un grand roux malingre au visage balafré de la joue au menton.

— Tue! Tue!

À chaque attaque, le moine encaissait sans broncher cette détermination à l'assassiner. Il parait au plus pressé, défendait, attaquait sans se départir de son calme et la sueur coulait le long de son visage buriné. À un moment, une lame lui entailla le dessus de la main qui tenait la dague.

Ils sont trop nombreux, je n'y arriverai pas.

— À l'assassin, cria-t-il d'abord sans conviction puis d'une voix de plus en plus forte.

Il para de justesse un coup au ventre et, du revers de sa dague, ouvrit la gorge de son adversaire qui s'était trop fendu pour lui porter le coup.

Trois! fit intérieurement le moine. Il avait cessé de crier "À l'assassin!". Personne ne viendrait et les gens restaient peureusement derrière leurs fenêtres, s'efforçant de distinguer dans le noir le féroce combat engagé dans la rue. Le moine ne s'en formalisa pas. Il avait appris de la vie à ne pas trop attendre le secours des autres lorsqu'il se trouvait dans le besoin.

De nouveau, une pluie de coups s'abattit sur lui mais de manière trop désordonnée. Avec un calme hallucinant, le moine bloqua l'attaque de ses adversaires et riposta aussitôt. Comme l'un de ses agresseurs se ruait seul sur lui, il dégagea et, glissant sa lame sous le bras de l'autre, le blessa profondément.

Les assassins hésitèrent. Le moine était un homme terrible les armes à la main. Rares étaient ceux qui possédaient comme lui le sentiment du fer, cette faculté de sentir en une fraction de seconde, au contact de la lame de l'adversaire, si celle-ci s'engageait par-dessous ou par-dessus et si l'autre s'apprêtait à attaquer, croiser, retourner ou dégager. Avec une adresse diabolique, il para un coup porté à son cœur et repoussa ses assaillants en claquant leur fer. Une détermination effrayante irradiait de toute sa personne. L'agresseur blessé à l'épaule recula, vacillant sur le sol glacé. Le moine se rua sur lui et l'embrocha sans un battement de cils. C'en était trop pour l'un des spadassins qui tout à coup fit volte-face malgré les imprécations de son chef. Le rouquin se retrouva seul face au moine et là celui-ci sut que cela allait être une autre affaire. C'est alors qu'un cri jaillit dans la nuit.

— Halte-là, le guet!

Le rouquin recula de plusieurs pas avant de tourner les talons et s'enfuir dans la nuit. Le moine fit de même mais dans une direction opposée. Manifestement, aucun des deux combattants ne se fiait aux archers du guet.

La pie jacassa lorsque la porte s'ouvrit, heureuse de revoir autour d'elle son petit monde. Volnay jeta un regard épouvanté au sang qui gouttait par terre.

— Que s'est-il passé? Tu es blessé?

— Un simple bobo, fit le moine avec une mâle assurance. On a essayé de m'assassiner au sortir de l'hôtel de Mme de Morange. Peux-tu m'aider à bander ma main?

Son fils se précipita. Le moine lui indiqua comment nettoyer la blessure avant de la bander.

— Des spadassins de bas étage, gronda-t-il, ce n'est pas faire honneur à un escrimeur de ma qualité qui en a refroidi cent en duel!

— Huit, père.

— Huit en duel officiel avec témoins mais bien plus en réalité! Enfin, seul le rouquin tirait correctement mais des rouquins Siltieri nous dirait que leurs cheveux ont été brûlés par les flammes de l'enfer!

Volnay étouffa un sourire.

— Hélène n'est toujours pas revenue? s'inquiéta le moine.

— Es-tu seulement passé chez toi?

— Oui et elle n'y est pas.

Le commissaire aux morts étranges haussa les épaules.

— Qu'as-tu appris là-bas? s'enquit-il enfin.

Pour une fois, le moine fut bref.

— Que Sophia est la fille du roi!

Volnay tressaillit. L'affaire commençait dans un cimetière et le menait maintenant tout près du roi, dans sa propre descendance! Mais où donc étaient-ils encore tombés?

— Notre maître joaillier est marié à une femme qui ne peut avoir d'enfant, récapitula-t-il. Celle-ci lui demande d'adopter un jour la fille de Belle Ange, elle-même maîtresse du roi. Recevant pour cela une pension, et après la mort de sa femme, il vend son commerce et abandonne son métier pour se consacrer à sa passion : les étoiles. Puis il laisse sa fille adoptive s'élever toute seule…

— Peut-être en voulait-il au monarque pour avoir introduit sans le vouloir son propre enfant dans son foyer, le privant de l'affection de sa femme? hasarda le moine.

— En tout cas, ce père adoptif s'intéresse à la sorcellerie et au roi! Souviens-toi que, lorsque nous avons visité l'astrologue, il nous a caché qu'il établissait le thème astral de Louis XV! Ce n'est donc pas un hasard si l'on retrouve cette fille de roi allongée nue sur une tombe! Et pour une messe noire!

— Pour un rituel d'envoûtement, le corrigea le moine. Souviens-toi du livre de l'astrologue. Le rituel nécessite une conjonction bien précise d'étoiles, la célébration d'une messe noire et le sacrifice d'une victime. Mais attention, il s'agit d'un envoûtement par le sang. La personne à envoûter doit être du même sang que la victime.

— Et Sophia est la fille de Louis XV!

Ils se regardèrent stupéfaits.

— C'est le roi que l'on veut envoûter! s'exclama Volnay.

XXIII

CHEVALIER SATANISTE
ET AUTRES DIABLERIES

Comme une pointe en diamant, les rayons du soleil vinrent se poser avec délicatesse sur l'Écureuil lorsque le commissaire aux morts étranges lui ouvrit la porte. Elle eut un sourire céleste quand Volnay l'invita à boire un café. Le moine arriva bientôt et lui baisa galamment la main.

— Je suis de plus en plus inquiet, Hélène n'est pas rentrée de la nuit, glissa-t-il à son fils.

Volnay lui jeta un regard moqueur.

— Et pourquoi donc cette jeune femme rentrerait-elle chez toi tous les soirs?

— Mon Dieu, c'est ce qu'elle fait depuis le début de cette enquête. Je n'ai aucune nouvelle d'elle et je ne sais où et comment la joindre.

— C'est elle qui en a décidé ainsi! Pour ma part, je l'ai quittée hier matin avant de partir voir Sartine. Elle ne m'a rien confié de ce qu'elle comptait faire.

Le moine refusa le café qu'on lui proposait et s'appliqua à lisser sa barbe d'un air pensif. Enfin Volnay donna le signal du départ pour le jardin des Tuileries. Deux statues représentant Mercure et la Renommée chevauchant un cheval ailé flanquaient l'entrée principale. Haut lieu de promenades mondaines, les entrées en étaient toujours gardées et n'importe qui n'était pas admis. L'Écureuil eut un sursaut en lisant l'écriteau à l'entrée du jardin *"Interdit aux chiens, aux filles, aux laquais et aux soldats"*. Remarquant son trouble, le policier lui tendit son bras et entra avec assurance avec elle et son père, passant sans un regard pour le factionnaire de service.

— Comme c'est beau, chuchota l'Écureuil à l'oreille de son compagnon. Je ne suis jamais venue ici.

Le moine observa avec désapprobation le maintien raide de Volnay alors que la jeune fille à son bras n'attendait de toute évidence que compliments et badinage.

Pourquoi lorsqu'il est avec une femme mon fils donne toujours l'impression de marcher sur des épines?

— Nous sommes en avance d'une heure, reprit l'Écureuil pour meubler la conversation.

— C'est mieux ainsi. Mon père et moi avons l'habitude d'arriver toujours au moment où l'on ne nous attend pas. Cela nous a parfois appris des choses intéressantes!

Jardins de galanterie aux beaux jours, les jardins sous la neige étaient presque déserts. Volnay observa l'allée centrale percée dans l'axe du palais des Tuileries et délimitée à l'est par un bassin rond, à l'ouest par un bassin octogonal. Louis XIV avait fait redessiner les jardins par André Le Nôtre qui avait introduit des terrasses dotées de rampes en courbe pour y accéder. Le commissaire aux morts étranges remarqua une silhouette connue emprunter l'une d'elles. Il s'immobilisa comme un chien en arrêt, les narines frémissantes.

— Je connais cet homme, murmura-t-il.

— Mon Dieu, dit le moine, n'est-ce pas Sartine qui vient?

— C'est bien lui, confirma son fils.

— Étonnant! Mais alors…

— Alors, cachons-nous!

Ils quittèrent précipitamment l'allée centrale, contournèrent les parterres qui refleuriraient au printemps et trouvèrent derrière un bosquet de sapins un bon point d'observation. Leur attention fut alors attirée par un homme à la large carrure marchant à grands pas entre des haies de buis. Ses bottes écrasaient la neige, faisant voler autour de lui des nuages d'une fine poudre blanche. L'Écureuil laissa échapper une exclamation :

— C'est lui!

— L'homme du cimetière! s'exclama le moine. Voici donc l'atout dans la manche de Sartine : un sataniste!

— Mieux vaut qu'il ne sache pas que nous savons! murmura son fils. Restons dissimulés à leurs yeux.

Ils observèrent en silence les deux hommes qui parlaient vivement. Sartine s'agitait nerveusement et ses gestes étaient de plus en plus brusques. Finalement, le lieutenant général de police tourna les talons et s'en fut à grands pas, fort mécontent.

— Les voilà qui se séparent! s'exclama le moine. Que faisons-nous maintenant?

— Laissons Sartine repartir, il doit avoir sa voiture non loin de là. Je vais suivre le sataniste avec Gaston et cette fois je lui mettrai la main dessus.

— Il m'a l'air dangereux, je viens avec toi.

— Tu es très repérable avec ta bure et je préfère que tu raccompagnes mon amie jusqu'à une voiture.

— Certes ton épée n'est pas pucelle mais je serais plus rassuré si…

— Ne t'inquiète pas, le coupa Volnay, je te rejoindrai chez moi. Restez là quelques instants avant de quitter les jardins.

L'Écureuil eut une moue attristée.

— Ne puis-je aller avec vous?

Le moine intervint.

— Mon enfant, vous n'avez pas idée de l'affaire où vous mettez les pieds.

Mais elle ne l'écoutait pas et s'accrochait au bras de Volnay.

— Vous reverrai-je?

Le policier la contempla un instant et dit :

— Oui.

Il reçut comme une offrande son corps mince contre le sien, la serrant à son tour avec ferveur contre lui puis il s'arracha à son étreinte et, à pas souples, prit la direction de la sortie du jardin.

— Eh bien eh bien… murmura le moine. Mon fils m'étonnera toujours.

Il le suivit des yeux alors qu'il s'éloignait avant de reporter son attention sur l'Écureuil.

— Je vois que vous vous entendez bien avec mon… euh… avec le commissaire aux morts étranges.

Elle rougit pudiquement.

— Oui, enfin je crois. Il n'est pas toujours facile à cerner.

Le moine approuva, amusé. Vive et éveillée, la jeune fille lui plaisait.

— Voyez-vous, fit-il en lui prenant le bras et en l'entraînant hors du jardin, dans l'exercice de son métier Volnay est un homme froid et rationnel. Mais en compagnie des femmes, il est capable de se montrer tout à fait ridicule !

— Pourquoi donc ?

Le moine haussa les sourcils.

— Mon... euh... Volnay aimerait pouvoir tout maîtriser dans sa vie, y compris ses sentiments.

Il soupira.

— Pour ma part, j'y ai renoncé depuis fort longtemps !

Le commissaire aux morts étranges se glissa hors des jardins des Tuileries. Déjà, l'épaisse silhouette du sataniste disparaissait à l'angle d'une rue. L'homme marchait très vite. Volnay courut pour le rattraper mais, lorsqu'il arriva au carrefour, l'autre avait disparu.

— Psitt !

Le commissaire aux morts étranges repéra une silhouette qui semblait changée en statue de glace. L'homme grelottait, dissimulé à moitié dans une porte cochère.

— Ah, les mouches de Sartine sont parfois bien utiles ! souffla Volnay.

Il le rejoignit rapidement.

— Alors, la mouche, dis-nous ce que tu as vu ! lança gaiement le policier.

— Il a pris la première rue à droite et va traverser la place Louis-le-Grand, dit Gaston en battant des bras pour se réchauffer. Venez ! Il va très vite !

Ils le retrouvèrent rue des Capucins, marchant lourdement botté et éperonné, l'épée aux côtés, comme un condottiere. Deux yeux de prédateur brillaient dans son visage anguleux d'où saillaient deux pommettes sèches. Volnay le suivit jusqu'à une enseigne représentant un bras tenant une épée. L'homme entra au rez-de-chaussée de la maison. Le commissaire aux morts étranges échangea un signe discret avec Gaston pour lui indiquer de l'attendre avant de se glisser à son tour dans les lieux.

Il se retrouva dans une salle d'armes où résonnait le bruit des fleurets entrechoqués. Le sol était parqueté mais patiné et usé par les semelles des combattants. Tout un pan de mur était couvert de glaces dans lesquelles se reflétaient les fleurets accrochés dans un râtelier. De grandes fenêtres dispensaient la lumière terne du jour. Dans un coin de la salle, trônait un cheval de bois pour apprendre l'escrime à cheval.

Maigre et nerveux, le maître d'armes portait une ample chemise de batiste aux manches larges, les poignets à boutonnière rentrés dans les gants. Il discutait avec le sataniste lorsqu'il aperçut Volnay. Il interrompit sa conversation pour s'approcher de lui.

— Monsieur, désirez-vous une leçon ? Mes deux élèves terminent leur engagement et je devrai m'occuper de monsieur qui vient d'arriver, à moins que tous deux vous ne souhaitiez croiser le fer ensemble ?

— J'en serai ravi, fit Volnay en s'inclinant légèrement.

Le maître d'armes revint vers le sataniste qui feignait l'indifférence. Celui-ci l'écouta et hocha brièvement la tête en signe d'assentiment. Il jeta ensuite un regard lourd sur Volnay avant de s'incliner pour le saluer. Le policier lui rendit son salut. Puis les deux hommes attendirent, les yeux fixés sur l'échange en cours, évitant de s'observer.

Les combattants s'affrontaient, vêtus d'un plastron bourré d'une laine épaisse maintenue entre deux grosses toiles recouvertes d'une épaisseur de cuir. Au centre du plastron, un cœur de cuir rouge était dessiné. Les fleurettistes battaient souvent l'air de leur fer, peinant à se trouver tant ils faisaient preuve de prudence, ne se risquant que pour esquiver des bottes maladroites sans les mener à leur terme. L'assaut achevé, le maître d'armes donna quelques conseils aux combattants. Une fois ceux-ci sortis, il revint vers Volnay et le sataniste, tenant à la main deux fleurets mouchetés par une bourre de tissu enveloppée de cuir, maintenue par une cordelette à l'extrémité de l'arme.

— Messieurs, dit-il, je ne vous connais pas, aussi vais-je vous observer dans un premier temps. Désirez-vous un plastron pour amortir les coups ?

— Pour moi, ce n'est pas la peine, dit le sataniste. Je ne crois pas que monsieur puisse me toucher.

— C'est drôle, fit Volnay, j'allais dire la même chose!

L'autre le considéra pensivement et fendit l'air de son épée avec une nonchalance affectée.

— Je pense que je peux vous donner une petite leçon...

Le maître d'armes intervint.

— Messieurs, ce n'est qu'un échange d'observation. Pas de touche au visage ou de bousculade. N'oubliez pas que l'escrime se résume en cinq points : le sentiment du fer, le coup d'œil, le jugement, la vitesse et la précision.

Il leva le bras.

— Messieurs, saluez! En garde! Allez!

Les fers teintèrent et s'entrechoquèrent. La garde du sataniste était parfaite. Tout de suite, le commissaire aux morts étranges comprit que son adversaire était redoutable. Combattant expérimenté, il alternait avec vivacité attaque et contre-attaque. Volnay tenta de prendre l'offensive mais se vit stoppé. L'autre battit alors brusquement sa lame et tenta un coup d'estoc avant de se fendre. Le policier recula prudemment, tenant sa garde en prime. Son adversaire attaqua de nouveau, tenta une botte, avançant toujours. Volnay porta sa garde en prime et se cantonna prudemment à une position défensive dans l'attente d'une ouverture. Le maître d'armes approuva ce choix tactique d'un bref hochement de tête.

Le sataniste attaquait maintenant sans relâche, le pressant de plus en plus. Volnay reculait tout en tentant de se préserver. D'un geste vif, son adversaire arracha la mouche de son épée et bondit en avant. Ses yeux avaient pris une teinte farouche.

— Monsieur! cria le maître d'armes.

Il n'eut pas le temps d'intervenir. Après un mouvement d'une rapidité inouïe, l'épée du sataniste se posa sur la gorge de Volnay.

— Monsieur, fit son adversaire, vous êtes mort!

Le commissaire aux morts étranges ne cilla pas. Son heure n'était pas venue et il le savait. D'un coup d'épée sec, le maître d'armes écarta la lame du sataniste.

— Monsieur, votre attitude est inqualifiable!

L'autre eut un rictus sardonique et, sans quitter Volnay des yeux, répondit :

— Pardonnez-moi, maître, c'était pour donner un peu de piquant à l'exercice !

Le policier fit un pas en avant, empêchant ainsi son adversaire de brandir son fleuret.

— Monsieur, dit-il, je suis commissaire au Châtelet et je vous déclare de prise de corps.

Un grand rire ébranla le sataniste pour se terminer dans ce qui ressemblait au hennissement d'un cheval.

— Vous voulez me faire prisonnier ? Eh bien attrapez-moi d'abord !

Il se jeta sur son adversaire pour lui asséner au menton un coup de la garde de son épée puis bouscula le maître d'armes et se précipita hors de la salle. Pendant ce temps, à terre, Volnay comptait les étoiles. Le maître d'armes alla chercher un flacon de sel et aida le policier à se mettre debout.

— Cet homme est fou, grommela-t-il.

— Est-ce un de vos clients ? demanda le commissaire aux morts étranges.

— C'est la première et dernière fois que je le vois, répondit fermement l'autre.

Il hésita et ajouta :

— En tout cas, c'est un redoutable bretteur. Je vous conseille de l'éviter car la prochaine fois, il pourrait bien vous tuer !

Volnay ignora le conseil et sortit rapidement. Dans la rue, il repéra Gaston qui revenait, tout essoufflé.

— Tu l'as perdu ?

— Diable commissaire, il court plus vite qu'un chien. Quand il s'est élancé dehors, j'ai… j'ai couru à sa poursuite mais il… il était trop rapide pour moi !

Il se cassa en deux les mains sur les genoux, soufflant bruyamment.

— Tu manges trop, fit Volnay. Cela t'alourdit. Jamais chat emmitouflé ne prit souris !

— Commissaire, les mouches n'ont pas pour fonction de courir mais de suivre ! Pas besoin d'être maigre pour espionner.

Le policier ne répondit pas. Sur ses épaules pesait le poids d'échecs répétés : la Vorace d'abord, Sophia puis le sataniste par deux fois. Ce dernier était un adversaire tout bonnement redoutable. Son assurance incroyable le disputait à son arrogance. Il semblait ne rien craindre de personne. Au cimetière, lors de l'enterrement de Sophia, il s'était sans vergogne signé à l'envers, révélant son identité de sataniste. Quelques minutes auparavant, il avait choisi d'affronter Volnay en combat singulier, s'offrant même le luxe de lui faire grâce de la vie.

Il virevolte trop, songea le policier. Un peu comme s'il voulait que l'on s'attache à ses pas plutôt qu'à ceux de son complice l'astrologue. À moins que son assurance ne provienne de la haute protection de quelqu'un.

— Dis-moi Gaston, dit-il, tu es seul ?

— Oui, commissaire.

— Et la mouche qui me suit ?

— Lorsque vous êtes entré dans la salle d'armes, je l'ai envoyée chercher du renfort.

Le commissaire aux morts étranges posa une main ferme sur l'épaule de Gaston.

— Dis-moi, mouche mon amie, que dirais-tu d'oublier ce qui vient d'arriver ? Ce ne serait bon ni pour toi ni pour moi que Sartine apprenne que nous avons laissé filer un suspect !

— Je n'osais pas vous le proposer commissaire. Rien n'est advenu, tout est à advenir !

Un sourire éclaira brièvement le visage de Volnay.

— Nous nous comprenons !

Gaston soupira de soulagement.

— Nous sommes des hommes de terrain, commissaire. Dans leurs bureaux du Châtelet, au coin du feu, ils ne se rendent pas compte des difficultés de nos professions !

Pour remercier la mouche de garder le secret sur leur malheureuse aventure, Volnay décida de lui offrir le meilleur repas de sa vie. Aussi, après être allés chercher le moine, les trois hommes s'attablèrent chez un traiteur non loin de là.

C'était un des rares traiteurs où l'on pouvait emporter les plats mais également manger sur place, en arrière-salle *et à sa propre table*, pour ne pas concurrencer les aubergistes. Le premier plat bouleversa Gaston : des yeux de veau farcis au gratin dont les prunelles avaient été avantageusement remplacées par des truffes noires entières. La mouche n'utilisait pas de fourchette mais mangeait en utilisant le pouce, l'index et le médius car, disait-il, les deux autres doigts servaient au diable lorsqu'il mangeait. Le moine lui remplit de nouveau sa flûte en remarquant :

— Tu avais soif mon ami la mouche!

— Ah, soupira Gaston, j'aime le champagne mais le coût m'en a fait perdre le goût!

Après les entremets, les larmes vinrent aux yeux de la mouche à la vue du canard aux huîtres, cuit à la braise et servi baignant dans une sauce liée au coulis de veau et de jambon, avec un peu de lard fondu, des truffes et de petits champignons parfumés.

— Ah, ce doit être très onéreux! commenta Gaston impressionné. Vous jetez la maison par les fenêtres pour moi!

Le commissaire aux morts étranges mangea peu mais les deux autres convives dévorèrent pour lui. Des pots de confitures sèches furent amenés pour dessert car Volnay, qui n'avait pas l'habitude de passer beaucoup de temps à table, estima que l'on pouvait se passer de fromage. La mouche pleura de bonheur en voyant les pots de mûres, framboises, prunes, pommes et poires glisser dans son assiette.

— Pourquoi pleures-tu? s'étonna Volnay.

— Vous êtes si bons avec moi alors que je vous cache tant de choses!

Le moine se moqua.

— Ne voilà-t-il pas que notre mouche devient sentimentale devant des pots de confitures…

— Sans oublier ce merveilleux veau et ce splendide canard aux huîtres, s'écria Gaston, le tout arrosé de cet excellent vin de Champagne!

Il essuya ses doigts poisseux sur sa manche. Volnay lui tapota le bras.

— C'est pour te remercier de ne rien dire au sujet de notre poursuite si mal engagée…

La mouche se frotta le nez avec sa manche.

— Oh pour ça, je suis plus fautif que vous! Non ce qui me peine, c'est cet homme après qui nous avons couru. Aujourd'hui, je l'ai bien vu à la lumière du jour et cette fois plus de doute possible, je l'ai reconnu!

— Alors?

— Il s'appelle Fauve et c'est un inspecteur de police!

Le commissaire aux morts étranges empila les bûches dans la cheminée tandis que son père tirait d'une boîte en noyer une petite fiche. Il la lut avec application après s'être pourvu d'une paire de bésicles.

— Inspecteur Fauve, dit *le chevalier de Fauve* car c'est le nom qu'il prend pour s'introduire officieusement dans certains cercles aisés. C'est d'ailleurs un spécialiste des états civils et des actes de naissance. Le faux en écriture est sa spécialité! Son secteur d'activité est les filles et les salles de jeu. Lorsque Sartine a mis en coupe réglée les maisons de jeu, le chevalier de Fauve lui a été bien utile. L'homme vit sur un certain pied. On dit que plusieurs femmes travaillent pour lui.

Il leva les yeux vers son fils pour apporter un commentaire éclairé.

— Ce n'est pas un cas rare, de nos jours, la probité des policiers laisse à désirer.

Un silence et le moine ajouta d'un ton dramatique :

— Le seul problème est que le chevalier de Fauve est mort, il y a deux ans, assassiné par un condamné qu'il convoyait et qui lui a brisé le crâne à coups de pierre.

— Difficile dans ces conditions de reconnaître un cadavre! remarqua Volnay.

— Le coup a dû être monté pour lui permettre de disparaître officiellement et de travailler dans l'ombre pour Sartine.

— Réfléchissons! décréta le commissaire aux morts étranges en se levant et en commençant à arpenter la pièce.

Cette nouvelle information permettait à son esprit de rebondir, d'échafauder d'autres hypothèses.

— Deux femmes à la messe noire : la Vorace et une inconnue. Trois hommes : l'astrologue, le curé dansant et… le chevalier de Fauve ou Sartine ? Comme à son habitude, Sartine sait tout. Il a suivi la trace de cette enfant dès sa naissance sachant qu'elle provenait de la couche du roi. Une bâtarde peut toujours servir… De plus, il semble remarquablement informé des pratiques de messes noires !

— Sartine… murmura le moine. Comme tu y vas, mon fils ! Disons plutôt le chevalier de Fauve, cela me semble plus plausible.

À cet instant, la porte s'ouvrit brutalement et toute une troupe d'archers du guet envahit la pièce, suivie du lieutenant général de police. Sous son manteau bordé d'hermine, celui-ci portait un habit de velours noir.

— Encore vous ! s'exclama le moine. Décidément, vous n'en finissez plus d'envahir ma maison ! Peut-être désirez-vous y prendre une chambre ?

— Vous ne croyez pas si bien dire ! Dites-moi où se trouve Sophia et je vous tiendrai pour quitte !

— Vous m'avez donné quarante-huit heures pour la retrouver, rappela Volnay indigné.

— Et moi, je crois que vous l'avez déjà ! répondit Sartine en se plantant devant lui.

— Vous vous trompez.

Le lieutenant général de police essaya de sonder le regard de son commissaire aux morts étranges mais, comme tant d'autres, il se perdit dans la profondeur de celui-ci, puits sans fond.

— Fouillez partout ! cria Sartine dépité. Ouvrez les coffres, les armoires, regardez dessous les lits, sondez les planchers et les murs !

Il y eut un vacarme dans toute la maison, ponctué par les cris du moine :

— Ne touchez pas à ce clavecin avec vos gros doigts, vous allez me le désaccorder. Reposez immédiatement ce vase ! Vous, laissez mes plantes tranquilles ou vous vous gratterez le cul toute la nuit !

On rapporta à Sartine des livres reliés en maroquin.

— Qu'est-ce que ceci ?

Le lieutenant général de police lut avec application le titre du livre :

— *Dissertation sur les apparitions des anges, des démons et des esprits et sur les revenants et vampires de Hongrie, de Bohême, de Moravie et de Silésie.*

Il releva la tête et fixa le moine avec ahurissement.

— Je m'attendais à tout, y compris à des facéties scatologiques, mais qu'est-ce donc que ces lectures ? Et qui est son auteur ?

— Dom Augustin Calmet est mort il y a deux ans, répondit le moine. Désolé, vous ne pourrez pas lui passer les brodequins et le livrer au bûcher ! Je le lis par curiosité mais j'avoue que ce n'est pas très sérieux…

— Et celui-ci ? reprit Sartine. *Caractères de magie tracés* de l'abbé de Rocheblanche !

— C'est un saint homme ! dit le moine sans rire.

— *Secrets merveilleux de la magie naturelle et cabalistique du Petit Albert*, continua Sartine impavide.

— Oh, de nos jours tout le monde sait que les salamandres habitent la région du feu, les sylphes celle de l'air, les gnomes le cœur de la terre et les ondins le fond de nos eaux !

— Et encore un autre ! s'exclama le lieutenant général de police. *Cosmopolite ou Nouvelle Lumière chimique pour servir d'éclaircissement aux trois principes de la nature exactement décrits dans les trois traités suivants…*

— *Le Traité du mercure, Le Traité du soufre* et *Le Traité du vrai sel des philosophes*, compléta le moine.

— Belle lecture ! commenta Sartine d'un ton sévère. Je vous félicite !

— Le contenu des livres permet d'en savoir plus sur le monde, expliqua le moine imperturbable. Bien sûr, on pourrait manger les livres pour mieux les digérer mais le plus sûr moyen de s'instruire est encore de les lire !

— Pas ces livres-là ! gronda Sartine.

Le moine secoua la tête.

— Je dénie toute forme de superstition ou d'obscurantisme. Je ne vois ni lutin, ni fée autour de moi. J'estime simplement que la nature recèle d'admirables secrets qu'il nous convient de percer.

— Vouloir percer les secrets de la nature est un outrage au ciel car si celui-ci désirait nous les révéler, il l'aurait fait!

— Je ne vois pas les choses comme vous, répondit paisiblement le moine. La nature me lance un défi, j'y réponds!

— Vous feriez mieux de cesser de lire toutes ces diableries et de demeurer à la place que Dieu vous a assignée!

— Sartine, gronda le moine, cinquante entrées différentes conduisent à la connaissance générale des mystères et vous n'en connaissez pas une seule!

Le lieutenant général de police eut un grognement exaspéré et se tourna vers Volnay.

— Dites-moi où est Sophia et nous en resterons là. Je sais que parfois vous agissez bizarrement mais, pour cette fois, je ne vous en tiendrai pas rigueur!

— Monsieur de Sartine, fit calmement Volnay, je vous ai dit que j'avais besoin d'un peu de temps pour la trouver. Pourquoi remettre en cause notre arrangement?

— Mais parce que je n'ai aucune confiance en vous!

— Je ne peux vous répondre pour l'instant, s'entêta le commissaire aux morts étranges.

— Très bien, fit Sartine en se tournant vers les archers du guet. Tous à la maison du commissaire!

Il toisa Volnay d'un air menaçant.

— Vous nous accompagnez ou préférez-vous que l'on défonce votre porte?

— Je préfère vous ouvrir, les voisins ne comprendraient pas!

Sous les quolibets de la pie, les hommes de Sartine envahirent la maison du commissaire aux morts étranges qu'ils se mirent en devoir de dévaster. Volnay eut un pincement au cœur en voyant les archers du guet saisir ses livres avec leurs grosses mains malhabiles.

— Sartine! Qu'ils ne touchent pas à mes livres! Sophia ne se cache pas entre les pages!

Le lieutenant général de police eut un grognement exaspéré.

— Vous, votre père et vos fichus livres! Vous feriez mieux de vous intéresser aux gens!

XXIV

ENLÈVEMENT DE SOPHIA
ET AUTRES DIABLERIES

La tempête passée, Volnay et son père entreprirent de ranger la maison du commissaire aux morts étranges. La pie jacassait à qui mieux mieux mais les deux hommes gardaient un silence renfrogné. La matinée s'achevait mal. Ils avaient surpris leur supérieur avec un inspecteur de police officiellement mort et suspecté de satanisme, Volnay avait perdu l'homme et Sartine venait de faire fouiller de fond en comble leurs maisons par ses hommes afin de retrouver Sophia. Quant à Hélène, ils en étaient sans nouvelles depuis la veille au matin. Le moine remettait en place une grande glace dans un cadre en bois sculpté et doré lorsque l'on cogna contre la porte.

— Je crois que pour cette enquête le monde entier gravite autour de nos deux maisons! se plaignit le moine. Si seulement, cela pouvait être Hélène…

— Je vais ouvrir, soupira son fils.

La porte ouverte, il se retrouva devant la gueule menaçante du pistolet du chevalier de Fauve!

— Puis-je entrer cher confrère?

Volnay recula. Il jeta un bref coup d'œil derrière lui, apercevant le moine glisser sa main sous sa bure, sans doute pour se saisir de sa dague. Comme devinant les mauvaises intentions des occupants de ces lieux, le chevalier de Fauve leva une main en l'air.

— Tout doux, messieurs, je suis venu ici de mon plein gré et je ne suis pas animé de mauvaises intentions. Bien au contraire!

— Prouvez-le, dit calmement Volnay.

— Mais tout de suite!

Le visage illuminé d'un large sourire, le chevalier de Fauve tendit son pistolet à Volnay qui s'empressa de le pointer sur lui.

— Amusant! commenta le moine en sortant sa dague. Mais est-il chargé?

— Il l'est, le rassura son fils.

Le chevalier de Fauve prit un air vaguement ennuyé.

— Puis-je m'asseoir?

Sans attendre de réponse, il ôta son manteau. Dessous, il portait un habit galonné et des manchettes en dentelles. Avec un soupir d'aise, il s'assit sur un fauteuil près du feu et se frotta les mains.

— Quel bonheur de se réchauffer!

Il jeta un regard circulaire à la pièce.

— Une charmante demeure, vraiment. Un peu en désordre toutefois… Ah, voici votre fameuse pie qui parle! On dit qu'elle est très impolie!

— Comment savez-vous où j'habite? le questionna Volnay.

— Oh, je suis un inspecteur de police et votre résidence n'est pas secrète.

— Pourquoi avoir fui ce matin?

Le chevalier de Fauve haussa les épaules.

— Parce que vous vouliez me prendre et que je ne le voulais pas. J'avais à vous parler mais, pour prouver ma bonne foi, il me fallait me livrer à vous de mon plein gré. J'aurais pu vous tuer ce matin, convenez-en. Et j'aurais pu faire de même à l'instant.

— Cela peut aussi constituer une manœuvre, remarqua le moine.

De Fauve porta un regard nonchalant sur lui.

— Vous vivez dans un monde de soupçon. Il vous faut apprendre à faire confiance. Surtout entre collègues…

— Un collègue mort, ironisa Volnay.

L'autre hocha la tête.

— Il y a deux ans, Sartine m'a demandé de mourir pour mieux infiltrer les milieux les plus noirs de la capitale. Pour cette raison, je le rencontre de temps à autre mais jamais au Châtelet, toujours dans un endroit public à Paris et brièvement.

Il avait l'accent de la vérité. Impressionnés, Volnay et son père échangèrent un regard surpris.

— Pourquoi cette mission ? demanda le commissaire aux morts étranges.

— Croyez-vous qu'il ne se passe rien derrière les murs des hôtels particuliers de Paris ou même chez le bourgeois ? Il y a dix ans, la comtesse de Montboissier et son amant, le duc d'Olonne avec sa maîtresse ainsi que le duc de La Tour d'Auvergne ont traité avec le diable par l'intermédiaire d'un certain Dubuisson, peintre en bâtiment. Celui-ci traça même le cercle dans lequel il allait faire apparaître le diable avec la pointe de l'épée du duc d'Olonne !

Ses yeux s'étrécirent.

— Paris est une ville remplie de secrets, de secrets magiques souvent et cela déplaît à M. le lieutenant général de police. Il veut purger cette ville de ses sorciers ou faux mages. C'est même devenu une obsession chez lui.

Sa grande carcasse se plia en avant et il baissa la voix.

— Il faut dire qu'il s'en passe de belles et que Sartine a raison d'être inquiet. Vous seriez surpris des noms de certaines personnes de haut rang qui se livrent à des pactes démoniques.

Il s'interrompit pour froncer les sourcils comme s'il se souvenait de quelque chose de déplaisant.

— Sartine m'a semblé prendre goût à mes rapports, reprit-il d'une voix soucieuse. Il m'en demande toujours davantage. Mais au fur et à mesure de nos rencontres, il me paraît de plus en plus renseigné sur tout ce qui relève de la magie noire comme si...

— Comme si, dans un même temps, il lisait des ouvrages interdits, acheva le moine.

L'inspecteur hocha la tête.

— C'est cela, oui. Ses questions sont de plus en plus précises et surtout il me questionne sur certains livres très particuliers et me demande comment se les procurer. Il y a deux semaines, il voulait savoir si la main d'un pendu tenant une bougie allumée formait une main de gloire avec de vrais pouvoirs et si la mèche de la bougie devait bien être tressée avec les cheveux du propriétaire de la main ! Les notes et manuscrits que je parviens à subtiliser l'intéressent au plus haut point. Il se met aussi à me demander des adresses...

Le moine hocha la tête.

— À trop vouloir sonder l'abîme, on peut s'y perdre…

Le chevalier de Fauve soupira.

— Ne m'en parlez pas! Ces derniers temps, Sartine m'a inquiété. Il ne m'a pas chargé d'enquêter sur l'affaire du cimetière. N'y voyez aucune envie ou jalousie, je n'ai pas pour habitude de mettre ma faucille dans le champ du voisin mais, du fait de mon implication dans le milieu, j'étais le mieux placé pour mener celle-ci, même parallèlement à la vôtre. Au lieu de cela, Sartine m'a occupé à des broutilles.

— Pourquoi alors vous êtes-vous rendu à l'enterrement de Sophia?

— J'ai pris sur moi. Je me disais que peut-être j'y retrouverais des figures connues…

— Vous vous êtes signé à l'envers…

— Pour m'en faire reconnaître au cas où…

— Et Sartine ne vous a jamais demandé d'enquêter?

— Non, il me gardait comme atout dans sa manche, comme il disait, mais en fait, lorsqu'il a daigné se souvenir de moi, c'était pour Sophia.

Le moine tressaillit.

— Oui, dit le chevalier de Fauve, il m'a parlé d'elle. Il voulait que je la retrouve à tout prix. Il ne comprenait pas comment elle pouvait être encore vivante. Je devais découvrir où elle se cachait car elle aurait, m'a-t-il dit, échappé miraculeusement à la mort.

Il se pencha vers eux, l'air grave.

— Sartine cherche cette enfant, elle occupe toutes ses pensées. Il veut la retrouver coûte que coûte!

Le moine s'appliquait à lisser le plumage de la pie à travers les barreaux de sa cage.

— Je me demande si nous avons bien fait de le laisser repartir, soupira-t-il. Que penses-tu de lui?

— Je ne suis pas certain de vouloir lui confier ma pie à garder mais son histoire me paraît crédible, répondit son fils qui arpentait la pièce.

— Oui, tout ceci ne m'étonne guère. La police se soucie fort peu de la noblesse ou des bourgeois, son but est de défendre le régime contre tous. Les faux sorciers sont une injure à son autorité comme tout ce qui peut influencer les esprits faibles et Dieu sait qu'ils sont légion ici-bas!

— Sartine nous aurait donc manipulés?

— Il l'a fait en nous taisant l'ascendance de Sophia alors qu'il la connaissait.

— Mais de là à commanditer une messe noire!

— Sartine est droit comme une faucille, se moqua le moine. Avec lui, rien ne m'étonne plus. Le chevalier de Fauve dit vrai au moins sur une chose. Sartine envoie ses inspecteurs et ses mouches provoquer les faux sorciers pour les démasquer puis il les fait arrêter discrètement par des lettres de cachet. Pour l'interrogatoire, un commissaire du Châtelet utilise une grille de questions…

Le commissaire aux morts étranges le coupa.

— Je redoute que l'on ne découvre Sophia. Tu as entendu le chevalier de Fauve à son sujet? Sartine est reparti il y a deux heures avec ses hommes. Il connaît l'existence de la ruelle de l'Or et a pu s'y rendre après être revenu bredouille de chez nous. Ses mouches ont dû nous suivre bien souvent chez la Dame de l'Eau. Je crains le pire!

Le moine sursauta.

— Tu as raison! Je vais ôter ma bure et ceindre mon épée. Va de l'avant, je te rejoindrai!

Enfouie sous la neige, la maison semblait abandonnée. Le commissaire aux morts étranges sortit son pistolet et poussa la porte. Du haut de l'escalier, il embrassa d'un coup d'œil la scène. En bas, près de la cheminée, la Dame de l'Eau gisait à terre. Des chaises étaient renversées, un vase brisé. Derrière une porte, on entendait les jappements rageurs du chien.

Volnay descendit précipitamment l'escalier. Il ranima la Dame de l'Eau en lui faisant respirer des sels.

— Que s'est-il passé? haleta le moine. Qu'avez-vous, ma Dame? Ont-ils enlevé Sophia?

Le commissaire aux morts étranges répéta la dernière question.

— Ils étaient deux hommes masqués, geignit la Dame de l'Eau en se tenant la tête. L'un en habit de velours rouge, l'autre en habit de velours noir avec une perruque poudrée.

— Sartine! s'exclama le moine.

Volnay devint pâle.

— Cela explique son étrange comportement et ses propos lorsqu'il m'a dit : *Vous n'êtes pas ouvert comme moi à l'invisible et à l'inattendu!* Il semblait effrayé à l'idée que Sophia soit un fantôme venu se venger de ses meurtriers!

— J'ai également vu le visage d'une femme à la fenêtre de leur voiture, ajouta la Dame de l'Eau.

— Comment était-elle? la pressa le commissaire aux morts étranges.

— Jeune et belle, des cheveux bruns tirant sur le roux, de beaux yeux verts...

— Hélène! s'écria Volnay. La complice de Sartine!

Le visage du moine devint d'une pâleur extrême.

— Non, je ne le crois pas! Pas elle! Pas elle!

C'était presque un cri désespéré. Le commissaire aux morts étranges lui posa la main sur l'épaule.

— Père, pour la première fois je commence à y voir vraiment clair dans cette histoire! Les choses prennent enfin un sens pour moi. Nous n'écoutons plus ce que les gens nous disent! Souviens-toi du jour où nous avons rencontré Hélène. Elle nous a dit qu'elle parlait l'araméen et était un peu sorcière.

"D'après les croyances populaires, on est sorcière de mère en fille."

— Et nous avons ri, se souvint le moine avec amertume.

— Toi, surtout!

— Hum...

Le moine se rembrunit.

— Qui plus est, et tu ne le sais pas, elle porte une fleur de lys à l'épaule.

— Quoi! Et tu ne m'en avais rien dit? Et d'abord comment l'as-tu vue?

Son père écarta les doigts de la main.

— Euh... cela fait beaucoup de questions.

— Comment l'as-tu vue? demanda froidement Volnay.

— Euh, par hasard, à la toilette…

— Et tu n'as pas jugé bon de m'en parler?

— Elle m'a raconté une histoire à faire pleurer et puis je crois qu'elle m'a un peu ensorcelé, je l'avoue.

Il pointa un doigt en l'air pour citer Cornelius Agrippa :

— "La femme ensorcelle l'homme quand, par un regard fort fréquent, elle dirige la pointe de celui-ci vers la pointe de l'autre et que ses yeux s'attachent fort, portant au cœur de l'autre une vapeur du plus pur sang engendré par la chaleur de son propre cœur."

— On appelle cela l'amour, fit remarquer la Dame de l'Eau.

Le moine s'empourpra.

— Évitez-moi ces imbécillités! trancha le commissaire aux morts étranges.

L'éclat de son œil était dur comme le diamant.

— Comme je l'ai dit, reprit-il, j'y vois désormais clair. Revenons en arrière, une nuit dans un cimetière. Sophia est allongée, inerte, sur la dalle froide. Cinq monstres l'entourent. Trois hommes, deux femmes. Ces trois hommes sont Sartine, le commanditaire, l'astrologue, le complice, et le curé dansant, l'exécutant. La prostituée donnant l'eucharistie, c'est la Vorace. La seconde femme participant à cette messe, sorcière à ses heures et agent de Sartine, s'appelle Hélène!

— Sartine, à la limite, je veux bien, murmura le moine, mais Hélène!

— Elle les a menés droit vers Sophia!

Le moine baissa la tête, accablé.

— Réfléchis! insista Volnay. C'est Sartine qui, dès le premier jour, nous a mis Hélène dans les pattes pour l'aider à prendre le contrôle de cette enquête, Sartine qui ne quitte pas Sophia des yeux depuis des années. Tu l'as toi-même reconnu dans la description de l'homme qui lui a donné un louis d'or. Et comme tu as pu le constater, Sartine cherche Sophia. Il a fait fouiller nos maisons et il s'est ensuite rendu à la ruelle de l'Or car ses mouches l'ont assez renseigné sur nos fréquentations là-bas.

— Et Sartine portait aujourd'hui un habit de velours noir…

— Tout se tient! renchérit Volnay. Lorsque j'ai voulu arrêter la Vorace et qu'elle s'est enfuie, Hélène n'a pas cherché à la retenir. Elle a dû ensuite avertir Sartine que nous étions sur la piste du curé dansant, ce qui a entraîné sa mort immédiate!

— Allons chez elle, décida le moine.

— Connais-tu son adresse? s'étonna son fils.

Une lueur moqueuse brilla dans les yeux du moine.

— Moi non mais sais-tu quelque chose qui échappe aux mouches?

Un sourire froid illumina le visage du commissaire aux morts étranges.

— Certes non! Suis-moi!

Ils sortirent de la maison et marchèrent en ligne droite vers Gaston qui recula, épouvanté par l'expression de leurs regards.

— Conduis-nous chez Hélène!

— Hélène? Mais je ne sais pas…

Volnay le saisit brutalement au col.

— Fini de jouer, mouche, oh ma mouche! Sous tes dehors de benêt, je sais que tu es le plus rusé de tous! Et tu dois parfaitement savoir où demeure cette jeune femme!

— Vous n'allez pas me faire du mal après m'avoir invité à votre repas, balbutia Gaston tout congestionné sous la poigne de fer du policier. Nous avons goûté aux mêmes plats…

— Mais nous n'avons pas partagé avec toi le pain de l'Eucharistie! remarqua finement le moine.

— Et je ne vous jetterai pas la pomme du péché! conclut la mouche résignée.

Il contempla le moine et le commissaire aux morts étranges. Une lueur farouche brillait dans leurs yeux. Rarement, il avait vu hommes aussi déterminés.

— Allons, murmura Volnay d'une voix rauque, hâte-toi de nous conduire.

Et dans sa voix perçait une sourde menace. La mouche n'hésita plus.

— Venez avec moi!

Ils le suivirent jusqu'à l'appartement d'Hélène, s'étonnant au passage du choix du faubourg Saint-Jacques et de la proximité des couvents.

— Siltieri aurait adoré habiter ici, commenta sans rire le moine. Je m'étonne qu'il n'ait pas encore visité cet endroit!

Rue des Marionnettes, ils s'engouffrèrent dans l'immeuble de la jeune femme et gravirent quatre à quatre les marches de l'escalier.

— Attends-nous à la porte et veille à ce que personne ne nous dérange, décréta le commissaire aux morts étranges.

L'appartement était meublé avec sobriété mais goût. Les meubles en acajou semblaient de ligne classique, avec peu de bronzes ou de dorures. Un rideau de vieux taffetas cramoisi masquait la grande fenêtre du salon. Volnay émit un petit cri étranglé en découvrant la table de la cuisine tout ensanglantée. Le moine s'empressa de le rejoindre.

— Chats noirs, crêtes de coq et rognons de bélier… murmura-t-il atterré devant l'étrange étalage.

— Voilà qui commence bien mal, constata le commissaire aux morts étranges.

— On lui donnerait le bon Dieu mais non sans confession, dit son père choqué.

Volnay alla jusqu'à la chambre et l'appela.

— Vois-tu ces livres?

Le moine mit ses bésicles et se pencha pour lire les titres.

— *De la vray magie noire vel Sigillum Salomonis*, *Agrippa*, *Clavicula Salomonis*… hum… tout cela sent le soufre!

Il baissa la tête, atterré. Son monde s'écroulait.

— C'était donc ça! Elle est allée à l'école du diable et en a appris la malice.

Son fils s'empara sur le bureau d'un cahier griffonné de figures et de chiffres.

— Des sorts, des formules, des conjurations, déchiffra le moine par-dessus son épaule. Où va se nicher le mal? Décidément, toujours là où on l'attend le moins!

Volnay eut une moue dubitative.

— Inutile d'aller plus loin, nous savons maintenant à qui nous avons affaire! Heureusement que tu n'as pas… enfin, tu vois ce que je veux dire…

— Comment? Euh, oui…

Son fils lui jeta un regard soupçonneux.

— Dis-moi, père, avec Hélène, tu n'as quand même pas…

— Qu'est-ce qui peut te faire penser ça! s'exclama trop vite le moine.

— Je ne sais pas, parfois il me semble que tu refuses d'accepter ton âge…

— Mais je n'ai aucune envie de vieillir, fils! s'écria le moine.

— Oui, dit Volnay, c'est bien ça le problème!

XXV

MESSE NOIRE
ET UNE DERNIÈRE DIABLERIE

L'obscurité régnait partout en maîtresse mais était-ce la nuit pour autant? se demandait avec inquiétude Sophia. Sa nourrice lui racontait que la lune rappelait à la vie des vampires dans leurs tombeaux, éveillant leur soif de sang. Alors, afin d'exorciser sa peur, Sophia ne cessait de parler à Hélène comme si seuls les mots pouvaient la maintenir loin de la folie et de la mort :

— Ma nourrice me disait que les monstres n'existaient pas et que ce n'était que des histoires auxquelles il ne fallait pas croire.

Dans le noir, les yeux vert et doré d'Hélène semblèrent se rétrécir pour n'être plus qu'une fente.

— Ta nourrice avait tort, Sophia, les monstres existent bien. Ils sont partout autour de nous et on ne sait même pas les distinguer des autres.

Elle se tourna à demi pour tenter de réduire la morsure des liens à ses poignets et ses pieds.

— Et dis-toi bien qu'ils prennent toujours l'apparence la plus aimable pour que tu ne te doutes de rien. Ils sont là pourtant, tout autour de nous…

Un sourire adoucit son visage.

— Heureusement, l'espoir demeure. Au mal s'oppose toujours le bien. C'est une question d'équilibre. Ils viendront…

— Qui cela? demanda Sophia. Le commissaire et son gentil moine?

— Oui, car ils sont braves et intelligents.

Hélène se tourna contre le mur et murmura.

— Du moins je le crois!

— Que croyez-vous donc?

L'homme entrait, habillé de velours rouge. Avec lui, un pan de lumière se glissa jusqu'aux deux prisonnières avant de disparaître lorsque la porte claqua. Le nouvel arrivant alluma une lanterne qui jeta des reflets tremblotants sur les murs froids.

— Toi d'abord, fit-il en s'agenouillant près de Sophia.

Il lui fit ingurgiter de force le contenu d'une petite fiole. Curieusement, l'enfant ne se débattit qu'une fois enlevée la fiole de ses lèvres. Il se contenta de la maintenir au sol, sous les imprécations d'Hélène, jusqu'à ce qu'elle s'endorme. Alors seulement, il se tourna vers la jeune femme et sa bouche dévoila un sourire de loup.

— Vous ensuite…

Il montra une certaine familiarité avec Hélène, comme s'il la connaissait depuis toujours, car, après avoir soigneusement vérifié les attaches de ses mains dans son dos, il retroussa sa robe d'une main experte et lui caressa les cuisses.

— Belle bête! apprécia-t-il.

Il rit et ajouta :

— Une fois, je n'ai pas vérifié l'état des liens d'une prisonnière et j'ai failli me faire arracher les yeux par cette femme. Cela a été la surprise de ma vie.

— Une fois, un homme m'a violée, rétorqua Hélène, cela ne m'a pas du tout surprise!

Il la regarda avec un froid détachement.

— Ne vous inquiétez pas, je m'occuperai plus tard à calmer vos ardeurs mais j'ai promis la primeur à un de mes amis qui a un gros sentiment pour vous.

Et il ajouta d'un ton tranquille :

— Nous vous tuerons ensuite.

Elle le suivit des yeux alors qu'il sortait de sa besace une coupe et un goupillon noir. Sans mot dire, il dénoua le lacet qui retenait ses chausses et urina dans la coupe. Il y ajouta du sel et ce qui semblait être du soufre. Ensuite, il trempa son goupillon dans la coupe et s'approcha de la jeune femme qui se contorsionna pour échapper à son étreinte. D'une main ferme, il la saisit par le cou et traça sur son front avec le goupillon le signe de croix à l'envers.

— Hélène, dit-il, je te rebaptise.

Dans un souffle, la jeune femme cracha :

— Je n'ai jamais été baptisée !

Surpris, l'autre la contempla avant d'éclater de rire.

Ils avaient fouillé sans succès l'appartement d'Hélène à la recherche d'indices pour les diriger dans leur quête désespérée.

— Ils n'ont pas amené Sophia chez Hélène et la maison de l'astrologue a brûlé, récapitula Volnay. Est-elle chez Sartine ? Ce serait prendre un risque énorme dans sa position et la chose se remarquerait…

Il médita un instant.

— Allons à l'abbaye en ruine !

— Mais pourquoi ?

— C'est le seul lieu où ils puissent se trouver, je n'en connais pas d'autre !

Le moine gémit de désespoir.

— Nous sommes complètement démunis !

Il claqua des doigts.

— Mais j'y pense, Hélène était avec nous lorsque nous sommes allés dans cette abbaye. Sachant que nous connaissons les lieux, ils n'y amèneront pas Sophia.

Son fils lui jeta un regard sombre.

— Je sais bien mais encore une fois je ne sais où aller et surtout n'oublie pas qu'ils ignorent que nous avons découvert l'enlèvement de Sophia.

— Voilà un sacré coup de dé ! conclut le moine atterré.

Le second homme s'approcha d'Hélène à pas lents, le sourire aux lèvres. Il était vêtu d'un costume de velours noir et portait une perruque poudrée.

— Vous ! souffla la jeune femme. Vous !

Son sourire s'effaça lentement et sa noirceur se dévoila. Il s'agenouilla et lui flatta la croupe.

— Mon compagnon a raison : belle bête ! Depuis le temps que je pense à vous et que je vous espère ! Soyez flattée d'avoir retenu l'attention d'un homme qui tient une si belle place dans la société. Que ferai-je de vous ensuite, Hélène? Peut-être mon cheval! J'ai lu que si je vous passais au cou des lanières de peau arrachées à des cadavres écorchés, je vous transformerai en une monture infatigable!

Et sans plus de commentaires, il commença à défaire son haut-de-chausses. Hélène ferma les yeux et ne les rouvrit que lorsqu'on la força à ouvrir la bouche.

— Non, balbutia-t-elle en montrant les dents.

Elle reçut une gifle qui lui ébranla une canine mais, par prudence, son agresseur changea d'avis et lui écarta les cuisses.

— Tu as raison, décida-t-il, nous nous passerons des préliminaires.

Il l'enfila d'un coup et s'activa en elle avec vigueur.

— Bouge un peu! haleta-t-il.

— Je vous laisse faire, répondit-elle d'un ton glacial. Vous remuez beaucoup mais la nature vous a peu doté, je ne sens rien!

Il la gifla.

— Bouge je te dis! Bouge femme!

Hélène resta inerte.

— Tu me tiens tête, hurla-t-il, aussi vais-je te corriger, impudente catin!

Il la frappa encore, lui fendant la lèvre et entaillant ses pommettes sans qu'elle laisse passer un son entre ses dents serrées. Comme émoustillé par le spectacle de la femme battue, l'homme s'activa en elle avec des petits cris de bête et éjacula dans un grognement satisfait.

Il resta allongé sur elle un instant puis, en soupirant, se leva et ajusta ses chausses. Il s'aperçut alors que la jeune femme ne l'avait pas quitté du regard.

— Vous serez le premier à mourir, lui annonça froidement Hélène.

Ils avaient réquisitionné trois chevaux à la première écurie venue et commencé une cavalcade folle à travers Paris puis la campagne enneigée. Le pauvre Gaston peinait à garder son équilibre sur sa pourtant placide monture et souffrait le martyre. À l'abbaye abandonnée, dans le vent glacial, ils se précipitèrent vers le réfectoire aux diaboliques peintures. Le commissaire aux morts étranges alluma son briquet et confectionna une torche improvisée.

— Rien, fit-il en examinant les lieux.

Ils passèrent à la cuisine puis cherchèrent le dortoir des moines avant de retourner à l'église. Dans le bras du transept, côté sud, s'ouvrait la sacristie. Ils poussèrent la porte puis décidèrent de revenir au cloître, explorant cette fois le côté ouest. Soudain, le commissaire aux morts étranges poussa une exclamation.

— Des traces de pas!

Il s'agenouilla dans la neige fraîche et les examina avec attention.

— Deux hommes qui portent un fardeau, déclara-t-il. Non! Que dis-je! Deux fardeaux car ils ont fait deux voyages.

Le moine leva les yeux, découvrant la double cheminée du chauffoir où l'on graissait les chaussures et où, à une lointaine époque, réchauffait l'encre tandis que les moines se faisaient tondre.

— S'il y a bien un lieu où amener une prisonnière et éviter qu'elle ne meure de froid, remarqua-t-il, c'est ici.

Son fils se releva souplement et, dans un même mouvement fluide, tira son pistolet et tourna doucement le loquet de la porte. La tiédeur relative de la pièce les saisit d'entrée. Dans l'âtre d'une cheminée refroidissaient des cendres.

— Bien vu! fit le moine en clignant des yeux pour accommoder à la demi-pénombre. Ils l'ont amenée là, ligotée et recouverte d'une couverture. Vois les traces d'un corps d'enfant dans la poussière et cette longue corde qui devait la tenir sans doute pieds et poings liés.

— Attends, père! s'écria soudain Volnay en désignant du doigt une autre corde et une seconde couverture. Regarde! Cela change tout!

Il se pencha et examina les traces.

— Là se trouvait un second corps allongé. Le corps d'un adulte. On tenait ici deux personnes prisonnières!

— Mais qui…

— Qui accompagnait Sophia ?

— Hélène ! Mais…

— La Dame de l'Eau l'a aperçue dans la voiture mais on la menaçait peut-être d'une arme.

— Mon Dieu, oui, s'écria le moine. Tu as raison comme de bien entendu ! Ce n'est pas ce que nous pensions. Oh mon Dieu…

— Quoi ?

La lumière de la torche venait de jeter un éclat doré au sol. Le moine se saisit délicatement de l'objet.

— Un anneau ! Et il y a une inscription à l'intérieur !

Il chaussa ses bésicles et le porta à ses yeux tandis que son fils l'éclairait.

— *AGLA*, lut-il avec application. Il s'agit d'une formule cabalistique formée de la première lettre des quatre mots hébreux *Atha Gabor Leonam Adonaï* : "Vous êtes puissant et éternel Seigneur."

D'un soupir, il exhala l'air de ses poumons.

— Il ne peut appartenir qu'à Hélène ! C'est elle qui s'en est dessaisie pour nous laisser une indication. Cela confirme bien qu'on la tenait prisonnière !

Il lança une longue imprécation et se frappa la tête.

— On nous manipule !

— C'est aussi mon impression.

— Le tableau chez Hélène était un peu chargé : toute cette charcuterie sanglante et ces livres blasphématoires ! Siltieri n'aurait pas mieux fait comme mise en scène. Nous avions envie d'y croire et nous y avons cru. Pauvre enfant ! Oh, mon Dieu !

— Arrête d'en appeler à Dieu, remarqua son fils, il ne peut rien pour nous.

— C'est vrai ! Nous sommes partis comme des benêts en nous disant : si c'est comme ci, ça ne peut être comme ça ! En vérité, même une souris de laboratoire irait plus vite que nous dans ses réflexions !

Le moine tourna sur lui-même comme si ses pensées s'affolaient.

— Nous avons décrété que le but de cette messe noire était de tuer le roi. C'est ce que l'on a voulu nous faire croire.

Brisons là toutes nos hypothèses! Une enquête est comme un jeu d'emboîtement de pièces en bois. Éparpillons les pièces, recomposons-les différemment et posons-nous de nouvelles questions. La personne visée par l'envoûtement d'une messe noire peut littéralement sécher et dépérir jusqu'à passer à trépas et nul docteur ne pourra la sauver. Seule une contre-messe a ce pouvoir en faisant à son tour sécher et mourir le célébrant et ses commanditaires.

Il agita théâtralement les bras en l'air.

— Seulement, une messe noire peut avoir d'autres desseins que ceux de tuer... Pense à la Montespan, fils, pense à la Montespan! L'histoire est là pour nous montrer le chemin de l'humanité et nous n'en tenons aucun compte!

Volnay le regarda avec effarement.

— Je vois où tu veux en venir : on peut ne pas chercher à tuer le roi mais à l'influencer dans son jugement et sa volonté! Mais es-tu bien sûr de toi?

— Oui car nous avons été manipulés de bout en bout, je me ruine le gosier à te le dire!

— Dieu! Si tu devines bien, nos déductions sont tardives. Prions le ciel pour qu'il ne soit pas trop tard!

— Ne prions pas, fit le moine, armons-nous et courons!

— Et où courir? l'arrêta son fils.

— Je crois le savoir et j'espère pour une fois ne pas me tromper!

Ils coururent enfourcher leurs chevaux et le moine indiqua brièvement à son fils où il fallait se rendre. Une fois sur leurs montures, ils les talonnèrent sans pitié.

— Et moi! cria Gaston essoufflé qui débouchait à l'air libre. Attendez-moi!

Les deux cavaliers ne se retournèrent même pas.

Les ombres grisées du crépuscule les rattrapèrent une heure après, lorsqu'ils aperçurent la silhouette menaçante du château. Au-dessus de leurs têtes roulaient de gros nuages noirs, un orage menaçait d'éclater. Le commissaire aux morts étranges se dressa sur ses étriers.

— Ce château a l'air désert, remarqua-t-il, mais ce n'est pas une ruine en dehors de la partie nord qui aurait besoin de quelques travaux!

— Comment allons-nous entrer?

— En sonnant à la grille comme des gens bien élevés!

Ils menèrent leurs chevaux écumants jusqu'à l'entrée. La foudre s'abattit tout près d'eux alors qu'ils arrivaient devant la grille du château.

— Fâcheux signe, murmura le moine, un Romain aurait rebroussé chemin!

— Mais pas nous! répondit Volnay la main crispée sur son épée.

Le murmure de la pluie et l'odeur de pierre mouillée et de végétation pourrissante les saisirent lorsqu'ils descendirent de monture. Le commissaire aux morts étranges héla le gardien. Une face de rat d'âge indéterminé s'encadra dans la lucarne de la tourelle qui jouxtait l'entrée du château.

— Laisse-moi faire, fils, murmura le moine.

— Que voulez-vous? cria l'homme.

— Entrer pardi, se moqua le moine, nous sommes des invités. Veuillez avoir l'amabilité de vous approcher pour le vérifier.

Le visage disparut dans un grognement. Ils attendirent. Bientôt la porte de la tourelle s'ouvrit. Le gardien descendit le petit escalier qui la desservait et s'approcha, le visage chafouin et l'air méfiant.

— Je ne vous annoncerai pas, déclara-t-il avec hauteur, car il n'y a personne d'autre que moi ici ce soir. Tous les domestiques ont reçu leur congé pour la journée.

— Ne soyez pas si prompt à décréter que nous n'entrerons pas, répliqua le moine, et regardez d'abord ceci.

Il fit mine de fouiller ses poches et jeta une bourse entre les barreaux de la grille. L'autre fit encore quelques pas en avant et se pencha pour la ramasser en marmonnant.

— Votre argent ne change rien à tout cela…

Mais lorsqu'il releva la tête, il se retrouva face au canon d'un pistolet et à l'œil féroce du moine.

— Il me tarde de tuer quelqu'un aujourd'hui, annonça celui-ci d'un ton rauque, alors ne me tente pas! Ouvre cette grille et laisse-nous entrer!

Le gardien bredouilla quelque chose mais se hâta d'ouvrir la grille. Une fois à l'intérieur, le moine lui colla son pistolet sur la tempe, le doigt crispé sur la détente.

— Combien d'hommes de main à l'intérieur ?

— Deux, monseigneur.

— Et les autres ?

— Trois.

— Merci !

Il frappa d'un coup sec et l'homme s'écroula à terre. Volnay eut une exclamation étouffée et lui jeta un regard froid.

— Comment faire maintenant pour l'interroger ? Sais-tu où se déroule la cérémonie ?

Le moine cilla brièvement.

— Euh… Une chapelle ! Il doit bien y avoir une chapelle ici !

— Je l'espère pour toi ! La prochaine fois que tu as envie de frapper quelqu'un, demande-moi d'abord !

Ils se ruèrent à l'intérieur du château. Les nuages noirs voilèrent les derniers reflets du jour et, d'un coup, le château se remplit de ténèbres. Les portes tremblèrent, les boiseries craquèrent et les charnières grincèrent. Des tentures masquaient les fenêtres. Ils avançaient dans une pénombre oppressante au rythme de leur cœur battant, heurtant parfois dans le noir des meubles dressés sur leur chemin comme autant d'obstacles. Ils débouchèrent sur un salon dont les rideaux tirés laissaient percevoir l'éclat des éclairs au-dehors. Ceux-ci illuminèrent brièvement des porcelaines à l'effigie du roi.

— Ah, notre bon roi est là aussi, marmonna le moine sarcastique.

Son fils lui fit signe de se taire et ils continuèrent leur progression en silence. Soudain, le moine s'arrêta net. Dans cette pièce les fenêtres n'étaient pas masquées. Derrière de lourds meubles, un bruit de respiration compressée et étouffée lui parvenait, accompagné de frémissements diaboliques. Une présence maléfique les attendait dans le noir. Le moine recula jusqu'à se trouver dos au mur et posa la main sur la garde de son épée en criant :

— Venez, mes petits chéris !

Un rouquin se rua vers eux, l'épée à la main.

— Tue!

Son cri se répercuta en écho, ses yeux étincelaient d'une haine brûlante.

— Ah, une vieille connaissance! gronda le moine en parant le coup. J'espère que tu as fait quelques progrès depuis notre dernière rencontre sinon va-t'en tenir l'écheveau à ta femme!

De son côté, Volnay croisait le fer avec un farouche spadassin. Il esquiva une série d'attaques poussives par de souples mouvements et tenta une botte audacieuse qui toucha son adversaire au flanc. Sans pitié, le commissaire aux morts étranges l'acheva sur place.

Le rouquin était d'un autre acabit. Il bloquait avec facilité les attaques du moine et se montrait redoutable en riposte. S'enhardissant, il tenta de presser son adversaire mais manqua sa contre-attaque. Aussitôt comme s'il avait attendu cela toute sa vie, le moine redoubla puis se fendit droit au cœur.

— Plus de morts, moins d'ennemis! conclut-il en essuyant son épée sur le corps de son adversaire.

— Nous devons être dans la bonne direction, constata Volnay en reprenant son souffle, sinon ils n'auraient pas été postés ici.

— Il faut toujours aller dans le sens du combat, dit judicieusement le moine. Plus il y a de monde, mieux c'est!

L'éclair au-dehors zébra le ciel, une lumière intense auréola l'autel. L'homme avait quitté son habit de velours rouge et abandonné le goupillon avec lequel il avait baptisé Hélène. Il portait désormais une chasuble blanche bordée de pives noires. Ses poignets s'ornaient de bracelets de perles noires et, à sa ceinture, scintillait la lame luisante d'un couteau. Ainsi paré, le chevalier de Fauve avait belle allure. À l'aide d'une sanguine, il traça un triangle sur le sol et plaça des cierges noirs des deux côtés du triangle. À la base de celui-ci, il inscrivit les lettres sacrées IHS accompagnées de deux croix.

Ceci fait, Mme de Morange entra, drapée dans un manteau de laine rouge mais les pieds nus. À l'invitation du chevalier de Fauve, elle ouvrit son manteau et se coucha nue et frissonnante sur les dalles froides de la chapelle, les bras en croix, un cierge noir dans chacune de ses mains. Son compère lui couvrit le ventre d'un napperon brodé sur lequel il disposa un crucifix, la tête du Christ à l'envers.

— Heureux les forts! clama-t-il. Heureux les méchants, les violents et les blasphémateurs, le royaume de Satan est à eux!

Le chevalier de Fauve prit ensuite un calice sur l'autel et s'approcha du corps inerte de Sophia. Il se saisit d'un de ses poignets qu'il tint au-dessus du récipient. Mme de Morange brailla d'une voix de tête :

— Lucifer, maître des esprits rebelles, je te prie de m'être favorable!

Les éclairs au-dehors jetaient des reflets incendiaires sur les corps nus de la mère et de sa fille. Bleue de froid, Mme de Morange geignit faiblement. La foudre tomba non loin de là.

— C'est un signe, cria le chevalier de Fauve d'une voix exaltée, un signe très encourageant! Continuons!

Il leva son couteau vers le ciel et se mit à psalmodier :

— Astaroth, Asmodée, princes d'amour, je vous conjure d'accepter le sacrifice de cette enfant! En échange, je voudrais que reviennent à sa mère l'affection du roi, la faveur des princes et des princesses de la cour et la satisfaction de tous ses désirs. Voilà, en témoignage de son respect, la vie et le sang de sa propre fille et de celle du roi. Puisse-t-il l'aimer jusqu'à la fin de ses jours!

Le chevalier de Fauve allait ouvrir les veines de l'enfant lorsque la porte s'ouvrit violemment. L'arme au poing, Volnay et le moine apparurent. D'un coup d'œil, le policier embrassa la scène : Mme de Morange étendue nue auprès de Sophia, inerte, Hélène recroquevillée dans un coin de la chapelle, le visage tuméfié, pieds et poings liés, et le chevalier de Fauve, le poignard à la main. Le sataniste contempla les deux arrivants d'un œil joyeux.

— Un moine défroqué! Voilà le participant qu'il nous manquait même si le policier est de trop!

Mme de Morange poussa un cri effrayé et se releva vivement pour courir se couvrir de son manteau.

— Eh, madame, ne courez pas si vite, se moqua le moine, ce n'est pas la première fois que je vous vois nue! Quant à mon fils, les femmes comme vous le laissent de marbre!

D'agacement, Volnay siffla doucement entre ses dents et agita son arme en direction du chevalier de Fauve.

— Lâchez ce poignard!

Un sourire torve envahit la face du chevalier de Fauve.

— Que croyez-vous donc qu'il puisse m'arriver? Les lois physiques n'existent plus, je suis à l'abri de vos balles dans le cercle sacré. Ici, il n'y a plus que vous, moi et le diable!

— Bougre de fou, dit le moine en levant son pistolet, je vais te montrer ce qui est sacré ici-bas, moi!

Vivement, le chevalier de Fauve souleva le corps de Sophia et posa la lame effilée de son poignard sur sa gorge.

— Lâchez vos armes ou, par l'Enfer, je vous jure bien que je l'égorge d'un coup!

Avec un geste léger, presque indétectable, Volnay fit signe à son père. De concert, les deux hommes se baissèrent lentement et posèrent leur pistolet à terre.

— Poussez-les loin de vous, fit le sataniste.

Le commissaire aux morts étranges devança son père et donna un coup de pied dans le premier pistolet. Celui-ci acheva sa course dans les pieds du chevalier de Fauve qui, satisfait, le ramassa. Le second coup de pied, plus violent sous le coup de la colère, fit glisser plus loin le second pistolet, à deux mètres à peine d'Hélène. Celle-ci jeta un regard inexpressif à l'arme puis à Volnay. Ses paupières cillèrent une fois, rapidement.

Pendant ce temps, le moine s'était nonchalamment écarté de son fils qui, lui-même, avait fait un pas de côté. Il devenait difficile au sataniste de les tenir ensemble dans sa ligne de mire.

— À votre place, je ne ferais pas cela!

Entré derrière eux, un homme grand et corpulent pointait deux pistolets chargés sur eux. Avec stupéfaction, Volnay reconnut Cornevin, le commissaire de quartier, vêtu d'un habit de velours noir.

— Vous!

— À mon avis, dit Cornevin au sataniste et à Mme de Morange, ils ont d'autres armes sur eux. Messieurs, couchez-vous sur le sol, je vous prie, les bras en croix.

Il s'approcha le premier de Volnay et trouva un petit pistolet à l'intérieur de sa botte droite. Il l'en ôta et s'approcha du moine. Celui-ci tenta de lui faucher les jambes mais l'autre évita le coup en traître.

— Tiens-toi tranquille, moine du diable! fit-il en lui appuyant méchamment son pied dans les reins.

Sur celui-ci, il trouva une dague dans la ceinture et un poignard tenu au creux des omoplates.

— En voilà des façons de se promener ainsi armé pour un homme de Dieu, plaisanta-t-il.

— J'en suis désolé, en convint le moine, mais l'on rencontre tant de mauvaises gens au-dehors!

— Tu n'avais qu'à rester chez toi!

Il pointa son pistolet en direction de la tête du moine. Mme de Morange fit un pas dans leur direction. Elle frissonnait de froid et de peur.

— Un instant, fit-elle, qu'allez-vous faire?

Le commissaire de quartier lui jeta un regard étonné.

— Le tuer, madame, lui et le commissaire aux morts étranges. Que voulez-vous que nous fassions d'autre?

Elle s'agita nerveusement.

— On risque d'entendre le coup de feu.

— Madame, il n'y a personne d'autre que des gens à nous dans votre hôtel particulier ou plutôt ce qu'il en reste. C'est sans danger mais pour vous rassurer, je peux les égorger.

— Oh oui, égorgez-moi! s'écria le moine. J'ai toujours rêvé de savoir ce que l'on ressentait en sentant son sang s'écouler hors de soi!

Le chevalier de Fauve émit un rire bruyant et contempla le moine non sans admiration.

— Il préfère cela à une balle dans la tête parce qu'il tentera sa chance quand vous vous pencherez sur lui pour le saisir au cou. Ce genre d'homme est plein de ressources et ne s'avoue jamais vaincu!

Son regard coula en direction de Volnay, toujours allongé, le souffle court.

— Quant à l'autre, reprit-il, regardez-le! Tous ses muscles sont bandés, il est prêt à se jeter sur vous!

— Une balle dans la tête alors, décida le commissaire de quartier. C'est plus prudent! Lequel d'abord, madame?

Le moine releva la tête et dit à Mme de Morange :

— Moi d'abord, s'il vous plaît, vous me devez bien cette grâce!

— Si vous étiez resté tranquille, rien de tout cela ne serait arrivé! lui cria-t-elle d'une voix aiguë. Vieux fou!

— Je ne suis pas vieux! se récria le moine.

Il tourna rapidement la tête vers son fils.

— Allez, on se retrouve de l'autre côté, s'il y a quelque chose. Sinon, sache que je t'aime!

Et il se rua dans les pieds du commissaire de quartier mais celui-ci avait prévu une tentative désespérée et il bondit de côté. Lorsqu'il leva ses deux pistolets, Volnay et le moine s'étaient relevés mais pas assez vite. Tranquillement, l'autre les ajusta et visa.

Le commissaire de quartier mourut sur le coup. Un nuage de fumée envahissait la chapelle et lorsqu'il commença à se dissiper, Volnay et son père virent Hélène abaisser très lentement son pistolet, le visage dépourvu de toute expression.

— Je vous avais dit que vous seriez le premier à mourir, dit-elle à Cornevin d'un ton atone.

Le chevalier de Fauve ne l'avait pas vue se saisir de l'arme que Volnay d'un coup de pied avait envoyée dans sa direction. Il poussa violemment Mme de Morange sur les deux intrus avant de se précipiter à l'extérieur. La dame alla atterrir sur le moine qui trébucha et tomba sur le sol.

— Madame, arrêtez de me mettre votre poitrine sous le nez, maugréa le moine en se relevant et en la repoussant.

Déjà son fils s'était lancé à la poursuite du chevalier de Fauve le long du corridor. Soudain, celui-ci s'arrêta et commença à reculer, laissant place à Sartine et à quatre archers du guet qui s'avançaient sur lui.

— Vous? balbutia Volnay essoufflé.

Sartine eut un sourire froid.

— Il semble que Gaston la mouche ait bien jugé de la situation en courant me prévenir au Châtelet après que vous avez déboulé hors de cette abbaye en criant qu'il fallait vous rendre au château de Mme de Morange! Nous avons crevé nos chevaux pour arriver à temps.

Quelques mètres derrière lui, Gaston apparut et adressa à Volnay un timide signe de la main.

— Où sont les autres? demanda sèchement le lieutenant général de police.

— À la chapelle, suivez-moi.

Sartine s'arrêta net en entrant dans le lieu sacré et en contemplant le spectacle qui s'offrait à ses yeux. Pieds et poings liés, Hélène à genoux tenait en joue Mme de Morange. Sophia gisait inerte sur le sol glacé.

— Dieu du ciel! jura Sartine.

— Pouvez-vous tenir Mme de Morange en joue? demanda calmement Hélène. Elle ne s'est pas encore rendu compte que mon arme n'est plus chargée mais la raison peut lui revenir! Et si vous vouliez bien demander qu'on me délie…

Sartine fit un geste de la main et un archer du guet alla libérer la prisonnière. Une fois debout, Hélène s'approcha lentement du corps du commissaire de quartier en inspirant doucement. Les yeux dans le vague, elle leva le pied et d'un geste sec lui écrasa les parties génitales du talon.

— Belle bête! murmura-t-elle d'un ton las.

Sartine eut un raclement de gorge gêné.

— Eh bien, eh bien…

Il ôta son manteau et en enveloppa maladroitement le corps de Sophia.

— Est-elle? demanda-t-il d'une voix hésitante.

— Elle est plongée dans le sommeil, le rassura le moine, comme la première fois. Mais je sais comment la réveiller.

Sartine se releva lentement, un éclair de haine dans les yeux. Il s'approcha doucement de Mme de Morange pétrifiée.

— Ainsi c'était vous! Vous!

Il tourna autour d'elle comme s'il allait la mordre et d'un geste brusque lui arracha son manteau. Mme de Morange eut une exclamation étouffée et couvrit sa poitrine de ses bras.

Le moine cracha de dégoût :

— Vous iriez jusqu'à sacrifier votre propre fille pour les hypo-
thétiques faveurs du roi!

Elle se tourna vers lui, la rage aux lèvres. Un rictus la défi-
gura un instant.

— Mieux vaut viser haut que voler bas par peur des branches!
Que savez-vous des honneurs et de la gloire? Oui, que pouvez-
vous donc savoir de tout ça, vous qui êtes tombé de si haut
pour ne jamais vous en relever?

Le moine secoua la tête en souriant.

— Vous n'y comprenez rien : je ne suis pas tombé, je suis
monté plus haut que je ne l'ai jamais été!

Son regard glissa vers le corps de Sophia inerte.

— Qu'est-ce qui vous a fait croire qu'en sacrifiant votre
enfant vous retrouveriez les faveurs du roi? Comment une telle
folie vous a-t-elle paru possible? Et comment passer de l'espé-
rance à la bêtise la plus noire?

Sans attendre la réponse, le commissaire aux morts étranges
fit un signe discret au sergent du guet qui entraîna Mme de
Morange, encadrée de deux archers. Le moine se tourna vers
lui :

— Tu as remarqué comme l'envie et la jalousie rendent les
femmes laides?

Son fils haussa nonchalamment les épaules. Il préférait
conserver pour lui son jugement sur les femmes. Sartine tourna
alors sa hargne vers le dernier prisonnier.

— Vous qui m'avez trahi, vos affaires sont faites!

Les fers au poignet, le chevalier de Fauve conservait toute
sa superbe. Grand seigneur, il s'avança vers son supérieur, lui
tendant la main :

— Allons Sartine, ne soyez pas fâché! Une poignée de
main…

Le lieutenant général de police recula d'un bond comme si
un serpent menaçait de le piquer. Le moine comprit sa réaction et se moqua :

— Ne craignez rien, Sartine, le pouvoir d'un sorcier et sa
damnation ne se transfèrent lors d'une poignée de main qu'à
la mort du sorcier!

Dehors la foudre tonna et le chevalier de Fauve tendit l'oreille.

— Oui, murmura-t-il, c'est le moment... Satan, mon véritable maître, est là et demande audience!

Ses yeux se teintèrent d'obscurité. Il étendit les mains vers les policiers, comme pour les saisir, les doigts bien écartés à la manière des ensorceleurs. Sa voix semblait s'être retirée dans quelque caverne obscure d'où elle résonna sinistrement :

— Le jeu n'est pas terminé! J'ai beaucoup appris ces deux dernières années et vous ignorez encore l'étendue de mes pouvoirs. J'ai renoncé à Dieu et à Jésus-Christ, aux saints et saintes, à l'Église apostolique et romaine, à tous les sacrements d'icelle, et à toutes les prières et oraisons qu'on pourrait faire pour moi. J'ai vu l'abîme et je m'y suis englouti. J'ai vu l'abîme et je suis devenu un dieu déchu!

Sa voix monta pour couvrir le bruit de la foudre au-dehors.

— Croyez-vous donc qu'on puisse gagner contre le diable en personne? Vous allez mourir! Vous allez tous mourir!

Une grimace sardonique dévora tout son visage et l'écume coula de sa bouche. Les archers du guet reculèrent et se signèrent vivement. Le sataniste rit et leva les bras en l'air comme s'il allait briser ses chaînes, s'écriant d'une voix terrible :

— J'en appelle à Asmodée, Kobal, Nergal, Ukobach, Bélial et Astaroth, grand-duc très puissant aux Enfers!

— Tu leur donneras le bonjour de ma part! fit le moine en lui envoyant son poing dans la figure.

Sartine avait pris place dans un des fauteuils du grand salon, le visage dans l'ombre. Sophia était couchée, endormie sur une bergère, enveloppée de couvertures. On attendait la mouche et un archer du guet, envoyés à la demeure du moine afin d'en rapporter un certain nombre de plantes pour la tirer de sa léthargie.

Le regard du moine courait alternativement de Sophia, qu'il considérait avec tendresse, à Hélène avec, pour celle-ci, un brin de compassion, de respect voire de fierté. Il lui semblait toutefois que, comme un ange tombé, la jeune femme paraissait secouer ses ailes sans pouvoir s'envoler.

— La mouche a volé vite jusqu'à moi ! constata Sartine qui n'avait cure de ce drame muet. Sans elle, je ne suis pas certain que vous vous en sortiez indemnes.

— La situation était sous contrôle, fit Volnay, et j'allais rattraper le dernier lascar.

— Mouiii, fit Sartine.

Il jeta un regard aiguisé à Hélène assise près de lui, l'arme toujours à la main. Personne n'avait osé la lui reprendre.

— Je constate également que mon auxiliaire vous a été d'une précieuse utilité !

— Monsieur, fit Hélène d'une voix atone, je ne suis pour rien dans ce dénouement. J'étais prisonnière de ces mauvaises gens. Ce sont le commissaire aux morts étranges et son moine qui m'ont permis de retourner le cours des choses.

— Mais vous tirez sans ôter vos liens, commenta joyeusement Sartine. Cela est fort utile…

— Vous savez bien qu'il est difficile de m'attacher…

Le lieutenant général de police la regarda, quelque peu désorienté de cette réponse. Finalement, il se tourna vers son commissaire aux morts étranges.

— Voici venu le temps des explications, Volnay. Et peut-être me raconterez-vous comment un de mes inspecteurs s'est trouvé mêlé à toute cette histoire ?

Le commissaire aux morts étranges eut un sourire froid.

— Votre inspecteur a depuis bien longtemps basculé dans l'obscur ! L'avez-vous vraiment chargé de pénétrer les milieux de la magie noire de Paris ?

Sartine hocha sombrement la tête.

— Le service du roi le commandait. Nous œuvrons pour renforcer l'attachement au roi de ses sujets. La croyance dans le diable les en détourne. L'imagination échauffée du peuple lui fait voir le malin à la place de son monarque ! Je ne crois pas en la sorcellerie mais le peuple y croit, de même que des gens de plus haute condition. De simples va-nu-pieds de prétendus sorciers leur conseillent de planter leur argent dans leurs jardins pour le faire pousser et leur font prendre des feuilles séchées pour des rouleaux d'or! Rendez-vous compte qu'on a même vu la marquise de Pompadour entrer déguisée chez une dame Bontemps qui vous dit l'avenir!

Il s'interrompit pour jeter un regard circulaire aux lieux enténébrés.

— J'aimerais bien comprendre comment vous en êtes arrivés d'un cimetière enneigé à la sinistre chapelle de ce château!

Volnay se racla la gorge et fit un pas en avant. Contrairement à son père, il était sobre et concis.

— Une nuit dans un cimetière, rappela-t-il, nous découvrons le corps d'une enfant de douze ans. Très vite, nous établissons son identité. Sophia Marly, fille d'un astrologue de la rue des Canettes, paroisse Saint-Sulpice.

Il jeta un regard peu amène à Sartine.

— Bien sûr, une autre personne aurait pu nous apprendre beaucoup plus vite son identité mais elle avait ses raisons pour ne pas le faire.

Sartine se rembrunit mais se garda de tout commentaire.

— Sophia était une fille naturelle du roi, nous l'ignorions. Il nous fallait mener une enquête pour trouver ses meurtriers mais sans savoir qui était vraiment la victime.

Son regard croisa celui d'Hélène et s'adoucit.

— Notre partenaire nous a permis de découvrir ce secret et cela a tout changé. Même bâtarde, Sophia restait une enfant de sang royal. Mme de Morange gardait sans doute un œil sur elle par l'intermédiaire du commissaire de quartier. Tout comme une autre personne pour des raisons tant politiques que personnelles...

Sartine blêmit et fit signe de poursuivre. Volnay reprit :

— Je ne sais quand l'idée est venue à Mme de Morange de se livrer à un envoûtement par le sang en sacrifiant sa propre fille. Après un beau mariage, elle était devenue une riche veuve mais, pour une ancienne maîtresse du roi, ce n'était décidément pas assez. Patience, cela nous le découvrirons plus tard. Revenons au début de notre histoire. Nous sommes sur les traces de la prostituée qui donnait la communion lors de la messe noire. Grâce à mon père, nous la retrouvons.

Le commissaire aux morts étranges joignit les mains et fronça les sourcils.

— Même si la Vorace se tue, l'inquiétude gagne les commanditaires de la messe noire. Le curé dansant reste un point faible pour eux. N'importe qui peut l'acheter et il peut prendre peur. On le pend donc et on met dans sa poche une liste de rues dont celle où habitait l'astrologue. C'est le désigner comme coupable du meurtre de sa fille.

Il fit un aparté.

— Ces assassins ignorent toutefois que le curé dansant porte sur lui la liste véritable de ses adresses de livraison, cousue à l'intérieur d'une doublure. Mon père retrouve celle-ci plus tard et l'une de ces adresses nous amène avec Hélène à une vieille abbaye abandonnée où vraisemblablement se tiennent d'abominables cérémonies.

— Heureux de l'apprendre! marmonna le lieutenant général de police.

— Nous rentrons bredouilles de l'abbaye, reprit Volnay, mais la découverte de ce lieu nous servira bien par la suite! Revenons pour l'instant à nos trois complices. Ils ont orienté nos soupçons sur l'astrologue. Toutefois, il ne faut pas le laisser tomber vivant entre nos mains car jamais il n'avouera ce meurtre et nos présomptions pourraient alors se porter sur d'autres. On incendie donc sa maison, brûlant du même coup la servante et son maître. On change de main la magnifique chevalière sertie d'un rubis que nous ne pouvions qu'avoir remarquée sur la personne de l'astrologue. Ruse brillante pour nous faire croire que l'astrologue est encore en vie et a mis en scène sa propre mort. C'est sans doute votre inspecteur de police, le chevalier de Fauve, qui a cette idée. Le plan est diabolique. Il repose également sur notre sens de l'observation.

Il eut un sourire bref qui n'atteignit pas ses yeux.

— J'avoue que celui-ci faillit être pris en défaut car ce détail m'échappa dans un premier temps. Sans doute pour renforcer nos soupçons, on dissimule deux livres dans la maison, dans des endroits où ils sont épargnés par les flammes. Ces livres horribles ne peuvent que désigner l'astrologue comme sataniste et donc commanditaire de la messe noire. Le moine met la main sur un de ces livres et, fort obligeamment, l'insoupçonnable commissaire de quartier trouve le second! Son visage est à moitié cuit. Je pense maintenant que c'est lui qui mit le feu à la maison de Marly.

— Il ne vous soutiendra pas le contraire, murmura Hélène. C'était un acompte, maintenant, il brûle en enfer.

Il y eut un silence lourd que rompit Volnay.

— Nos trois complices se sentent désormais en sécurité. Ils ont raison de l'être car nous sommes sur une fausse piste. Heureusement pour nous, Hélène va débloquer la situation en identifiant la véritable filiation de Sophia, nous permettant de remonter à sa mère, Mme de Morange. Coup de tonnerre dans le plan idéal de nos compères, le moine rend visite à Mme de Morange. Celle-ci panique et, pour gagner du temps, lui demande de revenir souper. Pendant ce laps de temps, avec ses complices, la décision est prise de le faire assassiner. L'assassinat échoue. Les complices doivent craindre le pire et puis… rien n'arrive. Nos comploteurs comprennent soudain que rien ne relie dans nos esprits Mme de Morange, la propre mère, à la tentative de meurtre de Sophia. Le trio reprend de l'assurance. La découverte de Sophia en vie les fait sans doute même exulter. Ils s'attachent alors à la récupérer. Eh oui, j'ai sauté cet épisode, c'est le commissaire de quartier en personne à qui je m'adresse pour déterrer le cercueil de l'enfant!

Son regard se fixa avec tendresse sur son père.

— En refusant d'autopsier Sophia, le moine est passé à côté d'une vérité flagrante mais lui a également sauvé la vie! Une fois sortie de sa léthargie, Sophia commence une double vie à l'intérieur et en dehors de sa maison jusqu'à ce que, enfin, nous comprenions la vérité, confirmée par l'ouverture du cercueil.

Il agita les mains en l'air en signe d'excuse.

— J'ai oublié de parler de la scène de l'enterrement et de ma première rencontre avec le chevalier de Fauve.

— Pourquoi le chevalier de Fauve s'est-il rendu dans ce cimetière? le questionna Sartine.

— Qui sait? La mort de Sophia était son œuvre, il a sans doute voulu contempler son achèvement. Que se passe-t-il dans la tête d'un criminel? Toujours est-il qu'il ne prenait pas beaucoup de risques en s'y rendant. Il ne s'est pas mêlé aux participants à l'enterrement. Seul ce malheureux signe de croix à l'envers l'a trahi…

— Grâce à ton sens de l'observation! renchérit son père.

— Merci! Reprenons le cours de notre enquête. Nous retrouvons Sophia grâce à son chien…

— Comment! s'exclama Sartine. Vous m'avez menti!

— Oui. Il faut vous avouer que nous n'étions plus très sûrs de vous à ce moment-là de l'histoire!

— Quoi?

— Diable, intervint le moine, mensonge, dissimulation de preuves et, plus tard, nous vous surprenons avec un de nos suspects, le sataniste que mon fils a aperçu dans le cimetière…

Sartine se rembrunit mais, au prix d'un immense effort, se contint.

— À cet instant, reprit Volnay, nos soupçons se portent toujours sur l'astrologue et nous vous y associons bien volontiers ainsi que…

Il lui jeta un bref coup d'œil.

— Hélène…

La jeune femme ne réagit pas. Elle semblait s'être absentée à l'intérieur d'elle-même.

— Il faut dire que, spontanément, le chevalier de Fauve, avec une immense audace, est venu se constituer prisonnier pour nous faire part de ses soupçons à votre encontre. Nous nous inquiétons alors du sort de Sophia que vous cherchez avec tant de rage et malheureusement nous arrivons trop tard à sa cachette. Là, on nous y fait la description d'agresseurs masqués mais dont l'un peut vous ressembler, monsieur le lieutenant général de police, et d'Hélène.

Volnay se tourna vers son père.

— Et c'est là que le moine intervient.

Le moine hocha modestement la tête. Volnay reprit sa respiration avant de continuer, remarquant que les yeux verts d'Hélène semblaient reprendre vie, envahis de lueurs mordorées.

— Une fois Sophia enlevée, nous décidons de nous rendre dans l'appartement d'Hélène.

Celle-ci tressaillit.

— Là encore, on l'a préalablement arrangé pour nous faire croire à sa culpabilité. Et nous nous laissons prendre même si, à réfléchir froidement, la mise en scène est un peu chargée! Mais où chercher Sophia? Nous hésitons entre chez vous, M. de Sartine, ou l'abbaye.

Le lieutenant général de police eut un sourire pincé.

— Nous allons à l'abbaye, reprit Volnay. C'est effectivement là que Sophia a été menée dans un premier temps, sans doute pour laisser le temps de vider le château de Mme de Morange de ses domestiques.

Hélène cilla brièvement.

— À l'abbaye, nous découvrons qu'on a gardé deux prisonnières, une enfant et un adulte. Qui donc peut être l'adulte sinon Hélène? Nous retrouvons d'ailleurs un anneau que mon père, toujours aussi observateur, reconnaît comme le sien.

Le moine rougit imperceptiblement. La main de Volnay plongea dans sa poche et il s'approcha de la jeune femme pour lui tendre l'anneau.

— Merci, fit-elle d'un ton neutre.

Elle garda quelques secondes l'anneau dans la paume de sa main avant de se décider à le remettre à son doigt.

— Et comment en êtes-vous arrivés au château de Mme de Morange? demanda Sartine intrigué.

— À une déduction logique de ma part sur l'identité des deux prisonnières, Sophia et Hélène, suit une déduction foudroyante de mon père!

C'était afficher que le duo d'enquêteurs qu'ils formaient était inséparable. Sartine le comprit et se renfrogna.

— J'en vins à la conclusion, intervint le moine, que nous nous étions fourvoyés. On nous a tellement manipulés dans cette affaire que cela nous a tourné le cerveau à l'envers! Et pourtant, nous détenions tous la solution du problème dès les premières pages, si j'ose dire, de notre enquête!

Sartine eut une moue interloquée.

— Comment ça?

Le moine eut un fin sourire.

— L'affaire des Poisons! La Montespan… Nous en avons tous parlé dès le début de notre énigme. Cela remonte au siècle dernier mais la nature humaine n'a pas changé. Le commanditaire de la messe noire de Sophia désirait la même chose que les courtisans participant aux messes noires sous Louis XIV. Quels que soient l'époque, leur pays, leur race ou position dans la société, nombre de gens n'ont soif que de pouvoir et de reconnaissance. Or, dans l'enquête sur les messes noires, sous Louis XIV, à deux reprises au moins, on parla de mère sacrifiant l'enfant dont elle venait d'accoucher! Mme de Morange, ancienne maîtresse du roi et mère de l'enfant, aura attendu plus longtemps… Quels benêts nous sommes de ne pas avoir trouvé plus tôt ce lien! Décidément, l'homme n'apprend jamais rien de l'histoire!

Il laissa planer un silence songeur puis ses yeux brillèrent de nouveau.

— Mais dès que j'eus compris, je comparais mes choix : courir avec mon fils à l'hôtel particulier de Mme de Morange ou au château de celle-ci. Comment je connaissais l'existence de ce dernier? Il faut vous dire que l'on parle beaucoup dans les dîners de Mme de Morange et c'est ainsi que j'appris son existence.

D'un geste en l'air, le moine esquissa un point d'interrogation.

— Alors, hôtel particulier ou château? La logique conduisait à choisir l'endroit le plus discret et isolé.

Il s'approcha d'Hélène qui le fixa sans mot dire.

— Là, nous sommes entrés en force mais nous nous sommes laissé surprendre par le commissaire de quartier et sans Hélène nous serions morts.

Le moine eut un sourire affectueux et sa main effleura l'épaule de la jeune femme qui ne réagit pas.

— Et voilà, conclut-il à regret, comment nous sommes partis du corps d'une enfant sur une pierre tombale à ce sombre château, démasquant une mère indigne, un inspecteur de police devenu fou et un commissaire de quartier vénal. Décidément, M. de Sartine, votre police n'est plus ce qu'elle était!

Le lieutenant général de police bondit sur ses pieds.

— Vous aimez faire pirouette mais je n'oublie pas tous vos tours et détours en cette enquête, c'est miracle que vous soyez encore vivant et les coupables arrêtés!

— Toute notre habileté consiste à retomber sur nos pieds, répliqua le moine en s'étirant nonchalamment. Mais dites-moi maintenant, que va-t-il arriver à Mme de Morange et le chevalier de Fauve ? Seront-ils bien jugés ?

Sartine eut une grimace sarcastique.

— Deux lettres de cachet feront le nécessaire. Quant au commissaire de quartier Cornevin, officiellement il est mort en héros au détour d'une sombre ruelle dans l'exercice de ses fonctions.

Le moine explosa.

— Vous ne changerez donc jamais, vous les serviteurs zélés de l'ordre royal ! La vérité vous fera toujours peur !

Le lieutenant général de police le toisa de haut.

— La vérité, nous la connaissons, nous, et c'est déjà amplement suffisant. Quelle utilité de raconter toute cette histoire devant un tribunal ? Je ne désire pas divulguer en public qu'on a essayé d'asservir la volonté du roi en sacrifiant une de ses bâtardes au cours d'une messe noire ! Et encore moins que le commanditaire de tout ceci est une ancienne maîtresse de notre monarque, le cerveau de l'affaire un de mes inspecteurs de police et l'exécutant un commissaire de quartier !

Le moine se leva, le visage pâle.

— La vérité est la dignité de l'homme et se doit d'être connue de lui, même si cela heurte quelques intérêts privés. La vérité montre à tous que ni le monde, ni nous-mêmes ne sommes ce que nous devrions être !

— C'est raisonner en philosophe, c'est-à-dire inutilement !

— Sartine, dit le moine, vous faites du mal à l'idée que je me fais du genre humain.

— C'est votre faute, répliqua le lieutenant général de police agacé, pourquoi parlez-vous tant ?

— Parce que les mots veulent dire des choses, répondit paisiblement le moine.

Malgré les protestations du moine, Sartine avait amené Sophia avec lui, une fois celle-ci éveillée. Il parlait de l'adopter. Prenant le moine à part, Hélène s'était longuement entretenue avec lui puis elle avait embrassé le père et le fils avant de s'en aller sans un mot de plus.

Séparés par le corps, demeurons indissolublement unis par nos âmes, pensa fugitivement le moine.

— Reverrons-nous un jour Hélène ? s'interrogea Volnay à haute voix après son départ.

— Qui sait ? Mais ceci est une autre histoire !

Au milieu de la nuit, Volnay et son père arrivèrent chez le commissaire aux morts étranges, accueillis par une pie plus bavarde que jamais. Le moine soupira. Il cherchait à exprimer la conclusion de toute cette histoire mais ne la trouvait point. Après un verre ou deux, il dit enfin :

— Notre planète tourne autour du soleil mais nous, pauvres humains, le seul axe autour duquel nous gravitons est nous-mêmes afin de tenter de mieux nous connaître.

— Est-ce là ton mot de la fin ? se moqua son fils.

— Non, en fait je le cherche en vain mais si tu me donnes quelques minutes, j'aurai bien une idée !

Pour une fois, son fils ne lui laissa pas le dernier mot.

— Père, je suis curieux de savoir ce qu'Hélène t'a dit. Vous vous êtes longtemps entretenus ensemble. On aurait dit deux amants qui se séparent…

— Que vas-tu imaginer, mon fils, j'ai vécu et tiré assez de leçons de la vie pour que celle-ci m'incite à la prudence…

— Tant mieux, dit Volnay, cela n'aurait pas été très malin au vu de votre différence d'âge…

— Je ne suis pas vieux ! le coupa le moine.

— Ce n'est pas ce que j'ai dit !

Son père l'arrêta. Il tenait sa fin.

— Quelle histoire merveilleuse digne des contes des *Mille et Une Nuits* ! s'exclama-t-il. *Si on la gravait à l'aiguille au coin de l'œil, elle servirait d'avertissement à quiconque peut apprendre par l'exemple !*

Hélène fit une petite révérence et on l'invita d'un sourire à se relever pour s'asseoir près du feu. Les deux fauteuils se trouvaient côte à côte, face à la cheminée, mais Hélène s'appliqua à garder le regard obstinément fixé sur les flammes. Assise à ses côtés, l'autre personne restait silencieuse, occupée à se remémorer tous les événements depuis la découverte du corps de Sophia dans le cimetière.

Après la venue du commissaire aux morts étranges, Sartine était accouru hors d'haleine à son hôtel particulier, le portrait de Sophia entre ses mains. Il lui avait appris qu'il s'agissait d'une des filles naturelles du roi que l'on venait de sacrifier lors d'une messe noire. L'affaire semblait d'une gravité exceptionnelle. Bien entendu, le commissaire aux morts étranges s'était saisi de l'affaire mais on savait l'homme tout aussi secret et incontrôlable que son collaborateur, le moine hérétique. Elle avait écouté en silence le lieutenant général de police affolé, prenant la mesure de la situation. Manifestement, la présence de sa meilleure et plus dévouée agente, Hélène, s'imposait. Aussi, en fin d'après-midi, Sartine s'était-il vu dans l'obligation d'amener Hélène avec lui chez Volnay et le moine, les obligeant à accepter sa présence pour cette enquête.

Sur un signe de tête de son hôte, Hélène commença le récit des derniers événements. Puis elle se tut, le regard toujours droit devant elle. Elle savait qu'elle aussi avait été manipulée au cours de cette enquête car ni Sartine ni la personne qui l'employait ne lui avait révélé ce qu'ils savaient au départ.

— Vous m'avez bien servi, dit finalement l'autre personne.

Plongée dans une demi-torpeur, Hélène ne répondit pas. Les flammes dansaient dans ses étranges prunelles, créant d'inquiétantes lueurs. Le feu lui remémorait des pensées que sa mère avait implantées dans sa tête avant de mourir pour un jour la venger.

Tout ceci n'est pas fini, pas encore…

Soudain, la fleur de lys sur son épaule la brûla.

— Je suis contente de vos services, ajouta encore la voix mélodieuse.

Hélène s'inclina.

— Madame la marquise de Pompadour est trop bonne.

TABLE

OUVRAGE RÉALISÉ
PAR L'ATELIER GRAPHIQUE ACTES SUD
ACHEVÉ D'IMPRIMER
SUR ROTO-PAGE
EN FÉVRIER 2013
PAR L'IMPRIMERIE FLOCH
À MAYENNE
POUR LE COMPTE DES ÉDITIONS
ACTES SUD
LE MÉJAN
PLACE NINA-BERBEROVA
13200 ARLES

DÉPÔT LÉGAL
1ʳᵉ ÉDITION : MARS 2013
N° impr. : 84213
(Imprimé en France)